THE
OFFICIAL BOTTLE
PRICE LIST

Books by Ralph M. and Terry H. Kovel

The Official Bottle Price List
The Complete Antiques Price List
Know Your Antiques
American Country Furniture 1780–1875
A Directory of American Silver, Pewter and Silver Plate
Dictionary of Marks—Pottery and Porcelain

THE OFFICIAL BOTTLE PRICE LIST

Second Edition

by Ralph and Terry Kovel

CROWN PUBLISHERS, INC., NEW YORK

To Bobbe,
who thought we forgot,
and
of course to
Lee and Kim

ACKNOWLEDGMENTS

To the following companies and collectors, our special thanks for their help in obtaining their pictures of bottles used in this book. Many of the bottles pictured in color were photographed at bottle shows and special exhibits.

Avon Products (Dudley English); James Beam Distilling Company; Jack Daniel Distillery (William C. Handlan); Roy Dwyer; Ezra Brooks Distilling Company (J. Glennon Walsh, Joseph P. Tremont, Howard M. Cutler); Fleischmann Distilling Corporation (John Mallory, James R. Charest); Glenmore Distilleries Company (Thomas Wipperman); William Grant & Sons (Mr. Anderson); Lionstone Distilleries, Ltd. (Even G. Kulsveen); Miniature Bottle Mart (Joan Natelli); Noel Tomas; Wheaton Commemoratives (John F. Heiner); Ancestor Shop, East; Robert Anderson; Jeff Anschutz; Sam and Kass Baker; Christopher Barry, Green River Glass Company; Ralph Baum; Doug Bedore; Leonard and Joyce Blake, Sign of the Fruit Jar; Charles Boehler; Roy Brown; A. B. Carpenter; Larry Cass; Bob and Phyllis Christ; Dave Clum; George Cooper; Norman and Jane Cramer; Ken Davis; Edmund De Haven; Roger Durflinger; Evans Bros., The Heritage Shop; Harry Frey; Bill Fry; Allen Galer; The Garbers; General Hershy's; Pete Gitney; Gordon's; Green Door Antiques; Jerry Hambleton; Donald Haury; The Havilands; Elizabeth Heathman; Norman Heckler; Heritage Shop; Byron L. Hughes; Ed Johannes; Duane Johnson; Roy Kalmer; Ray Klug; Knight's Tiny Shop; John May; T. W. McCandless; Richard McCarter; Lonkie McCullough; Meeks Antiques; Elvin and Cherie Moody; Steve Morey; Roland Morrison; Bob Nolt; George Parker; Thad Patay; Ray Priebe; William Rouppas; Phil Sherman; Mr. Sidens; George N. and Wilda Sides; Roy Sides and Family; Robert Spangler; Mark Suhanic; Summit House Antiques; Frank D. Swick; Eugene Szanca; Scott Tyson;

Ken, Louise, and Ron Vance, The Vance's Bottle Shop; Lee and Carleiita Warner; The Weathervane; Jim Whetzel, Jim's Bottle Shop; Leon Yaun.

Our special thanks go to The Ohio Bottle Club Show, Canton, Ohio, and the New Holland Bottle Club, New Holland, Pennsylvania.

To Debby Herman and the rest of the staff, an extra bit of appreciation for getting this all put together on time with as few mistakes as possible.

INTRODUCTION

Bottle collecting has become one of the top hobbies in the United States. Not only early historical flasks and figural bottles are collected, but also many types of modern bottles and reproductions. Bottle clubs and bottle shows have set the rules for this Official Bottle Price List. We have taken the terms from those in common usage and tried to organize the thousands of listings in easy-to-use form. Many abbreviations have been included that are part of the bottle collectors' language. The Tibbits' abbreviations appear throughout the book.

ABM means automatic bottle machine.

BIMAL means blown in mold, applied lip.

BIMALOP means blown in mold, applied lip, open pontil.

FB means free blown.

SC means sun colored.

SCA means sun colored amethyst.

OP means open pontil.

To make the descriptions of the bottles as complete as possible, in some categories, an identification number has been added to the description. The serious collector knows the important books about his specialty and these books have numbered lists of styles of bottles. Included in this book are identification numbers for Milk glass from Belknap, flasks from Van Rensselaer and McKearin, candy containers from Eikelberner, figurals from Umberger, bitters from Watson, and ink bottles from Covill. The full titles of the books used are included in the bibliography and listed in the introductory paragraph for each category.

Medicine bottles include all medicine or drugstore bottles, except those under the more specific headings of bitters or sarsaparilla. Modern liquor bottles are listed under the brand name if more than five of the bottles are in the collectible series. If you are not a regular at bottle shows, it may take a few tries to become accustomed to the method of listing. If you cannot find a bottle, try several related headings. For instance, hair dye is found under "household" bottles; many named bottles are found under "medicine," "food," "fruit jar," etc. If your fruit jar has several names, such as "Ball, Mason," look under "fruit jar, ball," or "fruit jar, mason."

The prices shown are in most cases the actual prices asked for bottles during the past year. A few bottles have been included to complete a listing. When this has been done, the prices are estimates based on known prices of the past two years. The estimated prices appear only for modern bottles in a series. Pre-World War I bottles are all listed at actual sale price.

Prices may vary in different parts of the country, so a range is given. Because of the idiosyncrasies of the computer, it was impossible to place a range of price on bottles that are illustrated. The price listed is an average.

Spelling is meant to help the collector. If the original bottle spelled the word "catsup" or "ketchup," that is the spelling that appears. If the period was omitted from "Dr." or the apostrophe from "Jones' sarsaparilla," that is the way it appears. A few bottles are included that had errors in the original spelling and that error is used in the list. "Whiskey" is used even if the bottle held Scotch or Canadian and should be spelled "whisky."

Every bottle illustrated in black and white is indicated by the word "illus." in the text. Every priced bottle pictured in color is indicated by the word "color" in the listing.

There are a very limited number of the color illustrated bottles shown without prices. They are so rare that no accurate prices are available. We thought the pictures should show the best ones to be an incentive to the collector. To guess at the price would be unfair to everyone.

We welcome any information about clubs, prices, or content for future books, but cannot give appraisals by mail. We have tried to be accurate, but we cannot be responsible if any errors in pricing appear.

DISCONTINUED AVON BOTTLES

The following decanters are no longer offered for sale. In keeping with Avon policy, should any of these decanters be reintroduced in the future, one of the following differentiations will occur: 1) In almost every case, the container or the closure (cap) will be different in color from the original issue; 2) In some cases, the decanter will appear identical to the original but will be identified with the letter "R" to mark it as a reissue. Please note that this policy applies to containers only. Product names may be reused in the future without notification.

ter Shave Caddy
ter Shave Lotion Stein (8 oz.—
  silvery)
oine Decanter (flask)
Man's World After Shave
  (globe)
tiseptic Mouthwash and
  Gargle—10 oz. glass bottle
pliqué Lipstick
on Birdfeeder Powdered
  Bubble Bath
on Classics After Shave
  —book decanters
on Defender (cannon)
on Gavel Decanter
on Pump Decanter—6 oz.
  After Shave
on Royal Orb
th Blossoms Soap and
  Sponge Set
th Seasons Foaming Bath Oil
th Urn
y Rum
y Rum Gift Decanter
dfeeder
ots and Saddle After Shave—
  Wild Country and Avon
  Leather
ocade Deluxe Gift Set—Beauty
  Dust, Cream Sachet, Perfume
  Rollette
ocade Scented Hair Spray
d Vase Cologne
neo Soap With Necklace
Rope
otain's Choice
sey's Lantern
arisma Tray
ristmas Cologne
ristmas Ornament Bubble
Bath

Christmas Sparkler Bubble Bath
Christmas Tree Bubble Bath
Citrus Klean-Air Concentrate
Clear Hair Dress for Extra
  Control
Close Harmony
Cologne Classic
Cologne Riviera
Cologne Trilogy—3 Men's
  Colognes
Competite Compact
Cotillion Cologne—2 oz.
Cotillion Cream Lotion
Daylight Shaving Time After
  Shave
Decisions, Decisions, Decisions
Decorator Soap Miniatures
  (apothecary jar)
Deluxe Compact and Deluxe
  Lipstick—silvery finish with
  4-A logo design
Demi-Cup
Dollars 'n' Scents
Dolphin Decanter Skin-So-Soft
Easter Bonnet Bunny
  Soap-on-a-Rope
Easter Dec-A-Doo Bubble Bath
Easter Quacker Soap-on-a-Rope
Eiffel Tower
Elusive Tray
Fashion Perfume Glacé
Festive Fancy Compact
Festive Fancy DemiStik
Festive Fancy Lipstick
First Christmas Perfumed
  Candle
First Edition After Shave
Flower Prints Lipstick—
  4 designs: Poppy, Daisy,
  Carnation, Sunflower
Foundation Supreme

Fragrance Bell—1 oz. Cologne
Freddy the Frog Bubble
  Bath Mug
Freddy the Frog Soap Dish
  and Soap
Futura
Gadabouts Compact—black case
  with Pressed Powder
Gadabouts Compact—yellow
  case with Pressed Powder
Gadabouts Lipstick—black case
Gadabouts Lipstick—yellow case
Gentlemen's Collection
Gift Decanter (Skin-So-Soft Urn)
Gift Fancy (fan rocker bottle)
Golden Angel Foaming Bath Oil
Golden Apple Perfumed Candle
Golden Heirloom—Deluxe
  Lipstick and Perfume Rollette
  Set
Here's My Heart Cologne Silk
Here's My Heart Cologne—2 oz.
Here's My Heart Cream Lotion
Here's My Heart Foaming Bath
  Oil
Her Prettiness Perfumed Talc
Hi-Light Gel Shampoo—Normal
  —3 oz.
Hi-Light Gel Shampoo—Oily
  —3 oz.
Hi-Light Shampoo—Normal
  —12 oz. liquid
Hi-Light Shampoo—Oily
  —12 oz. liquid
Inkwell After Shave Decanter
Jamaican Waterfall Klean-Air
  Concentrate
Jasmin After Bath Freshener
Jasmin Foaming Bath Oil
Jewelled Compact and Jewelled
  Lipstick

Jewelled Owl Pin Perfume Glacé
Leopard Captivator Compact
  —with Pressed Powder
Lilac Fragrance Kwickettes
Lily of the Valley After Bath
  Freshener
Little Champ Shampoo and Hair
  Trainer Set
Little Lamb Baby Lotion
Little Red Riding Hood Bubble
  Bath
Lonesome Pine Perfumed Gift
  Soap
Lovely Touch
Lucy Bubble Bath—4 oz.
Lucy Shampoo Mug
Mad Hatter Bubble Bath
Mallard Decanter After Shave
Manicure Beauti-Kit (7 manicure
  products)
Mary Non-Tear Shampoo
Master Organizer
Meadow-Fresh Klean-Air
  Concentrate
Men's After Shave Choice—set
  of three 2 oz. After Shaves
Miss Lollypop Cologne Mist
Miss Lollypop Cologne—2 oz.
Miss Lollypop Cream Sachet
Miss Lollypop Gift Set—Pretty
  Me Rollette and Lip Pop
Miss Lollypop Hand Cream
Miss Lollypop Ice Cream Puff
  —Perfumed Talc
Miss Lollypop Perfume Rollette
Miss Lollypop Perfumed Talc
Miss Lollypop Powder Mitt
Monkey-Shines Puppet Sponge
  and Soap
Mr. Presto-Chango Non-Tear
  Shampoo
Occur! Cologne Silk
Occur! Cologne—2 oz.
Opening Play Decanter
Original After Shave
Overnighter—Spicy After Shave
  and Squeeze Spray
  Deodorant Set
Pat 'n' Powder Mitt
Patterns Fashion Ring Perfume
  Glacé
Patterns Powder Shadow
  Collection
Patterns Tray
Perfumed Candle (amber/red)

Perfumed Keynote (glass key)
Pipe Dream
Polly Parrot Puppet Sponge
  And Soap
Pony Decanter
Pony Post
Pretty Peach Cologne Mist
  (ice cream soda)
Protective Hand Cream For Men
  (old design)
Protem Creme Shampoo
  —glass jar
Pyramid of Fragrance—Perfume,
  Cologne, Cream Sachet
Rapture Cologne Silk
Rapture Cream Lotion
Regence Cologne—2 oz.
Regence Perfume—1 oz.
Regence Perfumed Candle
  (line design)
Ring Fling Lipstick
Rose Geranium After Bath
  Freshener
Ruby Bud Vase Cologne
Ruff, Tuff and Muff—three
  1.5 oz. soaps
Santa's Helper—Bath Mitt and
  Gel Bubble Bath
Scentiments—Cream Sachet
  and Perfume Rollette Set
Schoolhouse Bubble Bath
Scimitar After Shave
Scrub Mug—Liquid Soap and
  Nail Brush
Sea Maiden
Silk & Honey Milk Bath—milk
  can container
Skin-So-Soft Deluxe Decanter
  (fluted)
Skin-So-Soft Decanter
Skin-So-Soft (glass) 8 oz.
Skin-So-Soft (glass) 4 oz.
Skin-So-Soft Smoothies—4 oz.
  SSS and 3 oz. Satin Talc Set
Skin-So-Soft Urn
Skin-So-Soft Vase
Small World Cologne
Small World Cologne Mist
Small World Cream Sachet
Somewhere Cologne Silk
Somewhere Cream Lotion
Space Ace Liquid Hair Trainer
  —rocket
Spicy Treasures—Spicy After
  Shave and Talc Set

Splash 'n' Spray Set
Stamp Decanter
Stay Fair Night Cream
Stein (silvery redesign—6 oz.)
Strawberry Fair Perfumed Soap
Structured for Man Cologne Set
  —3 colognes: Wood, Glass,
  Steel
Sudden Spring Klean-Air
  Concentrate
Sunseekers Lipstick
Swing Fling Compact
The Angler After Shave Decanter
The Wolf Non-Tear Shampoo
Tic Toc Turtle Bubble Bath
  —clock
Tiger Captivator Compact with
  Pressed Powder
To a Wild Rose Cologne—2 oz.
To a Wild Rose Foaming Bath Oil
To a Wild Rose Scented Hair
  Spray
Topaze Beauty Dust (Topaze
  Beauty Dust Refills are still
  available)
Topaze Cream Lotion
Touch of Beauty Hostess Soaps
  and Soap Dish
Tribute Cologne (frosted
  warrior)
Tribute Decanter (blue and
  silver warrior—After Shave)
Twenty Paces Cologne—Avon
  Leather and Wild Country—
  dueling pistol set
Two Loves—Cream Sachet and
  Perfume Rollette Set
Ultra Cover
Unforgettable Cream Lotion
Vanity Tray—with Perfumed
  Rollette and Patterns Lipstick
Viking Horn
Western Choice (steer horns)
Whipped Creams Hostess Soap
  —four 1.5 oz. soaps
Wild Country Body Powder
Wise Choice After Shave—
  owl decanter
Wishing Beauty Dust Refill
Wishing Cologne Mist
Wishing Perfumed Skin Softener
Zebra Captivator Compact with
  Pressed Powder

BOTTLE CLUBS

EDERATION OF HISTORICAL
BOTTLE CLUBS
/o Gene Bradberry, President
098 Faxon Avenue
Memphis, Tennessee 38122

NTERNATIONAL AVON
COLLECTORS CLUB
P. O. Box 1406
Mesa, Arizona 85201

LIONSTONE BOTTLE
COLLECTORS OF AMERICA
P. O. Box 75924 Dept. P.
Los Angeles, California 90075

NATIONAL AVON BOTTLE &
COLLECTABLES CLUB, U.S.A.,
INC.
P. O. Box 232
Amador City, Ccalifornia 95601

NATIONAL AVON CLUB
P. O. Box 5490
Overland Park, Kansas 66212

NATIONAL EZRA BROOKS
BOTTLE & SPECIALTIES CLUB
420 West 1st Street
Kewanee, Illinois 61443

NATIONAL JIM BEAM BOTTLE &
SPECIALTIES CLUB
6702 Stockton Avenue
El Cerrito, California 94530

PIONEER BOTTLE CLUB OF
FAIRHOPE
P. O. Box 294
Battles Wharf, Alabama 36533

ALABAMA ANTIQUE BOTTLE
COLLECTORS, SOCIETY
2657 Hanover Circle
Birmingham, Alabama 35205

ALABAMA BOTTLE COLLECTORS'
ASSOCIATION
2713 Hanover Circle S.
Birmingham, Alabama 35205

ALABAMA BOTTLE COLLECTORS'
SOCIETY
1768 Hanover Circle
Birmingham,Alabama 35205

NORTH ALABAMA BOTTLE &
GLASS CLUB
P. O. Box 109
Decatur, Aalabama 35601

HUNTSVILLE HISTORICAL BOTTLE
CLUB
113 Monte Sano Blvd. S.E.
Huntsville, Alabama 35801

HUNTSVILLE HISTORICAL BOTTLE
CLUB
5605 Woodridge S.W.
Huntsville, Alabama 35802

MONTGOMERY BOTTLE &
INSULATOR CLUB
851 Portland Avenue
Montgomery, Alabama 36111

MOBILE BOTTLE COLLECTORS
CLUB
Rt. #4 Box 28
Theodore, Alabama 36582

TUSCALOOSA ANTIQUE BOTTLE
CLUB
c/o Glenn House
1617 11th Street
Tuscaloosa, Alabama 35401

ALASKA BOTTLE CLUB
1304 W. 15th
Anchorage, Alaska 99501

AVON COLLECTORS CLUB
P. O. Box 1406
Mesa, Arizona 85201

INTERNATIONAL AVON
COLLECTORS CLUB (IAAC)
P. O. Box 1406
Mesa, Arizona 85201

ARIZONA TREASURES UNLIMITED
5506 W. McDowell Road
Phoenix, Arizona 85009

KACHINA-EZRA BROOKS BOTTLE
CLUB
4331 North 31st Drive
Phoenix, Arizona 85017

KACHINA-EZRA BROOKS BOTTLE
CLUB
2801 N. 34th Drive
Phoenix, Arizona 85009

PICK & SHOVEL ANTIQUES
BOTTLE CLUB OF ARIZONA
Box 7446
Phoenix, Arizona 85011

VALLEY OF THE SUN BOTTLE &
SPECIALTY CLUB
3117 West Bethany Home Road
Phoenix, Arizona 85017

ARIZONA EZRA BROOKS BOTTLE
CLUB
14 Walking Diamond Drive
Prescott, Arizona 86301

ARIZONA TERRITORY ANTIQUE
BOTTLE CLUB
P. O. Box 1221
Tucson, Arizona 85715

ARIZONA TERRITORY ANTIQUE
BOTTLE CLUB
P. O. Box 6364 Speedway Station
Tucson, Arizona 85716

SOUTHWEST ARKANSAS BOTTLE
CLUB
c/o Joe Parker
Star Route
Delight, Arkansas 71940

HEMPSTED COUNTY BOTTLE
CLUB
710 So. Hervey
Hope, Arkansas 71801

MADISON COUNTY BOTTLE
COLLECTORS CLUB
Rt. 2 Box 304
Huntsville, Arkansas 72740

LITTLE ROCK ANTIQUE BOTTLE
COLLECTORS
P. O. Box 5003
Little Rock, Arkansas 72205

GOLDEN GATE EZRA BROOKS
BOTTLE & SPECIALTIES CLUB
Mr. Kenneth Busse,President
438 Pacific Avenue
Alameda, California 94501

GOLDEN GATE HISTORICAL
BOTTLE SOCIETY
P. O. Box 129
Alameda, California 94501

CALIFORNIA LIONSTONE &
SPECIALTY CLUB
212 South El Molino Street
Alhambra, California 91801

NATIONAL AVON BOTTLE &
AVON COLLECTABLES CLUB
U.S.A., INC.
P. O. Box 65 or 232
Amador City, California 95601

SHASTA ANTIQUE BOTTLE
COLLECTORS ASSOCIATION
Route 1 Box 3147-A
Anderson, California 96007

GOLD STATE BOTTLE &
SPECIALTIES CLUB
P. O. Box 463
Aptos, California 95003

KERN COUNTY ANTIQUE BOTTLE
CLUB
402 Loch Lomond Drive
Bakersfield, California 93304

CHERRY VALLEY BEAM &
SPECIALTIES CLUB
P. O. Box 145
Beaumont, California 92223

NATIONAL ASSOCIATION OF JIM
BEAM & SPECIALTY CLUBS
490 El Camino Real
Belmont, California 94002

PENINSULA BOTTLE CLUB
P. O. Box 886
Belmont, California 94002

BENTON BEAMS & ANTIQUES
MaBelle V. Bramlettle
Benton,California 93512

JIM BEAM BOTTLE CLUB
139 Arlington
Berkeley, California 94707

BISHOP BELLES & BEAUX
BOTTLE CLUB
P. O. Box 1475
Bishop, California 93514

SAN BERNARDINO COUNTY
HISTORICAL BOTTLE CLUB
P. O. Box 127
Bloomington, California 92316

HANGTOWN BOTTLEERS
P. O. Box 208
Camino, California 95709

GOLDEN CADILLAC BOTTLE &
ANTIQUE CLUB
P. O. Box 1088
Cherry Valley, California 92223

BIDWELL BOTTLE CLUB
Box 546
Chico, California 95926

CHICO ANTIQUE BOTTLE CLUB
Route 2 Box 474
Chico, California 95926

AVON BOTTLE & SPECIALTY
CLUB
P. O. Box 23
Claremont, California 91711

PETALUMA BOTTLE & ANTIQUE
CLUB
9773 Minn. Avenue
Cotati, California 94928

NATIONAL JIM BEAM BOTTLE &
SPECIALTIES CLUB
6702 Stockton Avenue
El Cerrito, California 94530

MT. BOTTLE CLUB
422 Orpheus
Encinitas, California 92024

HUMBOLDT ANTIQUE BOTTLE
CLUB
P. O. Box 6012
Eureka, California 95501

RELIC ACCUMULATORS
P. O. Box 3513
Eureka, California 95501

TEEN BOTTLE CLUB
Route 1 Box 60-T E
Eureka, California 95501

NORTHWESTERN BOTTLE CLUB
ASSOCIATION
10190 Martinelli Road
Forestville, California 95436

MONTEREY BAY BEAM BOTTLE &
SPECIALTY CLUB
P. O. Box 258
Freedom California 95019

ANTIQUE BOTTLE CLUB
ASSOCIATION OF FRESNO
P. O. Box 1932
Fresno, California 93718

SOUTH BAY BOTTLE CLUB
1221 West 186th Street
Gardena, California 90248

GLASSHOPPERS FIGURAL
BOTTLE ASSOCIATION
Box 391
Harbor City, California 90710

HOLLYWOOD STARS EZRA
BROOKS BOTTLE CLUB
2200 Beachwood Drive Apt. 116
Hollywood, California 90068

SAN FRANCISCO BAY AREA
MINIATURE BOTTLE CLUB
c/o Darwin Williams
160 Lower Via Casitas #8
Kentfield, California 94904

QUEEN MARY BEAM &
SPECIALTY CLUB
P. O. Box 507
Lakewood, California 90714

MT. WHITNEY BOTTLE CLUB
P. O. Box 333
Lone Pine, California 93545

ORIGINAL SIPPIN COUSINS EZRA
BROOKS SPECIALTIES CLUB
1049 Freeland Street
Long Beach, California 90807

AMETHYST BOTTLE CLUB
3245 Military Avenue
Los Angeles, California 90034

EZRA BROOKS SPECIALTIES
CLUB
4908 1/2 Meridian Street
Los Angeles, California 90042

LILLIPUTIAN BOTTLE CLUB
5626 Corning Avenue
Los Angeles, California 90056

LIONSTONE BOTTLE
COLLECTORS OF AMERICA
P. O. Box 75924 Department P
Los Angeles, California 90075

MISSION BELLS (BEAMS)
1114 Coronada Terrace
Los Angeles, California 90026

SOUTH BAY BOTTLE CLUB
8324 Colegio Drive
Los Angeles, California 90045

SOUTHERN CALIFORNIA
MINIATURE BOTTLE CLUB
5626 Corning Avenue
Los Angeles, California 90056

LOS BANOS ANTIQUE BOTTLE
CLUB
635 Jefferson Avenue
Los Banos, California 93635

JIM'S GEMS
c/o Joe Dias
1241 Enslen Avenue
Modesto, California 95350

MODESTO OLD BOTTLE CLUB
(MOBC)
P. O. Box 1791
Modesto, California 95354

AVON BOTTLE & SPECIALTIES
COLLECTORS
Southern California Division
9233 Mills Avenue
Montclair, California 91763

SUNNYVALE ANTIQUE BOTTLE
COLLECTORS ASSOCIATION
1660 Yale Drive
Mountain View, California 94040

CURIOSITY BOTTLE ASSOCIATIO
Box 103
Napa, California 94558

JIM BEAM BOTTLE CLUB
P. O. Box 103
Napa, California 94558

CAMELLIA CITY JIM BEAM
BOTTLE CLUB
3734 Lynhurst Way
North Highlands, California 9566

WESTERN WORLD COLLECTORS
ASSOCIATION
P. O. Box 409
Ontario, California 91761

JEWELS OF AVON
2297 Maple Avenue
Oroville, California 95965

PARADISE GLASSHOPPERS
6982 Skyway
Paradise, California 95969

SAN LUIS OBISPO BOTTLE
SOCIETY
124 21st Street
Paso Robles, California 93446

NORTHWESTERN BOTTLE
COLLECTOR ASSOCIATION
1 Keeler Street
Petaluma, California 94952

PETALUMA BOTTLE & ANTIQUE
CLUB
P. O. Box 1035
Petaluma, California 94952

MT. DIABLO BOTTLE CLUB
4166 Sandra Circle
Pittsburg, California 94565

TEHAMA COUNTY ANTIQUE
BOTTLE CLUB
P. O. Box 541
Red Bluff, California 96080

TEHAMA COUNTY ANTIQUE
BOTTLE CLUB
Route 1 Box 775
Red Bluff, California 96080

NORTHERN CALIFORNIA JIM
BEAM BOTTLE & SPECIALTY
CLUB
2110 Elmira Drive
Redding, California 96001

GOLDEN GATE EZRA BROOKS
BOTTLE & SPECIALTY
CLUB OF NORTHERN CALIFORNIA
12517 San Pablo Avenue
Richmond, California 94805

LIVERMORE AVON CLUB
6385 Claremont Avenue
Richmond, California 94805

HIGH DESERT BOTTLE HUNTERS
P. O. Box 581
Ridgecrest, California 93555

BEAM BOTTLE CLUB OF
SOUTHERN CALIFORNIA
3221 N. Jackson
Rosemead, California 91770

BRONZE STAGECOACH EZRA
BROOKS BOTTLE & SPECIALTIES
CLUB
P. O. Box 1108
Roseville, California 95678

ANTIQUE BOTTLE CLUB
ASSOCIATION OF SACRAMENTO,
INC.
P. O. Box 467
Sacramento, California 92502

CENTRAL CALIFORNIA AVON
BOTTLE CLUB
5101 Stockton Blvd.
Sacramento, California 95820

GREATER CALIFORNIA
HISTORICAL BOTTLE CLUB
P. O. Box 55
Sacramento, California 95801

SAN BERNARDINO COUNTY
HISTORICAL BOTTLE CLUB
c/o Fontana Y.W.C.A.
17366 Merrill Avenue
Fontana, California 92335

SAN DIEGO ANTIQUE BOTTLE
CLUB
P. O. Box 536
San Diego, California 92112

SAN DIEGO EZRA BROOKS
BOTTLE & SPECIALTY CLUB
P. O. Box 16118
San Diego, California 92116

GLASS BELLES OF SAN GABRIEL
518 W. Neuby Avenue
San Gabriel, California 91776

SAN JOSE ANTIQUE BOTTLE
CLUB
1058 Timber Crest Drive
San Jose, California 95120

SAN JOSE ANTIQUE BOTTLE
COLLECTORS ASSOCIATION
P. O. Box 5432
San Jose, California 95150

SAN JOSE EZRA BROOKS BOTTLE
& SPECIALTIES CLUB
411 Lewis Road #340
San Jose, California 95111

SAN JOSE EZRA BROOKS BOTTLE
& SPECIALTY CLUB
2882 Manda Drive
San Jose, California 95124

MARIN COUNTY BOTTLE CLUB
c/o Jean Wyrick
31 Ridge Drive
San Rafael, California 94901

ANTIQUE BOTTLE CLUB OF
ORANGE COUNTY
P. O. Box 10424
Santa Ana, California 92711

ANTIQUE BOTTLE COLLECTORS
OF ORANGE COUNTY
223 E. Ponona
Santa Ana, California 92707

MINI SPIRITS BOTTLE CLUB
1230 Genoa Drive
Santa Ana, California 92704

ORANGE COUNTY MINIATURE
COLLECTORS
1230 Genoa Drive
Santa Ana, California 92704

SANTA BARBARA BEAM BOTTLE
CLUB
5307 University Drive
Santa Barbara, California 93111

SANTA BARBARA BOTTLE CLUB
1825 Garden Street
Santa Barbara, California 93101

SANTA BARBARA BOTTLE CLUB
5381 Paseo Cameo
Santa Barbara, California 93105

NORTHWESTERN BOTTLE
COLLECTORS ASSOCIATION
P. O. Box 1121
Santa Rosa, California 95402

STOCKTON HISTORICAL BOTTLE
SOCIETY
748 E. Mayfair Avenue
Stockton, California 95207

CHIEF SOLANO BOTTLE CLUB
4-D Boynton Avenue
Suisun, California 94585

TAFT ANTIQUE BOTTLE CLUB
P. O. Box 334
Taft, California 93268

TAFT ANTIQUE BOTTLE CLUB
522 "E" Street
Taft, California 93268

SAN LUIS OBISPO BOTTLE
SOCIETY
Rt. 1 Box 108
Templeton, California 93465

CALIFORNIA FRUIT JAR
COLLECTORS
Maxine Bush, Secretary
16646 Montego Way
Tustin, California 92680

MOTHERLODE ANTIQUE BOTTLE
CLUB OF CALAVERAS COUNTY
c/o Sharon Shewpack
P. O. Box 112
Vallecito, California 95251

NAPA-SOLANO BOTTLE CLUB
c/o Ginny Smith
1409 Delwood
Vallejo, California 94590

JUNIPER HILLS BOTTLE CLUB
Rt. 1 Box 18
Valyermo, California 93563

SEQUOIA ANTIQUE BOTTLE
SOCIETY
2105 S. Court Street
Visalia, California 93277

LOS ANGELES HISTORICAL
BOTTLE CLUB
747 Magnolia
West Covina, California 91790

LOS ANGELES HISTORICAL
BOTTLE CLUB
868 S. Duff Avenue
West Covina, California 91790

FIRST DOUBLE SPRINGS
COLLECTORS CLUB
13311 Illinois Street
Westminster, California 92683

WILLITS BOTTLE CLUB
c/o John Hathaway
Willits, California 95490

NAPA-SOLANG BOTTLE CLUB
P. O. Box 554
Yountville, California 94559

MARYSVILLE-YUBA CITY ANTIQUE
BOTTLE CLUB
475 South Barrett Road
Yuba City, California 95991

CHERRY VALLEY BOTTLE &
SPECIALTIES CLUB
12724 Ninth Street
Yucaipa, California 92399

ALAMOSA BOTTLE COLLECTORS
c/o Mrs. Robert Russell
Route 2 Box 170
Alamosa, Colorado 81101

HIGH-COUNTRY ANTIQUE
BOTTLE CLUB
311 14th Street
Alamosa, Colorado 81101

TIN CONTAINER COLLECTORS
ASSOCIATION
1496 S. Macon Street
Aurora, Colorado 80010

MILE HIGH EZRA BROOKS
BOTTLE CLUB
3685 Chase Court
Boulder, Colorado 80303

NORTHEASTERN ANTIQUE
BOTTLE CLUB
513 Curtis
Brush, Colorado 80723

AVON CLUB OF COLORADO
SPRINGS, COLORADO
707 N. Farragut
Colorado Springs, Colorado
80909

LIONSTONE WESTERN FIGURAL
CLUB
P. O. Box 2275
Colorado Springs, Colorado
80901

PEAKS & PLAINS ANTIQUE
BOTTLE CLUB
P. O. Box 814
Colorado Springs, Colorado
80901

FOUR CORNERS BOTTLE &
GLASS CLUB
P. O. Box 45
Cortez, Colorado 81321

ANTIQUE BOTTLE CLUB OF
COLORADO
P. O Box 63
Denver, Colorado 80201

ANTIQUE BOTTLE CLUB OF
COLORADO
2555 S. Raleigh
Denver, Colorado 80219

ROCKY MOUNTAIN JIM BEAM
BOTTLE & SPECIALTY CLUB
c/o George Hoeper
Alcott Station p. o. box 12162
Denver, Colorado 80212

HORSETOOTH ANTIQUE BOTTLE
COLLECTORS ASSOCIATION
P. O. Box 944
Fort Collins, Colorado 80521

NORTHEASTERN COLORADO
ANTIQUE BOTTLE CLUB
Route 1 Box 69
Ft. Morgan, Colorado 80701

NORTHERN COLORADO ANTIQUE
BOTTLE CLUB
227 W. Beaver Avenue
Ft. Morgan, Colorado 80701

WESTERN SLOPE BOTTLE CLUB
570 Grand Valley Drive
Grand Junction, Colorado 81501

TELLURIDE ANTIQUE BOTTLE
COLLECTORS
P. O. Box 344
Telluride, Colorado 81435

COLORADO MILE-HIGH EZRA
BROOKS BOTTLE CLUB
Mr. Gil Nation, President
7401 Decatur Street
Westminister, Colorado 80030

4-in-1 BOTTLE & DECANTER
CLUB
7401 Decatur Street
Westminster, Colorado 80030

CONNECTICUT SPECIALTIES
CLUB
c/o Steve Richardson
1135 Barnum Avenue
Bridgeport, Connecticut 06610

ANTIQUE BOTTLE CLUB OF
MIDDLETOWN, CONN.
P. O. Box 596
Middletown, Connecticut 06457

NUTMEG STATE BROOKS &
BEAM CLUB
c/o Roy Schmidt
25 Meadowood Drive
Middletown, Connecticut 06457

SOUTHERN CONNECTICUT
ANTIQUE BOTTLE CLUB
ASSOCIATION, INC.
60 Sassacus Drive
Milford, Connecticut 06460

SOUTHEASTERN NEW ENGLAND
ANTIQUE BOTTLE CLUB
656 Noank Road
Mystic, Connecticut 06355

SOMERS ANTIQUE BOTTLE CLUB,
INC.
P. O. Box 313
Somers, Connecticut 06071

CONNECTICUT SPECIALTIES
BOTTLE CLUB
P. O. Box 624
Stratford, Connecticut 06497

EAST COAST CLUB
c/o Art Swearsky
24 Gertrude Lane
West Haven, Connecticut 06516

MINIATURE BOTTLE MART
24 Gertrude Lane
West Haven, Connecticut 06516

TRI-STATE BOTTLE COLLECTORS
& DIGGERS CLUB
P. O. Box 6
Hockessin, Delaware 19707

MASON-DIXON BOTTLE
COLLECTORS ASSOCIATION
P. O. Box 505
Lewes, Delaware 19958

TRI-STATE BOTTLE COLLECTOR
& DIGGERS CLUB
c/o Thomas Morton
103 W. Park Place
Newark, Delaware 19711

APOLLO BEACH ANTIQUE
BOTTLE COLLECTORS
ASSOCIATION
P. O. Box 3354
Apollo Beach, Florida 33570

BAY CITY HISTORICAL BOTTLE
COLLECTORS
P. O. Box 3454
Apollo Beach, Florida 33570

M-T BOTTLE COLLECTORS
ASSOCIATION
P. O. Box 1581
Deland, Florida 32720

HARBOR CITY
1232 Causeway
Eau, Florida 32935

ISLAMORADA ORIGINAL FLORIDA
KEYS COLLECTORS CLUB
c/o Ella Ellis
P. O. Box 386
Islamorada, Florida 33036

ORIGINAL FLORIDA KEYS
COLLECTORS CLUB
P. O. Box 212
Islamorada, Florida 33036

ANTIQUE BOTTLE COLLECTORS
OF JACKSONVILLE
P. O. Box 1767
Jacksonville, Florida 32201

CENTRAL FLORIDA ANTIQUE
BOTTLE CLUB
1219 Plant Avenue
Lakeland, Florida 33801

ANTIQUE BOTTLE COLLECTORS
ASSOCIATION OF FLORIDA
4324 S.W. 13th Street
Miami, Florida 33144

ANTIQUE BOTTLE COLLECTORS
ASSOCIATION OF FLORIDA
14301 S. W. 87th Avenue
Miami, Florida 33158

FLORIDA NATIONAL EZRA
BROOKS BOTTLE & SPECIALTIES
CLUB
20706 S. Dixie Highway
Miami, Florida 33157

SOUTH FLORIDA JIM BEAM
BOTTLE & SPECIALTIES CLUB
5251 S.W. Second St.
Miami, Florida 33134

SOUTH FLORIDA JIM BEAM
BOTTLE & SPECIALTIES CLUB
9300 S. Dixie Highway
Miami, Florida 33156

WORLD WIDE MINIATURE BOTTLE
CLUB
11120 Killian Park Road
Miami, Florida 33156

MID-STATE ANTIQUE BOTTLE
COLLECTORS ASSOCIATION
3400 East Grant Avenue
Orlando, Florida 32806

MID-STATE ANTIQUE BOTTLE
COLLECTORS INC.
3122 Corrine Drive
Orlando, Florida 32803

ST. ANDREW BAY BOTTLE CLUB
ASSOCIATION
P. O. Box 12082
Panama City, Florida 32401

PENSACOLA BOTTLE & RELIC
COLLECTORS ASSOCIATION
1004 Fremont Avenue
Pensacola, Florida 32505

NORTHWEST FLORIDA REGIONAL
BOTTLE CLUB
P. O. Box 282
Port St. Joe, Florida 32456

SUNCOAST ANTIQUE BOTTLE
CLUB
P. O. Box 12712
St. Petersburg, Florida 33733

SANFORD ANTIQUE BOTTLE
COLLECTORS CLUB
P. O. Box 169
Sanford, Florida 32771

THE ANTIQUE BOTTLE
COLLECTORS OF SARASOTA
P. O. Box 11614
Bee Ridge Station
Sarasota, Florida 33578

WEST COAST FLORIDA EZRA
BROOKS BOTTLE CLUB
1360 Harbor Drive
Sarasota, Florida 33579

TAMPA ANTIQUE BOTTLE
COLLECTORS
P. O. Box 4232
Tampa, Florida 33607

PEACHSTATE BOTTLE &
SPECIALTY CLUB
1869 Shepherd Circle S.W.
Atlanta, Georgia 30311

BULLDOG DOUBLE SPRINGS
BOTTLE COLLECTOR CLUB OF
AUGUSTA, GEORGIA
1916 Melrose Drive
Augusta, Georgia 30906

GEORGIA-CAROLINA EMPTY
BOTTLE CLUB
2352 Devere Street
Augusta, Georgia 30904

GEORGIA BOTTLE CLUB
c/o Tom Zachary
2996 Pangborn Road
Decatur, Georgia 30033

SOUTHEASTERN ANTIQUE
BOTTLE CLUB
2996 Pangborn Road
Decatur, Georgia 30033

SOUTHEASTERN ANTIQUE
BOTTLE CLUB
8781 Channing Dr.
Jonesboro, Georgia 30236

MACON ANTIQUE BOTTLE CLUB
P. O. Box 5395
Macon, Georgia 31208

COASTAL EMPIRE BOTTLE CLUB
P. O. Box 3714 Station B
Savannah, Georgia 31404

ANTIQUE BOTTLE CLUB OF
HAWAII
P. O. Box 591
Ewa, Hawaii 96706

HAWAII BOTTLE COLLECTORS
CLUB
P. O. Box 8618
Honolulu, Hawaii 96815

GEM ANTIQUE BOTTLE CLUB,
INC.
P. O. Box 8051
Boise, Idaho 83707

BUHL ANTIQUE BOTTLE CLUB
Route 3
Buhl, Idaho 83316

ROCK & BOTTLE CLUB
c/o Mrs. M. E. Boothe
Route 1
Fruitland, Idaho 83619

EAGLE ROCK HISTORICAL
ASSOCIATION
P. O. Box 2321
Idaho Falls, Idaho 83401

PACATELLO ANTIQUE BOTTLE
CLUB ASSOCIATION
Route 2
Inkon, Idaho 83245

EM TEE BOTTLE CLUB
P. O. Box 62
Jerome, Idaho 83338

FABULOUS VALLEY ANTIQUE
BOTTLE CLUB
P. O Box 769
Osburn, Idaho 83849

FABULOUS VALLEY ANTIQUE
BOTTLE CLUB
P. O. Box 638
Osburn, Idaho 83849

POCATELLO ANTIQUE BOTTLE
COLLECTORS ASSOCIATION
915 Yellowstone
Pocatello, Idaho 83201

GREATER ST. LOUIS AREA BEAM
BOTTLE CLUB
c/o Jack Huggins
103 Powder Mill Road
Belleville, Illinois 62223

INTERNATIONAL EZRA BROOKS
BOTTLE CLUB
103 Powder Mill Road
Belleville, Illinois 62223

ILLINI JOM BEAM BOTTLE &
SPECIALTY CLUB
P. O. Box 13
Champaign, Illinois 61820

CHICAGO EZRA BROOKS BOTTLE
CLUB
2118 E. 100th Street
Chicago, Illinois 60617

FIRST CHICAGO BOTTLE CLUB
1419 W. Fullerton
Chicago, Illinois 60614

METRO EAST BOTTLE & JAR
ASSOCIATION
c/o Wyndham Losser
1702 North Keesler
Collinsville, Illinois 62234

LAND OF LINCOLN BOTTLE CLUB
P. O. Box 2079
Decatur, Illinois 62521

HEART OF ILLINOIS ANTIQUE
BOTTLE CLUB
2010 Bloomington Road
East Peoria, Illinois 61611

INTERNATIONAL EZRA BROOKS
CLUB
c/o Community Room
Industrial Savings & Loan
Association
5000 State Street
E. St. Louis, Illinois 62205

CHICAGO EZRA BROOKS BOTTLE
& SPECIALTY CLUB
8224 West 93rd Place
Hickory Hills, Illinois 60457

SWEET CORN CAPITOL BOTTLE
CLUB
c/o Bill Rankin
1015 W. Orange
Hoopeston, Illinois 60942

CHICAGO EZRA BROOKS BOTTLE
& SPECIALTY CLUB
1305 W. Marion Street
Joliet, Illinois 60436

JOLIET BOTTLE CLUB
c/o C. W. Sieber
12 E. Kenmore Avenue
Joliet, Illinois 60431

LOUIS JOLIET BOTTLE &
SPECIALTY CLUB
320 Pearle Street
Joliet, Illinois 60433

EZRA BROOKS BOTTLE &
SPECIALTIES CLUB
420 N. First Street
Kewanee, Illinois 61443

NATIONAL EZRA BROOKS
BOTTLE & SPECIALTIES CLUB
420 West 1st Street
Kewanee, Illinois 61443

KELLY CLUB
c/o Mary Kelly
147 North Brainard Avenue
La Grange, Illinois 60525

CENTRAL & MIDWESTERN
STATES BEAM & SPECIALTIES
CLUB
c/o Elmer Collins
44 S. Westmore
Lombard, Illinois 60148

FIRST CHICAGO BOTTLE CLUB
P. O. Box 254
Palatine, Illinois 60067

PEKIN BOTTLE COLLECTORS
ASSOCIATION
P. O. Box 535
Pekin, Illinois 61554

BLACKHAWK JIM BEAM BOTTLE
& SPECIALTIES CLUB
2003 Kishwaukee Street
Rockford, Illinois 61101

ILLINOIS BOTTLE CLUB
P. O. Box 181
Rushville, Illinois 62681

SAUK VILLAGE BOTTLE CLUB
21911 Merriell Avenue
Sauk Village, Illinois 60411

METRO-EAST BOTTLE AND JAR
ASSOCIATION
5305 A Hesse Avenue
Scott AFB, Illinois 62225

ILLINOIS BOTTLE CLUB
Route 1
Topeka, Illinois 61567

INDIANA EZRA BROOKS BOTTLE
CLUB
72 North 14th Street
Beech Grove, Indiana 49107

WE FOUND 'EM BOTTLE &
INSULATOR CLUB
P. O. Box 578
Bunker Hill, Indiana 46914

STEEL CITY EZRA BROOKS CLUB
3506 Revere Court
East Gary, Indiana 46405

FORT WAYNE BOTTLE CLUB
c/o Thurman Fuhrman
5622 Arbor Avenue
Ft. Wayne, Indiana 46807

FORT WAYNE HISTORICAL
BOTTLE CLUB
4040 South Drive
Fort Wayne, Indiana 46805

HOOSIER BOTTLE CLUB
c/o Fred Challis
P. O. Box 33126
Indianapolis, Indiana 46203

INDIANA EZRA BROOKS BOTTLE
CLUB
P. O. Box 24344
Indianapolis, Indiana 46224

FOUR FLAGS EZRA BROOKS
BOTTLE CLUB
c/o Mr. Peter Groote, President
P. O. Box 791
Mishawaka, Indiana 46544

FORT WAYNE HISTORICAL
BOTTLE CLUB
R. R. #1
Ossian, Indiana 46777

STEEL CITY EZRA BROOKS
BOTTLE CLUB
c/o Moose Lodge
2937 County Line Road
Portage, Indiana 46368

DES MOINES JIM BEAM &
SPECIALTY CLUB
c/o Edward Van Dyke
2417 48th Street
Des Moines, Iowa 50310

HAWKEYE DES MOINES AVON
CLUB
1406 60th
Des Moines, Iowa 50311

IOWA ANTIQUE BOTTLEERS
1506 Albia Road
Ottumwa, Iowa 52501

IOWA BOTTLEERS
902 N. Johnson
Ottumwa, Iowa 52501

LARKIN BOTTLE CLUB
c/o Clarence Larkin
107 W. Grimes
Red Oak, Iowa 51566

CHEROKEE STRIP EZRA BROOKS
BOTTLE & SPECIALTY CLUB
P. O. Box 631
Arkansas City, Kansas 67005

FLINT HILLS BEAM & SPECIALTY
CLUB
201 W. Pine
El Dorado, Kansas 67042

JAYHAWK BOTTLE CLUB
7919 Grant
Overland Park, Kansas 66212

NATIONAL AVON CLUB
P. O. Box 5490
Overland Park, Kansas 66212

ANTIQUE BOTTLE CLUB
c/o Bob Billamagna
2502 W. 32nd St. South
Apt. "D"
Wichita, Kansas 67217

WICHITA EZRA BROOKS BOTTLE
& SPECIALTIES CLUB
Mr. Larry Carter, President
8045 Peachtree Street
Wichita, Kansas 67207

LOUISVILLE BOTTLE
COLLECTORS
11819 Garrs Avenue
Anchorage, Kentucky 40223

KENTUCKY CARDINAL BEAM
BOTTLE CLUB
428 Templin
Bardstown, Kentucky 41104

KENTUCKY BLUEGRASS EZRA
BROOKS BOTTLE CLUB
6202 Tabor Drive
Louisville, Kentucky 40218

HISTORICAL BOTTLE
ASSOCIATION OF BATON ROUGE
1843 Tudor Drive
Baton Rouge, Louisiana 70815

DIXIE DIGGERS BOTTLE CLUB
P. O. Box 626
Empire, Louisiana 70050

CAJUN COUNTRY COUSINS
1004 Malcolm Street
Franklin, Louisiana 70538

CAJUN COUNTRY COUSINS EZRA
BROOKS BOTTLE & SPECIALTY
CLUB
P. O. Box 462
Franklin, Louisiana 70538

NEW ORLEANS ANTIQUE BOTTLE
CLUB
1016 Carnation Avenue
Metairie, Louisiana 70001

BAYOU TECHE BOTTLE CLUB
503 Oak Street
New Iberia, Louisiana 70560

NEW ORLEANS ANTIQUE BOTTLE
CLUB
1507 Exposition Blvd.
New Orleans, Louisiana 70118

NORTHEAST LOUISIANA BOTTLE
& INSULATOR CLUB
112 Pinewood Drive
West Monroe, Louisiana 71291

DIRIGO BOTTLE COLLECTOR'S
CLUB
c/o 59 Fruit Street
Bangor, Maine 04401

PAUL BUNYON BOTTLE CLUB
c/o Mrs. Francis Kearns
237 14th Street
Bangor, Maine 04401

WALDO COUNTY BOTTLENECKS
CLUB
Head-of-the-Tide
Belfast, Maine 04915

TRI-COUNTY BOTTLE
COLLECTORS ASSOCIATION
c/o John E. Irvin
RFD 3
Dexter, Maine 04930

DOVER FOXCROFT BOTTLE CLUB
c/o Wayne Champion
O Church Street
Dover Foxcroft, Maine 04426

IM BEAM COLLECTORS CLUB
O Lunt Road
Falmouth, Maine 04105

NEW ENGLAND BOTTLE CLUB
Parsonfield, Maine 04047

PINETREE BOTTLE CLUB
c/o Gene Swiger
9 School Street
South Portland, Maine 04100

MID COAST BOTTLE CLUB
c/o Miriam Winchenbach
Waldoboro, Maine 04572

MASON-DIXON BOTTLE
COLLECTORS ASSOCIATION
01 Market Street
Denton, Maryland 21629

BLUE & GRAY EZRA BROOKS
BOTTLE CLUB
106 Sunnybrook Drive
Fredrick, Maryland 21201

CATOCTIN BEAM BOTTLE CLUB
P. O. Box 384
Frederick, Maryland 21701

BALTIMORE ANTIQUE BOTTLE
HOUNDS
c/o Route 2 Box 379
Glenarm, Maryland 21057

THE BOTTLE PROSPECTORS
CLUB
c/o Brewster Town Hall
Brewster, Massachusetts 02631

ESSEX COUTY BOTTLE CLUB
7c Broad Street
East Lynn, Massachusetts 01902

NEW ENGLAND BEAM &
SPECIALTIES CLUB
5 Merritt Avenue
Groveland, Massachusetts 01830

NEW ENGLAND COLLECTORS
CLUB
c/o Al Goodrich
Groveland, Massachusetts 01830

BERKSHIRE ANTIQUE BOTTLE
ASSOCIATION
P. O. Box 294
Lee, Massachusetts 01238

NEW ENGLAND BOTTLE
COLLECTORS ASSOCIATION
7a Broad Street
Lynn, Massachusetts 01902

MERRIMACK VALLEY BOTTLE
CLUB
96 Elm Street
North Andover, Massachusetts
01845

SATUIT ANTIQUE BOTTLE CLUB
P. O. Box 27
North Scituate, Massachusetts
02060

THE BOTTLE PROSPECTOR'S
CLUB
143 Main Street
Yarmouth Port, Massachusetts
02675

TRAVERSE AREA BOTTLE &
INSULATOR CLUB
P. O. Box 205
Acme, Michigan 49610

MICHIANA BOTTLE CLUB
P. O. Box 135
Buchanan, Michigan 49120

AVON BOTTLE COLLECTOR'S
CLUB OF DETROIT
P. O. Box 8683
Detroit, Michigan 48224

WORLD WIDE AVON BOTTLE
COLLECTORS CLUB
P. O. Box 8683
Detroit, Michigan 48224

FLINT ANTIQUE BOTTLE CLUB
1460 Coutant Street
Flushing, Michigan 48433

YE OLD BOTTLE CLUB
Gaastra, Michigan 49027

MICHIGAN BOTTLE CLUB
145 Spruce Box 48
Hemlock, Michigan 48626

DICKINSON COUNTY BOTTLE
CLUB
717 Henford Avenue
Iron Mountain, Michigan 49801

YE OLDE CORKERS BOTTLE CLUB
c/o Shirley Wodzinski
Route 1
Iron River, Michigan 49935

MANISTEE COIN & BOTTLE CLUB
207 E. Piney Road
Manistee, Michigan 49660

HURON VALLEY BOTTLE CLUB
12475 Saline-Milan Road
Milan, Michigan 48160

WOLVERINE BEAM BOTTLE &
SPECIALTY CLUB OF MICHIGAN
36009 Larchwood
Mt. Clemens, Michigan 48043

FOUR FLAGS EZRA BROOKS
BOTTLE CLUB
P. O. Box 653
Niles, Michigan 49120

MICHIANA BOTTLE CLUB
c/o Morgan L. Thornburgh
1508 Fulkerson Road
Niles, Michigan 49120

EMMETT HISTORICAL BOTTLE
ASSOCIATION
108 Grove Street
Petoskey, Michigan 49770

NORTHERN MICHIGAN BOTTLE
CLUB
P. O. Box 421
Petoskey, Michigan 49770

METROPLITAN DETROIT BOTTLE
CLUB
c/o Alice Stephens
17721 Martin Rroad
Roseville, Michigan 48066

LIONSTONE COLLECTORS
BOTTLE & SPECIALTIES CLUB OF
MICHIGAN
c/o Walter Steck
3089 Grand Blanc Road
Swartz Creek, Michigan 48473

LAKE SUPERIOR ANTIQUE
BOTTLE CLUB
P. O. Box 67
Knife River, Minnesota 55609

MINNESOTA'S FIRST ANTIQUE
BOTTLE CLUB
5001 Queen Avenue North
Minneapolis, Minnesota 55430

NORTH STAR HISTORICAL
BOTTLE ASSOCIATION
3308 32nd Avenue South
Minneapolis, Minnesota 55406

ARNFALT COLLECTORS BEAM
CLUB
c/o Tony Arnfalt
New Richland, Minnesota 56072

THE MAGNOLIA STATE BOTTLE
CLUB
P. O. Box 6023
Handsboro, Mississippi 39501

MIDDLE MISSISSIPPI ANTIQUE
BOTTLE CLUB
P. O. Box 233
Jackson, Mississippi 39205

SOUTH MISSISSIPPI ANTIQUE
BOTTLE CLUB
c/o Aaron Rogers
203 S. 4th Avenue
Laurel, Mississippi 39440

MID-WEST ANTIQUE BOTTLE &
HOBBY CLUB
Community Building Downtown
Park
El Dorado Springs, Missouri
64744

ST. LOUIS ANTIQUE BOTTLE
COLLECTOR ASSOCIATION
306 N. Woodlawn Avenue
Kirkwood, Missouri 63122

MINERAL AREA BOTTLE CLUB
Knob Lick, Missouri 63651

HEART OF THE OZARKS
Ozark, Missouri 65721

N.W. MISSOURI BOTTLE & RELIC
CLUB
3706 Woodlawn Terrace
St. Joseph, Missouri 64506

ST. LOUIS ANTIQUE BOTTLE
ASSOCIATION
c/o Joseph Messler
32 W. Jackson
Webster Groves, Missouri 63119

ST. LOUIS EZRA BROOKS
CERAMICS CLUB
42 Webster Acres
Webster Groves, Missour 63119

BOZEMAN BOTTLE BUGS
c/o Mrs. Delmer Self
519 1/2 E. Lamme
Bozeman, Montana 59715

HELLGATE ANTIQUE BOTTLE
CLUB
P. O. Box 411
Missoula, Montana 59801

J. V. GUNN MIDWESTERN EZRA
BROOKS BOTTLE CLUB
P. O. Box 29198
Lincoln, Nebraska 68529

MINI-SEEKERS
Walter Jackman
"A" Acres, Rt. 8
Lincoln, Nebraska 68506

NEBRASKA BIG RED BOTTLE &
SPECIALTY CLUB
N. Street Drive-In
200 So. 18th Street
Lincoln, Nebraska 68508

NEBRASKA ANTIQUE BOTTLE &
COLLECTORS CLUB
1718 South 8th
Omaha, Nebraska 68108

MINERAL COUNTY ANTIQUE
BOTTLE CLUB
P. O. Box 349
Babbitt, Nevada 89415

EAGLE VALLEY GOPHERS
ANTIQUE BOTTLE CLUB
805 Winnie Lane
Carson City, Nevada 89701

VIRGINIA & TRUCKEE JIM BEAM
BOTTLE & SPECIALTIES CLUB
P. O. Box 1596
Carson City, Nevada 89701

NEVADA BEAM CLUB
c/o Terry duPont III
The B-Lazy-2
P. O. Box 426
Fallon, Nevada 89406

SOUTHERN NEVADA ANTIQUE
BOTTLE CLUB
1807 Commerce Street
Las Vegas, Nevada 89102

SO. NEVADA ANTIQUE BOTTLE
COLLECTORS, INC.
884 Lulu
Las Vegas, Nevada 89109

WEE BOTTLE CLUB
INTERNATIONAL (Minis)
304 Orland Street Apt. #56
Las Vegas, Nevada 89107

ANTIQUE BOTTLE CLUB
ASSOCIATION OF RENO-SPARKS
4965 Mason Road
Reno, Nevada 89500

RENO-SPARKS ANTIQUE BOTTLE
COLLECTORS ASSOCIATION
P. O. Box 6145
Reno, Nevada 89503

SILVER STATE EZRA BROOKS
CLUB
2030 Clear Acre Lane
Reno, Nevada 89502

TONOPAH ANTIQUE BOTTLE
CLUB
P. O. Box 545
Tonopah, Nevada 89049

BOTTLEERS OF NEW HAMPSHIRE
c/o RFD Bow Lake
Bow Lake, New Hampshire 03884

BOTTLEERS OF NEW HAMPSHIRE
125A Central Street
Farmington, New Hampshire
03835

NEW ENGLAND BEAM &
SPECIALTIES CLUB
P. O. Box 502
Greenville, New Hampshire 03048

NEW ENGLAND BOTTLE CLUB
P. O. Box 472
Henniker, New Hampshire 03242

YANKEE BOTTLE CLUB
511 Marloboro Street
Keene, New Hampshire 03431

YANKEE BOTTLE CLUB
c/o Kay Fox
Page Street
Keene, New Hampshire 03431

GRANITE STATE BOTTLE CLUB
c/o Alfred Davis
116 Academy Street
Laconia, New Hampshire 03246

JERSEY DEVIL BOTTLE DIGGERS
P. O. Box 64
Birmingham, New Jersey 08111

SOUTH JERSEY'S HERITAGE
BOTTLE & GLASS CLUB
P. O. Box 122
Glassboro, New Jersey 08028

NORTH JERSEY ANTIQUE BOTTL
CLUB ASSOCIATION
14 Birchwood Road
Hawthorne, New Jersey 07506

JERSEY DEVIL'S BOTTLE
DIGGERS
P. O. Box 131 Main Street
Juliustown, New Jersey 08042

SOUTH JERSEY HERITAGE
BOTTLE & GLASS CLUB
c/o Old Bottle & Book Barn
Harmony Road Route 295
Mickleton, New Jersey 08056

SUSSEX COUNTY ANTIQUE
BOTTLE COLLECTORS
Division of Sussex County
Historical Society
82 Main Street
Newton, New Jersey 07860

TRENTON JIM BEAM BOTTLE
CLUB
Route #31
Pennington Circle
Pennington, New Jersey 08534

TWIN BRIDGES BEAM BOTTLE &
SPECIALTY CLUB
P. O. Box 347
Pennsville, New Jersey 08070

LIONSTONE COLLECTORS CLUB
OF DELAWARE VALLEY
R. D. #3 Box 93
Sewell, New Jersey 08080

LAKELAND ANTIQUE BOTTLE
CLUB
24 Main Street
Succasunna, New Jersey 07876

TRENTON JIM BEAM BOTTLE
CLUB, INC.
324 Whitehead Road
Trenton, New Jersey 08638

THE JERSEY SHORE BOTTLE
CLUB
c/o RD #1 Box 72V
Toms River, New Jersey 08753

ARTIFACT HUNTERS
ASSOCIATION INC.
c/o 29 Lake Road
Wayne, New Jersey 07470

NORTH NEW JERSEY ANTIQUE
BOTTLE CLUB ASSOCIATION
P. O. Box 617
Westwood, New Jersey 07675

ROAD RUNNERS BOTTLE CLUB
OF ALBUQUERQUE
Mrs. Forella Tubb
3235 Reina Ct., N. E.
Albuquerque, New Mexico 8711

ROADRUNNER BOTTLE CLUB O
NEW MEXICO
6712 Carlton N.W.
Albuquerque, New Mexico 8710

AVE CITY ANTIQUE BOTTLE
LUB
oute 1, Box 155
arlsbad, New Mexico 88220

ORTHERN NEW YORK BOTTLE
LUB ASSOCIATION
. O. Box 257
dams Center, New York 13606

RYON BOTTLE BADGERS
. D. #5
msterdam, New York 12010

OUTHERN TIER BOTTLE &
NSULATOR COLLECTORS
SSOCIATION
6 Bigelow Street
inghamton, New York 13904

INGER LAKES BOTTLE CLUB
SSOCIATION
742 Sweeney Road R.D. 4
ortland, New York 13045

INGER LAKES BOTTLE CLUB
SSOCIATION
. O. Box 815
haca, New York 14850

HE GREATER CATSKILL
NTIQUE BOTTLE CLUB
iberty, New York 12754

MPIRE STATE BOTTLE
OLLECTORS ASSOCIATION
135 Wetzel Road
iverpool, New York 13088

VESTERN NEW YORK BOTTLE
OLLECTORS
339 Lake Avenue
ockport, New York 14094

CATSKILL MOUNTAINS JIM BEAM
OTTLE CLUB
/o William Gibbs
ix Gardner Avenue
Middletown, New York 10940

MPIRE STATE BOTTLE &
PECIALTY CLUB
/o William Bateman
ast Main Street
Milford, New York 13807

JPPER SUSQUEHANNA BOTTLE
LUB
. O. Box 183
Milford, New York 13807

COLLECTORS GUILD
925 Pine Avenue
Niagara Falls, New York 14301

UFFOLK COUNTY ANTIQUE
OTTLE ASSOCIATION
31 Harborview Drive
Northport, New York 11768

ST. LAWRENCE SEAWAY VALLEY
BEAM-BROOKS SPECIALTY CLUB
R. D. #2
Potsdam, New York 13676

GENESEE VALLEY BOTTLE
COLLECTORS ASSOCIATION
P. O. Box 9666
Midtown Post Office
Rochester, New York 14604

ROCHESTER NEW YORK BOTTLE
CLUB
7908 West Henrietta Road
Rush, New York 14543

CHAUTAUQUA COUNTY BOTTLE
COLLECTORS CLUB
Morse Hotel
Main Street
Sherman, New York 14781

RENSSELAER COUNTY ANTIQUE
BOTTLE CLUB
c/o Lester Keller
P. O. Box 564
Troy, New York 12180

EASTERN MONROE COUNTRY
BOTTLE CLUB
c/o Bethlehem Lutheran Church
1767 Plank Road
Webster, New York 14580

WEST VALLEY BOTTLETIQUE
West Valley, New York 14171

CAROLINA BOTTLE CLUB
c/o Industrial Piping Co.
Anonwood, Charlotte, North
Carolina 28210

ALBERMARLE BOTTLE &
COLLECTORS CLUB
c/o Sam Taylor, Secretary
Rt. 3 Box 687-A
Elizabeth City, North Carolina
27909

GOLDSBORO BOTTLE CLUB
117 North James Street
Goldsboro, North Carolina 27530

GREATER GREENSBORO MOOSE
EZRA BROOKS BOTTLE CLUB
217 S. Elm Street
Greensboro, North Carolina
27401

KINSTON COLLECTORS CLUB,
INC.
c/o 325 E. Lenoir
Kinston, North Carolina 28501

RUBBER CAPITOL JIM BEAM
CLUB
543 Stratford Avenue
Akron, Ohio 44303

OHIO BOTTLE CLUB
P. O. Box 585
Barberton, Ohio 44203

HERMAN'S BOTTLE CLUB
3640 Warrensville Center Rd. Apt.
#3
Cleveland, Ohio 44122

CENTRAL OHIO BOTTLE CLUB
P. O. Box 19864
Columbus, Ohio 43219

DIAMOND PIN WINNERS AVON
CLUB
5281 Fredonia Avenue
Dayton, Ohio 45431

INTERNATIONAL DECANTERS
CLUB
c/o Opal Redman
101 E. Third St.
Dayton, Ohio 45402

THE BUCKEYE BOTTLE CLUB
c/o Gilbert Gill
229 Oakwood Street
Elyria, Ohio 44035

OHIO EZRA BROOKS BOTTLE
CLUB
8741 Kirtland Chardon Road
Kirtland Hills, Ohio 44094

KIM CLUB FOR BOTTLE
COLLECTORS
22000 Shaker Blvd.
Shaker Heights, Ohio 44122

BUCKEYE BOTTLE DIGGERS
Route 1
Thornville, Ohio 43076

NORTHWEST OHIO BOTTLE CLUB
P. O. Box 822
Toledo, Ohio 43601

BAR-DEW ANTIQUE BOTTLE CLUB
817 E. 7th Street
Dewey, Oklahoma 74029

LITTLE DIXIE ANTIQUE BOTTLE
CLUB
P. O. Box 741
Krebs, Oklahoma 74501

SOUTHWEST OKLAHOMA
ANTIQUE BOTTLE CLUB
35 S. 49th Street
Lawton, Oklahoma 73501

SOONER EZRA BROOKS BOTTLE
CLUB
7309 South Klein
Oklahoma City, Oklahoma 73139

PONCA CITY OLD BOTTLE CLUB
2408 Juanito
Ponca City, Oklahoma 74601

ANTIQUE BOTTLES & RELIC CLUB
2517 E. 10 Street
Tulsa, Oklahoma 74104

McDONNEL DOUGLAS ANTIQUE
CLUB
5752 E. 25th Place
Tulsa, Oklahoma 74114

TULSA ANTIQUE BOTTLE & RELIC
c/o 2517 E. 10th Street
Tulsa, Oklahoma 74104

TULSA OKLAHOMA BOTTLE CLUB
5752 E. 25th Place
Tulsa, Oklahoma 74114

OREGON BOTTLE CLUB
ASSOCIATION
P. O. Box 175
Aurora, Oregon 97002

CENTRAL OREGON BOTTLE &
RELIC COLLECTORS
c/o Danny McCoy
5 Kansas
Bend, Oregon 97701

SOUTHERN OREGON BOTTLE
CLUB, INC.
P. O. Box 335
Canyonville, Oregon 97417

EMERALD EMPIRE BOTTLE CLUB
Rattlesnake Creek Road
Dexter, Oregon 97431

EMERALD EMPIRE BOTTLE CLUB
P. O. Box 292
Eugene, Oregon 97401

GOLD DIGGERS ANTIQUE BOTTLE
CLUB
P. O. Box 56
Gold Hill, Oregon 97525

PIONEER FRUIT JAR
COLLECTORS ASSOCIATION
P. O. Box 175
Grand Ronde, Oregon 97347

CENTRAL SOUTH OREGON
ANTIQUE BOTTLE CLUB
708 South F. Street
Lakeview, Oregon 97630

GOLD DIGGERS ANTIQUE BOTTLE
CLUB
1958 South Stage Road
Medford, Oregon 97501

OREGON BOTTLE COLLECTORS
ASSOCIATION
4207 S.E. Covell
Milwaukee, Oregon 97222

OREGON ANTIQUE BOTTLE CLUB
c/o William Blackburn
Route 3 Box 23
Molalla, Oregon 97038

MOLALLA BOTTLE CLUB
Route 1 Box 205
Mulino, Oregon 97042

FRONTIER COLLECTORS
504 N. W. Bailey
Pendleton, Oregon 97801

LEWIS & CLARK BOTTLE CLUB
ASSOCIATION
8435 S.W. 52nd Avenue
Portland, Oregon 97219

LEWIS & CLARK HISTORICAL
BOTTLE SOCIETY
4828 N. E. 33
Portland, Oregon 97211

EAST COAST DOUBLE SPRINGS
SPECIALTY BOTTLE CLUB
P. O. Box 419
Carlisle, Pennsylvania 17013

WASHINGTON COUNTY BOTTLE
& INSULATOR CLUB
R. D. #1 Box 342
Carmichaels, Pennsylvania 15320

FRIENDLY JIM'S BEAM CLUB
c/o James Bradley, Sr.
508 Benjamin Franklin H.W. East
Douglassville, Pennsylvania 19518

FORKS OF THE DELAWARE
BOTTLE CLUB
P. O. Box 693
Easton, Pennsylvania 18042

PENNSYLVANIA DUTCH JIM
BEAM BOTTLE CLUB
812 Pointview Avenue
Ephrata, Pennsylvania 17522

ERIE BOTTLE CLUB
P. O. Box 373
Erie, Pennsylvania 16512

ENDLESS MOUNTAIN ANTIQUE
BOTTLE CLUB
P. O. Box 75
Granville Summit, Pennsylvania
16926

INDIANA BOTTLE CLUB
240 Oak Street
Indiana, Pennsylvania 15701

PITTSBURGH BOTTLE CLUB
P. O. Box 401
Ingomar, Pennsylvania 15127

EAST COAST EZRA BROOKS
BOTTLE CLUB
2815 Fiddler Green
Lancaster, Pennsylvania 17601

PENNSYLVANIA BOTTLE
COLLECTOR'S ASSOCIATION
D. Eugene Heisey
RD 4
Manheim, Pennsylvania 17545

BEAVER VALLEY JIM BEAM CLUB
c/o Wilson J. Bragg
1216 Nimick Avenue
Monaca, Pennsylvania 15061

TRI-COUNTY ANTIQUE BOTTLE &
TREASURE CLUB
R. D. #2 Box 30
Reynoldsville, Pennsylvania 15851

TRI-COUNTY BOTTLE &
TREASURE CLUB
c/o Dwight A. Zimmerman
Box 320 Route 2
Reynoldsville, Pennsylvania 15851

DELAWARE VALLEY BOTTLE
CLUB
P. O. Box 19
Revere, Pennsylvania 18953

PENNSYLVANIA BOTTLE
COLLECTORS ASSOCIATION
743 Woodberry Road
York, Pennsylvania 17403

LITTLE RHODY BOTTLE CLUB
67 Roslyn Avenue
Providence, Rhode Island 02908

UNION BOTTLE CLUB
c/o Russell E. Clark
Linervilla Road
Buffalo, South Carolina 29321

SOUTH CAROLINA BOTTLE CLUB
2812 Duncan Street
Columbia, South Carolina 29210

GREER BOTTLE COLLECTORS
CLUB
Trade Street
Greer, South Carolina 29651

LOW COUNTRY ANTIQUE BOTTLE
COLLECTORS
P. O. Box 274
John's Island, South Carolina
29455

GREATER SMOKY MOUNTAIN
EZRA BROOKS BOTTLE CLUB
P. O. Box 3351
Knoxville, Tennessee 37917

GREATER SMOKY MOUNTAIN JIM
BEAM BOTTLE CLUB
7209 Cresthill Drive
Knoxville, Tennessee 37919

GREAT SMOKY MOUNTAIN BEAM
BOTTLE & SPECIALTY CLUB
Donald Payne
c/o B & T Distributing Company
P. O. Box 3351
Knoxville, Tennessee 37917

FEDERATION OF HISTORICAL
BOTTLE CLUBS
c/o Gene Bradberry
4098 Faxon Avenue
Memphis, Tennessee 38122

MEMPHIS ANTIQUE BOTTLE
CLUB
1070 Terry Circle
Memphis, Tennessee 38107

MEMPHIS BOTTLE COLLECTORS
CLUB
c/o 4083 Wildwood Drive
Memphis, Tennessee 38111

MIDDLE TENNESSEE BOTTLE
COLLECTORS CLUB
2804 Belmont Apt. 1
Nashville, Tennessee 37212

MIDDLE TENNESSEE BOTTLE
COLLECTORS CLUB
P. O. Box 12083
Nashville, Tennessee 37212

GULF COAST BEAM CLUB
P. O. Box 299
Baytown, Texas 77520

FOARD C. HOBBY CLUB
P. O. Box 625
Crowell, Texas 79227

TEXAS LONGHORN BOTTLE CLUB
16 Riverwood Road
Dallas, Texas 75217

AMERICAN ASSOCIATION OF
PERFUME COLLECTORS
P. O. Box 55074
Houston, Texas 77055

TEXAS LONGHORN BOTTLE CLUB
P. O. Box 5346
Irving, Texas 75060

FOURSOME (Jim Beam)
J. G. Lewis, Sr.
208 Azalea Drive
Longview, Texas 75601

FORT CONCHO BOTTLE CLUB
c/o Ave-N-Driv-Up Antique Bottle
Shop
703 West Avenue
N. San Angelo, Texas 76901

GULF COAST BOTTLE & JAR
CLUB
221 Camille
Pasadena, Texas 77503

ALAMO CHAPTER ANTIQUE
BOTTLE CLUB ASSOCIATION
c/o Robert Duff
101 Castano Avenue
San Antonio, Texas 78209

SAN ANTONIO ANTIQUE BOTTLE
CLUB
c/o 3801 Broadway
Witte Museum - Auditorium
San Antonio, Texas 78209

UTAH ANTIQUE BOTTLE CLUB
3 Villa Drive
Clearfield, Utah 84015

UTAH ANTIQUE BOTTLE CLUB
P. O. Box 15
Ogden, Utah 84402

UTAH ANTIQUE BOTTLE SOCIETY
4907 S. 2400-A
Roy, Utah 84067

GREEN MOUNTAIN BOTTLE CLUB
c/o Fred Brown
P. O. Box 269
Bradford, Vermont 05033

HISTORICAL BOTTLE DIGGERS
Route 3 Box 204
Broadway, Virginia 22815

DIXIE BEAM BOTTLE CLUB
Forest Hill Avenue
Clarksville, Virginia 23927

YE OLD BOTTLE CLUB
General Delivery
Clarksville, Virginia 23927

RICHMOND AREA BOTTLE
COLLECTORS ASSOCIATION
5901 Wonderland Lane
Mechanicsville, Virginia 23111

BOTTLE CLUB OF THE VIRGINIA
PENINSULA
P. O. Box 5456
Newport News, Virginia 23605

MILKBOTTLES ONLY
ORGANIZATION (MOO)
P. O. Box 5456
Newport News, Virginia 23605

OLD DOMINION BOTTLE CLUB
c/o 8434 Tidewater Drive
Norfolk, Virginia 23518

HAMPTON ROADS AREA BOTTLE
COLLECTORS ASSOCIATION
P. O. Box 3061
Portsmouth, Virginia 23701

RICHMOND AREA BOTTLE CLUB
ASSOCIATION
3064 Forest Hills Avenue
Richmond, Virginia 23225

HISTORICAL BOTTLE DIGGERS OF
VIRGINIA
129 Third Street
Stuarts Draft, Virginia 24477

WASHINGTON STATE ANTIQUE
BOTTLE CLUB ASSOCIATION
1200 112 S.W.
Everett, Washington 98201

KLICKITAL BOTTLE CLUB
ASSOCIATION
Goldendale, Washington 98620

CHINOOK EZRA BROOKS CLUB
721 Grade Street
Kelso, Washington 98626

EVERGREEN STATE BEAM
BOTTLE CLUB
1540 Maple Lane
Kent, Washington 98031

MT. RAINIER EZRA BROOKS
BOTTLE & SPECIALTIES CLUB
1540 Maple Lane
Kent, Washington 98031

PACIFIC NORTHWEST AVON
BOTTLE CLUB
c/o Bill & Bette Bouma
25425 68th South
Kent, Washington 98031

WASHINGTON BOTTLE
COLLECTORS ASSOCIATION
c/o 26020 135th S.E. #13
Kent, Washington 98031

SO. WHEDLEY BOTTLE CLUB
c/o Juanita Clyde
Langley, Washington 98260

SKAGIT BOTTLE & GLASS
COLLECTORS
1314 Virginia
Mt. Vernon, Washington 98273

CAPITOL BOTTLE COLLECTORS
Route 7 Box 445-96
Olympia, Washington 98501

WASHINGTON BOTTLE CLUB
ASSOCIATION
8319 49th Street East
Puyallup, Washington 98371

MT. RAINIER EZRA BROOKS
BOTTLE CLUB
c/o Samuel A. Rose, President
13320 S.E. 99th Street
Renton, Washington 98055

EVERGREEN STATE BEAM
BOTTLE & SPECIALTY CLUB
P. O. Box 99244
Seattle, Washington 98199

SEATTLE JIM BEAM BOTTLE
COLLECTORS' CLUB
8015 15th Avenue N. W.
Seattle, Washington 98107

SKAGIT GLASS & BOTTLE CLUB
Route 3 Box 110
Sedro Woolley, Washington 98248

ANTIQUE BOTTLE & GLASS
COLLECTORS
P. O. Box 163
Snohomish, Washington 98290

GREATER SPOKANE BOTTLE &
COLLECTORS ASSOCIATION
P. O. Box 920
Spokane, Washington 99210

INLAND EMPIRE BOTTLE &
COLLECTORS CLUB
12824 E. 4th
Spokane, Washington 99216

NORTHWEST BEAM &
SPECIALTIES CLUB
P. O. Box 4365 Station B
Spokane, Washington 92202

ANTIQUE ACRES EZRA BROOKS
CLUB
P. O. Box 559
Yelm, Washington 98597

JIM BEAM COLLECTORS
107 Mohawk Drive
Barrackville, West Virginia 26559

WILD & WONDERFUL WEST
VIRGINIA EZRA BROOKS BOTTLE
& SPECIALTY CLUB
1924 Pennsylvania Avenue
Weirton, West Virginia 26062

CAMERON BOTTLE DIGGERS
P. O. Box 276
314 South 1st Street
Cameron, Wisconsin 54822

FIGURAL BOTTLE ASSOCIATION
The Bottle Stopper
Eagle, Wisconsin 53119

BADGER BOTTLE DIGGERS
1420 McKinley Road
Eau Claire, Wisconsin 54701

MILWAUKEE JIM BEAM &
ANTIQUE BOTTLE CLUB
P. O. Box 56
6361 South 27th
Frankland, Wisconsin 53132

SOUTH CENTRAL WISCONSIN
BOTTLE CLUB
c/o Sherman Avenue Methodist
Church
2038 Sherman Avenue
Madison, Wisconsin 53704

MILWAUKEE JIM BEAM CLUB
3779 South 95th Street
Milwaukee, Wisconsin 53228

CENTRAL WISCONSIN BOTTLE
COLLECTORS
1640 Franklin Street
Stevens Point, Wisconsin 54481

MILWAUKEE JIM BEAM &
ANTIQUE BOTTLE CLUB
120 N. 15th Avenue
West Bend, Wisconsin 53095

CASPER ANTIQUE &
COLLECTORS CLUB
2555 E. 9th
Casper, Wyoming 82601

CHEYENNE ANTIQUE BOTTLE
CLUB
4417 East 8th Street
Cheyenne, Wyoming 82001

PAUL & FRAN'S - MODERN
FIGURALS
P. O. Box 388
Cheyenne, Wyoming 82001

INSUBOTT BOTTLE CLUB
P. O. Box 34
Lander, Wyoming 82520

SOUTHWESTERN WYOMING
AVON CLUB
P. O. Box 1688
Rock Springs, Wyoming 82901

FIRST CANADIAN BOTTLE &
SPECIALTY CLUB
P. O. Box 3232 Station B
Calgary 41, Alberta, Canada

CAMPBELL RIVER ANTIQUE
BOTTLE & RELIC CLUB
c/o Bill Patterson
#12 2705 (N Island) Hwy.
Campbell River, British Columbia,
Canada

DIGGERS CLUB
c/o Mrs. E. Klimes,
R. R. 2
Ladysmith, British Columbia,
Canada

NANAMINO OLD TIME BOTTLE
ASSOCIATION
P. O. Box 53
Nanamino, British Columbia,
Canada

THE OLD TIME BOTTLE CLUB OF
BRITISH COLUMBIA
c/o Mrs. Josie Riley
530 Cantrell Road
Richmond, British Columbia,
Canada

SKEENA ROCK & BOTTLE CLUB
c/o Mrs. Rod Miller
4735 Soucie Avenue
Terrace, British Columbia, Canada

OLD TIME BOTTLE CLUB OF
BRITISH COLUMBIA
1200 Woodland Drive
Vancouver 6, British Columbia,

Canada

SOOKE ROTO-ROOTERS
13 Maddock
Victoria, Bitish Columbia, Canada

VICTORIA GLASS & BOTTLE
COLLECTOR'S SOCIETY
402 Chester Avenue
Victoria, British Columbia, Canada

ARCADIA BOTTLE CLUB
c/o 16 Quarry Road
Halifax, Nova Scotia, Canada

PICTOU COUNTY HISTORICAL
BOTTLE CLUB
c/o George C. Dooley
P. O9 Box 308
Westville, Nova Scotia, Canada

BYTOWN BOTTLE COLLECTORS
CLUB
820 Dundee Avenue
Ottawa 14, Ontario, Canada

BYTOWN BOTTLE SEEKERS
c/o R. Rosewarne
102 First Avenue
Ottawa, Ontario, Canada

AUSTRALIAN BOTTLE
COLLECTORS' CLUB
39 Ellington Street
Ekibin, Queensland, 4121,
Australia

NASSUA INTERNATIONAL
ANTIQUE BOTTLE CLUB
c/o Joanne M. Kelly,
P. O. Box 6191
Nassau, New Providence Island,
Bahamas

CANAL ZONE BOTTLE CLUB
ASSOCIATION
P. O. Box 2232
Balboa, Canal Zone

JIM BEAMS BOTTLE CLUB
DENMARK
Mr. Kurt Vendelbo
Oresundsvej 130
2300 Copenhagen S, Denmark

BRITISH BOTTLE COLLECTORS'
CLUB
49 Elizabeth Road
Brentwood, Essex, England

BIBLIOGRAPHY

Authors' Note

Most of the books not published privately and listed in the bibliography can be obtained at local bookstores. We list below the specialized shops that carry many books not normally stocked.

WHERE TO BUY BOOKS

Antique Publications
Emmitsburg, Maryland 21727

Collector Books
P.O. Box 3009
Paducah, Kentucky 42001

Hotchkiss House
89 Sagamore Drive
Rochester, New York 14617

Mid-America Book Company
Leon, Iowa 50144

Old Time Bottle Publishing Co.
611 Lancaster Drive N.E.
Salem, Oregon 97301

Ole Empty Bottle House
Box 136
Amador City, California 95601
(Bottle Books)

The Little Glass Shack
3161 57th Street
Sacramento, California 95820

GENERAL

Adams, John P. *Bottle Collecting in New England*. New Hampshire Publishing Company, Somersworth, New Hampshire 03878, 1969. $3.95.

_____. *John P. Adams' Third Bottle Book*. New Hampshire Publishing Company, Somersworth, New Hampshire 03878, 1972. $3.95.

Bailey, Shirley R. *Bottle Town*. Privately printed, 1968. $3.50. (Order from author, 24 Westwood Terrace, Millville, New Jersey.)

Ballou, Hazel, and Alley, Kaylen. *The Beginners Book Collecting Jars and Bottles for Fun and Money*. Privately printed, 1966. $2.00. (Order from author, 1802 Margrave, Fort Scott, Kansas.)

Bates, Virginia T., and Chamberlain, Beverly. *Antique Bottle Finds in New England*. Privately printed, 1968. $3.95. (Order from William L. Bauhan, Inc., Noone House, Peterborough, New Hampshire.)

Beare, Nikki. *Bottle Bonanza: A Handbook for Glass Collectors.* Privately printed, 1965. $3.00 (Order from Hurricane House Publishers, Inc., 14301 S.W. 87th Avenue, Miami, Florida.)

Belknap, E. M. *Milk Glass.* New York: Crown Publishers, Inc., 1959. $6.00.

Blumenstein, Lynn. *Bottle Rush U.S.A.* Salem, Oregon: Old Time Bottle Publishing Company, 1966. $4.25.

_____. *Old Time Bottles Found in Ghost Towns.* Privately printed, 1966. $2.50.

_____. *"Redigging the West"* for Old Time Bottles. Privately printed, 1966. $4.25.

Bressie, Wes & Ruby. *Ghost Town Bottle Price Guide.* Privately printed, 1966. $3.00. (Order from author, Route 1, Box 582, Eagle Point, Oregon.)

Colcleaser, Donald E. *Bottles of Bygone Days.* Privately printed, 1965. $2.00. (Order from author, P.O. Box 2006, Napa, California.)

_____. *Bottles of Bygone Days, Part II.* Privately printed, 1966. $2.00.

_____. *Bottles Yesterday's Trash Today's Treasures.* Privately printed, 1967. $3.75.

Davis, Marvin and Helen. *Antique Bottles.* Privately printed, 1967. $3.00. (Order from author, 2320 Highway 66, Ashland, Oregon 97520.)

_____. *Bottles and Relics.* Privately printed, 1970. $4.50.

_____. *Old Bottle Collecting for Fun & Profit.* Privately printed, 1966. $2.25.

_____. *Pocket Field Guide for the Bottle Digger.* Privately printed, 1967. $2.00.

Devner, Kay. *At the Sign of the Mortar.* Privately printed, 1970. $2.75. (Order from author, 8945 E. 20th, Tucson, Arizona 85710.)

_____. *Backward Through a Bottle.* Privately printed, 1964. $2.00.

Eastin, June. *Bottles West, Volume 1.* Privately printed, 1965. $3.00. (Order from author, P.O. Box 703, Joshua Tree, California 92252.)

Ferraro, Pat and Bob. *A Bottle Collector's Book.* Privately printed, 1966. $3.00. (Order from author, Box 239, Lovelock, Nevada 89419.)

————. *The Past in Glass.* Privately printed, 1964. $3.00.

Fike, Richard E. *Guide to Old Bottles, Contents & Prices.* Privately printed, 1969. $2.75. (Order from author, 1135 Maxfield Drive, Ogden, Utah.)

————. *Guide to Old Bottles, Contents & Prices, Volume II.* Privately printed, 1969. $2.75.

————. *Handbook for the Bottle-ologist.* Privately printed, 1969. $2.75.

Freeman, Dr. Larry. *Grand Old American Bottles.* Watkins Glen, New York: Century House, 1964. $25.00.

Hughey, Karen L. *A Price Guide to Infants Nursing Bottles. Book 1.* Privately printed, 1972. (Order from The Ladies of the Lake, P.O. Box 540, Mackinac Island, Michigan 49757.)

Illinois Glass Company. *Old Bottle List Bonanza, Illustrated Catalogue & Price List.* Watkins Glen, New York: Century House, Americana Publishers.

Jones, May. *The Bottle Trail.* Privately printed, 1965. $2.25. (Order from author, P.O. Box 23, Nara Visa, New Mexico.)

————. *The Bottle Trail, Vol. 2.* Privately printed, 1963. $2.25.

————. *The Bottle Trail, Vol. 3.* Privately printed, 1963. $2.25.

————. *The Bottle Trail, Vol. 4.* Privately printed, 1966. $2.25.

————. *The Bottle Trail, Vol. 5.* Privately printed, 1965. $2.25.

————. *The Bottle Trail, Vol. 6.* Privately printed, 1966. $2.25.

————. *The Bottle Trail, Vol. 7.* Privately printed, 1967. $2.25.

————. *The Bottle Trail, Vol. 8.* Privately printed, 1967. $2.25.

Kaufmann, Don and June. *Dig Those Crazy Bottles: A Handbook of Pioneer Bottles.* Privately printed, 1966. (Order from author, 3520 Laramie Street, Cheyenne, Wyoming.)

Kendrick, Grace. *The Antique Bottle Collector, Including Latest Price Guide.* New York: Pyramid Books, 1971. $2.95.

_____. *"The Mouth-Blown Bottle."* Privately printed, 1968. $6.95.

_____. *Price Supplement to the Antique Bottle Collector.* Privately printed, 1965. $1.50.

Kenyon, Harry C. *Jersey Diggins, Volume 1.* Privately printed, 1969. $3.50. (Order from The Old Barn, Newfield, New Jersey.)

Kincade, Steve. *Early American Bottles and Glass.* Privately printed, 1964. $3.00. (Order from Clovis Printing Company, 619 Fifth Street, Clovis, California.)

Klamkin, Marian. *The Collector's Book of Bottles.* New York: Dodd, Mead & Company, 1971. $8.95.

Kovel, Ralph and Terry. *The Complete Antiques Price List.* New York: Crown Publishers, Inc., 1970. $5.95.

_____. *Know Your Antiques.* New York: Crown Publishers, Inc., 1967. $7.95.

Lane, Lyman and Sally, and Pappas, Joan. *A Rare Collection of Keene and Stoddard Glass.* New York: Crown Publishers, Inc., 1970. $4.95.

Leahy, Midge and Phil. *The Bottles of Leadville, Colorado.* Privately printed. 1967. $2.00. (Order from author, 4165 Stuart Street, Denver, Colorado.)

Lyons, Adrian D. *Your Friend's and My Friend's Bottle Book.* Privately printed. 1967. $3.00. (Order from author, The Mother Lode Bottle Shop, Maestown, California.)

Lyons, Bill and Jean. *Bottles from Bygone Days.* Privately printed, 1967. $4.25. (Order from author, Box 147, South Vienna, Ohio 45369.)

Maust, Don. *Bottle and Glass Handbook.* Uniontown, Pennsylvania: E. G. Warman Publishing Company, 1956. $3.00.

McConnell, Walter E. *Tri-State Bottles.* Privately printed, 1969. $3.00. (Order from author, RD #2, Box 116, Newton, New Jersey 07860.)

McKearin, George L. and Helen. *Two Hundred Years of American Blown Glass.* New York: Crown Publishers, Inc., 1950. $15.00.

Motter, Faye. *Stories in Bottles*. Privately printed, 1966. (Order from author, P.O. Box 37, Edina, Missouri.)

Munsey, Cecil. *The Illustrated Guide to Collecting Bottles*. New York: Hawthorn Books, Inc., 1970. $9.95.

Phillips, Helen V. *400 Old Bottles, Book #1*. Privately printed, 1967. (Order from author, 528 W. 5th Street, Cheyenne, Wyoming.)

Putnam, H. E. *Bottle Identification*. Privately printed, 1965. $2.50. (Order from author, P.O. Box 517, Jamestown, California.)

Putnam, P. A. *Bottled Before 1865*. Privately printed, 1968. $2.75. (Order from House of Putnam, P.O. Box 578, Fontana, California 92325.)

Rawlinson, Fred. *Old Bottles of the Virginia Peninsula, 1885–1941*. Privately printed, 1968. $4.30. (Order from FAR Publications, P.O. Box 5456, Newport News, Virginia 23605.)

Reed, Adele. *Bottle Talk*. Privately printed, 1966. $2.00. (Order from author, 272 Shepard Lane, Bishop, California 93514.)

_____. *Old Bottles and Ghost Towns*. Privately printed, 1962. $2.00.

Sellari, Carlo and Dot. *Eastern Bottles Price Guide, Volume 1*. Privately printed, 1969. $4.50.

_____. *Eastern Bottles Price Guide, Volume 2*. Privately printed. 1970. $4.50.

Tibbits, John C. *How to Collect Antique Bottles*. Privately printed, 1969. $4.00.

_____. *John Doe, Bottle Collector*. Privately printed, 1967. $4.00.

_____. *1200 Bottles Priced*. Privately printed, 1970. $4.50. (Order from The Little Glass Shack, 3161 56th Street, Sacramento, California 95820.)

Toulouse, Julian Harrison. *Bottle Makers and Their Marks*. Camden, New Jersey: Thomas Nelson, Inc., 1971. $15.00

Tufts, James W. *The Manufacture and Bottling of Carbonated Beverages*. Frontier Book Company, Publisher, Fort Davis, Texas 79734, 1969. $3.50.

Umberger, Art and Jewel. *It's a Corker!* Privately printed, 1966. $3.00. (Order from author, 819 W. Wilson, Tyler, Texas 75701.)

Unitt, Doris and Peter. *Bottles in Canada.* Peterborough, Ontario, Canada: Clock House Publications, 1972.

Walbridge, William S. *American Bottles Old & New, 1607 to 1920.* Frontier Book Company, Publisher, Fort Davis, Texas 79734, 1969. $4.00.

Watson, George, and Skrill, Robert. *Western Canadian Bottle Collecting.* Privately printed, 1971. $3.50.

Wood, Serry. *The Old Apothecary Shop.* Watkins Glen, New York: Century House, 1956. $2.00.

Yount, John T. *Bottle Collector's Handbook & Pricing Guide.* Educator Books, Inc., Drawer 32, San Angelo, Texas 76901, 1970. $3.95.

MODERN

Pictorial Bottle Review. *Collectors Edition Presents Beams, Avons, Ezra Brooks, Luxards, Garniers, Fancy and Figural Bottles.* B & K Enterprises, P.O. Box 42558, Los Angeles, California 90050, 1969.

Avon

Ahrendt, L. *Avon Bottle Collector's Guide.* Privately printed, $2.00. (Order from author, 5101 Stockton Road, Sacramento, California 95820.)

_____. *Avon Powder Boxes, Plastics & Toys.* Privately printed, 1969. $2.00.

_____. *Avon's California Perfume Company.* Privately printed, 1969. $3.00.

_____. *Mini Miniatures of Avon.* Privately printed, 1969. $2.00.

Flowers, Bryant. *The Flowers Collection. Avon Guide.* Privately printed, 1970. $5.00 (Order from author, P.O. Box 1613, Pampa, Texas 79065.)

Hanson, Hollis, Jr. *Hollis Hanson's Avon Guide on Rare and Fabulous Avons for the Advanced Collector.* Privately printed, 1970. $3.75. (Order from author, 350 E. Vassar, Fresno, California 93704.)

Hastin, Bud. *Avon Bottle Encyclopedia.* Privately printed, 1971. $8.95. (Order from author, Box 9868, Kansas City, Missouri 64134.)

International Avon Collectors Club. *International Avon Collectors Club, 1969–1970 Annual.* Privately printed, 1970. $5.00. (Order from author, P.O. Box 1406, Mesa, Arizona 85201.)

Newson, Ralph W., and Lamalfa, Jean V. *Fun with Avon Old & New: Bottle Collectors Notebook.* Privately printed, 1969. $3.75. (Order from Arjay Specialties, Box 4371, Panorama City, California 91412.)

_____. *Treasures of Avon.* Privately printed, 1969. $3.75.

Stuart, Lynn R. *Stuart's Book on Avon Collectables.* Privately printed, 1971. $4.20. (Order from author, P.O. Box 862, Gilbert, Arizona 85234.)

_____. *Collector's Guide to Avon Glass Figural Bottles, 1972 Edition.* Privately printed, 1972. $2.50. (Order from author, P.O. Box 862, Gilbert, Arizona 85234.)

Texas Collector's. *Texas Collector's Guide.* Privately printed, 1970. $5.00. (Order from author, Box 1479, Pampa, Texas 79065.)

Western Collector. *Avon-2: A Western Collector Handbook & Price Guide.* 1971. $4.95. (Order from Western Collector Books, 511 Harrison Street, San Francisco, California 94105.)

_____. *Western Collector's Handbook and Price Guide to Avon Bottles.* San Francisco, California: Western World Publishers, 1969. $3.95. (Order from Western Collector Books, 511 Harrison Street, San Francisco, California 94105.)

Beam

Cembura, Al, and Avery, Constance. *Jim Beam Bottles, 1970–1971 Identification and Price Guide.* Privately printed, 1970. $4.95. (Order from Al Cembura, 139 Arlington Avenue, Berkeley, California 94707.)

_____. *Jim Beam Bottles 1972–1973: Sixth Edition, Identification and Price Guide.* Privately printed, 1972. $5.95. (Order from author, 139 Arlington Avenue, Berkeley, California 94707.)

Bischoff

Avery, Constance and Leslie, and Cembura, Al. *Bischoff Bottles, Identification and Price Guide.* Privately printed, 1969. $4.75. (Order from Al Cembura, 139 Arlington Avenue, Berkeley, California 94707.)

Ezra Brooks

Western Collector. *Western Collector's Handbook and Price Guide to Ezra Brooks Decanters.* San Francisco, California: Western World Publishers, 1970. $4.95. (Order from Western Collector Books, 511 Harrison Street, San Francisco, California 94105.)

Garnier

Avery, Constance, and Cembura, Al. *Garnier Bottles.* Privately printed, 1970. $4.95 (Order from Al Cembura, 139 Arlington Avenue, Berkeley, California 94707.)

Schwartz, Jeri and Ed. *Just Figurals: A Guide to Garnier.* Privately printed, 1969. $4.25. (Order from author, North Broadway, Yonkers, N.Y. 10701.)

Luxardo

Avery, Constance, and Cembura, Al. *Luxardo Bottles: Identification and Price Guide.* Privately printed, 1968. $4.75. (Order from Al Cembura, 139 Arlington Avenue, Berkeley, California 94707.)

BITTERS

Bartholomew, Ed. *1001 Bitters Bottles.* Bartholomew House, Publishers, Fort Davis, Texas 79734, 1970. $4.95.

Watson, Richard. *Bitters Bottles.* New York: Thomas Nelson & Sons, 1965. $10.00.

_____. *Supplement to Bitters Bottles.* Camden, New Jersey: Thomas Nelson & Sons, 1968. $6.50.

CANDY CONTAINERS

Eikelberner, George, and Agadjanian, Serge. *American Glass Containers.* Privately printed, 1967. $7.50. (Order from Serge Agadjanian, River Road, Belle Mead, New Jersey 08502.)

_____. *More American Glass Candy Containers.* Privately printed, 1970. $6.00.

Matthews, Robert T. *Old Glass Candy Containers Price Guide.* Privately printed, 1966. $3.62. (Order from author, Glenelg, Maryland 21737.)

FIGURAL

Revi, Albert Christian. *American Pressed Glass and Figure Bottles.* New York: Thomas Nelson & Sons, 1964. $15.00.

Umberger, Jewel and Arthur L. *Collectible Character Bottles.* Privately printed, 1969. $12.50. (Order from Corker Book Company, 819 West Wilson, Tyler, Texas.)

Vincent, Pal. *The Moses Bottle.* Privately printed, 1969. $4.25. (Order from The Palabra Shop, Jct. Rtes. 26 and 122, Poland Spring, Maine 04274.)

Wearin, Otha D. *Statues That Pour: The Story of Character Bottles.* Denver, Colorado: Sage Books, 2679 South York Street, 1965. $6.00.

FLASKS

Barber, Edwin A. *Old American Bottles.* New York: David McKay Co., 1900. $3.50. (Reprint available from Frontier Book Co., Publisher, Fort Davis, Texas 79734.)

McKearin, George L. and Helen. *American Glass.* New York: Crown Publishers, Inc., 1959. $14.95.

Van Rensselaer, Stephen. *Early American Bottles & Flasks.* Southampton, New York: Cracker Barrel Press, 1921. $3.00.

_____. *Early American Bottles & Flasks—Revised.* Stratford, Connecticut, 1969. $15.00. (Order from J. Edmund Edwards, 61 Winton Place, Stratford, Connecticut 06497.)

FRUIT JARS

Bird, Douglas, and Corke, Marion and Charles. *A Century of Antique Canadian Glass Fruit Jars.* Privately printed, 1970. $6.95. (Order from Douglas Bird, 859 Valetta Street, London 74, Ontario, Canada.)

_____. *North American Fruit Jar Index.* Privately printed, 1968. $6.00.

Burris, Ronald B. *An Illustrated Guide for Collecting Fruit Jars with Price Guide.* Privately printed, 1966. $1.75. (Order from author, 2941 Campus Drive, Visalia, California 93277.)

_____. *Collecting Fruit Jars, Book #2, with Price Guide.* Privately printed, 1967. $2.00.

_____. *More Collectable Jars, Book #3, with Price Guide.* Privately printed, 1968. $2.50.

_____. *Rare and Unusual Fruit Jars, Book #4, with Price Guide.* Privately printed, 1970. $2.75.

Creswick, Alice, and Rodrigues, Arleta. *The Cresrod Blue Book of Fruit Jars.* Privately printed, 1969. $4.50. (Order from Cresrod Publishing Company, 0-8525 Kenowa SW, Grand Rapids, Michigan 49504.)

Harvest Publishing Company. *Harvest 2nd Fruit Jar Finders Price Guide.* Privately printed, 1970. $3.95. (Order from Harvest Publishing Company, Box 3015-M, Milwaukee, Wisconsin 53218.)

Hawkins, R. Doug. *For Preserving Fruit.* Privately printed, 1972. $4.00. (Order from author, 1209 S. Brundidge St., Troy, Alabama, 36081.)

Rodrigues, Arleta. *Fruit Jars—Canister to Kerr.* Privately printed, 1971. $4.50. (Order from James Publications, P.O. Box 2413, Castro Valley, California 94546.)

Rodrigues, Arleta, and Creswick, Alice. *A Collection of Yesterday's Fruit Jars from Great Aunt May's Cellar.* Privately printed, 1967. $6.50. (Order from Arleta Rodrigues, P.O. Box 2413, Castro Valley, California 94546.)

Schroeder, Bill. *1000 Fruit Jars Priced & Illustrated.* Privately printed, 1970. $3.95. (Order from author, Route 4, Paducah, Kentucky 42001.)

Toulouse, Julian Harrison. *Fruit Jars: A Collector's Manual.* Jointly published by Camden, New Jersey: Thomas Nelson & Sons, and Hanover, Pennsylvania: Everybody's Press, 1969. $15.00.

Umberger, Art and Jewel. *The Kitchen Cupboard: Fruit Jar Price Guide.* Privately printed, 1967. $3.00. (Order from author, 819 West Wilson, Tyler, Texas 75701.)

INKWELLS

Covill, William E., Jr. *Ink Bottles and Inkwells*. Taunton, Massachusetts: William S. Sullwold, Publishing, 1971. $17.50.

Nelson, Lavinia, and Hurley, Martha. *Old Inks*. Privately printed, 1967. $5.00. (Order from "Old Inks," 22 Bryant Road, Nashua, New Hampshire.)

Walter, Leo G., Jr. *Walter's Inkwells of 1885: Book #1*. Privately printed, 1968. $3.75. (Order from Stagecoach Antiques, 443 West Market Street, Akron, Ohio 44303.)

MEDICINE

Agee, Bill. *Collecting the Cures*. Privately printed, 1969. $3.00. (Order from author, 1200 Melrose, Waco, Texas 76710.)

Bartholomew, Ed. *1200 Old Medicine Bottles with Prices Current*. Frontier Book Company, Fort Davis, Texas 79734, 1970. $3.95.

Devner, Day. *Patent Medicine Picture*. Privately printed, 1968. $2.50. (Order from author, 8945 East 20th, Tucson, Arizona 85710.)

Freeman, Dr. Larry. *The Medicine Showman*. Watkins Glen, New York: Century House, 1957. $4.00.

Jensen, Al and Margaret. *Old Owl Drug Bottles & Others*. Privately printed, 1968. $3.50. (Order from author, 783 Alice Avenue, Mountain View, California 94040.)

Penland, Belle. *Bottles, Corks & Cures*. Privately printed, 1963. $2.65. (Order from author, P.O. Box 118, Twain, California 95984.)

Wilson, Bill and Betty. *Nineteenth Century Medicine in Glass*. Amador City, California: 19th Century Hobby & Publishing Company, 1971.

MILK

Rawlinson, Fred. *Make Mine Milk*. Privately printed, 1970. $3.85. (Order from FAR Publications, Box 5456, Newport News, Virginia 23605.)

Roth, Evelyn. *The Milky Way.* Privately printed, 1969. $2.50. (Order from author, 245 Shore Road, Ocean View, New Jersey 08230.)

Taylor, Gordon A. *Milk Bottle Manual: A Collector's Pictorial Primer and Pricing Guide.* Salem, Oregon: Old Time Bottle Publishing Company, 1971. $3.95.

MINIATURES

Snyder, Robert E. *Bottles in Miniature.* Privately printed, 1969. $4.00. (Order from author, 4235 West 13th, Amarillo, Texas 79106.)

_____. *Bottles in Miniature, Volume II.* Privately printed, 1970. $4.75.

_____. *Bottles in Miniature, Volume III.* Privately printed, 1972. $6.00.

Spaid, David M. *Mini World, 1971–1972 Identification and Price Guide.* Los Angeles, California: B & K Enterprises, 1971. $3.50.

POISON BOTTLES

Durflinger, Roger L. *Poison Bottles Collectors Guide, Vol. 1.* Privately printed, 1972. $3.95. (Order from author, 132 W. Oak Street, Washington C.H., Ohio 43160.)

Stier, Wallis W. *Poison Bottles: A Collectors' Guide.* Privately printed, 1969. $3.50. (Order from author, P.O. Box 243, Rockland, Idaho 83271.)

SARSAPARILLA

Shimko, Phyllis. *Sarsaparilla Bottle Encyclopedia.* Privately printed, 1969. $6.50. (Order from author, Box 117, Aurora, Oregon 97002.)

Umberger, Art and Jewel. *It's a Sarsaparilla! Price Guide.* Privately printed, 1968. $3.00. (Order from author, 819 W. Wilson, Tyler, Texas 75701.)

SODA AND MINERAL WATER

Fountain, John C., and Colcleaser, Donald. *Dictionary of Soda & Mineral Water Bottles.* Amador City, California: "Ole Empty Bottle House Publishing Company," 1968. P.O. Box 136. $3.75

Jones, J. L. *Soda and Mineral Water Bottles.* Greer, South Carolina: Palmetto Enterprises, 1972. $8.00.

Lincoln, Gerald David. *Antique Blob Top Bottles, Central & Southern New England.* Privately printed, 1970. $3.25. (Order from author, 700 Berlin Road, Marlboro, Massachusetts 01752.)

Markota, Peck and Audie. *Western Blob Top Soda and Mineral Water Bottles.* Amador City, California: Antique and Hobby Publishing Company, 1971. $5.00.

Schmeiser, Alan. *Have Bottles Will Pop.* Privately printed. 1968. $6.95. (Order from author, Dixon, California 95620.)

_____. *More Pop.* Privately printed, 1970. $10.00. (Order from author, 370 E. Mayes Street, Dixon, California 95620.)

WHISKEY AND BEER

Anderson, Sonja and Will. *Andersons' Turn-of-the-Century Brewery Dictionary.* Privately printed. $15.95. (Order from author, 1 Lindy Street, Carmel, New York 10512.)

_____. *Beers, Breweries & Breweriana.* Privately printed, 1969.

Fountain, John C., and Colcleaser, Donald. *Dictionary of Spirits and Whiskey Bottles.* Amador City, California: "Ole Empty Bottle House Publishing Company." 1969. P.O. Box 136. $3.75

Howe, John. *A Whiskeyana Guide: Antique Whiskey Bottles.* Privately printed, 1967. $3.00. (Order from author, 4894 Sandy Lane, San Jose, California 95124.)

Kaufmann, Don and June. *The United States Brewers' Guide, 1630–1864.* Privately printed, 1967. $1.75. (Order from author, 3520 Laramie Street, Cheyenne, Wyoming 82001.)

Peewee Valley Press. *Decanter Collector's Guide.* Privately printed, 1970. $2.75. (Order from author, P.O. Box 248, Peewee Valley, Kentucky 40056.)

Silva, Bev and Joe. *Research on San Francisco Whiskey Bottles.* Privately printed, 1967. $2.00. (Order from author, 6829 Mayhews Lndg. Road, Newark, California 94560.)

Wilson, Bill and Betty. *Spirits Bottles of the Old West.* Privately printed, 1968. $10.00. (Order from Antiques & Hobby Publishing Company, Box 136, Amador City, California 95601.)

NEWSPAPERS OF INTEREST TO BOTTLE COLLECTORS

The American Collector
(Formerly *The Gallery*)
3717 Mt. Diablo Boulevard
Lafayette, California 94549

Antique Monthly
P.O. Drawer 440
Tuscaloosa, Alabama 35401

Antique News
P.O. Box B
Marietta, Pennsylvania 17547

Antique Trader Weekly
P.O. Box 1050
Dubuque, Iowa 52001

The Antiquity
P.O. Box 307
Washington, New Jersey 07882

Collector's News
Grundy Center, Iowa 50638

Collector's Weekly
P.O. Box 1119
Kermit, Texas 79745

The Mid-America Reporter
Main Street
Leon, Iowa 50144

Tri-State Trader
P.O. Box 90-DM
Knightstown, Indiana 46148

West Coast Peddler
P.O. Box 4489
Downey, California 90241

NEWSLETTERS OF INTEREST TO BOTTLE COLLECTORS

The Lionstone Legend
P.O. Box 75924
Los Angeles, California 90075

*Milkbottles Only Organization
(MOO)*
Fred Rawlinson
P.O. Box 5456
Newport News, Virginia 23605

Miniature Bottle Mart
24 Gertrude Lane
West Haven, Connecticut 0651

MAGAZINES OF INTEREST TO BOTTLE COLLECTORS

Antiques Journal
P.O. Box 1046
Dubuque, Iowa 52001

Antiques Today
P.O. Box 1034
Kermit, Texas 79745

Bottle News
P.O. Box 1000
Kermit, Texas 79745

The Bottle Trader
P.O. Box 69
Gas City, Indiana 46933

Bottles & Relics
P.O. Box 654
Conroe, Texas 77301

Collector's World
P.O. Box 654
Conroe, Texas 77301

Hobbies
Lightner Publishing Corporation
1006 South Michigan Avenue
Chicago, Illinois 60605

*Journal of the Federation of
Historical Bottle Clubs*
10118 Schuessler
St. Louis, Missouri 63128

National Antiques Review
P.O. Box 619
Portland, Maine 04104

The National Bottle Gazette
P.O. Box 1011
Kermit, Texas 79745

Old Bottle Magazine
P.O. Box 243
Bend, Oregon 97701

Old Stuff
Johnson Hill's Press, Inc.
1233 Janesville Avenue
Fort Atkinson, Wisconsin 5353

Pictorial Bottle Review
B & K Enterprises, Inc.
P.O. Box 42558
Los Angeles, California 90050

Relics
P.O. Box 3668
Austin, Texas 78704

Spinning Wheel
Everybody's Press
Hanover, Pennsylvania 17331

Acid, Sheared Neck, Green, 22 In.High	22.50
Acid, Sulphuric, Label With Skull & Crossbones, Oval, Cobalt Blue, 8 1/2 In.	12.50
Apothecary, Acid Hydrochl., Vol., 1/2 Norm, Ground Stopper, Amber, 7 In.	8.00
Apothecary, Acid.Nitric.Crud, Ground Stopper, Clear, 7 In.High	7.00
Apothecary, Acid.Nitric, Ground Stopper, Clear, 4 3/4 In.High	6.00
Apothecary, Acid.Sulfur.Crud, Ground Stopper, Clear, 7 In.High	7.00
Apothecary, Aq.Cinam, Ground Stopper, Clear, 8 1/4 In.High	8.00
Apothecary, Blown, Amethyst	10.00
Apothecary, Blown, Stopper, 10 In.High	10.00
Apothecary, Carbon On Glass Label, Patent March, 1894, St.Louis, Ground Top	12.00
Apothecary, Cobalt Blue	3.50 To 15.00
Apothecary, Cobalt Blue, 9 In.Tall, 3 1/2 In.Diameter	15.00
Apothecary, Covered, Set Of Four Graduated	50.00
Apothecary, Crystal Glass, Ground Stopper, C.19th Century, Pontil	10.50
Apothecary, Cylindrical, Ground Neck & Stopper, Turn Mold, Clear	12.00
Apothecary, Embossed B & B, 1886 On Glass Lid, Amber	7.00
Apothecary, Emil Cermak Pharmacist, Omaha, 4 Oz.	1.25
Apothecary, Euchininum, Ground Stopper, Amber, 4 3/4 In.High	6.00
Apothecary, Glass Label, Glass Stopper, Narrow Mouth, Bimal, 1840, Clear	8.95
Apothecary, Gold & Red Panels, Enameled Flowers	65.00
Apothecary, Ground Glass Stopper, 8 In.High	2.50
Apothecary, Ground Neck, Square, Turned Purple, 9 3/4 In.High	11.00
Apothecary, Ground Stopper, Clear, 8 1/2 In.	9.00
Apothecary, Ground Stopper, 5 1/2 In.	5.00
Apothecary, Ground Stopper, 9 In.	4.00
Apothecary, Hydrogen Peroxide, 3 Percent Solution, Ground Stopper, Amber	10.00
Apothecary, Kalilauge, 1/1 Norm, Ground Stopper, Amber, 7 In.High	8.00
Apothecary, Kalium Bromatlosg, 1/10 Norm., Ground Stopper, Amber, 7 In.	8.00
Apothecary, Light Blue, Quart	12.00
Apothecary, Liquid Amon.Rhodan., Vol.1/10 Norm., Ground Stopper, Amber	8.00
Apothecary, Liquid Jodi.Vol., Ground Stopper, Amber, 7 In.High	8.00
Apothecary, Liquid Nater.Chlorat., Vol., Ground Stopper, Amber, 7 In.High	8.00
Apothecary, Liquid Nater.Thiosulfide, Vol., Ground Stopper, Amber, 7 In.High	8.00
Apothecary, Open Pontil, Glass Label, Ground Stopper, C.1840, 8 1/2 In.	19.95
Apothecary, Open Pontil, Ground Stopper, Aqua, 7 In.Tall	8.00
Apothecary, Painted Episcopal Crest, White Crackle Glaze, 4	50.00
Apothecary, Pottery, White, Black Lettering, 8 In.High	12.00
Apothecary, Pulv.Salicylic.C.Talco, Ground Stopper, Clear, 8 1/4 In.High	8.00
Apothecary, Reed's, Milk Glass, 5 In.	15.00
Apothecary, South Carolina Dispensary, Clear	22.50
Apothecary, Statue Of Liberty, American Eagle, Clear, 12 1/2 In.High	135.00
Apothecary, Teardrop Stopper, Mounted As Lamp, Blue, Pair	60.00
Apothecary, W.B.Jeron's, Chemist Market, Rasen, 8 In.High	3.00
Apothecary, 3 Piece Mold, Cornflower Blue	3.00
Apothecary, 3 Piece Mold, Stopper, Cobalt Blue	22.50
Apothecary, 31 Jecor Asell, Ground Stopper, Amber, 8 1/4 In.High	10.00
Aqua, Bottle, Pontil, Foldover Lip, 5 In. *Color*	XX.XX
Armagnac, Blue Water Canteen	25.00
Armagnac, Golden Eagle Pole	35.00
Armanetti, Fun Bottle	22.50
Atomizer, Amber Glass	3.00
Atomizer, Cameo, Richard, Dark Blue Flowers, Orange	135.00
Atomizer, Devilbiss, Signed, Iridescent, 6 1/2 In.	15.00
Atomizer, Round, Intaglio Cut Floral, Gold Cap, Lalique, Marny, France, Green	47.50
Atomizer, Val St.Lambert, Signed, Acid Cut Flowers In Cranberry, Mottled	125.00

Avon started in 1886 as the California Perfume Company. It was not until 1929 that the name Avon was used. In 1939 it became the Avon Products, Inc. Each year Avon sells many figural bottles filled with cosmetic products. Ceramic, plastic, and glass bottles are made in limited editions.

Avon, A Winner Boxing Gloves, 1960, Full & Boxed	10.00
Avon, After Shave, Blue Blazer, Paper Label	8.00
Avon, After Shave, Island Lime, Yellow	11.25
Avon, After Shave, Vigorate, Frosted	7.50
Avon, After Shave, Wooden Cap, 1961	17.50 To 18.75

Avon, After Shave, 4 Oz., 1958	5.99
Avon, After Shaving Lotion, 1939, Full & Box	24.95
Avon, After Shower Flask	45.00
Avon, After Shower Foam, 1965, Full	10.00
Avon, After Shower Foam, 1965, Full & Boxed	49.00
Avon, After Shower For Men, 1959	15.00
Avon, After Shower For Men, 1959, Tag & Label	22.00
Avon, Airplane, Full & Boxed	5.95
Avon, Alligator	1.25
Avon, Alpine	36.00
Avon, Alpine Flask, Full & Boxed, 1966	35.00 To 50.00
Avon, American Beauty Fragrance Jar, 1934	32.00 To 40.00
Avon, American Ideal Perfume	27.50
Avon, Angel, Full & Boxed	4.99
Avon, Angler, 1970, Full & Boxed	5.50
Avon, Anniversary Birthday Cake Award, 1951, Full & Boxed	125.00
Avon, Antiseptic Mouth Wash, 1959	5.00
Avon, Antiseptic Powder, 1958	2.00
Avon, Antiseptic, 1936, Full & Boxed	22.50
Avon, Apothecary Jar, 1965, Full & Boxed	12.00 To 14.50
Avon, Apple Blossom Beauty Dust, Full & Boxed	16.00
Avon, Apple Blossom Cologne, 6 Oz., 1936	75.00
Avon, Apple Blossom Cologne, 1942	59.50
Avon, Apple Blossom Toilet Water, 2 Oz., 1940	30.00
Avon, Apple Blossom Toilet Water, 1942	17.00
Avon, Armoire Bath Oil	3.99
Avon, Astringent Freshener, 1967, Full & Boxed	2.99
Avon, Astringent, 1936, Full & Boxed	11.25
Avon, Attention Cologne, 6 Oz., 1947	75.00
Avon, Attention Powder Sachet, 1943	8.00 To 20.00
Avon, Auto Horn, Full & Boxed	6.00
Avon, Avon Calling, Full & Boxed	7.50
Avon, Avonshire Blue	4.99
Avon, Award Sachet, 1962	4.00
Avon, Award, Bird Of Paradise Bracelet & Earrings, 1970	20.00
Avon, Award, Bird Of Paradise Pin, 1970	10.00
Avon, Award, Bird Of Paradise Scarf, 1970	10.00
Avon, Award, Blue Sachet, 1962	8.95
Avon, Award, Charm Bracelet, 6 Charms, 1969	75.00
Avon, Award, Christmas, 1971	17.50
Avon, Award, Compote, Cover, Coin Glass, 1886	37.50
Avon, Award, Pin, 1886-1936	50.00
Avon, Award, Presidential, 1967	12.50
Avon, Award, Sales, Cream Sachet, 1962	10.00
Avon, Award, Spoons Set, 7 Spoons, 1969	75.00
Avon, Baa Baa Black Sheep Set	50.00
Avon, Ballad Perfume	100.00
Avon, Barber Bottle, Full & Boxed	12.00 To 16.50
Avon, Barber Bottle, Spicy, 1963	25.00
Avon, Bath Classic Cologne Set, 1962, Full & Boxed	25.00
Avon, Bath Flower Soap Set, 1965, Full & Boxed	5.95
Avon, Bath Luxury, Set, 1966, Full & Boxed	4.99
Avon, Bath Oil For Men, 1965, Full & Boxed	10.00
Avon, Bath Seasons, Black With Silver, 1969	2.00
Avon, Bath Seasons, Jasmine, 1967	2.50
Avon, Bay Rum After Shave	7.95
Avon, Bay Rum After Shave Lotion, 4 Oz., 1964, 1/2 Full & Boxed	4.00
Avon, Bay Rum After Shave, Parchment Label, Full	6.00
Avon, Bay Rum Jug, Labels, 1962	4.00 To 8.50
Avon, Bay Rum Keg, 1965	8.50 To 12.00
Avon, Bay Rum Soap, Boxed	15.00
Avon, Bay Rum Talc	5.00 To 7.95
Avon, Bay Rum, C.P.C., Label	28.00
Avon, Bayberry Soap Set, Boxed	11.00
Avon, Beauty Basket Set, 1949	60.00
Avon, Beehive, Sweet As Honey	125.00

Avon, Bird Of Paradise Award Pin	9.00
Avon, Bird Of Paradise Award Scarf	8.00
Avon, Bird Of Paradise Tray, Full & Boxed	6.00
Avon, Birdhouse, 1969, Full & Boxed	4.99
Avon, Black After Shower, 1/2 Oz.	2.00
Avon, Blast Horn	6.99
Avon, Blue Blazer After Shave, Spray Can, Full	6.00
Avon, Blue Blazer After Shave, 6 Oz., 1963	19.50
Avon, Blue Blazer Alpine Decanter	45.00
Avon, Blue Blazer Deluxe Set, 1965, Full & Boxed	50.00
Avon, Blue Blazer Deodorant, Plastic, 1964	4.00
Avon, Blue Blazer Hair Dressing, 1964, Full & Boxed	4.00
Avon, Blue Blazer Men's Fragrance Wardrobe, Single, 1965	4.00
Avon, Blue Blazer Shaving Cream, Can, Full, 1964	6.00
Avon, Blue Blazer Soap & Sponge	10.00
Avon, Blue Blazer Soap On A Rope, 1964, Full & Boxed	6.00
Avon, Blue Blazer Talc	4.95
Avon, Blue Book, Full & Boxed	5.50
Avon, Blue Cream Sachet Award, Stand	8.00
Avon, Blue Iron, Plastic	9.50
Avon, Bo-Bo Elephant, Full & Boxed	4.00
Avon, Bonbon Decanter, 1972	2.10
Avon, Book, Clear, Full & Boxed	3.50
Avon, Book, Dark Amber, Full & Boxed	3.50
Avon, Book, Light Amber, Full & Boxed	5.50
Avon, Book, Set Of 4	14.00
Avon, Book, 1st Edition, Full & Boxed, 1967	4.95
Avon, Boot, Brown .... Color	3.00
Avon, Boot, Gold Top, Full & Boxed, 1966	3.00 To 5.00
Avon, Boot, Silver Top, 1965 .... Color	7.00
Avon, Boots & Saddle Kit, 1968, Full & Boxed	6.95
Avon, Bowling Pin, Plastic, 1960	3.00 To 8.00
Avon, Boxing Gloves, Maroon, Full & Boxed, 1960	19.50
Avon, Bravo, Full & Boxed	1.65
Avon, Breath Fresh, 1968	10.00
Avon, Bright Night Beauty Dust With Perfume, 1956	20.00
Avon, Bright Night Beauty Dust, Plastic	8.00
Avon, Bright Night Cologne Mist, 1953	6.00
Avon, Bright Night Cologne Mist, 1958, Full & Boxed	17.50
Avon, Bright Night Cologne, 1954, Full & Boxed	14.00
Avon, Bright Night Cream Sachet, Full & Boxed	5.00 To 7.95
Avon, Bright Night Perfume, Boxed	70.00
Avon, Bright Night Perfume, Felt Roll, 1954	90.00
Avon, Bright Night Perfume, Glass Stopper, Tag Label	57.50
Avon, Bright Night Perfume, Velvet Snap On Cover	35.00
Avon, Bright Night Powder Sachet, 1954, Full & Boxed	5.50 To 10.00
Avon, Bright Night Powder Sachet, 1955	6.00
Avon, Bright Night Toilet Water, 1954, Full & Boxed	10.00
Avon, Brocade Deluxe Set, 1967	12.00
Avon, Brocade Perfume Oil	3.00
Avon, Bubble Bath, 1949, Full & Boxed	18.00 To 20.00
Avon, Bud Vase, 1968, Full & Boxed	4.50
Avon, Buffalo Nickel	3.00
Avon, Bullet Perfume Oil	5.00 To 7.00
Avon, Bureau Organizer, 1965	35.00
Avon, Bureau Organizer, 1966	29.95 To 40.00
Avon, Buttons & Bows Beauty Dust	89.9
Avon, Buttons & Bows Cologne Mist, 1960	6.00
Avon, Buttons & Bows Cologne, 2 Oz., 1963, Full & Boxed	7.00
Avon, Buttons & Bows Cream Sachet	8.95
Avon, Buttons & Bows Roll On Deodorant, 1960, Full & Boxed	14.00
Avon, Cadillac, Gold, Full & Boxed	4.50 To 10.00
Avon, California Perfume Company, American Beauty Jar, 1914	75.00
Avon, California Perfume Company, American Ideal Face Powder, 1929	22.50
Avon, California Perfume Company, Astringent, Ribbed, 4 Oz., 1936	40.00
Avon, California Perfume Company, Baking Powder	24.95

Avon, California Perfume Company, Bandoline Hair Dress, 1920 .... 42.50
Avon, California Perfume Company, Bath Salts, 1929 .... 40.00
Avon, California Perfume Company, Black Walnut, 1/2 Oz. 10.00
Avon, California Perfume Company, Bleach Cream, 1929, 2 Oz. 20.00
Avon, California Perfume Company, Bleaching Cream, 2 Oz., 1934 .... 40.00
Avon, California Perfume Company, Book, 1915, Case 350.00
Avon, California Perfume Company, Carnation Powder Sachet, 1920, Box 50.00
Avon, California Perfume Company, Cleansing Cream, Ribbed, 1936 .... 55.00
Avon, California Perfume Company, Compact, Green, Gold, 1936 .... 15.00
Avon, California Perfume Company, Daphne Talc, Green, 1936 .... 20.00
Avon, California Perfume Company, Dusting Powder, Square, 1930 .... 35.00
Avon, California Perfume Company, Dusting Powder Tin, 1929 .... 26.25
Avon, California Perfume Company, Elite Foot Powder, 1925 .... 40.00
Avon, California Perfume Company, Extract Sweet Pea, White Paper Label 135.00
Avon, California Perfume Company, Face Lotion, Box .... *Color*   XX.XX
Avon, California Perfume Company, Face Lotion, 1906 .... 100.00
Avon, California Perfume Company, Flavoring Bottle, 1942, Savoury, 4 Oz. 10.00
Avon, California Perfume Company, Flavoring, Embossed, 1897 .... 30.00
Avon, California Perfume Company, Food Coloring, Red Label, 2 Oz. 15.00
Avon, California Perfume Company, Food Color Set, 6 Piece, 1935 .... 200.00
Avon, California Perfume Company, Fruit Flavor .... 20.00 To 30.00
Avon, California Perfume Company, Fruit Flavor Extract .... *Illus*   35.00
Avon, California Perfume Company, Fruit Flavors, Reversed A 30.00
Avon, California Perfume Company, Fruit Flavors, 1897 .... 25.00
Avon, California Perfume Company, Heliotrope Powder Sachet, 1915, Full 75.00
Avon, California Perfume Company, Heliotrope Sachet, 1886 .... 85.00
Avon, California Perfume Company, Jardin D'Amour, Label, 1934 .... 35.00
Avon, California Perfume Company, Lavender Water, Label, C.1915 .... 75.00
Avon, California Perfume Company, Little Folks Set, Rose Label, 1906 .... 50.00
Avon, California Perfume Company, Maple Flavor, 2 Oz. 10.00
Avon, California Perfume Company, Maple Flavor, 1932 .... 25.00
Avon, California Perfume Company, Marionette Perfume, 1 Dram, 1936 .... 85.00
Avon, California Perfume Company, Marionette Perfume, 8 Oz. 29.50
Avon, California Perfume Company, Milk Glass, Metal Cover 10.00
Avon, California Perfume Company, Perfection Cologne, 1/2 Oz., 1936 .... 40.00
Avon, California Perfume Company, Perfection Coloring Set, 1936, Tin Box 45.00
Avon, California Perfume Company, Perfection Food Coloring, 2 Oz., Box 60.00
Avon, California Perfume Company, Perfection Savory, 4 Oz., 1936 .... 50.00
Avon, California Perfume Company, Perfume Flaconette, Vernafleur, 1928 .... 72.50
Avon, California Perfume Company, Rouge, Turquoise, 1937 .... 10.00
Avon, California Perfume Company, Shampoo Cream 1908 .... 100.00
Avon, California Perfume Company, Starch Dressing, Full & Boxed, 1912 .... 22.50
Avon, California Perfume Company, Talc, Slide Top, 1930 .... 30.00
Avon, California Perfume Company, Tissue Cream, 2 Oz., 1934 .... 40.00

Avon, California Perfume Company, Fruit Flavor Extract

Avon, California Perfume Company, Tooth Tablet, Milk Glass, 1906	75.00
Avon, California Perfume Company, Tooth Tablet, 1908	150.00
Avon, California Perfume Company, Trailing Arbutus Perfume, 1929	75.00
Avon, California Perfume Company, Vanishing Cream, 2 Oz., 1934	50.00
Avon, California Perfume Company, Vernafleur Powder	10.00
Avon, California Perfume Company, White Lilac Perfume, 1915	50.00
Avon, California Perfume Company, Witch Hazel, Pre-Machine, Early 1900s	50.00
Avon, Cameo Cream Sachet, Label, 1962	5.00 To 6.95
Avon, Cameo Set, 1965, Full & Boxed	12.50 To 30.00
Avon, Cameo Soap On Rope, 1969, Full & Boxed	3.00
Avon, Cameo Soap Set, 1966, Full & Boxed	8.95
Avon, Candle, Amber, 1965, Full & Boxed	8.00 To 10.00
Avon, Candle, First Christmas, 1967	6.00
Avon, Candle, Milk Glass, Embossed, 1964	5.00 To 8.00
Avon, Candle, Red, 1965	12.00
Avon, Candle, Regence, Tall, 1968, Full & Boxed	12.00
Avon, Candle, Regence, 1967	8.00 To 11.50
Avon, Candle, Wassail Bowl, 1969	8.00
Avon, Candle, White, Gold Band, 1966	6.50
Avon, Candle, 1967, Perfumed, Full & Boxed	10.00
Avon, Candleholder, Amber	9.95
Avon, Candleholder, Crystalite, 1970, Full & Boxed	4.50
Avon, Candleholder, Floral, Full & Boxed	3.50
Avon, Candleholder, Frosted, 1967, Full & Boxed	10.00
Avon, Candleholder, Golden Apple, Full & Boxed	7.00
Avon, Candleholder, Red, Amber, 1965	9.00
Avon, Candlestick Cologne, 1966	5.00
Avon, Candlestick, Ruby Red, 1970, Full & Boxed	5.00
Avon, Candlestick, Silver, 1966, Full & Boxed	9.50
Avon, Cannon, Full & Boxed	14.95
Avon, Capitol Decanter	3.99
Avon, Captain's Choice, Canadian, Black Cap	9.95
Avon, Captain's Choice, 1964	5.00 To 7.50
Avon, Car, Cadillac, Full & Boxed	4.99
Avon, Car, Green	3.00
Avon, Car, Packard Roadster, Full & Boxed	4.00
Avon, Car, Straight Eight, Full & Boxed	2.99
Avon, Carafe, Cut Glass, Star Pattern	55.00
Avon, Carnation Powder Sachet, 1920	42.50 To 50.00
Avon, Casey's Lantern, Amber	15.95 To 18.00
Avon, Casey's Lantern, Green	12.00 To 18.00
Avon, Casey's Lantern, Red	Color 6.00 To 18.00
Avon, Charger	4.50
Avon, Charisma Tray	3.00
Avon, Charlie Brown Mug, Full & Boxed	4.50
Avon, Chessmen, White, Full & Boxed	6.00 To 10.00
Avon, Chief Scrubbem	4.50
Avon, Christmas Award, Full	45.00
Avon, Christmas Ornament Set, 1964	50.00
Avon, Christmas Ornament, Gold, 1967	2.50
Avon, Christmas Ornament, Green, 1967	4.00
Avon, Christmas Ornament, Red, 1967	3.00
Avon, Christmas Ornament, Silver, 1967	2.50
Avon, Christmas Ornament, Stockholders, 1959	50.00
Avon, Christmas Tree, Gold, 1968, Full & Boxed	5.00
Avon, Christmas Tree, Green, 1968, Full & Boxed	5.00
Avon, Christmas Tree, Red	2.50
Avon, Christmas Tree, Red, 1968, Full & Boxed	3.50
Avon, Christmas Tree, Set Of 4, Full & Boxed	15.75
Avon, Christmas Tree, Silver, 1968, Full & Boxed	3.50 To 5.00
Avon, Circus Wagon Soap, 1957, Full & Boxed	22.00 To 35.00
Avon, Classic Book, Blue, Full & Boxed	7.95
Avon, Classic Book, Clear, 1969, Full & Boxed	3.95
Avon, Classic Book, Dark Amber	4.79
Avon, Classic Book, Light Amber	5.50
Avon, Classic Book, Set Of 4	14.00 To 16.00

Avon, Classic Goddess	7.00
Avon, Clean Shot, 1970, Full & Boxed	2.99 To 5.99
Avon, Clock, Full & Boxed	3.50 To 5.50
Avon, Clover Leaf Tray, Boxed	10.95
Avon, Coach, Embossed After Shave, 2 Oz., White Cap, 1960	12.00
Avon, Cologne Atomizer, Boxed	8.95
Avon, Cologne Bell, 1965	12.50
Avon, Cologne Classic, 1967, Full & Boxed	4.50
Avon, Cologne For Men, 1943	50.00
Avon, Cologne Gem, Set, 1967, Full & Boxed	5.50
Avon, Cologne Plus Spicy	12.50
Avon, Cologne Riviera, 1968, Full & Boxed	6.50
Avon, Cologne Silk, 1966, 3 Oz., Full & Boxed	2.75
Avon, Cologne Spray Boat, Leather, Full Boxed	3.00
Avon, Cologne Trilogy, 1969, Full & Boxed	8.50
Avon, Color Garden Nail Polish Set, 1964, Full & Boxed	7.95
Avon, Cornucopia Decanter	3.50
Avon, Cotillion Beauty Dust, 1954	10.00
Avon, Cotillion Beauty Dust, 1959	6.00
Avon, Cotillion Beauty Dust, 1962	2.00
Avon, Cotillion Body Powder, Full & Boxed	13.00
Avon, Cotillion Body Powder, 1957, Full & Boxed	11.50
Avon, Cotillion Cologne Mist, 1959	90.00
Avon, Cotillion Cologne Mist, 1961, Yellow Bottom	6.00
Avon, Cotillion Cologne, Frosted, Full	5.00
Avon, Cotillion Cologne, 1947	72.50
Avon, Cotillion Cologne, 1950, 4 Oz., Full & Boxed	20.00
Avon, Cotillion Cologne, 1954, 4 Oz., Full & Boxed	7.50
Avon, Cotillion Cream Lotion & Cologne, 1951	35.00
Avon, Cotillion Cream Lotion, 1953	6.95
Avon, Cotillion Cream Sachet, 1957, Boxed	4.00
Avon, Cotillion Perfume, Garden Of Love, Ballard, Gold Round Box, 1948	60.00
Avon, Cotillion Perfume Oil	3.00
Avon, Cotillion Perfume, 1936, 1 Dram	25.00
Avon, Cotillion Perfume, 1964, Glass Stopper	25.00
Avon, Cotillion Powder Sachet, 1946	8.00
Avon, Cotillion Powder Sachet, 1947	7.00
Avon, Cotillion Powder Sachet, 1950	10.00
Avon, Cotillion Powder Sachet, 1954	4.50
Avon, Cotillion Powder Sachet, 1958	4.00
Avon, Cotillion Powder Sachet, 1958	7.95
Avon, Cotillion Powder Sachet, 1958, Pink, 1 1/4 Oz., Full & Boxed	6.00
Avon, Cotillion Powder Sachet, 1961, Boxed	8.00
Avon, Cotillion Powder Sachet, 1965	3.00
Avon, Cotillion Singing Bells, 1957, Full & Boxed	12.00 To 15.00
Avon, Cotillion Soap, 1954, Full & Boxed	20.00
Avon, Cotillion Toilet Water, 2 Oz., 1954, Full & Boxed	7.00
Avon, Country Club Men's Set, 1953, Full & Boxed	22.50
Avon, Courting Lamp, Full & Boxed	5.99
Avon, Covered Wagon, Boxed	3.00
Avon, Cranberry Powder Sachet	3.00
Avon, Cranberry Shaker, 1969	3.00
Avon, Cream Cake, 1949, Full & Boxed	4.99
Avon, Cream Hair Rinse, 1956, Full	5.00
Avon, Cream Rouge, 1942	8.00
Avon, Crystal Chandelier, 1969, Full & Boxed	5.50 To 7.50
Avon, Crystal Cologne, 1966, Full & Boxed	5.00
Avon, Crystal Glory, 1962, Full & Boxed	4.50 To 9.75
Avon, Crystalite Cologne, Full & Boxed	3.85
Avon, Cup, Demitasse, Blue & White, 1968	2.00
Avon, Cup, Demitasse, Rose, 1969	2.00
Avon, Cupid's Bow Set, 1956, Full & Boxed	47.50
Avon, Daisies Won't Tell Cologne Mist, 1962	4.00
Avon, Daisies Won't Tell Cologne, 1955, 2 Oz.	10.00
Avon, Daisies Won't Tell Cologne, 1962, 2 Oz.	7.00
Avon, Daisies Won't Tell Spray Cologne, 1957, Full & Boxed	7.00

Avon, Daisy Pick A Daisy Set, 1958	18.50
Avon, Daisy Pin, Perfume, 1969, Full & Boxed	5.50
Avon, Daisy Pretty Beginners Set, 1957	18.50
Avon, Daphne Talcum, 1936, Full & Boxed	8.00
Avon, Daylight Shaving Time, Full & Boxed, 1968	3.00 To 6.00
Avon, Decisions, Decisions, 1965	19.50 To 25.00
Avon, Decorator Soap Dish & Soap	4.99
Avon, Defender Cannon, 1966, Full & Boxed	16.00
Avon, Deluxe After Shave Powder, Brown	6.00
Avon, Deluxe Deodorant, Normal, Brown	6.00
Avon, Deluxe Oatmeal, Box	14.95
Avon, Dinner Bell, Full & Boxed, 1968	3.00 To 5.00
Avon, Dollars & Scents, Full & Boxed	13.50 To 25.00
Avon, Dolphin, 1968	Color 6.00
Avon, Dramatic Moments, Set, Full & Boxed	25.00
Avon, Dream Pipe	9.00
Avon, Dressing Table, Cream Sachet, 1962, Empty	7.50
Avon, Duck Decanter, Mallard, 1967, Full & Boxed	4.00 To 8.00
Avon, Dueling Pistols, Red Box, Pair	25.00 To 45.00
Avon, Duesenberg, Silver, Full & Boxed	8.00
Avon, Dune Buggy	3.99
Avon, Dusting Powder, Tin, 1936, 13 Oz.	10.00 To 18.75
Avon, Eiffel Tower, Full & Boxed	4.00
Avon, Electra, Boxed	3.00
Avon, Electric Charger	3.00
Avon, Electric Pre-Shave Lotion, 1958, 4 Oz., Full	6.00
Avon, Electric Pre-Shave, 4 Oz., 1967	1.50
Avon, Elegante Beauty Dust, Full & Boxed	12.95
Avon, Elegante Beauty Dust, 1956	15.00
Avon, Elegante Cologne, Full & Boxed, 1957	20.00
Avon, Elegante Cologne, 1957	8.00 To 13.00
Avon, Elegante Cologne, 4 Oz., 1956, Full & Boxed	30.00
Avon, Elegante Essence De Fleurs, 1956	8.00
Avon, Elegante Perfume, 1967	55.00
Avon, Elegante Powder Sachet, 1956, Boxed	15.00
Avon, Elegante Powder Sachet, 1957, Full & Boxed	7.00
Avon, Elegante Toilet Water, 2 Oz., 1956, Full & Boxed	25.00
Avon, Elegante Toilet Water, 1957, Full & Boxed	27.50
Avon, Elephant, Pink	1.00
Avon, Elite Powder, 1912, Full & Boxed	62.00
Avon, Elusive Tray	3.00
Avon, Embossed Leaves Cologne, 1966, Full & Boxed	3.99
Avon, Empress Lipstick & Compact Set	10.00
Avon, Essence, Flat Top Rocker	3.00
Avon, Excalibur, Full & Boxed, 1969	3.00
Avon, Face Powder, 1950, Full & Boxed	3.99
Avon, Fair Lady Set, Blue Caps, 1949	75.00
Avon, Fan Rocker, With Tassel, 1963	3.00
Avon, Fielder's Choice	2.99
Avon, Fife Hair Trainer, 1965, Full & Boxed	8.00
Avon, First Down Football, 1970, Full & Boxed	3.00
Avon, First Edition, 1967	4.00 To 7.00
Avon, First Recital Daisy Set, 1962	18.50
Avon, First Volunteer	5.99
Avon, Flamingo Decanter	3.99
Avon, Floral Medley Candles	4.50
Avon, Floral Talc Set, 1965, Full & Boxed	8.95
Avon, Flower Fantasy, 1963, Full & Boxed	8.00
Avon, Flowertime Cologne, 4 Oz., 1949, Full & Boxed	20.00
Avon, Flowertime Powder Sachet, 1949, Full & Boxed	8.50
Avon, Flowertime Talc & Cologne Set, 1949, Full & Boxed	32.00
Avon, Fluff Puff, 1967, Full & Boxed	5.50
Avon, Football, Rubber	5.25
Avon, For Your Loveliness, 1956, Full & Boxed	11.00
Avon, Forever Spring Beauty Dust, Green	14.95
Avon, Forever Spring Body Powder, 1951, Full & Boxed	13.50

Avon, Forever Spring Body Powder, 1957	10.00
Avon, Forever Spring Cologne, 1950, 4 Oz., Full & Boxed	20.00
Avon, Forever Spring Cologne, 1956, Bird On Top, Full	17.50
Avon, Forever Spring Cream Lotion	6.25
Avon, Forever Spring Cream Sachet, 1950, Full & Boxed	9.95
Avon, Forever Spring Perfume, 1950, Glass Stopper	57.50 To 65.00
Avon, Forever Spring Powder Sachet, 1950	8.00
Avon, Forever Spring Powder Sachet, 1956	6.00
Avon, Forever Spring Talc	4.99
Avon, Forever Spring Toilet Water, 1950, 2 Oz., Full & Boxed	20.00
Avon, Forever Spring Toilet Water, 1956, Bird On Top, Full	17.50
Avon, Fostoria Salt Cellar, 1969	6.00
Avon, Four A After Shave, Full & Boxed	22.50
Avon, Four A Award Bowl, Eilber, Emblem In Bottom, 9 In.	32.50
Avon, Four A Pearl Pin, Boxed	8.00
Avon, Four A Sapphire Pin, Boxed	12.00
Avon, Four A, Mirror Top, Full & Boxed	19.95
Avon, Four Leaf Clover Award Pin	10.00
Avon, Fox Hunt Set, 1966, Full & Boxed	15.00 To 25.00
Avon, Fragrance Bell, Label, 1965	7.95
Avon, Fragrance Bell, Tag & Label, 1965	11.95
Avon, Fragrance Chest Set, Silver Caps, 1966, Full & Boxed	15.00 To 25.00
Avon, Fragrance Favorites, 1965	7.00
Avon, Fragrance Fling Trio, 1968, Full & Boxed	7.95
Avon, Fragrance Flings, 1968	1.00
Avon, Fragrance Fortune	12.00
Avon, Fragrance Gem Set, 1963, Full & Boxed	9.95
Avon, Fragrance Hours	4.99
Avon, Fragrance Jar, Ribbon, 1948	22.50
Avon, Fragrance Jar, 1934	25.00
Avon, Fragrance Jar, 1943, Pink Ceramic	49.50
Avon, Fragrance Ornaments, 1965, Full & Boxed	25.00 To 42.50
Avon, Fragrance Rainbow Set, 1957	45.00
Avon, Fragrance Touch, 1969	4.00
Avon, Freddy The Frog Soap & Dish	4.50
Avon, French Perfume, 1 Oz., 1963, Full & Boxed	35.00
Avon, French Phone, Full & Boxed	18.00 To 22.50
Avon, Futura, Full & Boxed, 1969	16.50
Avon, Garden Of Love Powder Sachet, 1948	15.00 To 20.00
Avon, Gardenia Perfume, 1939, Three Drams	85.00
Avon, Gardenia Perfume, 1952, Three Drams, Full & Boxed	49.50
Avon, Gardenia Perfume, 1946, 1/2 Oz.	50.00
Avon, Gavel, Full & Boxed, 1967	9.00 To 14.50
Avon, Gentleman's Collection, 1968, Full & Boxed	9.00
Avon, Gentlemen's Collection, 1967	17.50
Avon, German Decision, Full & Boxed	19.50
Avon, Gold Leaf Pin, 1969, Full & Boxed	4.50
Avon, Golden Angel, 1968, Full & Boxed	4.50
Avon, Golden Apple	4.95 To 7.99
Avon, Golden Arch, Set	8.00
Avon, Golden Heirloom, 1968, Full & Boxed	35.00
Avon, Golden Promise Body Powder, 1948, Full Boxed	18.00
Avon, Golden Promise Body Powder, 1950, Full & Boxed	13.50
Avon, Golden Promise Cologne Body Powder, Montreal, 1948	20.00
Avon, Golden Promise Cologne, 4 Oz., 1948, Full & Boxed	13.00 To 20.00
Avon, Golden Promise Perfume, Glass Stopper, 1955	75.00
Avon, Golden Promise Powder Sachet, Gold Metal Cap, 1948	8.00 To 15.00
Avon, Golden Promise Powder Sachet, 1951, Yellow Cap, Full & Boxed	9.50
Avon, Golden Promise Precious Pear, 1953	60.00
Avon, Golden Promise Toilet Water, 2 Oz., 1948	17.50
Avon, Golden Slipper, 1959, Full & Boxed	180.00 To 200.00
Avon, Golden Vanity, With Mirror, 1965, Full & Boxed	19.50 To 23.00
Avon, Good Habit Rabbit, 1967, Full & Boxed	5.00
Avon, Grade A Egg Soap, Full & Boxed	2.00
Avon, Grecian Urn	4.00
Avon, Greek Goddess, 1969, Full & Boxed	6.50

Avon, Gun, 20 Paces, Full & Boxed	28.50
Avon, Hand Lotion, 1944, Full & Boxed	11.25
Avon, Hand Lotion, 1951	17.50
Avon, Hand On Bottle	3.96
Avon, Hansel & Gretel Soap, Box	11.95
Avon, Happy Hours, Memento Set, 1949, Full & Boxed	87.50
Avon, Happy Hours Talc	25.00
Avon, Harmony Rouge, Box	10.00
Avon, Hawaiian Delights, 1962, Boxed	7.00 To 10.00
Avon, Heirloom Set, Full & Boxed	35.00
Avon, Helmet, Blue Stripe	6.95
Avon, Helmet, Dull Gold, Full & Boxed	8.00 To 9.50
Avon, Helmet, Shiny Gold, Full & Boxed	16.50 To 26.00
Avon, Here's My Heart Beauty Dust, 1958	2.00
Avon, Here's My Heart Cologne Mist, 1955, Blue	11.00
Avon, Here's My Heart Cologne Mist, 1955, Green	20.00
Avon, Here's My Heart Cream Lotion, 1958, Full & Boxed	2.99
Avon, Here's My Heart Lotion Sachet	5.50
Avon, Here's My Heart Perfume	150.00
Avon, Here's My Heart Perfume Oil	2.00
Avon, Here's My Heart Powder Sachet, 1958	7.00
Avon, Here's My Heart Powder Sachet, 1960, Full & Boxed	6.99
Avon, Here's My Heart Soap Set, 1959, Full & Boxed	9.95 To 12.00
Avon, Here's My Heart Toilet Water	5.50
Avon, High Fashion Set, 1950, Boxed	22.50
Avon, Holiday Spice Set, 1965, Full & Boxed	9.50
Avon, Hormone Cream, 1951, Full & Boxed	3.99
Avon, Hostess Bouquet Soap, 1959, Full & Boxed	12.00
Avon, Humpty Dumpty Bubble Bath, 1963, Full & Boxed	8.00
Avon, Ice Cream Puff, 1968, Empty	2.50
Avon, Icicle, 1967, Full & Boxed	3.50
Avon, Indian Head, 1969, Full & Boxed	3.00
Avon, Inkwell, Pen, Full & Boxed	4.99 To 6.50
Avon, Insect Repellant, 1960	4.00
Avon, Insect Repellant, 1963, Full & Boxed	5.00
Avon, Island Lime Triangle, 1969	3.00
Avon, Island Lime, Dark Yellow Straw, 1966, Full & Boxed	49.00
Avon, Island Lime, Dark Yellow, 1968	4.50
Avon, Island Lime, Green Weave	7.95
Avon, Island Lime, Light Weave, 1966	5.00
Avon, Its A Blast, Full & Boxed	4.00
Avon, Jardin D'Amour Flaconette, 1929	65.00
Avon, Jardin D'Amour Powder Sachet, 1934	12.50
Avon, Jasmine Beauty Dust, 1946	15.95
Avon, Jasmine Dusting Powder, Metal Box	20.00
Avon, Jasmine Powder Sachet, 1946, Full & Boxed	14.95
Avon, Jewel Collection, 1964, Full & Boxed	40.00 To 58.00
Avon, Jeweled Owl Pin, Full & Boxed	4.50
Avon, Jeweled Slipper, Half Full	185.00
Avon, Jumpin'Jiminy	4.00
Avon, Just Two, Set, 1965, Full & Boxed	34.50 To 62.50
Avon, Just Two, Tags & Labels	40.00 To 49.50
Avon, Just Two, 1951, Full & Boxed	72.50
Avon, Keepsake, Cream Sache, 1970, Full & Boxed	4.00
Avon, Key Note, Full & Boxed	8.00 To 13.50
Avon, King Pin, 1969, Full & Boxed	2.99
Avon, Kwick Foam Shave Cream, 1958	5.99
Avon, Lace My Shoe	2.75
Avon, Lady Belle Styrofoam Bell, 1966	59.50
Avon, Lady Slipper Soap & Perfume, 1970, Full & Boxed	4.00
Avon, Lady Slipper Soap, 1965, Full & Boxed	7.00
Avon, Lavender & Lace, 1970, Full & Boxed	3.50
Avon, Lavender Powder Sachet	3.00 To 6.00
Avon, Leaf & Pearl Pin	5.00
Avon, Leather Classic, Boxed	5.00
Avon, Leather Spray Cologne Boot, 1967	3.00

Avon, **Leg Makeup**, 1948, Full & Boxed	11.25
Avon, **Leisure Hours**, Boxed	3.75
Avon, **Liberty Dollar**	3.00
Avon, **Lil Folks Time**, Soap, Box	9.95
Avon, **Lilac Soaps**, 1968, Full & Boxed	3.50
Avon, **Liquid Deodorant For Men**, 2 Oz., 1967	1.00
Avon, **Liquid Shampoo**, 1936, Full & Boxed	13.00
Avon, **Little Helper Iron Bubble Bath**, 1962	9.50
Avon, **Little Pro Soap**, Full & Boxed	5.00
Avon, **Lonesome Pine Soap**, 1966	7.00
Avon, **Looking Glass Mirror**, Full & Boxed	4.99
Avon, **Lotion Lovely**, Full & Boxed	4.00 To 5.99
Avon, **Lovebird**, 1969, Full & Boxed	39.00 To 4.95
Avon, **Lucy Mug**, Full & Boxed	4.50
Avon, **Luscious Perfume**	100.00
Avon, **Luscious Perfume**, 1 Dram, 1950	7.00
Avon, **Mad Hatter**, Full & Boxed	4.50
Avon, **Mailbox**, Full & Boxed	3.50
Avon, **Mama Bear**, 1966	3.00
Avon, **Man's World Globe**, 1969, Full & Boxed	4.95 To 6.00
Avon, **Manicure Beauty Kit**, 1968, Full & Boxed	8.00
Avon, **Manicure Tray**, 1965, White	6.50
Avon, **Marionette Perfume**, 1936, 1/2 Oz.	25.00
Avon, **Marionette Powder Sachet**, 1936	19.00
Avon, **Marionette Toilet Water**, 2 Oz., 1940	30.00
Avon, **Master Organizer**, 1970, Full & Boxed	29.50
Avon, **Men's Bureau Organizer**, 1966, Full & Boxed	45.00
Avon, **Men's Hair Lotion**, 1949, 1 Oz., Sample, Full & Boxed	17.50
Avon, **Men's Talc Can**, 1958	5.95
Avon, **Mickey Mouse Bubble Bath**, 1969	1.50
Avon, **Miss Lollypop Boot**	5.00
Avon, **Miss Lollypop Cologne Mist**	4.00
Avon, **Miss Lollypop Spray Head**, Full & Boxed	3.75
Avon, **Mitten Kitten Soap**	4.00
Avon, **Most Valuable Soap Set**, 1963, Full & Boxed	12.00
Avon, **Mother's Helper**, Blue Iron, Boxed	8.00
Avon, **Motorcycle**, Full & Boxed	6.00
Avon, **Mouse**, Full & Boxed	7.00 To 10.00
Avon, **Mr.Presto Chango**	4.50
Avon, **Mug**, Charlie Brown, 1969, Full & Boxed	3.00
Avon, **Mug**, Lucy, 1969, Full & Boxed	3.00
Avon, **Mug**, Peanuts	5.00
Avon, **Mug**, Snoopy, 1969, Full & Boxed	3.00
Avon, **Nail Beauty**, 1955	2.99
Avon, **Natoma Rose Talcum Can**, 1915	55.00
Avon, **Nearness Beauty Dust**, Cardboard, Full & Boxed	15.00
Avon, **Nearness Beauty Dust**, Plastic, Full & Boxed	10.00
Avon, **Nearness Body Powder**, Glass, Full & Boxed	15.00
Avon, **Nearness Body Powder**, 1954, Frosted, Blue Top	9.00
Avon, **Nearness Cologne Mist**, 1955	17.95
Avon, **Nearness Cologne Stick**, 1957	4.99
Avon, **Nearness Cologne**, 1/2 Oz., 1957, Full & Boxed	9.00
Avon, **Nearness Cologne**, 1954	15.00
Avon, **Nearness Cream Sachet**, Full & Boxed	5.00
Avon, **Nearness Perfume**, 1 Dram, 1954	5.00
Avon, **Nearness Powder Sachet**, 1954	7.00
Avon, **Nearness Shell Pin & Earrings Award Set**	29.50
Avon, **Nearness Talc Tin**	8.00
Avon, **Nearness Toilet Water**, 1954, Full & Boxed	15.00
Avon, **Nearness Toilet Water**, 1956, Full	17.00
Avon, **Nearness Two Pearls Set**, Box	27.50
Avon, **Nesting Dove**, Full & Boxed	4.50
Avon, **Occur Bud Vase**, Full & Boxed	3.00
Avon, **Occur Perfume Oil**, 1965	4.00
Avon, **Occur Powder Sachet**, 1960	7.00
Avon, **Occur Powder Sachet**, 1963	5.00

Avon, **Occur Soap Set**, Box	8.95
Avon, **Oland Gift Set**, Full & Boxed	9.95
Avon, **Old School Bell**, Full	14.95
Avon, **One Two Lace My Shoe**	5.00
Avon, **Orchard Blossom**, Cologne, 1940, 6 Oz.	52.00 To 60.00
Avon, **Orchard Blossom Cologne**, 6 Oz.	60.00
Avon, **Overnighter Set**, 2 Bottles, 1968, Full & Boxed	6.00
Avon, **Owl Pin**, Full & Boxed	7.50
Avon, **Packard Roadster**	*Color* 4.99
Avon, **Packy Elephant Soap**, Full & Boxed	7.00
Avon, **Paddle & Ball Set**, 1966, Full & Boxed	6.00
Avon, **Papa Bear**, 1966	3.00
Avon, **Parlor Lamp**, Full & Boxed	6.50
Avon, **Pasadena Cream Hair Lotion**	5.00
Avon, **Patterns Tray**	3.00
Avon, **Peach Cologne**, 1964	5.95
Avon, **Penguin Soap & Dish**	4.50
Avon, **Perfection Furniture Polish**, 1932	20.00
Avon, **Perfection Glace Necklace**, 1965	6.99
Avon, **Perfection Lemon Extract**, 2 Oz., 1942, Boxed	12.95
Avon, **Perfection Liquid Spots Out**, 1932, Full & Boxed	25.00
Avon, **Perfection Liquid Spots Out**, 1942, Full & Boxed	7.50
Avon, **Perfection Mothicide**, Can, 1955	5.00
Avon, **Perfection Mothicide**, 1943, 8 Oz.	15.00
Avon, **Perfection Powdered Cleaner**, 1942	9.00
Avon, **Perfection Prepared Starch**, 1930	20.00
Avon, **Perfection Silver Cream Polish**, 1930	15.00
Avon, **Perfection Silver Cream Polish**, 1943, 10 1/2 Oz.	15.00
Avon, **Perfume Flacon**, 1 Dram, 1966	4.00
Avon, **Perfume Pendant**, 1970, Boxed	12.00
Avon, **Perfume Pillowette**, 1965, Full & Boxed	9.50
Avon, **Perfume Rocker**, 1959, Full	4.50
Avon, **Perfume With Metal Leaves**, 1/2 Oz., 1966	6.00
Avon, **Persian Wood Bath Oil**, 6 Oz., Plastic, Full	5.50
Avon, **Persian Wood Beauty Dust**, Glass, 1956	12.50
Avon, **Persian Wood Beauty Dust**, 1957	10.50
Avon, **Persian Wood Beauty Dust**, 1960	5.95
Avon, **Persian Wood Body Powder**, Full & Boxed	7.95
Avon, **Persian Wood Cologne Mist**, 1957	9.00
Avon, **Persian Wood Cologne**, Embossed, Stopper, 1/2 Oz.Boxed	8.50
Avon, **Persian Wood Cologne**, 1959, 4 Oz.	12.50
Avon, **Persian Wood Cologne**, 1960, 4 Oz., Full & Boxed	13.99
Avon, **Persian Wood Cream Lotion**, Full	5.50
Avon, **Persian Wood Gift Fancy Set**, 1957, Boxed	14.00
Avon, **Persian Wood Perfume Oil**, Full	5.00
Avon, **Persian Wood Powder Sachet**, 1957	5.00
Avon, **Persian Wood Powder Sachet**, 1959	4.00
Avon, **Persian Wood Toilet Water**, 1959	11.00
Avon, **Petite Mouse**, 1970, Full & Boxed	6.00
Avon, **Petitpoint Perfume Glace**, 1967, Full & Boxed	10.00
Avon, **Petti Fleur**, 1969	3.00
Avon, **Pick A Daisy Set**, 1963	18.50
Avon, **Picture Frame**, Full & Boxed	6.00
Avon, **Pig In A Poke**, 1960, Full & Boxed	6.00
Avon, **Pillowettes**, Perfumed, 1965, Full & Boxed	15.00
Avon, **Pin Bottle**, see Avon, Bowling Pin	
Avon, **Pine Bath Salts**, 1936, Full	16.00
Avon, **Pipe Dream**, 1967, Amber	10.00 To 16.50
Avon, **Pistols Dueling**, Red, Full & Boxed	25.00 To 45.00
Avon, **Pitcher & Bowl Set**, Full & Boxed	6.25
Avon, **Pom Pom Cologne**, Milk White, 1 Oz., Full & Boxed	3.50
Avon, **Pony Post**, Short, 1968	*Color* 3.95
Avon, **Pony Post**, Tall, 1966	3.99 To 8.00
Avon, **Potbellied Stove**, Full & Boxed	3.50
Avon, **Powder Pak**, 1951, Full & Boxed	3.99
Avon, **Pre-Electric Shave**, Square, 4 Oz., 1962	4.00

Avon, Precious Pair Delights	1.99
Avon, President Horn Award, 1967, Full & Box	15.00
Avon, Pretty Peach Beauty Dust, Full & Boxed	7.00
Avon, Pretty Peach Cologne, 1964, Full & Boxed	4.00
Avon, Pretty Peach Cream Lotion	60.00
Avon, Pretty Peach Cream Sachet	2.00
Avon, Pretty Peach Hand Cream, Full & Boxed	5.00
Avon, Pretty Peach Pomade, Full & Box	12.00
Avon, Pretty Peach Soap & Sponge, 1964, Full & Boxed	8.00
Avon, Pretty Peach Soap On Rope, 1964, Full & Boxed	7.00
Avon, Pretty Peach Soda Cologne Mist, 1964	8.00
Avon, Pretty Peach Talc, Full	4.50
Avon, Pump Dispenser, 1965, Full & Boxed	9.50
Avon, Pyramid, 1969, Full & Boxed	9.00 To 12.50
Avon, Quaintance Beauty Dust, Full & Boxed	15.00
Avon, Quaintance Body Powder, 1949	12.50
Avon, Quaintance Body Powder, 1952	10.00
Avon, Quaintance Charmer Set, 1950, Boxed	15.00
Avon, Quaintance Cologne, 4 Oz., 1949	12.50
Avon, Quaintance Cream Lotion, 1949, Full & Boxed	9.00
Avon, Quaintance Cream Sachet, 1949, Full	10.00
Avon, Quaintance Dairy Perfume	65.00
Avon, Quaintance Dusting Powder, 1951	10.00
Avon, Quaintance Powder Sachet, 1948	7.00
Avon, Quaintance Powder Sachet, 1949, Full & Boxed	6.00 To 10.00
Avon, Quaintance Sachet	8.00
Avon, Rapture Award Pin	12.50
Avon, Rapture Beauty Dust	1.50
Avon, Rapture Perfume Oil	5.95
Avon, Rapture Powder Sachet	3.75 To 6.00
Avon, Rapture Rhapsody Set, Full & Boxed	35.00
Avon, Rapture Rhapsody, 1964, Tray & Bottles	25.00
Avon, Rapture Rhapsody, 1965, Full & Boxed	27.50
Avon, Refreshing Cologne, 1936, Full & Boxed	26.25
Avon, Refreshing Hours Set, 1962, Full & Boxed	17.50
Avon, Regence Candle, 1968, Full	6.00
Avon, Regence Gift Set, 1966	15.50
Avon, Regence Hand Mirror, 1966, Boxed	7.00
Avon, Regence Perfume Oil	3.00
Avon, Renaissance Cologne, Full & Boxed	2.50
Avon, Renaissance Trio Set, Full & Boxed	10.95
Avon, Rhapsody Tray & Set	37.95
Avon, Ribbed Perfume, 1952, 1 Dram	6.00
Avon, Rich Moisture Body Lotion, 1965	5.00
Avon, Ring Around Rosie Soap Set, Boxed, 1966	6.00 To 8.00
Avon, Ring Of Pearls	5.00
Avon, Riviera Cologne, Boxed	4.95
Avon, Rocker, Flat Top, 1959, Full & Boxed	3.50
Avon, Rocker, Perfume, 1 Oz.	27.00
Avon, Rose Fragrance Jar, Clear Stopper, 1948	25.00
Avon, Rose Fragrance Jar, Frosted Stopper, 1952	20.00
Avon, Rose Fragrance Jar, Frosted Stopper, 1958	15.00
Avon, Rose Fragrance Jar, 1937	25.00
Avon, Rose Geranium Bath Oil, 1945	16.00
Avon, Rose Geranium Bath Oil, 1357, Full & Boxed	19.50
Avon, Rose Geranium Liquid Soap Fragrance	12.50
Avon, Rose, Demi Cup, 1969, Full & Boxed	5.50
Avon, Royal Jasmine Bath Salts, 1954	12.95
Avon, Royal Orb, Red Letters, Neck Band	13.00
Avon, Royal Orb, 1965, Full & Boxed	11.00 To 22.50
Avon, Royal Orb, 1965	19.50
Avon, Royal Pine Bath Salts, 1951	12.00
Avon, Royal Pine, Set, 1954, Full & Boxed	27.50
Avon, Royal Swan	1.99
Avon, Royal Vase, Decanter, 1970, Full & Boxed	5.00
Avon, Safe Sam, Full & Boxed	6.00

Avon, **Sales Award Cream Sachet**, 1962 .... 7.00
Avon, **Santa's Chimney**, 1964, Full & Boxed 8.00
Avon, **Santa's Helper**, Full & Boxed 1.65
Avon, **Scentiment Set**, 1969, Full & Boxed 4.99
Avon, **School Daze** 8.00
Avon, **Scimitar**, Embossed S Coaches, 2 Oz., Full & Boxed 18.50
Avon, **Scimitar**, Embossed S Coaches, 2 Oz., Full & Boxed .... 10.00 To 18.50
Avon, **Scrub Mug**, Full & Boxed 4.50
Avon, **Sea Horse**, Full & Boxed 3.75
Avon, **Sea Maiden**, Full & Boxed 5.25
Avon, **Shaving Bowl**, Wooden, 1951, Full & Boxed 29.50
Avon, **Shaving Choice Set**, Blue & Silver Caps, Gold, 1967, Full & Boxed 7.00
Avon, **Sheriff's Badge Soap**, 1962, Full & Boxed 12.50
Avon, **Ship'In Bottle**, Full & Boxed 4.50
Avon, **Side Wheeler** 3.00
Avon, **Silk & Honey Beehive**, 1969 .... 5.00
Avon, **Silver Dollar**, 1970, Full & Boxed 4.00
Avon, **Silver Label Cologne**, 1949, 6 Oz. 9.95
Avon, **Six Shooter**, Full 9.50
Avon, **Skin Conditioner For Men**, Red Top 1.99
Avon, **Skin Conditioner For Men**, Tan Top, 1966 .... 4.50
Avon, **Skin-So-Soft Bath Urn**, 1965 .... 8.00
Avon, **Skin-So-Soft Cruet**, 1965 .... 5.00
Avon, **Skin-So-Soft**, Gold Band, 1965 .... 4.99
Avon, **Sleigh Mates**, 1966, Full & Boxed 4.99
Avon, **Smart Move Set**, Full & Boxed 27.50
Avon, **Smoker's Tooth Powder**, 1936, Full 11.25
Avon, **Smoker's Tooth Powder**, 1938, Full & Boxed .... 11.25 To 15.00
Avon, **Snail Perfume**, 1968, Full & Boxed .... 4.50 To 8.50
Avon, **Snoopy Doghouse**, Full & Boxed 2.00
Avon, **Somewhere Beauty Dust**, Jeweled 8.00
Avon, **Somewhere Beauty Dust**, 1961 .... 3.50
Avon, **Somewhere Cologne Mist**, 1961 .... 2.50
Avon, **Somewhere Cologne**, 2 Oz., 1961, Full & Boxed 5.50
Avon, **Somewhere Cream Lotion**, Green, Full & Boxed 15.00
Avon, **Somewhere Dusting Powder**, Full 10.00
Avon, **Somewhere Perfume**, 1 Oz., 1961 .... 125.00
Avon, **Somewhere Powder Sachet**, 1961 .... 7.00
Avon, **Somewhere Powder Sachet**, 1966 .... 12.50
Avon, **Somewhere Powder Sachet**, 1967 .... 12.00
Avon, **Sonnet Body Powder**, Full & Boxed 16.00
Avon, **Sonnet Toilet Water**, Full & Boxed 32.50
Avon, **Special Award**, Christmas Ornament 35.00
Avon, **Special Award**, 1964, Full & Boxed 39.95
Avon, **Spicy After Shave**, Amber, 1967 .... 1.00
Avon, **Spicy After Shave**, Clear, Full & Boxed 10.00
Avon, **Spicy After Shave**, 1965 .... 2.50
Avon, **Spicy Talc**, 1965 .... 2.50
Avon, **Spinning Top**, 1966, Full & Boxed 5.50
Avon, **Spirit Of St.Louis**, 1970 .... 50.00
Avon, **Splash & Spray Set**, 1968, Full & Boxed 14.00
Avon, **Sports Rally Aerosol Deodorant**, Can, Full 4.50
Avon, **Sports Rally Bracing Towelettes**, Full & Boxed 3.50
Avon, **Sports Rally Deodorant Soap**, Full & Boxed 4.50
Avon, **Sports Rally Deodorant**, 1966 .... 4.50
Avon, **Sports Rally Talc**, Full 4.50
Avon, **Spray Boots**, Full & Boxed 5.99
Avon, **Stagecoach**, 1960, Embossed, 2 Oz. 10.00
Avon, **Stagecoach**, 1960, Embossed, 4 Oz., Empty 15.00
Avon, **Stagecoach**, 1960, Embossed, 8 Oz., Empty 15.00
Avon, **Stanley Steamer** 3.99
Avon, **Station Wagon** 4.99
Avon, **Steer Horns**, 1967, Full & Boxed .... 12.00 To 25.00
Avon, **Stein**, Silver, 6 Oz., 1968 .... 2.00 To 5.00
Avon, **Stein**, Silver, 8 Oz., 1965 .... 5.00 To 10.00
Avon, **Sterling Six**, 1968 .... 3.00 To 6.50

Avon, Straight Eight, Full & Boxed	3.00
Avon, Strawberries & Cream, 1969	4.00
Avon, Strawberry Cooler	3.75
Avon, Strawberry Fair Soap, Full & Boxed	4.45
Avon, Strawberry Fragrance Soap, 1969, Full & Boxed	3.00
Avon, Strawberry Frosted Cooler	8.00
Avon, Structured For Men, 1969, Full & Boxed	16.50
Avon, Sun Lotion, Montreal, 1951	7.50
Avon, Sunny Hours Parasol Set	50.00
Avon, Sunny Sunfish, Soap, Box	7.95
Avon, Swan Lake, 3 Piece Set, 1948, Full & Boxed	110.00
Avon, Swinger	6.00
Avon, Swinger Golf Bag, 1969, Full & Boxed	5.50
Avon, Swinger, 1969, Full & Boxed	4.95
Avon, Syrup, Silver Plate Top, Spring Loaded	13.50
Avon, Tag Along Set	3.75
Avon, Telephone, Avon Calling, 1969, Full & Boxed	10.00
Avon, Temple Of Love, Box	14.00
Avon, Temple Of Love, Jar	15.00
Avon, Texas Sheriff Soap, Full & Boxed	18.00
Avon, Three Hearts On Cushion, Full & Boxed	28.50
Avon, Tic Toc Tiger, Full & Boxed	5.00
Avon, Tissue Cream, 1934	20.00
Avon, To a Wild Rose, see Avon, Wild Rose	
Avon, Tom Turtle Soap, Full & Boxed	7.00
Avon, Topaze Earrings Award	16.50
Avon, Topaze Jewel Set, 1961, Full & Boxed	14.50
Avon, Topaze Necklace Award	18.50
Avon, Topaze Perfume Oil, Full	3.00
Avon, Topaze Perfume, 1 Oz., 1959, Full & Boxed	95.00
Avon, Topaze Perfume, 1960	125.00
Avon, Topaze Powder Sachet, 1959	4.00
Avon, Topaze Spray Perfume, Full & Boxed	4.00
Avon, Topsy Turvy Clown, 1965	6.50
Avon, Touch Of Beauty, 1969, Soap	6.00
Avon, Touring T, Full & Boxed	2.75 To 4.50
Avon, Town Pump, 1968, Full & Boxed	4.00 To 6.00
Avon, Trailing Arbutus Perfume, 1934	37.50
Avon, Treasure Chest Soap Set, Boxed	15.00
Avon, Tribute After Shave, 4 Oz., 1967	1.00
Avon, Tribute Deodorant, 1963, Full & Boxed	3.99
Avon, Tribute Foam Shaving Cream & Lotion, Full & Boxed	13.50
Avon, Tribute Shaving Lotion, Full	4.50
Avon, Tribute Soap, Boxed	10.00
Avon, Trilogy Caddy	8.75
Avon, Tub Talk Telephone	5.00
Avon, Twenty Paces, Red Lining, Brown Box	22.50
Avon, Twin Tone Makeup Cream, White Milk Glass, Green Paper Lid, 1943	10.00
Avon, Two Loves Set, Full & Boxed	6.99
Avon, Unforgettable Beauty Dust	20.00
Avon, Unforgettable Heirloom, 1965, Full & Boxed	40.00
Avon, Unforgettable Perfume Oil	3.00
Avon, Unforgettable Powder Sachet	7.00
Avon, Urn, Milk Glass, 1963	8.00
Avon, Vanity Showcase, 1964	7.00
Avon, Vanity Tray, 1968, Full & Boxed	5.50
Avon, Vase, Royal Blue	3.50
Avon, Vernafleur Adherent, Powder Can, 1925	22.00
Avon, Vigorate, 1960, Frosted	4.50
Avon, Viking Horn, 1966, Full & Boxed	16.50
Avon, Vita Moist, 1966, Foreign, Full & Boxed	13.50
Avon, Volkswagen, Red	3.00
Avon, Warrior, Ribbed, European, Full & Boxed	4.99
Avon, Warrior, 1967, Silver	10.00
Avon, Wassail Bowl, 1969, Full & Boxed	7.50
Avon, Weather Or Not, Full & Boxed	4.95

Avon, Western Choice .... *Color*	20.00
Avon, White Marie Sachet, 1948, Full & Boxed	16.00
Avon, White Moire Cologne, 6 Oz., 1947	75.00
Avon, White Moire Cologne, 1948	40.00
Avon, White Moire Powder Sachet, Boxed	19.00
Avon, White Moire Set, 1948, Full & Boxed	75.00
Avon, Whitey The Whale, 1959	10.00
Avon, Wild Country Body Powder	8.50
Avon, Wild Country Cologne, 1967	2.00
Avon, Wild Country Dusting Powder, 1967	7.50
Avon, Wild Country Saddle Kit, Full & Boxed	30.00
Avon, Wild Country Soap On Rope, 1967	4.00
Avon, Wild Country Spray Cologne, 1968	7.00
Avon, Wild Country Spray Talc, 1969	2.00
Avon, Wild Rose Bath Oil, 1953	12.95
Avon, Wild Rose Beauty Dust, 1954	12.95
Avon, Wild Rose Cologne, 1950, Full & Boxed	15.00
Avon, Wild Rose Cologne Mist, 1954	11.00
Avon, Wild Rose Cream Lotion, 4 Oz., On Paper Label, 1954	4.00
Avon, Wild Rose Cream Lotion, Paper Label, 1958	4.00
Avon, Wild Rose Cream Sachet, 1950	6.95
Avon, Wild Rose Powder Sachet	3.75
Avon, Wild Rose Powder Sachet, 1950, Full & Boxed	9.50
Avon, Wild Rose Powder Sachet, 1963, Empty	8.00
Avon, Wild Rose Talc, 1957	2.50
Avon, Wild Rose Toilet Water, 1950, Full & Boxed	16.00
Avon, Windjammer Cologne, Painted Label	7.50
Avon, Windjammer Spray Talc, 1968	2.00
Avon, Wine Server Man's Cologne, Full & Boxed	24.00
Avon, Wise Owl, 1969, Full & Boxed	5.50
Avon, Wishing Beauty Dust	5.95
Avon, Wishing Cologne, Embossed, Stopper, 1/2 Oz., Boxed	8.50
Avon, Wishing Cologne, Printed Label, 1963	4.00
Avon, Wishing Come True, Gift Set, 1963, Full & Boxed	12.00
Avon, Wishing Perfume Oil, Full & Boxed	10.00
Avon, Wishing Powder Sachet, White Lid, 1963, Boxed	10.00
Avon, Wishing Powder Sachet, 1964, Yellow Lid	8.00
Avon, Wishing Skin Softener	3.50
Avon, Wooden Shaving Bowl, 1955	12.00
Avon, World's Greatest Dad	3.00
Avon, Wrist Watch, Plastic	2.96
Avon, Yankee Doodle Shower Soap, 1969, Full & Boxed	3.25
Avon, Yo-Yo Soap Set, Boxed	10.00
Avon, Young Hearts Cologne	17.50
Ballantine, Duck .... *Illus* 9.95 To 18.95	
Ballantine, Fisherman .... 14.95 To 18.95	
Ballantine, Golf Bag .... 9.95 To 18.95	
Ballantine, Knight, Silver .... *Illus*	15.00
Ballantine, Zebra .... *Illus*	14.00
Bank, Atlas Mason Jar, Miniature, 4 In.	4.50
Bank, Bear, Snowcrest, Clear, Abm	4.00
Bank, Cat, Grapette, Clear	4.00
Bank, Clown, Grapette	2.00
Bank, Clown, Snowcrest	4.00
Bank, Elephant, Grapette	2.00
Bank, Lincoln, Amethyst	6.00
Bank, Lincoln, Clear	3.00
Bank, Penguin, Snowcrest	4.00
Bank, Seal, Snowcrest	4.00
Bar, C.B.Seely's Sons, Inc., Embossed, Aqua, 29 Oz.	8.00
Bar, Cut Panels At Base & Neck, Cobalt Blue, 10 1/2 In.High	40.00
Bar, Eight Broad Panels, Cobalt Blue	40.00
Bar, Embossed Shield Border For Glass Label, Applied Ring Collar, Amber	18.00
Bar, Enamel Lettering, Black .... 12.50 To 35.00	
Bar, Ornate Silver Filigree, P.Monogram, Marked 999-1000	40.00
Bar, Pinch Style, Pewter Overlay Design Of Grapes & Leaves, Green ...	22.50

Ballantine, Knight, Silver
See Page 15

Ballantine, Zebra
See Page 15

Ballantine, Duck
See Page 15

Bar, Pressed Glass, Ashburton, 10 1/2 In.High	30.00
Bar, Pressed Glass, Horn Of Plenty, Flint, Quart	50.00
Bar, Sandwich Star, Blob Top, Flint, Quart	45.00

Barber bottles were used at either the barbershop or the home. They held hair tonic. These special, fancy bottles were popular in the last half of the nineteenth century.

Barber, Applied Lip, Hand Blown, Milk Glass, Fire Color, Pair	75.00
Barber, Bay Rum, Label	11.50
Barber, Bay Rum, Seward Bentley, Label, Applied Top	3.00
Barber, Bohemian Glass, Deer & Castle, Patent Dated 1900, Ruby	22.50
Barber, Bull's-Eye Swirl, Bulbous Base, H In Triangle Mark, 5 1/2 In.	10.00
Barber, Clambroth, Marked E.W.& Red Glass, Cutwork Panels On Neck	20.00
Barber, Clambroth, Porcelain Top	9.00
Barber, Cobalt	15.00
Barber, E.W.Inc., In Red, Opaque Glass, China Stopper, Pair	19.50
Barber, Emerald Green	15.00
Barber, Enameled Flower Decoration, Cobalt Blue, 9 In.Tall	25.00
Barber, Enameled Flower Design, Pontil, Bulged Neck, Bright Amethyst	33.00
Barber, Flowers, Green & White	35.00
Barber, Gold Flower, Porcelain Stopper, Amethyst	30.00
Barber, Hand Blown, Applied Lip, Pair	125.00
Barber, Hartshorn's Bay Rum, Boston, Mass, Dispenser Top, Label, Clear	1.00

Barber, Hobnail, Amber	45.00
Barber, Hobnail, Bulbous Base, Cylinder Neck, Clear, 5 In.High	8.00
Barber, Indented Panel, Milk Glass, 11 In.	20.00
Barber, Opalescent Hobs, Cranberry	50.00
Barber, P.G., Pewter Stopper, Paneled Neck, 7 In.	9.00
Barber, Paneled, Rolled Lip, China Stopper, C.1900	5.00
Barber, Porcelain Shaker Top, Clear, Pint	4.00
Barber, Sandwich Milk Glass, Hand Blown, Rolled Lip, Pontil, Pair	150.00
Barber, Spanish Lace, Slender Neck, 19th Century, Pair	36.00
Barber, T.Noonan And Co., Milk Glass White & Green	25.00
Barber, Water Witch Hazel In Blue, Opaque Glass, China Stopper, Pair	19.50
Barber, Yellow Amber	7.50
Barber, 8 Fluted Panels, Stopper, Clear, 9 3/4 In.High	9.50
Bardi, Donkey	3.95
Bardi, Drummer Boy	3.95
Bardi, Elephant	3.95
Bardi, Rifleman	3.95
Barrel, see also Food, Barrel	
Barrel, Golden Treasure, Light Aqua, 5 1/2 In. High *Illus*	35.00
Barrel, Joshua Wright, Aqua, 2 Quart	100.00
Barrel, That's The Stuff, Open Pontil, Yellow Amber	420.00
Barrel, Turner Brothers, New York, Amber	110.00
Barrel, Wormser Brothers, San Francisco, Amber	350.00
Barsottini, Alpine Pipe	10.00
Barsottini, Antique Auto	6.50
Barsottini, Antique Carriage	5.99
Barsottini, Apollo	14.95
Barsottini, Arch Of Trumph	12.75 To 15.00
Barsottini, Augustine Monk	11.95
Barsottini, Candlestick	11.00
Barsottini, Cannon	17.95
Barsottini, Carriage Lamp	8.99
Barsottini, Clock	22.00
Barsottini, Clock With Cherub	34.95
Barsottini, Clown	6.00
Barsottini, Coliseum	10.00
Barsottini, Donkey	6.00
Barsottini, Eiffel Tower	12.00
Barsottini, Elephant	6.00
Barsottini, Elk's Head	10.00
Barsottini, Father John	12.00
Barsottini, Florentine Steeple	8.00
Barsottini, Fruit Basket	7.95
Barsottini, Giraffe	20.00
Barsottini, Horse Head	10.50

Barrel, Golden Treasure, Light Aqua, 5 1/2 In. High

Barsottini, Lamplighter	24.00
Barsottini, Leaning Tower	7.50
Barsottini, Lido Antique Peddler	10.00
Barsottini, Little Bacchus	10.55
Barsottini, Lovebirds	11.95 To 17.00
Barsottini, Lucky Dice	9.25
Barsottini, Mandolin	8.00
Barsottini, Mezzotint	9.00
Barsottini, Monastery Cask	17.45
Barsottini, Monk With Wine Jug	13.00
Barsottini, Owl	12.95
Barsottini, Pistol, Brown	5.95 To 7.00
Barsottini, Pistol, Green	5.95 To 7.00
Barsottini, Rabbit With Carrot	10.95
Barsottini, Renaissance	9.00
Barsottini, Roman Coliseum	10.00 To 12.00
Barsottini, Roman Tribune	10.95 To 13.40
Barsottini, Roman Urn	9.00
Barsottini, Rooster	15.00
Barsottini, Santa Claus	10.95
Barsottini, William Tell	15.00

Beam bottles are made as containers for the Kentucky Straight Bourbon made by the James Beam Distilling Company. The Beam ceramics were first made in 1953. Executive series bottles started in 1955. Regal china specialties were started in 1955 and political figures in 1956. Customer specialties were first made in 1956, trophy series in 1957, state series in 1958.

Beam, see also Whiskey, Bell Scotch

Beam, Agnew, Elephant, Political, Dinner, 1970	1750.00 To 2100.00
Beam, Alaska Purchase, 1966	12.50 To 31.95
Beam, Alaska Star, 1958	67.50 To 85.00
Beam, Alaska Star, 1964, 1965	67.50 To 78.00
Beam, Amvets, 1970	3.95 To 8.45
Beam, Antioch, Centennial, 1967	*Illus* 5.50 To 10.95
Beam, Antique Trader, 1968, 1969	3.95 To 7.50
Beam, Aristide Bruante, Collector's Edition Vol. II , 1967	2.50
Beam, Arizona, States, 1968, 1969	*Illus* 3.75 To 4.95
Beam, Armanetti First Award Winner, 1969, 1970	13.95 To 22.50
Beam, Armanetti Fun Bottle, 1971	17.00 To 22.50
Beam, Armanetti Vase, 1968, 1969	7.00 To 9.50
Beam, Ashtray, Ivory, 1955	22.50
Beam, B.P.O.Does, 1971, Regal China	8.95

Beam, Antioch,
Centennial, 1967

Beam, Arizona, States,
1968, 1969

Beam, **B.P.O.Elk**, 1968, 1969, Regal China 8.95
Beam, **Bacchus**, Armanetti, 1970 ....*Illus* 22.00 To 25.00
Beam, **Baseball**, 1969, 1970, Regal China .... 3.75 To 6.95
Beam, **Beameister**, Import 2.00
Beam, **Beatty Burro**, Nevada, 1970 .... 10.00
Beam, **Bell Ringer**, Afore Ye Go, 1970, Regal China .... 7.00 To 8.50
Beam, **Bell Ringer**, Plaid, 1970, Regal China ....7.00 To 8.50
Beam, **Bell Scotch**, 1970, Regal China 8.95
Beam, **Bing Crosby**, 29th, 1970, Regal China .... 3.95 To 5.45
Beam, **Bing Crosby**, 30th, 1971, Regal China .... *Illus* 3.95 To 4.95
Beam, **Bing Crosby**, 31st, 1972, Regal China, 2 Mold 18.45
Beam, **Binion's Horseshoe**, 1970, Regal China .... 8.00 To 12.95
Beam, **Black Katz Cat**, 1968, Regal China .... 8.00 To 9.95
Beam, **Blue Boy**, 1966 Collector's Edition, Vol. II 14.50
Beam, **Blue Cherub**, 1960, Executive Edition, Vol., II .... 65.00 To 87.50
Beam, **Blue Crystal**, 1971 .... 3.95
Beam, **Blue Daisy**, 1967, Regal China .... 4.00 To 6.50
Beam, **Blue Fox**, Anniversary, 1967, Regal China .... 100.00 To 145.00
Beam, **Blue Goose**, 1971 .... 3.95 To 6.00
Beam, **Blue Jay**, 1969, Regal China .... 4.95 To 8.95
Beam, **Blue Slot Machine**, Harold's Club, 1967 .... 13.00 To 19.00
Beam, **Boot Hill**, Dodge City, 1972, Regal China .... 7.95 To 10.50
Beam, **Broadmoor Hotel**, 1968, Regal China .... 3.95 To 6.45
Beam, **Bronte**, Jug, Miniature, 1 Oz., Import 1.75
Beam, **Bronte**, Jug, 3/4 Quart, Import 5.50
Beam, **Buffalo Bill**, 1971, Regal China .... 6.00 To 8.95
Beam, **Cable Car**, 1968, 1969, Regal China 4.95

Beam, Bacchus,
Armanetti, 1970

Beam, Bing Crosby, 30th,
1971, Regal China

Beam, **Cal-Neva**, 1969, Regal China 8.95
Beam, **California Derby**, 1971, Golden Gate Fields .... 12.00 To 24.95
Beam, **California Mission Club**, 1970, Regal China .... 1999 TO 38.45
Beam, **Cameo**, Blue, 1965 .... 4.95
Beam, **Cannon**, 1970 .... 2.95 To 4.50
Beam, **Cardinal**, 1968, Trophy .... 36.50 To 42.50
Beam, **Cat**, Burmese, 1967, Brown, Yellow Eyes 10.95
Beam, **Cat**, Siamese, 1967, Light Brown, Blue Eyes 10.95
Beam, **Cat**, Tabby, 1967, Grey 10.95
Beam, **Cedars Of Lebanon**, 1971, Regal China 8.95
Beam, **Centennial**, Alaska Purchase, 1966 .... 12.50 To 31.95
Beam, **Centennial**, Antioch, 1967 .... 6.50 To 10.95
Beam, **Centennial**, Baseball, 1969, 1970, Regal China .... 3.75 To 6.95
Beam, **Centennial**, Cheyenne, 1967, Regal China .... 6.50 To 14.95
Beam, **Centennial**, Chicago Fire, 1971 .... 19.95

Beam, **Centennial**, Civil War, North, 1961 .... 32.00 To 39.95
Beam, **Centennial**, Civil War, South, 1961 .... 39.95 To 45.00
Beam, **Centennial**, Elks, 1969, 1970 .... 5.00 To 8.95
Beam, **Centennial**, Indianapolis, Sesquicentennial, 1971 .... 7.95
Beam, **Centennial**, Laramie, 1968 .... 6.95
Beam, **Centennial**, Lombard, Illinois, 1969, 1970 .... 3.95
Beam, **Centennial**, Portola Trek, 1969, San Diego 4.50
Beam, **Centennial**, Powell Expedition, 1969 .... 7.95
Beam, **Centennial**, Reno, 1968, 1969 .... 3.95 To 8.95
Beam, **Centennial**, Preakness, 1970, 1971 .... 7.95
Beam, **Centennial**, Riverside, 1970 .... 24.95
Beam, **Centennial**, San Diego, Portola Trek, 1969 .... 5.00
Beam, **Centennial**, San Diego, 1968, Regal China 7.95
Beam, **Centennial**, Santa Fe, 1960 .... 175.00 To 225.00
Beam, **Centennial**, St.Louis Arch, 1964 .... 24.00
Beam, **Centennial**, St.Louis Arch, 1967 .... 20.00
Beam, **Charisma**, 1970, Executive .... 8.95 To 13.95
Beam, **Cherub**, Blue, 1960, Executive Series .... 65.00 To 87.50
Beam, **Cherub**, Gray, 1958, Executive Series .... 140.00 To 165.00
Beam, **Cheyenne**, Centennial, 1967, Regal China .... 6.50 To 14.95
Beam, **Chicago Fire**, Centennial, 1971 .... 19.95
Beam, **Churchill Downs**, 95th, Pink Roses, 1969, 1970, Regal China ..... 3.95 To 6.50
Beam, **Churchill Downs**, 95th, Red Roses, 1969, 1970, Regal China ...... 6.95 To 8.95
Beam, **Churchill Downs**, 96th, Red Rose Decals, 1970, Regal China ...... 7.50 To 10.45
Beam, **Churchill Downs**, 97th, Red Roses, 1971, Regal China 7.95
Beam, **Churchill Downs**, 98th, 1972 .... 15.00
Beam, **Civil War**, North, Centennial, 1961 .... 32.00 To 39.95
Beam, **Civil War**, South, Centennial, 1961 .... 39.95 To 45.00
Beam, **Clear Crystal**, Bourbon, 1967 .... 8.00
Beam, **Clear Crystal**, Scotch, 1966 .... 4.95 To 8.00
Beam, **Clear Crystal**, Vodka, 1967 .... 8.00
Beam, **Cleopatra**, Rust, 1962 .... 3.95
Beam, **Cleopatra**, Yellow, 1962 .... 10.00 To 15.00
Beam, **Club**, Fox, Blue, 1967 .... 100.00 To 145.00
Beam, **Club**, Fox, Gold, 1969 .... 65.00 To 80.00
Beam, **Club**, Fox, Uncle Sam, 1971 .... 15.00 To 24.95
Beam, **Club**, Fox, White, 1969 .... 25.00 To 59.95
Beam, **Club**, Hawaii, Aloha 10.00
Beam, **Club**, Mission, California, 1970 .... 19.99 To 38.45
Beam, **Club**, National Convention Club, 1971 .... 8.95 To 14.95
Beam, **Club**, Pearl Harbor, 1972 .... 10.00
Beam, **Club**, Rocky Mountain, Denver, 1970 .... 18.00 To 19.95
Beam, **Club**, Twin Bridges, 1971 .... 27.95 To 39.95
Beam, **Coach Devaney**, Nebraska, 1972 .... 16.00
Beam, **Cocktail Shaker**, 1953 .... 3.95
Beam, **Coffee Warmer**, Black Handle, 1956 .... 3.95
Beam, **Coffee Warmer**, Black, 1954 .... 8.00
Beam, **Coffee Warmer**, Gold, 1954 .... 8.00
Beam, **Coffee Warmer**, Red, 1954 .... 8.00
Beam, **Coffee Warmer**, 1956, Stars .... 2.50 To 3.95
Beam, **Collector's Edition**, Blue Boy, Vol. II , 1967 .... 10.95
Beam, **Collector's Edition**, On The Terrace, Vol. II , 1967 .... 6.00
Beam, **Collector's Edition**, Soldier & Girl, Vol. II , 1967 .... 2.95
Beam, **Collector's Edition**, Vol.I, Set Of 6, 1966 .... 20.00
Beam, **Collector's Edition**, Vol. II , Set Of 6, 1967 .... 18.00
Beam, **Collector's Edition**, Vol. III , Set Of 8, 1968 .... 15.00
Beam, **Collector's Edition**, Vol. IV , Set Of 8, 1969 .... 9.95
Beam, **Collector's Edition**, Vol.V, Set Of 3, 1970 .... 15.00
Beam, **Collector's Edition**, Vol. VI , Set Of 6, 1971 .... 15.00
Beam, **Colorado**, 1959 .... 45.00
Beam, **Convention**, National, 1971 .... 8.45 To 14.95
Beam, **Convention**, 1972 .... 25.00
Beam, **Crystal**, Blue 3.95
Beam, **Crystal**, Bourbon, 1967 .... 8.00
Beam, **Crystal**, Emerald, 1968 .... 4.95 To 6.50
Beam, **Crystal**, Opaline 3.95

Beam, **Crystal**, Royal, 1959 .... 4.00 To 5.95
Beam, **Crystal**, Ruby 7.95
Beam, **Crystal**, Scotch, 1966 .... 4.95 To 8.00
Beam, **Crystal**, Vodka, 1967 .... 8.00
Beam, **Daisy**, Blue, 1967, Regal China .... 4.00 To 6.50
Beam, **Dancing Couple**, 1964, 1970 .... 75.00
Beam, **Dancing Scot**, Short, 1963 .... 30.00 To 35.00
Beam, **Dancing Scot**, Tall, 1964 .... 7.50 To 8.95
Beam, **Delaware Blue Hen**, 1972 .... 9.95 To 13.50
Beam, **Delft Blue**, 1963 .... 3.95 To 6.50
Beam, **Delft Rose**, 1963 .... 4.95
Beam, **Denver**, Rocky Mountain Club .... 18.00 To 24.95
Beam, **District Of Columbia**, Republican Dinner, Feb.10, 1972 .... 650.00
Beam, **Dodge City**, Boot Hill, 1972, Regal China .... 7.95 To 10.50
Beam, **Doe**, 1963 .... 26.50 To 39.00
Beam, **Doe**, 1967 .... 35.00
Beam, **Dog**, Black & White Setter, 1959, Regal China .... 54.95 To 44.95
Beam, **Duck**, 1957, Regal China .... 35.95 To 44.95
Beam, **Ducks And Geese**, Glass Special, 1955 .... 6.95
Beam, **Eagle**, 1966, 1967 .... 12.00 To 15.95
   Beam, **Elephant, see Beam, Political**
Beam, **Elks**, Centennial, 1968, 1969 .... 5.00 To 8.95
Beam, **Emerald Crystal** .... 4.95 To 6.50
Beam, **Executive**, 1955, Royal Porcelain .... 135.00 To 225.00
Beam, **Executive**, 1956, Royal Gold Round .... 110.00 To 159.95
Beam, **Executive**, 1957, Royal Di Monte .... 32.50 To 89.95
Beam, **Executive**, 1958, Gray Cherub .... 140.00 To 165.00
Beam, **Executive**, 1959, Tavern Scene .... 50.00 To 75.00
Beam, **Executive**, 1960, Blue Cherub .... 65.00 To 87.50
Beam, **Executive**, 1961, Golden Chalice .... 47.50 To 80.00
Beam, **Executive**, 1962, Flower Basket .... 39.50 To 57.95
Beam, **Executive**, 1963, Royal Rose .... 50.00 To 52.50
Beam, **Executive**, 1964, Royal Gold Diamond .... 42.50 To 54.95
Beam, **Executive**, 1965, Marbled Fantasy .... 59.50 To 84.95
Beam, **Executive**, 1966, Majestic .... 32.00 To 39.95
Beam, **Executive**, 1967, Prestige .... 17.50 To 25.00
Beam, **Executive**, 1968, Presidential .... 7.50 To 16.00
Beam, **Executive**, 1969, Sovereign .... 7.50 To 14.95
Beam, **Executive**, 1970, Charisma .... 8.95 To 13.95
Beam, **Executive**, 1971, Fantasia .... 14.95 To 34.95
Beam, **Executive**, 1972, Regency 14.95
Beam, **Fiji Islands**, 1971 .... 7.95 To 8.95
Beam, **First National Bank** 2450.00
Beam, **Fish**, Gold Speckled 65.00
Beam, **Fish**, 1957 .... 28.50 To 44.95
Beam, **Florida Shell**, Bronze, 1968, 1969 .... 3.95
Beam, **Florida Shell**, Mother-Of-Pearl, 1968, 1969 .... 3.95
Beam, **Football Hall Of Fame**, 1972 .... 11.95
Beam, **Foremost**, Black & Gold, 1956 .... 124.95 To 135.00
Beam, **Foremost**, Gray & Gold, 1956 .... 135.00
Beam, **Foremost**, Pink Speckled, 1956 .... 350.00
Beam, **Fox**, Blue, Anniversary, 1967, Club .... 100.00 To 145.00
Beam, **Fox**, Gold, 1969, Club .... 65.00 To 80.00
Beam, **Fox**, Green, 1965 .... 25.00 To 55.00
Beam, **Fox**, Green, 1967 .... 25.00 To 42.00
Beam, **Fox**, Uncle Sam, 1971, Club .... 15.00 To 24.95
Beam, **Fox**, White, 1969, Club .... 25.00 To 59.95
Beam, **Franklin Mint**, 1970, Regal China .... 3.95 To 9.95
Beam, **General Stark**, 1972 .... 19.50
Beam, **Genie**, Smoked Crystal, Glass 6.95
Beam, **Germany**, 1970 .... *Illus* 3.95 To 5.95
Beam, **Germany**, 1971, Hansel & Gretel 9.95
Beam, **Gold Fox**, 1969, Club .... 65.00 To 80.00
Beam, **Golden Chalice**, 1961, Executive .... 47.50 To 80.00
Beam, **Golden Gate Casino**, 1969, Las Vegas 65.00
Beam, **Golden Gate Casino**, 1970, Bridge .... 8.45 To 12.95

Beam, Germany, 1970
See Page 21

Beam, Golden Gates Fields, 1971, California Derby	12.00 To 24.95
Beam, Golden Nugget, 1969	57.50 To 65.00
Beam, Goose, Blue, 1971	3.95 To 6.00
Beam, Grand Canyon, 1969	12.50 To 17.95
Beam, Gray Cherub, 1958, Executive	140.00 To 165.00
Beam, Gray Horse, 1961	18.50
Beam, Gray Horse, 1967	12.00
Beam, Gray Slot Machine, 1968, 1969, Harold's Club	3.95
Beam, Grecian, 1961, Glass	3.95 To 4.95
Beam, Green China Jug, 1965	7.95
Beam, Green Fox, 1965	25.00 To 55.00
Beam, Hansel & Gretel, Germany, 1971	9.95
Beam, Harold's Club Covered Wagon, 1969, 1970	3.95 To 9.50
Beam, Harold's Club Man In Barrel No.1, 1957	375.00 To 425.00
Beam, Harold's Club Man In Barrel No.2, 1958	235.00 To 250.00
Beam, Harold's Club Nevada, Gray, 1963	155.00
Beam, Harold's Club Nevada, Silver, 1964	165.00
Beam, Harold's Club Pinwheel, 1965	62.50 To 69.95
Beam, Harold's Club Silver Opal, 1957	18.95
Beam, Harold's Club Slot Machine, Blue 1967	13.00 To 19.00
Beam, Harold's Club Vip, 1967, Gold, Green	45.00 To 64.95
Beam, Harold's Club Vip, 1968, Blue, Silver	47.50
Beam, Harold's Club Vip, 1969	75.00 To 90.00
Beam, Harold's Club Vip, 1970	75.00
Beam, Harold's Club Vip, 1971	39.95 To 45.00
Beam, Harrah's Club, Nevada Gray	450.00
Beam, Harrah's Club, Nevada Silver	675.00 To 875.00
Beam, Harry Hoffman, 1969, 1970	6.95
Beam, Harvey's, 1969, 1970, Velvet Suede Draw String Bag	14.95 To 19.95
Beam, Hawaii, Aloha, Club	10.00
Beam, Hawaii, King Kamehameha, 1972	8.95
Beam, Hawaii, 1959, 1960	64.95 To 72.00
Beam, Hawaii, 1967, Reissue	45.00 To 60.00
Beam, Hawaiian Open, Pro Am, 1972, United Airlines	9.95 To 12.50
Beam, Hemisfair, 1968	10.95 To 12.95
Beam, Hen, Blue, Delaware, 1972	9.95 To 13.50
Beam, Horse, Black, 1961	21.00
Beam, Horse, Black, 1967	19.50
Beam, Horse, Brown, 1961	21.00
Beam, Horse, Brown, 1967	19.50
Beam, Horse, Gray, 1961	21.00
Beam, Horse, Gray, 1967	18.95
Beam, Horseshoe Club, Customer Specialty, 1969 *Illus*	9.75
Beam, Humboldt County Fair, Velvet Suede Drawstring Bag, 1970	19.95
Beam, Hyatt House, 1971	45.00 To 50.00
Beam, Idaho, 1963	65.00 To 75.00

Beam, Illinois, 1968 .... 7.50 To 8.00
Beam, Indianapolis, Sesquicentennial, 1971 .... 7.95
Beam, Indianapolis 500, China Specialty, 1970 .... *Illus* 3.95
Beam, International Petroleum, Tulsa Oil, 1971 .... 7.95 To 8.45
Beam, Ivory Ashtray, 1955 .... 22.50
Beam, Jackalope, 1971 .... 7.00 To 10.00
Beam, John Henry, 1972 .... 50.00 To 59.95
Beam, Jug, Green, 1965 .... 7.95
Beam, Jug, Oatmeal, 1966 .... 40.00
Beam, Jug, Turquoise, 1966 .... 3.95
Beam, Kaiser International Open, 1971 .... 7.95 To 9.00
Beam, Kansas, 1960, 1961 .... 60.00 To 65.00
Beam, Katz Cat, Black, 1968 .... 8.95 To 10.95
Beam, Katz Cat, Yellow, 1967 .... 22.50 To 25.00
Beam, Katz Philharmonic .... 10.00 To 13.00
Beam, Kentucky Colonel, 1970 .... 3.75 To 9.95
Beam, Kentucky Derby, 95th, Pink Roses .... 3.95 To 6.50
Beam, Kentucky Derby, 95th, Red Roses .... 6.95 To 8.95
Beam, Kentucky Derby, 96th, Red Roses .... 7.50 To 10.45
Beam, Kentucky Derby, 97th, Red Roses .... 7.95 To 8.45
Beam, Kentucky Derby, 98th, 1972 .... 15.00
Beam, Kentucky, Black Head, 1967 .... 11.95 To 12.50
Beam, Kentucky, Brown Head, 1967 .... 18.00

Beam,
Horseshoe Club,
Customer Specialty,
1969
See Page 22

Beam,
Indianapolis 500,
China Specialty, 1970

Beam, Kentucky, White Head 22.50
Beam, King Kamehameha, 1972 .... 8.95
    Beam, Kitten, see Beam, Cat
Beam, Laramie, Centennial, 1968 .... 6.95
Beam, Las Vegas Golden Gate, 1969 .... 65.00
Beam, Las Vegas Nugget, 1969 .... 57.50 To 65.00
Beam, Las Vegas, 1969 .... 4.00
Beam, Lilac, Lombard, Illinois, 1969, 1970 .... 3.95
Beam, London Bridge, 1971 .... 4.95 To 7.95
Beam, Majestic, 1966, Executive .... 32.00 To 39.95
Beam, Man In Barrel No.1, 1957 .... 375.00 To 425.00
Beam, Man In Barrel No.2, 1958 .... 235.00 To 250.00
Beam, Marbeled Fantasy, 1965, Executive .... 59.50 To 84.95
Beam, Marbelized Crystal, 1972 .... 3.95
Beam, Marina City, 1962 .... 32.50 To 40.00
Beam, Mark Antony, Glass Specialty, 1962 .... 8.95 To 18.50
Beam, Michigan, 1972 .... 10.95
Beam, Milwaukee Club Stein, 1972 .... 39.95 To 46.00
Beam, Minnesota Viking, 1972 .... 10.00
Beam, Mint 400, Metal Car Stopper, 1970 .... 7.95 To 9.95
Beam, Mint 400, Motorcycle Stopper, 1970 .... 7.95 To 9.95
Beam, Mission Club, California, 1970 .... 19.99 To 38.45

Beam, Moila Shrine, 1972	64.95
Beam, Montana, 1963	85.00 To 92.00
Beam, Mt.Rushmore, South Dakota, 1969, 1970	3.75 To 6.95
Beam, Musicians On Wine Cask, 1964	10.95
Beam, Muskie, Wisconsin, 1971	8.95
Beam, National Convention, 1971	8.45 To 14.95
Beam, Nebraska Centennial, 1967	9.95 To 12.95
Beam, Nebraska, Coach Devaney, 1972	16.00
Beam, Nevada, Burro, 1970	10.00
Beam, Nevada, 1963, 1964	57.00 To 64.95
Beam, New Hampshire, Eagle, 1971	18.00
Beam, New Hampshire, 1967, 1968	7.50 To 9.95
Beam, New Hampshire, General Stark, 1972	18.00
Beam, New Jersey, Blue	69.50 To 79.00
Beam, New Jersey, Gray, 1963, 1964	65.00 To 79.00
Beam, New Jersey, Yellow, 1963, 1964	50.00 To 55.00
Beam, New Mexico, 1972	3.95
Beam, New York World's Fair, 1964	22.50 To 25.00
Beam, Nixon Bottle & Plate Set	1600.00
Beam, North Dakota, 1964	75.00 To 85.00
Beam, Oatmeal Jug, 1966	32.50
Beam, Ohio, 1966	9.95 To 11.00
Beam, Ohio, Hall Of Fame, 1972	11.95
Beam, Oldsmobile, 1972	23.95
Beam, Olympian, 1960	5.00
Beam, Olympica, 1971, Marbelized Glass	4.00 To 5.45
Beam, On The Terrace, Collectors Edition, Vol.1, 1967	6.50
Beam, Opaline Crystal	3.95
Beam, Oregon, 1959	35.00 To 42.00
Beam, P.G.A., 1971	3.95 To 7.65
Beam, Paul Bunyan, 1970, 1971	*Illus* 7.00
Beam, Pearl Harbor, 1972	10.00
Beam, Pennsylvania, State Series, 1967	*Illus* 5.00
Beam, Pheasant, Reissue	12.00 To 14.95
Beam, Pheasant, 1960	14.00 To 16.95
Beam, Pimlico Preakness, 1970, 1971	*Illus* 7.95
Beam, Pin Bottle, Wood Stopper, Labels, Fifth	6 95 To 10.95
Beam, Pin Bottle, Wood Stopper, Labels, Pint	4.00 To 4.95
Beam, Pin, Short, Wood Stopper, 1952	4.00
Beam, Pineapple, Silver Base, Hawaii Open Pro Am, 1972	9.95 To 12.50
Beam, Pinwheel, Harold's Club, Customer Specialty, 1965	62.50 To 69.95
Beam, Political, 1956, Donkey, Ashtray	10.95 To 16.00
Beam, Political, 1956, Elephant, Ashtray	10.95 To 16.00
Beam, Political, 1960, Donkey, Campaigner	14.95
Beam, Political, 1960, Elephant, Campaigner	14.95
Beam, Political, 1964, Donkey, Boxer	14.50
Beam, Political, 1964, Elephant, Boxer	14.95
Beam, Political, 1968, Donkey, Clown	6.00 To 8.00
Beam, Political, 1968, Elephant, Clown	6.00 To 8.00
Beam, Political, 1972, Donkey, Football	6.00 To 8.00
Beam, Political, 1972, Elephant, Football	6.00 To 8.00
Beam, Ponderosa, Lake Tahoe, 1969	3.95 To 6.95
Beam, Pony Express, Regal China Specialty, 1968	*Illus* 3.75 To 6.50
Beam, Poodle, Gray, 1970	5.95 To 7.00
Beam, Poodle, White, 1970	5.95 To 7.00
Beam, Portola Trek, San Diego Centennial, 1969	4.50
Beam, Powell Expedition, Centennial, 1969	6.95 To 8.95
Beam, Preakness, Centennial, 1970, 1971	7.95
Beam, Presidential, 1968, Executive	7.50 To 16.00
Beam, Prestige, 1967, Executive	17.50 To 25.00
Beam, Prima Donna, 1969	9.00
Beam, Pro Am, Hawaii, 1972	9.95 To 12.50
Beam, Rabbit, Texas, 1971	7.95
Beam, Ram, 1958	60.00 To 115.00
Beam, Redfin Submarine, 1970	3.95 To 7.95
Beam, Redwood, 1967	6.75 To 9.95

Beam, Paul Bunyan, 1970, 1971
See Page 24

Beam, Pennsylvania,
State Series, 1967
See Page 24

Beam, Pony Express,
Regal China Specialty, 1968
See Page 24

Beam, Pimlico Preakness,
1970, 1971
See Page 24

Beam, Regency, 1972	14.95
Beam, Reno, Centennial, 1969, 1970	3.95 To 8.95
Beam, Richard's New Mexico	3.75 To 4.95
Beam, Riverside, Centennial, 1970	24.95
Beam, Robin, 1969	4.95 To 8.95
Beam, Rocky Mountain Club, Denver, 1970	18.00 To 24.95
Beam, Royal Crystal, 1959	4.00 To 5.95
Beam, Royal Di Monte, 1957, Executive	32.50 To 89.95
Beam, Royal Emperor, 1958	3.95 To 5.95
Beam, Royal Gold Diamond, 1964, Executive	42.50 To 54.49
Beam, Royal Gold, Round, 1956, Executive	100.00 To 159.95
Beam, Royal Jade	4.95
Beam, Royal Opal, 1957, Glass	6.50 To 8.95
Beam, Royal Porcelain, 1955, Executive	135.00 To 225.00
Beam, Royal Reserve	3.95 To 5.00
Beam, Royal Rose, 1963, Executive	50.00 To 52.50

Beam, Ruby Crystal	7.95
Beam, Ruidoso Downs, Flat Ears, 1968, 1969	3.95 To 6.50
Beam, Ruidoso Downs, Pointed Ears, 1968, 1969	3.95 To 6.50
Beam, Sahara Invitational, 1971	8.00 To 9.95
Beam, San Diego, Centennial, 1968	*Illus* 7.95
Beam, Santa Fe, Centennial, 1960	175.00 To 225.00
Beam, Scotch Bell, 1970	8.95
Beam, Seattle Seafair, 1972	11.95 To 16.95
Beam, Seattle World's Fair, 1962, Space Needle	22.50
Beam, Shell, Bronze, 1968, 1969, Florida	3.95
Beam, Shell, Pearl, 1968, 1969, Florida	3.95
Beam, Short Pin, 1952	4.00
Beam, Short Scot, 1963	7.50
Beam, Shriners, 1970	3.95 To 8.45
Beam, Slot Machine, Blue, Harold's, 1967	13.00 To 19.00
Beam, Slot Machine, Gray, Harold's, 1968, 1969	3.95
Beam, South Carolina, State Series, 1970	*Illus* 7.00
Beam, South Dakota, 1969, 1970, Mt.Rushmore	3.75 To 6.95
Beam, Sovereign, 1969, Executive	7.50 To 14.95
Beam, Space Needle, 1962, Seattle World's Fair	22.50
Beam, Speckled Pink, 1956, Foremost	350.00
Beam, St.Louis Arch, Centennial, 1964	24.00
Beam, St.Louis Arch, Centennial, 1967	20.00
Beam, Submarine, Redfin, 1970	3.95 To 7.95
Beam, State, Alaska Purchase, 1966	12.50 To 31.50
Beam, State, Alaska, Star, 1958	67.50 To 85.00
Beam, State, Alaska, Star, 1964, 1965	65.00 To 78.00
Beam, State, Arizona, 1968, 1969	3.75 To 4.95
Beam, State, Colorado, 1959	45.00
Beam, State, Florida, Bronze Shell, 1968, 1969	3.95
Beam, State, Florida, Pearl Shell, 1968, 1969	3.95

Beam, San Diego,
Centennial, 1968

Beam, South Carolina,
State Series, 1970

Beam, State, Hawaii, 1959, 1960	64.95 To 72.00
Beam, State, Hawaii, 1967, Reissue	45.00 To 60.00
Beam, State, Idaho, 1963	65.00 To 75.00
Beam, State, Illinois, 1968	7.50 To 8.00
Beam, State, Kansas, 1960, 1961	60.00 To 65.00
Beam, State, Kentucky, Black Head, 1967	11.95 To 12.50
Beam, State, Kentucky, Brown Head, 1967	18.00
Beam, State, Maine, 1970, 1971	7.00
Beam, State, Montana, 1963	85.00 To 92.00
Beam, State, Nebraska, 1967	9.95 To 12.95
Beam, State, Nevada, 1963, 1964	57.00 To 64.95
Beam, State, New Hampshire, 1967, 1968	7.50 To 9.95

Beam, State, New Jersey, Blue .... 69.50 To 79.00
Beam, State, New Jersey, Gray, 1963, 1964 .... 65.00 To 79.00
Beam, State, New Jersey, Yellow, 1963, 1964 .... 50.00 To 55.00
Beam, State, North Dakota, 1964 .... 75.00 To 85.00
Beam, State, Ohio, 1966 .... 9.95 To 11.00
Beam, State, Oregon, 1959 .... 35.00 To 42.00
Beam, State, Pennsylvania, 1967 .... 5.00
Beam, State, South Carolina, 1970 .... 7.00
Beam, State, South Dakota, Mt.Rushmore, 1969, 1970 .... 3.75 To 6.95
Beam, State, West Virginia, 1963 .... 100.00 To 139.95
Beam, State, Wyoming, 1965 .... 65.00 To 72.95
Beam, Submarine, Redfin, 1970 .... 3.95 To 7.95
Beam, Tavern Scene, 1959, Executive .... 50.00 To 75.00
Beam, Texas Hemisfair, 1968 .... 10.95 To 12.95
Beam, Texas Jackrabbit, 1971 .... 7.95
Beam, Thailand, 1969 .... 3.00 To 5.50
Beam, Tombstone, 1970 .... 3.95 To 8.45
Beam, Travel Lodge, 1972 .... 7.95 To 10.95
Beam, Trophy, Blue Jay, 1969 .... 4.95
Beam, Trophy, Cardinal, 1968 .... 36.50 To 42.50
Beam, Trophy, Cat, Burmese, 1967 .... 10.95
Beam, Trophy, Cat, Siamese, 1967 .... 10.95
Beam, Trophy, Cat, Tabby, 1967 .... 10.95
Beam, Trophy, Doe, Reissue, 1967 .... 35.00
Beam, Trophy, Doe, 1963 .... 26.50 To 39.00
Beam, Trophy, Dog, 1959 .... 54.95 To 69.95
Beam, Trophy, Duck, 1957 .... 35.95 To 44.95
Beam, Trophy, Eagle, 1966, 1967 .... 12.00 To 15.95
Beam, Trophy, Fish, 1957 .... 28.50 To 44.95
Beam, Trophy, Fox, Green, 1965 .... 25.00 To 55.00
Beam, Trophy, Fox, Green, 1967 .... 25.00 To 42.00
Beam, Trophy, Horse, Black, 1961 .... 21.00
Beam, Trophy, Horse, Black, 1967 .... 19.50
Beam, Trophy, Horse, Brown, 1961 .... 21.00
Beam, Trophy, Horse, Brown, 1967 .... 19.50
Beam, Trophy, Horse, Gray, 1961 .... 21.00
Beam, Trophy, Horse, Gray, 1967 .... 18.95
Beam, Trophy, Pheasant, Reissue .... 12.00 To 14.95
Beam, Trophy, Pheasant, 1960 .... 14.00 To 16.95
Beam, Trophy, Poodle, Gray, 1970 .... 5.95 To 7.00
Beam, Trophy, Poodle, White, 1970 .... 5.95 To 7.00
Beam, Trophy, Rabbit, Texas, 1971 .... 8.95
Beam, Trophy, Ram, 1958 .... 90.00 To 115.00
Beam, Trophy, Robin, 1969 .... 4.95 To 8.95
Beam, Trophy, Texas Jackrabbit, 1971 .... 8.95
Beam, Trophy, Wisconsin Muskie, 1971 .... 8.95
Beam, Trophy, Woodpecker, 1969 .... 4.95
Beam, Twin Bridges, Club, 1971 .... 27.95 To 39.95
Beam, Uncle Sam Fox .... 15.00 To 24.95
Beam, Veterans Of Foreign Wars, 1971 .... 7.95 To 8.45
Beam, Viking, Minnesota, 1972 .... 10.00
Beam, Western Golf Association, 1971 .... 8.50
Beam, West Virginia, 1963 .... 100.00 To 139.95
Beam, White Fox, 1969 .... 25.00 To 59.95
Beam, Woodpecker, 1969 .... 4.95 To 8.95
Beam, Wyoming, 1965 .... 62.00 To 72.95
Beam, Yellow Katz Cat, 1967, Regal China 25.00
Beam, Yosemite, 1967 .... 3.95 To 7.45
Beam, Yuma Rifle Club, 1968 .... Illus 30.00 To 40.00
Beam, Zimmerman Blue Beauty, 1969, 1970 .... 15.00 To 22.00
Beam, Zimmerman Cherub, Lavender 4.00
Beam, Zimmerman Cherub, Salmon 4.00
Beam, Zimmerman Glass, 1969, 1970 .... 7.00
Beam, Zimmerman Peddler, 1971 .... 17.00 To 22.50
Beam, Zimmerman Two Handle Jug, 1955 .... 125.00
Beam, Zimmerman Z, 1970 .... Illus   12.00

Beam,
Yuma Rifle Club, 1968
See Page 27

Beam,
Zimmerman Z, 1970
See Page 27

Beer was bottled in all parts of the United States by the time of the Civil War. Stoneware and the standard beer bottle shape of the 1870s are included in this category.

Beer, A.B.G.M.Co., Cobalt	12.00 To 33.50
Beer, A.H.Smith & Co., Ltd., Don Brewery, Sheffield, 8 In.	3.00
Beer, A.Strasser, Savannah, Ga., Amber	28.00
Beer, A.Templeton, Louisville, Creamale	40.00
Beer, Acme, Stubby	6.00
Beer, Acme, Stubby, No Deposit	2.00
Beer, Anheuser Busch, L.C.A.Roessler, Charleston, S.C., Eagle On Star, Amber	10.00
Beer, Arnas, 3 Mold, Whittled, Double Applied Lip, Honey Amber	3.50
Beer, Atlas Prager, Medium	5.50
Beer, Berghoff, Blob, Fort Wayne, Ind., Amber	4.00
Beer, Black Glass	5.00
Beer, Blatz, Embossed, Aqua	3.50
Beer, Blatz, Old Heidelberg, Stubby	5.00
Beer, Blatz, Pilsner	2.75
Beer, Blatz, Shield	4.00
Beer, Born & Co., Columbus, Ohio, Blob Top, Amber, Quart	8.00
Beer, Budweiser Lager	2.00
Beer, Budweiser, Medium	3.50
Beer, Budweiser, Salt & Pepper Shakers, Miniature	4.50
Beer, Buffalo Brewing Co., Sacramento, Calif., Embossed Buffalo Leaping	12.00
Beer, Bunker Hill Brewery, Blob Top, Fluted Neck & Below Slug Plate, Amber	7.00
Beer, C.Conrad Co.'s Original Budweiser, Embossed Patent No.6376	10.00
Beer, C.G.Co., Bubbly, Applied Lip & Ring, Blue, 9 3/4 In.	3.00
Beer, Canada, Blob, Embossed, Barrel, Amber	20.00
Beer, Coor's, Ceramic	5.00
Beer, Czechoslovakia, Embossed Near Bottom 1930, Dark Green	3.50
Beer, Eagle Brewery, Embossed Eagle	12.50
Beer, Eagle, Blob Top, Quart	9.00
Beer, English, Embossed 1930 On Bottom	3.50
Beer, English, Screw In Stopper, Embossed Brand Name	4.50
Beer, Falls City	10.00
Beer, Falstaff, Embossed, Aqua	3.50
Beer, Fort Pitt, Stubby	5.00
Beer, Foxhead	10.00
Beer, Galt, Canada, Blob, Amber	18.00
Beer, German, Wire Harness, Porcelain Top, Amber	1.75
Beer, Goebel's Old Stag, Stone, Embossed Barley Vines, Tan & Brown	19.00
Beer, Grain Belt	1.00
Beer, Hanley, Lawton, & Crews, Youngs Botanic Brewery, Ltd., 7 In.	3.00
Beer, Hoster, Columbus, Ohio, Blob Top, Amber, Quart	8.00
Beer, Jax	10.00

Aqua, Bottle, Pontil, Foldover Lip, 5 In.

Avon, Boot, Brown   Avon, Boot, Silver Top, 1965

Avon, California, Perfume Company,
Face Lotion, Box

Avon, Casey's Lantern, Red

Avon, Pony Post, Short, 1968

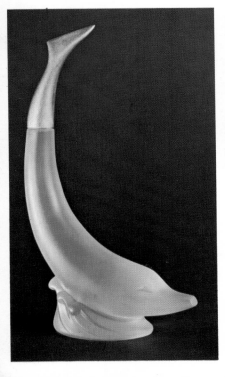

Avon, Dolphin, 1968

Bitters, H.L.Mishler's Keystone, Anti-Dispeptic

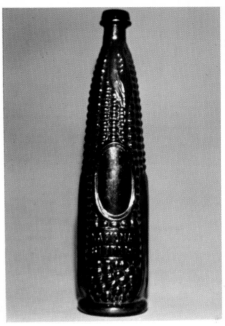

Bitters, National, Ear Of Corn

Bitters, Log Cabin, Box, Opener, Booklet

Avon, Packard Roadster

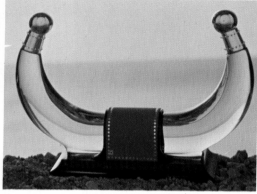

Avon, Western Choice

Bitters, Foerester's Teutonic,
Amber, Iron Pontil

Bitters, Tippecanoe,
Chapin, 6 Cone
Sour Mash, 1867

Bitters, Tippecanoe,
H.H.Warner
And Company

Bitters,
1860 Plantation,
4 Log, Patented 1862

Bitters,
1860 Plantation,
6 Log, Patented 1862

Collector's Art, Robin

Collector's Art, Blue Jay

Collector's Art, Koala Bears

Collector's Art, Rabbits

Collector's Art, Cardinal   Collector's Art, Parakeet   Collector's Art, Hummingbird

Codd, Milton Aerated Waterworks,
N.S.Aqua, 8 1/2 In.

Ezra Brooks, Charolais, 1973

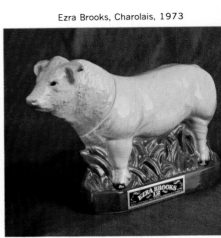

Ezra Brooks, Club Bottle, Map, 1973

Ezra Brooks, Penny Farthington,
High, Wheeler, 1973

Ezra Brooks, Totem Pole, 1972

Ezra Brooks, Ski The Idaho Potato, 1973

Ezra Brooks, West Virginia
Mountain Lady, 1972

Figural, Mermaid,
Silver Top, Bennington

Figural, Bear,
Applied Face, 11 In., Pontil

Figural, Clock, Milk Glass, Pontil, 12 In.

Figural, Clock, Bininger,
Clear, Engraved, 5 1/2 In.

Figural, Clock, Bininger
Regulator, Amber, Emboss

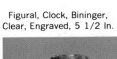

Beer, John Grof, Milwaukee, Embossed, 8 Panels, Blob Top, Amber	22.00
Beer, John Hauck, Amber, Quart	6.00
Beer, John Ryan, Porter & Ale, Pontil, Cobalt Blue	35.00
Beer, John Stanton, Troy, N.Y., Blob, Green	20.00
Beer, L.G.Co., Applied Lip & Ring, Bubbly, Blue, 9 3/4 In.High	3.00
Beer, Liquid Bread, C.1885, Cobalt Blue	35.00
Beer, Lone Star	10.00
Beer, Louis Weber, Blob Top, Aqua	8.00
Beer, Maitland Brewing, Sydney, Australia, Sun Purpled	35.00
Beer, Mcavey Brew Co., Malt Marrow Chicago, Ills., C.1880 Embossed, Squat	4.00
Beer, Milk Glass	7.50
Beer, Miniature, San Miguel, Philippines	2.00
Beer, National Lager, H.Rohrbacker Agt.Stockton, Cal., Blob Top	9.00
Beer, National, Eagle, Quart	25.00
Beer, Old Pabst	2.00
Beer, Old Schlitz	2.00
Beer, P.F.Heering, Sealed, Amber	45.00
Beer, Paul Polh, Chicago, Ill., Pony, Square Blob, Honey Amber	10.00
Beer, Porter Ale, Free-Blown, Pontil, Olive Green, Large Size	80.00
Beer, Prager	4.00
Beer, Ranier, Seattle Brewing & Malting Company, Blob Top, Amber	10.00
Beer, Reno Brewing Co.Blob, Amber	8.00
Beer, Royal Ruby, Anchor Glass, Abm, Quart	6.25 To 12.00
Beer, Royal Ruby, 7 Oz.	8.00
Beer, Royal Ruby, 8 Oz.	10.00
Beer, Royal Ruby, 12 Oz.	7.00
Beer, Royal Ruby, 13 Oz.	6.00
Beer, San Francisco, Fredericksburg, Picture Of Brewery, Clear, Pint	8.00
Beer, San Miguel, Philippines, Miniature	2.00
Beer, Schlee & Son, Columbus, Ohio, Aqua	6.00
Beer, Schlitz, Embossed, Blob Top, Amber, Quart	20.00
Beer, Schlitz, Royal Ruby, Label, 7 Oz.	18.00
Beer, Schlitz, Royal Ruby, Quart	7.50
Beer, Schlitz, Royal Ruby, Throw Away	6.50
Beer, Schlitz, Whittle Marks, Heavy Script, Amber, Pint	6.00
Beer, Schwartzenbrach Brewing Co.	2.50
Beer, Scotch Stone Ale, Mcintire & Townsend, St.John, N.B., Pottery, Quart	6.00
Beer, Seitz, Easton, Pa., S On Back, Green	12.00
Beer, St.Louis Lager, Label, Amber, 10 In. *Illus*	20.00
Beer, Stoddard Type, Amber, Pint	11.00
Beer, Stone, Marked Buchan	8.50
Beer, Stora Bryggereits Pilsenerol, Blob, Amber	8.00
Beer, Stout, Whittled, Graphite Pontil, 1840-60, Olive Amber, 1/2 Pint	42.00
Beer, Stout, 3 Mold, Open Pontil, 1800-20, Black Glass, 3/4 Pint	50.00
Beer, Stubby, Olive Green	15.00

Beer, St.Louis Lager, Label, Amber, 10 In.

Beer, The Stoll Brewing Co., Troy, N.Y., Blob Top, Apple Green	12.50
Beer, Valley Forge	10.00
Beer, William Gerst, Amber, Quart	6.00
Beer, Ziher & Sykes, Embossed, Aqua	3.50
Bellows, Footed, Applied Swags, Pink & White Stripes	170.00
Bellows, Footed, Clear Applied Swags, White Looping, Cranberry	150.00
Bennington Type, Book, Flint Enamel	38.00
Bennington, Toby, Marked, 1849	370.00
Bimal, Dark Amber, 7 3/4 In.High	7.00
Bininger, Barrel, Amber, Pint	130.00
Bininger, Barrel, Quart	120.00
Bininger, Jug, Handled, Amber, Pint	110.00
Bininger, Jug, Handled, Amber, Quart	135.00
Bininger, Jug, Handled, No.19 Broad St.	100.00

Bischoff Company has made fancy decanters since it was founded in 1777 in Trieste, Italy. The modern collectible Bischoff bottles have been imported to the United States since about 1950. Glass, porcelain, and stoneware decanters and figurals are made.

Bischoff, African Head, Ceramic, 1962	16.00 To 20.00
Bischoff, Alpine Pitcher, Porcelain, 1969	12.00
Bischoff, Amber Flowers Decanter, Glass, 1952	30.00 To 35.00
Bischoff, Amber Leaves Decanter, Glass, 1952	30.00 To 35.00
Bischoff, Amphora, Majolica, 1950	25.00
Bischoff, Aqua & Gold Decanter, Water Scene, 1956	50.00
Bischoff, Aqua & Silver Decanter, Gondola, 1954	29.00 To 35.00
Bischoff, Ashtray, Miniature, Ceramic, 1962	4.00 To 4.50
Bischoff, Bell House, Ceramic, 1960	30.00
Bischoff, Bell Tower, Ceramic, 1959	30.00
Bischoff, Black Cat, Glass, 1969	30.00
Bischoff, Boy, Chinese, Ceramic, 1962	30.00 To 40.00
Bischoff, Boy, Spanish, Ceramic, 1961	30.00 To 40.00
Bischoff, Cameo Pitcher Decanter, Ceramic, 1962	20.00
Bischoff, Candlestick, Antique, Glass, 1958	18.00
Bischoff, Candlestick, Fruit, Ceramic, 1964	20.00 To 25.00
Bischoff, Candlestick, Gold, Glass, 1958	18.00
Bischoff, Cat, Black, 1969	10.00
Bischoff, Chariot Urn, 2 Compartments, Ceramic, 1966	25.00
Bischoff, Christmas Tree Decanter, 1957	60.00
Bischoff, Clown, Black Hair, Ceramic, 1963	41.00
Bischoff, Clown, Red Hair, Ceramic, 1963	41.00
Bischoff, Coach Bottle, 1948	42.00
Bischoff, Cobalt Blue & Gold Decanter, Gondola, 1956	50.00
Bischoff, Cobalt Blue & Silver Decanter, 1954	40.00 To 45.00
Bischoff, Coronet Decanter, Amber Glass, 1952	30.00 To 37.50
Bischoff, Dachshund, Glass, 1966	31.90
Bischoff, Deer, Ceramic, 1969	22.00
Bischoff, Dog, Alabaster Glass, 1969	18.00
Bischoff, Dog, Dachshund, 1966	40.00
Bischoff, Dolphin, Double	16.00
Bischoff, Duck, Glass, 1964	45.00
Bischoff, Egyptian Ashtray, Ceramic, 1961	7.95
Bischoff, Egyptian Dancer Pitcher, Ceramic, 1961	22.00
Bischoff, Egyptian Decanter, 2 Handled, 2 Compartments, 1960	30.00
Bischoff, Egyptian Man Vase, Ceramic, 1961	25.00
Bischoff, Egyptian Musician Pitcher, 2 Musicians, Ceramic, 1963	19.00
Bischoff, Egyptian Pitcher, 3 Musicians, 1959	25.00 To 30.00
Bischoff, Emerald Decanter, Roses, 1952	45.00
Bischoff, Festival, Jeweled Vase Decanter, 1957	50.00
Bischoff, Fish, Glass, 1969, Ruby	15.00
Bischoff, Fish, 1964	50.00
Bischoff, Floral Canteen, Ceramic, 1969	18.00
Bischoff, Flower Decanter, Gold, Pink, Blue, Green Flowers, 1956	50.00
Bischoff, Flower Decanter, Ruby, 1953	35.50
Bischoff, Fruit Canteen, Ceramic, 1969	18.00
Bischoff, Geese Decanter, Amber, 1952	26.00

Bischoff, Geese Decanter, Ruby, 1952	26.00
Bischoff, Girl, Chinese, Ceramic, 1962	40.00
Bischoff, Girl, Spanish, Ceramic, 1961	30.00 To 40.00
Bischoff, Gold Dust & Green Decanter, 1958	42.50
Bischoff, Grapes Decanter, Ruby, 1953	35.50
Bischoff, Grecian Vase Decanter, Ceramic, 1969	11.00
Bischoff, Green & Silver Decanter, 1954	30.00 To 35.00
Bischoff, Green Striped Decanter, 1958	35.00
Bischoff, Horse Head, Amber	15.00
Bischoff, Jungle Scene, Amber, Glass, 1952	34.00
Bischoff, Jungle Scene, Ruby, Glass, 1952	34.00
Bischoff, Kamotsuru, see Kamotsuru	
Bischoff, Kord, see Kord	
Bischoff, Lavender & Gold Decanter, Roses, 1954	20.00 To 25.00
Bischoff, Lavender & Silver Decanter, Daisies, 1954	33.00
Bischoff, Mask, Ceramic, Gray, 1963	18.00 To 21.00
Bischoff, Nigerian Mask, 1963	18.00 To 21.00
Bischoff, Oil & Vinegar Cruets, Ceramic, Black, White, 1959	22.50
Bischoff, Opaline, Aqua Glass Decanter, 1957	50.00
Bischoff, Red Bell Shaped Decanter, 1957	45.00
Bischoff, Red Rose Decanter, Handpainted Flowers, 1957	50.00
Bischoff, Rose Decanter, Gold, 1952	25.00
Bischoff, Rose Decanter, Green, 1954	30.00
Bischoff, Rose Decanter, Pink, 1953	27.50
Bischoff, Ruby Etched Decanter, Glass, 1953	40.00
Bischoff, Ruby Etched Decanter, 1952	35.00
Bischoff, Silver Spotted Decanter, 1958	35.00
Bischoff, Sleigh Bottle, 1949	42.00
Bischoff, Striped Decanter, 1958	35.00
Bischoff, Topaz & Gold Decanter, 1955	26.00
Bischoff, Topaz & Silver Decanter, 1955	40.00
Bischoff, Topaz Basket Decanter, 1958	35.00 To 35.00
Bischoff, Vase, Gold, Painted Flowers, 1955	16.00
Bischoff, Vase, Modern, Ceramic, Black & Gold, 1959	35.00
Bischoff, Venetian Decanter, Blue, 1953	25.00
Bischoff, Venetian Decanter, Green, 1953	25.00
Bischoff, Venetian Decanter, Violet, 1953	25.00
Bischoff, Watchtower, Ceramic, 1960	10.00
Bischoff, Wedding Procession Vase, Ceramic, 1962	20.00 To 25.00
Bischoff, White & Yellow Vase, 1959	20.00
Bischoff, White Pitcher, Gold Handle, 1960	22.00
Bischoff, White Swags, Jeweled Vase Decanter, 1957	50.00
Bischoff, Wild Geese Decanter, Ruby, Glass, 1952	28.00
Bischoff, Wild Geese Pitcher, Ceramic, 1969	26.00

Bitters bottles held the famous 19th-century medicine called bitters. It was often of such a high alcohol content that the user felt healthier with each sip. The word bitters must be embossed on the glass or a paper label must be affixed for the collector to call the bottle a bitters bottle. Most date from 1840 to 1900. The numbers used in the entries in the form W-0 refer to the books Bitters Bottles and Supplement to Bitters Bottles by Richard Watson.

Bitters, see also Sarsaparilla

Bitters, A.B.M.Peychand's Bitter Cordial, Round, Amber	18.00
Bitters, Abbott, Baltimore, Round, Amber, 8 In.	4.50
Bitters, Abbott, Stain, Golden Amber	10.00
Bitters, Abbott's Aromatic, Label, Embossed	7.00
Bitters, Abbott's, Abm	3.00
Bitters, Adirondack Stomach, Clear	13.00
Bitters, Ads Iron Tonic, Aqua	6.00
Bitters, Ads Iron Tonic, Clear	6.00
Bitters, African Stomach, Spruance Stanley & Co., Amber	55.00
Bitters, African Stomach, Amber, W 3	40.00
Bitters, African Stomach, Amber, W-3	22.50 To 45.00
Bitters, African Stomach, Round, Amber, 9 1/2 In.	60.00
Bitters, African Stomach, Whittled Appearance, Light Amber	50.00

Bitters, Alpine Herb, W-6	55.00
Bitters, Amargo	25.00
Bitters, American Stomach, Buffalo, N.Y., Clear .... *Illus*	125.00
Bitters, Andrew's Vegetable Jaundice, Aqua .... 160.00 To	260.00
Bitters, Angelica Bitter Tonic	20.00
Bitters, Angostura Bark, Eagle, Amber, W-11	55.00
Bitters, Angostura Bark, Figural Eagle, Embossed, Amber	115.00
Bitters, Angostura, Green	5.00
Bitters, Angostura, Miniature, Bimal, Green	7.00
Bitters, Argyle, E.B.Whitlock, Embossed, W-13	60.00
Bitters, Aromatic Orange Stomach, Nashville, Amber, W-384	95.00
Bitters, Arp's Stomach, Embossed	75.00
Bitters, Ash Tonic, Apple Green	70.00
Bitters, Atwell's Wild Cherry, Label, Aqua	20.00
Bitters, Atwood's Genuine Physical Jaundice, Aqua, W-16 .... 12.00 To	60.00
Bitters, Atwood's Genuine, Aqua	15.00
Bitters, Atwood's Genuine, N.Wood Sole Proprietor, Aqua, W-15 .... 20.00 To	60.00
Bitters, Atwood's Jaundice, Aqua, W-17 .... 5.00 To	9.00
Bitters, Atwood's Jaundice, Bubbles, Aqua	4.95
Bitters, Atwood's Jaundice, Corker, Aqua	5.00
Bitters, Atwood's Jaundice, Free Sample, 3 In. .... *Illus*	15.00
Bitters, Atwood's, Blown In Mold, Open Pontil, Cloudy	12.00
Bitters, Atwood's, Formerly, Abm, 90 Percent Label	8.00
Bitters, Atwood's, M.Carter & Son, Label	12.00

Bitters, American Stomach, Buffalo, N.Y., Clear   Bitters, Atwood's Jaundice, Free Sample, 3 In.

Bitters, Atwood's, Moses Atwood, 8 Sided, Aqua	1.00
Bitters, Atwood's, Open Pontil, Aqua	26.00
Bitters, Augauer, Label, Embossed, W-21	45.00
Bitters, Aunt Charity's, 73 Percent Label, Clear	10.00
Bitters, Austin's Oswego, Embossed	40.00
Bitters, Ayer's Restorative, Cloudy, Aqua, W-386	25.00
Bitters, B & L Invigorator, Cylinder, Clear, 11 In.High	12.50
Bitters, B & L Invigorator, Label & Contents	15.00
Bitters, Baker's Orange Grove, Amber, W-23 ....90.00 To	145.00
Bitters, Baker's Orange Grove, Golden Amber	150.00
Bitters, Baker's Orange Grove, Reddish Amber	98.50
Bitters, Baker's Orange Grove, Stain, Dark Amber	115.00
Bitters, Baker's Orange Grove, Yellow Amber .... 125.00 To	150.00
Bitters, Baker's Premium, Aqua, W-24	50.00
Bitters, Baniama, Aqua	15.00
Bitters, Barters	6.00
Bitters, Bavarian, Embossed, W-28	75.00

Bitters, **Begg's Dandelion**, Embossed, W-30 .... 55.00 To 65.00
Bitters, **Bell's Cocktail**, Amber, W-32 .... 145.00 To 210.00
Bitters, **Belmont Tonic Herb**, Amber, W-33 .... 65.00
Bitters, **Bengal**, Embossed 40.00
Bitters, **Bennet's Celebrated Stomach**, Jos.N.Souther & Co., Orange Amber 185.00
Bitters, **Bennett Pieter's Co.**, Red Jacket, Square, 9 1/2 In. 12.50
Bitters, **Berkshire**, Big, Amber, W-38 .... 300.00
Bitters, **Big Bill Best**, Burst Bubble On Outside Corner, Amber 75.00
Bitters, **Big Bill Best**, Label, Contents, Amber, W-41 .... 80.00
Bitters, **Big Bill's Best**, Embossed 125.00
Bitters, **Billing's Mandrake Tonic**, Aqua 8.00
Bitters, **Bishop's Wahoo**, Amber, W-43 .... 170.00
Bitters, **Bisleri Ferro China**, Contents & Labels, Amber 25.00
Bitters, **Bismarck**, Amber, W-44 .... 45.00
Bitters, **Bitter Apple Tonic**, Clear 6.00
Bitters, **Bitterquelle** 5.00
Bitters, **Bitterquelle**, Dark Green .... 2.75 To 9.00
Bitters, **Bitterquelle**, Green 2.75
Bitters, **Bitterquelle**, 90 Percent Label 6.50
Bitters, **Bonset**, Embossed 140.00
Bitters, **Boonekamp**, Lady's Leg, Labels 28.00
Bitters, **Boonekamp**, UAH embossed Bottom, Full Content & Labels 65.00
Bitters, **Bostetter's**, Amber 5.00
Bitters, **Boston Malt**, Olive Green 23.00
Bitters, **Botanic Stomach**, Embossed, W-51 .... 90.00
Bitters, **Bourbon Whiskey**, Claret, Barrel, W-52 .... 150.00 To 165.00
Bitters, **Bourbon Whiskey**, Green 175.00
Bitters, **Bourbon Whiskey**, Puce 120.00
Bitters, **Boyce's Tonic**, Aqua, W-53 .... 12.00
Bitters, **Boyce's Tonic**, Sample, Aqua 12.00
Bitters, **Brauter Bitter**, Label, Amber, 10 In. 12.00
Bitters, **Brophy's**, Embossed, W-397 .... 35.00
Bitters, **Brown Chemical Co.**, Iron Bitters, Amber, 8 1/7 In.High, W-399 .... 33.00
Bitters, **Brown's Celebrated Indian Herb**, Amber, W-57 .... 170.00 To 225.00
Bitters, **Brown's Celebrated Indian Queen**, Black 350.00
Bitters, **Brown's Celebrated Indian Queen**, Honey Amber, W-57 .... 320.00
Bitters, **Brown's Iron**, Amber, W-399 .... 15.00 To 30.00
Bitters, **Brown's Iron**, Honey Amber 30.00
Bitters, **Brown's Iron**, Label, Amber, 9 In. .... *Illus* 27.50
Bitters, **Brown's Iron**, Light Amber 17.50
Bitters, **Brown's Sarsaparilla**, Embossed 80.00
Bitters, **Buhrer's Gentian**, Amber, 8 1/2 In.High, W-402 .... *Illus* 75.00
Bitters, **Bull Wild Cherry**, Embossed, W-59 .... 85.00
Bitters, **Burdock Blood**, Aqua, W-60 .... 7.00 To 13.50
Bitters, **Burdock Blood**, Clear 10.00
Bitters, **Burdock Blood**, Deep Aqua 15.00
Bitters, **Burdock Blood**, T.Milburn & Co., Toronto, Ont., Sun Colored Amethyst 20.00
Bitters, **Burdock Blood**, Toronto, Ont. 17.50
Bitters, **Byrne Stomach**, Amber, W-63 .... 370.00
Bitters, **C.Gates & Co.**, Life Of Man, Aqua 40.00
Bitters, **C.H.Swains**, Bourbon, Amber, 10 In., W-326 .... *Illus* 200.00
Bitters, **Cabin**, see also Bitters, Drake's Plantation
Bitters, **Caldwell's Herb**, Amber, W-65 .... 140.00
Bitters, **California Fig**, Amber, W-66 .... 40.00
Bitters, **California Fig & Herb**, Amber, W-67 .... 65.00 To 65.00
Bitters, **Canton**, Star, Embossed, Lady's Leg, Deep Amber, W-69 .... 175.00
Bitters, **Carmeliter**, Dollar Sign, Brown 80.00
Bitters, **Carmeliter**, Dollar Sign, Green 175.00
Bitters, **Carmeliter Stomach**, Olive Green, W-71 .... 40.00
Bitters, **Carmeliter Stomach**, Yellow Amber, W-71 .... 38.00
Bitters, **Caroni**, Amber, W-72 .... 16.00 To 20.00
Bitters, **Caroni**, Cylinder, Black, 8 In. 12.50
Bitters, **Carpathian Herb**, Embóssed, Hollander Drug Co., Pa., Amber, 9 In. 50.00
Bitters, **Carpathian Herb**, Hollander Drug Co., Braddock, Pa. 50.00
Bitters, **Carpathian Herb**, Hollander Drug Co., Square, 9 In., Amber 50.00

Bitters, Brown's Iron,
Label, Amber, 9 In.
See Page 33

Bitters, C.H.Swains, Bourbon,
Amber, 10 In., W-326
See Page 33

Bitters, Buhrer's Gentian, Amber,
8 1/2 In.High, W-402
See Page 33

Bitters, **Carpathian Herb**, Square, Amber, 9 In.High	50.00
Bitters, **Carter's Spanish Mixture**, Pontil	65.00
Bitters, **Cascaro**, Amber	12.50 To 25.00
Bitters, **Celebrated Berlin Stomach**, Stain, W-79	25.00
Bitters, **Celebrated Crown**, Embossed, W-80	90.00
Bitters, **Celery**, S.City W Co., Steuben Co.Wine Co.Chicago, Clear	14.00
Bitters, **Clark's Compound Mandrake**, Whittled	35.00
Bitters, **Clarke's Sherry Wine**, Aqua	55.00
Bitters, **Clarke's Sherry Wine**, Aqua, 9 1/2 In.Tall	18.00
Bitters, **Clarke's Sherry Wine**, Rectangular, Only 25 Cents, Aqua, W-87	50.00
Bitters, **Clarke's Sherry Wine**, Sharon, Mass., Aqua	50.00
Bitters, **Clarke's Sherry Wine**, Stain, 8 In.High	21.00
Bitters, **Clarke's Vegetable Sherry Wine**, Aqua, 1/2 Gallon	90.00
Bitters, **Clover**, Aqua	17.50
Bitters, **Cole Bros.Vegetable Indian**, Aqua, W-413	42.50
Bitters, **Colleton**, Stain, Aqua, W-91	130.00
Bitters, **Columbo Peptic**, ABM	15.00
Bitters, **Colombo Peptic**, Bimal, Amber	22.50
Bitters, **Columbo Peptic**, Square, L.E.Jung, New Orleans, Amber, 9 In., W-93	50.00
Bitters, **Corwitz Stomach**, Miniature, Chestnut, Pontil	60.00
Bitters, **Corwitz Stomach**, 8 Oz., Amber	45.00
Bitters, **Courtney's Dixiana Owensboro**, Ky., Amber	65.00
Bitters, **Cuban**, J.L.Davis & Son, Family Tonic, Brown *Illus*	75.00
Bitters, **Cumberland**, W-18	125.00
Bitters, **Curacao**, Chamberlain & Co., Des Moines, Amber *Illus*	50.00
Bitters, **Curtis & Perkins Wild Cherry**, Aqua, W-102	40.00 To 95.00
Bitters, **Damiana**, Baja, California, Aqua, W-103	35.00 To 50.00
Bitters, **Dandelions**, XXX inside Stain, W-104	49.50

Bitters, Demuth's Stomach, Amber, W-106	35.00
Bitters, Devil-Cert Stomach, Fred Kalina, Pittsburgh, Pa., Quart	65.00
Bitters, De Vonaire Orange	4.00
Bitters, De Witt's Stomach, Amber, W-426	12.50
Bitters, De Witt's Stomach, Rectangular, Amber, W-107	52.00
Bitters, Donnell's Stomach, Amber	12.00
Bitters, Doyle's Hop	35.00
Bitters, Doyle's Hop, Amber, W-110	16.00 To 30.00
Bitters, Doyle's Hop, Bimal, Honey Amber	28.00
Bitters, Doyle's Hop, Dark Amber	22.50
Bitters, Doyle's Hop, Golden Amber	24.50
Bitters, Doyle's Hop, Honey Amber	26.00
Bitters, Doyle's Hop, Labels Front & Back, W-110	26.00
Bitters, Doyle's Hop, 60 Percent Labels	45.00
Bitters, Dr.A.H.Smith's Old Style, Amber, W-309	60.00
Bitters, Dr.A.S.Hopkins Union Stomach, Olive Amber .... *Illus*	70.00
Bitters, Dr.Atherton's Dew Drop, Citron, W-14	130.00
Bitters, Dr.Ball's Vegetable Stomach, Open Pontil, Aqua	27.50
Bitters, Dr.Ball's Vegetable Stomachic, Stained, Open Pontil, Aqua	70.00
Bitters, Dr.Baxter's Mandrake, Amethyst	12.00
Bitters, Dr.Baxter's Mandrake, Aqua, W-29	5.00 To 18.00
Bitters, Dr.Baxter's Mandrake, Bimal, Dug, Aqua	7.00
Bitters, Dr.Baxter's Mandrake, Clear	7.50
Bitters, Dr.Baxter's Mandrake, 12 Sided, Clear	8.00

Bitters, Curacao,
Chamberlain & Co.,
Des Moines, Amber
See Page 34

Bitters, Cuban, J.L.Davis & Son,
Family Tonic, Brown
See Page 34

Bitters, Dr.A.S.Hopkins Union Stomach,
Olive Amber

Bitters, Dr.Bell's	140.00
Bitters, Dr.Bell's Blood Purifying, The Great English Remedy	115.00
Bitters, Dr.Boerhave's Holland, Embossed, W-48	40.00 To 45.00
Bitters, Dr.Boyce Tonic, 12 Sided, Aqua, W-53	32.50
Bitters, Dr.Buzzell's Bilious, Label, 10 In. .... *Illus*	48.00
Bitters, Dr.C.D.Warner's German Hop, 1880, W-355	55.00
Bitters, Dr.C.M.Ayer Restorative, Cloudy, Aqua, W-386	60.00
Bitters, Dr.C.M.Ayer's Restorative, Embossed	40.00
Bitters, Dr.C.W.Roback's Stomach, Iron Pontil, Golden Amber	175.00
Bitters, Dr.C.W.Roback Stomach, Ohio, Amber .... *Illus*	130.00
Bitters, Dr.Campbell's Scotch, Stain	150.00
Bitters, Dr.M.M.Fenner's Capitol, Fredonia, New York, Aqua, W-122	35.00

Bitters, Dr.Buzzell's Bilious,
Label, 10 In.
See Page 35

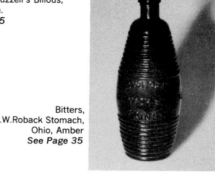

Bitters,
Dr.C.W.Roback Stomach,
Ohio, Amber
See Page 35

Bitters, **Dr.Fisch's**, Amber, W-124	94.00 To 175.00
Bitters, **Dr.Fisch's**, W.W.Ware 1866, Amber, W-124	149.00
Bitters, **Dr.Fisch's**, W.H.Ware 1866, Medium Amber	155.00
Bitters, **Dr.Flint's Quaker**, Aqua, W-126	24.00
Bitters, **Dr.Geo.Pierce's Indian Restorative**, W-258	70.00
Bitters, **Dr.Gould's**, Label	15.00
Bitters, **Dr.Grussie Altherr's Krauter Bitters**, Lady's Leg, Honey Amber	75.00
Bitters, **Dr.H.C.Stewart's Tonic**, Col., Ohio, Amber	*Illus* 25.00
Bitters, **Dr.H.S.Flint & Co.Quaker**, 1872, Aqua, 10 In.	*Illus* 35.00
Bitters, **Dr.Harter's Wild Cherry**, Blown In Mold, Applied Lip, Dark Amber	22.50
Bitters, **Dr.Harter's Wild Cherry**, Dayton, Ohio, 5 In., W-158	25.00
Bitters, **Dr.Harter's Wild Cherry**, Dayton, Ohio, Amber, 4 3/4 In.High	25.00
Bitters, **Dr.Harter's Wild Cherry**, Dayton, Ohio, 3 7/8 In.High	40.00
Bitters, **Dr.Harter's Wild Cherry**, St.Louis	25.00
Bitters, **Dr.Harter's**, Miniature	28.00
Bitters, **Dr.Henley's Wild Grape Root**, Deep Aqua, W-164	50.00
Bitters, **Dr.Hoofland's German**, Aqua, 8 In., W-174	22.50
Bitters, **Dr.Hoofland's German**, Dug, Iridescence, Aqua, 7 In.	17.50
Bitters, **Dr.Hoofland's German**, Light Ice Blue	45.00
Bitters, **Dr.Hoofland's German**, Liver Complaint, Cloudy	18.00
Bitters, **Dr.Hopkins's Union Stomach**, Amber	15.00
Bitters, **Dr.Hopkins's Union Stomach**, Yellow Amber, W-177	37.50

Bitters, Dr.H.C.Stewart's Tonic, Col., Ohio, Amber

Bitters, Dr.H.S.Flint &
Co.Quaker, 1872,
Aqua, 10 In.

Bitters, Dr.J.Hostetter's, Black Glass 55.00
Bitters, Dr.J.Hostetter's, Crude, Dark Olive Green, 9 X 3 X 3 In. 75.00
Bitters, Dr.J.Hostetter's, L & W On Base, Amber 10.00
Bitters, Dr.J.Hostetter's Stomach, ABM 4.00
Bitters, Dr.J.Hostetter's Stomach, Amber, W-179 .... 5.00 To 17.50
Bitters, Dr.J.Hostetter's Stomach, Black 95.00
Bitters, Dr.J.Hostetter's Stomach, Brown, 9 In. .... *Illus*   8.00
Bitters, Dr.J.Hostetter's Stomach, Crude, C.1868, Citron Yellow 20.00
Bitters, Dr.J.Hostetter's Stomach, Crude, Dark Olive Green 70.00
Bitters, Dr.J.Hostetter's Stomach, Crude, Graphite Pontil, Stained 125.00
Bitters, Dr.J.Hostetter's Stomach, Crude, Green 65.00
Bitters, Dr.J.Hostetter's Stomach, Dark Amber 12.50
Bitters, Dr.J.Hostetter's Stomach, Dug, Not ABM 6.50
Bitters, Dr.J.Hostetter's Stomach, Embossed, Amber 15.00
Bitters, Dr.J.Hostetter's Stomach, I.G.Co.L 50 On Base, Dug, Brown 12.00
Bitters, Dr.J.Hostetter's Stomach, Label, Green 60.00
Bitters, Dr.J.Hostetter's Stomach, Labels, Amber 12.50
Bitters, Dr.J.Hostetter's Stomach, Open Pontil, Stained, Yellow 25.00
Bitters, Dr.J.Hostetter's Stomach, S.Mc Kee & Co.On Base, Dug, Amber 5.50
Bitters, Dr.J.Hostetter's Stomach, S.Mc Kee & Co.On Base, Golden Amber 15.00
Bitters, Dr.J.Hostetter's Stomach, S.Mc Kee On Bottom, Amber 7.00
Bitters, Dr.Huntington's Golden Tonic, Amber, W-182 .... 80.00
Bitters, Dr.J.G.B.Siegert & Hijos, 3 Mold, Whittled, Green 5.00
Bitters, Dr.J.Kauffman's Angeline, Labeled, Contents, Clear 15.00
Bitters, Dr.Jacob's, Aqua, W-190 ....90.00 To 130.00
Bitters, Dr.Job Sweet's Strengthening, Label, Aqua 55.00
Bitters, Dr.Job Sweet's, Embossed, Label, Aqua 55.00
Bitters, Dr.John Bull's Compound Cedron, Louisville, Ky. 175.00
Bitters, Dr.Kaufmann's Sulphur, Clear 7.50
Bitters, Dr.Kaufmann's Sulphur, Label, Aqua .... 12.00 To 15.00
Bitters, Dr.Langley's Root & Herb, Aqua .... 20.00 To 30.00
Bitters, Dr.Langley's Root & Herb, Whittled, Aqua 22.00
Bitters, Dr.Langley's Root & Herb, 76 Union St.Aqua 22.50
Bitters, Dr.Loew's, Embossed 110.00
Bitters, Dr.Lovegoods Family, Amber, W-220 .... 350.00
Bitters, Dr.M.M.Fenner's Capitol, Aqua 35.00
Bitters, Dr.Mampe's Herb Stomach, Square, Sun Colored Amethyst .... 35.00 To 62.00
Bitters, Dr.Mampe's Herb Stomach, W-225 .... 39.00
Bitters, Dr.Manly Hardy's Genuine Jaundice, Open Pontil, Aqua, W-155 .... 20.00
Bitters, Dr.Mowe's Vegetable, Embossed, W-235 .... 70.00 To 85.00
Bitters, Dr.Petzolds, Amber, 10 1/2 In.High 85.00
Bitters, Dr.Petzolds Dug, 8 Oz., W-176 .... 175.00
Bitters, Dr.Pierce's Indian Restorative, Aqua, W-258 .... 47.50

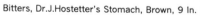

Bitters, Dr.J.Hostetter's Stomach, Brown, 9 In.

Bitters, Dr.Pierce's Indian Restorative, Aqua, 9 In.High 28.75
Bitters, Dr.Renz's Herb, Stain, Green, W-273 .... 55.00
Bitters, Dr.Roback's Stomach, Barrel, W-280 .... 100.00 To 135.00
Bitters, Dr.Russell's Pepsin Calisaya, Emerald Green 90.00
Bitters, Dr.Russell's Pepsin Calisaya, Apple Green 65.00
Bitters, Dr.S.B.H.& Co., Abm, Green 3.00
Bitters, Dr.S.B.H.& Co., Amethyst 7.00
Bitters, Dr.S.B.H.& Co., Aqua 5.00
Bitters, Dr.S.B.H.Man-A-Lin, Label, Contents 6.00
Bitters, Dr.S.S.Perry's Female Strengthening, Clear .... Illus   95.00
Bitters, Dr.Sawen's Life Invigorating, Amber, W-295 .... 25.00
Bitters, Dr.Sawen's Life Invigorating, Amber With Green Tint 90.00
Bitters, Dr.Sawen's Life Invigorating, Utica, N.Y. 30.00
Bitters, Dr.Shaw's Mt.Vernon, Me.Compound Hepatica, Embossed, Aqua 90.00
Bitters, Dr.Siegert's, 3 Piece Mold, Embossed, Olive Green 5.00
Bitters, Dr.Skinner's Sherry Wine, Aqua, Open Pontil, W-307 .... 100.00
Bitters, Dr.Smith's Columbo Tonic, Label, Light Amber 30.00
Bitters, Dr.Stanley's South American Indian, Square, Light Amber, 7 7/8 In. 65.00
Bitters, Dr.Stephen Jewett's Celebrated Health Restoring, Aqua .... 45.00 To 125.00
Bitters, Dr.Stewart's Tonic, Amber, 8 In. .... Illus   40.00
Bitters, Dr.Stewart's Tonic, Rectangular, Labels, Amber, 8 In., W-500 .... 70.00
Bitters, Dr.Stewart's Tonic, Variant A, Labels, W-500 .... 50.00
Bitters, Dr.Sweet's Strengthening, W-328 .... 30.00
Bitters, Dr.Thos.Hall's California Pepsin Wine, Amber 40.00
Bitters, Dr.Von Hopf's Curacao, Light Amber, W-343 .... 80.00
Bitters, Dr.Von Hopf's Curacao, Pint 65.00
Bitters, Dr.Von Hopf's Curacao, Embossed, Chamberlain Co., Iowa, Amber 65.00
Bitters, Dr.W.L.Wilbur's Aromatic, Amber, W-365 .... 35.00
Bitters, Dr.Warren's Bilious, Aqua, W-513 .... 75.00

Bitters, Dr.S.S.Perry's
Female Strengthening, Clear

Bitters, Dr.Stewart's Tonic,
Amber, 8 In.

Bitters, Dr.Wheeler's Tonic Sherry Wine, Aqua, 8 In., W-518 .... 37.50
Bitters, Dr.Wilson's Herbine, Label, Aqua, W-368 .... 25.00 To 32.50
Bitters, Dr.Wood's Sarsaparilla & Wild Cherry, Open Pontil, W-372 .... 125.00
Bitters, Dr.Young's Wild Cherry 75.00
Bitters, Dr.Young's Wild Cherry, Hourglass Back, Amber 160.00
Bitters, Dragon Brand Orange, Label, Bimal 15.00
    Bitters, Drake's Plantation, see also Bitters, Cabin
Bitters, Drake's Plantation, 3 Log, Amber, W-111 .... 35.00
Bitters, Drake's Plantation, 4 Log, Amber, W-111 .... 37.50 To 45.00
Bitters, Drake's Plantation, 4 Log, Golden Yellow 55.00
Bitters, Drake's Plantation, 5 Log, Amber 72.00
Bitters, Drake's Plantation, 6 Log, Amber, W-111 .... 45.00
Bitters, Drake's Plantation, 6 Log, Bubbles, Light Amber 55.00
Bitters, Drake's Plantation, 6 Log, Light Honey Amber 50.00

Bitters, **Drake's Plantation**, 6 Log, Puce ....75.00 To 125.00
Bitters, **Drake's Plantation**, 6 Log, 4 Plain Panels 97.50
Bitters, **Duffy's**, Baltimore, Md., Crude, Yellow Amber 10.00
Bitters, **E.Baker's Premium**, Clear, W-24 .... 40.00 To 60.00
Bitters, **E.Dexter Loveridge**, Wahoo, Amber 100.00
Bitters, **E.E.Hall**, Aqua 90.00
Bitters, **E.E.Hall**, Barrel, Amber, W-151 .... 85.00
Bitters, **Ear Of Corn**, National, Patent 1867, Amber 170.00
Bitters, **Economy**, Amber 5.00
Bitters, **Edw.Wilder's Stomach**, Roofed Shoulders, Clear, W-366 .... 60.00 To 78.00
Bitters, **Electric Brand**, Blown In Mold, Applied Lip, Amber, Quar .... 15.00 To 20.00
Bitters, **Electric Brand**, Cloudy, Amber 10.00
Bitters, **Electric Brand**, Contents, Label, Amber, W-115 .... 15.00
Bitters, **Electric**, Embossed H.E.Bucklen & Co., Chicago, Ill., Amber, 9 In. 35.00
Bitters, **Electric**, Label, Amber, W-114 .... 10.00
Bitters, **Emerson's Botanic**, Label, Aqua 20.00
Bitters, **Emerson's Excelsior Botanic**, Sun Colored .... *Illus* 60.00
Bitters, **Ernst Arp** 29.00
Bitters, **Ernst L.Arp Kiel**, Labeled, Whittled, Cross In Circle, Aqua, Quart 30.00
Bitters, **Excelsior**, Embossed, New York, W-119 .... 85.00
Bitters, **Excelsior**, Globed, Rectangular, Seedy Amber 100.00
Bitters, **Excelsior**, Rectangular, Seedy Amber 100.00
Bitters, **F.Brown Sarsaparilla & Tomato Bitters**, Stain, Open Pontil, Aqua 45.00
Bitters, **Faith Whitcomb's**, Stain, Aqua 52.50
Bitters, **Fenner's Capitol**, Aqua 35.00
Bitters, **Fernet Brancha**, Abm, Green 5.00
Bitters, **Fernet Branca Milano**, Green 5.00
Bitters, **Fernet Vittone**, Abm, Green 6.00
Bitters, **Ferro China Bisleri Milano**, Bright Green 11.00
Bitters, **Ferro China Bisleri**, Black Glass 5.00
Bitters, **Ferro Quina Stomach**, Embossed, W-123 .... 80.00
Bitters, **Ferro Quina Stomach**, Orange Amber 65.00
Bitters, **Fish Bitters**, Crude Top, Dark Amber 175.00
Bitters, **Fish**, Bruise In Base, Amber, W-125 .... 60.00
Bitters, **Fish**, Golden Amber, Darker Stripe Down Length Of Bottle 145.00
Bitters, **Fish**, The, Clear, W-125 .... 380.00
Bitters, **Fish**, Variant A, Dark Amber 175.00
Bitters, **Fish**, W.H.Ware, Pat.1866, Dark Amber, 12 In. .... *Illus* 175.00
Bitters, **Fisher's Compound Mandrake**, Labeled Kennebunk, Maine, Amber 22.50
Bitters, **Flint's Quaker**, Aqua, W-126 .... 19.00 To 25.00
Bitters, **Foerester's Teutonic**, Amber, Iron Pontil .... *Color* XX.XX
Bitters, **Fratelli Brance Milano**, Green 5.00
Bitters, **Frazier's Root**, Aqua 7.00
Bitters, **Frazier's Root**, Label, Aqua 7.00
Bitters, **Fred Kalina Stomach**, Pittsburgh, Pa., Quart .... *Illus* 75.00

Bitters,
Emerson's Excelsior Botanic,
Sun Colored

Bitters, Fish, W.H.Ware,
Pat.1866, Dark Amber, 12 In.

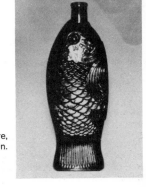

Bitters, Fred Kalina Stomach, Pittsburgh, Round, Fancy Design, Clear	45.00
Bitters, Frso Anti-Bilious Bitters Compound, Label, Clear	12.00
Bitters, Geo.Benz & Sons, Appetine, Embossed	300.00
Bitters, Geo.Benz & Sons, St.Paul, Dark Brown, Miniature *Illus*	200.00
Bitters, Geo.C.Hubbel, Cabin Shape, Embossed, Aqua	30.00
Bitters, German Hop, D.C.Warner Stamped Out	45.00
Bitters, German Hop, 1872, Reading, Mich., Amber, W-130	30.00 To 55.00
Bitters, German Tonic, Improved Pontil, Aqua, W-131	250.00
Bitters, Gilbert's Sarsaparilla, Octagonal, Amber, W-4325	105.00
Bitters, Gilka, Shaped Kantorowiz, Green	92.00
Bitters, Globe Tonic, Amber, W-134	47.00 To 60.00
Bitters, Globe Tonic, Light Amber	70.00
Bitters, Godwin Indian Vegetable & Sarsaparilla Bitters, Aqua	140.00
Bitters, Goff's Herb, Aqua	8.00
Bitters, Goff's Herb, Bimal, Aqua	7.50
Bitters, Goff's Herb, Camden, N.H., Aqua, W-137	10.00
Bitters, Goff's, Clear, W-136	4.00
Bitters, Goff's, Label & Contents, Embossed	12.00
Bitters, Goff's, Label, Contents, Boxed	14.00
Bitters, Golden, Stain, Aqua, W-138	72.50
Bitters, Goodwin Indian Vegetable & Sarsaparilla, Pontil, Aqua, W-140	140.00
Bitters, Grange, Embossed Anchor, Satin Finish, Amber, 1/2 Pint	12.00
Bitters, Great Western Tonic, Embossed, Labels, W-143	95.00
Bitters, Greeley's Bourbon Whiskey, Barrel, Puce, W-145	140.00
Bitters, Greeley's Bourbon Whiskey, Copper	130.00
Bitters, Greeley's Bourbon, Amber, W-144	50.00 To 90.00
Bitters, Greeley's Bourbon, Barrel, Light Puce	175.00
Bitters, Greeley's Bourbon, Barrel, Rose Amber, 9 In.High	150.00
Bitters, Greeley's Bourbon, Barrel, Smokey Amber	120.00
Bitters, Greeley's Bourbon, Embossed, Puce	130.00
Bitters, Greeley's Bourbon, Embossed, Smokey Green	145.00
Bitters, Greeley's Bourbon, Label, Barrel, Amber	200.00
Bitters, Greeley's Bourbon, Label, Smokey	230.00
Bitters, Greeley's Bourbon, Label, Smokey Amber	230.00
Bitters, Greeley's Bourbon, Pink Amber	120.00
Bitters, Griel's Herb, Griel & Young, Mfgrs., Lancaster, Pa.	110.00
Bitters, Gwilym Evans Quinine, Bluish Aqua	110.00
Bitters, H.E.Swan, Pressed Glass, Horn Of Plenty, 11 In.High	45.00
Bitters, H.E.Swan, Pressed Glass, Horn Of Plenty, 7 In.High	26.66
Bitters, H.H.Warner's Tippecanoe, Amber	65.00
Bitters, H.Kake's Indian Specific, Open Pontil	65.00
Bitters, H.L.Moshler's Keystone, Anti-Dispeptic *Color*	XX.XX
Bitters, H.P.Herb Wild Cherry, Amber, W-148	120.00 To 165.00
Bitters, Hall's Barrel, Amber, W-152	95.00
Bitters, Hansard's Genuine Hop, Pottery, 7 1/2 In. *Illus*	60.00

Bitters, Fred Kalina,
Stomach, Pittsburgh,
Pa., Quart
See Page 39

Bitters, Geo.Benz & Sons,
St.Paul,
Dark Brown, Miniature

Bitters,
Hansard's Genuine Hop,
Pottery, 7 1/2 In.

Bitters, Hansard's Genuine Hop, Swansea & Llanelly, Stone, Tan & Cream 60.00
Bitters, Harter's Wild Cherry, Label, Amber, W-158 .... 32.50 To 35.00
Bitters, Hartwig Kantorowicz Nachfolger, Amber 22.50
Bitters, Hartwig Kantorowicz Posen Hamburg, Germany, Milk Glas .... 55.00 To 75.00
Bitters, Hartwig Kantorowicz, Embossed Fish In Star, Amber 225.00
Bitters, Henderson's Carolina, Amber, W-162 .... 12.50
Bitters, Henley's IXL , Light Green 68.00
Bitters, Henley's Wild Grape Root, Aqua, W-164 .... 30.00
Bitters, Hentz Curative, W-165 .... 35.00 To 80.00
Bitters, Hentz's Curative, Free Sample, Aqua 20.00
Bitters, Herb, Aqua 14.00
Bitters, Hi Hi Bitters Co., Rock Island, Illinois, Amber, W-167 .... 65.00
Bitters, Hi Hi Bitters, Rock Island, Six Star 100.00
Bitters, Hibbard's Wild Cherry, Aqua 90.00
Bitters, Hibernia, Braunschweiger & Bumstead, W-446 .... 75.00
Bitters, Highby Tonic, Amber 20.00
Bitters, Hoffland's German, Contents, Aqua 15.00
Bitters, Hoffman's Golden 18.00
Bitters, Holtzermann's Patent Stomach, Amber, W-172 .... 120.00
Bitters, Home, St.Louis, Dug, Amber 45.00
Bitters, Home, St.Louis, Embossed, W-173 ....60.00 To 110.00
Bitters, Hop & Iron, Square, Amber, 8 1/2 In., W-175 .... 30.00 To 45.00
Bitters, Hop, Dated 1872, Hop Vine Embossed, Lablels, Amber, 9 1/2 In. 35.00
Bitters, Hopkin's Union Stomach, Amber 15.00
Bitters, Hua, Lady's Leg 15.00
Bitters, Hubbel Golden, Stain, Aqua 80.00
Bitters, Hunki Dori 65.00
Bitters, Huntington's Golden Tonic, Amber, W-182 .... 62.50 To 78.00
Bitters, Imperial Kidney, Liver, Nerve, Blood & Stomach, Amber 100.00
Bitters, Iron Tonic, Label, Amber, W-186 .... 15.00 To 22.50
Bitters, Iron, Brown Chemical Co., Square, Amber, 8 1/2 In. 25.00
Bitters, J.M.Leonard, Wild Cherry, Bangor, Me., Label, 3 Mold, 7 1/2 In.High 15.00
Bitters, J.W.Walker's, V.B.On Base 5.50
Bitters, Jacob Pinkerton Wahoo & Calisaya, Stain, Amber, W-349 .... 70.00
Bitters, Jenkin's Stomach, L.& W.On Base ....75.00 To 125.00
Bitters, John Roots', Buffalo, 1834, Label, Green Blue .... *Illus* 300.00
Bitters, Johnson's Calisaya, Burlington, Bt., Amber .... 40.00 To 77.00
Bitters, Johnson's Calisaya, Square, Bubbles, Light Honey Amber 85.00
Bitters, Jordan's Celebrated Stomach, Clear 6.00
Bitters, Jos Triner, Amber 3.00
Bitters, Kaiser Wilhelm, Co., Sandusky, Ohio, 10 1/2 In. .... *Illus* 35.00
Bitters, Kaiser Wilhelm, Embossed, W-197 .... 75.00 To 95.00
Bitters, Kantorowicz, Gilka Shape, Green 125.00
Bitters, Kaufmann's Sulphur, Aqua .... 9.00 To 15.00
Bitters, Kelly's Old Cabin, Amber, W-199 .... 300.00 To 350.00

Bitters, John Roots', Buffalo,
1834, Label, Green Blue

Bitters, Kaiser Wilhelm Co.,
Sandusky, Ohio, 10 1/2 In.

Bitters, Kennedy's East India, Square, Clear Turning Purple, 8 7/8 In.	27.50
Bitters, Keystone, Stain, Amber, W-201	85.00
Bitters, Kimball's Jaundice, Amber, W-202	150.00
Bitters, Kimball's Jaundice, Olive Amber	110.00
Bitters, Kimmell's Tonic Herb, Label, Clear	10.00
Bitters, King Solomon's, Olive Amber	64.00
Bitters, King Solomon's, Seattle, Washington, Amber, W-457	95.00
Bitters, Koehler's Stomach, Embossed	40.00
Bitters, Lacour's, Amber	40.00
Bitters, Lady's Leg, Amber	40.00 To 55.00
Bitters, Lady's Leg, Coppertone, 12 In.High	40.00
Bitters, Lady's Leg, Emerald Green, 13 In.	55.00
Bitters, Lady's Leg, Graphite Pontil, Olive Green	65.00
Bitters, Lady's Leg, Red Amber, Turn Mold	22.00
Bitters, Lady's Leg, Underberg Hua On Base, Red Amber	25.00
Bitters, Lancaster Glass Works, Barrel, Embossed Base, Amber	150.00
Bitters, Lanley's Aqua, W-206	25.00
Bitters, Langley's Root & Herb, Aqua, Open Pontil, W-206	17.50 To 20.00
Bitters, Langley's Root And Herb, Blown In Mold, Applied Lip, Aqua	25.00
Bitters, Langley's, Amber, Quart	40.00 To 55.00
Bitters, Langley's, Backward Nines, Aqua	25.00
Bitters, Langley's, Slug Plate, Aqua, 6 1/4 X 2 3/8 In.	20.00
Bitters, Langley's, 76 Union St., O.P., Aqua, 8 1/2 In.High	50.00
Bitters, Langley's, 99 Union St., Aqua	20.00 To 25.00
Bitters, Lash's Bitters Co., Round, Amber	25.00
Bitters, Lash's Bitters, Nature's Tonic Laxative, Amber	9.00
Bitters, Lash's Kidney & Liver, Amber, W-208	14.00
Bitters, Lash's Kidney & Liver, Sample	12.00
Bitters, Lash's Kidney & Liver, ABM , Labels	12.00
Bitters, Lash's Natural Tonic Laxative, Signature, ABM m1913	7.95 To 9.00
Bitters, Lash's, Ginger Cordial, Contents, 80 Percent Label	11.50
Bitters, Lash's, Miniature, Stain, Blown In Mold	14.00
Bitters, Lashe's, Monogram L.C.B.O., Wide Mouth, Oval, Clear	7.00
Bitters, Lediard's, W-211	110.00
Bitters, Leipziger Burgunder Wein, Dark Green, W-212	48.00
Bitters, Leipziger Burgunder Wein, Olive Green	35.00
Bitters, Lewis Red Jacket, Amber, W-213	52.50
Bitters, Life Of Man, C.Gates & Co., Embossed, Aqua, W-214	35.00
Bitters, Lippman's Great German, Amber, W-215	60.00
Bitters, Litthauer Stomach, Label, Milk Glass, W-216	55.00 To 75.00
Bitters, Litthauer Stomach, Ohio, Label, Milk Glass Illus	80.00
Bitters, Loew's Celebrated Stomach, Apple Green, W-217	180.00
Bitters, Log Cabin Hops & Buchu	132.50
Bitters, Log Cabin, Box, Opener, Booklet Color	XX.XX
Bitters, Louisiana Pelican Aromatic On Hostetter's, 73 Percent Label	18.50
Bitters, Loveridge's Wahoo, Embossed, Part Label, Amber, W-348	85.00
Bitters, Loveridge's Wahoo, Flask, Amber, Pint	275.00
Bitters, Loveridge's Wahoo, 1863, Amber, 11 In. Illus	150.00
Bitters, Lowell's Invigorating, Aqua, W-221	30.00
Bitters, Lutz's German Stomach, Label Under Glass, Amber	110.00
Bitters, Lyman's Dandelion, C.Sweet & Bro., Bangor, Me., Aqua, W-460	90.00
Bitters, Malt, Boston, U.S.A.On Base, Blob Top, Dark Green, W-224	29.75
Bitters, Malt, Light Green, W-224	48.00
Bitters, Mandrake, see Bitters, Dr. Baxter	
Bitters, Marshall's, Square, Amber, 8 3/4 In., W-227	24.00 To 45.00
Bitters, Mischler's, Amber, W-229	50.00
Bitters, Mishler's Herb, Label, Amber, W-229	32.50
Bitters, Mishler's Herb, Yellow Amber, W 229	30.00
Bitters, Morning Star, Amber, W-232	160.00 To 170.00
Bitters, Morning Star, Improved Pontil	200.00
Bitters, Moulton's Oloroso, Blue, Aqua	150.00
Bitters, Mt.Cider, Embossed, Green	150.00
Bitters, N.K.Brown, Iron & Quinine, Burlington, Vt., Aqua	49.00
Bitters, National, Ear Of Corn Color	XX.XX
Bitters, National, Ear Of Corn, Amber, W-236	185.00 To 210.00
Bitters, National, Ear Of Corn, Dark Amber, 12 1/2 In. Illus	225.00

Bitters,
Litthauer Stomach,
Ohio, Label, Milk Glass
See Page 42

Bitters, Loveridge's Wahoo, 1863, Amber, 11 In.
See Page 42

Bitters, National, Ear Of Corn,
Dark Amber, 12 1/2 In.
See Page 42

Bitters, Nibol, Kidney And Liver, Embossed, W-473	95.00
Bitters, Norton's Eureka, Amber	7.50
Bitters, O K Plantation, 1840, Patented 1863, Amber .... *Illus*	750.00
Bitters, Old Atwood's	4.00
Bitters, Old Dr.Gooodhue's Root & Herb, 3 O's In Goodhue, Label	30.00
Bitters, Old Dr.Warren's Quaker, Aqua, W-357	32.00 To 45.00
Bitters, Old Home, Embossed, W-241	110.00
Bitters, Old Homestead Wild Cherry, Amber, W-242	90.00 To 110.00
Bitters, Old House	1.40
Bitters, Old Sachem Bitters & Wigwam Tonic, Puce, W-244	150.00
Bitters, Old Sachem, Regular, Embossed, Honey	130.00
Bitters, Old Sachem, Regular, Embossed, Red Amber	125.00
Bitters, Old Solomon's Indian Wine, Amber	27.50

Bitters, O K Plantation, 1840, Patented 1863, Amber

Bitters, Orange Grove	35.00
Bitters, Original Pocahontas, Aqua, W-259	570.00
Bitters, Orruro, Amb, Round, Olive Green	17.50
Bitters, Orruro, Green, W-248	12.50
Bitters, Oswego 25 Cents, Oval, Amber .... 47.50 To 55.00
Bitters, Oxygenated, Aqua, W-249 .... 45.00 To 90.00
Bitters, Oxygenated, Open Pontil, Aqua	45.00
Bitters, Paine's Celery Compound, Labels	5.75
Bitters, Paine's Celery Compound, Square Sided, Amber	4.50
Bitters, Pankin's Hepatic, New York, Amber	125.00
Bitters, Parker's Celebrated Stomach, I.G.Co., On Base, Amber	75.00
Bitters, Parker's Celebrated Stomach, Large Monogram, W-480	60.00
Bitters, Parmelee's Hop Iron Buchin, Amber	26.00
Bitters, Pepsin Calisaya, Dr.Russel Medicine Co., Green, 8 In., W-253	30.00
Bitter, Pepsin, Green, W-251	40.00
Bitters, Perrine's Apple Ginger	80.00
Bitters, Perrine's Apple Ginger, Philadelphia	90.00
Bitters, Peruvian, Amber, W-254 .... 25.00 To 45.00
Bitters, Peruvian, Embossed, Clear	25.00
Bitters, Peruvian, Embossed, Honey Amber	35.00
Bitters, Peruvian, Shield, P.B.Co., Square, Amber, 9 In.	37.50
Bitters, Petzold's Genuine German, Amber, W-256 .... 95.00 To 130.00
Bitters, Peychaud's American Aromatic Bitter Cordial, Amber	15.00
Bitters, Peychaud's American Bitter Cordial, Honey Amber	15.00
Bitters, Phoenix, John Moffatt, Frosted, 1/2 Pint, W-257	45.00
Bitters, Phoenix, John Moffatt, N.Y., Aqua	22.00
Bitters, Phoenix, Open Pontil, Olive Green	135.00
Bitters, Phoenix, Open Pontil, 1 Dollar Size, Aqua	50.00
Bitters, Phoenix, Pontil, Iridescent, Aqua, 5 1/4 In.	40.00
Bitters, Phoenix, Pontil, Stain, Aqua, 5 1/4 In.High	40.00
Bitters, Pineapple	125.00
Bitters, Pineapple, Honey Amber	92.00
Bitters, Pipifax, Globbed, Square, Broken Bubble, Light Amber	20.00
Bitters, Plantation, Puce	55.00
Bitters, Plantation, 4 Log, Amber .... 37.50 To 40.00
Bitters, Plantation, 4 Log, Golden Amber	42.50
Bitters, Plantation, 4 Log, Label, Amber, W-111	57.50
Bitters, Plantation, 4 Log, Patented 1862 .... *Color* XX.XX
Bitters, Plantation, 4 Log, Stain, Citron, W-111	85.00
Bitters, Plantation, 6 Log, Citron, W-111	90.00
Bitters, Plantation, 6 Log, Patented 1862 .... *Color* XX.XX
Bitters, Polo Club Stomach, Amber, W-260	60.00
Bitters, Pond's Genuine Laxative, Paper Labels, Brown .... *Illus* 37.50
Bitters, Pond's Kidney & Liver, Abm, Amber	18.00
Bitters, Pond's, ABM , Yellow Amber	20.00
Bitters, Pond's, Amber, W-261	17.50
Bitters, Pond's, Embossed, Paper Label	25.00
Bitters, Poor Man's Family, Aqua, 6 1/2 In., W-262 .... *Illus* 35.00
Bitters, Prickley Ash Bitters Co., Amber, 9 1/2 In., W-263 .... 22.00 To 42.00
Bitters, Prune Stomach & Liver, Amber, W-264	60.00
Bitters, Purdy's Cottage, Embossed, W-266	285.00
Bitters, Pure Apple Brandy, Clear	15.00
Bitters, Quaker, see Bitters, Dr. Flint	
Bitters, Quaker, Embossed, Aqua	22.50
Bitters, Rainbow Tonic, Labeled	12.00
Bitters, Ramsey's Trinidad	90.00
Bitters, Ramsey's Trinidad, Olive Green, W-268 .... 50.00 To 90.00
Bitters, Red Jacket, Square, Amber .... 12.00 To 60.00
Bitters, Reed's, see also Bitters, Lady's Leg	
Bitters, Reed's 1878 Gilt Edge Tonic, Amber	30.00
Bitters, Reed's 1878 Gilt Edge Tonic, Dug	14.00
Bitters, Reed's 1878 Gilt Edge Tonic, Open Bubble	14.00
Bitters, Reed's, Lady's Leg, Embossed, W-272	115.00
Bitters, Renault, Label, Round, Graduated Collar, Pewter Cap, Amber, W-105	9.95
Bitters, Renault, Label, Round, Graduated Collar, Pewter Cap, Amber, 1 Oz.Size	3.95
Bitters, Rex Co., Chicago, Sun Color, 11 1/2 In. .... *Illus* 85.00

Bitters, Pond's Genuine Laxative,
Paper Labels, Brown
See Page 44

Bitters,
Poor Man's Family,
Aqua, 6 1/2 In., W-262
See Page 44

Bitters, Rex Co., Chicago, Sun Color, 11 1/2 In.
See Page 44

Bitters, Rex Kidney & Liver, Amber, W-274	22.00
Bitters, Rex Kidney & Liver, 10 Percent Label, Light Haze	20.00
Bitters, Rex, ABM , Smokey Amber	18.50
Bitters, Richardson's Vegetable Purifying, Aqua	15.00
Bitters, Rising Sun, John C.Hurst, Philada., Square, Red Amber, W-277	75.00
Bitters, Rivauds Cocktail, Amber, W-278	260.00
Bitters, Roback's Barrel, Amber, W-280	100.00 To 135.00
Bitters, Roback's Stomach, Amber	120.00
Bitters, Roback's Stomach, Cloudy, Amber	120.00
Bitters, Roback's Stomach, Improved Pontil, Amber, W-280	160.00
Bitters, Rocky Mountain Tonic, Embossed	120.00
Bitters, Rose's Magador, Amber	65.00
Bitters, Roxana Brand, Full Content & Labels	25.00
Bitters, Royal Pepsin Stomach, Amber, 9 1/2 In.High .... *Illus*	75.00

Bitters, Royal Pepsin Stomach, Amber, 9 1/2 In.High

Bitters, Royal Pepsin, Large Size 85.00
Bitters, Rush's, Amber, W-289 .... 22.50 To 38.00
Bitters, Russ's St.Domino, Amber, W-290 .... 27.50 To 55.00
Bitters, S.A.Spencer, Dr.Jacob's, Embossed, W-190 .... 90.00 To 130.00
Bitters, S.B.Goff's Herb 12.00
Bitters, S.O.Richardson, Open Pontil, Aqua, W-275 .... 35.00
Bitters, S.O.Richardson, South Reading, Mass., Aqua 25.00
Bitters, S.O.Richardson's, Flared Lip, Stained 30.00
Bitters, S.O.Richardson's, Open Pontil, Aqua 35.00
Bitters, S.O.Richardson's, Stain, Aqua 35.00
Bitters, S. T. Drake's, see Bitters, Drake's
Bitters, Sachem Bitters & Wigwam Tonic, Puce 150.00
Bitters, Sanborn's Kidney & Liver Vegetable Laxative, Rectangular, Amber 70.00
Bitters, Sanitarium-Hi-Ku, Green 150.00
Bitters, Santox Stomach, Amber 12.50
Bitters, Sarasina Stomach, W-294 .... 65.00 To 110.00
Bitters, Sarasina, W-496 .... 30.00
Bitters, Saxlehner's Bitterquelle, Crude, Olive Green, 9 In. 5.00
Bitters, Saxlehner's Bitterquelle, Dark Green 6.00
Bitters, Saxlehner's Bitterquelle, Whittled, Amber 2.50
Bitters, Saxlehner's Bitterquelle, Whittled, Green 2.50
Bitters, Sazerac Aromatic, Lady's Leg, Golden Amber 300.00
Bitters, Sazerac Aromatic, Milk Glass, W-296 .... 275.00 To 300.00
Bitters, Schroeder's Lady's Leg, Amber, W-294 .... 175.00
Bitters, Schroeder's, Louisville, Kentucky, Lady's Leg 190.00
Bitters, Severa Stomach, Amber 20.00
Bitters, Sherk's Bitter Tincture Of Roots, Aqua .... 160.00 To 500.00
Bitters, Simon's Centennial, Aqua, W-304 .... 160.00
Bitters, Simon's Centennial, Washington's Bust, Broken Bubble, Aqua 95.00
Bitters, Sir Robert Edgar's English Life, Amber .... Illus 130.00
Bitters, Sir Robert Edgar's English Life, U.S.A., Brown .... 25.00 To 60.00
Bitters, Smith's Celebrated Old Style, Amber, W-309 .... 20.00
Bitters, Smith's Celebrated Old Style, Stain, Amber 260.00
Bitters, Smith's Druid, Barrel, Amber, W-308 .... 325.00
Bitters, Smith's Green Mountain Renovator, East Georgian, Vermont, 7 In. 300.00
Bitters, Somon Centennial, Aqua 20.00
Bitters, Sonoma Wine, Amber 55.00
Bitters, St.Gotthard Herb, Amber 75.00
Bitters, St.Jacob's, Embossed .... 25.00 To 45.00
Bitters, Star Kidney & Liver, Amber, W-315 .... 85.00
Bitters, Steele's Niagara, Amber, W-316 .... 75.00 To 125.00
Bitters, Stephen Jewett's, Aqua, W-193 .... 3.00
Bitters, Stomach & Tonic, Clear 25.00
Bitters, Stomach, Amber 20.00
Bitters, Stoughton, Label, Amber 300.00
Bitters, Suffolk Pig, Amber 350.00
Bitters, Suffolk Pig, Philbrook & Tucker, Whittled, Amber 20.00
Bitters, Sweet's Strengthening, Aqua, W-328 .... 5.00
Bitters, Table, Honeycomb Pattern, Ground Pontil, Clear, 6 1/2 In.High 15.00
Bitters, Taft's Tonic, Aqua .... 50.00 To 75.00
Bitters, The Globe Tonic 60.00
Bitters, The Globe Tonic, Yellow Amber 10.00
Bitters, Tiny Bird, Label .... Color XX.XX
Bitters, Tippecanoe, Chapin, 6 Cone Sour Mash, 1867 .... 30.00
Bitters, Tippecanoe, Cobalt Blue .... Color XX.XX
Bitters, Tippecanoe, H.H.Warner And Company 70.00
Bitters, Tippecanoe, H.H.Warner Co., Pat.Nov.20, '83, Rochester, N.Y. 85.00
Bitters, Tippecanoe, Label, Amber 70.00
Bitters, Tippecanoe, Pat.Nov.20, 1883, Warner Co., Amber .... Illus 65.00
Bitters, Tippecanoe, Sample, Brown 11.00
Bitters, To-Ni-Ta Mucous Membrane, Amber 12.50
Bitters, Toneco Stomach, Contents, Label, Clear, W-330 .... 15.00
Bitters, Toneco, ABM 7.50
Bitters, Tonic, Label, Aqua, W-331 .... 50.00
Bitters, Tonola, Aqua, W-332 .... 50.00
Bitters, Tonola, Cloud, Aqua ....

Bitters, Sir Robert Edgar's English Life,
U.S.A., Brown
See Page 46

Bitters, Tippecanoe, Pat.Nov.20, 1883,
Warner Co., Amber
See Page 46

Bitters, Traveler's, Embossed Traveler, Rectangular, Dates 1834/1870, Amber	900.00
Bitters, Triner's Bitter Wine, Amber	5.00
Bitters, Tucker Sarracenia Life, Amber	75.00
Bitters, Turner Bros., N.Y., Barrel, Yellow Amber	65.00
Bitters, Turner Brothers, New York, Barrel, Amber	105.00
Bitters, Udolpho Wolfe's Aromatic Schnapps, Green, Pint	15.00
Bitters, Udolpho Wolfe's Aromatic Schnapps, Green, Quart	12.00
Bitters, Udolpho Wolfe's Aromatic Schnapps, Stain, Amber	6.00
Bitters, Udolpho Wolfe's Schiedam Aromatic Schnapps, Emerald Green	15.00
Bitters, Underberg Bitters, Full Label	12.00
Bitters, Underberg, Embossed On Base	25.00
Bitters, Underberg, Miniature, Germany	2.00
Bitters, Union, E.Wormer's & Co., Pittsburgh, Pa., Quart	45.00
Bitters, Vermo Stomach Bitters, Tonic, & Appetizer, Clear, W-342	23.00
Bitters, Vermo Stomach, Square, Clear, 9 1/2 In.	32.50
Bitters, Vermont, Clear	30.00
Bitters, Vicar Bitter & Tonic Co., Dark Amber .... *Illus*	125.00
Bitters, Von Hopf's Curacoa, Amber, W-344	20.00
Bitters, W.C., Amber, W-347	170.00
Bitters, W.C.Bitters, Bruise, Amber, W 347	160.00
Bitters. W.C.Chilton & Co., Romain's Crimean, Amber	93.00
Bitters, W.F.Severa	30.00
Bitters, Wahoo & Calisaya, Amber, W-349	80.00 To 100.00

Bitters, Vicar Bitter & Tonic Co., Dark Amber

Bitters, Wahoo & Calisaya, Stain	35.00
Bitters, Wait's Kidney & Liver, Amber	22.50
Bitters, Walker's Vinegar, Aqua	7.50
Bitters, Walker's Vinegar, Contents, Aqua	5.00
Bitters, Walkinshaw's Curative, Amber, W-352	85.00
Bitters, Wallace's Tonic Stomach, W-353	45.00
Bitters, Warner's German Hop, Amber	45.00
Bitters, Warner's Safe Cure, Sample, Amber	30.00
Bitters, Warner's Safe Tonic, Embossed, 7 1/4 X 3 X 1 1/2 In.	275.00
Bitters, Warner's Tippecanoe, Amber	65.00
Bitters, Warner's Tippecanoe, Log Shaped, Amber	80.00
Bitters, Watson's Caroni, Olive	24.00
Bitters, Webb's A No.1 Tonic	22.00
Bitters, West India Stomach, Amber, W-359	34.50 To 75.00
Bitters, Wild Cherry Jaundice, 90 Per Cent Label, Bangor, Me., Aqua	15.00
Bitters, Wild Cherry, Amber, W-148	150.00
Bitters, Wilder's Stomach, 5 Story Building, Windows, Beaded Corners, Clear	125.00
Bitters, Wilkinshaw's Curative, Amber	85.00
Bitters, Willard's Golden Seal, Aqua, W-367	37.50
Bitters, Willard's Golden Seal, Oval, Pinhead On Lip, Aqua	48.00
Bitters, William Allen's Congress, Stain, Aqua	45.00
Bitters, Wine, Cobalt, 12 In.High	20.00
Bitters, Wishart's Pine Tree Cordial, Patent 1859, Aqua *Illus*	48.00
Bitters, Wood's Tonic Wine, Aqua	65.00
Bitters, Wryghte, London, Whittled, Skirted Sides, Emerald Green	150.00
Bitters, Yerba Buena, Amber, Large	32.50
Bitters, Yerba Buena, Amber, W-375	55.00
Bitters, Yerba Buena, Globbed Top, Amber, Large Size	40.00
Bitters, Yerba Buena, Globbed Top, Dark Amber, Small Size	100.00
Bitters, Zoeller's Stomach, Contents, Labels, Amber, W-378	65.00 To 95.00
Bitters, Zoeller's Stomach, The Zoeller Medical Co., Pittsburgh, Pa., Amber	65.00
Bitters, Zu Zu, Amber, W-379	60.00
Black & White Scotch, Scotty, Black *Illus*	30.00
Black & White Scotch, Scotty, White *Illus*	30.00

Bitters, Wishart's Pine Tree Cordial,
Patent 1859, Aqua

Black & White Scotch,
Scotty, Black

Black & White Scotch,
Scotty, White

Black Glass, Cylindrical, Long Bulged Neck, Pontil, 1770, Quart	39.00
Black Glass, Cylindrical, Pontil, 1770, Pint	29.00
Black Glass, Dip Mold, Quart	12.00
Black Glass, English, Matt Churchward-Aish, Sealed, Bubbly, C.1800	90.00
Black Glass, Graphite Pontil, Applied Top, 2 In, Kick Up, 9 1/2 In.High	15.00
Black Glass, Triangular	25.00
Blacking, Bixby, Amber, 4 In.High	2.00
Blown, Applied Neck Ring, Deep Push Up, Light Green	7.00
Blown, Decanter, 4 Section, Etched, Blown Stopper, Clear, 10 1/2 In. High	45.00
Blown, Jar, Expanded Collar, Olive Green	70.00
Blown, Keene, 2 Mold, Rectangular, Palm Panel, Clear, 8 3/4 In.	32.50
Blown, Pillar Mold, Pontil, Neck Longer Than Bottle, Ribbed, Flint	28.00
Blown, Pinch, Applied Swags, Scalloped Foot, Clear	25.00
Blown, Pontil, Olive Amber	30.00
Blown, Tapered Sides, Collared Neck, Amethyst	90.00

Borghini ceramic containers are filled in Pisa, Italy. The more recent imports are stamped with the words 'Borghini collection made in Italy, 1969.'

Borghini, Alpine House	4.00
Borghini, Black Stone	3.95
Borghini, Cat, Black	7.00
Borghini, Clown	25.00
Borghini, Dog	25.00
Borghini, Girl, Nubian	6.00
Borghini, Horse's Head	25.00
Borghini, Santa Maria	4.00
Brandy, Baltimore Club	2.50
Brandy, Bardinet, Embossed	3.00
Brandy, Brandy Cordial On Medallion, Pontil, Amber, Quart	250.00
Brandy, California Brandy On Label, Wicker Case, Amber, Quart	2.00
Brandy, Christian Bros., Bank, Seals	14.00
Brandy, Flat Barrel, Aqua, Pint	6.00
Brandy, Homer California Ginger, Round, Stain, Amber	10.00
Brandy, John Richards, Bordeaux, 1815 Cognac, Seal, Aqua, 11.High	35.00
Brandy, Mogavi, Kick Up, Cork	6.00
Brandy, Old Mr.Boston, Five Star, Flask	1.10
Brandy, Porcelain Keg, White With Banding, Contents	6.00
Bronte, Jug, Large Size	5.00
Bronte, Miniature, 2 Tone Color	1.95
Brooks, see Ezra Brooks	
Burgermeister Beer Decanter	39.50
Buton, Poker Dice Bottle	200.00
C.A.Richards & Co., Boston, Amber	5.00
Cabin Still, see Old Fitzgerald	
Calabash, Baltimore Glass Works & Sheaf, Open Pontil, Amber, Quart	45.00
Calabash, Clasped Hands & Eagle, Improved Pontil, Amber, Quart	170.00
Calabash, Commemorative, Washington & Tree, 1732-1932 Embossed, Clear	6.00
Calabash, Hunter & Fisherman, Amber, Quart	75.00 To 110.00
Calabash, Hunter & Fisherman, Aqua, Quart	40.00
Calabash, Hunter & Fisherman, Stain, Aqua, Quart	30.00
Calabash, Jenny Lind & Factory, Aqua, Quart	30.00
Calabash, Jenny Lind & Factory, Stain, Light Green, Quart	75.00
Calabash, Mc Kearin G I-35, Washington & Tree, Aqua, Quart	45.00
Calabash, Mc Kearin G I-36, Washington & Tree, Aqua, Quart	40.00
Calabash, Mc Kearin G I-100, Jenny Lind & Kossuth, Aqua, Quart	40.00
Calabash, Mc Kearin G I-101, Aqua, Quart	15.00
Calabash, Mc Kearin G I-102, Jenny Lind & Glass Factory, Green, Quart	280.00
Calabash, Mc Kearin G I-103, Jenny Lind & Glass Factory, Aqua, Quart	30.00
Calabash, Mc Kearin G I-104, Jenny Lind & Factory, Blue Green, Quart	230.00
Calabash, Mc Kearin G I-107, Jenny Lind & Glass Factory, Aqua, Quart	45.00
Calabash, Mc Kearin G I-112, Kossuth & Frigate Mississippi, Green, Quart	290.00
Calabash, Mc Kearin G I-113, Kossuth & Tree, Light Green, Quart	45.00
Calabash, Mc Kearin G Iv-42, Clasped Hands & Eagle, Aqua, Quart	40.00
Calabash, Roosevelt & T.V.A.Dam, Aqua, Quart	5.00
Calabash, Sheaf & Tree, Stain, Open Pontil, Aqua, Quart	17.50

Calabash, Sheaf Of Wheat & Star, Handle, Amber, Quart 170.00
Calabash, Sheaf Of Wheat & Star, Open Pontil, Aqua 45.00
Calabash, Soldier & Large Star, Aqua, Quart 55.00
Canadian Mist, Mountie 18.95

*Candy containers of glass were very popular after World War I. Small
glass figural bottles held dime-store candy. Today many of the same shapes
hold modern candy in plastic bottles. The numbers used in the entries in the
form E-0 refers to the book American Glass Containers by George
Eikelberger and Serge Agadjanian.*

Candy Container, Airplane, ABM , Clear 5.00
Candy Container, Airplane, Army Bomber 15-P7 .... 18.00
Candy Container, Airplane, Spirit Of Goodwill, Closure, Paint, Propellor 32.00
Candy Container, Airplane, Tin Wings, Patent 113053 .... 22.00
Candy Container, Airplane, 5 In. .... *Illus* 12.00
Candy Container, Army Bomber 8.00
Candy Container, Army Car 12.00
Candy Container, Automobile, Contents 5.00
Candy Container, Automobile, Coupe With Long Hood, U.S.A. 45.00
Candy Container, Automobile, Miniature 8.00
Candy Container, Automobile, Miniature, Streamlined, Cardboard Closure 12.00
Candy Container, Automobile, No.58 .... 12.00
Candy Container, Automobile, Sedan With 12 Vents, Tin Top 45.00
Candy Container, Automobile, Station Wagon 22.00
Candy Container, Automobile, Touring Car, Streamlined 14.00
Candy Container, Baby Chick, Painted, No.145 .... 25.00
Candy Container, Baseball Player With Bat 50.00
Candy Container, Car, Volkswagen, Beetle Sedan 8.00
Candy Container, Battleship, Closure .... 4.50 To 12.00
Candy Container, Battleship, Miniature 5.00
Candy Container, Battleship, 5 1/2 In.Long .... *Illus* 7.00
Candy Container, Bear, Seated, Closure 19.00
Candy Container, Billiken, Screw Top, 75 Percent Gold Paint, Clear 35.00
Candy Container, Boat, Clear, 2 1/2 In. 3.00
Candy Container, Boat, Cruiser 15.00
Candy Container, Boat, Frosted, 3 In. 5.00
Candy Container, Boat, Miniature, Battleship 18.00
Candy Container, Boot, Santa Claus, Cardboard Top .... 6.00 To 15.00
Candy Container, Bottle Carrier & Bottles, Painted, No.3 .... 30.00
Candy Container, Bulldog, Round Base, Tin Cover, Painted 22.00
Candy Container, Bulldog, Screw Closure 13.00
Candy Container, Bulldog, Sitting, Painted Round, Base 20.00
Candy Container, Bus, Victory Lines Special, Painted, Cardboard Closure 18.00
Candy Container, Car, Antique Racing, Abm, Clear 5.00
Candy Container, Car, Electric 25.00
Candy Container, Car, Open 30.00
Candy Container, Car, Station Wagon .... 6.00 To 22.00
Candy Container, Car, Volkswagen 15.00
Candy Container, Chicken On Nest .... 4.00 To 25.00
Candy Container, Chicken, No.149 .... 6.00 To 10.00
Candy Container, Clock 12.00
Candy Container, Cruiser .... 6.00 To 10.00
Candy Container, Cruiser, No.98 .... 4.00
Candy Container, Crystal Palace, Clear 40.00
Candy Container, Dog 6.00
Candy Container, Dog By Barrel 35.00
Candy Container, Dog, Hound Pup, No Hat 10.00
Candy Container, Dog, Hound Pup, Screw Top, Cobalt Blue 18.00
Candy Container, Dog, Hound, Closure, Contents, Clear 4.00
Candy Container, Dog, No.183 .... 2.00
Candy Container, Dog, No.184 .... 5.00
Candy Container, Dog, Painted, U.S.A., Brown, 4 In. .... *Illus* 23.00
Candy Container, Dog, Scottie .... 3.00 To 8.00
Candy Container, Dog, Scottie, Head Up, Tipped Left 5.00
Candy Container, Dog, Scottie, Head Up, Tipped Right 5.00
Candy Container, Dog, Sitting 6.00

Candy Container,
Airplane, 5 In.
See Page 50

Candy Container, Battleship, 5 1/2 In.Long
See Page 50

Candy Container, Dog, Painted, U.S.A., Brown, 4 In.
See Page 50

Candy Container, Drum Mug, Painted, No.543	20.00
Candy Container, Electric Iron	8.00
Candy Container, Elephant, G.O.P.	15.00
Candy Container, Fire Engine, Fire Dept In Circle	12.00
Candy Container, Fire Engine, Miniature	10.00
Candy Container, Fire Engine, Red Paint	5.00
Candy Container, Fire Engine, Train	8.00
Candy Container, Girl With Geese	11.00
Candy Container, Grandfather Clock	8.00
Candy Container, Gun, Hand, Tin Cap	18.00
Candy Container, Gun, Long Barrel	25.00
Candy Container, Gun, No.247	8.00
Candy Container, Gun, No.252	8.00
Candy Container, Gun, No.271	8.00
Candy Container, Gun, No.279	8.00
Candy Container, Gun, Revolver, Clear	10.00
Candy Container, Gun, Revolver, Clear To Slightly Amethyst	15.00
Candy Container, Gun, Revolver, Clear, Tin Cap	18.00
Candy Container, Gun, Revolver, Tin Cap, Amber	35.00
Candy Container, Gun, Screw Cap, 13 1/2 In.Long	38.00
Candy Container, Gun, Stough's Whistlin Jim, Waisted Type Grip, Tin Cap	20.00
Candy Container, Gun, V.G.Co., Revolver, Tin Cap	15.00
Candy Container, Horn, Millstein 1948, Pink Plastic Part	12.00

Candy Container, Horse With 2 Wheeled Cart	3.00 To 12.00
Candy Container, Iron	10.00 To 18.00
Candy Container, Jeep	6.00 To 20.00
Candy Container, Jumbo Pencil, No.567	25.00
Candy Container, Kewpie	28.00
Candy Container, Kewpie Beside Barrel, Closure	30.00 To 32.00
Candy Container, Kewpie, Marked, Clear	37.00
Candy Container, Lamp, Inside Ribbed Base	12.00
Candy Container, Lantern	4.50 To 8.00
Candy Container, Lantern, Abm, Clear	5.00
Candy Container, Lantern, Barn Type	32.00
Candy Container, Lantern, Beaded	22.00
Candy Container, Lantern, Beaded Globe	8.00
Candy Container, Lantern, Beaded, Painted	22.00
Candy Container, Lantern, Clear, Cap	8.00
Candy Container, Lantern, Dec.20, '84	5.00
Candy Container, Lantern, Flint Globe	20.00
Candy Container, Lantern, Pear Shaped Globe	5.00
Candy Container, Lantern, Red Top & Bail	4.00
Candy Container, Lantern, T.H.Stouch, Jeannette, Pa.	12.00
Candy Container, Lantern, Tin Base & Top, Bail Handle, Clear	10.00
Candy Container, Lantern, 4 1/2 In. Illus	12.50
Candy Container, Learned Fox	40.00
Candy Container, Lemon, Three Mold, C.1930, Clear	7.00
Candy Container, Liberty Bell With Hanger	18.00
Candy Container, Liberty Bell, Amber	15.00
Candy Container, Liberty Bell, Blue	15.00 To 30.00
Candy Container, Liberty Bell, Green	15.00
Candy Container, Lighthouse	8.00
Candy Container, Locomotive	32.00
Candy Container, Locomotive, Contents	5.00
Candy Container, Locomotive, No.888	10.00
Candy Container, Locomotive, No.1028	12.00
Candy Container, Locomotive, Stough's E3's Hooker	6.00
Candy Container, Locomotive, Victory Glass Co., 1928	8.00
Candy Container, Military Hat	20.00
Candy Container, Military Hat, Paper Top, No.131	8.00
Candy Container, Mug, No.542	25.00
Candy Container, Old Santa, No.671	65.00
Candy Container, Opera Glass, Plain Panels, Gilt, Tin Screw Cap	28.00
Candy Container, Opera Glasses, Closure	40.00
Candy Container, Opera Glasses, Painted, No.558	7.00
Candy Container, Orange, Three Mold, C.1930, Clear	7.00
Candy Container, Pear, Three Mold, C.1930, Clear	25.00
Candy Container, Pencil	6.00 To 9.00
Candy Container, Peter Rabbit	10.00
Candy Container, Pistol, Brown	7.00
Candy Container, Plum, Three Mold, C.1930, Clear	21.00
Candy Container, Policeman's Night Stick, Tin Cap, Clear	7.00
Candy Container, Pony & Cart	7.00
Candy Container, Pug Dog, Filled, 4 In. Illus	9.00
Candy Container, Pup, Hound	6.50 To 12.00
Candy Container, Rabbit	18.00
Candy Container, Rabbit Coming Out Of Egg, Screw Closure	10.00 To 12.00
Candy Container, Rabbit Eating Carrot	35.00
Candy Container, Rabbit In Eggshell, Painted, No.608	30.00
Candy Container, Rabbit With Basket, Tin Bottom Illus	23.00
Candy Container, Rabbit With Market Basket, Metal Screw Cap, 4 1/2 In.	8.50
Candy Container, Rabbit, By Stough	13.50
Candy Container, Rabbit, Full, 6 In. Illus	19.75
Candy Container, Rabbit, Paws Extended, Metal Screw Cap, 5 1/4 In.	30.00
Candy Container, Rabbit, Running On Log	12.00
Candy Container, Rabbit, Sitting, Basket On Arm, Tin Top	9.50
Candy Container, Rabbit, Sitting, 6 1/2 In.	7.00
Candy Container, Rabbit, Three Mold, C.1930, Clear	60.00
Candy Container, Radio, Tune In, Tin Bottom	

Candy Container, Lantern, 4 1/2 In.
See Page 52

Candy Container,
Pug Dog, Filled, 4 In.
See Page 52

Candy Container,
Rabbit, Full, 6 In.
See Page 52

Candy Container,
Rabbit With Basket,
Tin Bottom
See Page 52

Candy Container, **Revolver**, Cork, Painted, Black & Silver	25.00
Candy Container, **Revolver**, Diamond In Grip, Tin Cap	10.00
Candy Container, **Santa Claus**	8.50
Candy Container, **Santa Claus**, Painted, Label	15.00
Candy Container, **Santa Claus**, Peaked Cap, Metal Screw Closure On Base	22.50
Candy Container, **Santa Leaving Chimney**, No.673	25.00
Candy Container, **Santa**, Plastic Head	25.00 To 30.00
Candy Container, **Santa**, 5 In.	16.50
Candy Container, **Santa's Boot**	6.00 To 15.00
Candy Container, **Santa's Boot**, Miniature	4.00
Candy Container, **Dog Scottie**, Head Up	4.00
Candy Container, **Dog Scottie**, Open Bottom	9.00
Candy Container, **Dog Scottie**, Open Top	5.00
Candy Container, **Dog Sitting**	3.50
Candy Container, **Dog Sitting**, Lid	7.50
Candy Container, **Rabbit Sitting**	8.50 To 10.00
Candy Container, **Rabbit Standing With Basket**	25.00
Candy Container, **Spark Plug**, Clear, 3 In.	*Illus* 35.00
Candy Container, **Spark Plug**, Light Green	35.00
Candy Container, **Speedboat**, 5 In.Long	*Illus* 7.00
Candy Container, **Spirit Of Goodwill**, Painted, No.8	35.00

Candy Container, Station Wagon, 5 In.Long .... *Illus*	6.00 To 15.00
Candy Container, Steam Engine	6.50
Candy Container, Strutting Turkey	12.50
Candy Container, Suitcase	30.00
Candy Container, Suitcase, Clear	18.00
Candy Container, Suitcase, Metal Closure, Milk Glass	28.00
Candy Container, Suitcase, No.707	10.00
Candy Container, Suitcase, Wire Handle, Metal Closure	14.75
Candy Container, Tank, Army	6.00 To 9.00
Candy Container, Tank, Army, Contents	6.00
Candy Container, Tank, Driver, Victory Glass Toys	8.00
Candy Container, Tank, 2 Cannons, Cardboard Closure	15.00
Candy Container, Tank, 2 Guns, Cardboard Closure	9.50
Candy Container, Telephone, Dial	3.00 To 15.00
Candy Container, Telephone, Receiver	20.00
Candy Container, Telephone, Tin Lid, Victory Glass Co., Jeannette, Pa.	8.50
Candy Container, Telephone, Upright	10.00
Candy Container, Telephone, Upright, Ribbed, Black Wood Receiver, Pa.	19.00
Candy Container, Telephone, Victory Glass Co., Dial Type, Cardboard Closure	9.00
Candy Container, Telephone, Wooden Receiver	12.00
Candy Container, Train	9.00
Candy Container, Train Engine, No.1028	5.00

Candy Container, Spark Plug, Clear, 3 In.
See Page 53

Candy Container, Speedboat, 5 In.Long
See Page 53

Candy Container,
Station Wagon,
5 In.Long

Candy Container, Train, Double Window	5.00
Candy Container, Train, Single Window	8.00
Candy Container, Trunk, Closure & Handle	10.00
Candy Container, Wheelbarrow, No.842	35.00
Candy Container, Willy's Jeep .... *Illus*	8.50
Candy Container, Willy's Jeep, Driver	15.00

Candy Container, Willy's Jeep

Candy Container, Windmill	22.50
Candy Container, Windmill, Dutch, Cardboard Closure	30.00
Candy Container, Windmill, Dutch, Metal Sail, Cardboard Closure	20.00
Candy Container, Windmill, Metal Blades, No.843	30.00
Canning Jar, see Fruit Jar	
Canteen, G.A.R., Raised Emblem & Writing, Brass & Cork Stopper, Quart	35.00
Carafe, Cambridge, Pressed Feather Pattern	18.00
Carafe, Cranberry Glass, Inverted Thumbprint, Square Top	37.50
Carafe, Cut Glass, Pineapple Pattern	27.00
Carafe, Cut Glass, Russian Pattern	48.00
Carafe, Keene, N.H., Blown, 3 Mold, Waffle & Sunburst, Ribs, C.1825, Clear	400.00
Carafe, Rubina, Acid Etched Floral, Deep Ruby At Top, 8 In.Tall	55.00
Carboy, Open Pontil, Straw Jacket, Blob Top, 3 Mold, Olive Green, 4 Gallon	45.00

Case bottles are those of the traditional shape known by this name. The bottles have flat sides and are almost square. Some taper and are narrower at the bottom. Case bottles can be of any age from the mid-1600s to the present day.

Case Free-Blown, Clear, Pint	8.00
Case Gin, Blankenheym & Nolet, Olive Green	12.00
Case Gin, Blankenheym & Nolet, 10 1/2 In.Tall	17.50
Case Gin, Blob Seal, Rolled Collar Lip, Miniature, Olive Green	65.00
Case Gin, Crude Applied Lip, Olive Green, Pint	12.00
Case Gin, Flared Mouth, Open Pontil	30.00
Case Gin, H.& B.& C., Black Glass, 6 In.	65.00
Castor, Pressed Glass, Drape, Hexagonal, 2 Lip, Clear	4.00
Ceramic, Jug, Chas.Hyman & Son, 2 Color Brown Glaze, Quart	12.00
Ceramic, Jug, False Bottom, Brown Glaze With Yellow Streaks, Quart	2.00
Ceramic, Jug, Happy Days, 2 Tone Glaze, Quart	20.00
Ceramic, Ring, Brown Glaze	32.50
Chemical, AH On Bottom, 4 In. .... *Illus*	3.00
Chemical, Ammonium Hydroxide, Nh-40h	4.00
Chemical, Astyptodyne Chemical Co., Label, Clear	3.50
Chemical, Bugine, Iron City Chemical Co., Applied Lip, Clear	4.00
Chemical, C.W.Merchant Chemist, Lockport, N.Y., Graphite Pontil, Aqua	45.00
Chemical, Con Acid Hydrochloric, Glass Stopper	5.00
Chemical, Dioviburnia Dios Chemical Co., Label	5.00
Chemical, Dioxogen, The Oakland Chemical Co., Amber	4.00
Chemical, Embossed, Amber	2.00
Chemical, From The Laboratory Of G.W.Merchant Chemist, N.Y., Emerald	39.00
Chemical, J.K.Palmer, Chemists, Boston, Pontil, Cylinder, Dark Olive Amber	15.00
Chemical, Keasrey & Mattison Co., Chemists, Ambler, Pa., Light Blue	5.00
Chemical, Laboratory, Double Neck, Pontil	7.00

Chemical, **Liquizone**, Manufactured By The Liquid Ozone Co. 4.00
Chemical, **Reese's**, Embossed Internal & External, Emerald & Cobalt, Pair 19.00
Chemical, **Rumford Chemical Works**, Bimal, Teal Blue 4.00
Chemical, **Rumford Chemical Works**, Blue, 5 1/2 In. .... *Illus* 7.50
Chemical, **Rumford Chemical Works**, Dated On Base 1868, Blue Gre .... 6.00 To 7.00
Chemical, **Rumford Chemical**, Blue Green, 8 In.High 10.00
Chemical, **Spt Ammon Arom**, Glass Stopper 5.00
Chemical, **W.B.Jeron's**, Chemist Market, Rasem, 8 In. 3.00
Chest, **Enamel Decoration**, Inset Neck, Pewter Collar 75.00
Chestnut, **American**, Free-Blown, Crude Lip, Olive Green, 10 1/2 In.High 62.00
Chestnut, **Clear**, 8 In. 4.00

Chemical, AH On Bottom, 4 In.
See Page 55

Chemical,
Rumford Chemical Works,
Blue, 5 1/2 In.

Chestnut, **Green Collar**, Amber, Pint 45.00
Chestnut, **Green**, 8 1/2 In. 59.00
Chestnut, **Handle**, Pontil, Light Golden Amber 55.00
Chestnut, **Medium Amber** 70.00
Chestnut, **Midwestern**, 12 Diamond-Quilted Over 24 Vertical Ribs, Clear 225.00
Chestnut, **New England**, Light Green, 8 1/2 In. 65.00
Chestnut, **Open Pontil**, Aqua 10.00
Chestnut, **Open Pontil**, Stain, Green, 10 In. 25.00
Chestnut, **Open Pontil**, Stain, Green, 9 In. 17.00
Chestnut, **Sand Check**, Olive Amber, Quart 30.00
Chestnut, **Sheared Neck**, Aqua 25.00
Clevenger **Bros.Glass Works, Apollo 9**, Handmade, Amethyst 14.50
Cobalt **Blue, Foreign Inscription In Gold**, Monogrammed & Design 50.00

*Coca-Cola was first made in 1886. Since that time the drink has been
sold in all parts of the world in a variety of bottles. The 'waisted' bottle
was first used in 1916.*
Coca-Cola, **Amber** .... 5.00 To 18.00
Coca-Cola, **Anniversary**, Gold, 6 1/2 In. 15.00
Coca-Cola, **Arrows**, Brown 22.50
Coca-Cola, **Augusta**, Me., Raised Name, Green 3.00
Coca-Cola, **Baltimore**, Md., Raised Name, Green 3.00
Coca-Cola, **Bangor**, Me., Raised Name, Green 3.00
Coca-Cola, **Beidenharn Candy Co.**, Vicksburg, Miss. 25.00
Coca-Cola, **Big Chief Embossed** 3.50
Coca-Cola, **Big Chief Soda**, 4 Sided, 4 Embossed Indians' Heads, Tulsa, Okla. 5.00
Coca-Cola, **Birmingham**, Ala., Aqua 7.50
Coca-Cola, **Blown In Mold**, Applied Lip, Straight Sided, Amber 8.50
Coca-Cola, **Bottling Co.**, Cleveland, Ohio .... *Illus* 12.00
Coca-Cola, **Bueno**, Farmington, New Mexico, Pat'd Dec.29, 1925, 9 Oz. 4.00
Coca-Cola, **Chattanooga**, Amber 13.50
Coca-Cola, **Christmas**, Dated Dec.25, 1923 .... 3.50 To 4.50
Coca-Cola, **Christmas**, Dated Dec.25, 1923, Dug 3.50

Coca-Cola, Christmas, Dated Dec.25, 1923, Washington, D.C. 3.50
Coca-Cola, Coke Flavors 3.50
Coca-Cola, Columbia, Ind., Raised Name, Green 3.00
Coca-Cola, Columbus, Ohio, Amber 10.00
Coca-Cola, Cuero Turkey, Embossed 4 Turkeys 25.00
Coca-Cola, Cumberland, Amber 15.00
Coca-Cola, Dated Nov.1915 .... 3.50
Coca-Cola, Dated Nov.1915, Dug 3.50
Coca-Cola, Dug, Amber .... 9.75 To 14.75
Coca-Cola, Embossed Casc, Indian Head In Circle, Aqua 10.00
Coca-Cola, Embossed Coca-Cola Trade Mark Registered, Aqua 30.00
Coca-Cola, Embossed Coca-Cola, Ozs.& Rown Inside Diamond Emblem, Amber 25.00
Coca-Cola, Embossed Property Of Coca-Cola Bottling Co., Avon Park, Aqua 3.50
Coca-Cola, Embossed Property Of Coca-Cola Bottling Co., Fla., 1923, Aqua 3.50
Coca-Cola, Embossed Wheeling, W.Va., Amber 5.00
Coca-Cola, Gold 18.00
Coca-Cola, Green 5.00
Coca-Cola, Huntsville, Ala., Amber 7.50
Coca-Cola, Hutchinson, Bottling Co., Birmingham .... Illus 140.00
Coca-Cola, Hutchinson, Chattanooga, Tennessee .... Illus 75.00
Coca-Cola, Jackson, Tenn., Arrow Around Coca-Cola, Amber 11.50

Coca-Cola, Bottling Co.,
Cleveland, Ohio
See Page 56

Coca-Cola, Hutchinson,
Chattanooga, Tennessee

Coca-Cola, Hutchinson,
Bottling Co., Birmingham

Coca-Cola, Jackson, Tenn., Arrow Around Coca-Cola, Aqua 5.00
Coca-Cola, Mae West Type, Embossed Coca-Cola Trademark Registered, Amber 7.00
Coca-Cola, Miniature, Aqua, 1 9/16 In.High 3.00
Coca-Cola, Miniature, Brass, Ring In Top To Hang 5.00
Coca-Cola, Miniature, Capped & Filled, Marked, 3 In.Tall .... .75
Coca-Cola, Miniature, Filled & Capped .... .75
Coca-Cola, Miniature, Filled & Capped, Case Of 24 .... 11.50
Coca-Cola, Miniature, Filled & Capped, 12 .... 5.00
Coca-Cola, Miniature, Marked On 2 Sides & Metal Cap, Filled & Capped .... .75
Coca-Cola, Miniature, 1 1/2 In.High .... .25
Coca-Cola, Mold Made, Embossed Crown Carbonating Co., Hamlet, N.C. 10.00
Coca-Cola, Nashville, Tenn., Amber 10.50
Coca-Cola, New Albany, Miss., Brown 50.00
Coca-Cola, No.D105529 .... .40
Coca-Cola, November, 1915 .... 3.50
Coca-Cola, Paper Label 12.50
Coca-Cola, Pittsburgh Embossed, Bimal, Amber 7.50
Coca-Cola, Portland, Me., Raised Name, Green 3.00
Coca-Cola, Pre-1912, Clear 7.95

Coca-Cola, Property Of Coca-Cola Bottling Co., Avon Park, Florida, Aqua	3.50
Coca-Cola, Providence, R.I., Raised Name, Green	3.00
Coca-Cola, Ring Lite	4.00
Coca-Cola, Seltzer, 10 Sided, Siphon, Green	30.00
Coca-Cola, Soda Water, Clear	2.25
Coca-Cola, Soda Water, Green	3.00
Coca-Cola, Soda Water, 5 Stars In Square In Middle	1.25
Coca-Cola, Square	3.50
Coca-Cola, Straight Sided, Bimal, Amber	8.50
Coca-Cola, Straight Sided, Dug, Abm, Aqua	2.50
Coca-Cola, Straight Sided, Script Writing, C.1905	3.50
Coca-Cola, Straight Sided, Script Writing, Dug	3.95
Coca-Cola, Tester, Green, 11 In.Tall	7.50
Coca-Cola, Uncle Sam Embossed On All Four Sides, Square	25.00
Coca-Cola, 1900	5.00
Coca-Cola, 1915	6.00
Coca-Cola, 1915, Green	5.00
Coca-Cola, 1915, Ice Blue	28.50
Coca-Cola, 1915, Quart	3.00
Coca-Cola, 4 Panel Bottom, 6 Panel Top, Clear	8.00
Coca-Cola, 6 Stars In Panels, Embossed Soda Water Property Of Coca-Cola	15.00
Codd, British, Embossed, Marble In Neck	7.25
Codd, C.N.Ballinger, Monmouth, Embossed, Bimal, Marble Stopper	4.95
Codd, E.P.Shaw & Co., Wakefield, Hound Trademark, Marble In Neck	5.00
Codd, Embossed D Whiddet Tower Works, Herne Bay, 7 1/4 In.High	4.15
Codd, Embossed Star Brand Super Strong With Star, Forms Eyes & Head, Aqua	7.95
Codd, Milton Aerated Waterworks, N.S.Aqua, 8 1/2 In. _Color_	XX.XX
Cognac, Baccarat-Signed, Applied Scroll & Fleur-De-Lis, Stopper, Clear	28.00
Cognac, John Richards' Bordeaux, Ujeux, 1815, Seal, Aqua, 11 In.High	35.00
Collector's Art, Bluebird	16.95
Collector's Art, Blue Jay _Color_	11.95
Collector's Art, Canary	11.95
Collector's Art, Cardinal	11.50
Collector's Art, Cardinal _Color_	11.50
Collector's Art, Hummingbird _Color_	11.95
Collector's Art, Koala Bear _Color_	11.95
Collector's Art, Meadowlark	12.95
Collector's Art, Parakeet _Color_	11.95
Collector's Art, Rabbits _Color_	11.95
Collector's Art, Robin _Color_	11.95
Collector's Weekly, Flask, No.1	27.50
Collector's Weekly, Flask, No.2	14.95
Collector's Weekly, Flask, No.3	13.50
Collector's Weekly, Flask, No.4	11.50
Collector's Weekly, Flask, No.5	10.00
Collector's Weekly, Flask, No.6	10.00
Cologne, Acorn Shape, Fancy Design, Open Pontil, Clear	25.00
Cologne, Acorn Shape, Open Pontil, Clear	25.00
Cologne, Arch Shape, Fancy Design, Open Pontil, Aqua	20.00
Cologne, Arch With Figure, Fancy Design, Open Pontil, Aqua	27.50
Cologne, Baccarat, Gold Edging & Trim, Cut Faceted Stopper, Label, Cranberry	45.00
Cologne, Baccarat, Sapphire Blue Swirl, Stopper	38.00
Cologne, Barber Type, Label, 1913 In Metal Stopper	18.00
Cologne, Barrel Shape, Fancy Design, Open Pontil	22.50
Cologne, Barrel Shape, Sheared Lip, 2 3/4 In.High	17.50
Cologne, Basket, O.P., 3 In.High	16.00
Cologne, Blown, Ribbed, Clear Tam-O-Shanter Stopper, Cobalt Blue	75.00
Cologne, Bristol, White, 11 In.	22.00
Cologne, Bust, Fancy Design, Open Pontil, Clear	27.50
Cologne, Button Arched, Stopper, Pressed Glass	6.50
Cologne, Cambridge, Marked, Cut Stopper & Base, Numbered, Black Amethyst	10.50
Cologne, Carnival Glass, Grape & Cable, Purple	175.00
Cologne, Charley Ross, Clear, 4 1/2 In.High _Illus_	50.00
Cologne, Christian De Paris, Fancy Design, Open Pontil, Aqua	22.50
Cologne, Church & Figures, Open Pontil, Clear	27.50
Cologne, Church With Figures, Fancy Design, Open Pontil, Clear	27.50

Cologne, Clam Shape, Open Pontil, Aqua	32.50
Cologne, Cut Glass, Prismatic Neck, Wafer Top, Hobstars, Facet Stopper	4.00
Cologne, Cut Glass, Signed Hawkes, Hobstar & Fine Diamond, 5 1/2 In.High	55.00
Cologne, Cut Glass, Signed Hawkes, Sterling Top, Floral Motif On 4 Panels	28.00
Cologne, Demijohn, Pontil, Aqua	20.00
Cologne, Dog In Doghouse, Fancy Design, Open Pontil, Clear	22.50
Cologne, Dresden Type, Embossed & Enameled Flowers, Stopper, 7 In.High	15.00
Cologne, Embossed Lady, Pontil, Aqua, 3 1/2 In. _Illus_	30.00

Cologne, Charley Ross,
Clear, 4 1/2 In.High
See Page 58

Cologne, Embossed Lady,
Pontil, Aqua, 3 1/2 In.

Cologne, Emerald Green, 8 1/4 In.Tall	6.00
Cologne, Faces, Fancy Design, Open Pontil Clear	22.50
Cologne, Fancy Design, Woven Basket, Open Pontil, Aqua	10.00
Cologne, Flat Barrel, Fancy Design, Open Pontil, Clear	10.00
Cologne, Flowers, Fancy Design, Label, Open Pontil, Aqua	32.50
Cologne, Girl In Basket, Clear	10.00
Cologne, Girl In Basket, Fancy Design, Clear	10.00
Cologne, Gold Decoration, Cobalt Blue	27.00
Cologne, Hoyt's, Labeled Trial Size	3.00
Cologne, Hoyt's, Labeled, Medium Size	4.50
Cologne, Indian Figures, Fancy Design, Stain, Open Pontil, Aqua	50.00
Cologne, Lion, Fancy Design, Open Pontil, Aqua	85.00
Cologne, Monument, Fancy Design, Open Pontil, Clear	27.50
Cologne, Moonstone, Blue	5.00
Cologne, N.Y.Label, Fancy Design, Open Pontil, Aqua	30.00
Cologne, Open Pontil, Aqua	20.00
Cologne, Open Pontil, Fancy Design, Clear	25.00
Cologne, Palm Motif, Large Pontil, Clear	45.00
Cologne, Pineapple, Fancy Design, Open Pontil, Clear	27.50
Cologne, Pineapple Shape, Clear	27.50
Cologne, Pittsburgh, Open Pontil, Crude, Deep Cobalt	95.00
Cologne, Pressed Glass, Maiden's Blush	35.00
Cologne, Ribbed, Label, Open Pontil, Aqua	27.50
Cologne, Rope Corners, Fancy Design, Clear	5.00
Cologne, Sandwich Glass, Mc Kearin Plate, No.22, Amethyst, 7 1/4 In.High	75.00
Cologne, Sandwich Glass, Ribbed, Pontil, Clear	40.00
Cologne, Sandwich Glass, 12 Panel, Clear	18.00
Cologne, Sandwich Type, 12 Sides, Ring Pontil, Sapphire Blue	55.00
Cologne, Sandwich, 12 Sides, Teal Blue, 6 In.High	50.00
Cologne, Satin Glass, Lizard Chasing Fly	100.00
Cologne, Scroll Design, Open Pontil, Clear	20.00
Cologne, Sheared Top, Pontil, Light Olive Green, 8 3/4 In.High	10.00
Cologne, Ship, Fancy Design, Open Pontil, Clear	27.50
Cologne, Silver Overlay, Stopper, 3 3/4 In.High	10.00
Cologne, Spatter Glass, Marked Ricksicker's Sweet Clover In Gold, Clear	35.00
Cologne, Square, Foreign Embossing, Open Pontil, Clear, 4 In.	13.00

Cologne, **Star Design**, Open Pontil, Aqua 25.00
Cologne, **Stars**, Fancy Design, Open Pontil, Aqua 25.00
Cologne, **Sterling Overlay Carnation Pattern**, Bulbous, Emerald Green 45.00
Cologne, **Steuben**, Verre De Soie, Ground Stopper 35.00
Cologne, **Stone Monument**, Fancy Design, Clear 1.00
Cologne, **Stopper**, Cut Glass 75.00
Cologne, **Stopper**, Flint, Amethyst 20.00
Cologne, **Stovepipe**, Clear, 4 1/2 In.High .... *Illus* 35.00
Cologne, **Sunburst**, Clear, 2 3/4 In.Long 85.00
Cologne, **Tall Monument**, Fancy Design, Open Pontil, Clear 42.50
Cologne, **Urn & Flowers**, Fancy Design, Open Pontil, Aqua 25.00
Cologne, **Urn Shaped**, Fancy Design, Open Pontil, Clear 32.50
Cologne, **Urn With Colored Label**, Fancy Design, Open Pontil, Clear 30.00
Cologne, **Val St.Lambert**, Feathered Ground, Cranberry Relief Flowers 45.00
Cologne, **Vase Shape**, Fancy Design, Open Pontil, Aqua 32.50
Cologne, **Violin Shape**, Open Pontil, Aqua .... 30.00 To 37.50
Cologne, **Violin Shape**, Open Pontil, Clear 20.00
Cologne, **Woman Shaped**, Clear 25.00
Cologne, **Yellow S Motif**, France, P.V., Stopper, 8 In.Tall 25.00
Condiment, **Three Mold**, Blown Glass 50.00
Cordial, **Cascara**, Park Davis & Co., Label, Amber, 9 In. 5.00
Cosmetic, **Cherry Toothpaste**, Lid, Woman & Lion, C.1840 .... 21.00
Cosmetic, **Colgate & Co.**, Perfumer, 3 Mold, Stopper, Clear 5.50
Cosmetic, **Ely's Cream Balm**, Amber, 2 1/2 In.High 3.50
Cosmetic, **Gargling Oil** 7.00
Cosmetic, **George Lorenz**, Emerald Green 8.50
Cosmetic, **Hagan's Magnolia Balm** 9.00
Cosmetic, **Hind's Honey & Almond Cream**, Portland, Me. .... *Illus* 2.50
Cosmetic, **J.& L.Mouth Wash**, 4 In. 4.00
Cosmetic, **Lilac Toilet Lotion**, Label, Price 35 Cents, 5 1/2 In. 8.00
Cosmetic, **M.B.& Co. Rose Attar**, Milk Glass, 5 1/2 In.High 15.00
Cosmetic, **Mme.Dejoux Oriental Lotion**, Detroit, Label .... *Illus* 18.00
Cosmetic, **Noxzema**, Jar, Half Gallon 100.00
Cosmetic, **Powder**, Milk Glass, White, Covered, Gold 8.00
Cosmetic, **Rawleigh's Sweet Clover Lotion**, Label, Clear .... *Illus* 6.00
Cosmetic, **Rubifoam For The Teeth**, Embossed, Sample, Label, Clear 2.50
Cosmetic, **Sweet Georgia Brown Cleansing Cream**, Patent Date 1898, Label 3.50
Cosmetic, **Watkin's Nail Polish**, Metal Cover, Cobalt 2.00
　　C.P.C., California Perfume Company, see Avon
Cranberry Glass, **Overlay**, Cut White To Cranberry, 8 1/2 In.High 80.00
Creative World, **Fortunate Fisherman** 15.50
Creative World, **Queen Anne Clock** 19.95
Creative World, **Shakespeare Folio** .... 17.95 To 26.50
Cut Glass, **Carafe**, Captain's, Hobstars, Flat Bottom 59.00
Cut Glass, **Cologne**, Hobstar & Pinwheel, 5 1/2 In. 45.00
Cut Glass, **Fancy Stopper**, 4 1/2 In. 18.50
Cut Glass, **Fancy Stopper**, 6 1/2 In. 18.50
Cut Glass, **Signed Fleur-De-Lis & Hawkes**, Etched Wheat On Front, Quart 85.00
Cut Glass, **Talcum**, Silver Plate Top 4.50
Cut Glass, **Vinegar**, Glass Stopper 5.00
Cut Glass, **Water** 60.00
Cut Glass, **Water**, Diamond & Fan 25.00
Cut Glass, **Water**, Signed Libbey 45.00
Cut Glass, **Water**, Strawberry, Diamond, & Fan 40.00

Dant figural bottles first were released in 1968 to hold J.W.Dant
alcoholic products. The company has made the Americana series, field birds,
special bottlings, and ceramic bottles.
Dant, **Alamo** 2.00
Dant, **Bobwhite** .... *Illus* 5.95
Dant, **Boeing 747** 11.95
Dant, **Boston Tea Party** .... *Illus* 4.00
Dant, **Eagle**, Facing Left 5.95
Dant, **Field Bird**, California Quail 5.95
Dant, **Field Bird**, Chukar Partridge 4.00
Dant, **Field Bird**, Mountain Quail 6.00

Cologne, Stovepipe,
Clear, 4 1/2 In.High
See Page 60

Cosmetic,
Mme.Dejoux Oriental Lotion,
Detroit, Label
See Page 60

Cosmetic, Hind's Honey &
Almond Cream, Portland, Me.
See Page 60

Cosmetic,
Rawleigh's Sweet Clover Lotion,
Label, Clear
See Page 60

Dant, Bobwhite
See Page 60

Dant, Boston Tea Party
See Page 60

Dant, **Field Bird**, Prairie Chicken		4.00
Dant, **Field Bird**, Ruffed Grouse		4.00
Dant, **Field Bird**, Woodcock		4.00
Dant, **Fort Sill Centennial**, 1969	*Illus*	10.00
Dant, **Mt.Rushmore**	*Illus*	10.50
Dant, **Ring-Necked Pheasant**	*Illus*	5.95

Dant, Fort Sill Centennial, 1969
See Page 61

Dant, Mt.Rushmore
See Page 61

Dant, Ring-Necked Pheasant
See Page 61

Dant, San Diego	3.00
Dant, Tea Party	2.00
Dant, Wild Turkey	16.00
Dant, 500-Mile Race	4.95

Decanters were first used to hold the alcoholic beverages that had been stored in kegs. At first a necessity, the decanter later was merely an attractive serving vessel.

Decanter, see also Beam, Bischoff, Kord, etc.

Decanter, Amberina, Diamond-Quilted, Cut Stopper, Ruffled Top, Deep Fuchsia	110.00
Decanter, Amberina, Stopper	95.00
Decanter, Applied Seal, The Old Mill, Whitlock & Co., Handle, Amber, Quart	575.00
Decanter, Baccarat, Signed, Etched, C.1910, 10 In.High	65.00
Decanter, Bar, Old Valley Whiskey, Gold Lettering	40.00
Decanter, Bar, Stopper, Eight Panels Around Side, Amethyst	160.00
Decanter, Barrel Shape	9.00
Decanter, Bellflower Decoration, Stopper, Ribbed, Green	50.00

Decanter, Blown In Mold, Polished Pontil, 3 Applied Rings On Neck, Quart	35.00
Decanter, Blown In Mold, Ring Neck, Clear	25.00
Decanter, Blown, Applied Glass Ring At Neck, Enameled Floral, Gold, Clear	45.00
Decanter, Blown, Applied Rings On Neck, Pinwheel Stopper, 10 3/4 In.Tall	15.00
Decanter, Blown, Cut Fluting Around Base, Gold Decoration	30.00
Decanter, Blown, Engraved, 18th Century, Tulips At Base Of Neck	95.00
Decanter, Blown, Gold Design, Stopper	22.50
Decanter, Blown, Hobnail, Handle	30.00
Decanter, Blown, Ribbed, Applied Handle, Clear, 9 3/4 In.Tall	75.00
Decanter, Blown, Swags & Vertical Ribs, Stopper, Clear	30.00
Decanter, Blown, 3 Mold, Diamond Pattern, Sunburst Stopper, C.1825-35, Clear	225.00
Decanter, Bohemian Glass, Copper Wheel Engraved Panels & Grapes, Red Flash	45.00
Decanter, Bohemian Glass, Cut Amber	45.00
Decanter, Bohemian Glass, Cut Ruby	49.00
Decanter, Bohemian Glass, Engraved Monkeys, Ruby	49.00
Decanter, Bohemian Glass, Etched Leaves, Inverted Pontil, Ruby, 14 In.	27.50
Decanter, Bohemian Glass, Etched Vintage, Silver Label, Stopper, Ruby, Pair	105.00
Decanter, Bohemian Glass, Frosted Center, Red Birds, Blown, Stopper, Ruby	30.00
Decanter, Brandy, Etched Leaves, Stopper, Clear	15.00
Decanter, Bull's-Eye With Diamond Point, Flint, Green	38.00
Decanter, Carnival Glass, Golden Wedding, Quart	5.00
Decanter, Carnival Glass, Grape, Marigold, Matching Round Stopper	60.00
Decanter, Carnival Glass, Grapes, Smokey	135.00
Decanter, Carnival, Imperial Grape, Purple, 12 In.	195.00
Decanter, Clear & Chartreuse Overlay, Clear Cut Cherry Branches, Pair	175.00
Decanter, Copeland Spode, Coronation, Green, Quart	12.50
Decanter, Cord & Tassel, Doughnut Stopper	15.00
Decanter, Coronation, Royal Doulton, Blue	35.00
Decanter, Coronation, Royal Doulton, Green	35.00
Decanter, Cut Glass, Blown Stopper, Panel Cutting, 13 3/4 In.Tall	60.00
Decanter, Cut Glass, Diamond Pattern, Sterling Rim, English	55.00
Decanter, Cut Glass, Engraved Initials	40.00
Decanter, Cut Glass, Handle, Steeple Blown Stopper, Pair	135.00
Decanter, Cut Glass, Pyramid, Hobstars, Vesicas Of Cane, Strawberry Diamond	135.00
Decanter, Cut Glass, Shallow Cut, Clear	7.50
Decanter, Cut Glass, Sharp Nailhead, Stopper, 13 3/4 In.High	100.00
Decanter, Cut Glass, Silver Plate Top, Handle, B.Grieg Fettes Colege 1893	125.00
Decanter, Cut Glass, Square, Buttons & Cross-Hatching, Edinburgh, Scotland	70.00
Decanter, Design & Applied Rings On Neck, Mushroom Stopper, O.P., 1/2 Pint	45.00
Decanter, Diamond Sunburst, Clear, Small Size	125.00
Decanter, Embossed Blob Seal New Bedford Whaling Company 1853, Hand Blown	15.00
Decanter, Enameled Lily Of The Valley, Pewter Rim, Green	65.00
Decanter, Erickson, Hollow Stopper, Clear & Sunlight Yellow Flames	35.00
Decanter, Etched, Bulbous, Pair	50.00
Decanter, Faceted Stopper, Etched Greek Key Band, Pair	25.00
Decanter, Finche's Golden Wedding, Enameled, Clear, Pint	1.00
Decanter, Flint Glass, Waffle & Thumbprint, Stopper, Quart	85.00
Decanter, Fluted, H.F. & B., New York, Yellow Amber, Pint	160.00
Decanter, Four Compartment, 12 In.High	15.00
Decanter, Free-Blown, Aqua, Quart, 12 In.	5.00
Decanter, Free-Blown, Open Pontil, Clear, Pint	3.00
Decanter, Free-Blown, Open Pontil, Clear, 1/2 Pint	3.00
Decanter, French Opalescent, 12 In.Tall	32.50
Decanter, Geometric Design, Olive Amber, Quart	510.00
Decanter, Gin, Etched Leaves, Stopper, Clear	15.00
Decanter, Globular Swirl, Amber, Pint	200.00
Decanter, Gold Decoration, 12 In.Tall	22.50
Decanter, Grape Design, Ruby Glass	80.00
Decanter, Imperial Grape, Purple, Carnival Glass	85.00
Decanter, Impressed Star Pattern, 13 1/2 In.High	17.50
Decanter, Kate Greenaway, Four Boys, Amber, 10 In.High	110.00
Decanter, Mary Gregory, Hand Blown, White Figure Of Girl, Clear, 9 In.High	75.00
Decanter, Mc Kearin G I-29, Blown In Mold, Quart	85.00
Decanter, Mc Kearin G I-29, 3 Mold, Blown, Flint, 1/2 Pint	80.00
Decanter, Mc Kearin G III -16, Keene, Pint *Illus*	450.00
Decanter, Mc Kearin G III -19, Keene, Quart *Illus*	600.00

Decanter,
McKearin G III-19,
Keene, Quart
See Page 63

Decanter,
McKearin G III-16,
Keene, Pint
See Page 63

Decanter, Mc Kearin G III -2, Blown, 3 Mold, Clear, 1/2 Pint 185.00
Decanter, Mc Kearin No.6, Plate No.83, Arch Pattern, Three Mold, Stopper 65.00
Decanter, Mc Kearin 44, Flint, Neck Rings, Blown, C.1800, Pint 20.00
Decanter, Old Rye, Etched Leaves, Stopper, Clear 15.00
Decanter, Overlay, White Cut To Cranberry, Gold & Floral Enamel, Stopper 75.00
Decanter, Pattern Glass, Excelsior, Pint 25.00
Decanter, Pillar Mold 6.25
Decanter, Pressed Glass, Fine Cut 4.00
Decanter, Pressed Glass, Loop Pattern, Stopper, 13 1/2 In.High 15.00
Decanter, Pressed Glass, Pittsburgh Pillar, Bar, Cobalt Blue Stripes 50.00
Decanter, S Repeat, Amethyst, 10 In.High 45.00
Decanter, Sandwich Glass, Fern Design, Stopper, 13 In.High 22.50
Decanter, Sandwich Star, Flint 35.00
Decanter, Santa, Signed Susie, Ceramic .... ·8.50
Decanter, Signed Czeck., Waffle Cut, Ball Stopper 25.00
Decanter, Single Applied Ring At Neck, Heavy Fluting, Blue 22.50
Decanter, Square, Open Pontil, Green 12.50
Decanter, Washington, Bar Lip 35.00
Decanter, Waterford, Diamond Faceted, Neck Bands, 18th Century 125.00
Decanter, Wedgwood, England, Cobalt With White 95.00
Decanter, Whiskey, Grape & Cable, Purple, Carnival Glass 550.00
Decanter, Whiskey, Pressed Glass, Diamond Point, Faceted Stopper 22.00
Decanter, Whiskey, Pressed Glass, Honeycomb, Ribbed, Cut Ball Stopper 45.00
Decanter, White Spiral Stripes, Cobalt Blue, Pair 160.00
Decanter, Wine, Art Glass, White Raised Dots, Gold & Black Bands, Clear 11.50
Decanter, Wine, Carnival Glass, Imperial Grape, Green 50.00
Decanter, Wine, Cranberry Glass, Enameled Daisies, Clear Applied Handle 40.00
Decanter, Wine, Crystal Stopper, Amethyst 37.50
Decanter, Wine, Pressed Glass, Horn Of Plenty, Pint 95.00
Demijohn, Applied Lip, Open Pontil, Dark Green, 14 In.High 21.00
Demijohn, Applied Top, Cobalt Blue, 15 In.Tall 150.00
Demijohn, B.F.C., Yellow Amber, Gallon 12.50
Demijohn, Bulbous, Pontil, Olive Amber, 2 Quart 85.00
Demijohn, Kidney Shape, Olive Amber, 3 Gallon 50.00
Demijohn, Kidney Shape, Three Mold, Sheared Lip, Green, 18 In.High 17.50
Demijohn, Open Pontil, Amber, Quart 17.50
Demijohn, Open Pontil, Light Green, 3 Gallon 15.00
Demijohn, Open Pontil, Olive Green, Gallon 35.00
Demijohn, Open Pontil, 2 On Front, Apple Green 50.00
Demijohn, Rough Pontil, Olive Green, 15 In.High 45.00
Demijohn, Stoddard Type, Applied Top, Bubbles, Amber, 12 In.High 12.00
Demijohn, Three Mold, Teal Green, 12 In.High 16.00
Demijohn, Wicker Case, Amber, Gallon 9.00
Demijohn, Wicker Case, Aqua, Gallon 7.00
Demijohn, 3 Mold, Open Pontil, Olive, 4 Gallon 27.50

Dickel, Golf Club, Large Size	3.95
Dickel, Powder Horn, Amber, 12 3/4 In.High	4.95 To 6.00
Double Springs, Boy, Peasant	9.95
Double Springs, Bull	13.95
Double Springs, Bull, Red, 1968	9.00
Double Springs, Bulldog	14.95
Double Springs, Cadillac, 1913	12.00 To 26.95
Double Springs, Car, Model T Ford	19.95 To 21.95
Double Springs, Car, Stutz Bearcat, 1919	29.00
Double Springs, Chicago Water Tower	24.98 To 39.98
Double Springs, Coyote, Gold, National Gun Owners Association	19.95
Double Springs, Georgia Bulldog	14.95 To 16.95
Double Springs, Girl, Peasant	9.95
Double Springs, Golfer, Duffer	9.95
Double Springs, Hold That Tiger	16.95
Double Springs, Matador	9.00 To 11.95
Double Springs, Mercer	21.95
Double Springs, Milwaukee Buck	12.95
Double Springs, Model T Ford, 1910	19.95 To 21.95
Double Springs, Owl, Brown	9.95
Double Springs, Owl, Red	9.95
Double Springs, Pierce Arrow	17.00 To 22.95
Double Springs, Rolls-Royce, 1912	12.00 To 21.95
Double Springs, Scotsman, White Mc Kay	8.00 To 10.95
Double Springs, Stanley Steamer, 1911	17.00 To 22.95
Double Springs, Stutz Bearcat, 1919	18.00 To 26.95
Double Springs, Tiger On Football	14.95
Double Springs, W.C.Fields	19.95
Double Springs, Water Tower	39.00
Double Springs, Wild Catter	5.00
Dresser, Hickman	8.00
Dresser, Limoges, Ball Shape, Painted Flowers, 6 In.High, Pair	20.00
Dresser, Milk Glass, Actresses' Heads, 8 In.	37.50
Dresser, Milk Glass, Bulbous, Embossed Lions' Heads, Pair	40.00
Dresser, Pressed Glass, Block & Sawtooth, Cut Stopper	10.00
Drioli, African Woman	30.00
Drioli, Gondola	30.00
Drug, A.M.Cole, Virginia City, Nevada	5.00
Drug, Bailey Drug Store, Embossed, Corker, Aqua	2.00
Drug, Blown, 18th Century, 3 3/4 In.High	15.00
Drug, Chapin & Whiton Druggists, Open Pontil, Stain	15.00
Drug, Columbus Pharmaceutical, Amber *Illus*	7.00
Drug, Diagonal Mold, Octagonal, Light Olive Green, 2 7/8 In.High	32.00
Drug, Dr.S.H.Thompson Sterile Tube, Patent June, 1922, Label, Clear	20.00
Drug, Fellows & Co.Chemists, St.John, New Brunswick	4.00
Drug, Fruit Syrup, Brown & White, Gallon	5.25

Drug, Columbus Pharmaceutical, Amber

Drug, Jar, Doctor's, Pontil, Lid, Amethyst, 9 1/2 In.High	9.50
Drug, Maine Pharmacy	.75
Drug, Medical Dept., U.S.Navy, Square, Clear	3.00
Drug, Nevada Drugstore, Embossed	5.00
Drug, Nevada, Embossed, BIMAL	5.00
Drug, O'Rourke & Hurley, Prescription Chemists, Little Falls, N.Y., Cobalt	12.50
Drug, O'Rourke & Hurley, Prescription Chemists, Little Falls, N.Y., Green	12.50
Drug, Owl, Abm	4.00
Drug, Owl, Milk Glass	25.00
Drug, Roberts, Goldfield, Nevada	15.00
Drug, South Carolina Dispensary & Tree, Whiskey Shape, Amber, Quart	310.00
Drug, South Carolina Dispensary, Light Green, 1/2 Pint	110.00
Drug, Store, Embossed, Cobalt	5.00
Drug, Store, Embossed, Emerald Green	6.00
Drug, Tarrant Druggist, New York, Open Pontil, Rectangular, 5 Sides, Clear	9.50
Drug, Teal Rumford Chemical Works, BIMAL , Dug, Teal	4.00
Drug, The Oakland Chemical Co., Round, Embossed, Amber, 4 1/2 In.Tall	2.50
Drug, U.S.A.Hospital, Light Amber	35.00
Durg, W.H.Stowell Druggist & Assayer, No.3 Main St., Eureka, Nevada	8.00
Drug, Wide Mouth, Purpled	.50
Dyottsville Glass Works, Patent On Shoulder, I.O., Citron	12.50
Embalming Fluid, National Casket Co., Clear, 12 In. _Illus_	12.00
Error, Aromatic Schnapps, Backward S, Dark Olive, 8 In.High	35.00
Error, Beam Convention, Dates Incorrect	20.95
Error, California Tooth Wash, S Backward In Wash, Clear, 4 1/2 In.High	30.00
Error, Coca Cola, Macon, Ga., N Backwards In Macon, Aqua, 7 In.Tall	10.00
Error, Dr.Daniel's Wonder Worker, Wonder Misspelled, Clear	7.00
Error, Dr.J.S.Clark's, Comma Instead Of Apostrophe, Aqua, 8 1/2 In.	8.00
Error, E.Morgan & Sons, Sole Proprietors, Providence, R.I., 12 Panels, Aqua	10.00
Error, Hopkins Union Stomach, Yellow Amber, W-177	37.50
Error, J.H.Cutter Old Bourbon, Reverse S In Louisville, Kentucky, Embossed	150.00
Error, John Bull Sarsaparilla, Louisville, Stain Inside, Aqua	25.00
Error, Mason's Patent Nov.30th, 1858, Backward S In Mason, Amber	8.00
Error, Mineral Water, Embossed Misspelled Bedford Springs Co., Aqua	15.00
Error, Rochester Germicide, Print Upside Down, 1888, Amber	10.00
Error, Rocheter Misspelled On Base, Tippecanoe, Log Figural, Dark Amber	80.00
Error, Rush's Sarsaparilla, Misspelled	8.00
Error, Swayzee's Imppoved Mason, Quart _Illus_	5.00
Error, Tippecanoe, Roschester Misspelled, Amber	65.00
Error, Try Me Rock, Tarde Mark Registered, Green, Pint	10.00
Error, Warner's Tippecanoe, Mispelled Rochester On Base	70.00

Ezra Brooks fancy bottles were first made in 1964. The Ezra Brooks Distilling Company is from Frankfort, Kentucky.

Ezra Brooks, American Legion, 1972	12.95 To 29.95
Ezra Brooks, American Original Classic Firearms, Series I, 1969	18.95
Ezra Brooks, Antique Cannon, 1969 _Illus_	4.50 To 7.00
Ezra Brooks, Antique Phonograph, 1970	9.00 To 11.95
Ezra Brooks, Arizona Desert Scene, 1969	4.95 To 12.95
Ezra Brooks, Astronaut, Foremost, 1970	6.95 To 14.95
Ezra Brooks, Bareknuckle Fighter, 1972	10.95 To 12.95
Ezra Brooks, Beaver, 1972 _Illus_	12.00
Ezra Brooks, Bertha, Elephant, 1970	14.50 To 31.95
Ezra Brooks, Big Daddy, Florida, 1969	6.95 To 14.95
Ezra Brooks, Bird Dog, 1971	4.95 To 11.95
Ezra Brooks, Bordertown Club, 1970 _Illus_	24.00
Ezra Brooks, Brahma Bull, 1972	10.95 To 11.95
Ezra Brooks, Bucket Of Blood, 1972	7.95 To 31.95
Ezra Brooks, Buffalo Hunt, 1970	9.95 To 24.95
Ezra Brooks, Bulldog, Georgia, 1972 _Illus_	12.00 To 17.95
Ezra Brooks, California Quail, 1970	4.95 To 12.50
Ezra Brooks, Car, Ontario Race Car, 1970	7.00 To 9.95
Ezra Brooks, Car, Race Indy, 1970	12.00 To 17.50
Ezra Brooks, Car, Sprint, 1971	9.95 To 14.95
Ezra Brooks, Ceremonial Dancer, 1970	18.50 To 29.95
Ezra Brooks, Charolais, 1973 _Color_	XX.XX

Embalming Fluid,
National Casket Co., Clear, 12 In.
See Page 66

Error,
Swayzee's Imppoved Mason, Quart
See Page 66

Ezra Brooks, Antique Cannon, 1969
See Page 66

Ezra Brooks, Bordertown Club, 1970
See Page 66

Ezra Brooks,
Beaver, 1972
See Page 66

Ezra Brooks,
Bulldog, Georgia, 1972
See Page 66

Ezra Brooks, Cheyenne 'Shootout', 1970 .... 6.95 To 10.00
Ezra Brooks, Chicago Water Tower, 1969 .... 8.50 To 14.00
Ezra Brooks, Cigar Store Indian, 1968 .... 2.95 To 9.95
Ezra Brooks, Clown, 1972 .... 10.00
Ezra Brooks, Club Bottle, Birthday, 1972 .... 15.00 To 16.95
Ezra Brooks, Club Bottle, Distillery, 1970 .... 24.95 To 34.95
Ezra Brooks, Club Bottle, Map, 1973 .... *Color*   XX.XX
Ezra Brooks, Dead Wagon, 1970 .... 8.95 To 12.00
Ezra Brooks, Delta Belle, 1969 .... 5.50 To 12.95
Ezra Brooks, Drum & Bugle Corps, 1972, Conquistador's 17.50
Ezra Brooks, Dueling Pistol, Flintlock, 1968 .... 6.50 To 9.95
Ezra Brooks, Duesenburg, 1971 .... 9.95 To 11.95
Ezra Brooks, Fighting Cock, South Carolina, 1970 .... 11.95 To 13.50
Ezra Brooks, Fire Engine, 1971 .... 7.95 To 12.95
Ezra Brooks, Firearms, Set Of 4, American Classic Series I, 1969 .... 18.95
Ezra Brooks, Flask, Historic, Set Of 4, 1970 .... 6.00 To 13.95
Ezra Brooks, Flintlock Dueling Pistol, 1968 .... 6.50 To 9.95
Ezra Brooks, Florida, Big Daddy, 1969 .... 6.95 To 14.95
Ezra Brooks, Florida Gator, 1972 .... 17.95
Ezra Brooks, Fordson Tractor, 1971 .... *Illus* 12.00 To 15.95
Ezra Brooks, Foremost Astronaut, 1970 .... 6.95 To 14.95
Ezra Brooks, Fresno Grape, 1970 .... 13.95 To 29.95
Ezra Brooks, Gamecock, South Carolina, 1970 .... 11.95 To 13.50
Ezra Brooks, Gator, Florida, 1972 .... *Illus*   17.95
Ezra Brooks, Georgia Bull Dog, 1972 .... 12.00 To 17.95
Ezra Brooks, Go Big Red, No.I, 1970 .... 20.00 To 35.00
Ezra Brooks, Go Big Red, No. II , 1971 .... 19.95 To 29.95
Ezra Brooks, Go Big Red, No. III , 1972 .... 17.00
Ezra Brooks, Gold Eagle, 1971 .... 16.50 To 27.95
Ezra Brooks, Gold Horseshoe, 1970 .... 24.95 To 59.95
Ezra Brooks, Gold Prospector, 1970 .... 5.95 To 12.50
Ezra Brooks, Gold Seal, 1972 .... 12.00
Ezra Brooks, Golden Grizzly Bear, 1968 .... 3.50 To 8.95
Ezra Brooks, Golden Rooster, No.1, 1969 .... 59.95 To 107.95
Ezra Brooks, Grandfather's Clock, 1970 .... 5.95 To 11.95
Ezra Brooks, Greater Greensboro Open, 1972 .... *Illus* 17.50 To 24.95
Ezra Brooks, Grizzly Bear, Golden, 1968 .... 3.50 To 8.95
Ezra Brooks, Hambletonian, 1971 .... 10.00 To 13.50
Ezra Brooks, Harold's Club Dice, 1968 .... 3.50 To 8.95
Ezra Brooks, Hereford, 1972 .... 10.95 To 14.95
Ezra Brooks, Historic Flasks, 1970, Not Ceramic, Set Of 4 .... 6.00 To 13.95
Ezra Brooks, Hollywood Cops, 1972 .... *Illus* 20.00 To 24.95
Ezra Brooks, Horseshoe, Gold, 1970 .... 24.95 To 59.95
Ezra Brooks, Indian Ceremonial, 1970 .... 18.50 To 29.95
Ezra Brooks, Indian, Cigar Store, 1968 .... 2.95 To 9.95
Ezra Brooks, Indianapolis 500 Race Car, 1970 .... 12.00 To 17.50
Ezra Brooks, Iowa, Old Capitol, 1971 .... 35.00 To 50.00
Ezra Brooks, Iron Horse, Train, 1969 .... 4.95 To 12.95
Ezra Brooks, Jack-O-Diamonds, 1969 .... 4.95 To 12.95
Ezra Brooks, Japanese Pistols, 1968 .... 49.95 To 70.00
Ezra Brooks, Jayhawk, Kansas, 1969 .... 8.50 To 14.95
Ezra Brooks, Jester's Court, 1972 .... 16.95
Ezra Brooks, Jumping Man, Mr.Merchant, 1970 .... 11.00 To 17.95
Ezra Brooks, Kachina Doll, 1971 .... *Illus* 75.00 To 375.00
Ezra Brooks, Kansas Jayhawk, 1969 .... 8.50 To 14.95
Ezra Brooks, Kansas Wheat Shocker, 1971 .... 10.00 To 13.50
Ezra Brooks, Katz Cat, Pair, 1969, Katz Seal Point .... 19.95 To 22.50
Ezra Brooks, Katz Cat, Philharmonic, Conductor, 1970 .... 9.95 To 13.50
Ezra Brooks, Killer Whale, 1972 .... *Illus*   16.95
Ezra Brooks, King Of Clubs, 1969 .... *Illus*   4.95 To 6.95
Ezra Brooks, Legionnaire, American, 1972 .... 12.50 To 29.95
Ezra Brooks, Liberty Bell, 1970 .... 6.95 To 19.95
Ezra Brooks, Lighthouse, Maine, 1971 .... 18.00 To 25.00
Ezra Brooks, Lion On The Rock, 1971 .... *Illus* 4.95 To 12.95
Ezra Brooks, Liquor Square, 1972 .... 17.50
Ezra Brooks, Lobster, Maine, 1970 .... 27.50 To 39.00

Ezra Brooks, Fordson Tractor, 1971
See Page 68

Ezra Brooks,
Kachina Doll, 1971
See Page 68

Ezra Brooks,
Greater Greensboro Open, 1972
See Page 68

Ezra Brooks,
Gator, Florida, 1972
See Page 68

Ezra Brooks, Hollywood Cops, 1972
See Page 68

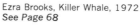

Ezra Brooks, Killer Whale, 1972
See Page 68

Ezra Brooks, Lion On The Rock, 1971
See Page 68

Ezra Brooks,
Maine Lighthouse,
1971

Ezra Brooks,
Man O' War,
1969

Ezra Brooks, Longhorn 29.99
Ezra Brooks, Longhorn Steer, Texas, 1971 .... 19.95 To 24.00
Ezra Brooks, Maine Lighthouse, 1971 ....*Illus* 18.00 To 25.00
Ezra Brooks, Maine Lobster, 1970 .... 27.50 To 39.00
Ezra Brooks, Man O' War, 1969 ....*Illus* 8.00 To 10.50
Ezra Brooks, Man O'War War, Gold, Fired 49.95
Ezra Brooks, Man On Mountain, New Hampshire, 1970 .... 16.00 To 24.95
Ezra Brooks, Military Tank, 1972 .... 14.00 To 19.95
Ezra Brooks, Missouri Mule, 1972 .... 10.00 To 14.95
Ezra Brooks, Motorcycle, 1972 .... 10.50
Ezra Brooks, Mountaineer, West Virginia, 1971 .... 90.00 To 140.00
Ezra Brooks, Mr.Foremost, 1969 .... 9.50 To 30.95
Ezra Brooks, Mr.Merchant, 1970 .... 11.00 To 17.95
Ezra Brooks, New Hampshire, Old Man Of The Mountain, 1970 .... 16.00 To 24.95
Ezra Brooks, New Hampshire Statehouse, 1970 .... 15.95 To 18.50
Ezra Brooks, New Hampshire, Statehouse, Gold, Fired 49.95
Ezra Brooks, Nugget Classic, 1970 .... 15.00 To 29.95
Ezra Brooks, Oil Gusher, 1969 .... 5.95 To 11.00
Ezra Brooks, Old Capitol Iowa, 1971 .... 35.00 To 50.00
Ezra Brooks, Old Man Of The Mountain, New Hampshire, 1970 .... 16.00 To 24.95
Ezra Brooks, Ontario Race Car, 1970 .... 7.00 To 9.95
Ezra Brooks, Overland Express Stagecoach, 1969 .... 4.95 To 10.00
Ezra Brooks, Panda, Giant, 1972 .... 10.50 To 11.95
Ezra Brooks, Penny Farthington, High, Wheeler, 1973 .... *Color*   XX.XX
Ezra Brooks, Philharmonic Katz Cat, 1970 .... 9.95 To 13.50
Ezra Brooks, Phoenix Bird, 1971 .... 35.00 To 95.00
Ezra Brooks, Phonograph, Antique, 1970 .... 9.00 To 11.95

Ezra Brooks, Pirate, 1971 .... 8.00 To 11.50
Ezra Brooks, Pistol, Japanese, 1968 .... 49.95 To 70.00
Ezra Brooks, Potbellied Stove, 1968 .... 6.50 To 9.95
Ezra Brooks, Queen Of Hearts, 1969 .... 3.95 To 12.95
Ezra Brooks, Race Car, Indy, 1970 .... 12.00 To 17.50
Ezra Brooks, Razorback, 1970 .... 9.95
Ezra Brooks, Red Dice, Harold's Club, 1968 .... 3.50 To 8.95
Ezra Brooks, Reno Arch, 1968 .... 5.50 To 19.95
Ezra Brooks, Rooster No.1, Gold ....59.95 To 107.95
Ezra Brooks, Sailfish, 1971 .... 8.95 To 11.45
Ezra Brooks, Salmon, Washington .... 44.95 To 89.95
Ezra Brooks, San Francisco Cable Car, 1968 .... 2.95 To 8.00
Ezra Brooks, Sea Captain, 1971 .... 11.45 To 12.50
Ezra Brooks, Seal, Gold, 1972 .... *Illus*   12.00
Ezra Brooks, Senator, 1972 .... 15.00
Ezra Brooks, Sherman Tank, Patton, Military, 1972 .... 14.00 To 19.95
Ezra Brooks, Silver Dollar, White Base 10.95
Ezra Brooks, Silver Dollar, 1970 .... *Illus* 5.50 To 17.95
Ezra Brooks, Silver Spur, 1971 .... 12.50 To 24.95
Ezra Brooks, Ski Boot, 1972 .... 11.00
Ezra Brooks, Ski The Idaho Potato, 1973 .... *Color*   XX.XX
Ezra Brooks, Slot Machine, 1971 .... 19.95
Ezra Brooks, Snowmobile, 1972 .... 11.95
Ezra Brooks, South Carolina Fighting Cock, 1970 .... 11.95 To 13.50
Ezra Brooks, Sprint Car Racer, 1971 .... *Illus* 9.95 To 14.95
Ezra Brooks, Spur, Silver, 1971 .... 12.50 To 24.95

Ezra Brooks, Seal,
Gold, 1972

Ezra Brooks,
Silver Dollar, 1970

Ezra Brooks, Sprint Car Racer, 1971

Ezra Brooks, Stagecoach, Overland Express, 1969 .... 4.95 To 10.00
Ezra Brooks, Stock Market Ticker Tape, 1970 .... 6.00 To 10.00
Ezra Brooks, Stove, Potbellied, 1968 .... 6.50 To 9.95
Ezra Brooks, Tank, Military, 1972 .... 14.00 To 19.95
Ezra Brooks, Tecumseh, 1969 .... Illus 4.50 To 11.00
Ezra Brooks, Telephone, 1971 .... 7.00 To 12.95
Ezra Brooks, Texas Longhorn Steer, 1971 .... 19.95 To 24.00
Ezra Brooks, Ticker Tape, 1970 .... 6.00 To 10.00
Ezra Brooks, Tonopah, Mule, 1972 .... 18.00
Ezra Brooks, Totem Pole, 1972 .... Color   XX.XX
Ezra Brooks, Tractor, Fordson, 1971 .... 12.00 To 15.95
Ezra Brooks, Trout & Fly, 1970 .... 6.95 To 9.95
Ezra Brooks, Turkey, White, 1971 .... 11.95 To 29.99
Ezra Brooks, Vermont Skier, 1972 .... 12.00
Ezra Brooks, Washington Salmon .... 44.95 To 89.95
Ezra Brooks, Water Tower, Chicago, 1969 .... 8.50 To 14.00
Ezra Brooks, West Virginia Mountain Lady, 1972 .... Color   XX.XX
Ezra Brooks, West Virginia Mountaineer, 1971 .... 90.00 To 140.00
Ezra Brooks, Wheat Shocker, Kansas, 1971 .... Illus 10.00 To 13.50

Ezra Brooks, Tecumseh, 1969

Ezra Brooks, Wheat Shocker, Kansas, 1971

Ezra Brooks, White Turkey, 1971 .... 11.95 To 29.99
Ezra Brooks, Wichita Centennial, Century II .... 12.50 To 21.95
Ezra Brooks, Winston Churchill, 1969 .... 2.50 To 10.00
Ezra Brooks, Zimmerman's Hat .... 9.95 To 15.95
Face Cream, see Medicine
Famous Firsts, Alpine Bell 9.95
Famous Firsts, America, Yacht 24.95
Famous Firsts, Balloon 19.95

Famous Firsts, Butterfly	19.50
Famous Firsts, Coffee Mill	22.50
Famous Firsts, Dewitt Clinton Engine, 1969	21.50 To 22.95
Famous Firsts, French Telephone, 1969	26.50
Famous Firsts, Garibaldi	17.50
Famous Firsts, Hen	13.50
Famous Firsts, Marmon Wasp	23.00
Famous Firsts, Napoleon	17.50
Famous Firsts, Phonograph	21.50
Famous Firsts, Renault Racer	10.95 To 23.00
Famous Firsts, Robert E.Lee Riverboat	21.50
Famous Firsts, Scale	21.50
Famous Firsts, Sewing Machine	21.50
Famous Firsts, Spirit Of St.Louis	35.00
Famous Firsts, St.Pols Bell	9.95
Famous Firsts, Wasp	10.95

Figural bottles are specially named by the collectors of bottles. Any bottle that is of a recognizable shape, such as a human head, or a pretzel, or a clock, is considered to be a figural. There is no restriction as to date or material.

Figural, Abraham Lincoln, Bank, Metal Slotted Screw Top, Embossed	15.00
Figural, Acrobat, Clear	25.00 To 30.00
Figural, Acrobat, Miniature	25.00
Figural, Andrew Jackson	28.00
Figural, Animal Reading Book, Clear, 5 In.	25.00
Figural, Apostle, Amber	95.00
Figural, Baby, Crying, Clear	22.50
Figural, Balloon, Captive, Dated 1878, Case	40.00
Figural, Banana, Ceramic, German	17.50
Figural, Banana, Metal Screw Cap, Clear, 7 5/8 In.High	11.00
Figural, Barrel, Carnival Glass	30.00
Figural, Barrel, Clear, 3 In.	4.00
Figural, Barrel, Hawley Glass Works, Amber	35.00
Figural, Barrel, Mist Of The Morning, Stain, Citron	320.00
Figural, Barrel, That's The Stuff, Open Pontil, Yellow Amber	420.00
Figural, Bather On Rocks	50.00
Figural, Bear, Amethyst	45.00
Figural, Bear, Applied Face, Pontil, Dark Gray, 11 In. .... *Illus*	235.00
Figural, Bear, Applied Face, 11 In., Pontil .... *Color*	XX.XX
Figural, Bear, Dark Green, 12 In. .... *Illus*	75.00
Figural, Bear, Enameled, White	7.00
Figural, Bear, Kummel, Dark Olive, 11 In.	25.00
Figural, Bear, Milk Glass, 11 1/2 In. .... *Illus*	175.00

Figural, Bear,
Applied Face,
Pontil, Dark Gray,
11 In.

Figural, Bear,
Dark Green,
12 In.

Figural, Bear,
Milk Glass,
11 1/2 In.

Figural, **Bear**, Painted Black	10.00
Figural, **Bear**, Sitting, Amber	40.00
Figural, **Bear**, Standing, Clear	12.00
Figural, **Bell**, Cane Pattern, Wooden Handle In Closure, Clear	8.00
Figural, **Bell**, Schoolhouse, 6 1/4 In.High	8.50
Figural, **Bell**, Stained, Pontil, Clear, 3 In.	6.00
Figural, **Bennington Type**, Book, Green & Yellow Mottling, Departed Spirit	230.00
Figural, **Bennington Type**, Book, Mottled	115.00
Figural, **Billiard Balls & Cues**, Pontil, Clear, 16 1/4 In.	110.00
Figural, **Billiard Balls & Cues**, Pontil, Frosted & Clear, 14 In.	65.00
Figural, **Billy Club**, Amber, 10 In.	15.00
Figural, **Billy Club**, Clear, 12 In.	3.00
Figural, **Billy Club**, Corked Screw Top, Dark Amber	35.00
Figural, **Bird**, Spain, Milk Glass, 8 In.Tall	10.00
Figural, **Bird**, Spain, Milk Glass, 10 In.Tall	12.00
Figural, **Bopeep**	6.00
Figural, **Boat**, U.S.N.Dreadnaught	35.00
Figural, **Boot**, Ceramic Brown, 6 In.	30.00
Figural, **Boot**, Marked, Clear, 4 3/4 In.High	8.50
Figural, **Bottle In Basket With Handle**, Spanish, Clear, Quart	2.00
Figural, **Boxing Glove**, Pat.1889, Screw Cap, Clear	33.00
Figural, **Boy & Girl Climbing Tree**, Depose, Bird Nest Stopper	75.00
Figural, **Boy & Girl Climbing Tree**, Depose, Pontil, Red Paint, Clear	48.00
Figural, **Boy Holding Drum**, Clear, 14 In.	5.00
Figural, **Boy On Barrel**, Clear, 5 In.	12.50
Figural, **Boy Sitting On Hat**, Hallo, That's Father's Hat, Japanese	10.00
Figural, **Broom**, Ceramic, Colored, 6 In.	8.00
Figural, **Brush**, Dust Remover, Whiskey Giveaway, Boysen's Falstaff, Omaha	22.50
Figural, **Bullfighter**, Enamel, Clear, 13 In.	1.00
Figural, **Bunch Of Grapes**, Clear, 2 In.	2.00 To 3.00
Figural, **Bunch Of Grapes**, Clear, 6 In.	1.00
Figural, **Bundle Of Cigars**, Amber, 5 In.	25.00
Figural, **Bunker Hill Monument**, Fire Opalescent	75.00
Figural, **Bunker Hill**, Clear, 12 In.	25.00 To 35.00
Figural, **Bust**, Cleveland, Clear Frosted, 10 In.	52.50
Figural, **Bust**, Crying Baby, Embossed T.P.S.& Co., N.Y., June 2, 1874, Clear	55.00
Figural, **Bust**, Harrison, Pedestal, Puce & Frosted, 12 In.	100.00
Figural, **Bust**, M.J.Owens, Frosted, Clear, 5 In.	17.50
Figural, **Bust**, Political Contemporary Of Garfield, Clear	75.00
Figural, **Bust**, Teddy Roosevelt, Clear, 5 In.	27.50
Figural, **Bust**, Washington, Screw Top, Blue, 4 In.	2.00
Figural, **Bust**, Woman, Clear, 3 In.	15.00
Figural, **Bust**, Woman, Clear, 12 In.	2.00
Figural, **Cabin**, Clevenger Booze, Amber	20.00
Figural, **Cabin Shape**, Constitutional Beverage, Amber	55.00
Figural, **Cannon Barrel**, R. & G.A. Wright, Philadelphia, Blue	510.00
Figural, **Cannon**, R. & G.A.Wright, Philadelphia, Amethyst, 8 In.	400.00
Figural, **Cannon**, Water Stain, Olive Amber	40.00
Figural, **Canteen**, Glass Label, Clear, 5 In.	20.00
Figural, **Canteen**, Glass Label, Clear, 6 In.	37.50
Figural, **Car**, Cable, Tan, France	20.00
Figural, **Carrie Nation**, Screw Cap, Clear	8.00 To 10.00
Figural, **Cat**, Clear, 11 In. *Illus*	30.00
Figural, **Cat**, Smiling, Vaseline Yellow, 8 In.	25.00
Figural, **Charlie Chaplin**, Ceramic	45.00
Figural, **Cherub Holding Bottle**, French, Clear, 15 In. *Illus*	55.00
Figural, **Chicken & Egg**, Viarengo	1.00
Figural, **Chicken On Nest With Egg**, Clear Cork, 10 In.	12.00
Figural, **Child & Cornucopia**, 5 1/2 In.	17.50
Figural, **Choirboy**, L'Abee Francois	25.00
Figural, **Christmas Tree**, Clear, 14 1/2 In. *Illus*	250.00
Figural, **Christmas Tree**, Star Stopper, Bimal, Red & Green Tinsel, 14 In.	35.00
Figural, **Cigar**, Amber	20.00
Figural, **Cigar**, Clear, 6 1/2 In.High	13.00
Figural, **Cigar**, Screw Cap, Amber, 5 In.	17.00
Figural, **Cigars**, Flask, Metal, 6 In. *Illus*	20.00

Figural, Cat, Clear, 11 In.
See Page 74

Figural, Cherub Holding Bottle,
French, Clear, 15 In.
See Page 74

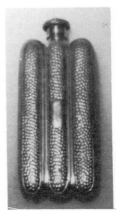

Figural, Christmas Tree,
Clear, 14 1/2 In.
See Page 74

Figural, Cigars,
Flask, Metal, 6 In.
See Page 74

Figural, **Clam**, Blue, 5 In.	45.00
Figural, **Clam**, Clear, 3 In.	7.00
Figural, **Clam**, Milk Glass, 4 In.	75.00
Figural, **Clam**, Screw Cap, Paint	24.00
Figural, **Clock**, Bininger, Amber	300.00
Figural, **Clock**, Bininger, Clear, Engraved, 5 1/2 In. .... Color	XX.XX
Figural, **Clock**, Bininger, Regulator, Amber, Embossed .... Color	XX.XX
Figural, **Clock**, Bininger, Regulator, Pontil, Dark Amber Brown	350.00
Figural, **Clock**, Bininger, Regulator, 19 Broad St., N.Y. .... Illus	335.00
Figural, **Clock**, Clear, 7 In.	15.00
Figural, **Clock**, Glass Label, Clear, 5 In.	25.00
Figural, **Clock**, Grandfather's, Pontil, Milk Glass, 12 In. .... Illus	350.00
Figural, **Clock**, Milk Glass, Pontil, 12 In. .... Color	XX.XX
Figural, **Clock**, Raised Clock Face, Happy Time, Dutch Lunch Sauce, Tin Top	16.00
Figural, **Clock**, Regulator, Engraved, Pontil, 6 In. .... Illus	375.00
Figural, **Clown On Flat Round Flask**, Japanese	10.00
Figural, **Clown**, Clear, 6 1/2 In.	20.00
Figural, **Clown**, Clear, 7 In.	22.50
Figural, **Clown**, Grapette Co., Clear	2.50
Figural, **Clown**, Grapette Products Co., Camden, Ark., C.1930, Clear, 7 In.	2.95
Figural, **Clown**, Stopper, Cranberry Glass	65.00
Figural, **Clown**, 2 Face, 12 In.	85.00
Figural, **Coachman**, Amber, 9 In.	170.00
Figural, **Coachman**, Bennington, Signed Lyman & Fenton .... Illus	295.00
Figural, **Coachman**, Van Dunck's, Amber	115.00
Figural, **Coffeehouse**, Tall, Label, Stamp, Yellow Striped	4.00
Figural, **Collapsed Bottle**, Green	1.00
Figural, **Cricket Ball**, W.L.S.	5.00
Figural, **Crown Lavender Salts**, English Registry Mark .... Color	XX.XX
Figural, **Crying Baby**, Clear, 6 In.	25.00 To 65.00
Figural, **Cucumber**, Green, 4 In.	25.00
Figural, **Czar**, Bonbon, Tin Lid On Base, 16 1/4 In.	150.00

Figural, Clock,
Bininger's Regulator,
19 Broad St., N.Y.
See Page 75

Figural, Clock,
Grandfather's Pontil,
Milk Glass, 12 In.
See Page 75

Figural, Clock, Regulator,
Engraved, Pontil, 6 In.
See Page 75

Figural,
Coachman, Bennington,
Signed Lyman & Fenton
See Page 75

Figural, **Czar**, Clear Standing, Tin Lid On Base, 16 1/2 In.		150.00
Figural, **Dagger**, Clear, 10 In.		6.00
Figural, **Dagger**, Stag Handle, Ceramic, German, 12 In.Long		17.50
Figural, **Derringer**, Clear, 5 In.		6.00
Figural, **Derringer**, Clear, 6 In.		6.00
Figural, **Dog**, Aidee, Pressed Glass		2.50
Figural, **Dog**, Casanova		10.00
Figural, **Dog**, Clear, 4 In.		20.00
Figural, **Dog**, Clear, 10 In.		3.00
Figural, **Dog**, Cohodos		6.00
Figural, **Dog**, Crying, Frosted		35.00
Figural, **Dog**, Depression Glass, Green		25.00
Figural, **Dog**, Poodle, Screw Cap, Blue		10.50
Figural, **Dog**, 2 1/2 In.	*Illus*	2.50
Figural, **Dominoes**, Frosted & Clear, 12 3/4 In.		90.00
Figural, **Double Dice**, Milk Glass, Stopper		30.00
Figural, **Double Dice**, Stopper, Milk Glass		35.00
Figural, **Dueling Pistol**, Gold Paint, Clear, 10 In., Pair		7.00
Figural, **Ear Of Corn**, Amber, 10 In.		75.00
Figural, **Ear Of Corn**, Clear, 7 In.		75.00
Figural, **Ear Of Corn**, Screw Cap		20.00
Figural, **East Terrace**, Windsor Castle, Crown Devon, England		6.00
Figural, **Eiffel Tower**, Benoit Serres		6.00
Figural, **Elephant**, ABM , Clorox, 1930s, Amber		35.00
Figural, **Elephant**, Amber, 10 In.		7.50
Figural, **Elephant**, Castle Products, Newark, N.J., Clear	*Illus*	5.00
Figural, **Elephant**, Grapette Products Co., Camden, Ark., C.1930, Clear, 7 In.		2.95

Figural, Dog, 2 1/2 In.
See Page 76

Figural, Elephant,
Castle Products,
Newark, N.J., Clear
See Page 76

Figural, **Elephant**, No.839, German, Orange, 7 In.Tall	18.00
Figural, **Elephant**, Old Sol, ABM, Amber	8.00
Figural, **Elephant**, Sitting, Clear	18.50
Figural, **Elephant**, Sitting, No.1377, German, Blue, 7 In.Tall	22.00
Figural, **Elephant**, Standing, Amber	15.00
Figural, **Elephant's Head**, Frosted & Clear, 12 In.	35.00
Figural, **Elk's Tooth**, Screw Top, Elk's Emblem, Clear	30.00
Figural, **Eye**, Milk Glass, 4 In.	42.50
Figural, **Fantasia**, Clear	25.00
Figural, **Fantasia**, Frosted	45.00
Figural, **Feed The Baby**, Frosted Face, Marble, Clear	4.00
Figural, **Fiddle**, Green	12.00
Figural, **Fish & Elephant**, Bols Blown Glass	9.00
Figural, **Fish Bitters**, Cobalt Blue, 12 In. *Color*	XX.XX
Figural, **Fish**, Bennington Type	100.00
Figural, **Fish**, Ceramic, Brown, 7 In.	31.00
Figural, **Fish**, Clear, 3 In.	12.50
Figural, **Fish**, Clear, 14 In.	2.00
Figural, **Fish**, Cod Liver Oil, Amber, 6 In.High	8.00
Figural, **Fish**, Cod Liver Oil, Machine Made, Deep Honey Amber	8.00
Figural, **Fish**, Cod Liver Oil, Machine Made, Reddish Amber	8.00
Figural, **Fish**, Cork Top, Amber, 7 In.	5.00
Figural, **Fish**, Cork Top, Amber, 12 In.	6.00
Figural, **Fish**, Embossed, Screw Top	2.50
Figural, **Fish**, Enamel, Clear, 9 In.	10.00
Figural, **Fish**, Pontil, Clear, 3 In.	12.50
Figural, **Fish**, Rockingham Type Glazed Pottery, 9 In.	10.00
Figural, **Fish**, Screw Top, Amber, 12 In.	4.00
Figural, **Fish**, Whimsey, Clear, 9 In.	5.00
Figural, **Football**, Ceramic, Brown, 4 1/2 In.High	18.00
Figural, **French Cavalier**, Miniature	25.00
Figural, **Frog**, Green, 4 1/2 In.Tall	30.00
Figural, **Fruit Form**, Clear	3.00
Figural, **Fruit Form**, Stain, Clear	2.00
Figural, **Gambia**, Matteo Magazzin, Cherry Wobble, Labels	10.00
Figural, **Garibaldi**, Clear, 12 In.High	10.50
Figural, **George Washington Bust**, Jacquin, Cobalt Blue, 4 In.High	15.00
Figural, **George Washington**, Screw Cap, Clear	8.00
Figural, **Gift**, Ceramic, Colored, 4 In.	5.00
Figural, **Girl In Rocking Chair**, Clear, 5 In.	40.00
Figural, **Girl**, Frosted, Clear, 8 In.	10.00
Figural, **Girl**, 3 1/2 In.High	10.00
Figural, **Glad & Sad Faces**, Clear	30.00

Figural, **Goat**, Standing, Clear	8.00
Figural, **Goat**, Viarengo	42.50
Figural, **Gold Water**, German	25.00
Figural, **Golf Bag**, Aidee	1.75
Figural, **Golfer**, With Club, Eamses, German, 8 In.Tall	21.00
Figural, **Grandfather's Clock**, Pontil, Clear, 12 In.	22.50
Figural, **Granger Bust**	60.00
Figural, **Great-Grandfather's Grandson**, Monkey Holding Mirror, Japanese	10.00
Figural, **Grover Cleveland Bust**	200.00
Figural, **Gun**, Ground Mouth, Screw Cap, Amber	27.00
Figural, **Ham**, Clear, 6 In.	10.00
Figural, **Hand With Gun**, Depose, Frosted & Clear, 14 1/4 In.	110.00
Figural, **Hand With Mirror**, Pontil, Frosted & Clear, 14 In.	110.00
Figural, **Hand**, Ceramic, Brown, 6 In.	27.00
Figural, **Hand**, Glad, German, Blue	30.00
Figural, **Hand**, Glad, Pat.Pending, German, Flesh Color	40.00
Figural, **Hand**, Screw Top, Clear, 6 In.	10.00
Figural, **Happy And Sad Faces**, Clear, 12 In.	14.00
Figural, **Happy Man**, Light Green, 8 In.	4.00
Figural, **Hard Roll**, Ceramic, German	17.50
Figural, **Hare & Kangaroo**, Bols Blown Glass	9.00
Figural, **Harrison Bust On Pedestal**, Frosted, Puce, 12 In.	100.00
Figural, **Hatchet**, Clear, 6 In.	9.00
Figural, **Hatchet**, Metal, 6 In.	10.00
Figural, **Hawk**, El Lorito Benetuser, Milk Glass .... *Illus*	35.00
Figural, **Heart**, Amber, 7 1/2 In.	8.00
Figural, **Heart**, John Hart & Company .... *Color*	XX.XX
Figural, **Hessian Soldier**	55.00
Figural, **Horn**, John Parkers Advertising	7.00
Figural, **Horn**, Pressed Glass, Ground Top, Turning Amethyst, 8 1/2 In.High	27.50
Figural, **Horse**, Cazanove	10.00
Figural, **Horseshoe**, Flask, Ceramic	23.00
Figural, **Hot Tamale**, Chunky Version	10.00
Figural, **Hot Tamale**, Long Version	15.00
Figural, **Hourglass**, 3 3/4 X 6 3/4 In.	275.00
Figural, **House**, Rynbende	4.50
Figural, **Humpty Dumpty**, Clear	4.00
Figural, **Hunter**, Green, Germany	8.00

Figural, Hawk, El Lorito Benetuser, Milk Glass

Figural, **Husted Santa Claus**	75.00
Figural, **Inca Pisca**, Black	10.00
Figural, **Indian Maiden With Shield & Spear**, H.Pharazyn, Phila., Amber	920.00
Figural, **Indian Queen**, see Bitters, Brown's Celebrated Indian Queen	
Figural, **Jester**	50.00
Figural, **Joan Of Arc**	20.00

Figural, Joan Of Arc At Stake, Depose	90.00
Figural, Joan Of Arc On Horseback, Miniature	25.00
Figural, John Bull, Amber, 12 In.	85.00
Figural, John L.Sullivan Figure, Frosted, Clear & Colored, 15 In.	160.00
Figural, Kiss Snookum's, German	45.00
Figural, Knight On Horseback	9.00
Figural, Kummel Bear, Black, 11 In.	22.50 To 25.00
Figural, Lapwing, Bols Blown Glass	9.00
Figural, Learned Fox	35.00 To 45.00
Figural, Learned Fox, Amethyst	30.00
Figural, Lifesaver, When Sinking, Take Hold, German, Brown	25.00
Figural, Lighthouse, Screw Top, Clear, 10 In.	1.00
Figural, Lincoln Bank, Clear, 8 In.	1.00
Figural, Locomotive, Rocher Freres, 1951	12.00
Figural, Madonna, Hand Blown, Pontil, Dated 1932, Amber, 13 In.Tall	4.00
Figural, Madonna, Hand Blown, Pontil, Dated 1932, Cobalt Blue, 13 In.Tall	3.50
Figural, Madonna, Light Green, 13 In.	3.00
Figural, Madonna, Pontil, Clear, 13 In.	1.00
Figural, Madonna, Yellow 10 In.	1.00
Figural, Mammy, Robj	25.00
Figural, Man From Valley Of The Moon, Man Astride A Barrel	10.00
Figural, Man On Barrel, Bennington Type, Marked Jim Crow, Rockingham Glaze	118.00
Figural, Man, Ceramic, Brown, 8 In.	20.00
Figural, Man, Milk Glass, 11 In.	90.00
Figural, Man, Smiling, Van Dunck's Genever, Brown, 9 In. *Illus*	180.00
Figural, Man's Bust, Pontil, Clear, 12 In.	30.00
Figural, Man's Bust, Stained, Clear, 11 In.	2.00
Figural, Matador	20.00
Figural, Mermaid, Ceramic, Brown, 8 In.	40.00
Figural, Mermaid, Poison, Silver Top, 9 In. *Illus*	125.00
Figural, Mermaid, Silver Top, Bennington *Color*	XX.XX
Figural, Misshapen Bottle, Clear, 8 In.	1.00
Figural, Monk, Ceramic, 11 In. *Illus*	35.00
Figural, Monk, Fat, Certosino, Labels	7.00
Figural, Monk, Milk Glass, Holland *Illus*	18.00
Figural, Monkey With Banana, Mobana	2.50
Figural, Monkey With Glasses, Clear	28.00
Figural, Monkey, Green, 13 In.Tall	5.00
Figural, Monkey, Green, 13 1/2 In.Tall	5.00
Figural, Monument With Busts, Clear, 14 In.	4.00
Figural, Monument, Black, 12 In.	50.00
Figural, Monument, Clear, 12 In.	18.00
Figural, Monument, Milk Glass, 8 In.	65.00
Figural, Monument, Milk Glass, 9 In.	50.00
Figural, Moses In Cradle, Clear, 5 In.	35.00
Figural, Moses, Facsimile, ABM , Fed.Law, Amber, Quart	8.00
Figural, Moses, Honeymoon, Green, Quart	12.00 To 30.00
Figural, Moses, Poland Water, Amber, 11 In.High	180.00
Figural, Moses, Stopper Type, Large Size, Amber	10.00
Figural, Moses, Stopper Type, Large Size, Clear	5.00
Figural, Moses, 1925, Facsimile	4.00
Figural, Mr.Cocktail, German, Brown, 9 1/2 In.Tall	50.00
Figural, Mr.Pickwick, Clear, 9 In.	4.00 To 7.00
Figural, Mrs.Carrie Nation, Clear, 9 In.	4.00
Figural, Naked Girl, Clear, 12 In.	5.00
Figural, Naked Woman, Frosted, Clear, 14 In.	25.00
Figural, Napoleon, Croizet	25.00
Figural, Napoleon, Robj	25.00
Figural, Negro Boy, Miniature, 1 In.	2.75
Figural, Negro Waiter, Satin Glass, Black Head, Sheared Neck	150.00
Figural, Negro, Frosted, 14 In.	45.00
Figural, Nugget, Amethyst, 3 In.	22.50
Figural, Oilcan, Giveaway, Made In Germany, Oil Of Joy	15.00
Figural, Old Hickory Whiskey, Ceramic, 11 1/2 In.High *Illus*	20.00
Figural, Old Man, Ceramic, White, 5 In.	19.00
Figural, Owl, Clear, 5 In.	10.00

Figural, Man, Smiling, Van Dunck's Genever, Brown, 9 In.
See Page 79

Figural, Mermaid,
Poison, Silver Top, 9 In.
See Page 79

Figural, Monk, Ceramic, 11 In.
See Page 79

Figural, Monk, Milk Glass, Holland
See Page 79

Figural,
Old Hickory Whiskey,
Ceramic, 11 1/2 In.High
See Page 79

Figural, Owl,
Milk Glass,
6 In.High

Figural, Owl, Milk Glass, 6 In.High	*Illus*	75.00
Figural, Owl, Mustard Jar, Prepared Flaccus Bros., 6 In.	*Color*	XX.XX
Figural, Owl, Pink, 9 1/2 In.High		30.00
Figural, Oyster Shell, Screw Cap, Paint		25.00
Figural, Oyster, Aqua, 5 In.		17.50
Figural, Oyster, Enamel, Clear, 6 In.		12.00
Figural, Pagoda, Fancy, Clear, 6 1/4 In.High		9.00
Figural, Parrot, El Lorito, 4 In.		20.00
Figural, Parrot, Standing, Clear		12.00
Figural, Passenger Car, Roches Freres, 1951		10.00
Figural, Paul Bunyan		8.00
Figural, Pear, Blown, Branch Is Mouth, 6 In.High		38.00
Figural, Pig, Applied Handle, Bristol Glass		45.00

Figural, Pig, Bourbon In A Hog's ---, Amber, 7 In.	110.00
Figural, Pig, Clear	45.00
Figural, Pig, Contents, Clear, 4 In.	22.50
Figural, Pig, Depose, Clear, 7 In.	7.50
Figural, Pig, Flattened Sides, Clear, 9 1/2 In.Long	37.50
Figural, Pig, Good Old Rye In A Hog .... *Color*	XX.XX
Figural, Pig, John Gaubotz, St.Louis, Mo., Incised Railroad Routes, Stoneware	400.00
Figural, Pig, Something Good In A Hog's---, Clear, 4 In. .... 15.00 To 22.50
Figural, Pig, Something Good In A Hog's ---, He Won't Squeal, Clear, 4 In.	27.50
Figural, Pig, Theodore Netter Distilling, Co. .... *Color*	XX.XX
Figural, Pig, Whimsey, Pontil, Clear, 7 In.	7.50
Figural, Pipe, Clear & Amber	17.50
Figural, Pistol, Amber	22.50
Figural, Pistol, Amber, 7 In.	20.00
Figural, Pistol, Amber, 10 In.	25.00
Figural, Pistol, Amber, 11 In.	40.00
Figural, Pistol, Blue, 8 In.	55.00
Figural, Pistol, Clan Tartan, His	6.00
Figural, Pistol, Clear, 3 In.	11.00
Figural, Pistol, Clear, 6 In.	6.00
Figural, Pistol, Clear, 7 In.	17.00
Figural, Pistol, Clear, 8 In.	4.00
Figural, Pistol, Clear, 9 In.	6.00
Figural, Pistol, Clear, 10 In.	19.00
Figural, Pistol, Green, 8 In.	22.50
Figural, Pistol, Screw Cap, Clear	12.00
Figural, Pistol, Threaded Ground Top, Clear	9.50
Figural, Poodle, Screw Top, Blue, 8 In.	10.00
Figural, Potato, Brown Enamel, Clear, 6 In.	10.00
Figural, Potato, Clear, 6 In.	4.00
Figural, Potato, Patent Applied For, Screw Cap, Paint	23.00
Figural, Powder Horn, Clear, 9 In.	12.00
Figural, Powder Horn, Clear, 10 In.	7.00
Figural, Pretzel	25.00
Figural, Pretzel, Ceramic, 6 In.	15.00
Figural, Pretzel, German	20.00
Figural, Pretzel, German, 7 In.	17.00
Figural, Pretzel, 5 1/2 In. .... *Illus*	20.00

Figural, Pretzel, 5 1/2 In.

Figural, Quo Vadis With Painted Embossing, Clear, Quart	2.00
Figural, Raised Bulldog On Corner, Frosted	50.00
Figural, Revolver, Clear	10.00
Figural, Roast Turkey, Amber	40.00
Figural, Rolling Pin, Bimal, Corker, Clear, 14 In.	9.00
Figural, Rolling Pin, Clear	3.00
Figural, Rolling Pin, Nailsea Type, Blue, 13 In.	37.50
Figural, Sad Hound, Blue	40.00
Figural, Sad Hound, Painted, Milk Glass, Light Blue, 11 In.	35.00
Figural, Sailor, Clear, 12 In.	14.00
Figural, Sandeman, Manhattan, Black	30.00
Figural, Sandeman, Manhattan, Blue	40.00

Figural, Santa Claus At Chimney, Amber, 5 In.	30.00
Figural, Santa Claus, Husted, Clear, 13 In. .... *Illus*	95.00
Figural, Santa Claus, Stain, Clear, 12 In. .... 6.00 To 20.00	
Figural, Sausage, Pottery, Brown, 5 In.	15.00
Figural, Scallop, Clear, 5 In.	9.00
Figural, Scotchman, Little, German, Brown, 9 In.Tall	50.00
Figural, Scotchman, Little, Playing Bagpipe, German	45.00
Figural, Scotchman, Old & Little, Holding Dog & Cane, German	45.00
Figural, Scroll In Hands, English Salt Glaze, C.1800, People's Rights	95.00
Figural, Senorita, Milk Glass	20.00
Figural, Sewing Basket, Depose, Clear	14.00
Figural, Shoe Fly, Diamond-Quilted, Clear, 4 In.	5.00
Figural, Shoe With Toe Showing, Amethyst, 4 In.	65.00
Figural, Shoe With Toe Showing, Frosted, Clear, 6 In.	17.50
Figural, Shoe, Applied Lip, BIMAL , Clear, 4 3/4 In.Long	7.50
Figural, Shoe, Clear, 4 In.	2.00
Figural, Shoe, Laced, Rockingham	47.50
Figural, Silver Plated Canteen, Here's A Smile For Those I Love	6.00
Figural, Single Dice, Milk Glass	20.00
Figural, Slipper, Clear, 6 In.	7.00
Figural, Slipper, Flower In Buckle, Clear, 3 1/2 In.Long	3.00
Figural, Sloth On Tree, Clear, 4 In.	12.00
Figural, Smiling Cat, Blue	40.00
Figural, Soldier, Clear, 8 In. High .... *Illus*	30.00
Figural, Soldier, Hessian, Clear	40.00
Figural, Spanish Lady, Embossed Made In Spain, Clear, 12 In.High	10.00
Figural, St. Anthony With Baby, Bonbon, Tin Lid, 16 In.	150.00

Figural, Santa Claus,
Husted, Clear, 13 In.

Figural, Soldier, Clear, 8 In. High

Figural, Stack Of Dominoes, Amethyst	48.00
Figural, Stanley, Footed .... *Illus*	24.00
Figural, Statue Of Idol, Ceramic, Green, 11 In.	1.00
Figural, Statue Of Liberty, Base, Milk Glass, 9 1/2 In. .... *Illus*	75.00
Figural, Statue Of Liberty, Clear, 12 1/2 In.High	125.00
Figural, Statue Of Liberty, Metal Top, Milk Glass .... *Illus*	350.00
Figural, Statue Of Liberty, Metal Top, 15 1/2 In. .... *Color*	XX.XX
Figural, Statue Of Liberty, Milk Glass, 10 In.High	45.00
Figural, Stove, Stain, Clear, 5 In.	5.00
Figural, Stuffed Turkey, Amber, 5 In.	22.50
Figural, Tacos, Ceramic, Austria, Pat.App'd F', 7 In. .... *Illus*	12.00
Figural, Tamale, Long & Slender, Merry Xmas 1912, German	20.00
Figural, Tamale, Short & Fat, German	15.00
Figural, Tank, Bank, Tankar System Saves, 5 In. .... *Illus*	10.00
Figural, Teapot, Blown Spout Is Neck Of Bottle, Honey Amber	37.50
Figural, Teapot, Casanova	7.00
Figural, Teardrop, Open Pontil, Emerald Green, 7 In.	32.00

Figural, Stanley, Footed
See Page 82

Figural, Statue Of Liberty,
Base, Milk Glass, 9 1/2 In.
See Page 82

Figural, Tacos, Ceramic,
Austria, Pat.App'd F', 7 In.
See Page 82

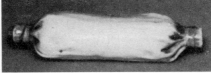

Figural, Statue Of Liberty,
Metal Top, Milk Glass
See Page 82

Figural, Tank, Bank, Tankar System Saves, 5 In.
See Page 82

Figural, Teddy Roosevelt, Clear, 5 In.	27.50
Figural, Toilet	12.50
Figural, Top Hat & Umbrella, What A Nite Drunk, German	45.00
Figural, Tower Bridge, London, Crown Devon, England	6.00
Figural, Town Pump, German	22.00
Figural, Turkey, Ceramic, German, Brown	17.50
Figural, Turtle, Clear	12.50
Figural, Turtle, Clear, 5 In.	4.00
Figural, Turtle, Embossed Merry Xmas, Paint, Clear	17.50
Figural, Two Men With Bottle, Wet Or Dry, Japanese	10.00
Figural, Uncle Sam, Clear, 9 In. ..... *Illus*	75.00
Figural, Venetian Clown, Multicolors On White, Cased, 15 1/2 In.High	15.00
Figural, Venus Di Milo	6.00
Figural, Viking Ship, Larson's	5.99
Figural, Violin, Amethyst	45.00
Figural, Violin, Applied Lip, Pink	30.00
Figural, Violin, Aqua, 7 1/4 In.	5.00
Figural, Violin, Clear, 6 1/4 In.Tall	5.00
Figural, Violin, Cobalt Blue	4.50
Figural, Violin, Cobalt Blue, 8 In.Tall	1.25
Figural, Violin, Cobalt Blue, 12 In.Tall	1.25
Figural, Violin, Enameled Flowers, Amethyst, 10 In. ..... *Illus*	20.00
Figural, Violin, Flared Lip, Premachine, Amber, 12 In.High	15.00

Figural, Uncle Sam, Clear, 9 In.
See Page 83

Figural, Violin,
Enameled Flowers, Amethyst, 10 In.
See Page 83

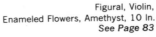

Figural, **Violin**, Flask, Amber, Pint	170.00
Figural, **Violin**, Flask, Aqua, Pint	40.00
Figural, **Violin**, Green, 9 3/4 In.High	20.00
Figural, **Violin**, Holder, Light Blue, 9 1/2 In.Tall	12.00
Figural, **Violin**, Improved Pontil, Aqua	25.00
Figural, **Violin**, Light Blue	8.00
Figural, **Violin**, Music Bar On One Side, Light Blue	8.00
Figural, **Violin**, Pale Blue, 6 In.	7.50
Figural, **Violin**, Stained, Aqua, 10 In.	6.00
Figural, **Violin**, West, Pittsburgh, Amber	50.00
Figural, **W.C.Fields**	19.95
Figural, **W.L.S.Ivanoff**, Jan. ABM	7.00
Figural, **Washington Bust**, Dark Blue	10.00
Figural, **Washington Bust**, Light Blue	15.00
Figural, **Washington**, BIMAL, Clear	7.00
Figural, **Washington**, Clear, 9 In.	2.00
Figural, **Washington**, Clear, 10 In.	5.00
Figural, **Washington**, Silver Painted, Clear, 9 1/2 In.High	10.00
Figural, **Watch**, Clear, 3 In.	6.00
Figural, **Wheel Shape**, The Hub Flask, Whiskey, Clear, 6 In.High	12.50
Figural, **Whiskbroom**, Daisy & Button	12.50
Figural, **Whiskbroom**, Flask, Clear, Pint	12.50
Figural, **Whiskbroom**, Flask, Clear, 1/2 Pint	12.50
Figural, **Whiskbroom**, Flask, Pint	18.00
Figural, **Whiskbroom**, Marked Knapp, Partial Cologne Label, Clear	31.00
Figural, **Whiskbroom**, Sun Colored Amethyst, Pint	35.00
Figural, **Whiskbroom**, 6 1/8 In.High	17.00
Figural, **White Stag**, Handle, German	20.00
Figural, **Wild Boar**, Cobalt Blue, 1/2 Pint	60.00
Figural, **Woman**, Head Is Stopper, Frosted	30.00
Figural, **Woman's Bust**, Clear, 3 In.	15.00
Figural, **Woman's Torso**, Clear, 7 In.	10.00
Figural, **World's Fair**, 1939, Milk Glass *Color*	XX.XX
Figural, **World's Fair**, 1939, Milk Glass, Quart	4.00
Figural, **Zeppelin**	25.00
Fire Extinguisher, **Bomb**, Wall Bracket, Liquid Filled, Labels, 5 In.Diameter	15.00
Fire Extinguisher, **C.& N.W.Railroad In Raised Letters**, Blue Fluid Filled	32.50
Fire Extinguisher, **Carbona**, 12 Sided, Amber	10.00
Fire Extinguisher, **Comet Automatic**, Metal Frame, Red	12.50
Fire Extinguisher, **Free-Blown Crackle Glass**, Barrel, Amberina To Yellow	150.00
Fire Extinguisher, **Free-Blown Crackle Glass**, Barrel, Chartreuse, 6 In.	37.50
Fire Extinguisher, **Free-Blown Crackle Glass**, Barrel, Crystal, 6 In.	37.50
Fire Extinguisher, **Free-Blown Crackle Glass**, Barrel, Emerald, 6 In.	37.50
Fire Extinguisher, **Free-Blown Crackle Glass**, Barrel, Yellow Amber, 6 In.	37.50
Fire Extinguisher, **Free-Blown Crackle Glass**, Turquoise, 6 In.	37.50
Fire Extinguisher, **Globe Shape**, Beehive Design, Embossed Korbeline, Amber	35.00

Fire Extinguisher, Harden's Hand Grenade Extinguisher, Blue	20.00 To 25.00
Fire Extinguisher, Harden's Hand Grenade, Ribbed, Embossed Star, Blue	24.00
Fire Extinguisher, Harden's Hand, Contents, footed, blue	25.00
Fire Extinguisher, Harden's, May 27, '84, 8 In.High .... *Illus*	40.00
Fire Extinguisher, Harden's, Turquoise, 7 In. .... *Illus*	35.00
Fire Extinguisher, Hayward, Honey Amber, Patent 1871	35.00
Fire Extinguisher, Hayward's, Light Green	22.50
Fire Extinguisher, Hayward's, 1871 Patent, Square Faced, Sapphire Blue	36.00
Fire Extinguisher, Hazelton's, Keg, Brown, 11 1/2 In. .... *Illus*	125.00
Fire Extinguisher, N.Y. Hayward Hand Grenade .... *Color*	XX.XX
Fire Extinguisher, Pear Shape, Red Flashed	5.00
Fire Extinguisher, Pear Shape, Red Flashed, Contents	10.00
Fire Extinguisher, Phoenix, 22 In.Tube, Hangs On Wall	8.00
Fire Extinguisher, Pronto, Partial Label, Cap & Hanger, Amber	27.50
Fire Extinguisher, Red Comet, Full, Decal, Holder	20.00
Fire Extinguisher, Shur-Stop, Holder	7.00

Fitzgerald, see Old Fitzgerald

Flasks have been made since the 18th century in America. The free blown, mold blown, and decorated flasks are all popular with collectors. The numbers that appear with some of the entries are those used in the Mc-Kearin book, American Glass. The numbers used in the entries in the form Van R-O or Mc Kearin G I-O refer to the books Early American Bottles & Flasks *by Stephen Van Rensselaer 'and* American Glass *by George P. and Helen Mc Kearin.*

Fire Extinguisher, Harden's,
May 27, '84, 8 In.High

Fire Extinguisher, Harden's,
Turquoise, 7 In.

Fire Extinguisher, Hazelton's, Keg,
Brown, 11 1/2 In.

Flask, A Little More Grape Capt.Bragg, Aqua	65.00
Flask, A Merry Christmas, Label, Clear, 1/2 Pint	50.00
Flask, A.L.Chamberlain & Co., Fairhaven, Ct.Embossed, Amber, 1/2 Pint	25.00
Flask, Acid Etched Scenes & Margaret Waddel, 1850, Squat, Deep Amber	100.00
Flask, Anchor & Cabin, Spring Garden Glass Works, Aqua, Pint	60.00
Flask, Anchor & Sheaf Of Wheat, Baltimore Glass Works, Aqua, Quart	75.00
Flask, Anchor On Base, Amber, 1/2 Pint	4.50
Flask, Anchor, Amber, 1/2 Pint	12.50
Flask, Applied Rigaree, Olive Amber, Pint, Blown	220.00
Flask, Applied Swags, Clear, Blown	10.00

Flask, **Applied Swags**, Pulled Collar, Dark Olive Green 200.00
Flask, **Applied Tapered Top**, O.P., Olive Amber, 1/2 Pint 32.50
Flask, **Avenue Hotel**, Amber, 1/2 Pint 5.00
Flask, **Baltimore & Corn For The World**, Embossed, Aqua, Quart 100.00
Flask, **Baltimore Glass Works & Resurgam Eagle**, Amber, Pint 190.00
Flask, **Baltimore Glass Works & Sheaf**, Aqua, Quart 45.00
Flask, **Baltimore Glass Works**, 7 1/2 In. .... *Color* XX.XX
Flask, **Barrel Shape**, Aqua, Pint 10.00
Flask, **Basket Weave**, Clear, 1/2 Pint 8.50
Flask, **Bennington**, Double Eagle, Pint, 7 1/2 In. 35.00
Flask, **Bininger**, Green, Pint 48.00
Flask, **Broad Flutes**, Cobalt Blue, 1/2 Pint 350.00
Flask, **Broad Flutes**, Pewter Collar, Green 110.00
Flask, **Bryan & Sewall**, Silver Screw Cap, Embossed, Clear, 1/2 Pint 55.00
Flask, **Bulbous Top & Bottom**, Square Center, Clear, 13 In. 12.50
Flask, **Bull's-Eye**, Applied Mouth, Dark Green 12.00
Flask, **Byron & Scott**, Open Pontil, Olive Amber, 1/2 Pint .... 120.00 To 150.00
Flask, **C.A.Richards**, Boston, Aqua, Pint 30.00
Flask, **Calabash**, Clasped Hands & Eagle, Stained, Aqua, Quart 25.00
Flask, **Calabash**, Clasped Hands, Eagle, Pontil, Yellow Green, Quart 65.00
Flask, **Calabash**, Hunter & Fisherman, Aqua, Quart 55.00
Flask, **Calabash**, Sheaf Of Wheat & Star, Dark Amber, Quart 400.00
Flask, **Calabash**, Sheaf Of Wheat & Star, Sheets & Duffy, Stain, Aqua, Quart 40.00
Flask, **Calabash**, Sheaf Of Wheat & Star, Stain, Aqua, Quart 25.00
Flask, **Calabash**, Union & Eagle, Dark Amber 110.00
Flask, **Cannon & Clasped Hands**, Aqua, Pint 60.00
Flask, **Cannon & Flag**, Aqua, Pint 50.00
Flask, **Cannon**, Graphite Pontil, 1/2 Pint 65.00
Flask, **Ceramic**, Brown Glaze, 1/2 Pint 9.00
Flask, **Ceramic**, Loyal Order Of Moose, Light Brown, 1/2 Pint 3.00
Flask, **Chapin & Gore**, Chicago, Sour Mash, 1867, Applied Collar, Amber, Pint 60.00
Flask, **Charley Ross**, Clear 28.00
Flask, **Chestnut**, Applied String Rim, Handle, Amber 38.00
Flask, **Chestnut**, Aqua, 9 1/2 In.High 35.00
Flask, **Chestnut**, Broad Flutes, Aqua, Pint .... 60.00 To 70.00
Flask, **Chestnut**, Diamond Checker, Golden Amber 350.00
Flask, **Chestnut**, Diamond Pattern, Milk Glass 20.00
Flask, **Chestnut**, Flattened, Applied Handle, Pontil, Amber, Quart 23.00
Flask, **Chestnut**, Flattened, Seal, Chestnut Grove, Whiskey, C.W., Amber, Quart 19.00
Flask, **Chestnut**, Fluted, Amber, Pint 170.00
Flask, **Chestnut**, Fluted, Amethyst 140.00
Flask, **Chestnut**, Free-Blown, Pontil, Flat Lip, Olive Green, 7 In.High 43.00
Flask, **Chestnut**, Handled, Open Pontil, Amber, 8 In.High 25.00
Flask, **Chestnut**, Kent, Vertical Ribs, 18 Ribs Swirled To Right, Green 75.00
Flask, **Chestnut**, Mantua, 16 Ribs Swirled To Left, Aqua, 6 1/2 In. 70.00
Flask, **Chestnut**, Midwestern, 25 Ribs Swirled To Left, Sheared Neck, Green 80.00
Flask, **Chestnut**, New England, Free-Blown, Open Pontil, Yellow Green 60.00
Flask, **Chestnut**, New England, Open Pontil, Olive Green, 10 In. 60.00
Flask, **Chestnut**, New England, Open Pontil, Olive Green, 5 1/4 In. 60.00
Flask, **Chestnut**, Ohio, Broad Flutes, Clear, Small Size 40.00
Flask, **Chestnut**, Ohio, Dark Amber, 1/2 Pint 180.00
Flask, **Chestnut**, Ohio, Swirled To Right, Pulled Collar, Pint 60.00
Flask, **Chestnut**, Ohio, Swirled To Right, 1/2 Pint 175.00
Flask, **Chestnut**, Open Pontil, Olive Amber, 6 In.High 45.00
Flask, **Chestnut**, Open Pontil, Olive Green, 5 In. 60.00
Flask, **Chestnut**, Open Pontil, Olive Green, 10 In. 60.00
Flask, **Chestnut**, Reddish Amber 35.00
Flask, **Chestnut**, Sand Check, Persian, Olive Amber, Quart 30.00
Flask, **Chestnut**, Sheared Neck, Deep Amber 100.00
Flask, **Chestnut**, Sheared Neck, 16 Ribs, Mantua, Aqua, 6 1/4 In. 75.00
Flask, **Chestnut**, Steigel Type, 16 Diamond, Clear, 5 1/4 In. 30.00
Flask, **Chestnut**, Swirled To Left, Open Pontil, Sheared Lip, Blue Green 90.00
Flask, **Chestnut**, Swirled To Right, Blue Aqua, 1/2 Pint 60.00
Flask, **Chestnut**, Swirled To Right, Broad Swirls, Olive Green 125.00
Flask, **Chestnut**, Swirled To Right, Turned Over Collar, Aqua 50.00
Flask, **Chestnut**, Zanesville, 10 Diamond, 1/4 In.Ground Off Top, Yellow Green 290.00

Flask, Chestnut, Zanesville, 24 Vertical Ribs, Reddish Amber, 5 3/4 In.	100.00
Flask, Chestnut, Zanesville, 24 Vertical Ribs, Sheared Neck, Deep Amber	125.00
Flask, Chestnut, Zanesville, 24 Vertical Ribs, Sheared Neck, Golden Amber	160.00
Flask, Chestnut, Zanesville, 24 Vertical Ribs, Sheared Neck, Green	100.00
Flask, Chestnut, 16 Vertical Ribs, Sheared Neck, Amethyst, 6 1/2 In.	110.00
Flask, Clasped Hand & Cannon, Aqua, Pint	55.00
Flask, Clasped Hands & Eagle, Aqua, Pint	32.50
Flask, Clasped Hands & Eagle, Aqua, Quart	35.00
Flask, Clasped Hands & Eagle, Aqua, 1/2 Pint	20.00 To 35.00
Flask, Clasped Hands & Eagle, Stain, Aqua, Quart	37.50
Flask, Clasped Hands & Eagle, Stain, Burst Bubble, Aqua, Pint	7.50
Flask, Clasped Hands & Eagle, Stain, Green, Quart	140.00
Flask, Clasped Hands & Eagle, Yellow Green, 6 1/2 In. *Illus*	100.00
Flask, Clasped Hands, Eagle, & Pittsburg, Aqua, Quart	40.00
Flask, Clasped Hands, Eagle, & Union, 1/2 Pint	40.00
Flask, Cleve, Steve & Cock, Barrel Shape, Clear, Pint	90.00
Flask, Clock & Web, Clear, 1/2 Pint	14.50
Flask, Clyde Glass Works, Aqua, Quart	40.00
Flask, Coffin, Diamond-Quilted, Bubbles, Applied Top, 5 In.High	4.50
Flask, Coffin, Diamond-Quilted, Shot Glass Stopper, Blown In Mold, Clear	10.00
Flask, Coffin, John Judge & Co., Boston, Full Measure Quart, Clear, 11 In.	7.00
Flask, Coffin, Label Monogram Geneva, Dark Green, Pint	16.00
Flask, Coffin, Miniature, Amethyst, 4 In.	4.00
Flask, Coffin, Pumpkin Seeds, Crude, Opal	5.00
Flask, Coffin, Quart, Deep Aqua	8.00
Flask, Coffin, Quilted Design, Amethyst, 4 In.	8.00
Flask, Coffin, Z.O.K.H.& G.On Bottom, Aqua, Quart	7.50
Flask, Cognac Monnet, Dragon Design, Clear	25.00
Flask, Corncob Ribbings, Pulled Neck, Clear, Small Size	110.00
Flask, Cornucopia & Basket, Olive Green, Pint	65.00
Flask, Cornucopia & Eagle	72.50
Flask, Cornucopia & Urn, Olive Amber	50.00 To 65.00
Flask, Cornucopia & Urn, Open Pontil, Olive Amber, Pint	45.00
Flask, Cornucopia & Urn, Pontil, Olive Green, 6 1/2 In. *Illus*	75.00

Flask, Clasped Hands & Eagle,
Yellow Green, 6 1/2 In.

Flask, Cornucopia & Urn, Pontil,
Olive Green, 6 1/2 In.

Flask, Cornucopia, Historical	65.00
Flask, Cornucopia, Whittled, Open Pontil, Olive Green, Pint	75.00
Flask, Crude, C.1830, Dark Olive Green, Pint	35.00
Flask, Cut Glass, Sterling Top, 5 3/4 In.	50.00
Flask, Dancing Girl & Hessian Soldier, Aqua, Pint	60.00
Flask, Dancing Sailor & Seated Musician, Olive Amber, 1/2 Pint, Van R-75	235.00
Flask, Decorated Papier-Mache Over Glass, Pint	4.00
Flask, Demishape, Flat, Wicker Covered, Deep Aqua, 9 In.High	10.00
Flask, Diamond Checker, Ribs At Base, Inset Neck, Clear	40.00

Flask, Diamond Pattern, Amber, 1/2 Pint 310.00
Flask, Diamond Pattern, Clear, 1/2 Pint 8.50
Flask, Diamond Sunburst, Three Mold, Olive Green 275.00
Flask, Diamond-Quilted, P.B.W.On Bottom, Clear, Quart 20.00
Flask, Dog & Stag, Clear, Quart 13.00
Flask, Dot On Front & Back, Domed Base, Whittled, Amber, Pint 20.00
Flask, Double Eagle & Cunningham, Pittsburg, Pa., Aqua, Pint 90.00
Flask, Double Eagle Over Oval, Sheared Neck, Amber, Pint 70.00
Flask, Double Eagle, Amber, Pint 52.50
Flask, Double Eagle, Amber, 1/2 Pint 55.00
Flask, Double Eagle, Aqua, Pint .... 32.50 To 40.00
Flask, Double Eagle, Aqua, Quart .... 30.00 To 45.00
Flask, Double Eagle, Aqua, 1/2 Pint .... 35.00 To 50.00
Flask, Double Eagle, C & I In Front & Back, Aqua, 1/2 Pint 60.00
Flask, Double Eagle, Cunningham & Co., Aqua, Pint 35.00
Flask, Double Eagle, Cunningham & Imsen In Ovals, Aqua, Pint 55.00
Flask, Double Eagle, Embossed Pittsburgh, Pa., Dark Olive Amber, Pint 250.00
Flask, Double Eagle, Inside Bubble Burst, Light Green, Pint 110.00
Flask, Double Eagle, Light Green, Quart 59.00
Flask, Double Eagle, Marked Pittsburgh, Green, Quart 170.00
Flask, Double Eagle, Marked Stoddard, N.H.In Oval, Olive Amber, Pint 10.00
Flask, Double Eagle, Marked, Olive Amber, Pint 100.00
Flask, Double Eagle, Olive Amber, Pint .... 65.00 To 100.00
Flask, Double Eagle, Open Pontil, Amber, 1/2 Pint .... 40.00 To 60.00
Flask, Double Eagle, Open Pontil, Olive Amber, Pint .... 35.00 To 65.00
Flask, Double Eagle, Pittsburg, Pa., Amber, Pint 40.00
Flask, Double Eagle, Pittsburgh, Aqua, Pint 30.00
Flask, Double Eagle, Pittsburgh, Deep Green, Quart 65.00
Flask, Double Eagle, Pittsburgh, Light Blue, Quart 45.00
Flask, Double Eagle, Pittsburgh, Olive Amber, Pint 60.00
Flask, Double Eagle, Pittsburgh, Open Pontil, Olive Amber, 1/2 Pint 125.00
Flask, Double Eagle, Pittsburgh, Pa., Aqua, Quart 50.00
Flask, Double Eagle, Rough Pontil, Stain 19.00
Flask, Double Eagle, Stoddard, N.H., Olive Amber, Pint 110.00
Flask, Double Eagle, Stoddard, N.H., Open Pontil, Amber, Pint 30.00
Flask, Double Eagle, Stoddard, N.H., Open Pontil, Amber, Pint, ... 30.00 To 80.00
Flask, Double Eagle, Stoddard, N.H., Open Pontil, Amber, Quart 80.00
Flask, Double Success To Railroad, Pontil, Olive Amber, Pint 200.00
Flask, Drinking, Leather Top, Silver Plate Bottom & Cap 6.50
Flask, Drum, Prohibition, Label 35.00
Flask, Duck Will You Take A Drink, Pale Green, Pint 110.00
Flask, Duck Will You Take A Drink, Pale Green, Quart 160.00
Flask, Eagle & Baltimore, G.W., Aqua, Pint 35.00
Flask, Eagle & Clasped Hands, Aqua, Pint 50.00
Flask, Eagle & Cornucopia, Keene 105.00
Flask, Eagle & Cornucopia, Pontil, Olive Amber, Pint 75.00
Flask, Eagle & Cornucopia, With X, Open Pontil, Olive Amber, Pint 72.50
Flask, Eagle & Cunningham & Co., Pittsburgh, Pa., Aqua, Quart 100.00
Flask, Eagle & Flag, Embossed, Aqua, Pint 65.00
Flask, Eagle & For Pike's Peak Traveler, Aqua, 1/2 Pint 40.00
Flask, Eagle & For Pike's Peak, Traveler, Aqua, Quart 40.00
Flask, Eagle & For Pike's Peak, Traveler, Pittsburgh, Pa., Pint .... 30.00 To 45.00
Flask, Eagle & Girl On Bicycle, A & DHA , Aqua, Pint 85.00
Flask, Eagle & Man Drinking, Olive Yellow, Quart 625.00
Flask, Eagle & Stars, Reverse Grapes .... *Color*   XX.XX
Flask, Eagle & Tree, Sheared Lip, Tubular Pontil, Aqua, Pint 80.00
Flask, Eagle & Union, Pittsburgh, Pa., Aqua, Quart 30.00
Flask, Eagle In Circle, Strap, Amethyst, 1/2 Pint 24.00
Flask, Eagle On Wreath, Willington Glass Co., Olive Green, 1/2 Pint 175.00
Flask, Eagle With Banner, Dark Amber, 1/3 Pint 70.00
Flask, Eagle-Willington, Olive Green, Quart 100.00
Flask, Eagle, Baltimore Glass Works, Aqua, Pint 50.00
Flask, Eagle, Pittsburgh, Aqua, Pint 50.00
Flask, Eagle, With Banner, Dyottville Glass Works, Philadelphia, Aqua, Pint 140.00
Flask, Elongated & Vertically Ribbed, Light Green, Pint 20.00
Flask, Elongated, Pontil, White & Clear Looping, Nailsea 65.00

Flask, Elongated, Vertically Ribbed, Light Green, Pint	20.00
Flask, Embossed Indian Head, Clear, 1/4 Pint	15.00
Flask, Embossed Star, Ground Threaded Top, Amber, Pint, 7 In.High	10.00
Flask, Expanded Pattern Mold, Sheared Mouth, Pontil, Crude, Aqua, Pint	12.00
Flask, Extended Base Expands At Center, Collared, Applied Handle, Amber	300.00
Flask, Flat Sides, Applied Handle, Olive Amber	35.00
Flask, Flat Sides, Extended Collar, Deep Amber, Pint	30.00
Flask, Flora Temple, Amber Quart	100.00 To 175.00
Flask, Flora Temple, Aqua, Pint	230.00
Flask, Flora Temple, Handled, Label, Amber, Pint	200.00
Flask, Flora Temple, Handled, Puce, Pint	170.00 To 240.00
Flask, Flora Temple, Handleless, Light Green, Pint	200.00
Flask, Flora Temple, Harness Trot, Handle, Ring Collar, Puce Amber, Pint	230.00
Flask, For Pike's Peak & Eagle, Pittsburgh, Pa., Facing Left, Blue	75.00
Flask, For Pike's Peak Traveler & Hunter, Amber, Pint	420.00
Flask, For Pike's Peak, Prospector Walking To Left, Eagle, Aqua, Pint	45.00
Flask, For Pike's Peak, Stained, Aqua, 1/2 Pint	10.00
Flask, For Pike's Peak, Traveler & Eagle, Aqua, 1/2 Pint	45.00
Flask, For Pike's Peak, Traveler & Hunter, Amber, Pint	420.00
Flask, For Pike's Peak, Traveler & Hunter, Aqua, Pint	55.00
Flask, For Pike's Peak, Traveler & Hunter, Olive Amber, Pint	380.00
Flask, Free-Blown, Applied Rigaree, Olive Amber, Pint	220.00
Flask, General Macarthur & God Bless America, Pontil, Green, 1/2 Pint	10.00
Flask, General Macarthur, 1942, Flags, Blue, 1/2 Pint	15.00
Flask, General Washington, Eagle & 10 Stars, Light Green, Pint	200.00
Flask, Geo.W.Robinson, No.75 Main St., W.Virginia, Aqua, 1/2 Pint	38.00
Flask, Geometric Design, Brass Screw Cap, Clear, 1/2 Pint	12.00
Flask, George D.Robinson, Aqua, 1/2 Pint	12.50
Flask, George Washington, 1932, Clear, Gallon	7.00
Flask, Girl On Bicycle, Girl For Joe, Stain, Aqua, Pint	80.00
Flask, Girl Riding Bicycle & Eagle, Aqua, Pint	80.00
Flask, Globular, Collared Neck, Aqua	50.00
Flask, Globular, Collared Neck, Aqua, 1/2 Gallon	25.00
Flask, Globular, Collared Neck, Dark Amber	30.00
Flask, Globular, Flat Sides, Collared Neck, Aqua	30.00
Flask, Globular, Fluted, Swirled To Left, Aqua	60.00
Flask, Globular, Long Neck, Deep Olive Green	80.00
Flask, Globular, Ohio, Broad Swirls, To Left, Green Aqua	60.00
Flask, Globular, Punched, Expanded Collar, Short Neck, Aqua	15.00
Flask, Globular, Short Neck, Aqua	40.00
Flask, Globular, Swirled To Left, Aqua	85.00
Flask, Globular, Turned Over Collar, Dark Amber	80.00
Flask, Globular, Turned Over Collar, Dark Green	40.00
Flask, Globular, Turned Over Collar, Dark Green, 1 1/2 Quart	40.00
Flask, Grandfather's, Legendary, Broken Swirl, Reddish Amber	125.00
Flask, Granite Glass Co.& Stoddard, N.H., Pint	95.00
Flask, Granite Glass Co., Reverse Stoddard N.H., Amber, Pint	145.00
Flask, Grapes, Reverse Eagle, Aqua, Quart	110.00
Flask, Hambone, Amber	40.00
Flask, Handled, Graphite Pontil, Cylindrical, Amber	25.00
Flask, Hands Clasping, Reverse Eagle *Color*	XX.XX
Flask, Harris Jamaica Ginger On Label, Clear, 1/2 Pint	3.00
Flask, Hessian Soldier & Dancer, Chapman, Baltimore, Blue, Pint	675.00
Flask, Hunter & Dog, Honey Amber	165.00
Flask, Hunter & Dog, Puce, Pint	440.00
Flask, Hunter & Dog, Stained, Aqua, 1/2 Pint	25.00
Flask, Hunter & Fisherman, Calabash, Aqua	30.00
Flask, Hunter, Fisher, Amber	115.00
Flask, Hunter, Holding Gun & Bottle, German	35.00
Flask, In Remembrance, Clear Milk Glass, 1/2 Pint	10.00
Flask, In Remembrance, Milk Glass, Blue, 1/2 Pint	10.00
Flask, Indian Hunter & Eagle, Aqua, Quart	55.00
Flask, Indian Shooting Bow & Arrow & Eagle, Aqua, Quart	90.00
Flask, Indianapolis Glass Works, Aqua, 1/2 Pint	32.50
Flask, Inside Screw Cap, Amber, 1/2 Pint	13.00
Flask, Isabella Glass Works & Sheaf, Open Pontil, Aqua, Pint	80.00

Flask, Isabella Glass Works Factory, Aqua, Quart	80.00
Flask, Isabella Glass Works, Sheaf Of Wheat, Aqua, Pint	100.00
Flask, Isabella Glass Works, Sheaf Of Wheat, Pint	80.00
Flask, Isabella Glass Works, 7 1/2 In. .... *Color*	XX.XX
Flask, Jackson & Co.Olive Green, 1/2 Pint	52.50
Flask, Jenny Lind, East Liverpool, Ohio	50.00
Flask, Jenny Lind, Eisterville Glass Works, Embossed, Amber	15.00
Flask, Jenny Lind, Open Pontil	85.00
Flask, Jft & Co., Phila., Fluted, Applied Handle, Deep Amber	275.00
Flask, Jno.F.Horne, Knoxville, Tenn., Anchor, Banded, Amber, Quart	38.00
Flask, Jockey On Running Horse, Aqua, Pint	49.00
Flask, Jos.A.Magnus & Co., Cincinnati	13.50
Flask, Keene, Open Pontil, Sheared Neck, Green, Pint	40.00
Flask, Kidney Shape, Wicker Covered & Handle, Deep Aqua, 7 1/4 In.High	10.00
Flask, Klondike, Ming Glass	60.00
Flask, Kossuth, Aqua, 11 In. .... *Illus*	95.00
Flask, L.G.Co. On Base, Lyndeboro Glass Co., Yellow Amber, Pint	10.00
Flask, L.G.Co. On Base, Lyndeboro, Tapered Applied Top, Amber, 1/2 Pint	15.00
Flask, Lady In Tall Champagne Glass, German	35.00
Flask, Lady's Picture In Color Under Glass, Clear .... *Illus*	75.00
Flask, Lady's Railway Companion, Beaded Case	25.00
Flask, Lewis 66, The Strauss Pritz Co., Cincinnati, Ohio, Clear, Pint	5.00
Flask, Lewis 66, The Strauss Pritz Co., Cincinnati, Ohio, Clear, 1/2 Pint	5.00
Flask, Liberty, Eagle & Willington Glass Co., Olive Amber, Pint	90.00
Flask, Liberty, Eagle & Willington Glass Co., Olive Green, Pint	85.00
Flask, Liberty, Eagle & Willington Glass Co., Olive Green, 1/2 Pint	85.00
Flask, Lilienthal & Co., Banded, Pint	90.00
Flask, Liquor, Camphor Glass, Silver Deposit, Hunting Scene	12.00
Flask, Louis Tussog, German	15.00
Flask, Louisville, Ky., Glass Works, Aqua, Pint	35.00
Flask, Lyndeboro, L.G.Co.On Base, Amber, Pint	25.00
Flask, Lyndeboro, L.G.Co.On Base, Marked, Teal Green, Pint	27.50
Flask, Lyndeboro, L.G.Co.On Base, Stain Inside, Amber, 1/2 Pint	12.50
Flask, Lyndeboro, L.G.Co.On Base, Yellow Green	25.00
Flask, Lyndeboro, Marked L.G.Co. On Base, Patent On Front, Light Blue, Pint	31.00
Flask, Lyndeboro, Patent On Shoulder, L.G.Co. On Base, Aqua, 1/2 Pint	27.50
Flask, M Embossed On Base, Honey Amber, Pint	15.00
Flask, Macy & Jenning, New York, C.1887, Handled, Cylindrical, Amber	12.50
Flask, Man Holding Drink, Brown, German	35.00
Flask, Man Playing Banjo & Dancer, Dark Amber, 1/2 Pint	300.00
Flask, Man With Satchel & Eagle With Banner, Green, Pint	180.00
Flask, Marked M.Volry's Patent, Sept.25, 1866, Pewter Base & Screw Top	5.00
Flask, Masonic & Eagle, Amber	180.00

Flask, Kossuth,
Aqua, 11 In.

Flask,
Lady's Picture In Color
Under Glass, Clear

Flask, **Masonic & Keene Eagle**, Pontil, Stain, Aqua, Pint	280.00
Flask, **Masonic**, Keene, Cloud, Open Pontil, Olive Amber	180.00
Flask, **Masonic**, Keene, Pontil, Cloudy, Olive Amber, Pint	180.00
Flask, **Mc Kearin C-11**	78.00
Flask, **Mc Kearin G C-8**, Success To The Railroad & Eagle, Olive Amber, Pint	170.00
Flask, **Mc Kearin G I-2**, Washington & Eagle, Aqua, Pint 120.00 To	160.00
Flask, **Mc Kearin G I-3**, General Washington, Aquamarine, Pint	500.00
Flask, **Mc Kearin G I-5**, Washington & Eagle, Aqua, Pint	950.00
Flask, **Mc Kearin G I-6**, Clear, Pint	475.00
Flask, **Mc Kearin G I-7**, Aqua, Pint	390.00
Flask, **Mc Kearin G I-10**, Washington & Eagle, Light Green, Pint	160.00
Flask, **Mc Kearin G I-11**, Washington & Eagle, Aqua, Pint 280.00 To	325.00
Flask, **Mc Kearin G I-14**, General Washington & Eagle, Medium Green, Pint	400.00
Flask, **Mc Kearin G I-14**, Washington & Eagle, Aqua, Pint	140.00
Flask, **Mc Kearin G I-16**, Washington & Eagle, Pontil, Aqua, Pint	45.00
Flask, **Mc Kearin G I-17**, Aqua, Pint	90.00
Flask, **Mc Kearin G I-18**, Washinton & Baltimore Monument, Cornflower, Pint	1200.00
Flask, **Mc Kearin G I-18**, Washington & Monument, Clear Green, Pint	100.00
Flask, **Mc Kearin G I-20**, Fells Point & Monument, Clear, Pint 70.00 To	90.00
Flask, **Mc Kearin G I-20**, Washington & Baltimore Monument, Amethyst, Pint	675.00
Flask, **Mc Kearin G I-20**, Washington & Baltimore Monument, Aqua, Pint	40.00
Flask, **Mc Kearin G I-20**, Washington & Baltimore Monument, Green, Pint	475.00
Flask, **Mc Kearin G I-20**, Washington & Baltimore Monument, Puce, Pint	975.00
Flask, **Mc Kearin G I-21**, Washington & Baltimore Monument, Clear, Quart	55.00
Flask, **Mc Kearin G I-24**, Historical, Aqua	115.00
Flask, **Mc Kearin G I-25**, Washington & Classical Bust, Stain, Aqua, Pint	60.00
Flask, **Mc Kearin G I-25**, Washington, Bridgetown, N.J., Aqua, Quart	80.00
Flask, **Mc Kearin G I-26**, Historical, Amethystine	375.00
Flask, **Mc Kearin G I-26**, Washington & Spread Eagle, Aqua, Quart	100.00
Flask, **Mc Kearin G I-28**, Albany Glass Works, Aquamarine	175.00
Flask, **Mc Kearin G I-28**, Aqua	160.00
Flask, **Mc Kearin G I-28**, Washington & Albany Ship, Deep Green, Pint	425.00
Flask, **Mc Kearin G I-30**, Aqua	175.00
Flask, **Mc Kearin G I-30**, Washington & Albany Glass, Works, Aqua, 1/2 Pint	160.00
Flask, **Mc Kearin G I-31**, Washington & Jackson, Dark Olive Green, Pint	150.00
Flask, **Mc Kearin G I-31**, Washington & Jackson, Olive Green, Pin 100.00 To	150.00
Flask, **Mc Kearin G I-32**, Washington & Jackson, Sheared Lip, Olive, Pint	130.00
Flask, **Mc Kearin G I-34**, Olive Amber, 1/2 Pint 140.00 To	200.00
Flask, **Mc Kearin G I-37**, Taylor & Washington, Dyottville, Aqua, Quart	65.00
Flask, **Mc Kearin G I-37**, Washington & Taylor, Blue, Quart	500.00
Flask, **Mc Kearin G I-37**, Washington & Taylor, Green, Quart	90.00
Flask, **Mc Kearin G I-37**, Washington & Taylor, Pontil, Stain, Aqua, Quart	30.00
Flask, **Mc Kearin G I-38**, Aqua, Pint	50.00
Flask, **Mc Kearin G I-38**, Deep Amethyst, Pint	450.00
Flask, **Mc Kearin G I-38**, Washington & Taylor, Amethyst, Pint 500.00 To	550.00
Flask, **Mc Kearin G I-38**, Washington & Taylor, Dark Olive Green, Pint	300.00
Flask, **Mc Kearin G I-38**, Washington & Taylor, Medium Green, Pint	200.00
Flask, **Mc Kearin G I-38**, Washington & Taylor, Stained, Aqua	35.00
Flask, **Mc Kearin G I-39**, Historical, Light Emerald	110.00
Flask, **Mc Kearin G I-39**, Washington & Taylor, Light Green, Quart	60.00
Flask, **Mc Kearin G I-39**, Washington & Taylor, Stain, Aqua, Quart	25.00
Flask, **Mc Kearin G I-40**, Washington & Taylor, Green, Pint	130.00
Flask, **Mc Kearin G I-40**, Washington & Taylor, Stain, Aqua, Pint	25.00
Flask, **Mc Kearin G I-40a**, Washington & Taylor, Aqua	65.00
Flask, **Mc Kearin G I-40a**, Washington & Taylor, Moss Green, Pint	310.00
Flask, **Mc Kearin G I-41**, Washington & Taylor, Blue, Pint	950.00
Flask, **Mc Kearin G I-41**, Washington & Taylor, Stain, Aqua, 1/2 Pint	40.00
Flask, **Mc Kearin G I-42**, Sheared Neck, Aqua, Quart 40.00 To	60.00
Flask, **Mc Kearin G I-42**, Washington & Taylor, Stain, Aqua, Quart	30.00
Flask, **Mc Kearin G I-43**, Washington & Taylor, Aqua, Quart 40.00 To	80.00
Flask, **Mc Kearin G I-43**, Washington & Taylor, Light Green, Quart	60.00
Flask, **Mc Kearin G I-43**, Washington & Taylor, Stain, Light Green	30.00
Flask, **Mc Kearin G I-44**, Washington & Taylor, Olive Green, Pint	250.00
Flask, **Mc Kearin G I-45**, Washington & Taylor, Grass Green, Quart	250.00
Flask, **Mc Kearin G I-45**, Washington & Taylor, Stain, Aqua, Quart	35.00
Flask, **Mc Kearin G I-46**, Washington & Taylor, Aqua, Quart	45.00

Flask, Mc Kearin G I-46, Washington & Taylor, Clear, Quart 50.00
Flask, Mc Kearin G I-47, Aqua, Quart 50.00
Flask, Mc Kearin G I-47, Dyottville, Green, Quart 135.00
Flask, Mc Kearin G I-47, Washington, Father Of His Country, Green, Quart 100.00
Flask, Mc Kearin G I-48, Eagle & Flag, Aqua, Quart 160.00
Flask, Mc Kearin G I-48, Light Blue Green, Pint 600.00
Flask, Mc Kearin G I-48, Washington & Plain Reverse, Aquamarine, Pint 225.00
Flask, Mc Kearin G I-48, Washington & Plain Reverse, Olive Green, Pint 100.00
Flask, Mc Kearin G I-50, Washington & Taylor, Stain, Aqua, Pint 25.00
Flask, Mc Kearin G I-51, Washington & Taylor, Smokey Yellow, Quart 360.00
Flask, Mc Kearin G I-54, Washington & Taylor, Stain, Citron, Quart 200.00
Flask, Mc Kearin G I-54, Washington, Rolled Lip, Pontil, Green, Quart 100.00
Flask, Mc Kearin G I-55, Aqua, Pint 40.00
Flask, Mc Kearin G I-55, Historical, Dark Amber 160.00
Flask, Mc Kearin G I-55, Collared Lip, Smokey Amber, Pint 315.00
Flask, Mc Kearin G I-55, Washington & Taylor, Green, Pint 45.00
Flask, Mc Kearin G I-57, Aqua, Quart .... 35.00 To 45.00
Flask, Mc Kearin G I-58, Aqua, Pint 40.00
Flask, Mc Kearin G I-59, Aqua, 1/2 Pint .... 50.00 To 70.00
Flask, Mc Kearin G I-62, John Q.Adams & Eagle, J.T.& Co., Aqua 350.00
Flask, Mc Kearin G I-64, General Jackson & Eagle, Aqua, Pint 325.00
Flask, Mc Kearin G I-65, Aqua, Pint 410.00
Flask, Mc Kearin G I-65, Olive Green, Pint 1800.00
Flask, Mc Kearin G I-66, Clear With Amethyst Tint, Pint 650.00
Flask, Mc Kearin G I-68, General Jackson & Leaves & Acorns, Green, Pint 450.00
Flask, Mc Kearin G I-68, General Jackson, Leaves & Acorns, Aqua, Pint 650.00
Flask, Mc Kearin G I-71, Major Ringgold & Rough & Ready, Aqua, Pint 60.00
Flask, Mc Kearin G I-71, Taylor & Ringgold, Aqua, Pint .... 60.00 To 70.00
Flask, Mc Kearin G I-73, Taylor & Baltimore Monument, Stain, Aqua, Pint 50.00
Flask, Mc Kearin G I-73, Taylor & Monument, Amethyst, Pint 825.00
Flask, Mc Kearin G I-74, Z.Taylor & Corn For The World, Aqua, Pint 365.00
Flask, Mc Kearin G I-74, Z.Taylor & Corn For The World, Clear, Pint 425.00
Flask, Mc Kearin G I-74, Z.Taylor & Corn Stalk, Brilliant Green Pint 750.00
Flask, Mc Kearin G I-75, Taylor & Corn, Aquamarine, Pint 260.00
Flask, Mc Kearin G I-76, Deep Aqua, Pint 750.00
Flask, Mc Kearin G I-77, Taylor & Eagle, Masterson, Aqua, Quart 550.00
Flask, Mc Kearin G I-78, Aquamarine, Pint 350.00
Flask, Mc Kearin G I-79, Historical, Aqua 165.00
Flask, Mc Kearin G I-80, Lafayette & Dewitt Clinton, Amber, Pint 340.00
Flask, Mc Kearin G I-80, Lafayette, Dewitt Clinton, Olive Amber, Pint 440.00
Flask, Mc Kearin G I-81, Lafayette & Dewitt Clinton, Olive Amber 1/2 Pint 550.00
Flask, Mc Kearin G I-83, Lafayette & Liberty, Olive Amber, 1/2 Pint 270.00
Flask, Mc Kearin G I-85, Lafayette & Liberty Pole, Amber, Pint 300.00
Flask, Mc Kearin G I-85, Lafayette & Liberty Pole, Olive Green, Pint 300.00
Flask, Mc Kearin G I-89, Lafayette & Masonic, Olive Amber, 1/2 Pint 600.00
Flask, Mc Kearin G I-90, Lafayette & Eagle, Aqua, Pint .... 140.00 To 175.00
Flask, Mc Kearin G I-90, Lafayette, Firecracker, Aquamarine 110.00
Flask, Mc Kearin G I-91, Lafayette & Eagle, Aqua, Pint 120.00
Flask, Mc Kearin G I-93, Clear Green, Pint 525.00
Flask, Mc Kearin G I-93, Lafayette & Eagle, Green 75.00
Flask, Mc Kearin G I-93, Masonic, Lafayette & Eagle, Clear Green, Pint 500.00
Flask, Mc Kearin G I-94, Benjamin Franklin, Dark Brown, Pint 975.00
Flask, Mc Kearin G I-94, Franklin & Dyott, Aqua, Pint .... 140.00 To 150.00
Flask, Mc Kearin G I-95, Franklin & Dyott, Aqua, Pint 125.00
Flask, Mc Kearin G I-96, Franklin & Dyott, Aqua, Quart 160.00
Flask, Mc Kearin G I-97, Franklin & Franklin, Aqua, Quart 180.00
Flask, Mc Kearin G I-99, Calabash, Jenny Lind Glass House, Dark Green 350.00
Flask, Mc Kearin G I-99, Jenny Lind & Glassworks, Yellow Green, Quart 325.00
Flask, Mc Kearin G I-102, Jenny Lind & Glass Factory, Green, Quart 280.00
Flask, Mc Kearin G I-103, Jenny Lind, Calabash, Aqua 25.00
Flask, Mc Kearin G I-107, Jenny Lind & Fisterville G.W., Aqua, Quart 25.00
Flask, Mc Kearin G I-107a, Calabash, Jenny Lind & Factory, Blue Green, Quart 25.00
Flask, Mc Kearin G I-108, Aqua 315.00
Flask, Mc Kearin G I-108, Aquamarine, Pint 425.00
Flask, Mc Kearin G I-110, Jenny Lind & Lyre, Aqua, Quart 400.00
Flask, Mc Kearin G I-111, Kossuth & Sloop, Stain, Aqua, Pint .... 85.00 To 160.00

Figural, Crown Lavender Salts,
English Registry Mark

Figural, Heart, John Hart & Company

Figural, Owl, Mustard Jar,
Prepared Flaccus Bros., 6 In.

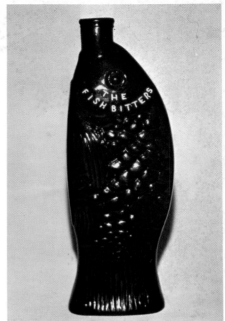

Figural, Fish Bitters, Cobalt Blue, 12 In.

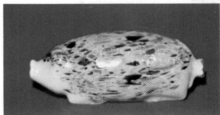

Figural, Pig, Good Old Rye In A Hog

Figural, Pig, Theodore Netter Distilling, Co.

Figural, Statue Of Liberty, Metal Top, 15 1/2 In.

Whiskey, Greeting, Theodore Netter

Fire Extinguisher, N.Y. Hayward Hand Grenade

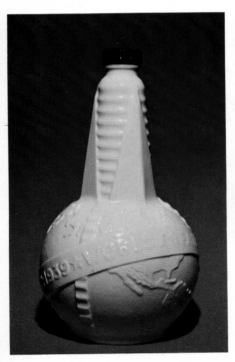

Flask, Isabella Glass Works, 7 1/2 In.

Flask, Baltimore Glass Works, 7 1/2 In.

Figural, World's Fair, 1939, Milk Glass

Flask, Eagle & Stars, Reverse Grapes

Flask, Hands Clasping, Reverse Eagle

Food, Ann Page Raspberry Preserve, 4 In.

Flask, The Father Of His Country, General Taylor

Food, Family Nectar, Clear, Pure

Food, Atlantic Prepared Mustard, R.T.French, 5 In.

Food, Catsup, Lutz, 9 In.

Food, Royal Baking Powder Company,
Box, Salesman's

Food, Shrewsbury Brand Choicest Products, 9 In.

Fruit Jar,
Flaccus Type, Pale Blue

Fruit Jar, Flaccus Type,
White Milk Glass

Fruit Jar,
Flaccus, Green

Fruit Jar,
Flaccus, Amber

Fruit Jar, Canton Electric Fruit Jar, Quart

Fruit Jar,
Potter & Bodine,
Airtight, Pint, 1858

Fruit Jar,
Potter & Bodine,
Airtight, Quart, 1858

Gin Case, 4 Bottles In Box,
Nineteenth Century

Ink, Butler, Cin., Ohio   Ink, Keller's, Detroit   Ink, Eureka School

Ink, Cadmium Steel Black   Ink, English, Green   Ink, English, Aqua

Ink, Carter's,
Mr.& Mrs.Carter, Patent, 1914, Germany

Ink, Carters, 10 1/2 In.   Ink, Carters,
                                   Cobalt Blue, 7 1/2

Ink, Green,   Ink, Umbrella,
'R', Open Pontil   Cobalt, Open Pontil

Ink, L.H.Thomas, Oct.16, 1883, Paper Label

Ink, Umbrella, Dark Amber   Ink, Honey Amber,   Ink, Turtle, J.I.M., Clear
2 1/2 In.

Soda, J.Wise,   Ink, 3 In., Cobalt Blue
Allentown, Pa., 6 1/2 In.

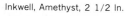

Inkwell, Amethyst, 2 1/2 In.

Jack Daniel, Distiller, Old No.7, Battleship Maine

Flask, Mc Kearin G I-111, Sloop & Kossuth, Clear Green, Pint 650.00
Flask, Mc Kearin G I-112, Kossuth, Calabash, Aqua 170.00
Flask, Mc Kearin G I-113, Kossuth & Tree, Light Green 80.00
Flask, Mc Kearin G I-114, Byron & Scott, Amber, 1/2 Pint 175.00
Flask, Mc Kearin G I-114, Byron & Scott, Olive Amber, 1/2 Pint 120.00
Flask, Mc Kearin G I-114, Byron & Scott, Open Pontil, Olive Amber, 1/2 Pint 120.00
Flask, Mc Kearin G I-116, Bust & Fairview Works, Dark Green, Pint 1550.00
Flask, Mc Kearin G I-118, Columbia & Eagle, Green Aqua, 1/2 Pint 275.00
Flask, Mc Kearin G I-121, Historical, Aqua 150.00
Flask, Mc Kearin G II -1, Double Eagle, Aqua, Pint 140.00
Flask, Mc Kearin G II -4, Double Eagle, Dark Olive Green, Pint 525.00
Flask, Mc Kearin G II -6, Cornucopia & Eagle, Aqua, Pint 150.00
Flask, Mc Kearin G II -7, Clear Blue Green, Pint 1300.00
Flask, Mc Kearin G II -8, Washington & Eagle, Fl In Oval, Aqua 500.00
Flask, Mc Kearin G II -9, Spread Eagle & Eagle In Flight, Yellow, Pint 750.00
Flask, Mc Kearin G II -10, 'Ihmsen' & Agriculture, Aqua, Pint 325.00
Flask, Mc Kearin G II -10, Green Aqua, Pint 525.00
Flask, Mc Kearin G II -11, Aqua, 1/2 Pint 200.00
Flask, Mc Kearin G II -11, Cornucopia & Eagle, Aqua, 1/2 Pint 200.00
Flask, Mc Kearin G II -11, Cornucopia & Eagle, Clear, 1/2 Pint 200.00
Flask, Mc Kearin G II -11, Cornucopia & Eagle, Light Green, 1/2 Pint 60.00
Flask, Mc Kearin G II -11, Inverted Cornucopia & Eagle, Aqua, 1/2 Pint 180.00
Flask, Mc Kearin G II -15, Aqua, 1/2 Pint 450.00
Flask, Mc Kearin G II -16, Aqua 90.00
Flask, Mc Kearin G II -18, Cornucopia & Eagle, Zanesville, Aqua, 1/2 Pint 250.00
Flask, Mc Kearin G II -19, Midwestern, Pottery, Eagle, Morning Glory, Buff 55.00
Flask, Mc Kearin G II -19, Pottery, Pint .... 110.00 To 150.00
Flask, Mc Kearin G II -22, Eagle & Lyre, Deep Aquamarine, Pint 345.00
Flask, Mc Kearin G II -22, Eagle & Lyre, Louisville, Green, Pint 950.00
Flask, Mc Kearin G II -24, Deep Olive Yellow, Pint 600.00
Flask, Mc Kearin G II -24, Double Eagle, Louisville, Corrugated, Aqua, Pint 80.00
Flask, Mc Kearin G II -24, Corrigated, Sapphire, Pint 250.00
Flask, Mc Kearin G II -24, Double Eagle, Louisville, Kentucky, Green, Pint 450.00
Flask, Mc Kearin G II -24, Double Eagle, Stain, Aqua, Pint 40.00
Flask, Mc Kearin G II -24, Eagle, Blue, Pint 900.00
Flask, Mc Kearin G II -25, Blue Aqua, Pint 150.00
Flask, Mc Kearin G II -25, Greenish Aqua, Pint 100.00
Flask, Mc Kearin G II -26, Historical, Aqua, Variant, 4 Stars 165.00
Flask, Mc Kearin G II -29, Double Eagle, Light Green, Pint 225.00
Flask, Mc Kearin G II -31, Double Eagle, Aqua, Quart 110.00
Flask, Mc Kearin G II -32, Double Eagle, Aqua, Pint 160.00
Flask, Mc Kearin G II -32, Pale Green, Pint 120.00
Flask, Mc Kearin G II -33, Louisville Glass Works & Eagle, Aqua, 1/2 Pint 100.00
Flask, Mc Kearin G II -36, Eagle, Aquamarine, Pint 150.00
Flask, Mc Kearin G II -36, Eagle Louisville G.W., Sand Check, Aqua, Pint 60.00
Flask, Mc Kearin G II -38, Eagle & Dyottville, Aqua, Pint 120.00
Flask, Mc Kearin G II -40, Double Eagle, Pontil, Aqua, Pint 60.00
Flask, Mc Kearin G II -41, Eagle & Tree, Aqua, Pint 95.00
Flask, Mc Kearin G II -42, Eagle & Franklin Frigate, Stain, Aqua, Pint 100.00
Flask, Mc Kearin G II -44, Eagle & Cornucopia, T.W.D. In Oval, Aqua 30.00
Flask, Mc Kearin G II -45, Cornucopia & Eagle, Aqua, 1/2 Pint 120.00
Flask, Mc Kearin G II -46, Cornucopia & Eagle With Shield, Aqua, 1/2 Pint 100.00
Flask, Mc Kearin G II -47, Eagle & Tree, Aquamarine, Quart 160.00
Flask, Mc Kearin G II -48, Eagle & Flag, Aqua, Quart 150.00
Flask, Mc Kearin G II -49, Aqua 18.00
Flask, Mc Kearin G II -50, Eagle & Stag, Aqua, 1/2 Pint .... 160.00 To 200.00
Flask, Mc Kearin G II -52, Eagle & Flag, Aqua, Pint ....75.00 To 100.00
Flask, Mc Kearin G II -53, Aqua, Pint 130.00
Flask, Mc Kearin G II -54, Eagle & Flag, Dark Amber, Pint 475.00
Flask, Mc Kearin G II -54, Eagle & Flag, Stain, Aqua, Pint 60.00
Flask, Mc Kearin G II -54, Olive Amber, Pint 450.00
Flask, Mc Kearin G II -55, Aqua, Quart 70.00
Flask, Mc Kearin G II -55, Eagle & Grapes, Stain, Aqua, Quart .... 35.00 To 50.00
Flask, Mc Kearin G II -56, Aquamarine, 1/2 Pint 100.00
Flask, Mc Kearin G II -60, Aqua, 1/2 Pint 200.00
Flask, Mc Kearin G II -60, Black Amber, 1/2 Pint 625.00

Flask, Mc Kearin G II -60, Eagle & Charter Oak, Amber, 1/2 Pint .... 260.00 To 500.00
Flask, Mc Kearin G II -61, Olive Green, Quart 110.00
Flask, Mc Kearin G II -62, Willington & Eagle, Green, Pint 120.00
Flask, Mc Kearin G II -63, Willington, Clear Deep Green, 1/2 Pint 100.00
Flask, Mc Kearin G II -65, Westford, Olive Amber, 1/2 Pint 100.00
Flask, Mc Kearin G II -68, Eagle, Yellow Amber, Pint 150.00
Flask, Mc Kearin G II -69, Cornucopia & Eagle, Light Green, 1/2 Pint 200.00
Flask, Mc Kearin G II -70, Amber, Pint 125.00
Flask, Mc Kearin G II -70, Double Eagle, Olive Amber, Pint 170.00
Flask, Mc Kearin G II -70, Double Eagle, Open Pontil, Olive Amber, 1/2 Pint 140.00
Flask, Mc Kearin G II -70, Olive Green, Pint 160.00
Flask, Mc Kearin G II -71, Eagle, Cornucopia, Amber, Pint 90.00
Flask, Mc Kearin G II -71, Olive Amber 175.00
Flask, Mc Kearin G II -72, Eagle & Cornucopia, Dark Olive Green, Pint 70.00
Flask, Mc Kearin G II -72, Eagle & Cornucopia, Olive Amber, Pint .... 35.00 To 65.00
Flask, Mc Kearin G II -73, Aqua, Pint 70.00
Flask, Mc Kearin G II -73, Cornucopia & Eagle, Olive Amber, Pint .... 55.00 To 75.00
Flask, Mc Kearin G II -73, Cornucopia & Eagle, Stain, Olive Amber 67.50
Flask, Mc Kearin G II -73, Cornucopia & Eagle, Keene Mark 110.00
Flask, Mc Kearin G II -73, Eagle, Cornucopia With X, Olive Green, Pint 90.00
Flask, Mc Kearin G II -76, Concentric Eagle, Green Yellow, Quart 1300.00
Flask, Mc Kearin G III -1, Aquamarine, 1/2 Pint 650.00
Flask, Mc Kearin G III -1, Green, 1/2 Pint 375.00
Flask, Mc Kearin G III -2, Aqua, 1/2 Pint .... 55.00 To 75.00
Flask, Mc Kearin G III -4, Cornucopia & Urn, Olive Amber, Pint 55.00
Flask, Mc Kearin G III -4, Open Pontil, Olive Green 65.00
Flask, Mc Kearin G III -7, Cornucopia, Urn, 6 Bars, Amber, 1/2 Pint 58.00
Flask, Mc Kearin G III -7, Cornucopia & Urn, Green, 1/2 Pint 55.00
Flask, Mc Kearin G III -7, Olive Amber, 1/2 Pint .... 50.00 To 55.00
Flask, Mc Kearin G III -7, Olive Green, 1/2 Pint .... 65.00 To 80.00
Flask, Mc Kearin G III -8, Cornucopia & Urn, Olive Green, 1/2 Pint 50.00
Flask, Mc Kearin G III -10, Cornucopia & Urn, Amber, 1/2 Pint 65.00
Flask, Mc Kearin G III -10, Cornucopia & Urn, Olive Green, 1/2 Pint 55.00
Flask, Mc Kearin G III -10, Cornucopia, Olive Amber, 102 Pint 75.00
Flask, Mc Kearin G III -12, Cornucopia & Produce, Amber, 1/2 Pint 35.00
Flask, Mc Kearin G III -12, Cornucopia & Urn, Olive Amber, 1/2 Pint 60.00
Flask, Mc Kearin G III -13, Cornucopia & Urn, Aqua, 1/2 Pint 38.00
Flask, Mc Kearin G III -15, Light Emerald Green 95.00
Flask, Mc Kearin G III -16, Cornucopia & Urn, Aqua, Pint .... 45.00 To 80.00
Flask, Mc Kearin G III -17, Cornucopia & Urn, Emerald Green, Pint 170.00
Flask, Mc Kearin G III -17, Cornucopia & Urn, Stain, Aqua, Pint 35.00
Flask, Mc Kearin G III -17, Emerald Green, Pint 175.00
Flask, Mc Kearin G III 73, Cornucopia & Eagle With X, Olive Green, Pint 80.00
Flask, Mc Kearin G IV -1, Eagle, Masonic, Blue Green, Pint 190.00
Flask, Mc Kearin G IV -1, Historical, Green 245.00
Flask, Mc Kearin G IV -1, Justus Perry, Masonic, Green, Pint 22.00
Flask, Mc Kearin G IV -1, Masonic Eagle, Iron Pontil, Clear Green Pint 175.00
Flask, Mc Kearin G IV -1, Masonic, Aquamarine 300.00
Flask, Mc Kearin G IV -1, Masonic, Eagle, Open Pontil, Light Green, Pint 200.00
Flask, Mc Kearin G IV -1, Masonic, Justus Perry, Blue Green, Pint 220.00
Flask, Mc Kearin G IV -2, Baltimore Fells Point, Light Puce, 1/2 Pint 450.00
Flask, Mc Kearin G IV -2, Masonic, Aquamarine, Pint 400.00
Flask, Mc Kearin G IV -3, Green, Pint 850.00
Flask, Mc Kearin G IV -3, J K B, Masonic, Eagle, Yellow Green, Pint 760.00
Flask, Mc Kearin G IV -3, Masonic & Eagle, Jkb, Green, Pint 850.00
Flask, Mc Kearin G IV -3, Masonic & Eagle, Stain, Aqua, Pint 270.00
Flask, Mc Kearin G IV -3, Peacock Green, Pint 375.00
Flask, Mc Kearin G IV -4, Corn For The World, Aqua 75.00
Flask, Mc Kearin G IV -4, Masonic Eagle, JKB , Light Green, Pint 400.00
Flask, Mc Kearin G IV -5, Masonic, Yellow Green 450.00
Flask, Mc Kearin G IV -9, Masonic Eagle, Deep Aqua, Pint 325.00
Flask, Mc Kearin G IV -12, Masonic Eagle, Deep Blue Green, Pint 675.00
Flask, Mc Kearin G IV -17, Masonic & Keene, Stain, Aqua, Pint 280.00
Flask, Mc Kearin G IV -17, Masonic, Amber 225.00
Flask, Mc Kearin G IV -17, Masonic, Eagle, Keene In Oval, Olive Green, Pint 178.00
Flask, Mc Kearin G IV -17, Masonic, Keene Eagle, Stain, Open Pontil, Pint 280.00

Flask, Mc Kearin G IV -18, Masonic & Eagle, Olive Amber, Pint	170.00
Flask, Mc Kearin G IV -19, Masonic & Eagle, Olive Amber, Pint	190.00
Flask, Mc Kearin G IV -19, Masonic, Amber	225.00
Flask, Mc Kearin G IV -20, Masonic, Amber	225.00
Flask, Mc Kearin G IV -21, Masonic & Eagle, Olive Amber, Pint	190.00
Flask, Mc Kearin G IV -24, Masonic, Amber	235.00
Flask, Mc Kearin G IV -24, Masonic, Olive Green, 1/2 Pint	190.00
Flask, Mc Kearin G IV -24, Keene Masonic, Olive Amber, 1/2 Pint	225.00
Flask, Mc Kearin G IV -27, Masonic, Aquamarine	125.00
Flask, Mc Kearin G IV -28, Clear Green, 1/2 Pint	225.00
Flask, Mc Kearin G IV -28, Masonic, Deep Aquamarine	350.00
Flask, Mc Kearin G IV -28, Masonic, Medium Green, 1/2 Pint	350.00
Flask, Mc Kearin G IV -31, Eagle & Farmer's Arms, Light Green, Pint	850.00
Flask, Mc Kearin G IV -32, Amber, Pint	150.00
Flask, Mc Kearin G IV -32, Historical, Yellow	265.00
Flask, Mc Kearin G IV -32, Masonic & Eagle, Blue Green, Pint	210.00
Flask, Mc Kearin G IV -32, Green, Pint	525.00
Flask, Mc Kearin G IV -34, Masonic & Franklin Frigate, Stain, Aqua, Pint	40.00
Flask, Mc Kearin G IV -34, Masonic, Pale Green	160.00
Flask, Mc Kearin G IV -37, American Eagle & Masonic Arch, Aqua, Pint	100.00
Flask, Mc Kearin G IV -37, Masonic & Eagle, Stain, Aqua, Pint	85.00
Flask, Mc Kearin G IV -37, Masonic, Clear	105.00
Flask, Mc Kearin G IV -37, Masonic, Pale Green	100.00
Flask, Mc Kearin G IV -38, Masonic, Aquamarine	25.00
Flask, Mc Kearin G IV -39, Clasped Hands & Eagle, Stain, Light Green, Quart	130.00
Flask, Mc Kearin G IV -40, Clasped Hands & Eagle, Masonic, Aqua, Pint	20.00
Flask, Mc Kearin G IV -42 Type, Eagle Side, Yellowish Emerald Green, Quart	115.00
Flask, Mc Kearin G IV -42, Calabash, Aqua	50.00
Flask, Mc Kearin G IV -42, Eagle & Clasped Hands, Calabash, OP , Quart	40.00
Flask, Mc Kearin G IV -42, Eagle & Clasped Hands, Calabash, Quart	40.00
Flask, Mc Kearin G IV -42, Masonic, Aquamarine	25.00 To 48.00
Flask, Mc Kearin G V-1, Success To The Railroad, Aqua, Pint	210.00
Flask, Mc Kearin G V-2, Locomotive, Olive	360.00
Flask, Mc Kearin G V-3, Double Success To The Railroad, Olive Amber, Pint	200.00
Flask, Mc Kearin G V-3, Success To R.R., Olive Amber, Pint	150.00
Flask, Mc Kearin G V-4, Olive	360.00
Flask, Mc Kearin G V-4, Olive Green, Pint	175.00
Flask, Mc Kearin G V-5, Double Success To The Railroad, Olive Amber, Pint	170.00
Flask, Mc Kearin G V-5, Success To The Railroad, Amber, Pint	135.00
Flask, Mc Kearin G V-5, Success To The Railroad, Olive Green, Pint	160.00
Flask, Mc Kearin V-6, Dark Amber	190.00
Flask, Mc Kearin G V-6, Success To The Railroad, Olive Amber, Pint	210.00
Flask, Mc Kearin G V-8, Success To The Railroad & Eagle, Olive Amber, Pint	190.00
Flask, Mc Kearin G V-9, Railroad & Eagle, Open Pontil, Olive Amber, Pint	160.00
Flask, Mc Kearin G V-10, Dark Amber, Shade To Very Light At Shoulder	245.00
Flask, Mc Kearin G V-10, Lowell Railroad & Eagle, Olive Green, 1/2 Pint	200.00
Flask, Mc Kearin G V-10, Lowell Railroad, Olive Amber, 1/2 Pint	200.00
Flask, Mc Kearin G VI -1, Baltimore, A Little More Grape Capt.Gragg, Aqua	275.00
Flask, Mc Kearin G VI -2, Pale Yellow Green, 1/2 Pint	30.00
Flask, Mc Kearin G VI -2, Sloop & Baltimore Monument, Amethyst, 1/2 Pint	800.00
Flask, Mc Kearin G VI -2, Yellow Green, 1/2 Pint	525.00
Flask, Mc Kearin G VI -4, Aqua, Pint	80.00
Flask, Mc Kearin G VI -4, Corn & Baltimore Monument, Citron, Quart	375.00
Flask, Mc Kearin G VI -4, Corn For The World & Baltimore, Amber, Quart	300.00
Flask, Mc Kearin G VI -4, Corn For The World, Aqua, Quart	90.00
Flask, Mc Kearin G VI -4, Corn For The World, Flat Collar, Aqua, Quart	90.00
Flask, Mc Kearin G VI -4, Golden Amber, Quart	300.00
Flask, Mc Kearin G VI -7, Corn For The World & Monument, Green, 1/2 Pint	650.00
Flask, Mc Kearin G VI -106, Traveler's Companion, Aquamarine, 1/2 Pint	250.00
Flask, Mc Kearin G VII -29, Sunburst, Open Pontil, Bluish Green, 3/4 Pint	260.00
Flask, Mc Kearin G VIII -1, Sunburst, Olive Amber, Pint	700.00
Flask, Mc Kearin G VIII -1, Sunburst, Yellow Green, Pint	275.00
Flask, Mc Kearin G VIII -2, Clear Grass Green	315.00
Flask, Mc Kearin G VIII -2, Deep Yellow Green, Pint	300.00
Flask, Mc Kearin G VIII -2, Sunburst, Green, Pint	325.00
Flask, Mc Kearin G VIII -2, Sunburst, Yellow Green, Pint	300.00

Flask, Mc Kearin G VIII -3, Sunburst, Olive Amber, Pint 350.00
Flask, Mc Kearin G VIII -8, Sunburst, Keene, Olive Amber, Pint .... 250.00 To 290.00
Flask, Mc Kearin G VII -9, Olive Amber 250.00
Flask, Mc Kearin G VIII -9, Sunburst, Keene, Amber, 1/2 Pint 250.00
Flask, Mc Kearin G VIII -10, Sunburst, Keene, Olive, Green, 1/2 Pint 175.00
Flask, Mc Kearin G VIII -10, Sunburst, Olive Amber, 1/2 Pint 250.00
Flask, Mc Kearin G VIII -11, Sunburst, Green, 1/2 Pint 600.00
Flask, Mc Kearin G VIII -16, Sunburst, Corrugated, Yellow Olive, 1/2 Pint 175.00
Flask, Mc Kearin G VIII -18, Sunburst, Olive Green, 1/2 Pint 290.00
Flask, Mc Kearin G VIII -20, Sunburst, Sand Check, Aqua, Pint 80.00
Flask, Mc Kearin G VIII -21, Sunburst, Aqua, Pint 90.00
Flask, Mc Kearin G VIII -22, Sunburst, Amber, Pint 1100.00
Flask, Mc Kearin G VIII -24, Oval Sunburst, Medial Rib, Aqua, 1/2 Pint 150.00
Flask, Mc Kearin G VIII -25, Oval Sunburst, Aqua, 1/2 Pint 160.00
Flask, Mc Kearin G VIII -25, Sunburst, Pale Green, 1/2 Pint 175.00
Flask, Mc Kearin G VIII -26, Sunburst, Light Green, Pint 375.00
Flask, Mc Kearin G VIII -27, Clear, 1/2 Pint 230.00
Flask, Mc Kearin G VIII -27, Sunburst, Clear, 1/2 Pint 200.00
Flask, Mc Kearin G VIII -28, Sunburst, Aqua, 1/2 Pint 190.00
Flask, Mc Kearin G VIII -29, Medium Blue Green, 3/4 Pint 160.00
Flask, Mc Kearin G VIII -29, Sunburst, Bluish Green, 3/4 Pint 260.00
Flask, Mc Kearin G VIII -29, Sunburst, Clear Green, 3/4 Pint 225.00
Flask, Mc Kearin G IX -1, Historical, Aqua 55.00
Flask, Mc Kearin G IX -1, Scroll, Aqua, Quart 40.00
Flask, Mc Kearin G IX-1, Violin, Clear Green, Quart 225.00
Flask, Mc Kearin G IX -1, Violin, Deep Amber, Quart 225.00
Flask, Mc Kearin G IX -2a, Scroll, Yellow Green, Quart 140.00
Flask, Mc Kearin G IX -6, Scroll, Aqua, Pint 120.00
Flask, Mc Kearin G IX -6, Scroll, Aqua, Quart 100.00
Flask, Mc Kearin G IX -8, Light Green 59.00
Flask, Mc Kearin G IX -10, Scroll, Aqua, Pint 15.00
Flask, Mc Kearin G IX -10, Scroll, Cornflower Blue, Pint 220.00
Flask, Mc Kearin G IX -10, Scroll, Iridescent Blue, Pint 180.00
Flask, Mc Kearin G IX -10, Scrolled Violin, Aqua, Pint 50.00
Flask, Mc Kearin G IX -11, Aqua 48.00
Flask, Mc Kearin G IX -11, Bubbles In Neck, Aqua, Pint 30.00
Flask, Mc Kearin G IX -11, Deep Blue Band At Waist, Sapphire Blue 150.00
Flask, Mc Kearin G IX -11, Medium Emerald Green 135.00
Flask, Mc Kearin G IX -11, Scroll, Open Pontil, Aqua, Pint .... 35.00 To 40.00
Flask, Mc Kearin G IX -11, Scroll, Script Lietters M C, Blue Aqua, Pint 40.00
Flask, Mc Kearin G IX -11, Scroll, Violin, Open Pontil, Light Blue 45.00
Flask, Mc Kearin G IX -13, Iron Pontil, Double Collared Mouth, Pint 40.00
Flask, Mc Kearin G IX -14, Scroll, Stain, Aqua, Pint 30.00
Flask, Mc Kearin G IX -17, Blue Aqua 33.00
Flask, Mc Kearin G IX -20, Scroll, Aqua, Pint 32.50
Flask, Mc Kearin G IX -25, Light Turquoise 44.00
Flask, Mc Kearin G IX -29, Scroll, Aqua, 2 1/2 Quart .... 175.00 To 230.00
Flask, Mc Kearin G IX -31, Scroll, Aqua, 1/2 Pint 35.00
Flask, Mc Kearin G IX -32, Scroll, Aqua, 1/2 Pint .... 40.00 To 50.00
Flask, Mc Kearin G IX -33, Scroll, Double Collared Mouth, Cloudy, 1/2 Pint 15.00
Flask, Mc Kearin G IX -34, Scroll, Aqua 75.00
Flask, Mc Kearin G IX -34, Scroll, Stained, Aqua, 1/2 Pint 35.00
Flask, Mc Kearin G IX -34, Violin, Aquamarine, 1/2 Pint 100.00
Flask, Mc Kearin G IX -36, Aqua 70.00
Flask, Mc Kearin G IX -36, Powder Blue, 1/2 Pint 35.00
Flask, Mc Kearin G IX -37, Aqua 55.00
Flask, Mc Kearin G IX -37, Long Outward Flared Neck, Bluish Aqua, 1/2 Pint 32.50
Flask, Mc Kearin G IX -38, BP & B On One Side, Yellow Green, 1/2 Pint 40.00
Flask, Mc Kearin G IX -43, Scroll & J.R.& Son, Corset Shape, Aqua, Pint 250.00
Flask, Mc Kearin G IX -43, Scroll, Corset Waist, Aqua, Pint 250.00
Flask, Mc Kearin G IX -44, Aquamarine, Pint 240.00
Flask, Mc Kearin G IX -46, Aqua, Quart 275.00
Flask, Mc Kearin G IX -47, Deep Aqua, Pint 650.00
Flask, Mc Kearin G IX -47, Fleur-De-Lis & Union Factory, Aqua, Pint 550.00
Flask, Mc Kearin G IX -50, Light Blue Green, Quart 600.00
Flask, Mc Kearin G IX -51, Scroll, Heart Medallion, Blue Aqua, Quart 825.00

Flask, Mc Kearin G IX , Scroll, Aqua, Pint .... 27.50 To 35.00
Flask, Mc Kearin G IX , Scroll, Aquamarine, Pint 30.00
Flask, Mc Kearin G IX , Scroll, Banded Neck Aqua, Pint 30.00
Flask, Mc Kearin G IX , Scroll, Banded Neck, Aqua, Quart 35.00
Flask, Mc Kearin G IX , Scroll, Medium Green, Pint 70.00
Flask, Mc Kearin G IX , Scroll, Pale Blue 30.00
Flask, Mc Kearin G X-1, Game, Stag & Tree, Ground Lip, Aqua, Pint 45.00
Flask, Mc Kearin G X-1, Stag & Tree, Stain, Aqua, Pint 100.00
Flask, Mc Kearin G X-3, Aqua, 1/2 Pint 100.00
Flask, Mc Kearin G X-3, Sheaf Of Rye & Grapes, Stain, Aqua, 1/2 Pint 45.00
Flask, Mc Kearin G X-4, General Taylor, Puce, Pint 650.00
Flask, Mc Kearin G X-5, General Taylor, Aqua, Pint 170.00
Flask, Mc Kearin G X-6, Red Amber, 1/2 Pint 490.00
Flask, Mc Kearin G X-8, Aqua, 1/2 Pint 70.00
Flask, Mc Kearin G X-8, Blue, 1/2 Pint 1150.00
Flask, Mc Kearin G X-8, Sloop & Star, Stain, Aqua, 1/2 Pint 85.00
Flask, Mc Kearin G X-8, Sloop & 8-Pointed Star, Light Green, 1/2 Pint 250.00
Flask, Mc Kearin G X-8, Sloop & 8-Pointed Star, Medium Green, 1/2 Pint 275.00
Flask, Mc Kearin G X-12, Stong Man & Two Gentlemen, Clear, 1/2 Pint 170.00
Flask, Mc Kearin G X-14, Murdock & Cassell & Zanesville, Ohio, Green, Pint 525.00
Flask, Mc Kearin G X-15, Aqua, Pint 30.00
Flask, Mc Kearin G X-15, Summer & Winter, Aqua, Pint 35.00
Flask, Mc Kearin G X-15, Summer & Winter, Dark Puce Almost Amethyst, Pint 550.00
Flask, Mc Kearin G X-15, Summer & Winter, Stain, Aqua, Pint 22.50
Flask, Mc Kearin G X-17, Summer & Summer, Aqua, Pint 35.00
Flask, Mc Kearin G X-18, Summer & Summer, Aqua, Quart 30.00
Flask, Mc Kearin G X-19, Summer & Winter, Aqua, Quart .... 50.00 To 75.00
Flask, Mc Kearin G X-19, Summer & Winter, Stain, Aqua, Quart 50.00
Flask, Mc Kearin G X-20, Steamboat & Sheaf Of Wheat 160.00
Flask, Mc Kearin G X-22, Log Cabin, Hard Cider, Aqua, Pint 850.00
Flask, Mc Kearin I-50, Historical, Aqua 50.00
Flask, Medium Swirl, Pulled Neck, Amethyst, 1/2 Pint 160.00
Flask, Mercury 8.25
Flask, Merry Christmas Label Under Glass, Clear, 1/2 Pint 50.00
Flask, Midwestern, Swirled To Left 60.00
Flask, Milk Glass, Blue Zigzag Overlay 100.00
Flask, Milk Glass, Klondyke 35.00
Flask, Moorman, C.P., Whittle, Pint 150.00
Flask, Mounted Soldier & Dog, Aqua, Quart 45.00
Flask, Mounted Soldier & Dog, Citron, Quart 340.00
Flask, Nailsea, Double, White Looping, 10 In. .... *Illus* 95.00
Flask, Nailsea, Reclining, Purple & White Loopings, Cork Stopper 50.00
Flask, Narrow Flutes, Extended Neck, Applied Handle, Green, 1/2 Pint 150.00
Flask, Narrow Flutes, Pulled Neck, Green, Small Size 50.00

Flask, Nailsea, Double, White Looping, 10 In.

Flask, **Narrow Stripes On Each Side**, Collared Neck, Olive Green 220.00
Flask, **New England**, Globular, Yellow Olive, 6 3/4 In. 70.00
Flask, **New England**, Ludlow, Chestnut, Yellow Olive Green, 6 1/2 In. 45.00
Flask, **Norwegian Lion & Shield Embossed**, Swirled Ribs, Aqua 55.00
Flask, **Ohio**, Globular, Aqua, 1/2 Pint 100.00
Flask, **Ohio**, Globular, Club Shape, Broken Right Swirl, Aqua, 8 In.High 650.00
Flask, **Ohio**, Globular, Swirled To Left, Dark Amber 300.00
Flask, **Ohio**, Grandfather, Globular, Swirled To Right, Amber 350.00
Flask, **Ohio**, Swirl, Open Pontil, Long Neck, Aqua 65.00
Flask, **Ohio**, Swirled To Left, Aqua 80.00
Flask, **Ohio**, Swirled To Left, Light Green, Pint 70.00
Flask, **Ohio**, Swirled, Collared Neck, Aqua 80.00
Flask, **One Strap**, Amber, Pint 21.00
Flask, **Onion**, Collared, Scarred Base, Amber, Pair 22.50
Flask, **Onion**, Dutch, Open Pontil, Olive 29.00
Flask, **Opal Loopings**, Amethyst, Small Size 200.00
Flask, **Open Pontil**, Applied Top, Aqua, Quart 45.00
Flask, **Oval**, Broad Flutes, Extended Neck, Light Green 40.00
Flask, **Oval**, Expanded Ribs, Medium Green 30.00
Flask, **Oval**, Opal Application Around Center, Opal Neck, Amber 100.00
Flask, **Oval**, White Opal Swirls, Double Applied Spandrels 25.00
Flask, **Oval**, White Stripings, Cranberry 50.00
Flask, **Patent**, Amber, Pint 17.50
Flask, **Peace**, Raised Clasped Hands, Eagle & U.S.In Shield, Dated 1838 .... 125.00
Flask, **Persian**, Saddle, Open Pontil, Green, Quart 10.00
Flask, **Personal**, Initials C.A.M., Pontil, Aqua 16.00
Flask, **Peter Small**, Phila., Amber, Quart 17.50
Flask, **Pewter Screw Type Stopper**, C.1866 .... 12.00
Flask, **Picnic**, Clear, Small 2.50
Flask, **Picnic**, Amber, 1/2 Pint 35.00
Flask, **Picnic**, Fine Old Rye Whiskey On Label, Clear, 1/2 Pint 3.00
Flask, **Picnic**, Grandfather's Clock Embossed, Star, Clear, 1/2 Pint 17.50
Flask, **Picnic**, Merry Christmas & Happy New Year, Embossed 23.00
Flask, **Picnic**, Merry Christmas On Label, Clear, 1/4 Pint 7.00
Flask, **Picnic**, Star & Grandfather's Clock, Clear, 1/2 Pint 15.00
Flask, **Picnic**, Sunburst Pattern, Amethyst 12.00
Flask, **Picnic**, Web Design With Clock, Clear, 1/2 Pint 15.00
Flask, **Pike's Peak Traveler & Hunter**, Olive Amber, Pint 380.00
Flask, **Pike's Peak**, Aqua, Pint 40.00
Flask, **Pike's Peak**, Aqua, Quart 100.00
Flask, **Pike's Peak**, For Not Embossed, Perched Eagle, Aqua, 1/2 Pint 60.00
Flask, **Pistol**, Brass, 4 1/4 In.Long 45.00
Flask, **Pitkin Type**, Light Green, Pint 75.00
Flask, **Pitkin Type**, Swirled, Aqua, Pint 70.00
Flask, **Pitkin Type**, Swirled, Blue Green, Pint 90.00
Flask, **Pitkin**, Corncob, Swirled To Left, Clear Green, Pint 225.00
Flask, **Pitkin**, Corncob, Swirled To Left, Olive Green, 1/2 Pint 170.00
Flask, **Pitkin**, Corncob, Swirled To Right, Amber, Pint 320.00
Flask, **Pitkin**, Corncob, Swirled To Right, Light Green, Pint 200.00
Flask, **Pitkin**, Double Post, Pontil, Olive Green, 1/2 Pint 180.00
Flask, **Pitkin**, Left Swirl, Cannot Stand By Itself, Aqua, 1/2 Pint 325.00
Flask, **Pitkin**, Left Swirl, Double Pattern, Vertical Ribs, Green, 1/2 Pint 250.00
Flask, **Pitkin**, Left Swirl, Light Olive Green, Less Than 1/2 Pint 275.00
Flask, **Pitkin**, Left Swirl, Vertical Ribs, Dark Olive Green, 1/2 Pint 250.00
Flask, **Pitkin**, Light Green, Pint 140.00
Flask, **Pitkin**, Midwestern, Double Post, Light Green, Pint 100.00
Flask, **Pitkin**, Midwestern, Globular, Swirl, Open Pontil, Aqua 42.50
Flask, **Pitkin**, Midwestern, 20 Vertical & Swirled Ribs, Green 305.00
Flask, **Pitkin**, New England, Swirled To Left, Open Pontil, Olive Green 180.00
Flask, **Pitkin**, Olive Amber, 1/2 Pint 180.00
Flask, **Pitkin**, Open Pontil, Olive Green, 1/2 Pint 180.00
Flask, **Pitkin**, Ribbed Swirl, Green, Pint 180.00
Flask, **Pitkin**, Right Swirl, Coarse Pattern, Vertical Ribs, Olive Green, Pint 325.00
Flask, **Pitkin**, Right Swirl, Double Pattern, Vertical Ribs, Olive Green, Pint 325.00
Flask, **Pitkin**, Right Swirl, Green, 1/2 Pint 250.00
Flask, **Pitkin**, Right Swirl, Olive Green, Pint 325.00

Flask, Pitkin, Right Swirl, Short Neck, Yellow Green, Pint	325.00
Flask, Pitkin, Right Swirl, Vertical Ribs, Light Olive Green, 1/2 Pint	250.00
Flask, Pitkin, Right Swirl, Vertical Ribs, Olive Amber, 1/2 Pint	250.00
Flask, Pitkin, Stain, Aqua, Pint	75.00
Flask, Pitkin, Swirled To Left, Olive Green, 1/2 Pint	140.00
Flask, Pitkin, Swirled To Right, Corn Cob, Medium Green, 1/2 Pint	170.00
Flask, Pitkin, Swirled To Right, Corn Cob, Olive Green, 1/2 Pint	130.00
Flask, Pitkin, Swirled To Right, Emerald Green	175.00
Flask, Pitkin, Swirled, Amber	240.00
Flask, Pitkin, Swirled, Olive Green	175.00 To 200.00
Flask, Pitkin, 32 Ribs, Broken Swirl, New England, Olive, 6 1/2 In.	150.00
Flask, Pitkin, 32 Ribs, Broken Swirl, Olive Green To Golden, 5 3/4 In.	200.00
Flask, Pittsburgh, Double Eagle, Aqua	40.00
Flask, Pittsburgh, Double Eagle, Sheared Lip, Open Pontil, Apple Green	85.00
Flask, Plated, Health To The Fairest, 1/2 Pint	9.00
Flask, Pocket, Bininger's Traveler's Guide, Embossed, Amber	250.00
Flask, Pocket, Digestive Cordial, Amber, 1/4 Pint	60.00
Flask, Pocket, Leather, Silver Design	18.00
Flask, Pocket, Pull-Up, Opaque White Applied Loopings, N.Y., C.1770, Green	175.00
Flask, Pocket, Sheared Lip, Pontil, Aqua	40.00
Flask, Pocket, Silver Plate, Embossed	8.00
Flask, Pottery, Brown Glaze, 1/2 Pint	15.00
Flask, Pottery, Flat Oval, Pint, 7 In.High	15.00
Flask, Pottery, Footed Base Marked 504, Wicker Design, Gray & Red Brown	30.00
Flask, Powder, Beaded Design	20.00
Flask, Powder, Gourd	25.00
Flask, Powder, Man & Dog, Man Shooting Gun	25.00
Flask, Prohibition, Buckskin Covering, Pint	4.00
Flask, Pumpkin Seed, Amethyst	6.00
Flask, Pumpkin Seed, BIMAL , Dug, Clear, 1/2 Pint	3.00
Flask, Pumpkin Seed, Flattish, Clear, 4 3/4 In.High	4.00
Flask, Pumpkin Seed, Flattish, 6 1/2 In.Tall	4.50
Flask, Pumpkin Seed, Screw Top, Amber	11.00
Flask, Pumpkinseed, Amber, 10 Oz.	25.00
Flask, Pumpkinseed, Clear, 1/2 Pint	7.50
Flask, Pumpkinseed, Spider Web, Clear, 1/2 Pint	6.50
Flask, Quilted, Poison, Olive Green, 1/2 Pint	170.00
Flask, Quilted, 1/2 Pint	8.00
Flask, Railroad & Eagle, Pontil, Olive Amber, Pint	160.00
Flask, Ravenna Glass Co., Traveler's Companion With Star, Aqua, Pint	35.00
Flask, Ravenna Glass Co., Traveler's Companion, Amber Quart	310.00
Flask, Roth & Co., San Francisco, Embossed, Amber	110.00
Flask, Rye-Rake-Fork, Baltimore Glass Works, Aqua, Quart	95.00
Flask, S.C.Dispensary With Palm Tree, Clear, Pint	30.00
Flask, S.M.& Co., N.Y., Pontil, Brown .... *Illus*	175.00

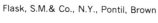

Flask, S.M.& Co., N.Y., Pontil, Brown

Flask, S.Mc Kee & Co., On Bottom, 1/2 Pint	15.00
Flask, Saddle, Applied Threads Around Neck, Green	10.00
Flask, Saddle, Olive Amber	20.00
Flask, Saddle, Persian, Crude Lip, Rough Pontil, Amber, 8 1/2 In.	10.00
Flask, Saddle, Swirled To Right, Broad Swirls, Sapphire Blue	80.00
Flask, Sailboat & Sunburst, Sheared Lip, Aqua, 1/2 Pint	45.00
Flask, Sailing Vessel & Columbian Jubilee, Amber, Pint	10.00
Flask, Scattered White Splotches, Medium Green	80.00
Flask, Scent, Ribbed, Embossed Heart & Star, Clear, 1/2 Pint	135.00
Flask, Scroll, Amber	15.00
Flask, Scroll, Aqua, Pint	40.00 To 50.00
Flask, Scroll, Aqua, Quart	60.00
Flask, Scroll, Aqua, 1/2 Pint	36.00 To 60.00
Flask, Scroll, B.P.& B., Aqua, 1/2 Pint	110.00
Flask, Scroll, Blown, 2 Stars On Each Side, Midwestern, C.1830-45, Aquamarine	125.00
Flask, Scroll, Cobalt Blue, Pint	500.00
Flask, Scroll, Dark Amber, Quart	175.00
Flask, Scroll, Deep Amber, 1/2 Pint	150.00 To 200.00
Flask, Scroll, Emerald Green, 1/2 Pint	350.00
Flask, Scroll, Graphite Pontil, Cornflower Blue, Quart	300.00
Flask, Scroll, Green, 1/2 Pint	175.00
Flask, Scroll, Lemon Green, 1/2 Pint	225.00
Flask, Scroll, Medium Amber, 1/2 Pint	125.00
Flask, Scroll, Medium Blue, Pint	350.00
Flask, Scroll, Olive Green, Pint	200.00
Flask, Scroll, Sheared Lip, Aqua, 1/2 Pint	48.00
Flask, Scroll, Tubular Pontil, 4 Stars, Sheared Mouth, Aqua, Pint	70.00
Flask, Scroll, Yellow Green, Pint	225.00
Flask, Seeing Eye, Amber, Pint	140.00
Flask, Sheaf Of Wheat & Kensington Glass Works, Aqua, Quart	130.00
Flask, Sheaf Of Wheat & Tree With Bird, Calabash, Aqua	50.00
Flask, Sheaf Of Wheat & Westford Glass Co., Amber, Pint	80.00
Flask, Sheaf Of Wheat & Westford Glass Co., Deep Amber	115.00
Flask, Sheaf Of Wheat & Westford Glass Co., Green, Pint	70.00
Flask, Sheaf Of Wheat & Westford Glass Co., Olive Amber, Pint	75.00
Flask, Sheaf Of Wheat & Westford Glass Co., Pint, Green	70.00
Flask, Sheaf Of Wheat & Westford Glass Co., Rolled Lip, Amber, Pint	120.00
Flask, Sheaf Of Wheat & 8 Pointed Star, Traveler's Companion, Red Amber	125.00
Flask, Sheaf Of Wheat, Calabash, Aqua	40.00
Flask, Sheaf, Traveler's Companion, Amber, Quart	120.00
Flask, Snap Case, Amber, 1/2 Pint, 6 1/4 In.High	17.50
Flask, Soldier & Dancer, Stain, Aqua, Pint	55.00
Flask, Soldier & German Inscription, Pontil, Aqua, 1/2 Pint	40.00
Flask, South Carolina Dispensary With Palm Tree, Amber, 1/2 Pint	100.00
Flask, South Carolina Dispensary With Palm Tree, Aqua, Pint	72.50
Flask, South Carolina Dispensary With Palm Tree, Clear, Pint	20.00
Flask, Spiritus Frumenti, Spider & Web, Metal Labels, Amber, 1/2 Pint	15.00
Flask, Spring Garden Glass Works & Cabin, Aqua, Pint	55.00
Flask, Spring Garden Glass Works With Anchor & Cabin, Aqua, Pint	60.00
Flask, Spring Garden Glass Works, Anchor & Cabin, Aqua, Pint	60.00
Flask, Spring Garden Glass Works, Aqua, Pint	50.00 To 85.00
Flask, Spring Garden, George Washington & Cabin, Stain, Aqua, Pint	35.00
Flask, Springfield Glass Works & Cabin, Aqua, 1/2 Pint	70.00
Flask, Stag & Hunting Equipment, Amethyst, 1/2 Pint	95.00
Flask, Stag & Hunting Equipment, Open Pontil, Amethyst, 1/2 Pint	95.00
Flask, Stag & Wild Boar, Amethyst, 1/2 Pint	70.00
Flask, Stanley & Co., Spruance, Pint	150.00
Flask, Stanley & Co., Spruance, 1/2 Pint	135.00
Flask, Star Center, Sheaf Of Wheat, Pitchfork, & Rake, Olive Amber, Quart	75.00
Flask, Stoddard Double Eagle, N.H. In Oval, Amber, Pint	130.00
Flask, Stoddard, Applied Lip, Bubbles, Red Amber, Pint	12.50
Flask, Stoddard, Double Eagle, Amber, Pint	90.00
Flask, Stoddard, Double Eagle, Amber, Quart	80.00
Flask, Stoddard, Double Eagle, Olive Amber, 1/2 Pint	62.00
Flask, Stoddard, Double Eagle, Open Pontil, Amber, Pint	80.00
Flask, Stoddard, Olive Green, Pint	22.00

Flask, **Stoddard**, Patent Embossed, Olive Green, Pint 30.00
Flask, **Stoddard**, Stubby, Pontil, Olive Amber 35.00
Flask, **Stoddard**, Stubby, Pontil, Olive Green 18.00
Flask, **Stoddard**, Three-Part Mold, Embossed Week's Glass Works 92.50
Flask, **Stoneware**, Pint 10.00
Flask, **Strap**, Childs & Co.Wines & Liquors, Honey Amber, Quart 22.00
Flask, **Strap**, Mulls Grape Tonic Rock Island III, Amber, 7 5/8 In. 10.00
Flask, **Strickland**, Pocket, Amber 40.00
Flask, **Stripes On Each Side**, Light Green 80.00
Flask, **Success To The Railroad**, Pontiled, Olive Green 60.00
Flask, **Sunburst**, Pontil, Bluish Green, 3/4 Pint 260.00
Flask, **Swirl To Right**, Globular, Open Pontil, Light Green, Quart 60.00
Flask, **Swirled Pitkin**, Amber 240.00
Flask, **Swirled To Left**, Broad Swirls, Pewter Collar, Amber, 1/2 Pint 70.00
Flask, **Teardrop**, Pontil, Sheared Lip, Olive Green 50.00
Flask, **The Father Of His Country**, General Taylor .... *Color* XX.XX
Flask, **Traveler's Companion & Ravenna Glass Co.**, Aqua, Pint 65.00
Flask, **Traveler's Companion & Sheaf**, Amber, Quart ....40.00 To 110.00
Flask, **Traveler's Companion & Star**, Aqua, 1/2 Pint 55.00
Flask, **Traveler's Companion & 8-Pointed Star**, Light Aqua, 1/2 Pint 60.00
Flask, **Traveler's Companion With Star**, Amber, Pint 180.00
Flask, **Traveler's Companion**, Aqua, 1/2 Pint 55.00
Flask, **Traveler's Companion**, Ravenna, Amber, Quart 310.00
Flask, **Traveler's Companion**, Ravenna, 8-Pointed Star, Blue 70.00
Flask, **Tyrolean Type**, Swirled To Right, One Flat Side, Pewter Cap, Blue 125.00
Flask, **U.S.A.Hospital Dep't**, Bubbles, Olive 40.00
Flask, **Union & Cannon With Flag**, Pint 60.00
Flask, **Union & Cannon**, Aqua, Quart ....60.00 To 70.00
Flask, **Union & Clasped Hands**, Aqua 47.50
Flask, **Union & Eagle**, Aqua, Quart ....25.00 To 40.00
Flask, **Union & W.Franks & Sons**, Aqua, 8 In. .... *Illus* 100.00
Flask, **Union Dual**, Clear, 1/2 Pint 3.00
Flask, **Union With Eagle**, Dark Amber, 1/2 Pint 60.00
Flask, **Union**, Aqua, Pint 25.00
Flask, **Union**, Calabash, Embossed ARS , Masonic Emblem, Aqua, Quart 65.00
Flask, **Union**, Clasped Hands & Crest, Eagle With 13 Stars, Blue, Blown 50.00
Flask, **Union**, Clasped Hands & Eagle With Pittsburg, Pa., Aqua, Pint 35.00
Flask, **Union**, Clasped Hands In Shield, Eagle & Banner, Aqua, Pint 25.00
Flask, **Union**, Clasped Hands, Aqua, Quart 20.00
Flask, **Union**, Clasped Hands, Eagle & A.& Co.Reverse 55.00
Flask, **Union**, Clasped Hands, Eagle, Pittsburg, Pa., Open Pontil, Aqua, Pint 35.00
Flask, **Union**, Clasped Hands, Light Blue, 1/2 Pint 35.00
Flask, **Union**, Clasped Hands, Noel Tomas, Aqua, Pint 50.00
Flask, **Union**, Clasped Hands, 13 Stars, Dove With Ribbon, Aqua, Pint 75.00
Flask, **Union**, Eagle, Calabash, Aqua, Quart 37.50
Flask, **Union**, Eagle, H & S, Masonic Emblem, 13 Stars, Aqua, Pint 75.00

Flask,
Union & W.Franks & Sons,
Aqua, 8 In.

Flask, **Union**, Embossed Old Rye, Pittsburgh, Single Collar, Aqua, Pint	70.00
Flask, **Union**, Oval, Clear	2.00
Flask, **Union**, 12 Star, Dove	75.00
Flask, **Vergas Spiced Brandy**, Aqua, Pint	4.00
Flask, **Vertical Lines Over Entire Sides**, Amber, Pint	17.50
Flask, **Vertical Rib**, Amber, 1/2 Pint	12.50
Flask, **Vertically Ribbed**, Amber, Pint	17.50
Flask, **Vertically Ribbed**, Improved Pontil, Stain, Aqua, Pint	25.00
Flask, **Vinol**, ABM , Amber	5.00
Flask, **Vinol**, Private Mold, Amber	5.00
Flask, **Violin With Merry Christmas Label**, Clear, 1/2 Pint	5.00
Flask, **Warranted Oval**, Squarish, Amethyst, 14 Oz.	3.00
Flask, **Warranted**, Side Bands, Amethyst, Pint	3.25
Flask, **Warranted**, Side Bands, Amethyst, 6 Oz.	2.95
Flask, **Warranted**, Side Bands, Amethyst, 7 Oz.	2.95
Flask, **Warranted**, 1/2 Pint	3.00
Flask, **Washington & Jackson**, Amber	130.00
Flask, **Washington & Jackson**, Cloudy, Open Pontil, Olive Amber, Pint	130.00
Flask, **Washington & Taylor**, Aqua, Quart	50.00
Flask, **Washington & Taylor**, Blob Top, Pontil, Aqua, Pint	75.00
Flask, **Washington & Taylor**, Bridgeton, N.J., Aqua, Pint	50.00
Flask, **Washington & Taylor**, Cobalt, Quart	40.00
Flask, **Washington & Taylor**, Embossed, Aqua, Pint	75.00
Flask, **Washington & Taylor**, Flared & Sheared Lip, Tubular Pontil, 1/2 Pint	85.00
Flask, **Washington & Taylor**, Open Pontil, Aqua, Quart	35.00
Flask, **Washington & Taylor**, Open Pontil, Stain, Aqua	45.00
Flask, **Washington & Taylor**, Tapered Lip, Aqua, Quart	70.00
Flask, **Washington & Taylor**, Wine Color	525.00
Flask, **Washington**, Sheaf Of Rye, Double Collared Lip, Aqua, 1/2 Pint	85.00
Flask, **West Willington Glass Co.& Sheaf Of Wheat**, Red Amber, Quart	175.00
Flask, **Westford Glass Works & Sheath Of Wheat**, Olive Amber, 1/2 Pint	95.00
Flask, **Wharton's Whiskey**, Pocket, Blue, 1/4 Pint	200.00
Flask, **Whiskey**, Civil War Officer's, Field, Pewter Cap, Leather Covered	12.50
Flask, **Whiskey**, For Pocket Or Purse, Silver Plate Screw Cap	7.50
Flask, **Whiskey**, Sterling Bottom & Closure, 8 In.	20.00
Flask, **Whitney Glass Works On Base**, Amber, 1/2 Pint	17.50
Flask, **Whitney Glass Works**, Applied Collar, Marked On Base, Red Amber, Pint	20.00
Flask, **Wicker Covered & Handle**, Aqua, Gallon, 15 1/2 In.High	12.00
Flask, **Wicker Covered**, Flat, Aqua, 6 7/8 In.High	5.00
Flask, **Will You Take A Drink**, Will A Duck Swim, Aqua, Pint	140.00
Flask, **Willington & Eagle**, Green, Pint .... 100.00 To	130.00
Flask, **Wm.Jackson & Co.Olive Green**, Quart	55.00
Flask, **Woman With Staff**, Clear, 1/2 Pint	40.00
Flask, **Women's Suffrage**	9.75
Flask, **X Embossed On Base**, Golden Amber, Pint	18.00
Flask, **Z O. GWK & Co.**, Aqua, 1/2 Pint	22.50
Flask, **Zanesville**, Swirl, 18 Ribs, Open Pontil, Aqua, Pint	90.00
Flask, **1/2 Girl Sitting On Grass**, Japanese	10.00
Flask, **18 Diamond-Quilted**, Midwestern, Green, 6 1/4 In.	100.00
Flask, **1928**, Green, 1/4 Pint	6.00

*Food bottles include all of the many grocery store containers, such as catsup,
horseradish, jelly, and other foodstuffs. A few special items, such as
vinegar, are listed under their own headings.*

Food, **A.L.Murdock's Liquid Food**	3.00
Food, **Almond Cream**, Label, 5 1/2 In.	8.00
Food, **Ann Page Raspberry Preserve**, 4 In .... *Color*	XX.XX
Food, **Armour & Co.Packers**	2.00
Food, **Asco Pimento Stuffed Olives**, 6 Fluid Ozs. .... *Illus*	10.00
Food, **Atlantic Prepared Mustard**, R.T.French, 5 In. .... *Color*	XX.XX
Food, **Baker's Flavoring Extracts**, Baker Extract Company, Abm, 5 In.High	.45
Food, **Banana Flavor**, Contains 48 Percent Alcohol, 6 1/2 In.	8.00
Food, **Barrel Shape**, Green, 2 Quart	9.00
Food, **Beechnut**, Jar, Embossed Beechnut, Ground Edge	7.00
Food, **Biedenharn Candy Co.**, Vicksburgh, Miss., Dug	22.00
Food, **Brook's Fruit Squashes**, Melbourne, Australia, Sun Purpled	35.00

Food, Butler's Tomato Ketchup, Paper Label .... *Illus*	6.00
Food, Butterworth, Figural	1.00
Food, California Perfume Co., see Avon, California Perfume Co.	
Food, Capers, Emerald, 6 1/2 In.High	7.00
Food, Capers, Green	9.00
Food, Catsup, Embossed U.S.Q.M.A., World War I	13.50
Food, Catsup, Lutz, 9 In. .... *Color*	XX.XX
Food, Catsup, Paneled, Green	1.00
Food, Charles Gulden, Sauce, Bulbous, Amethyst	3.00
Food, Chicos' Spanish Peanut, Metal Base	10.00
Food, Colton's Select Flavors, Embossed, Corker	1.50
Food, Cottage Cheese, Embossed, Dated, 5 In.High	2.00
Food, Crimson Rambler Syrup, Label, Dated 1919	5.00
Food, Cudahy Packing Co.	2.00
Food, E.R.Durkee & Co., N.Y., Belt & Mailed Gauntlet Design, 1877, Clear	4.95
Food, Eddie & Eddie Pure Food, Embossed, Round, Pint	.50
Food, Eno's Fruit Salt	5.00
Food, Essence Of Coffee & Chicory, Australia, Green	15.00
Food, Family Nectar, Clear, Pure .... *Color*	XX.XX
Food, Flaccus Bros.Mustard, W.Va., Label, Milk Glass .... *Illus*	300.00
Food, Foss, Liquid Fruit Flavors, Portland, Me., Rectangular, Amb, Amethyst	.45
Food, French's Medford Mustard	.75
Food, French's Mustard, Clear, Pint	1.75
Food, Gebhardt Eagle Chili Powder, Embossed Eagle	1.00

Food, Asco Pimento Stuffed Olives,
6 Fluid Ozs.
See Page 102

Food, Butler's Tomato Ketchup,
Paper Label

Food, Flaccus Bros.Mustard,
W.Va., Label, Milk Glass

Food, Gold-Brand Pure Leaf Lard, Geo.Naphey & Son, Phila., 1889, Clear, Quart	12.00
Food, Groft's Swiss Milk Cocoa, Pint	10.00
Food, Heinz Ketchup, Labels, Red, 26 1/2 In.Tall	225.00
Food, Heinz Tomato Ketchup, Bulbous, Clear	7.50
Food, Heinz, Embossed Seal Front, Base Embossed'93 Pat.June 17, 1890	5.00
Food, Helmes Railroad Mills, Bimal Ground Mouth, Glass Lid, Band, Amber	8.00
Food, Herb, Free Cut, Square Base, Inside Fluting Waterfall Type, 4 In.	38.00
Food, Hires Household Extract, Square, C.1900, Aqua	2.00
Food, Hires, Extract, Root Beer, Square, Aqua	2.00
Food, Hirsch's Chili Sauce, Tin Top, Label, Clear, 8 In.	4.00

Food, **Hirsch's Ketchup**, Clear Cork, Label, 10 In. 5.00
Food, **Horlick's Malted**, Racine, Wis., U.S.A., Slough, Bucks, Eng., Clear, 3 Qt. 6.00
Food, **Hunt's Catsup**, Decanter 1.50
Food, **Hyman's Catsup**, Tin Top, Label, Clear, 8 In. 2.00
Food, **Indian Root Beer Extract**, Bimal, Amber 2.50
Food, **J.V.Sharp**, Williamstown, N.J., Aqua, 9 In.High .... *Illus* 22.00
Food, **Jar**, Cottage Cheese, Embossed 1.50
Food, **Jar**, Cottage Cheese, Painted 1.00
Food, **Jar**, Violin Shape, Improved Pontil, Aqua 25.00
Food, **Jeanmaime Farina**, Pontil, Clear 10.00
Food, **Joshua Wright**, Barrel, Aqua, 2 Quart 100.00
Food, **Jumbo Peanut Butter**, Clear, 1 Lb. 2.00
Food, **Jumbo Peanut Butter**, Lid, Pint 5.50
Food, **Jumbo Peanut Butter**, Lid, 1/2 Pint 5.00
Food, **Jumbo Peanut Butter**, Pail Shape, Zinc Cap, Wire Bail, Clear, 1 1/2 Lbs. 4.00
Food, **Jumbo Peanut Jar**, Embossed Elephant 4.00
Food, **Karo**, Wire Bail .... .90
    Food, Ketchup, see also Catsup
Food, **L.Rose & Co.**, Embossed Roses, Aqua, 14 In.High 18.00
Food, **L.Rose & Co.**, Leith, Lime Juice, Embossed Leaves & Flowers, Green 7.50
Food, **L.Rose & Co.**, Lime Juice, Aqua, 14 In. 5.00
Food, **L.Rose & Co.**, Lime Juice, Bimal, Aqua, 14 1/2 In. 10.00
Food, **L.Rose & Co.**, Lime Juice, Stain, Aqua, 14 In. 1.00
Food, **Lemon Extract**, Label, Pontil, Aqua, 6 In. .... *Illus* 15.00
Food, **Lime Juice**, L.Rose & Co., Aqua, 14 In. 5.00
Food, **Log Cabin**, Extract, Amber, 6 1/2 In. 60.00
Food, **Log Cabin**, Extract, Warner, Amber 54.00
Food, **Log Cabin Syrup** 7.50
Food, **Louis Freres' Mustard**, Open Pontil 14.00
Food, **Lutz Bros.Tomato Catsup**, Allegheny, Pa., 8 1/2 In. .... *Illus* 18.00
Food, **Maclaren's Cheese** 2.00
Food, **Mcallister's Mocking Bird Food**, N.Y., Pint 10.00
Food, **Mellin's**, Aqua, Pint 2.00
Food, **Mellin's**, Sample 2.00
Food, **Mosheri Bros.Gilt Edge Baking Powder**, Milk Bottle Shape 20.00
Food, **Mrs.Chapin's Mayonnaise**, Pint 1.50
Food, **Murdock Liquid Food**, 12 Sided, Amber 8.50
    Food, Mustard, see also Food, Barrel, Mustard
Food, **Nut House**, Store Jar, Embossed House & Writing, Ball Shape, Clear 15.00
Food, **Old Judge Coffee** 3.00
Food, **Olive Oil**, Cathedral Type, Aqua, 9 In.High 7.50
    Food, Peppersauce, see Peppersauce
    Food, Pickle, see also Pickle
Food, **Pineapple Flavoring**, Contains 48 Percent Alcohol, 6 1/2 In. 8.00
Food, **Planter's Peanut**, Embossed, 5 Cent, Mr.Peanut, Nut Finial 35.00
Food, **Planter's Peanut**, Embossed, 1940 Leap Year Jar 10.00
Food, **Planter's Peanut**, Mr.Peanut On 4 Corners, Purpling 40.00
Food, **Planter's Peanut**, Mr.Peanut On 4 Corners, Square 20.00
Food, **Planter's**, Block Letters, Hexagonal, Metal Closure, Amethyst 26.50
Food, **Pre-Digested Food Co.**, Puscola, Brown, 5 In. .... *Illus* 6.00
Food, **Premium Coffeyville**, Kas., Pint 10.00
Food, **Premium Coffeyville**, Kas., Quart 10.00
Food, **Ridgway's 'Ad' Coffee**, Brown, 8 In. .... *Illus* 10.00
Food, **Rojek's Sour Cream Jar**, Painted 1.75
Food, **Rose's Lime Juice**, Clear, 9 In.High .... *Illus* 25.00
Food, **Rose's Lime Juice**, Light Green, 8 In.High 5.00
Food, **Rosella Preserves**, Melbourne, Australia, Kiwi Bird, Sun Purpled 25.00
Food, **Ross's Brand Lime Juice**, Vertically Embossed Star, Green, 14 In.High 5.00
Food, **Royal Baking Powder Company**, Box, Salesman's .... *Color* XX.XX
Food, **Sauer's Pure Lemon Extract**, Boxed .... *Illus* 3.00
Food, **Shrewsbury Brand Choicest Products**, 9 In. .... *Color* XX.XX
Food, **Shriver's Oyster Ketchup**, Amber 40.00
Food, **Simpson Spring Co's.Fruit Syrups**, Mass., Square Bottom, Bimal, Clear 2.00
Food, **Soy Sauce**, Chinese 5.50
Food, **Squire Dingee** 7.00
Food, **Three Mold**, Honey Amber 12.00

Food, J.V.Sharp, Williamstown,
N.J., Aqua, 9 In.High
See Page 104

Food, Lutz Bros.Tomato Catsup,
Allegheny, Pa., 8 1/2 In.
See Page 104

Food,
Lemon Extract,
Label, Pontil,
Aqua, 6 In.
See Page 104

Food,
Ridgway's 'Ad' Coffee,
Brown, 8 In.
See Page 104

Food, Rose's Lime Juice,
Clear, 9 In.High
See Page 104

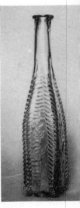

Food, Pre-Digested Food Co.,
Puscola, Brown, 5 In.
See Page 104

Food, Sauer's Pure Lemon Extract, Boxed
See Page 104

Food, Tom's Peanut, Embossed	15.00
Food, Tomato Sauce, A.F.C., Australia, Sun Purpled	25.00
Food, Valentine's Meat Juice, Teardrop, Corker, Amber, 3 1/4 In.	8.00
Food, Virginia Dare, Embossed	2.50
Food, Wan-Eta Cocoa, Amber, Quart	3.50 To 10.00
Food, White House Brand Vinegar, Handle, Abm, Clear, Pint	6.00
Food, White House Brand Vinegar, Handle, Amb, Clear, Quart	6.00
Food, White House Vinegar On Bottom, Decanter, Green, 7 In.	10.00
Food, White House Vinegar, Cobweb Pattern, & Flowers Embossed, Handle, Clear	6.00

Food, White House Vinegar, Handle, Embossed, Corker, Clear, Pint	6.00
Food, White House Vinegar, Jug, March 6, 1909, Quart	9.00
Food, Wm.Underwood & Co., Boston, Pontil, Aqua	12.50
Free-Blown, Captain's, Pontil, Olive Green	80.00
Free-Blown, Etched N.V., Open Pontil, 18th Century, Olive Amber, 2 Quart	170.00
Free-Blown, Jug, Handled, Pontil, Amber, Quart	110.00
Free-Blown, Open Pontil, Light Green	15.00
Free-Blown, Saddle, English, Flattened, Sheared Lip, Golden Amber	100.00

Fruit jars made of glass have been used in the United States since the 1850s. Over one thousand different jars have been found with varieties of closures, embossing, and colors. The date 1858 on many jars refers to a patent, not the age of the bottle. Be sure to look in this listing under any name or initial that appears on your jar. If not otherwise indicated the jar is clear glass, quart size. The numbers used in the entries in the form T-O refer to the book A Collectors' Manual of Fruit Jars *by Julian Harrison Toulouse.*

Fruit Jar, A.& D.H.Chambers, Union, 2 Quart	18.00
Fruit Jar, A.& D.H.Chamber's Wax Sealer, Aqua, 1/2 Gallon	10.00
Fruit Jar, A.G.Smalley, Amber, Quart	20.00
Fruit Jar, A.G.Smalley & Co., Clear, Quart	3.00
Fruit Jar, A.G.W.L.Pittsburgh, Base Embossed, Wax Sealer	10.00
Fruit Jar, A.Kline, Pint	35.00
Fruit Jar, A.Kline, Quart	14.00 To 22.00
Fruit Jar, A.Kline, Stopper, 2 Quart	20.00
Fruit Jar, A.Stone & Co., Aqua, Quart	120.00
Fruit Jar, A.Stone & Co., Philad'a, Aqua, Chipped *Illus*	250.00
Fruit Jar, A.Stone & Co., Philad'a, Aqua, 7 In. *Illus*	350.00
Fruit Jar, Acme, Clear, Pint	1.00 To 3.00
Fruit Jar, Acme, Clear, Quart	1.00 To 3.00
Fruit Jar, Acme, 1/2 Gallon	5.00
Fruit Jar, Adams & Co.Manufacturers, Pittsburgh, Pa.	375.00
Fruit Jar, Agnew, Clear, Quart	18.00
Fruit Jar, Airtight, Closure, Aqua, Quart	175.00
Fruit Jar, Airtight, Whittled, Aqua, 7 In.High *Illus*	250.00
Fruit Jar, All Right, Dated Tin Lid, Aqua, 1/2 Gallon	95.00
Fruit Jar, Alta-Crest, Dacro, Blue Lettering, March 28, 1929, Pint	5.00
Fruit Jar, Amazon Swift Seal, Bail, Glass Lid, Aqua, Quart	1.00
Fruit Jar, Anchor H Emblem	1.50
Fruit Jar, Anchor Hocking, Lightning, Embossed Anchor, Pint	6.00
Fruit Jar, Anchor Hocking, Lightning, Embossed Anchor, Quart	6.00
Fruit Jar, Atlas E-Z Seal, Amber, Quart	15.00 To 22.00
Fruit Jar, Atlas E-Z Seal, Aqua, 1/2 Gallon	3.00
Fruit Jar, Atlas E-Z Seal, Aqua, Pint	.75 To 4.00
Fruit Jar, Atlas E-Z Seal, Aqua, 1/2 Pint	.75 To 4.00
Fruit Jar, Atlas E-Z Seal, Aqua, Quart	.75 To 2.00
Fruit Jar, Atlas E-Z Seal, Blue, Pint	8.00
Fruit Jar, Atlas E-Z Seal, Blue, Quart	8.00 To 15.00
Fruit Jar, Atlas E-Z Seal, Blue, 1/2 Pint	3.25 To 4.50
Fruit Jar, Atlas E-Z Seal, Clear, Pint	2.00
Fruit Jar, Atlas E-Z Seal, Clear, 1/2 Gallon	1.50
Fruit Jar, Atlas E-Z Seal, Clear, 1/2 Pint	1.00 To 15.00
Fruit Jar, Atlas E-Z Seal, Cornflower Blue, Pint	10.00
Fruit Jar, Atlas E-Z Seal, Cornflower Blue, Quart	20.00
Fruit Jar, Atlas E-Z Seal, Glass Lid, Clear, Quart	1.50
Fruit Jar, Atlas E-Z Seal, Milk Glass Lid, Amber, Quart	22.00
Fruit Jar, Atlas E-Z Seal, Olive Green, Quart	9.00
Fruit Jar, Atlas E-Z Seal, Squatty, Aqua, Pint	2.00 To 9.75
Fruit Jar, Atlas E-Z Seal, Squatty, Blue, Pint	4.00
Fruit Jar, Atlas E-Z Seal, Squatty, Green, Pint	9.75
Fruit Jar, Atlas E-Z Seal, Vaseline Color, Pint	10.00
Fruit Jar, Atlas E-Z Seal, Vaseline Color, Quart	10.00
Fruit Jar, Atlas Good Luck, Clear, Pint	2.25
Fruit Jar, Atlas Good Luck, Embossed 4-Leaf Clover, Glass Lid, 1/2 Gallon	5.00
Fruit Jar, Atlas Good Luck, Clear, Quart	1.50 To 3.00
Fruit Jar, Atlas H-A Mason	1.50

Fruit Jar, **Atlas Junior Mason**	4.00
Fruit Jar, **Atlas Mason Improved Patent**, Milk Glass Insert, Olive, Pint	18.50
Fruit Jar, **Atlas Mason Patent 1858**	27.5
Fruit Jar, **Atlas Mason Patent**, Genuine Boyd's Mason Back Mason, Aqua	3.00
Fruit Jar, **Atlas Mason**, Aqua	1.25
Fruit Jar, **Atlas Mason**, Clear, 1/2 Pint	2.00
Fruit Jar, **Atlas Mason's Improved**, Aqua, Pint	8.00
Fruit Jar, **Atlas Mason's Patent Nov.30**, 1858, Aqua, 1/2 Gallon	2.00
Fruit Jar, **Atlas Mason's Patent**, Apple Green, Quart	4.50
Fruit Jar, **Atlas Mason's Patent**, Light Green	3.00
Fruit Jar, **Atlas Mason's Patent**, Quart	2.00
Fruit Jar, **Atlas Special Mason**, Quart	4.75
Fruit Jar, **Atlas Special**, Light Green, 4 In.High .... *Illus*	12.00
Fruit Jar, **Atlas Strong Shoulder Mason**, Aqua, Pint	1.00

Fruit Jar, A.Stone & Co.,
Philad'a, Aqua, Chipped
See Page 106

Fruit Jar, A.Stone & Co.,
Philad'a, Aqua, 7 In.
See Page 106

Fruit Jar, Air-Tight, Whittled,
Aqua, 7 In.High
See Page 106

Fruit Jar, Atlas Special,
Light Green, 4 In.High

Fruit Jar, **Atlas Strong Shoulder Mason**, Cornflower Blue, 1/2 Gallon	12.00
Fruit Jar, **Atlas Strong Shoulder Mason**, Screw On Lid, Aqua, Quart .... 1.00 To	2.00
Fruit Jar, **Atlas Strong Shoulder Mason**, Whittled, Bubbly, Aqua, 1/2 Gallon	4.50
Fruit Jar, **Atlas Strong Shoulder**, Aqua, 1/2 Gallon	2.00
Fruit Jar, **Atlas Wholefruit**, Aqua, Pint	.75
Fruit Jar, **Atlas Wholefruit**, Aqua, 1/2 Pint	.75
Fruit Jar, **Atlas Wholefruit**, Clear, Pint	1.00
Fruit Jar, **Atlas Wholefruit**, Clear, Quart .... 1.50 To	2.00
Fruit Jar, **Atlas**, Amber, Quart	25.00

Fruit Jar, Atlas, Apple Green, 1/2 Gallon	5.00
Fruit Jar, Atlas, Glass Top, Aqua, 1/2 Pint	7.50
Fruit Jar, Automatic Sealer, Aqua, Quart	50.00
Fruit Jar, Automatic Sealer, Closure, Aqua, 1/2 Gallon	95.00
Fruit Jar, B.B.G.M.Co., Aqua, Quart	12.00 To 25.00
Fruit Jar, B.B.G.M.Co. Monogram On Side, 2-Piece Insert, Aqua, Quart	25.00
Fruit Jar, B.B.Wilcox, Quart	20.00
Fruit Jar, B.H.B., Amber, 1/2 Pint	15.00
Fruit Jar, Bagley, Quart	7.50
Fruit Jar, Ball Deluxe	2.50
Fruit Jar, Ball Eclipse, Quart	1.50
Fruit Jar, Ball Eclipse, Wide Mouth, Aqua, Pint	.75
Fruit Jar, Ball Eclipse, Wide Mouth, Aqua, 1/2 Pint	.75
Fruit Jar, Ball Eclipse, Wide Mouth, Clear, Quart	1.00
Fruit Jar, Ball Eclipse, Wide Mouth, Glass Top, Clear, Quart	3.00
Fruit Jar, Ball Eclipse, Wide Mouth, Glass Top, Clear, 1/2 Gallon	4.00
Fruit Jar, Ball Ideal, Aqua	2.00
Fruit Jar, Ball Ideal, Blue	1.25
Fruit Jar, Ball Ideal, Blue, Pint	.75
Fruit Jar, Ball Ideal, Blue, Quart	1.00
Fruit Jar, Ball Ideal, Blue, 1/2 Gallon	7.50
Fruit Jar, Ball Ideal, Blue, 1/2 Pint	75 To 1.00
Fruit Jar, Ball Ideal, Clear	.35
Fruit Jar, Ball Ideal, Clear, Pint	15.00
Fruit Jar, Ball Ideal, Clear, Quart	25 To 1.50
Fruit Jar, Ball Ideal, Clear, 1/2 Gallon	1.50
Fruit Jar, Ball Ideal, Clear, 1/2 Pint	2.00 To 2.75
Fruit Jar, Ball Ideal, Clear, 1/3 Pint	2.75
Fruit Jar, Ball Ideal, Clear, 3 Pint	15.00
Fruit Jar, Ball Ideal, Dated, Aqua	2.75
Fruit Jar, Ball Ideal, Dated, Blue, Pint	1.00
Fruit Jar, Ball Ideal, Dated, Blue, 1/2 Pint	1.00
Fruit Jar, Ball Ideal, Dated, Clear, 1/2 Gallon	2.00
Fruit Jar, Ball Ideal, Dated 1908, Bail & Lid	1.25
Fruit Jar, Ball Ideal, Green, Quart	7.50
Fruit Jar, Ball Ideal, Pat'd July 14, 1908, Aqua, Pint	1.50 To 3.00
Fruit Jar, Ball Ideal, Pat'd July 14, 1908, Aqua, Quart	1.50 To 3.00
Fruit Jar, Ball Ideal, Pat'd July 14, 1908, Aqua, 1/2 Gallon	. 3.00
Fruit Jar, Ball Ideal, Pat'd July 14, 1908, Quart	1.00 To 2.00
Fruit Jar, Ball Ideal, Patent July 14, 1908, Clear, Pint	1.50
Fruit Jar, Ball Ideal, Patent July 14, 1908, Clear, Quart	1.50
Fruit Jar, Ball Ideal, Square, Aqua, Pint	2.50 To 3.00
Fruit Jar, Ball Ideal, Square, Aqua, Quart	3.00
Fruit Jar, Ball Ideal, Square, Clear, Quart	1.50
Fruit Jar, Ball Improved Mason	2.50
Fruit Jar, Ball Improved Mason's Patent, 1858, 4-9 On Bottom, Aqua	3.00
Fruit Jar, Ball Improved, Aqua, Pint	3.00 To 8.00
Fruit Jar, Ball Improved, Aqua, Quart	2.00 To 3.00
Fruit Jar, Ball Improved, Aqua, 1/2 Pint	1.40
Fruit Jar, Ball Improved, Mason's Patent 1858, Aqua, Pint	8.00
Fruit Jar, Ball Improved, SCA , Pint	5.00
Fruit Jar, Ball Improved, Yellow, Quart	14.00
Fruit Jar, Ball Mason Patent, Blue, 1/2 Gallon	6.00
Fruit Jar, Ball Mason, Aqua, Quart	50 To 2.00
Fruit Jar, Ball Mason, Aqua, 1/2 Gallon	2.00 To 6.00
Fruit Jar, Ball Mason, Blue, Pint	67 To 3.00
Fruit Jar, Ball Mason, Green, Quart	8.50
Fruit Jar, Ball Mason, Light Green	1.50
Fruit Jar, Ball Mason, Salt & Pepper Shaker, Boxed	1.25
Fruit Jar, Ball Mason, 1/2 gallon	1.00
Fruit Jar, Ball Mason, 5 On Bottom, Light Green	3.00
Fruit Jar, Ball·Mason, 6 On Bottom, Dark Aqua	3.00
Fruit Jar, Ball Mason's Patent 1858, Aqua, Quart	2.00
Fruit Jar, Ball Mason's 1858, Clear, Quart	2.00
Fruit Jar, Ball Perfect Mason, Amber, 1/2 Gallon	22.00 To 25.00
Fruit Jar, Ball Perfect Mason, Apple Green, Quart	8.00

Fruit Jar, Ball **Perfect Mason**, Apple Green, 1/2 Gallon	10.00
Fruit Jar, Ball **Perfect Mason**, Aqua	.50
Fruit Jar, Ball **Perfect Mason**, Aqua, 1/2 Pint	1.40
Fruit Jar, Ball **Perfect Mason**, Blue, Pint	.25
Fruit Jar, Ball **Perfect Mason**, Blue, Quart	.25
Fruit Jar, Ball **Perfect Mason**, Blue, 1/2 Pint	8.00
Fruit Jar, Ball **Perfect Mason**, Graduated, Aqua, Quart	3.00
Fruit Jar, Ball **Perfect Mason**, Purpling, Quart	3.00
Fruit Jar, Ball **Perfect Mason**, Salt & Pepper, Zinc Lids	10.00
Fruit Jar, Ball **Perfect Mason**, 2 On Bottom, Dark Aqua	3.00
Fruit Jar, Ball **Perfect Seal**, Blue	1.25
Fruit Jar, Ball **Perfect Seal**, Yellow Amber, Pint	13.00
Fruit Jar, Ball **Sanitary**, Sure Seal, Blue, Pint	2.00
Fruit Jar, Ball **Sanitary**, Sure Seal, Blue, Quart	2.00
Fruit Jar, Ball **Sanitary**, Sure Seal, Clear, Pint	2.00
Fruit Jar, Ball **Sanitary**, Sure Seal, Clear, Quart	2.00
Fruit Jar, Ball **Sanitary**, Sure Seal, Green, Pint	2.00
Fruit Jar, Ball **Sanitary**, Sure Seal, Green, Quart	2.00
Fruit Jar, Ball **Sanitary**, Sure Seal, Wide Mouth, Aqua, 3 Quart	3.00
Fruit Jar, Ball **Script**, Mason's Patent Nov.30th 1858, Aqua, Quart	5.00
Fruit Jar, Ball **Script**, Mason's Patent, Quart	1.50
Fruit Jar, Ball **Square Mason**, Clear	1.00
Fruit Jar, Ball **Standard**, Aqua	5.00
Fruit Jar, Ball **Standard**, Aqua, Quart	2.00
Fruit Jar, Ball **Standard**, Clear	1.50 To 2.75
Fruit Jar, Ball **Standard**, Wax Sealer, Aqua, 1/2 Gallon	3.00
Fruit Jar, Ball **Standard**, Wax Sealer, Blue	6.00 To 20.00
Fruit Jar, Ball **Sure Seal**, Blue, Pint	3.00
Fruit Jar, Ball **Sure Seal**, Blue, Quart	2.00 To 3.00
Fruit Jar, Ball **Sure Seal**, Blue, 1/2 Gallon	2.50
Fruit Jar, Ball **Sure Seal**, Blue, 1/2 Pint	15.00
Fruit Jar, Ball **Sure Seal**, Bottle Shape, 3-Cup Size	8.00
Fruit Jar, Ball **Sure Seal**, Clear, Pint	2.00
Fruit Jar, Ball **Sure Seal**, Clear, 1/2 Pint	15.00
Fruit Jar, Ball **Sure Seal**, Glass Lid, Wire Bail, Blue, Quart	4.00
Fruit Jar, Ball **Sure Seal**, Green, Pint	2.00
Fruit Jar, Ball **Sure Seal**, Green Quart	2.00
Fruit Jar, Ball **Sure Seal**, Pint	1.00
Fruit Jar, Ball **Sure Seal**, Quart	2.25
Fruit Jar, Ball **Sure Seal**, Wide Mouth, Aqua, 2 Pint	3.00
Fruit Jar, Ball **Sure Seal**, Wide Mouth, Aqua, 2 Quart	3.00
Fruit Jar, **Ball**, Amber, 2 Quart	20.00
Fruit Jar, **Ball**, Aqua, Quart	1.00 To 2.00
Fruit Jar, **Ball**, Aqua, 1/2 Gallon	2.00
Fruit Jar, **Ball**, Clear, Pint	2.00
Fruit Jar, **Ball**, Clear, 1/2 Pint	1.50
Fruit Jar, **Ball**, Clear, 2 Pint	2.00
Fruit Jar, **Ball**, Clear, 3 Pint	2.00
Fruit Jar, **Ball**, Mason's Patent, Clear	2.00
Fruit Jar, **Ball**, Patented 1908, Glass Lid, Clamp, Green, 1/2 Gallon	1.50
Fruit Jar, **Bamberger's Sure Seal**, Quart	7.50
Fruit Jar, **Banner Trade Mark**, Warranted, Pint	5.00
Fruit Jar, **Banner Trade Mark Warranted**, Quart	5.00
Fruit Jar, **Banner**, Blue, 1/2 Pint	15.00
Fruit Jar, **Banner**, Circled By Dates, Closure, Aqua, 1/2 Gallon	45.00
Fruit Jar, **Banner**, Clear	12.00
Fruit Jar, **Banner**, Clear, 1/2 Pint	15.00
Fruit Jar, **Banner**, Pat'd Feb.9, 1864, Aqua, Quart	70.00
Fruit Jar, **Banner**, Pat'd Feb.9th, 1864, Reissue Jan.22, 1867, Aqua	40.00
Fruit Jar, **Banner**, Quart	5.00
Fruit Jar, **Banner**, Trademark, Wide Mouth, Glass Lid, Wire Bail, Clear, Quart	5.00
Fruit Jar, **Banner**, 1/2 Pint	5.00
Fruit Jar, **BBGM co.**, Mono, Aqua, 1/2 Gallon	18.00
Fruit Jar, **Bean Cake**, Chinese Characters, Pint	6.00
Fruit Jar, **Beaver**, Amber	325.00
Fruit Jar, **Beaver**, Amethyst, Quart	15.00

Fruit Jar, **Beaver**, Beaver Chewing Twig, Made In Canada, Quart	16.00
Fruit Jar, **Beaver**, Embossed, Clear, Pint	35.00
Fruit Jar, **Beaver**, Embossed, Clear, Quart	10.00
Fruit Jar, **Beaver**, Embossed, Clear, 1/2 Gallon	12.00
Fruit Jar, **Beaver**, Embossed, Glass Lid, Zinc Band, Clear, Quart	10.00
Fruit Jar, **Beaver**, Embossed, Glass Lid, Zinc Band, Clear, 1/2 Gallon	12.00
Fruit Jar, **Beaver**, Embossed, Glass Lid, Zinc Band, Midget, Clear, Pint	35.00
Fruit Jar, **Beechnut**, Pint	4.00
Fruit Jar, **Beehive**, Quart, Aqua	52.50
Fruit Jar, **Bernardin**, Pint	1.00
Fruit Jar, **Best Fruit Keeper**, Aqua, Quart	35.00
Fruit Jar, **Best Wide Mouth**	2.00
Fruit Jar, **Best**, Squat, Wide Mouth, Amber, Quart	150.00
Fruit Jar, **Best**, Squatty, Ground Mouth, Zinc Band, Glass Lid, Clear, Quart	15.00
Fruit Jar, **Best**, Squatty, Ground Mouth, Zinc Band, Glass Lid, Clear, 1/2 Gal.	20.00
Fruit Jar, **Blue Ball**, 1/2 Gallon	1.50
Fruit Jar, **Boldt Mason**, Aqua, Pint	35.00
Fruit Jar, **Boldt Mason**, Green, Pint	40.00
Fruit Jar, **Bostwick Perfect Sealer**, The In Script, Bulbous, Clear	30.00
Fruit Jar, **Boyd Mason**, Aqua, Quart	2.00
Fruit Jar, **Boyd Mason**, Light Aqua, Quart	2.00
Fruit Jar, **Boyd Perfect Mason**, Aqua, Quart	2.00
Fruit Jar, **Boyds Mason**	1.50
Fruit Jar, **Brockway**	2.75
Fruit Jar, **Brockway**, Clear, Quart	2.00
Fruit Jar, **Brockway**, Clear-Vu, Pint	1.50
Fruit Jar, **Brockway**, Clear-Vu, Quart	1.50
Fruit Jar, **Brown & Co.**, Clear, Quart	10.00
Fruit Jar, **Buckeye**, Light Aqua, Quart	150.00
Fruit Jar, **Burlington**, The Glass Lid, Screw Band, 1/2 Gallon	20.00 To 25.00
Fruit Jar, **C G Co.Monogram**, Mason's 1858, Aqua, Quart	7.00
Fruit Jar, **C.B.& Co.**, Pint	12.00
Fruit Jar, **C.B.K.**, Pint	12.00
Fruit Jar, **C.F.Spencer's Patent**, Rochester, N.Y., Wax Sealer, 2 Quart	45.00
Fruit Jar, **C.Riessner & Co.**, 2 Quart	20.00
Fruit Jar, **C.S.& Co.**, Patent 1841, Aqua, Pint	22.50
Fruit Jar, **C.S.& Co.**, Wax Sealer, Quart	10.00 To 12.00
Fruit Jar, **C.S.& Co.**, Wax Sealer, 1/2 Pint	12.00
Fruit Jar, **C.W.Merchant**, Lockport, N.Y., Emerald Green, 1/2 Pint	40.00
Fruit Jar, **Calcutt's**, Aqua, Pint	35.00
Fruit Jar, **California Mission**, Aqua, Pint	6.00
Fruit Jar, **California Mission**, Aqua, Quart	3.00 To 7.00
Fruit Jar, **California Mission**, Aqua, 1/8 Gallon	8.50
Fruit Jar, **California Mission**, Aqua, 1/2 Pint	22.50
Fruit Jar, **California Mission**, Clear, Quart	4.00 To 6.00
Fruit Jar, **California Mission**, Clear, 1/2 Gallon	8.00
Fruit Jar, **Canadian Jewel**	1.50 To 3.00
Fruit Jar, **Canadian Mason**, Quart	1.00
Fruit Jar, **Canton Domestic**, Quart	45.00
Fruit Jar, **Canton Domestic**, 1/2 Gallon	60.00
Fruit Jar, **Canton Electric Fruit Jar**, Quart *Color*	XX.XX
Fruit Jar, **Canton**, Screw-On Glass Lid With Lugs, Clear, Quart	135.00
Fruit Jar, **Canton**, The, Domestic, Clear, 11 In.High *Illus*	65.00
Fruit Jar, **Cason Crystal**, Clear, Quart	17.50
Fruit Jar, **Chambers**, Union Made, Quart	15.00
Fruit Jar, **Champion**, The Closure, Aqua, Quart	65.00
Fruit Jar, **Chief**, Clear, Quart	5.00
Fruit Jar, **Christmas Mason**, Pint	22.50 To 40.00
Fruit Jar, **Christmas Mason**, The Ball Jar On Reverse, 2 Pint	37.50 To 40.00
Fruit Jar, **Clark's Peerless**, Aqua, Pint	4.95
Fruit Jar, **Clark's Peerless**, Aqua, Quart	10.00
Fruit Jar, **Clark's Peerless**, Cornflower Blue, Pint	12.00
Fruit Jar, **Clark's Peerless**, Pint	3.50 To 6.50
Fruit Jar, **Clark's Peerless**, Quart	3.50 To 8.00
Fruit Jar, **Clarke**, Cleveland, Ohio *Illus*	25.00
Fruit Jar, **Clarke**, 1/2 Gallon	50.00

Fruit Jar, Canton, The,
Domestic, Clear, 11 In.High
See Page 110

Fruit Jar, Clarke,
Cleveland, Ohio
See Page 110

Fruit Jar, Cleveland Fruit Juice, Clear, 1/2 Gallon	2.00
Fruit Jar, Cleveland Fruit Juice, Quart	1.50
Fruit Jar, Climax Trade Mark, Pat'D July 14, 1908 On Base, Quart	4.50
Fruit Jar, Climax, Blue	12.00
Fruit Jar, Climax, Blue, 1/2 Pint	15.00
Fruit Jar, Climax, Clear, 1/2 Pint	15.00
Fruit Jar, Clyde, Clear, Quart	8.50 To 12.00
Fruit Jar, Clyde, Mason Improved, Pint	6.00
Fruit Jar, Clyde, Quart, Clear	3.50 To 7.00
Fruit Jar, Clyde, The, Ground Mouth, Clear, Pint	3.00
Fruit Jar, Clyde, The, Ground Mouth, Clear, Quart	8.00
Fruit Jar, Clyde, The, In Script, Machine Made, Pint	5.00
Fruit Jar, Clyde, The, In Script, Pint	5.00
Fruit Jar, Clyde, The, Pint	6.00
Fruit Jar, Coffeyville	18.00
Fruit Jar, Cohansey Glass Mfg.Co., Pat.July 16, 1872, Embossed, Amber	7.00
Fruit Jar, Cohansey, Amber, Pint	15.00
Fruit Jar, Cohansey, Aqua, Pint	20.00
Fruit Jar, Cohansey, Aqua, Quart	13.00
Fruit Jar, Cohansey, Aqua, 1/2 Gallon, Whittled	18.00
Fruit Jar, Cohansey, Aqua, 1/2 Pint	40.00
Fruit Jar, Cohansey, Aqua, 1/2 Pint, Whittled	40.00
Fruit Jar, Cohansey, Aqua, 2 Quart	15.00
Fruit Jar, Cohansey, Arched, Glass Lid, Ground Lip, Wire Ring, Aqua, Quart	15.00
Fruit Jar, Cohansey, Barrel, Closure, Aqua, 1/2 Gallon	15.00 To 40.00
Fruit Jar, Cohansey, Barrel, Whittled, Quart	45.00
Fruit Jar, Cohansey, Blue, Quart	12.00
Fruit Jar, Cohansey, Clear, Quart	10.00 To 15.00
Fruit Jar, Cohansey, Glass Mfg.Co., Pat.Feb.12, 1867 On Bottom, Pint	20.00
Fruit Jar, Cohansey, Name Arched, Glass Lid, Wire Clamp, Aqua, Quart	18.00
Fruit Jar, Cohansey, Name Arched, Pint	17.50
Fruit Jar, Cohansey, On Base & Lid, Stain, Amber	19.00
Fruit Jar, Cohansey, Pat.Feb.12, 1867, Wide Mouth, Aqua, Quart	35.00
Fruit Jar, Cohansey, Wax Sealer, Barrel, Patent Mar.1877, Aqua, Quart	60.00
Fruit Jar, Cohansey, 1/2 Gallon	15.00
Fruit Jar, Columbia, Aqua, Pint	20.00
Fruit Jar, Columbia, Aqua, Quart	22.00
Fruit Jar, Columbia, Closure, Clear, 1/2 Gallon	25.00
Fruit Jar, Columbia, Embossed Base & Lid, Clear, 1/2 Gallon	12.00
Fruit Jar, Columbia, Quart	18.00
Fruit Jar, Columbia, Side Embossing, Pint	25.00
Fruit Jar, Common Sense, Gregory's Patent Aug.17th, 1869, Whittled, Aqua	330.00
Fruit Jar, Congress & Empire, Olive Green, C Pint	22.00

Fruit Jar, **Conserve**, Clear, Pint .... 3.50 To 8.00
Fruit Jar, **Conserve**, Quart 5.00
Fruit Jar, **Cork Sealer**, Iron Pontil, Dark Aqua, Quart 70.00
Fruit Jar, **Cork Sealer**, 10 Petal, Iron Pontil, Aqua, Quart 100.00
Fruit Jar, **Cross, Mason's Improved**, Aqua, Pint 1.50
Fruit Jar, **Crown** 1.50
Fruit Jar, **Crown Imperial**, Midget, Aqua 20.00
Fruit Jar, **Crown Imperial**, Midget, Clear 20.00
Fruit Jar, **Crown Midget**, Aqua .... 12.00 To 14.00
Fruit Jar, **Crown Midget**, Clear .... 10.00 To 12.00
Fruit Jar, **Crown**, Embossed 2.00
Fruit Jar, **Crown**, Ground Top .... 5.00 To 14.50
Fruit Jar, **Crown**, Improved Corona, Aqua 3.00
Fruit Jar, **Crown**, Pint 3.75
Fruit Jar, **Crown**, Quart 1.50
Fruit Jar, **Crown**, T.Eaton Co., Toronto & Winnipeg, Aqua, Quart 5.50
Fruit Jar, **Crystal Jar C.G.**, Closure, Clear, 1/2 Gallon 20.00
Fruit Jar, **Crystal Jar**, Clear, Quart .... 20.00 To 25.00
Fruit Jar, **Crystal Jar**, Embossed, Amber, Quart 17.00
Fruit Jar, **Crystal Jar Mason**, Clear, Pint 8.00
Fruit Jar, **Crystal**, Aqua, Quart 30.00
Fruit Jar, **Crystal**, C.G., Clear, 1/2 Gallon .... 20.00 To 23.00
Fruit Jar, **Crystal**, Clear, Quart 16.00
Fruit Jar, **Crystal**, Glass Lid, 1/2 Gallon 23.00
Fruit Jar, **Crystal**, Glass Screw Lid, Aqua, 1/2 Gallon 45.00
Fruit Jar, **Crystal**, Glass Screw Lid, Quart 22.00
Fruit Jar, **Crystal**, Patent Date On Base & Cover, Bubble Break, Aqua, Quart 20.00
Fruit Jar, **Crystal**, Patent Dec.17, 1878, Glass Screw Cap, Clear, Quart 17.50
Fruit Jar, **Crystal**, Pint 35.00
Fruit Jar, **Cunningham & Co.**, Embossed Kline Top, Whittled, Aqua, 1/2 Gallon 18.00
Fruit Jar, **Cunningham & Co.**, Pointil, 2 Quart 165.00
Fruit Jar, **Cunningham & Ihmsen**, Base Embossed, Wax Sealer 10.00
Fruit Jar, **Cunningham & Ihmsen**, Tin Lid, Blue, Quart 40.00
Fruit Jar, **Curtice Brothers Preservers**, N.Y., 7 In. .... *Illus* 50.00
Fruit Jar, **D.G.Co.**, Monogram, Glass Lid, Screw Band, Ground Mouth, Aqua, Quart 35.00
Fruit Jar, **Daisy**, Dark Amber 10.00
Fruit Jar, **Daisy**, F.E.Ward, Pint 4.00
Fruit Jar, **Daisy**, The F.E.Ward & Co., Quart .... 4.00 To 12.00
Fruit Jar, **Daisy**, The Pint .... 7.00 To 10.00
Fruit Jar, **Dandy**, Amber, 1/2 Gallon 75.00
Fruit Jar, **Dandy**, The, Amber, Quart 55.00
Fruit Jar, **Dandy**, The, Aqua, Pint 22.50
Fruit Jar, **Dandy**, The, Aqua, Quart 22.50
Fruit Jar, **Dandy**, The, Closure, Violet Color, Quart 30.00
Fruit Jar, **Dandy**, The, Quart 9.00
Fruit Jar, **Dandy**, The, 1/2 Gallon 61.00
Fruit Jar, **Darling**, The, Aqua, 1/2 Gallon 20.00
Fruit Jar, **Darling**, The, Imperial, ADM Monogram, Imperial 1/2 Gallon 28.00
Fruit Jar, **Darling**, The, Imperial Below ADM Monogram, Aqua, Pint 25.00
Fruit Jar, **Dated 1886**, Amber, Pint 35.00
Fruit Jar, **Deerfoot Farms** 10.00
Fruit Jar, **Dexter**, Aqua, 8 In.High .... *Illus* 47.00
Fruit Jar, **Dexter**, Closure, Aqua, Quart 30.00
Fruit Jar, **Dexter**, Quart 32.00
Fruit Jar, **Dexter**, Wreath Of Fruit, Aqua, Quart 30.00
Fruit Jar, **Dexter**, 1/2 Gallon 22.00
Fruit Jar, **Diamond Improved**, Quart 2.50
Fruit Jar, **Diamond**, Pint 3.00
Fruit Jar, **Diamond**, Quart 3.00
Fruit Jar, **Dillon & Co.**, Embossed Base, Wax Sealer 10.00
Fruit Jar, **Dillon & Co.**, Fairmont, Indiana, Wax Sealer, Green, Quart 9.00
Fruit Jar, **Dillon & Co.**, On Base, 1/2 Gallon 9.00
Fruit Jar, **Doolittle In Script**, Aqua, 1/2 Gallon 35.00
Fruit Jar, **Doolittle**, Aqua, Quart .... 10.00 To 25.00
Fruit Jar, **Doolittle**, Embossed Lid, Clear, Quart .... 20.00 To 35.00
Fruit Jar, **Doolittle**, Patent Dec.24, 1901, Clear, Pint 25.00

Fruit Jar,
Curtice Brothers Preservers,
N.Y., 7 In.
See Page 112

Fruit Jar, Dexter,
Aqua, 8 In.High
See Page 112

Fruit Jar, Doolittle, Patent 1900, Aqua, Quart	28.00
Fruit Jar, Double Safety, Amethyst, Quart	2.50
Fruit Jar, Double Safety, Clear, Pint	1.50 To 2.00
Fruit Jar, Double Safety, Clear, Quart	2.00
Fruit Jar, Double Safety, 1/2 Pint	3.50 To 4.50
Fruit Jar, Drey Ever Seal, Clear, Quart	1.00 To 1.75
Fruit Jar, Drey Ever Seal, Dated 1858 With Cross	1.75
Fruit Jar, Drey Improved Ever Seal, Glass Lid, Clear, Pint	1.00
Fruit Jar, Drey Mason, Clear, Quart	1.00 To 2.00
Fruit Jar, Drey Perfect Mason, Clear, Quart	2.00
Fruit Jar, Drey Perfect Mason, Sun Color	1.50
Fruit Jar, Drey, Square Mason, Clear, Pint	1.75
Fruit Jar, Drey, Square Mason, Clear, Quart	2.00
Fruit Jar, Duraglas On Base, Amber, Quart	4.00
Fruit Jar, E.C.Flaccus, Wax Sealer, Embossed, Clear, Quart	25.00
Fruit Jar, Eagle & Shield Embossed Lid, Tin Closure, Clear	58.00
Fruit Jar, Eagle & Shield, Embossed On Lid, Clear, 48 Oz.	110.00
Fruit Jar, Eagle, Aqua, Quart	45.00
Fruit Jar, Eagle, Closure, Aqua, 1/2 Gallon	45.00
Fruit Jar, Eagle, Quart	40.00 To 55.00
Fruit Jar, Eagle, 1/2 Gallon	35.00
Fruit Jar, Eagle, 2 Quart	50.00
Fruit Jar, Eclipse, The, Ground Top	20.00
Fruit Jar, Eclipse, Zinc Lid, Aqua, Quart	50.00
Fruit Jar, Economy Sealer, Aqua, 1/2 Gallon	15.00
Fruit Jar, Economy Sealer, Ghost Letters, Greenish, Quart	10.00
Fruit Jar, Economy, Clear, Quart	2.00
Fruit Jar, Economy, Closure & Clamp, Quart	6.00
Fruit Jar, Economy, Closure & Clamp, 1/2 Gallon	6.00
Fruit Jar, Economy, Lid & Clip, Pint	2.00
Fruit Jar, Economy, Lid & Clip, Quart	2.00
Fruit Jar, Economy, Purpling, Pint	5.00
Fruit Jar, Economy, Quart, Sun Purpled	2.00
Fruit Jar, Electric, Aqua, Pint	7.50
Fruit Jar, Electric, Aqua, 1/2 Gallon	45.00
Fruit Jar, Electric, Aqua, 7 1/2 In.High *Illus*	30.00
Fruit Jar, Electric, Globe, Aqua, Quart	40.00 To 65.00
Fruit Jar, Electric, Globe, Cover & Clamp, Aqua, 2 Quart	35.00
Fruit Jar, Electric, Globe, Long Bubbles, Quart	37.50
Fruit Jar, Electric, Globe, Stained, Pint	13.00
Fruit Jar, Electric, Globe, Whittle, Bubbles, Quart	27.50
Fruit Jar, Electric, Globe, Cover & Clamp, Aqua, 2 Quart	35.00
Fruit Jar, Electrolux, Pint	40.00
Fruit Jar, Empire, Clear, Pint	40.00
Fruit Jar, Empire, Clear, 1/2 Pint	10.00

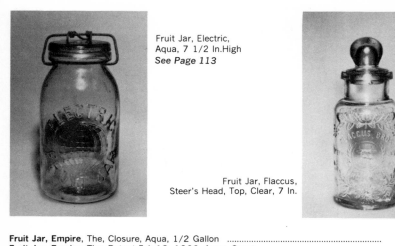

Fruit Jar, Electric,
Aqua, 7 1/2 In.High
See Page 113

Fruit Jar, Flaccus,
Steer's Head, Top, Clear, 7 In.

Fruit Jar, Empire, The, Closure, Aqua, 1/2 Gallon	30.00
Fruit Jar, Empire, The, Patent Feb.13, 1866, Aqua, Quart	15.00
Fruit Jar, Empire, Quart	3.00
Fruit Jar, Empire, 1/2 Gallon	4.50
Fruit Jar, Eureka In Script, Aqua, Pint	10.00
Fruit Jar, Eureka, Aqua	50.00
Fruit Jar, Eureka, Clear, Pint	4.00 To 8.00
Fruit Jar, Eureka, Clear, 18 Oz.	10.00
Fruit Jar, Eureka, In Script, Clear, Pint	8.00
Fruit Jar, Eureka, Light Green, Pint	12.00
Fruit Jar, Eureka, Quart	6.00 To 9.00
Fruit Jar, Eureka, Whittled, Quart	40.00
Fruit Jar, Everlasting, Aqua, 1/2 Gallon	9.00
Fruit Jar, Everlasting, Improved, Closure, Quart	12.50
Fruit Jar, Everlasting, Improved, In Circle, Dated, Amethyst, Quart	12.00
Fruit Jar, Excelsior Spring, Emerald Green, Pint	20.00
Fruit Jar, F.& J.Bodine, Closure, Aqua, Quart	55.00
Fruit Jar, F.& J.Bodine, Phila., 2 Quart	60.00
Fruit Jar, F.& J.Bodine, Philadelphia, Whittled, Ground Mouth, Aqua, Quart	75.00
Fruit Jar, F.A.& Co., Pontil, Pint	135.00
Fruit Jar, F.B.Co., Quart	8.00
Fruit Jar, F.B.Co., Wax Sealer, Amber, Quart	55.00
Fruit Jar, F.C.G.Co., Base Embossed, Wax Sealer	10.00
Fruit Jar, F.C.G.Co., Wax Sealer, Air Bubbles, Aqua, Quart	10.00 To 12.00
Fruit Jar, F.C.G.Co., Wax Sealer, Air Bubbles, Aqua, 1/2 Gallon	12.00
Fruit Jar, F.C.G.Co., Wax Sealer, Aqua, Quart	12.00
Fruit Jar, F.Dexter, Aqua, 2 Quart	25.00
Fruit Jar, Famous, Wide Mouth, Pint	11.00
Fruit Jar, Farley	5.00
Fruit Jar, Farm Family	4.00
Fruit Jar, Flaccus Type, Pale Blue	*Color* XX.XX
Fruit Jar, Flaccus Type, White Milk Glass	*Color* XX.XX
Fruit Jar, Flaccus, Amber	*Color* XX.XX
Fruit Jar, Flaccus, Clear, Quart	22.00 To 35.00
Fruit Jar, Flaccus, Glass Stopper, Clear	90.00
Fruit Jar, Flaccus, Green	*Color* XX.XX
Fruit Jar, Flaccus, Steer's Head, Flowers, & Berries, Clear, Pint	27.00 To 45.00
Fruit Jar, Flaccus, Steer's Head, Top, Clear, 7 In.	*Illus* 54.00
Fruit Jar, Flaccus, Table Delicacies, Wheeling, Square, Clear	75.00
Fruit Jar, Foster Sealfast, Clear, Quart	1.50 To 2.00
Fruit Jar, Foster Sealfast, Glass Lid, Wire Bail, Clear, Pint	3.00 To 4.00
Fruit Jar, Four Seasons Mason, Pint	3.00
Fruit Jar, Four Seasons Mason, Quart	5.00
Fruit Jar, Franklin-Dexter, Aqua, Quart	35.00

Fruit Jar, **Franklin-Dexter**, Aqua, Two Quart	25.00
Fruit Jar, **Franklin-Dexter**, 1/2 Gallon	25.00 To 30.00
Fruit Jar, **Franklin**, Closure, Aqua, Quart	60.00
Fruit Jar, **Franklin**, Quart	35.00
Fruit Jar, **Franklin**, 2 Quart	40.00
Fruit Jar, **Free-Blown**, Open Pontil, Clear, Pint	12.50
Fruit Jar, **Fruit-Keeper**, C.G.Co., Aqua, Quart	20.00
Fruit Jar, **Fruit-Keeper**, Pint	25.00 To 30.00
Fruit Jar, **Fruit-Keeper**, Quart	25.00
Fruit Jar, **Fruit-Keeper**, 1/2 Gallon	30.00
Fruit Jar, **G.J.Co.**, Aqua, Quart	15.00
Fruit Jar, **G.J.Gilchrist Fruit & Food**	17.50
Fruit Jar, **Garden Queen**	4.00
Fruit Jar, **Gaynor Mason**, The, Clear, Quart	10.00
Fruit Jar, **Gaynor**, Glass Top, Clear	4.25
Fruit Jar, **Gem**, Aqua, 1 1/2 Pint	8.00
Fruit Jar, **Gem**, Aqua, Quart	7.50
Fruit Jar, **Gem**, Cross, Aqua, Pint	4.00
Fruit Jar, **Gem**, Cross, Aqua, Quart	8.00
Fruit Jar, **Gem**, Cross, Aqua, 2 Quart	4.00
Fruit Jar, **Gem**, Cross, 1/2 Gallon	10.00
Fruit Jar, **Gem**, Cross, Midget	12.00
Fruit Jar, **Gem**, Improved	3.00
Fruit Jar, **Gem**, Improved, Made In Canada, Clear Lid, Yellow Amber, Quart	40.00
Fruit Jar, **Gem**, Midget	16.00
Fruit Jar, **Gem**, Midget, 1/2 Pint	15.00
Fruit Jar, **Gem**, New, Amthyst, 1/2 Gallon	5.00
Fruit Jar, **Gem**, Quart	8.00
Fruit Jar, **Gem**, The Aqua, Quart	3.00
Fruit Jar, **Gem**, The Aqua, 1/2 Gallon	6.00
Fruit Jar, **Gem**, The, C.F.J., Quart	7.50
Fruit Jar, **Gem**, The, Pint	7.00
Fruit Jar, **Gem**, Wallaceburg	5.00
Fruit Jar, **Gem**, 1/2 Gallon	8.00
Fruit Jar, **Genuine Boyd's Mason Back Mason**, Aqua, 1/2 Gallon	3.00
Fruit Jar, **Genuine Boyd's Mason**, Boyd's In Script, Aqua, Pint	4.50
Fruit Jar, **Genuine Mason**, Green, Pint	16.00
Fruit Jar, **Gilberds Improved**, Closure, Aqua, 1/2 Gallon	80.00 To 85.00
Fruit Jar, **Gilberds Improved**, Whittled, Aqua, Quart	90.00 To 95.00
Fruit Jar, **Gilberds**, Improved, Aqua, Quart	75.00
Fruit Jar, **Gilberds Improved**, Quart	76.50 To 100.00
Fruit Jar, **Gilberds Improved**, Star, Amber, Quart	90.00
Fruit Jar, **Gilchrist Jar Co.**	30.00
Fruit Jar, **Gilchrist**, Aqua, Quart	25.00
Fruit Jar, **Gilchrist**, Monogram, Porcelain Dome Liner, Quart	10.00
Fruit Jar, **Gilchrist**, Quart	22.00
Fruit Jar, **Gillano & Co.**, Pint	8.00
Fruit Jar, **Gimble Brothers**, Quart	14.00
Fruit Jar, **Glass Lid**, Wire Clamp, 5 Lbs.2 Gallon	5.50
Fruit Jar, **Glassboro Improved**, Aqua, 1/2 Gallon	18.00
Fruit Jar, **Glassboro Improved**, Quart	15.00
Fruit Jar, **Glassboro**, Pint	15.00
Fruit Jar, **Globe**	17.00
Fruit Jar, **Globe Tobacco**, Amber, 2 Quart	20.00
Fruit Jar, **Globe Wide Mouth**, Aqua, Quart	20.00
Fruit Jar, **Globe**, Amber, Pint	28.50 To 35.00
Fruit Jar, **Globe**, Amber, Quart	22.50 To 35.00
Fruit Jar, **Globe**, Amber, 1/2 Gallon	35.00
Fruit Jar, **Globe**, Aqua, Quart	12.00 To 14.00
Fruit Jar, **Globe**, Aqua, 1/2 Gallon	10.00 To 15.00
Fruit Jar, **Globe**, Aqua, 2 Quart	17.50
Fruit Jar, **Globe**, Electronic, Closure, Aqua, 1/2 Gallon	45.00
Fruit Jar, **Globe**, Honey Amber, Quart	25.00 To 32.50
Fruit Jar, **Glocker**, Quart	10.00
Fruit Jar, **Glosstop**, Quart	3.00
Fruit Jar, **Golden State Mason**, Quart	6.00

Fruit Jar, **Golden State Mason**, S In Triangle, Amethyst 8.00
Fruit Jar, **Golden State Mason**, 1/2 Gallon 8.00
Fruit Jar, **Golden State**, Pint 9.00
Fruit Jar, **Good House Keeper's** 2.75
Fruit Jar, **Good House Keeper's**, 1/2 Pint 4.50
Fruit Jar, **Good Luck** 2.00
Fruit Jar, **Good Luck**, 1/2 Gallon 4.50
Fruit Jar, **Green Mountain**, Aqua, Quart 12.00
Fruit Jar, **Green Mountain**, Clear, 2 Quart 20.00
Fruit Jar, **Green**, Improved, Imperial Quart 6.00
Fruit Jar, **Griffin** 40.00
Fruit Jar, **Griffin**, Closure, Aqua, Quart 85.00
Fruit Jar, **Gwh Monogram**, Quart 8.00
Fruit Jar, **H.& C.**, Quart 12.00
Fruit Jar, **H.& R.**, Wax Sealer, Quart 8.00
Fruit Jar, **H.W.Pettit**, Aqua, Pint 4.50
Fruit Jar, **H.W.Pettit**, Pint 6.00
Fruit Jar, **H.W.Pettit**, Westville, N.J. 6.00
Fruit Jar, **H.W.Pettit**, Westville, N.J., Embossed Base, Blue, Quart 6.00
Fruit Jar, **Haines**, Quart, T-3 .... 35.00
Fruit Jar, **Haines's Patent**, Closure, Aqua, 1/2 Gallon 45.00
Fruit Jar, **Haller**, Mrs.G.E., Aqua 125.00
Fruit Jar, **Hamilton**, Clear 25.00
Fruit Jar, **Hansee's Palace Home**, Cover, Clear .... *Illus* 50.00
Fruit Jar, **Hansee's Palace Home**, Pint, Clear 35.00
Fruit Jar, **Hansee's Palace Home**, Sun Colored, Quart 17.50
Fruit Jar, **Hansee's Palace**, Quart .... 32.00 To 45.00
Fruit Jar, **Hansee's**, Pint 37.00
Fruit Jar, **Hartell Letchworth**, Aqua, Quart .... 50.00 To 60.00
Fruit Jar, **Hartell Letchworth**, 3 Lug Base, Aqua, Quart 45.00
Fruit Jar, **Hartell Letchworth**, 6 Lug Base, Aqua, Quart 45.00
Fruit Jar, **Hartell**, Embossed Lid 1858, 2 Quart 18.00
Fruit Jar, **Hartell's**, Aqua, 1/2 Gallon 30.00
Fruit Jar, **Hartell's**, Bubbly, Quart 22.50
Fruit Jar, **Harvest Mason**, Clear, Quart 9.00
Fruit Jar, **Hazel Preserve**, Pint 6.00
Fruit Jar, **Hazel Preserve**, 1/2 Pint 8.00
Fruit Jar, **Hazel**, Embossed On Milk Glass Lid, Clear, Quart 10.00
Fruit Jar, **Hazel**, HA , Clear, 1/2 Gallon 4.00
Fruit Jar, **Hazel**, HA , Preserve Jar, Quart 6.00
Fruit Jar, **Hazel**, Preserve Jar, Pint 2.50
Fruit Jar, **Hazel**, Preserve Jar, 1/2 Pint 5.50
Fruit Jar, **Heart**, Clear, Quart 9.00
Fruit Jar, **Helme's Railroad Mills**, Glass Insert, Embossed 4.00

Fruit Jar,
Hansee's Palace Home,
Cover, Clear

Fruit Jar,
J.J.Squire, Pat'd Oct.,
1864, Aqua, 8 In.
See Page 117

Fruit Jar, **Helme's Railroad Mills**, Screw Top, ABM , Glass Insert, Amber 5.00
Fruit Jar, **Hero Improved**, Aqua, Quart 14.50
Fruit Jar, **Hero Improved**, Aqua, 2 Quart 17.50
Fruit Jar, **Hero Improved**, Quart .... 12.50 To 15.00
Fruit Jar, **Hero**, Aqua, Quart 12.00
Fruit Jar, **Hero**, Nov.26, 1867 On Base, Quart 22.50
Fruit Jar, **Hero**, The, Aqua, Quart .... 8.00 To 12.00
Fruit Jar, **Hero**, The, Aqua 2 Quart 12.00
Fruit Jar, **Hero**, The, Bail Type, Quart .... 18.00 To 28.00
Fruit Jar, **Hero**, The, Cross, Midget 9.00
Fruit Jar, **Hero**, The, Quart 17.00
Fruit Jar, **Hero**, Tin Insert, Aqua, Quart 15.00
Fruit Jar, **Heroine**, The, Quart 10.00
Fruit Jar, **Holleanna Mason**, Round, Zinc Lid, Clear, Quart .... 15.00 To 20.00
Fruit Jar, **Hom-Pak Mason** 2.00
Fruit Jar, **Honest Mason**, Pat.1858, Turning Pink, 1 1/2 Quart 10.00
Fruit Jar, **Honest Mason**, 1858, Zinc Cap, Clear 17.50
Fruit Jar, **Hormel** .... 1.50 To 2.50
Fruit Jar, **Howe**, The, Closure, Aqua, Quart 45.00
Fruit Jar, **Howe**, The, Embossed, Scranton, Pa., Aqua, Quart 35.00
Fruit Jar, **Howe**, The, Scranton, Pa. 40.00
Fruit Jar, **HWP** , Aqua, Pint 12.00
Fruit Jar, **Imperial Improved**, Quart, Green 6.00
Fruit Jar, **Independent**, Pint 65.00
Fruit Jar, **Iowana**, The, Closure, Quart 4.00
Fruit Jar, **Ivanhoe** 1.50
Fruit Jar, **Ivanhoe**, Pint 3.00
Fruit Jar, **J & B**, Pat'd June 14th, 1898, Aqua, Quart 26.00
Fruit Jar, **J.Elwood Lee**, Conshohocken, Pa., Ground Mouth, Screw Band, Amber 30.00
Fruit Jar, **J.J.Squire**, Pat'd Oct., 1864, Aqua, 8 In. .... *Illus* 7.50
Fruit Jar, **J.P.Smith Sons & Co.**, Pittsburgh, Wax Sealer, Quart 26.00
Fruit Jar, **J.T.Kinney**, Closure, Aqua, Quart 80.00
Fruit Jar, **Jeanett.**, Clear, Quart .... 1.50 To 2.00
Fruit Jar, **Jelly**, Square, Fancy Design, Screw Glass Lid, Wire Bail, Pint 7.00
Fruit Jar, **Johnson & Johnson**, Amber, Quart 15.00
Fruit Jar, **Johnson & Johnson**, Amber, 1/2 Pint 15.00
Fruit Jar, **Johnson & Johnson**, Cobalt, Quart 100.00
Fruit Jar, **Johnson & Johnson**, N.Y., Pat.May 21, 1895, Dark Amber, 1/2 Gallon 20.00
Fruit Jar, **Johnson & Johnson**, 1/2 Pint 15.00
Fruit Jar, **K 444 On Bottom**, Clear 3.00
Fruit Jar, **KBG** , Fancy Monogram, Mason's 1858, Zinc Lid, Aqua, Quart 12.00
Fruit Jar, **KC** , Mason 2.75
Fruit Jar, **KC** , Mason, Clear, Pint 1.75
Fruit Jar, **Kerr Anniversary**, Cobalt 9.00
Fruit Jar, **Kerr Anniversary**, Quart, Gold 15.00
Fruit Jar, **Kerr**, Economy, Amethyst, 1/2 Gallon 8.00
Fruit Jar, **Kerr Economy**, Clear .... 1.50 To 1.75
Fruit Jar, **Kerr Self Sealing**, Quart, Cornflower Blue 20.00
Fruit Jar, **Kerr**, Amber, Quart 7.50
Fruit Jar, **Kerr**, Glass Top 1.50
Fruit Jar, **Kerr**, 1/2 Pint 1.00
Fruit Jar, **Kerr**, 1915, Clear, Quart .... 1.00 To 2.00
Fruit Jar, **Keystone Trademark**, Registered, Quart .... 5.00 To 7.00
Fruit Jar, **Keystone**, Improved, Whittled, Aqua, Two Quart 12.00
Fruit Jar, **Keystone**, Pint 3.00
Fruit Jar, **Keystone**, Quart 3.00
Fruit Jar, **Keystone**, Trademark, Reg., Quart, Clear .... 3.50 To 6.00
Fruit Jar, **Kieffer's**, 1/4 Pint 25.00
Fruit Jar, **King**, Aqua, 2 Quart 72.50
Fruit Jar, **King**, Crown & Flags, Clear, Quart 7.50
Fruit Jar, **King**, In Banner, Quart 8.00
Fruit Jar, **King**, Oval, Aqua, Quart 10.00
Fruit Jar, **King**, Pint 10.00
Fruit Jar, **King**, 1/2 Pint 15.00
Fruit Jar, **Kinsella**, 1874, True Mason, Zinc Lid 6.00
Fruit Jar, **Kline**, Aqua, 2 Quart 20.00

Fruit Jar, **Kline**, Hollow Stopper, Aqua, Quart 120.00
Fruit Jar, **Kline**, Oct.27, 1863 On Stopper, 1/2 Gallon 30.00
Fruit Jar, **Knowlton Vacuum**, Aqua, Quart .... 11.00 To 20.00
Fruit Jar, **Knowlton Vacuum**, Green, 1/2 Gallon 16.00
Fruit Jar, **Knowlton Vacuum**, Lid, Quart .... 8.00 To 12.00
Fruit Jar, **Knowlton Vacuum**, Pint .... 18.00 To 25.00
Fruit Jar, **Knowlton Vacuum**, 1/2 Gallon .... 12.00 To 18.00
Fruit Jar, **Knowlton Vacuum**, 2 Piece Lid, Star In Center 15.00
Fruit Jar, **Knox**, Glass Lid, Metal Band, 1/2 Pint 5.00
Fruit Jar, **Knox**, 2 Piece Knox Metal Lid, Pint 2.50
Fruit Jar, **Knox**, 2 Piece Knox Metal Lid, Quart 2.50
Fruit Jar, **Knox**, 2 Piece Knox Metal Lid, 1/2 Gallon 4.00
Fruit Jar, **Kohrs** 3.00
Fruit Jar, **L.& W.**, Clamp Top, Quart, Wax Sealer 37.50
Fruit Jar, **Lafayette**, Amethyst 75.00
Fruit Jar, **Lafayette**, Aqua, Quart .... 55.00 To 75.00
Fruit Jar, **Lafayette**, Closure, Aqua, 1/2 Gallon 75.00
Fruit Jar, **Lafayette**, Pat.Sept.2, 1884, Aug.4, 1885, Aqua .... *Illus* 67.50
Fruit Jar, **Lafayette**, 3 Piece Closure, Dug 18.00
Fruit Jar, **Lamb Mason**, Metal Top, Glass Insert, Clear .... 1.00 To 3.00
Fruit Jar, **Lamb Mason**, Pint 1.50
Fruit Jar, **Leader**, The, Amber, Quart .... 60.00 To 70.00
Fruit Jar, **Leader**, The, Aqua, Quart 29.00
Fruit Jar, **Leader**, The, Clear, Quart 17.00
Fruit Jar, **Leader**, The, Closure, Amber, 1/2 Gallon 28.00
Fruit Jar, **Leader**, The, Reproduction Clamp, Amber, Quart 55.00
Fruit Jar, **Leader**, The, Reproduction Clamp, Yellow, Quart 70.00
Fruit Jar, **Leader**, Whittled, Reproduction Lid, Amber, 1/2 Gallon 75.00
Fruit Jar, **Leotric**, Aqua, Pint 3.00
Fruit Jar, **Leotric**, In Circle, Pint 3.50
Fruit Jar, **Leotric**, In Circle, Quart 3.50
Fruit Jar, **Leotric**, Pint .... 3.50 To 5.00
Fruit Jar, **Leotric**, Quart .... 3.00 To 5.00
Fruit Jar, **Leotric**, Whittled, Quart 7.00
Fruit Jar, **Lightning Compact**, Amber 20.00

Fruit Jar, Lafayette, Pat.Sept.2, 1884, Aug.4, 1885, Aqua

Fruit Jar, **Lightning Mason**, 1858, Aqua, Quart 2.00
Fruit Jar, **Lightning Trademark**, Amber, Quart 20.00
Fruit Jar, **Lightning Trademark**, Putnam, Embossed On Base, Aqua .... 3.00 To 12.00
Fruit Jar, **Lightning Trademark**, Quart 2.00
Fruit Jar, **Lightning Trademark**, Reg.U.S.Pat.Off.Putnam On Base, Blue, Pint 20.00
Fruit Jar, **Lightning Trademark**, Reg.U.S.Pat.Office, Aqua, Pint 4.00
Fruit Jar, **Lightning Trademark**, Reg.U.S.Pat.Office, Aqua, Quart 4.00
Fruit Jar, **Lightning Trademark**, 2 Quart 5.00
Fruit Jar, **Lightning**, Amber 18.00
Fruit Jar, **Lightning**, Amber, Gallon 22.50

Fruit Jar, **Lightning**, Amber, Pint 28.00
Fruit Jar, **Lightning**, Amber, Quart .... 17.00 To 35.00
Fruit Jar, **Lightning**, Amber, 1/2 Gallon 25.00
Fruit Jar, **Lightning**, Anchor Hocking, Pint 3.00
Fruit Jar, **Lightning**, Aqua, Pint .... 1.00 To 2.00
Fruit Jar, **Lightning**, Aqua, Quart .... 1.00 To 2.00
Fruit Jar, **Lightning**, Aqua, 1/2 Gallon 2.50
Fruit Jar, **Lightning**, Aqua, 1/2 Pint 10.00
Fruit Jar, **Lightning**, Clear, Pint 1.00
Fruit Jar, **Lightning**, Clear, 1/2 Pint 10.00
Fruit Jar, **Lightning**, Clear, Quart 1.00
Fruit Jar, **Lightning**, Clear, 1/2 Gallon 2.50
Fruit Jar, **Lightning**, Cornflower Blue, Pint 14.00
Fruit Jar, **Lightning**, Cornflower Blue, Quart .... 20.00 To 25.00
Fruit Jar, **Lightning**, Cornflower Blue, 1/2 Gallon 25.00
Fruit Jar, **Lightning**, Honey Amber 18.00
Fruit Jar, **Lightning**, Honey, Amber, Pint 31.00
Fruit Jar, **Lightning**, Honey, Pint 31.00
Fruit Jar, **Lightning**, Puce Green, 2 Quart 28.00
Fruit Jar, **Lightning**, Squat, 1/2 Gallon 3.50
Fruit Jar, **Lightning**, Trademark Putnam, Aqua, Quart 3.00
Fruit Jar, **Lightning**, Wire Basket, Amber, Quart 27.50
Fruit Jar, **Lockport Mason**, Aqua, Pint .... 3.00 To 5.00
Fruit Jar, **Lockport Mason**, Franklin, Aqua, Quart 40.00
Fruit Jar, **Lockport Mason**, Pint 2.00
Fruit Jar, **Lustre**, Glass Lid, Wire Bail, Quart 7.00
Fruit Jar, **Lustre**, Pint .... 3.00 To 5.00
Fruit Jar, **Lustre**, Quart .... 3.50 To 5.00
Fruit Jar, **Lustre**, Quart, Blue 4.00
Fruit Jar, **Lustre**, R.E.Tongue & Bros.Co., Inc., Phila., Wire Closure, Quart 6.00
Fruit Jar, **Lyman**, W.W., Quart 16.00
Fruit Jar, **Lyman**, W.W., 1/2 Gallon 30.00
Fruit Jar, **M.F.J.C**⌐, Wax Sealer, Quart 8.00
Fruit Jar, **M.G.Co.**, Base Embossed, Wax Sealer 10.00
Fruit Jar, **Macomb Pottery**, Quart 8.00
Fruit Jar, **Magic** 70.00
Fruit Jar, **Magic**, Amber, Quart 140.00
Fruit Jar, **Marion**, The, Apple Green, Pint 15.00
Fruit Jar, **Marion**, The, Dated, Quart 6.00
Fruit Jar, **Marion**, The, Fancy Letters, Aqua, 1/2 Gallon 9.00
Fruit Jar, **Marion**, The, Mason's Patent Nov.30th, 1858, Aqua, Quar .... 7.00 To 8.75
Fruit Jar, **Mason Jar Of 1872**, No Band, Aqua, Quart 8.00
Fruit Jar, **Mason Jar Of 1872**, Quart .... 15.00 To 25.00
Fruit Jar, **Mason Midget**, Cross On Back 7.50
Fruit Jar, **Mason Midget**, 1/2 Pint 8.00
Fruit Jar, **Mason Midget**, 1858, CFJ On Front 7.50
Fruit Jar, **Mason 1858 Moor Bros.** 10.00
Fruit Jar, **Mason**, Amber, Pint 15.00
Fruit Jar, **Mason**, Amber, 1/2 Gallon 35.00
Fruit Jar, **Mason**, Black Letters, Amber, Pint 30.00
Fruit Jar, **Mason**, Both Sides Embossed, Green, Pint 2.50
Fruit Jar, **Mason**, Both Sides Embossed, Green, Quart 2.50
Fruit Jar, **Mason**, Christmas, Improved, Pint, Aqua .... 22.50 To 40.00
Fruit Jar, **Mason Midget**, 1/2 Pint 8.00
Fruit Jar, **Mason**, Patent November 30, 1858, Amber, Pint 25.00
Fruit Jar, **Mason**, Patent November 30, 1858, Cobalt Blue, Pint 50.00
Fruit Jar, **Mason**, Patent 1858, Vaseline, Pint 30.00
Fruit Jar, **Mason**, Pottery, Jan.24, 1899 .... 10.00
Fruit Jar, **Mason**, Star Monogram, Pint 6.00
Fruit Jar, **Mason**, Star, Clear, Pint 2.50
Fruit Jar, **Mason**, Star, Clear, Quart 2.50
Fruit Jar, **Mason's CFJ Co.**, Improved, Aqua, Pint 1.50
Fruit Jar, **Mason's CFJ Co.**, Improved, Aqua, 2 Quart 2.50
Fruit Jar, **Mason's CFJ Co.**, Improved, Clyde, N.Y., Midget 17.50
Fruit Jar, **Mason's CFJ Co.**, Improved, Clyde, N.Y., Reverse, Clear, Pint 5.00
Fruit Jar, **Mason's CFJ Co.**, Improved, Clyde, N.Y., Reverse, Clear, Quart 5.00

Fruit Jar, Mason's CFJ Co., Improved, Clyde, N.Y., Whittled, Quart 10.00
Fruit Jar, Mason's CFJ Co., Improved, Reverse Clyde, N.Y., 1/2 Gallon 5.00
Fruit Jar, Mason's CFJ Improved, Amber, 1/2 Gallon .... 20.00 To 70.00
Fruit Jar, Mason's CFJ Improved, Clear .... 1.75 To 3.50
Fruit Jar, Mason's CFJ Improved, Midget 8.00
Fruit Jar, Mason's CFJ , 1858, Aqua, Quart 2.00
Fruit Jar, Mason's CFJ , 1858, Midget, Amber 8.50
Fruit Jar, Mason's Cross Improved, Aqua, Pint 1.50
Fruit Jar, Mason's Cross, C.J.Co.Monogram, Quart 2.25
Fruit Jar, Mason's Cross, C.J.Co.Monogram, 2 Quart 2.25
Fruit Jar, Mason's Cross, Quart 1.25
Fruit Jar, Mason's Crystal, Clear, Quart 30.00
Fruit Jar, Mason's Hero Cross, Patent 1858, Amber, Quart 35.00
Fruit Jar, Mason's Improved Midget 7.50
Fruit Jar, Mason's Improved Midget, Cross On Front 7.50
Fruit Jar, Mason's Improved Patent, Aqua, Pint 8.00
Fruit Jar, Mason's Improved Patent, Aqua, Quart 3.00
Fruit Jar, Mason's Improved, Beach & Claridge, 1/2 Gallon 10.00
Fruit Jar, Mason's Improved, Cross, Aqua, 2 Quart 2.00
Fruit Jar, Mason's Improved, Cross, Quart .... 2.25 To 3.00
Fruit Jar, Mason's Improved, Cross, 1/2 Gallon .... 2.25 To 3.00
Fruit Jar, Mason's Improved, Monogram, Ground Top, Aqua 3.50
Fruit Jar, Mason's Improved, Whittled, Midget 6.50
Fruit Jar, Mason's Improved, 1880 Patent, Zinc & Glass Lid, Aqua 3.00
Fruit Jar, Mason's Keystone Monogram, Quart 2.25
Fruit Jar, Mason's Keystone Monogram, 2 Quart 2.25
Fruit Jar, Mason's Keystone, Tin Insert, Pat.Jan.19, 1869, Aqua, Quart 25.00
Fruit Jar, Mason's Keystone, Whittled 6.50
Fruit Jar, Mason's LGW Improved, Pint 13.00
Fruit Jar, Mason's Patent Nov.30, 1858 .... 2.00
Fruit Jar, Mason's Patent Nov.30th, 1858, Amber, Quart 45.00
Fruit Jar, Mason's Patent Nov.30th, 1858, Amber, 1/2 Gallon .... 20.00 To 55.00
Fruit Jar, Mason's Patent Nov.30th, 1858, Aqua, Pint, Ground Top 5.00
Fruit Jar, Mason's Patent Nov.30th, 1858, Aqua, Quart 3.75
Fruit Jar, Mason's Patent Nov.30th, 1858, Aqua, 2 Quart 4.75
Fruit Jar, Mason's Patent Nov.30th, 1858, Blue, Quart .... *Illus*   6.00
Fruit Jar, Mason's Patent Nov.30th, 1858, Clear, Pint 4.00
Fruit Jar, Mason's Patent Nov.30th, 1858, Clear, Quart 3.00
Fruit Jar, Mason's Patent Nov.30th, 1858, Cross, Aqua, Quart 2.00
Fruit Jar, Mason's Patent Nov.30th, 1858, Cross, Honey Amber 35.00
Fruit Jar, Mason's Patent Nov.30th, 1858, Cross Monogram, Amber, Quart 37.50
Fruit Jar, Mason's Patent Nov.30th, 1858, Cross, Pint 2.50
Fruit Jar, Mason's Patent Nov.30th, 1858, Embossed, Aqua, 1/2 Gallon 4.50
Fruit Jar, Mason's Patent Nov.30th, 1858, K.B.G.Co., Quart 5.00
Fruit Jar, Mason's Patent Nov.30th, 1858, Light Green 3.00
Fruit Jar, Mason's Patent Nov.30th, 1858, Maltese Cross, Aqua, Pint 4.00
Fruit Jar, Mason's Patent Nov.30th, 1858, Maltese Cross On Front, Aqua 3.00
Fruit Jar, Mason's Patent Nov.30th, 1858, Maltese Cross, Yellow Green, Quart 45.00
Fruit Jar, Mason's Patent Nov.30th, 1858, Midget, Amber 7.50
Fruit Jar, Mason's Patent Nov.30th, 1858, Midget, Black Amethyst 7.00
Fruit Jar, Mason's Patent Nov.30th, 1858, Midget, Cobalt Blue, Pint 10.00
Fruit Jar, Mason's Patent Nov.30th, 1858, Monogram, 1/2 Gallon 2.00
Fruit Jar, Mason's Patent Nov.30th, 1858, Pat.Nov.26, 67 On Bottom, Aqua 3.00
Fruit Jar, Mason's Patent Nov.30th, 1858, Pat, Nov.26, 67 On Bottom, Clear 3.00
Fruit Jar, Mason's Patent Nov.30th, 1858, Port On Back, Aqua, Quart 3.00
Fruit Jar, Mason's Patent Nov.30th, 1858, Port On Back, Pint 6.00
Fruit Jar, Mason's Patent Nov.30th, 1858, Port On Back, 1/2 Gallon 6.00
Fruit Jar, Mason's Patent Nov.30th, 1858, Sunburst, Moon & Star, 1/2 Gallon 70.00
Fruit Jar, Mason's Patent Nov.30th, 1858, Tudor Rose Reverse, 1/2 Gallon 35.00
Fruit Jar, Mason's Patent Nov.30th, 1858, U.G.Co., Rev., Clear, Quart 12.50
Fruit Jar, Mason's Patent With Hero Cross, Ground Top, Green, Quart 12.50
Fruit Jar, Mason's Patent 1858, Aqua, Quart 3.00
Fruit Jar, Mason's, Trademark On Slant, Aqua, Quart 10.00
Fruit Jar, Mastodon, Wax Sealer, Embossed Side, Aqua, Quart 25.00
Fruit Jar, Mcdonald New Perfect Seal, Aqua, Quart 4.50
Fruit Jar, Metro Easi-Pak 2.50

Fruit Jar, **Meyer's Test**, Aqua, Quart 100.00
Fruit Jar, **Meyer's Test**, Quart 85.00
Fruit Jar, **Michigan Mason**, Aqua, Quart 20.00
Fruit Jar, **Miller's Fine Flavor**, Lightning Type, Closure, 1/2 Gallon, Aqua 15.00
Fruit Jar, **Miller's Fine Flavors**, Square, Aqua, 2 Quart 17.50
Fruit Jar, **Millville Atmospheric**, Aqua, 1/2 Gallon .... 13.00 To 18.00
Fruit Jar, **Millville Atmospheric**, Clear, Quart .... 16.00 To 18.00
Fruit Jar, **Millville Atmospheric**, Glass Screw Clamp, Aqua, Quart 20.00
Fruit Jar, **Millville Atmospheric**, June 18th, 1861, Bubbles, 1/2 Gallon 35.00
Fruit Jar, **Millville Atmospheric**, Pint .... 20.00 To 22.50
Fruit Jar, **Millville Atmospheric**, Whitall's Pat.June 18, 1861, Aqua, Quart 25.00
Fruit Jar, **Millville Atmospheric**, 1/2 Gallon 22.50
Fruit Jar, **Millville Atmospheric**, 1 1/2 Quart 20.00
Fruit Jar, **Millville Atmospheric**, 1861, 2 Quart .... *Illus* 22.50

Fruit Jar,
Mason's Patent Nov.30th,
1858, Blue, Quart
See Page 120

Fruit Jar,
Millville Atmospheric,
1861, 2 Quart

Fruit Jar, **Millville Improved**, Closure, Aqua, Quart 40.00
Fruit Jar, **Millville Improved**, Quart 40.00
Fruit Jar, **Millville Improved**, Stain, Aqua, Quart 3.00
Fruit Jar, **Millville**, Aqua, Pint 15.00
Fruit Jar, **Millville**, Aqua, Quart .... 5.00 To 20.00
Fruit Jar, **Millville**, Pint .... 20.00 To 28.00
Fruit Jar, **Millville**, Quart .... 15.00 To 20.00
Fruit Jar, **Millville**, Square Shoulder, Dome Lid, Over Size Clamp, Quart 40.00
Fruit Jar, **Millville**, Square Shoulder, 1/2 Gallon 45.00
Fruit Jar, **Millville**, 1/2 Pint .... 32.00 To 60.00
Fruit Jar, **Mission Mason**, Aqua, Quart .... 3.00 To 7.00
Fruit Jar, **Mission Mason**, Pint 5.50
Fruit Jar, **Mission Mason**, Quart .... 4.00 To 6.00
Fruit Jar, **Model Mason**, Amethyst, Quart 12.00
Fruit Jar, **Model Mason**, Clear, Quart 10.00
Fruit Jar, **Monarch**, Pint 3.00
Fruit Jar, **Monarch**, Quart 3.00
Fruit Jar, **Moore's Pat.Dec.3rd**, 1 1/2 Quart 48.00
Fruit Jar, **Moore's**, Patent, Dec.3, 1861, Quart 50.00
Fruit Jar, **Moore's Patent**, Aqua, Quart .... 20.00 To 40.00
Fruit Jar, **Moore's Patent**, Closure, Aqua, 1 1/2 Quart 40.00
Fruit Jar, **Moore's Patent**, Millville Clamp, Quart 25.00
Fruit Jar, **Mother's Jar**, Blue, Quart 40.00
Fruit Jar, **Mother's Jar**, Quart 35.00
Fruit Jar, **Mountain Mason** 8.00
Fruit Jar, **Mountain Mason**, Clear, Pint 5.00
Fruit Jar, **Mrs.Chapin's**, Clear, Pint 1.75
Fruit Jar, **Mrs.Holler**, Clear Lid, Aqua, Quart 120.00
Fruit Jar, **Mrs.Holler**, Closure, Aqua, Quart 145.00

Fruit Jar, Mrs.Holler, Stoned Lid, Aqua, 1/2 Gallon 125.00
Fruit Jar, Mudge's Patent Canner, Lifter, 2 Cylinder, Quart 75.00
Fruit Jar, Myer's Test, Closure, Aqua, 1/2 Gallon 95.00
Fruit Jar, N.O.Fansler, Cleveland, Ohio, Quart 45.00
Fruit Jar, National, Clear, 1/2 Gallon 6.50
Fruit Jar, Newmark, Extra Special Mason, Pint 9.00
Fruit Jar, NW Electroglas 3.00
Fruit Jar, Ohio Quality Mason, Clar, Pint .... 3.00 To 7.50
Fruit Jar, Ohio Quality Mason, Clear, Quart .... 9.50 To 12.00
Fruit Jar, Old Judge Coffee, Clear, Quart .... 1.50 To 3.00
Fruit Jar, Old Judge Coffee, Clear, 1/2 Gallon 3.00
Fruit Jar, Open Pontil, Rolled Lip, Deep Aqua, Quart 50.00
Fruit Jar, Opler Brothers, Inc., New York, Clear, Quart 6.00
Fruit Jar, Owen, Aqua, 1/2 Gallon 4.00
Fruit Jar, P.Lorillard & Co., Amber, Pint 8.00
Fruit Jar, P.Lorillard Co., Metal Closure, Patent July 16, 1872, Amber 15.00
Fruit Jar, Paneled, Folded Neck, Emerald Green 425.00
Fruit Jar, Patent, June 9, 1860, Cinc., O., Aqua, Quart 40.00
Fruit Jar, Pearl, The, Aqua, Quart 28.00
Fruit Jar, Peerless, Aqua, Quart 95.00
Fruit Jar, Peerless, 2 Quart 45.00
Fruit Jar, Penn, The Wax Sealer, Footed Base, Quart 100.00
Fruit Jar, Peral, The, 3 Dates At Base, Aqua, Quart 40.00
Fruit Jar, Perfect Seal 3.00
Fruit Jar, Perfect Seal, Aqua, Quart 3.00
Fruit Jar, Perfect Seal, Pint 3.00
Fruit Jar, Perfect Seal, Vine 3.00
Fruit Jar, Perfection 18.00
Fruit Jar, Perfection, Pint 30.00
Fruit Jar, Perfection, 1887, 1/2 Gallon 45.00
Fruit Jar, Pet, Closure, Aqua, Quart 45.00
Fruit Jar, Petal, Tin Top, Blue .... *Color* XX.XX
Fruit Jar, Pine Deluxe 2.00
Fruit Jar, Pine Mason, 1/2 Gallon 3.00
Fruit Jar, Pittsburgh, Quart 22.00
Fruit Jar, Potter & Bodine, Airtight, Pint, 1858 .... *Color* XX.XX
Fruit Jar, Potter & Bodine, Airtight, Quart, 1858 .... *Color* XX.XX
Fruit Jar, Premium Coffeyville, Closure, Violet Color, 1/2 Gallon 15.00
Fruit Jar, Premium, Clear, Quart 15.00
Fruit Jar, Presto Supreme, Clear .... .50
Fruit Jar, Presto, Pint 2.50
Fruit Jar, Presto, Quart 2.50
Fruit Jar, Princess, Clear, Pint 8.00
Fruit Jar, Protector, Aqua, 2 Quart 30.00
Fruit Jar, Protector, Arches, Aqua, Quart 30.00
Fruit Jar, Protector, Arches, Aqua, 1/2 Gallon 25.00
Fruit Jar, Protector, Arches, Quart .... 11.00 To 25.00
Fruit Jar, Protector, 2 Quart .... 25.00 To 30.00
Fruit Jar, Protector, 6 Sided, Aqua, 7 In. .... *Illus* 25.00
Fruit Jar, Puritan, Aqua, Quart 85.00
Fruit Jar, Putnam, Amber, Quart 12.00
Fruit Jar, Pyramid, Pint 10.00
Fruit Jar, Quality Mason, Ohio, Clear, Pint 6.00
Fruit Jar, Queen, Aqua, 1/2 Pint 5.00
Fruit Jar, Queen, Aqua, Quart 9.00
Fruit Jar, Queen, Aqua, 2 Quart 12.00
Fruit Jar, Queen, Clear, Pint .... 1.00 To 4.00
Fruit Jar, Queen, Clear, Quart .... 1.00 To 2.00
Fruit Jar, Queen, Clear, 1/2 Gallon 13.00
Fruit Jar, Queen, Clear, 1/2 Pint 5.00
Fruit Jar, Queen, Glass Lid, Side Clamps, 1/2 Pint 12.00
Fruit Jar, Queen, Improved, Aqua, Quart 2.50
Fruit Jar, Queen, Purpling, Pint 3.00
Fruit Jar, Queen, The, Aqua, Quart 12.00
Fruit Jar, Queen, The, CFJ Co., Reverse 12.00
Fruit Jar, Queen, The, Quart 10.00

Fruit Jar, Protector, 6 Sided, Aqua, 7 In.
See Page 122

Fruit Jar, Queen, The, 2 Quart	15.00
Fruit Jar, Queen, Wide Mouth, Adjustable, Clear, Pint	1.00
Fruit Jar, Queen, Wide Mouth, Adjustable, Clear, Quart	1.00
Fruit Jar, Quick Seal, Aqua, Quart	3.00 To 5.00
Fruit Jar, Quick Seal, Bail, Glass Lid, Aqua, Quart	1.00
Fruit Jar, Quick Seal, Blue, Pint	2.00
Fruit Jar, Quick Seal, Blue, Quart	2.00
Fruit Jar, Quick Seal, Clear, Pint	2.00
Fruit Jar, Quick Seal, Clear, Quart	2.00
Fruit Jar, Quick Seal, Green, Pint	2.00
Fruit Jar, Quick Seal, Green, Quart	2.00
Fruit Jar, Rath's, Quart	3.00
Fruit Jar, Red Key Mason, Aqua, Pint	9.50
Fruit Jar, Red Key Mason, Aqua, Quart	6.00 To 8.00
Fruit Jar, Red Key Mason, Pint	6.00
Fruit Jar, Red Key Mason, Quart	6.00 To 7.00
Fruit Jar, Red Key Mason, 1/2 Gallon	12.00
Fruit Jar, Red Wing, Minn., Patent 1899, Quart, Crockery	8.50
Fruit Jar, Red Wing, Minn., Patent 1899, 1/2 Gallon, Crockery	8.50
Fruit Jar, Reed's Patties In Script, Eugene O.Reed, Chicago, 3 Quart	25.00
Fruit Jar, Reliable Tight Seal	2.75
Fruit Jar, Root Mason	2.50
Fruit Jar, Root Mason, Aqua, Quart	3.50
Fruit Jar, Root, Quart	3.00
Fruit Jar, Root, Queen, Side Clamps, 1/2 Gallon	4.00
Fruit Jar, Rose, The, Amethyst, 1/2 Gallon	27.50
Fruit Jar, Rose, The, 2 Piece Closure, Clear, Quart	25.00
Fruit Jar, Royal Brockway	1.50
Fruit Jar, Royal Of 1876, Aqua, Quart	85.00
Fruit Jar, Royal Of 1876, Closure, Aqua, 1/2 Gallon	40.00
Fruit Jar, Royal, Aqua, Pint	4.50
Fruit Jar, Royal, Aqua, Quart	4.50
Fruit Jar, Royal, Aqua, 1/2 Gallon	90.00
Fruit Jar, Royal, Clear, Quart	4.00
Fruit Jar, Royal, Clear, 1/2 Gallon	90.00
Fruit Jar, Royal, Clear, 1/2 Pint	5.00
Fruit Jar, Royal, Clear, Pint	1.50
Fruit Jar, Royal, In Crown, Clear, Quart	2.50
Fruit Jar, S.G.Co., Mason's 1858, Pint	6.00
Fruit Jar, S.K.& Co., Wax Sealer, 5-Point Star On Base, Quart	18.00
Fruit Jar, S.Mc K ee, Wax Sealer, Embossing On Shoulder, Aqua, 1/2 Gallon	30.00
Fruit Jar, S.Mc K ee & Co., Wax Sealer, 1/2 Gallon	15.00
Fruit Jar, S.Royal, Trademark, Full Measure, Registered, Clear, Quart	3.00
Fruit Jar, Sachram	4.00
Fruit Jar, Safe Seal, Blue, Pint	2.00

Fruit Jar, Safe Seal, Blue, Quart	2.00
Fruit Jar, Safe Seal, Clear, Pint	2.00
Fruit Jar, Safe Seal, Clear, Quart	2.00
Fruit Jar, Safe Seal, Green, Pint	2.00
Fruit Jar, Safe Seal, Green, Quart	2.00
Fruit Jar, Safety Seal, Made In Canada, Clear	3.00
Fruit Jar, Safety Valve, Amethyst, Quart	13.00
Fruit Jar, Safety Valve, Aqua, 1/2 Pint	9.00 To 15.00
Fruit Jar, Safety Valve, Aqua, 2 Quart	25.00
Fruit Jar, Safety Valve, Bubbly, 1/2 Pint	20.00 To 22.50
Fruit Jar, Safety Valve, Clear, Pint	6.00
Fruit Jar, Safety Valve, Clear, 1/2 Gallon	12.00 To 25.00
Fruit Jar, Safety Valve, Clear, 1/2 Pint	5.00
Fruit Jar, Safety Valve, Greek Key, Pat.Appl.For May 21, 1895, Aqua, 2 Quart	19.00
Fruit Jar, Safety Valve, Green, Quart	12.00
Fruit Jar, Safety Valve, Hc, Pat'd May 21, 1895, Sun Color, 1/2 Pint	20.00
Fruit Jar, Safety Valve, Patent 1895, 1/2 Pint	8.00
Fruit Jar, Safety Valve, 1/2 Pint, Aqua	8.50
Fruit Jar, Safety, Amber, Pint	75.00
Fruit Jar, Safety, Amber, Quart	60.00
Fruit Jar, Safety, Amber, 1/2 Gallon	50.00
Fruit Jar, Safety, Wide Mouth Mason, Aqua, Quart	9.00
Fruit Jar, Salesman's Sample, Unperforated Lid, Jar Rubber	6.00
Fruit Jar, Samco Genuine Mason, Clear, Quart	67 To 1.75
Fruit Jar, Samco Genuine, Clear, Pint	1.75
Fruit Jar, Samco, Super	2.00
Fruit Jar, San Francisco Glass Works, Wax Sealer, Quart, Aqua	200.00
Fruit Jar, San Jose, Quart	35.00
Fruit Jar, Sanitary, Wide Mouth Mason, Quart	15.00
Fruit Jar, Saratoga Congress Spring, Emerald Green, Pint	20.00
Fruit Jar, Saratoga Congress Spring, Emerald Green, Quart	22.00
Fruit Jar, Saratoga Spring, Star, Amber, Pint	26.00
Fruit Jar, Saratoga Spring, Star, Olive Green, Quart	28.00
Fruit Jar, Schaffer, The, Rochester, N.Y., Closure, Aqua, 1/2 Gallon	65.00
Fruit Jar, Schram Automatic Sealer, Glass Lid, Wire Bail, Clear, Pint	4.00
Fruit Jar, Schram, Aqua, Pint	3.00
Fruit Jar, Schram, Automatic Sealer, Clear, 1/2 Gallon	3.00
Fruit Jar, Schram, Pint	3.00
Fruit Jar, Schram, Turning Purple, 1/2 Gallon	5.00
Fruit Jar, Sealfast, Clear, 1/2 Pint	5.00
Fruit Jar, Security Seal, Light Purple, Quart	5.00
Fruit Jar, Security Seal, Quart	3.50
Fruit Jar, Selco Surety Seal	4.00
Fruit Jar, Shepherd's Hook Mason, Aqua, Quart	5.00
Fruit Jar, Sierra, Pint	15.00
Fruit Jar, Silicon, Aqua, Pint	10.00
Fruit Jar, Smalley Full Measure, Amber, Quart	20.00 To 27.50
Fruit Jar, Smalley Self Sealer	3.50
Fruit Jar, Smalley Self Sealer, Pint	2.50
Fruit Jar, Smalley Self Sealer, Wide Mouth, Pint	3.50
Fruit Jar, Smalley Self Sealer, Wide Mouth, Quart	4.00
Fruit Jar, Smalley Self Sealer, Wide Mouth, 1/2 Gallon	5.00
Fruit Jar, Smalley, Amber, Quart, Milk Glass Insert	20.00
Fruit Jar, Smalley, Aqua, Ground Top, Quart	3.50
Fruit Jar, Smalley, Aqua, Ground Top, 1/2 Gallon	4.50
Fruit Jar, Smalley, ASG , Boston & New York On Bottom, Pint	5.00
Fruit Jar, Smalley, ASG , Handle, Quart	18.00
Fruit Jar, Smalley, ASG Mon., Patent 1896, Square, Aqua, Quart	8.00
Fruit Jar, Smalley, Clear Quart	12.00
Fruit Jar, Smalley, The, Pint	3.00
Fruit Jar, Smalley, The, Self Sealer, Wide Mouth, Quart	5.00
Fruit Jar, Smalley, 1/2 Gallon	15.00
Fruit Jar, Smalley, 1/2 Pint	10.00
Fruit Jar, Smalley's Nu-Seal Trade Mark, In Diamond, Quart	4.00
Fruit Jar, Smalley's Nu-Seal, 1/2 Pint	5.50
Fruit Jar, Smalley's Royal, Quart, Clear	4.00

Fruit Jar, Smith Son Co., Wax Sealer, Aqua, Quart	8.00
Fruit Jar, Snowflake, Disc Protector Lid, Embossed, Porcelain Disc, Midget	90.00
Fruit Jar, Snowflake, Mason's Patent Nov.30th, 1858, Quart	10.00
Fruit Jar, Spencer's Patent, Aqua, Quart	40.00
Fruit Jar, Standard Mason, 5 On Bottom, Aqua	3.00
Fruit Jar, Standard W.Mcc & Co., Whittled, Quart	12.00
Fruit Jar, Standard, Wax Sealer, Clear, Quart	3.00
Fruit Jar, Standard, Wax Sealer, Embossed Side, Aqua, 1/2 Gallon	8.00
Fruit Jar, Star Below Star, Clear Quart	20.00
Fruit Jar, Star Below Star, Embossed, Glass Lid, Zinc Band, Green, Quart	25.00
Fruit Jar, Star Below Star, 2 Piece Star Insert, Aqua, Quart	18.00
Fruit Jar, Star Glass Co., Wax Sealer, Albany, Ind., Light Green	22.00
Fruit Jar, Star Glass Co., Wax Sealer, Aqua, Quart	18.00
Fruit Jar, Sterling Mason, Clear, Quart	1.50 To 2.50
Fruit Jar, Stone Mason, Quart	10.00
Fruit Jar, Stone, A. & Co., Aqua, Quart	120.00
Fruit Jar, Stone, Philadelphia, Glass Top, Inside Thread, Quart	60.00
Fruit Jar, Straight Side, Metal Top, Clear, 6 In.	3.00
Fruit Jar, Sun, Aqua, Pint	45.00
Fruit Jar, Sun, Aqua, Quart	15.00 To 40.00
Fruit Jar, Sun, Aqua, 1/2 Gallon	45.00
Fruit Jar, Sun, H.J.Barstow On Bottom, 1890 & 1895, Trademark, Aqua, Pint	27.50
Fruit Jar, Sun, Pint	45.00 To 55.00
Fruit Jar, Sun, Quart	40.00 To 45.00
Fruit Jar, Sun, Safety Valve Clamp, Quart	12.50 To 22.50
Fruit Jar, Sure Seal, Aqua, Pint	3.00
Fruit Jar, Sure Seal, Aqua, Quart	5.00
Fruit Jar, Sure Seal, Blue, Pint	2.00
Fruit Jar, Sure Seal, Blue, Quart	2.00 To 4.00
Fruit Jar, Sure Seal, Clear, Pint	1.25 To 2.00
Fruit Jar, Sure Seal, Clear, Quart	2.00
Fruit Jar, Sure Seal, Green, Pint	2.00
Fruit Jar, Sure Seal, Green, Quart	2.00
Fruit Jar, Swayzee's Improved Mason, Aqua, Quart	4.00
Fruit Jar, Swayzee's Improved Mason, Fleur-De-Lis, Green, 1/2 Gallon	10.00
Fruit Jar, Swayzee's Improved, Clear, Quart	3.00 To 5.25
Fruit Jar, T.Eaton Co., Toronto & Winnipeg, Aqua, Quart	5.50
Fruit Jar, T.F.H-A On Base	2.00
Fruit Jar, Telephone, Quart	3.00
Fruit Jar, Telephone, The Wide Mouth, Quart	4.00
Fruit Jar, Telephone, The, Pint	6.00
Fruit Jar, Telephone, The, Pint, Aqua	6.00
Fruit Jar, Telephone, The, Whitney Glass Works, Quart, Light Blue, Green Lid	7.50
Fruit Jar, Texas Mason, Pint	6.00 To 10.00
Fruit Jar, Texas Mason, Quart	6.00 To 10.00
Fruit Jar, Victor, Patent 1899, Glass Snap Lock Band, Aqua, Pint	32.00
Fruit Jar, Widemouth Telephone, The, Glass Lid, Wire Bail, Green, Quart	8.00
Fruit Jar, Winslow Improved Valve Jar, Glass Lid, Aqua, 1/2 Gallon	100.00
Fruit Jar, Tight Seal, Aqua, Pint	1.00
Fruit Jar, Tight Seal, Aqua, Quart	3.00 To 5.00
Fruit Jar, Tight Seal, Blue, Pint	2.00
Fruit Jar, Tight Seal, Blue, Quart	2.00
Fruit Jar, Tight Seal, Clear, Pint	2.00
Fruit Jar, Tight Seal, Clear, Quart	2.00
Fruit Jar, Tight Seal, Green, Pint	2.00
Fruit Jar, Tight Seal, Green, Quart	2.00
Fruit Jar, Tile, Widemouth, Aqua, Quart	5.00
Fruit Jar, Tillyer, Aqua, Quart	52.00 To 65.00
Fruit Jar, Tillyer, Ghost Letters On Reverse, Quart	50.00
Fruit Jar, Toulouse's, Quart	12.00
Fruit Jar, Triomphe, 1/2 Pint	5.00
Fruit Jar, True's Imperial Brand, Pint	5.00
Fruit Jar, Union, A.& D.H.Chambers, Wax Sealer, Quart	15.00
Fruit Jar, Union, Wax Sealer, Embossed Side, Aqua, 1/2 Gallon, T-1	25.00
Fruit Jar, Union, Wax Sealer, Quart, T-1	35.00
Fruit Jar, Vacu-Top, Clear, Pint	5.00

Fruit Jar, **Vacu-Top**, Quart	2.50
Fruit Jar, **Vacu-Top**, Variation	4.00
Fruit Jar, **Vacuum Seal**, Machine Made, Clear, Pint	3.00
Fruit Jar, **Vacuum Seal**, Machine Made, Embossed Patent Dates, Clear, Quart	4.00
Fruit Jar, **Vacuum Tite**, Metal Lid, Rubber Dome & Pump, Clear, Quart	60.00
Fruit Jar, **Van Vliet**, Quart	300.00
Fruit Jar, **Van Vliet**, Quart, Aqua	275.00
Fruit Jar, **Veteran**, Clear, Pint	11.00
Fruit Jar, **Veteran**, Clear, Quart	12.00
Fruit Jar, **Victory Across Shield On Lid**, Clear, Quart	3.00
Fruit Jar, **Victory**, Aqua, Quart	9.00
Fruit Jar, **Victory**, Aqua, 1/2 Pint	4.00
Fruit Jar, **Victory**, Clear, Pint	4.25
Fruit Jar, **Victory**, Clear, Quart	6.00
Fruit Jar, **Victory**, Clear, 1/4 Pint	5.00
Fruit Jar, **Victory**, Clear, 1/2 Pint	5.00
Fruit Jar, **Victory**, Clear, 2 Quart	18.00
Fruit Jar, **Victory**, Glass Lid, Twin Clamps, Clear, 1/2 Gallon	6.00
Fruit Jar, **Victory**, Hom-Pak	4.00
Fruit Jar, **Victory**, Milk Glass Lid, Twin Clamps, Clear, Pint	8.00
Fruit Jar, **Victory**, Pat.Feb.12, 1864, Aqua, Quart	15.00
Fruit Jar, **Victory**, Pat'd.Feb.1894, Quart, T-1	22.00
Fruit Jar, **Victory**, Patent Date, Clear, Quart	27.00
Fruit Jar, **Victory**, Patent 1864 & 1867, Pint	15.00
Fruit Jar, **Victory**, Patent 1864 & 1867, Quart	15.00
Fruit Jar, **Victory**, 1864 & 1867 Patent, Aqua, 2 Quart	12.00
Fruit Jar, **Victory**, 1/4 Pint, Side Clamps	6.50
Fruit Jar, **W.G.B.T.**, 1/2 Pint	1.50
Fruit Jar, **WAN-ETA Cocoa**, Amber, Pint	6.00
Fruit Jar, **WAN-ETA Cocoa**, Amber, Quart	3.50 To 6.00
Fruit Jar, **WAN-ETA Cocoa**, Aqua, Quart	4.00 To 6.00
Fruit Jar, **WAN-ETA Cocoa**, Amber, 1/2 Pint	5.00 To 6.00
Fruit Jar, **WAN-ETA Cocoa**, Quart	3.75
Fruit Jar, **Wax Sealer**, Aqua, 1/2 Gallon	4.00
Fruit Jar, **Wax Sealer**, Cobalt Blue, 1/2 Gallon	145.00
Fruit Jar, **Wax Sealer**, Open Pontil, Aqua	35.00
Fruit Jar, **Wax Sealer**, Sept.18, 1860, Aqua, 1/2 Gallon	55.00
Fruit Jar, **Wax Sealer**, Whittled, Aqua, Quart	18.00
Fruit Jar, **Wears On Banner Below Crown**, Pint	4.00
Fruit Jar, **Wears On Banner Below Crown**, Quart	9.00
Fruit Jar, **Wears**, The, Clear, Quart	6.00
Fruit Jar, **Wears**, The, Pat'd Feb 23 '09 On Base, Closure, Clear, Pint	14.00
Fruit Jar, **Wears**, The, Pat'd Feb 23 '09 On Base, Closure, Clear, Quart	9.00
Fruit Jar, **Weck**, Embossed Strawberry, Quart	6.00
Fruit Jar, **Weideman**, Quart	3.00 To 4.00
Fruit Jar, **Weir**, Amber Lid, Quart	15.00
Fruit Jar, **Weir**, Brown & White, Pint	9.00
Fruit Jar, **Weir**, Patent 1901, Brown & White, 1/2 Gallon	8.50
Fruit Jar, **Wheaton**, 1/2 Pint	2.00
Fruit Jar, **Whitall-Tatum**, Pontil, Clear, Quart	35.00
Fruit Jar, **Whitall-Tatum**, 2 Quart	40.00
Fruit Jar, **Whitall-Tatum**, Pontil, Pint	28.00
Fruit Jar, **Whitall's Patent June 18**, 1861, Wax Sealer, Aqua, 1/2 Gallon	27.50
Fruit Jar, **Whitall's**, Patent, Aqua, Quart	16.00
Fruit Jar, **White Bear**, Aqua, Quart	7.00
Fruit Jar, **White Bear**, Quart	15.00
Fruit Jar, **White Crown Mason**, Patent 1910, 2 Piece Lid, Aqua, Quart	5.00
Fruit Jar, **White Crown Mason**, Pint	7.25
Fruit Jar, **White Crown**, Milk Glass Insert Band, Quart	8.00
Fruit Jar, **Whitney Mason Patent 1858**, Aqua, Quart	6.00
Fruit Jar, **Whitney Mason**, Patent 1858, Green, Quart	15.00
Fruit Jar, **Whitney Mason**, Patent 1858, 3 Dots Under Mason	3.00
Fruit Jar, **Whitney Mason**, Patent 1858, 5 Dots Under Name	3.00
Fruit Jar, **Whitney Mason**, Patent, 1858, Pint	1.00
Fruit Jar, **Wilcox**, 1/2 Gallon	35.00
Fruit Jar, **Willoughby**, Aqua, Quart	50.00

Fruit Jar, **Winslow Improved Valve Jar**, Aqua, Quart	85.00
Fruit Jar, **Winslow**, Aqua, Quart	37.50
Fruit Jar, **Winslow**, The, Improved Valve, 1870, Aqua, Pint .... *Illus*	325.00
Fruit Jar, **Winslow**, 2 Quart	35.00
Fruit Jar, **Wire Closure**, Glass Lid, Pint	1.00
Fruit Jar, **Wm.Frank & Sons**, Base Embossed, Wax Sealer	10.00
Fruit Jar, **Woodbury Improved**, Aqua, Quart	15.00
Fruit Jar, **Woodbury Improved**, Pint	20.00
Fruit Jar, **Woodbury Improved**, Quart .... 20.00 To	25.00
Fruit Jar, **Woodbury**, Aqua, Quart .... *Illus*	40.00
Fruit Jar, **Woodbury**, Clear, Pint	25.00
Fruit Jar, **Woodbury**, Clear, Quart	25.00
Fruit Jar, **Woodbury**, Clamp & Cap, Aqua, Quart	20.00
Fruit Jar, **Woodbury**, Embossed With Glass Works On Base, Quart	17.50
Fruit Jar, **Woodbury**, Fancy C.W.W.On Front, N.J.On Bottom, 1/2 Gallon	20.00
Fruit Jar, **Yeoman's Fruit Bottle**, Aqua, 1/2 Gallon	30.00
Fruit Jar, **Yeoman's Fruit Bottle**, Aqua, 10 In. .... *Illus*	38.00
Fruit Jar, **Yeoman's**, Fruit Bottle, Whittled, Aqua, Quart	40.00
Fruit Jar, **4 Seasons Mason**, Pint	3.00

Fruit Jar, Winslow, The,
Improved Valve, 1870,
Aqua, Pint

Fruit Jar, Woodbury,
Aqua, Quart

Fruit Jar, Yeoman's Fruit Bottle,
Aqua, 10 In.

Fruit Jar, **1858 With Reverse HT After No.**, 1/2 Gallon	8.00
Fruit Jar, **1858**, Hourglass Monogram Reverse, Closure, Aqua, 1/2 Gallon	8.00
Fruit Jar, **1858**, Sun, Moon, Star, Ball Reverse, Closure, Aqua, 1/2 Gallon	45.00
Fruit Jar, **1908**, Blue, Pint	.95
Fruit Jar, **1908**, Blue, Quart	.95
Galliano, **Soldier**	8.95
Galliano, **Soldier**, 1 Gallon	42.00

*Garnier bottles were first made in 1899 to hold Garnier liqueurs. The
firm was founded in 1859 in France. Figurals have been made through the
twentieth century, except for the years of prohibition and World War II .*

Garnier, **Accordion Player**, Label, Stamp, Full	22.50
Garnier, **Alguiere**, Pitcher	16.50
Garnier, **Aztec**, 1965 .... 11.95 To	16.50
Garnier, **Bellhop**, Label, Stamp, Full	22.50

Garnier, Betty Boop, Label, Stamp, Full	22.50
Garnier, Bluebird, 1970	4.99
Garnier, Butterfly	4.99
Garnier, California Quail	8.95
Garnier, Car, Alfa Romeo, 1970	3.95
Garnier, Car, Fiat Nuevo	3.95
Garnier, Car, Fiat, 500, 1970	3.95
Garnier, Car, Renault, 1911, 1970	3.95
Garnier, Card	4.99
Garnier, Cardinal, 1969	4.95 To 8.95
Garnier, Chalet, 1955	15.00
Garnier, Chick, Labels	22.50
Garnier, Christmas Tree, 1956 *Illus*	50.00
Garnier, Collie	14.50
Garnier, Creme De Menthe, Green	.99
Garnier, Dog, Label, Stamp	22.50
Garnier, Elephant & Rider, 1961	22.50
Garnier, Faceless Soldier	35.00
Garnier, Figural, Frosted Hand Holding Bottle, Bulged Neck, Marked Depose	50.00
Garnier, Flower Basket	16.50
Garnier, Franesa, Rabbit With Accordian, Pressed Glass	15.00
Garnier, German Shepherd	14.50
Garnier, Hen & Chicks, Label, Stamp	25.00
Garnier, Lady, Full Dress, Southern Sales	12.00
Garnier, Lady, Heart On Dress	9.00
Garnier, Liqueur, 1939, Tapered, Maryland Stamp, Brown	7.00
Garnier, Man, Bowler Hat	22.50
Garnier, Man, Brown Cap, 1/2 Full	22.50
Garnier, Manhattan, Man, Cane, Blue Coat, Pressed Glass	15.00
Garnier, Meadowlark	4.95
Garnier, Milord, Drunk	5.95
Garnier, New Mexico Roadrunner, 1969	8.95
Garnier, Owl	22.50
Garnier, Partridge	4.95
Garnier, Pressed Seal, Screw Top	9.00
Garnier, Road Runner, 1969	4.95
Garnier, Round Log, 1958	10.00
Garnier, Saint Tropez, 1961	9.95
Garnier, Scarecrow, 1960	13.50
Garnier, Skier, Label, Stamp, Full	22.00
Garnier, Spaniel	14.50
Garnier, Taxicab, Yellow, 1960	15.00
Garnier, Three Monkeys, Label, Stamp, Full	22.50
Garnier, Trout, 1967	16.50
Garnier, Turk, Full	22.50
Garnier, Valley Quail, 1969	4.95
Garnier, Vase *Illus*	13.00
Gemel, Double, Aqua	15.00
Gemel, Marked 1885 *Illus*	78.00
Gemel, Nailsea, Double, Pink & White	175.00
Gemel, Opal Stripes, Clear	50.00

Gin was first made in the 1600s and gin bottles have been made ever since.
Gin has always been an inexpensive drink, that is why so many of these
bottles were made. Many were of a type called case bottles today.

Gin, Beveled Corners, Ribbing, Olive Amber, Quart	8.00
Gin, Bininger, Old London Dock Gin, Green	85.00
Gin, Bininger, Old London Dock, Amber, 8 Oz.	27.50
Gin, Bininger, Old London Dock, Bubbles, Olive Green	40.00
Gin, Bininger, Old London Dock, Green	85.00
Gin, Bininger, Old London Dock, Honey Amber	35.00
Gin, Bininger, Old London Dock, Olive Green 9 1/2 In.High	45.00
Gin, Bininger, Old London Dock, Square, Yellow, Pint	65.00
Gin, Blown, Square Face, Open Pontil, Flanged Mouth, Olive Green, 9 In.	30.00
Gin, Blown, Square Face, Open Pontil, Flanged Mouth, Olive Green, 10 In.	30.00
Gin, Bol's, Label, Stamp, Brown, 5 In.	5.00

Garnier, Christmas Tree, 1956
See Page 128

Garnier, Vase
See Page 128

Gemel, Marked 1885
See Page 128

Gin, Case,
A.Van Hoboken & Co.,
Rotterdam, Olive Green

Gin, Booth's	2.75
Gin, Bouvier's Buchu Gin, Embossed, Label, Miniature, Clear	15.00
Gin, Brown, H.Obernauer, Pittsburg, Pa., Embossed, Amber, 10 In.Square	20.00
Gin, Case, A.M.Bininger & Co., 375 Broadway, N.Y., Square, Puce, Quart	47.50
Gin, Case, A.Van Hoboken & Co., Rotterdam, Olive Green .... *Illus*	50.00
Gin, Case, Added Collar, Avocado Green, Quart	10.25
Gin, Case, Added Collar, Avocado Green, 1/2 Gallon	11.95
Gin, Case, Applied Top, Refired Pontil, Dark Olive Green, Quart	7.50
Gin, Case, Avon Hoboken, AM In Seal On Sides, Rotterdam, Amber, 11 In.	4.00
Gin, Case, Avon Hoboken, AM In Seal On Sides, Rotterdam, Amber, 19 3/4 In.	4.00
Gin, Case, Avon Hoboken, Rotterdam, Large Size	45.00
Gin, Case, Bimal, Applied Cobalt Seal Daniel Visser, Clear	25.00
Gin, Case, Black Glass, 6 In.High	20.00
Gin, Case, Black Glass, 9 In.High	12.50
Gin, Case, Blankenheym & Nolet, Embossed, Olive	12.00
Gin, Case, Blown, Paddled Sides, Applied Top, Dark Green, 8 3/4 In.High	7.00
Gin, Case, Daniel Visser & Zonen, Schiedam On Blue Seal, Clear	25.00
Gin, Case, Dekuyper, ABM	8.00
Gin Case, E.Kiderlen, Embossed, Olive Green, 8 3/4 In.	10.00
Gin, Case, E.Kiderlen, Embossed, Rotterdam, 8 In.	15.00
Gin, Case, E.Kiderlen, Rotterdam, 12 In.High	13.00
Gin, Case, Fabriek Van Levert & Co., Amsterdam, Applied Top, Olive Green	9.00
Gin, Case, Free-Blown, Flared Lip, Open Pontil, Green, Quart	21.00
Gin, Case, Free-Blown, Open Pontil, Flattened Lip, Olive	39.00
Gin, Case, Free-Blown, Pontil, Olive Green, 1 1/2 Quart	33.00
Gin, Case, Free-Blown, Squashed Lip, Olive Amber	35.00

Gin, Case, Free-Blown, Tubular Pontil, C.1775, Olive Green	50.00
Gin, Case, J.& R.Duster, London, Embossed, Part Label, Amber	7.50
Gin, Case, J.H.Henkes, Holland, Olive Green, 9 In.	2.50
Gin, Case, L.J.F.Brands, Schiedam, Applied Seal, Green, 10 1/2 In.High	25.00
Gin, Case, Miniature, HDB & C On Blob Seal, Rolled Lip, Olive Green	65.00
Gin, Case, Olive Green, Pint	7.00
Gin, Case, Olive Green, Quart	7.00
Gin, Case, Olive Green, 6 1/2 In.High	7.00
Gin, Case, Olive Green, 9 1/2 In.Tall	4.00
Gin, Case, Olive Green, 10 1/2 In.Tall	4.00
Gin, Case, Open Pontil, Crude Lip	32.00
Gin, Case, Open Pontil, Light Green	15.00
Gin, Case, Pottery, Square, Flattened Sides, Pint	14.00
Gin, Case, Rucker's Dry, Taper, Aqua, Quart	7.00
Gin, Case, Square, Turning Purple	10.00
Gin, Case, T On Bottom, Olive, 7 1/2 In.	25.00
Gin, Case, Taper, Amber	20.00
Gin, Case, Taper, Green, Quart	10.00
Gin, Case, V.Hoytema & Co., Black Glass	18.00
Gin, Case, V.Hoytema & Co., Flanged Lip, Bubbly, Olive Amber, 9 In.High	11.00
Gin, Case, VI On Applied Seal, Dark Green, 12 In.High	48.00
Gin, Case, W.H.& Co. In Seal, Light Lime Green, 11 In.High	55.00
Gin, Case, 3 Mold, Olive Green	15.00
Gin, Case, 4 Bottles In Box, Nineteenth Century *Color*	XX.XX
Gin, Case, 8 In.	8.00
Gin, Case, 9 1/2 In.	10.00
Gin, Charles' London Cordial, Aqua	30.00
Gin, Cosmopoliet, J.J.Melcher's WZ Schiedam, Beveled Corners	85.00
Gin, Cosmopoliet, J.J.Melcher's WZ Schiedeam, Embossed Man, Green	37.50
Gin, David Viszer & Ionen Schiedam, Olive Green *Illus*	35.00
Gin, Dr.C.Bouvier's Buchu, Square, Clear, Quart	11.00
Gin, Dutch, Free-Blown, Paddle Molded	26.00
Gin, E.Gordon's Dry, Blob Top, Wolf's Head In Bottom, Aqua	10.00
Gin, Gayoso America Dry, Shaped Like A Gordon's	7.00
Gin, Geneva On Label, Green, Quart	4.00
Gin, Gordon's Dry, London, England, ABM , Aqua, Quart	3.00
Gin, Gordon's Dry, London, England, ABM , Sea Green, Quart	3.00
Gin, Gordon's, Embossed, Corker	1.50
Gin, Gordon's, Frosted, Martini Shaker	4.50
Gin, Gordon's London Dry, Square, Aqua, Quart	5.00
Gin, Gordon's London Dry, Square, Clear, Quart	5.00
Gin, Green, Quart	6.00
Gin, H.Obernaur, Pittsburgh, 10 In.Square, Amber	15.00
Gin, J.A.Gilka, Script, Berlin Schutzen Str.No.9, Red Amber	25.00
Gin, Jockey Club House, Improved Pontil, Olive Green, Quart	160.00
Gin, Juniper Leaf, Label, Amber, Quart	27.50
Gin, London Swan Gin, Label, Aqua, Quart	12.50
Gin, London, Dry, Sir Robert Burnett Co., Rectangular, ABM , Aqua, Pint	3.00
Gin, Melcher's, Geneva On Label, Green, Quart	4.00
Gin, Milk Glass, Quart	6.00
Gin, Moses, Poland Spring, Green	3.00
Gin, Old Mr.Boston, English Market, Flask	1.10
Gin, Paul Jones, Frankfort Distilleries	5.00
Gin, Philantrop, Black Glass, 11 In.High	75.00
Gin, Porcelain Keg, Contents, White With Banding	19.00
Gin, Seal, Part Label, 3 Piece Mold, Deep Green	36.00
Gin, Slant Sides, Machine Molded	2.75
Gin, Slope Side, Green	20.00
Gin, Square Face, Open Pontil, Olive Green	25.00
Gin, Steinhagen, Germany	3.00
Gin, Vandenburgh, Blob Top, Seal	35.00
Gin, Vandervalk's Holland, Jug, Handled, Clear	2.00
Ginger Ale, Canada Dry, Carnival	7.50
Ginger Ale, Coppahaunk Springs, Waverly, Indian Embossed, Aqua	5.00
Glenmore, Amaretto Di Saronno, Siena Guard, 1970 *Illus*	12.00
Glenmore, Yellowstone *Color*	XX.XX

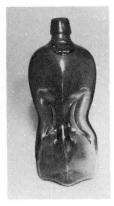

Gin, David Viszer
& Ionen Schiedam, Olive Green
See Page 130

Glenmore,
Amaretto Di Saronno,
Siena Guard, 1970
See Page 130

Globular, Club Form, 24 Swirled Ribs, Aqua, 9 In.	80.00
Globular, Golden Amber, 3/4 Quart	500.00
Globular, Swirl, Amber, Pint	200.00
Globular, Swirled To Left, Amber, 1/2 Quart	225.00 To 250.00
Globular, Swirled To Left, Honey Amber, 1/2 Quart	225.00
Globular, Swirled To Right, Amber, 1/2 Quart	400.00
Globular, Swirled To Right, Honey Amber, 1/2 Quart	225.00 To 275.00
Globular, Swirled To Right, Yellow Green, 1/2 Quart	525.00

Glue bottles are often included with information about ink bottles. The numbers in the form C-0 refer to the book Ink bottles and Inkwells by William E. Covill, Jr.

Glue, Bay State, Label, Round, Aqua, C-1758	5.00
Glue, Carter's Nickel Mucilage, Aqua	5.00
Glue, David's Mucilage, Cone, Label, Paneled Sides, Open Pontil, Aqua, C-1773	12.50
Glue, Igloo Type Fountain, Similar To C-1313, Clear	12.00
Glue, Maynard & Noyes Mucilage, Cone, Label, Aqua	2.00
Glue, Morgan's Patent July 1867, Applicator, Similar To C-1314, Clear	27.50
Glue, Morgan's Patent 1867, Igloo Type, Porcelain, Similar To C-1313, Clear	10.00
Glue, Sanford's Ink Library Paste, Embossed Vertically, Amber, 1/2 Pint	15.00
Glue, Spaulding's, Round, Pontil, Aqua	10.00
Glue, Superior Adhesive, Label, Cone Shape, Aqua, C-1766	6.00
Glue, Swan Mucilage, Cone, Label, Similar To C-1767, Aqua	2.00
Glue, Taylor's Mucilage, Cone, Label, Aqua, C-1767	3.00
Glue, William A.Davis U.S.Treasury Mucilage, Embossed Clear	7.50
Grant, Lady Scot	16.00
Grant, Scotsman	16.00
Grenadier, Soldier, Baylor's 3rd Continental	16.95 To 19.95
Grenadier, Soldier, Captain, Confederate States	12.95
Grenadier, Soldier, Captain, U.S.Infantry, Union Army	12.95
Grenadier, Soldier, Continental Marines	16.95 To 19.95
Grenadier, Soldier, Corporal, Grenadier	12.95
Grenadier, Soldier, Dragoon, 17th Regiment	9.95 To 12.95
Grenadier, Soldier, Eugene	16.95 To 19.95
Grenadier, Soldier, General George A.Custer	12.95 To 15.45
Grenadier, Soldier, General Jeb Stuart	12.95 To 15.45
Grenadier, Soldier, Joan Of Arc	10.95
Grenadier, Soldier, King's African Corps	12.95
Grenadier, Soldier, King's African Rifle Corps, Quart	29.95
Grenadier, Soldier, Lannes	16.95 To 19.95
Grenadier, Soldier, Lassal	16.95 To 19.95
Grenadier, Soldier, Murat	16.95 To 19.95
Grenadier, Soldier, Napoleon	79.95 To 88.50
Grenadier, Soldier, Ney	16.95 To 19.95
Grenadier, Soldier, Officer, Grenadier Guards	12.95
Grenadier, Soldier, Officer, Scots Fusileer	11.95

Grenadier, Soldier, Sergeant Major, Coldstream	11.95
Grenadier, Soldier, 1st Officer Guard	12.95
Grenadier, Solder, 1st Pennsylvania	16.95 To 19.95
Grenadier, Soldier, 2nd Maryland	19.95 To 49.95
Grenadier, Soldier, 3rd, New York	16.95 To 19.95
Grenadier, Soldier, 18th Continental	16.95 To 19.95
Hair Products, see Medicine	
Hand Blown, Jar, Stopper, Light Blue, 13 In.	22.00
Hand Lotion, see Medicine	
Harvey's, Decanter, Coalport	7.95
House Of Koshu, Faithful Retainer	23.00
House Of Koshu, Geisha, Blue	30.00 To 33.00
House Of Koshu, Geisha, Pink	30.00 To 33.00
House Of Koshu, Golden Pagoda	12.00
House Of Koshu, Hotei	9.95
House Of Koshu, Lion Man, Red	14.00
House Of Koshu, Lion Man, White	14.00
House Of Koshu, Maiden	12.00
House Of Koshu, Noh Mask	16.00
House Of Koshu, Okame Mask	16.00
House Of Koshu, Pagoda, Golden	12.00
House Of Koshu, Pagoda, White	16.95
House Of Koshu, Playboy	12.00
House Of Koshu, Princess	12.00
House Of Koshu, Sake God, Colorful Robe	10.95
House Of Koshu, Sake God, White	10.95
House Of Koshu, Smokisan	6.00
House Of Koshu, Three Monkeys	6.00
House Of Koshu, Two Lovers	3.00
Household, Blacking, A.A.Cooley, Hartford, Conn., Sheared Lip, O.P., Green	55.00
Household, Blacking, Sheared Lip, Square, Open Pontil, Dark Green, 4 1/2 In.	35.00
Household, Blacking, Square, Pontil, Similar To Mc Kearin 227, Olive Green	45.00
Household, Bug Killer, Kil-Lol Chemical Co., N.Y., Aqua *Illus*	5.00
Household, Clorox, Elephant Figural, 930s, Amber	35.00
Household, Dead Stuck For Bugs, Embossed Bug, Cassel, Germany, Aqua	9.95
Household, Dead Stuck For Bugs, Embossed Bug, Sun Color, 8 3/4 In. High	5.00
Household, Dick's Ant Destroyer, Embossed, Ground Lip	12.00
Household, Dirigo Metal Polish, Label, Wooden Case, Contents	3.00
Household, Hong Kong Chinese Bluing, Embossed Chinaman, Miniature	9.00
Household, M.S.A.Co.Nitro Solvent, Rectangular, BIMAL, Aqua	3.00
Household, Mouse Exterminator, Embossed, Dated 1918, Wire Legs	7.50
Household, Price's Patent Candle Co., Wedge, Cobalt	35.00
Household, Prof.Degrath's Electric Oil, 2 1/2 In.	9.50
Household, Shoe Polish, see Shoe Polish	
Household, Stove Polish, Liquid, Embossed	.50
Household, Thumbs Sunshine Polish	2.00

Household, Bug Killer, Kil-Lol Chemical Co., N.Y., Aqua

Household, Upton's Refined Liquid	17.00
I.W.Harper, Amber	4.00
I.W.Harper, Amber, Non Federal Law	12.50
I.W.Harper, Bar Bottle, Enameled, Polished Pontil, Clear, Quart	26.00
I.W.Harper, Bar Bottle, Pinch, White Enamel	18.00
I.W.Harper, Barrel Shape, Sample, Clear	18.00
I.W.Harper, Blob Lip, Amber, Quart	15.00
I.W.Harper, Ceramic Jug, Sampe, 2-Tone Brown Glass	11.00
I.W.Harper, Decanter, Old I.W.Harper In Gold, Cut Glass	25.00
I.W.Harper, Gold Medal Whiskey, Stone, Anchors Embossed, Quart	25.00
I.W.Harper, Gold Medai, Ceramic, Yellow Glaze, Quart	14.00
I.W.Harper, Jug, Ceramic, Sample, Brown & Gray Glaze	12.00
I.W.Harper, Man, Blue	9.00 To 12.95
I.W.Harper, Man, Gray	16.50
I.W.Harper, Man, White	49.95 To 55.00
I.W.Harper, Pinch Bottle, Enameled, Clear, Pint	8.00
I.W.Harper, Wicker Case, Amber, Quart	4.00

*Ink bottles were first used in the United States in 1816. Early ink
bottles were of ceramic and were often imported. Inks can be identified by
their shape. They were made to be hard to tip over. The numbers used in
the entries in the form C-0 refer to the book Ink bottles and inkwells
by William E. Covill, Jr.*

Ink, A.& E., Cone, Aqua	4.00
Ink, A.& F., Turtle, Aqua, C-610	42.50
Ink, A.W.Brinkerhoff, Pat'd May 7th 1872, Embossed, Funnel Type	35.00
Ink, A.W.Brinkerhoff, Pat'd 1872, Round, Funnel Opening, Clear, C-1359	11.00
Ink, Alling's, Blue Green	90.00
Ink, Alling's High School Ink, Rochester, N.Y., Round, Similar To C-581, Aqua	10.00
Ink, Alling's, Master, Label, Pouring Spout, Aqua, 7 1/2 In.High, C-787	20.00
Ink, Alling's, Patent Apl.25.1871, Triangular, Blue Green, C-704	55.00
Ink, AMB , Cobalt Blue, 2 1/8 In.High	5.00
Ink, American Fountain Pen, Label, Round, Aqua, C-158	11.00
Ink, Amethyst, 2 1/2 In. _Color_	XX.XX
Ink, Arnold, Pottery, Tan, Quart	8.00
Ink, Barne's Jet Black, Cone, Label, Similar To C-97, Light Green	5.00
Ink, Barne's Jet Black, Label, Round, Aqua, C-320	7.50
Ink, Barrel Shape, Embossed Pat March 1st 1870, Clear, 2 In.High	12.00
Ink, Barrel, Clear, 1870	15.00
Ink, Barrel, Open Pontil, Clear, C-668	37.50
Ink, Barrel, Polished Pontil, Similar To C-672, Clear	17.50
Ink, Barrel, Rough Lip, Clear, C-673	12.50
Ink, Barrel, Similar To C-658 In Size & Shape, Clear	10.00
Ink, Basalt, Round, Black	5.00 To 15.00
Ink, Beehive Fountain, Aqua, 1 In.High, C-649	65.00
Ink, Bell Shape, Panels, Open Pontil, Aqua, C-146	32.50
Ink, Bell Top, Round, Rough Lip, Similar Shape To C-231, Clear	5.00
Ink, Bell Top, Round, Similar To C-231, Aqua	12.00
Ink, Bennington Type, Pottery, 2 In.	10.00
Ink, Bertinquiot, Domed, Open Pontil, Olive Amber, C-575	120.00
Ink, Bertinquiot, Embossed, Pontil, Olive Amber	150.00
Ink, Bertinquiot, Embossed, Raised Ring At Base Of Neck, Olive Amber	375.00
Ink, Bertinquoit, Pontil, Dark Green	150.00
Ink, Bertinquiot, Pontil, Light Amber	150.00
Ink, Billing's Label, Round, Similar To C-584, Aqua	7.00 To 10.00
Ink, Billing's Mauve, Round, Similar To C-586, Aqua	17.50
Ink, Billing's Mauve, Round, Similar To C-588, Stain	10.00
Ink, Billing's Mauve, Round, Similar To C-589, Aqua	9.00
Ink, BIMAL, Aqua, 1 3/4 In.Square, 2 13/16 In.High	9.00
Ink, BIMAL, Aqua, 2 7/8 In.High	10.00
Ink, BIMAL, Clear, 3 3/16 In.High	8.00
Ink, BIMAL, Long Neck 2 3/4 In.High, Cobalt Blue	22.00
Ink, BIMAL, Pouring Lip, Aqua, 8 1/16 In.High	12.00
Ink, BIMAL, Pouring Lip, Aqua, 9 3/8 In.High	15.00
Ink, BIMAL, Pouring Lip, Whittle Marks, Bubbles, Emer.Green, 9 5/8 In.High	35.00
Ink, BIMAL, Stain, Honey Amber, 2 3/8 In.High	18.00

Ink, BIMAL, 3 3/16 In.High	10.00
Ink, BIMAL, 10 Sided, Clear, 3 1/16 In.High	10.00
Ink, Bixby, Amber	4.50 To 6.00
Ink, Bixby, Aqua	3.00
Ink, Bixby, Cone	8.00
Ink, Bixby, Cone, Aqua	8.00
Ink, Bixby, Jet Black, Cone, Label, Similar To C-97, Aqua	2.00
Ink, Bixby, On Bottom, Embossed Patented Mch 83 '26, On Shoulder, Aqua	8.00
Ink, Bixby, Patent March 6, 1883, Amber	8.00 To 10.00
Ink, Bixby, Patent 83, Aqua	6.00
Ink, Bixby, Pat. MCH 83 On Bottom, Deep Aqua, 4 In.High	4.00
Ink, Bixby, S.M.& Co., New York, Embossed Across 4 Sides	44.00
Ink, Bixby, S.M.& Co., N.Y., Petaled Dome, Similar To C-290, Aqua	35.00
Ink, Bixby, Yellow Amber	15.50
Ink, Black Writing Fluid, Umbrella, Similar To C-131, Olive Amber	75.00
Ink, Black Writing Ink, Cone, Label, Similar Shape To C-97, Aqua	2.00
Ink, Blown, Cork Stand, Similar To C-1056, Aqua	9.00
Ink, Blown, Covered, Pontil, Clear, C-1063	5.00
Ink, Blown, Funnel Opening, Polished Pontil, Blue, C-1038	22.00
Ink, Blown, Inkwell, Pontil, Similar To C-1036, Amber	40.00
Ink, Blown, Polished Pontil, Similar To C-1052, Clear	5.00
Ink, Blown, Pontil, Clear, C-1028	5.00
Ink, Blown, Square, Enamel Decoration, Pontil, Opaque White, C-1075	30.00
Ink, Blown, 2 Mold, Rectangular, Flared Lip, Aqua, 2 3/8 In.	7.00 To 10.00
Ink, Blue Writing Fluid, Cone, Label, Similar To C-73, Aqua	3.00
Ink, Boat Shape, Ribbed, Clear, C-1107	5.00
Ink, Bonney, Cone, Fancy Design, Aqua, C-155	100.00
Ink, Box, Writing Sand & Concentrated Ink, Labeled, C-1731 & 1740	27.50
Ink, Brown Instrument Co., The, Phila., Pa., Embossed, BIMAL, Clear, Square	8.00
Ink, Bulk, ABM, Cobalt, 32 Oz.	8.00
Ink, Butler, Cin., Ohio	Color XX.XX
Ink, C.C.Doty's Best, Round, Similar To C-595, Aqua	25.00
Ink, Cadmium Steel Black	Color XX.XX
Ink, Cardinal, Turtle Shaped With Embossed Bird, Aqua	22.50
Ink, Cardinal, Turtle, Aqua	45.00
Ink, Carter's Black Letter Ink, Red Label	Illus 20.00
Ink, Carter's Black Letter Ink, Yellow Label	Illus 18.00
Ink, Carter's Black Letter, Cone, Label, Similar Shape To C-43, Aqua	2.00
Ink, Carter's Black Letter, Cone, Label, Similar Shape To C-47, Clear	2.00
Ink, Carter's Black Letter, Label, Round, Similar To C-245, Aqua	4.00
Ink, Carter's Black Writing Fluid, Master, Label, C-822	10.00
Ink, Carter's C3 No.3, Embossed On Base, Blue Black Ryto Ink, Cobalt Blue	35.00
Ink, Carter's French Railroad Copying, Ceramic	Illus 65.00
Ink, Carter's India, Square, Label, Contents, Box, Clear	32.50
Ink, Carter's Master, Cobalt	21.50
Ink, Carter's No.1 Embossed, 32 Fluid Oz., Pouring Spout, Cobalt Blue	25.00
Ink, Carter's No.1, Embossed On Base, Fluid Oz.On Shoulder, Clear	3.00
Ink, Carter's No.2, Embossed, 16 Fluid Oz., Red Stopper, Nov.15, 1899, Cobalt	50.00
Ink, Carter's No.3, Embossed, Cobalt Blue, 6 1/8 In.High	50.00
Ink, Carter's No.5, Clear	1.50
Ink, Carter's No.35, Embossed On Base, Label, Aqua	20.00
Ink, Carter's Raven Black, Cone, Label, Similar To C-42, Aqua	3.00
Ink, Carter's Raven Black, Cone, 2 Labels, Similar To C-42, Green	12.50
Ink, Carter's Writing Fluid, Pottery, With Calendar	Illus 120.00
Ink, Carter's 1897 Embossed On Base, BIMAL, Stain, Cobalt Blue, 2 1/2 In.	6.00
Ink, Carter's 1897, Made In U.S.A., Embossed, BIMAL, Green, 2 1/2 In. High	18.00
Ink, Carter's, Amber, 10 In.High	12.00
Ink, Carter's, Aqua, Quart	8.50
Ink, Carter's, Aqua, 7 1/2 In.	3.50
Ink, Carter's, Cathedral, Cobalt Blue, Quart	33.50 To 45.00
Ink, Carter's, Cathedral, Cobalt, Pint, Labels	50.00 To 72.00
Ink, Carter's, Cathedral, Cobalt, 1/2 Pint	57.50 To 75.00
Ink, Carter's, Cathedral, Cobalt, 6 In.	Illus 75.00
Ink, Carter's, Cathedral, Dark Cobalt Blue, 1/2 Pint	89.00
Ink, Carter's, Cathedral, Label, Cobalt, 8 In.High	Illus 110.00
Ink, Carter's, Cathedral, Label, Pouring Spout, Pint	50.00

Ink, Carter's, Cathedral, Label, Pouring Spout, Quart	50.00
Ink, Carter's, Cathedral, Light Blue, 1/2 Pint	89.00
Ink, Carter's, Clover Design In Panels, 6 Sided, Similar To C-5555, Blue	65.00
Ink, Carter's, Cloverleaf, Cobalt	55.00
Ink, Carter's, Cobalt Blue, 7 1/2 In. .... *Color*	XX.XX
Ink, Carter's, Cobalt, Pint	10.00
Ink, Carter's, Cone, Amber	7.00 To 8.00
Ink, Carter's, Cone, Aqua	2.75 To 3.50
Ink, Carter's, Cone, Emerald Green	10.00
Ink, Carter's, Cone, Label, Similar To C-45, Aqua	3.00
Ink, Carter's, Cone, Rich Teal Blue	15.00
Ink, Carter's, Embossed On Base, Black & Red Label, Black Letter Ink, Aqua	20.00
Ink, Carter's Embossed On Base, 2 Twice Above, Paper Label, 7 7/8 In.High	47.00
Ink, Carter's, Embossed, BIMAL , Dark Amber, 2 1/2 In.High	22.00
Ink, Carter's, Embossed, BIMAL , Deep Aqua, 2 1/2 In.High	15.00
Ink, Carter's, Embossed, Blue Black Ink Registered Nov.21, 1871 Label, Green	25.00
Ink, Carter's, Embossed, Carter's Black Letter Ink, Label, Aqua	18.00
Ink, Carter's, Embossed, Full Quart, Whittle Marks, Quart	11.00
Ink, Carter's, Embossed, Ground Stopper, Clear, 2 13/16 In.High	30.00
Ink, Carter's, Embossed, Pat.Feb.14, '99, BIMAL , Clear Turning Amethyst	10.00
Ink, Carter's, Embossed, Pouring Spout, Blue Green, 9 1/2 In.High	45.00
Ink, Carter's, Embossed, Spout, Emerald Green, 9 13/16 In.High	45.00
Ink, Carter's, Embossed, 5 Panels, Cobalt Blue, 2 13/16 In.High	23.00
Ink, Carter's, Etched, Cobalt Blue, Pint	40.00
Ink, Carter's, Ma Carter, Screw Cap	26.00
Ink, Carter's, Master, ABM , Cobalt Blue, 32 Oz., 9 1/2 In.High	15.00
Ink, Carter's, Master, ABM , Contents, Label, Cobalt, Quart	7.00
Ink, Carter's, Master, Cathedral, Blue, 6 In.High, C-820	50.00 To 80.00
Ink, Carter's, Master, Cathedral, Blue, 8 In.High, C-820	50.00
Ink, Carter's, Master, Pouring Spout, Similar To C-804, Aqua, 6 In.High	6.00
Ink, Carter's, Master, Pouring Spout, Similar To C-804, Green, 7 1/2 In.High	22.50
Ink, Carter's, Master, Pouring Spout, Similar To C-806, Light Green, 8 In.	17.50
Ink, Carter's, Master, Similar To C-810, Clear, 8 In.High	6.00
Ink, Carter's, Mr.& Mrs.Carter	65.00
Ink, Carter's, Mr.& Mrs.Carter, Patent, 1914, Germany .... *Color*	XX.XX
Ink, Carter's, Mr.& Mrs., Red Mark, Germany, Pair	110.00
Ink, Carter's, No.1 On Base, Round, Cobalt, Quart	11.00
Ink, Carter's, No.47, Square	1.50
Ink, Carter's, Round, Clear, C-250	2.00
Ink, Carter's, Similar To C-805, Light Green, 5 1/2 In.High	10.00
Ink, Carter's, Square, Light Green	4.00
Ink, Carter's, Square, Penholders, Similar To C-510, Aqua	15.00
Ink, Carter's, Stopper, Similar To C-810, Clear, 10 In.High	3.00
Ink, Carter's, Umbrella, Aqua, Pint	6.00
Ink, Carter's Writing Fluid, Pottery, Paper Label, Light Brown	120.00
Ink, Carter's, 4 Panels, Square, Similar To C-402, Aqua	6.00
Ink, Carter's, 10 1/2 In. .... *Color*	XX.XX
Ink, Carter's, 35 Embossed On Base .... *Illus*	20.00
Ink, Cast Iron Frame, Pat'D Nov.25 1879, Good Luck, Clear	50.00
Ink, Cathedral, Quart	40.00
Ink, Caw's Black Fluid Ink, Embossed, Stained, Blue Green, 2 5/8 In.High	15.00
Ink, Caw's Black Fluid, Master, Pouring Spout, Stain, Green, 9 In., C-827	55.00
Ink, Caw's Ink New York, Embossed On Front Panel, Square, Aqua, 2 1/4 In.	12.00
Ink, Caw's Ink New York, Embossed On Front Panel, Square, Aqua, 2 3/16 In.	12.00
Ink, Caw's, Embossed On Shoulder, Aqua, 3 In.High	15.00
Ink, Caw's, New York, Square, Aqua, 2 1/2 In.	4.00
Ink, Caw's, Schoolhouse, BIMAL , Aqua	3.50
Ink, Caw's, Square, Similar To C-410, Aqua	5.00
Ink, Chas.M.Higgins & Co., New York, Wooden Slide Cover Box, 16 Oz.	75.00
Ink, Chas.M.Higgins & Co., USA 803 Embossed, Stopper, Clear, 5 13/16 In	18.00
Ink, Chemical Writing Fluid, Umbrella, Label, Pontil, Similar To C-125, Green	45.00
Ink, Chinese, BIMAL	10.00
Ink, Clark's Excelsior, Conn. .... *Illus*	125.00
Ink, Combined Writing Copying Inkete, Aqua, 6 1/4 In.High	35.00
Ink, Commercial Black, Umbrella, Label, Aqua, C-160	7.50
Ink, Cone, Amber	3.50 To 7.00

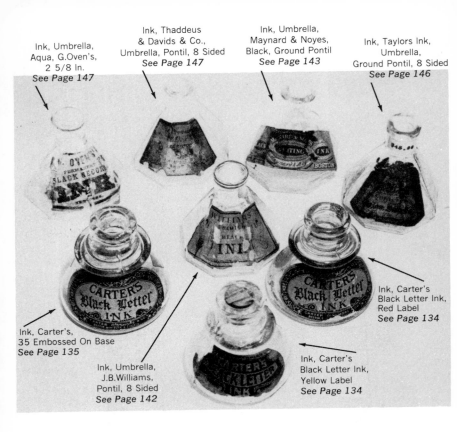

Ink, Umbrella,
Aqua, G.Oven's,
2 5/8 In.
See Page 147

Ink, Thaddeus
& Davids & Co.,
Umbrella, Pontil, 8 Sided
See Page 147

Ink, Umbrella,
Maynard & Noyes,
Black, Ground Pontil
See Page 143

Ink, Taylors Ink,
Umbrella,
Ground Pontil, 8 Sided
See Page 146

Ink, Carter's,
35 Embossed On Base
See Page 135

Ink, Umbrella,
J.B.Williams,
Pontil, 8 Sided
See Page 142

Ink, Carter's
Black Letter Ink,
Yellow Label
See Page 134

Ink, Carter's
Black Letter Ink,
Red Label
See Page 134

Ink, Carter's French Railroad
Copying, Ceramic
See Page 134

Ink, Carter's Writing Fluid, Pottery, With Calendar
See Page 134

Ink, Carter's, Cathedral,
Cobalt, 6 In.
See Page 134

Ink, Carter's, Cathedral,
Label, Cobalt, 8 In.High
See Page 134

Ink, Clark's Excelsior, Conn.
See Page 135

Ink, Keene,
Hammond's Black Record Ink,
Amber, Pontil
See Page 142

Ink, Keene,
Superior Black Ink,
Pontil, Shoulder Crack
See Page 142

Ink, W.S.Brakenbridge,
Norwich, Ct., Pontil,
Chipped Lip
See Page 149

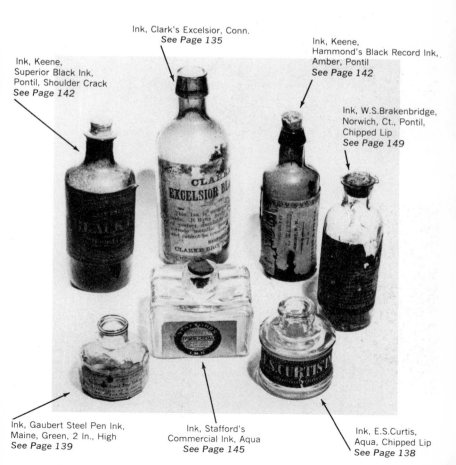

Ink, Gaubert Steel Pen Ink,
Maine, Green, 2 In., High
See Page 139

Ink, Stafford's
Commercial Ink, Aqua
See Page 145

Ink, E.S.Curtis,
Aqua, Chipped Lip
See Page 138

Ink, Cone, Aqua	1.50 To 3.00
Ink, Cone, BIMAL , Amber	6.00
Ink, Cone, BIMAL , Bubbles, Emerald Green, 2 In.High	48.00
Ink, Cone, Cobalt	6.50 To 20.00
Ink, Cone, Double Collar, Sheared Lip, Aqua	4.00
Ink, Cone, Double Collar, Sheared Lip, Green	5.00
Ink, Cone, Gaubert Steel Pen Ink, Black, No.13, Arch Row, Augusta, Me., Green	50.00
Ink, Cone, L.H.Thomas, Embossed, Label, Aqua	11.50
Ink, Cone, Miniature, 12 Panels, Ground Pontil, Aqua, 2 3/16 In.High	22.00
Ink, Cone, Miniature, 12 Panels, Rough Pontil, Aqua, 2 3/16 In.High	27.00
Ink, Cone, Miniature, 12 Panels, Rough Pontil, Green, 2 1/4 In.High	50.00
Ink, Cone, Octagonal, Sheared Lip, Aqua	5.00
Ink, Cone, Open Pontil, Blue, C-27	310.00
Ink, Cone, Open Pontil, Rough Lip, Blue, C-16	200.00
Ink, Cone, Open Pontil, Similar To C-18, Emerald Green	140.00
Ink, Cone, Open Pontil, Similar To C-18, Olive Amber	70.00
Ink, Cone, Open Pontil, Similar To C-18, Olive Green	80.00
Ink, Cone, Paneled Sides, Open Pontil, Aqua, Large, C-138	25.00
Ink, Cone, Paneled, Embossed D, 8 Panels, BIMAL , Amber, 2 5/8 In.	48.00
Ink, Cone, Paneled, Finger Dent In 2 Panels, 8 Sided, Deep Green, 2 3/8 In.	90.00
Ink, Cone, Paneled, Neck Off To Right, 8 Sided, Rolled Lip, Aqua	30.00
Ink, Cone, Paneled, Rough Pontil, Stain, Aqua, 2 1/2 In.High	22.00
Ink, Cone, Paneled, 8 Sided, BIMAL , Reddish Amber, 2 3/4 In.High	45.00
Ink, Cone, Paneled, 8 Sided, Deep Aqua, 2 1/4 In.High	9.00
Ink, Cone, Paneled, 8 Sided, Pontil, Sheared Top, Golden Amber, 2 1/4 In.High	125.00
Ink, Cone, Pontil, Medium Green, 2 5/8 In.High	75.00
Ink, Cone, Rough Pontil, Emerald Green, 2 1/4 In.High	145.00
Ink, Cone, Squat, 12 Panels, Pontil, Aqua, 1 5/8 In.High	27.00
Ink, Cone, 8 Panels, Pontil, Olive Green, 2 1/4 In.High	90.00
Ink, Congress Record, Domed, Label, Amber, C-592	15.00
Ink, Conqueror Red Ink, Label, Pen Rest, Contents	20.00
Ink, Continental Black, Round, Desk, Label, Aqua, C-722	10.00
Ink, Continental Ink On Label, Square, Similar To C-441, Aqua	4.00
Ink, Continental, Cone, Label, Similar To C-97, Aqua	3.00
Ink, Coventry	85.00
Ink, Coventry, Clark's Excelsior Black Ink, Conn., Label, 6 1/8 In.High	125.00
Ink, Cross Fountain Pen Ink, Label, Round, Light Green, C-157	17.50
Ink, Cross Pen Co., Embossed CPC , 12 Panels Below Shoulder, Aqua	20.00
Ink, Cross Pen, Aqua	7.50
Ink, Cucumber	4.00
Ink, Cylinder, Round, Open Pontil, Dug, Stained, Aqua, 2 1/2 In.High	7.50
Ink, D.& B., Open Pontil, Aqua, 1 1/2 In.High, C-191	13.00
Ink, D & D, Round, Clear	1.50
Ink, Daniel Johnson & Co., Pottery, Embossed, Penholder, Gray	115.00
Ink, David U S Treasury, Label, Round, Aqua, C-273	7.50
Ink, Davids & Black, N.Y., Master, Spout, Pontil, Similar To C-752, Green	55.00
Ink, Davids & Black, New York, Embossed, Emerald Green, 9 9/16 In.High	110.00
Ink, Davids Black Marking Ink, Cylindrical, Pat'd Feb.16th 1886, Cobalt	45.00
Ink, Davids Excelsior Violet, Thaddeus Davids Co., Round, 2 1/2 In.	8.00
Ink, Davids Magic Black, Master, 2 Labels, Similar Shape To C-840, Amber	10.00
Ink, Davids, Embossed, Pat'D Sept.14, '80 On Base, Clear, 2 3/16 In.High	35.00
Ink, Davids, Turtle, Stain, Similar To C-616, Aqua	7.50
Ink, Davis Automatic Inkstand, Pat.March 19, '89, Pressed, Chandelier, Clear	45.00
Ink, De Halsey, Embossed, Patents, Olive Amber, 2 1/16 In.High	175.00
Ink, Denby Pottery, Master, Spout, Brown, 7 1/2 In.	10.00
Ink, Diamond Brand Brilliant Red Ink For Rubber Stamps, BIMAL , Aqua	18.00
Ink, Diamond Ink Co., Milwaukee, Clear	4.00
Ink, Diamond, Paperweight Inkwell, Clear, C-1531	17.50
Ink, Dickerman's Government Ink, Label, Round, Aqua, C-274	7.50
Ink, Domed, Open Pontil, Large Size, Aqua, C-13	20.00
Ink, Dovell's Patent, Cone, Label, Similar To C-57, Aqua	11.00
Ink, E.Dietzgen Co., Paperweight, Cast Iron Base, Clear	10.00
Ink, E.S.Curtis, Aqua, Chipped Lip *Illus*	18.00
Ink, E.Water's, Troy, N.Y., Open Pontil, Aqua, Pint, 5 In., C-773	100.00 To 110.00
Ink, Ebony	8.50
Ink, Embossed Bird On Top, Aqua, 2 In.High *Illus*	65.00

Ink, Embossed X On Base, Olive Amber, 2 1/2 In.High	145.00
Ink, Emry Davis, The, Round, Similar To C-270, Stain, Clear	2.00
Ink, Encre Japonair, Pottery, Master, Spout, 8 2/8 In.	9.00
Ink, English, Aqua .... *Color*	XX.XX
Ink, English, Green .... *Color*	XX.XX
Ink, Estes, N.Y., Master, Iron Pontil, Similar To C-756, Aqua, Quart, 8 In.High	110.00
Ink, Eureka School .... *Color*	XX.XX
Ink, Excelsior Office Fluid, Master, Pouring Spout, Amber, 10 In., C-828	10.00
Ink, F.K.C., Square, Open Pontil, Similar To C-479, Clear	21.00
Ink, Farley's, Open Pontil, Olive Amber, 3 1/2 In.High, C-528	270.00
Ink, Farley's, Umbrella, Label, Open Pontil, Similar To C-131, Amber	80.00
Ink, Farley's, 8 Sided, Open Pontil, Olive Amber, 3 In.High, C-527	300.00
Ink, Farley's, 8 Sided, Open Pontil, Similar To C-526, Olive Amber	160.00
Ink, Figural, Barrel Shape, Golden Treasure, Aqua, 3 In.	22.50
Ink, Fine, Umbrella, Label, Open Pontil, Similar To C-125, Aqua	22.50
Ink, Fountain Type, Clear, 5 In., C-1299 .... *Illus*	5.50
Ink, Fountain, Banana Shape, Aqua, C-711	22.50
Ink, Fountain, Swan Finial, Pontil, Clear, C-1100	80.00
Ink, Foxboro Recorder, Square, Clear, C-432	14.00
Ink, Fred D.Alling, Rochester, N.Y.Building Shape, 2 1/2 In.	8.00
Ink, Free-Blown, Covered, Open Pontil, Blue, C-1064	40.00
Ink, Free-Blown, Funnel Opening, Pontil, Similar Shape To C-1367, Yellow	15.00
Ink, Free-Blown, Funnel Opening, Pontil, Similar To C-1367, Amber	5.00
Ink, Free-Blown, Funnel Opening, Pontil, Similar To C-1367, Blue, 1 1/2 In.	17.50
Ink, Free-Blown, Funnel Opening, Pontil, Similar To C-1367, Deep Aqua	10.00
Ink, Free-Blown, Funnel Opening, Pontil, Similar To C-1367, Light Amber	7.50
Ink, Free-Blown, Funnel Opening, Round, Open Pontil, Aqua, C-1071	4.00
Ink, Free-Blown, Funnel Opening, Round, Open Pontil, Similar To C-1347, Clear	2.00
Ink, Free-Blown, Open Pontil, Round, Clear, C-1055	12.50
Ink, Free-Blown, Open Pontil, Similar To C-1028, Stain, Clear	10.00
Ink, Free-Blown, Round, Open Pontil, Olive Amber, C-1032	230.00
Ink, Free-Blown, Round, Open Pontil, Similar To C-1035, Blue	17.50
Ink, Free-Blown, Round, Pontil, Light Green, C-1070	20.00
Ink, Free-Blown, Round, Pontil, Similar To C-113, Light Green	5.00
Ink, French's Violet Ink, Philadelphia Ink Co., Pat Oct.17, 1865, Clear	25.00
Ink, Funnel Opening Off To One Side, 10 Panels, Clear, 2 1/2 In.High	28.00
Ink, Funnel Opening, Embossed Safety Inkstand, Pat.Apl.3, '66	30.00
Ink, Funnel Opening, Round, Paneled Base, Similar To C-1356, Clear	4.00
Ink, Funnel Opening, Round, Similar To C-1346, Clear	2.00
Ink, Funnel Opening, Round, Similar To C-1348, Clear	2.00
Ink, Funnel Opening, Round, Similar To C-1350, Clear	2.00
Ink, Funnel Opening, Round, Similar To C-1358, Amber	15.00
Ink, Funnel Opening, Similar To C-1345, With Filler Cap, Round Clear	5.00
Ink, Funnel Opening, 24 Ribs, Applied Handle .... *Illus*	375.00
Ink, Funnel Opening, 25 Ribs, Round, Pontil, Clear, C-1338	30.00
Ink, G.& R.'s American Writing Fluid, Cone, Open Pontil, Aqua, C-2	110.00
Ink, G.Brickett's, Label, Open Pontil, Olive Amber, 5 In.High, C-189	50.00
Ink, G.M.W.& A.A.S., Domed, Oval, Pen Rest, Similar To C-635, Stain, Aqua	25.00
Ink, Gaubert Steel Pen Ink, Maine, Green, 2 In., High .... *Illus*	50.00
Ink, Geometric Pattern, Rayed Base, Clear	12.00
Ink, Geometric Pattern, Three Mold, Olive Amber	100.00
Ink, Geometric, Open Pontil, Clear, C-1190	325.00
Ink, Geometric, Open Pontil, Similar To C-1175, Olive Amber	80.00
Ink, Geometric, Open Pontil, Similar To C-1184, Olive Amber	120.00
Ink, Geometric, Open Pontil, Similar To C-1185, Small Size, Olive Amber	100.00
Ink, Geometric, Open Pontil, Similar To C-1194, Olive Amber	90.00
Ink, Geometric, Open Pontil, Similar To C-1196, Large Size, Olive Amber	100.00
Ink, Geometric, Open Pontil, Similar To C-1200, Olive Green, Large Size	85.00
Ink, Geometric, Open Pontil, Similar To C-1271, Olive Amber	80.00
Ink, Geometric, Open Pontil, Small Size, Olive Amber, C-1188, 1189	100.00
Ink, Geometric, Pontil, Olive Amber	100.00
Ink, Geometric, Urn Shape, Open Pontil, Clear, C-1193	525.00
Ink, Gray's Novelty Ink Stand, Fountain, Rough Lip, Aqua, C-705 & 706	42.50
Ink, Green Bixby	4.00
Ink, Green, 'R', Open Pontil .... *Color*	XX.XX
Ink, H.A.Bartlett & Co., Phila., Label, Aqua, 2 1/2 In. .... *Illus*	20.00

Ink, Funnel Opening,
24 Ribs, Applied Handle
See Page 139

Ink, Embossed Bird On Top, Aqua, 2 In.High
See Page 138

Ink, H.A.Bartlett & Co.,
Phila., Label, Aqua, 2 1/2 In.
See Page 139

Ink, Fountain Type, Clear, 5 In., C-1299
See Page 139

Ink, H.G.Hotchkiss, N.Y., Master, Pouring Spout, Blue, 10 In.High, C-860	20.00
Ink, Haley Ink Co., Embossed, Tin Pouring Spout, Aqua, 10 1/4 In.High	65.00
Ink, Haley Ink Co., Master, Clear, Pint	8.00
Ink, Haley Ink Co., Round, Aqua, C-279	17.50
Ink, Haley Ink Co., Sheared Lip, Tin Pour Lip, BIMAL , Aqua, Quart	25.00
Ink, Hard Cider-Tippecanoe Extract, Barrel, Polished Pontil, Clear, C-667	150.00
Ink, Harrison's Columbia, Patent, 8 Sided, Flat Lip, Pontil, Aqua	55.00
Ink, Harrison's Columbian, Embossed In 3 Lines, Rolled Lip, Sapphire Blue	135.00
Ink, Harrison's Columbian, Embossed Vertically, 8 Sided, Aqua	90.00
Ink, Harrison's Columbian, Embossed, Cobalt Blue, 7 In. *Illus*	175.00
Ink, Harrison's Columbian, Embossed, Light Blue *Illus*	100.00
Ink, Harrison's Columbian, Embossed, Sapphire Blue *Illus*	135.00
Ink, Harrison's Columbian, Embossed, 8 Sided, Aqua *Illus*	90.00
Ink, Harrison's Columbian, Embossed, 8 Sided, 2 1/8 In.High	50.00
Ink, Harrison's Columbian, Embossed, 12 Sided, Aqua	160.00
Ink, Harrison's Columbian, Graphite Pontil, Cobalt Blue	90.00
Ink, Harrison's Columbian, Label, Open Pontil, Aqua, C-534	60.00
Ink, Harrison's Columbian, Master, 12 Sided, Pontil, Stain, Aqua, Gallon, C-762	180.00
Ink, Harrison's Columbian, Octagonal, Open Pontil, Aqua, 1 3/4 In.High	63.50
Ink, Harrison's Columbian, Open Pontil, Aqua, 2 1/2 In.	55.00
Ink, Harrison's Columbian, Open Pontil, Rough Lip, Aqua, 3 1/2 In.High, C-537	30.00
Ink, Harrison's Columbian, Open Pontil, Similar To C-534, Aqua, 2 1/4 In.	50.00
Ink, Harrison's Columbian, Open Pontil, Similar To C-535, Aqua, 2 1/2 In.	45.00
Ink, Harrison's Columbian, Open Pontil, Similar To C-535, Aqua, 3 In.High	55.00
Ink, Harrison's Columbian, Open Pontil, Similar To C-764, Blue, 3 1/2 In.	250.00
Ink, Harrison's Columbian, Open Pontil, 3 1/2 In.High	49.00

Ink, Harrison's Columbian,
Embossed, Cobalt Blue, 7 In.
See Page 140

Ink, Harrison's Columbian,
12 Sided, 7 3/16 In.

Ink, Harrison's Columbian,
Embossed, Sapphire Blue
See Page 140

Ink, Harrison's Columbian,
Embossed, Light Blue
See Page 140

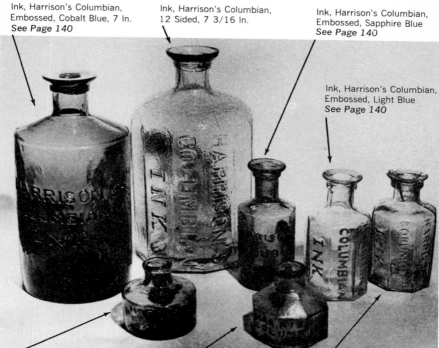

Ink, Harrison's Columbian,
Sapphire Blue, 2 In.High

Ink, Harrison's Columbian,
8 Sided, 2 In.High

Ink, Harrison's Columbian,
Embossed, 8 Sided, Aqua
See Page 140

Ink, Harrison's Columbian, Pontil, Cobalt, Pint		225.00
Ink, Harrison's Columbian, Round, Open Pontil, Similar To C-194, Blue		190.00
Ink, Harrison's Columbian, Sapphire Blue, 2 In.High	*Illus*	135.00
Ink, Harrison's Columbian, 8 Sided, Open Pontil, Similar To C-529, Aqua		65.00
Ink, Harrison's Columbian, 8 Sided, Open Pontil, Similar To C-529, Green		140.00
Ink, Harrison's Columbian, 8 Sided, Open Pontil, Similar To C-530, Aqua		65.00
Ink, Harrison's Columbian, 8 Sided, Open Pontil, Similar To C-531, Aqua		55.00
Ink, Harrison's Columbian, 8 Sided, Open Pontil, Similar To C-531, Green		170.00
Ink, Harrison's Columbian, 8 Sided, 2 In.High	*Illus*	50.00
Ink, Harrison's Columbian, 12 Sided, Master, Similar To C-761, Aqua, Quart		65.00
Ink, Harrison's Columbian, 12 Sided, 7 3/16 In.	*Illus*	160.00
Ink, Higgin's, Aqua, 7 7/8 In.High		4.00
Ink, Higgin's, Embossed, Round, Clear, 32 Oz.		10.00
Ink, Hohenthal Brothers & Co., Indelible, N.Y., Pour Spout, Pontil, Amber		325.00
Ink, Honey Amber, 2 1/2 In.	*Color*	XX.XX
Ink, Hooker's, Square, Off-Center Mouth, Penholders, Similar To C-499, Aqua		42.50
Ink, Horizontally Ribbed, Open Pontil, Similar To C-1169, Olive Green		170.00
Ink, Hotchkiss, Lyons, N.Y., Master, Pouring Spout, Blue, 9 1/2 In., C-860		15.00
Ink, House, Aqua, C-505		60.00
Ink, House, Aqua, C-681		130.00
Ink, House, Aqua, Stain, C-693		35.00
Ink, House, Clear, Stain, C-680		90.00
Ink, House, Cobalt		37.50
Ink, House, Lip Bruise, Clear, C-677		160.00
Ink, House, Rough Lip, Similar To C-684, Aqua		110.00
Ink, Igloo, Rough Lip, Similar To C-647, Amber		170.00

Ink, **Igloo**, Rough Lip, Similar To C-647, Blue		160.00
Ink, **Igloo**, Similar Shape To C-647, Aqua		17.50
Ink, **Inkwell**, Brass, Traveling		15.00
Ink, **Inkwell**, Sandwich, Ribbed, Similar To C-1172, Rough Lip, Clear		80.00
Ink, **Inkwell**, Sandwich, Ribbed, Similar To C-1173, Rough Lip, Blue		180.00
Ink, **Inkwell**, Three Openings, Porcelain, White		12.50
Ink, **Inkwell**, Tin, Paper Label On Base, Black Paint With Gold Stripe, C-1674		20.00
Ink, **J.& I.E.M.**, Embossed On 6 Of 10 Panels, X On Base, Aqua, 2 1/8 In.Tall		45.00
Ink, **J.& I.E.M.**, Embossed With Bird, Turtle Type, Blue Green, 1 1/2 In.High		90.00
Ink, **J.& I.E.M.**, Embossed, Mold Line Between I & E, Wax Stopper, Aqua		75.00
Ink, **J.& I.E.M.**, Honey Amber		85.00
Ink, **J.& I.E.M.**, Igloo, Similar To C-632, Aqua		20.00
Ink, **J.& I.E.M.**, Line Between I & E, Bimal, Aqua		18.00
Ink, **J.& I.E.M.**, Turtle		12.00
Ink, **J.& I.E.M.**, Turtle, Aqua		13.50
Ink, **J.& I.E.M.**, Turtle Shape, Yellow		165.00
Ink, **J.& I.E.M.**, Turtle, Cobalt Blue		325.00
Ink, **J & I E M**, Turtle, Dated 1865		25.00
Ink, **J & I E M**, Turtle, Dated, Aqua		17.00
Ink, **J.& I E M**, Turtle, Label, Similar To C-626, Aqua		15.00
Ink, **J & I E M**, Turtle, Label, Similar To C-628, Amber		90.00
Ink, **J & I E M**, Turtle, Lip Bruise, Similar To C-627, Aqua		7.00
Ink, **J & I E M**, Turtle, Similar To C-627, Lip Bruise, Clear		85.00
Ink, **J & I E M**, Turtle, Similar To C-628, Blue		200.00
Ink, **J.& I.E.Moore**, Embossed, Pouring Lip, Aqua, 7 15/16 In.		55.00
Ink, **J.B.Williams**, Umbrella, Pontil, 8 Sided	*Illus*	48.00
Ink, **J.Bourne & Son**, London England, Vitreous Stone, Light Brown		16.00
Ink, **J.Bourne**, 1/2 Pint		6.00
Ink, **J.Field**, Embossed On Side, Square, Aqua, 2 3/16 In.High		50.00
Ink, **J.J.Butler**, Cin., O., Label, Round, Aqua, C-594		30.00
Ink, **J.K.Palmer Chemist Boston**, Master, Spout, Pontil, Olive Amber, C-107		55.00
Ink, **J.Kidder**, Square, Open Pontil, Similar To C-482, Stain, Aqua		22.50
Ink, **J.M.& S.**, Igloo, Similar To C-632, Rough Lip, Aqua		12.50
Ink, **J.M.& S.**, Igloo, Similar To C-633, Aqua		22.50
Ink, **J.S.Dunham**, Umbrella, Open Pontil, Aqua, C-116		280.00
Ink, **J.W.Pennell**, 8 Sided, Aqua		35.00
Ink, **James P.Scott's**, Embossed, Ground Pontil, Aqua, 2 7/8 In.High		45.00
Ink, **Jet Black Eagle**, Round, Similar To C-539, Aqua		17.50
Ink, **Jet Black High School**, Aqua, 3 In.	*Illus*	50.00
Ink, **John G.Tilton & Co.**, Umbrella, Open Pontil, Similar To C-125, Aqua		25.00
Ink, **John Holland Cincinnati**, Square, Similar To C-437, Stain, Aqua		17.50
Ink, **Josiah Jonson's Japan Writing Fluid**, London, Teakettle, Pottery, C-1242		115.00
Ink, **Joy's**, Embossed, Pouring Lip, Aqua, 9 9/16 In.		108.00
Ink, **Keene Geometric**, Open Pontil, Olive Amber		85.00
Ink, **Keene**, Geometric		85.00 To 125.00
Ink, **Keene**, Hammond's Black Record Ink, Amber, Pontil	*Illus*	125.00
Ink, **Keene**, Hammond's Black Record Ink, By J.Harris, Amber		125.00
Ink, **Keene**, Superior Black Ink, Pontil, Shoulder Crack	*Illus*	75.00
Ink, **Keller's Inks & Mucilage Paste & Sealing Wax,** Grayish Pottery		35.00

Ink, Jet Black High School, Aqua, 3 In.

Ink, Keller's Superior Writing Fluid, Detroit, Pottery, Blue Gray To White	27.00
Ink, Keller's, Detroit .... *Color*	XX.XX
Ink, Kensington, Flint Glass, Log Cabin, Fire Polished Base, 3 1/4 In.High	450.00
Ink, Kirtland's Ink, W.& H., Igloo, Stain, Rough Lip, Aqua, C-622	25.00
Ink, Kit, Francis Kidder's Original Indelible, 2 Bottles In Box, Pontils	50.00
Ink, Ky.G.W.Embossed On Bottom, Square, Beveled Edges, Aqua, 1 1/2 In.High	23.50
Ink, L.& W., Embossed On Base, Aqua 2 1/2 In.High	40.00
Ink, L.H.Thomas, Cone, Similar To C-77, Aqua	35.00
Ink, L.H.Thomas, Master, Aqua, 6 1/2 In.High, C-907	15.00
Ink, L.H.Thomas, Oct.16, 1883, Paper Label .... *Color*	XX.XX
Ink, L.H.Thomas, Spout, Label, Aqua, Quart	35.00
Ink, Label, Stopper, Cobalt Blue, Quart	55.00
Ink, Lead, Small, C-1645	6.00
Ink, Levison's, Schoolhouse, 2 1/2 In.	150.00
Ink, Levison's, St.Louis, Neck In Center Of Bottle, Schoolhouse, Amber	80.00
Ink, Locomotive, Trade Mark, Patented Oct.1874, Aqua, C-715	400.00
Ink, Log Cabin, Kensington, C-677 .... *Illus*	450.00
Ink, M.C.Hotchkiss Lyons, N.Y., Embossed, Pouring Lip, Amber	100.00
Ink, Made In Spain, Embossed On Bottom, Pen Holder, Deep Green, 2 1/8 In.	15.00
Ink, Maltese Cross In Panels, Turtle, Similar To C-640, Aqua .... 20.00 To 27.50	
Ink, Martell's Black, Cone, Label, Similar Shape To C-97, Aqua	3.00
Ink, Master, Corker, Spout, 1886, Amber	6.00
Ink, Master, Cylindrical, Tapered Collar, Depressed Pontil, Olive Green	45.00
Ink, Master, Fluted Shoulder, Aqua To Light Green	9.00
Ink, Master, Patent Date 1886, Amber	5.00
Ink, Master, Pour Lip, Green, Pint	12.00
Ink, Master, Pouring Lip, Olive Green, 9 11/16 In.High	27.00
Ink, Master, Pouring Lip, Open Pontil, Emerald Green, 3/4 Quart .... 17.50 To 20.00	
Ink, Master, Pouring Spout, Open Pontil, Round, Amber	45.00
Ink, Master, Pouring Spout, Similar Shape To C-735, Stain, Burst Bubble, Blue	15.00
Ink, Master, Pouring Spout, Similar Shape To C-861, Green, 10 In.High	15.00
Ink, Master, Pouring Spout, Similar To C-861, Olive Amber, 9 1/2 In.High	20.00
Ink, Master, Pouring Spout, Similar To C-935, Green, 6 1/2 In.High	10.00
Ink, Master, Pouring Spout, Similar To C-937, Olive Green, 7 1/2 In.High	12.50
Ink, Master, Pouring Spout, Similar To C-937, Olive Green, 7 1/4 In.High	15.00
Ink, Master, Round, Pouring Spout, Open Pontil, Amber	45.00
Ink, Master, Similar Shape To C-917, Light Green, 10 In.High	13.00
Ink, Master, 12 Sided, Spout, Iron Pontil, Emerald Green, 2 Quart, C-780	320.00
Ink, Maynard & Noyes Black Ink, Umbrella, 8 Sided, Aqua	48.00
Ink, Maynard & Noyes Black, Umbrella, Ground Pontil .... *Illus*	48.00
Ink, Maynard & Noyes, Master, June 24, 1866, Pouring Lip, Olive Green	225.00
Ink, Maynard & Noyes, Master, Pouring Spouts, Similar To C-925, Olive Amber	20.00
Ink, Maynard & Noyes, Umbrella, Label, Similar To C-10, Stain, Rough Lip, Aqua	90.00
Ink, Mc Kearin G II -2, Coventry, Medium Green, 1 11/16 In.High	125.00
Ink, Mc Kearin G II -2, Coventry, Olive Green, 1 10/16 In.High	135.00
Ink, Mc Kearin G II -2, Geometric	110.00
Ink, Mc Kearin G II -15, Dark Olive Amber, 1 5/8 In.High	175.00
Ink, Mc Kearin G II -15, Olive Amber, 1 9/16 In.High	175.00
Ink, Mc Kearin G II -16a, Coventry, Medium Green, 2 1/2 In.High	125.00
Ink, Mc Kearin G II -16a, Coventry, Olive Amber, 1 3/8 In.High	125.00
Ink, Mc Kearin G II -18, Coventry, Olive Amber, 1 11/16 In.High	135.00
Ink, Mc Kearin G II -18b, Keene, Medium Green, 1 5/8 In.High	160.00
Ink, Mc Kearin G II -18c, Keene, Olive Amber, 1 5/8 In.High	160.00
Ink, Mc Kearin G II -18d, Coventry, Dark Olive Green, 1 1/2 In.High	125.00
Ink, Mc Kearin G II -18d, Coventry, Medium Dark Green, 1 11/16 In.High	135.00
Ink, Mc Kearin G II -18f, Keene, Medium Dark Green, 2 15/16 In.High	135.00
Ink, Mc Kearin G III -29, Keene, Olive Green, 1 3/8 In.High	145.00
Ink, Mc Kearin G 120, No.2, Geometric, Rough Pontil, Olive Amber	99.00
Ink, Milk Glass, Teakettle, Pink & Gold Flowers	195.00
Ink, Moore's Writing Fluid, Round, Label, Bruise, Aqua, C-296	2.00
Ink, Morgan's Patent July 16 1867, Embossed, Pewter Cap, 12 Sides, Clear	50.00
Ink, Morgan's Patent July 16 1867, Embossed, 12 Panels, Domed, Clear	35.00
Ink, Muspratt's, Igloo, Label, Rough Lip, Aqua, C-934	16.00
Ink, N.C.Brakenridge, Umbrella, Norwich, Conn., Open Pontil, Label, Aqua	35.00
Ink, N.Y. On Base, Umbrella, Similar To C-165 & 166, Aqua	12.50
Ink, Oblong Shape, Pen Rests, Sheared Lip, Aqua	22.00

Ink, Oliver Typewriter, The, BIMAL , Clear	7.00
Ink, Opdyke Bros., Embossed, Barrel Shape, Aqua, 2 1/2 In.High	55.00
Ink, Open Pontil, Frosted	6.00
Ink, Open Pontil, Olive Amber, 2 1/2 In.High, C-217	35.00
Ink, Open Pontil, Olive Amber, 4 In.High, C-209	50.00
Ink, Open Pontil, Similar To C-210, Olive Green, 2 In.High	42.50
Ink, Oval, Penholder, Rough Lip, Aqua, C-703	10.00
Ink, P.J.Arnold, Master, Pottery, 9 1/8 In.	8.00
Ink, Paneled Shoulder, Round, Similar To C-877, Aqua	8.00
Ink, Paperweight Inkwell, Pontil, Light Green, C-1060	15.00
Ink, Parker's, Diamond Shape, Cap, ABM	1.00
Ink, Parker's, Diamond Shape, Embossed, Cobalt	10.00
Ink, Patent Applied For, Boat, Similar To C-719, Stain, Aqua	10.00
Ink, Patent 1876, Light Blue, 5 In. *Illus*	150.00
Ink, Patented July 1895, Round, Similar To C-366, Aqua	5.00
Ink, Patented, March 12, 1870, Barrel, Clear, C-672	15.00
Ink, Paul's Safety Bottle & Ink Co., N.Y., Embossed, Label, Clear	10.00
Ink, Paul's Safety, Quart	10.00
Ink, Pestle Shape, Quill Holder, Redware & Papier-Mache, C-1536 & 1537	75.00
Ink, Petaled Dome, Similar To C-605, Aqua	10.00
Ink, Petroleum P.B. & Co., Barrel, Similar To C-665, Stain, No Lip, Aqua	10.00
Ink, Pitkin Type, Swirled Ribs, Open Pontil, Bruise, Similar To C-1153, Amber	130.00
Ink, Pitkin Type, Swirled Ribs, Open Pontil, Similar Shape To C-1160, Amber	160.00
Ink, Pitkin Type, Swirled Ribs, Open Pontil, Similar To C-1134, Olive Amber	200.00
Ink, Pitkin Type, Swirled Ribs, Open Pontil, Similar To C-1158, Olive Amber	190.00
Ink, Pitkin Type, Swirled Ribs, Open Pontil, Similar To C-1159, Olive Green	200.00
Ink, Pitkin Type, 36 Melon Ribs, Open Pontil, Olive Amber, C-1130	510.00
Ink, Pitkin, Square, Bright Clear Olive Amber	185.00
Ink, Pitkin, 36 Ribs Swirled Left, Green, 1 1/2 In.High	350.00
Ink, Pitkin, 36 Ribs Swirled Left, Round, Olive Green, 1 7/16 In.High	350.00
Ink, Pitkin, 36 Ribs Swirled Left, 2 1/4 In.Square, Olive Green, 1 3/8 In.	350.00
Ink, Pitkin, 36 Ribs Swirled Left, 2 1/4 In.Square, Olive Green, 1 9/16 In.	350.00
Ink, Pitkin, 36 Ribs Swirled Right, Olive Green, 1 7/8 In.High	350.00
Ink, Pitkin, 36 Ribs Swirled Right, Round, Olive Green, 1 1/2 In.High	375.00
Ink, Pomeroy's, BIMAL , Aqua, 1/2 Pint	8.00
Ink, Pontil, Cylindrical, Medium Green, 6 1/4 In.	16.00
Ink, Porcelain, Brass Cover, 2 Holes For Quills, Pouring Spout, White	75.00
Ink, Poss's, Label, Open Pontil, Aqua	30.00
Ink, Pottery, Round	8.00
Ink, Pottery, Wide Mouth, Tan, Pint	6.00
Ink, Pour Lip, BIMAL , Cobalt, 16 Oz.	4.50
Ink, Pressed, Brass Hinged Cover & Pen Rack, English Mark Of 1874, Clear	25.00
Ink, Pressed, Hobnail Pattern, Clear, Square, 2 1/2 In.High	85.00
Ink, Rectangular, Penholder, Similar To C-498, Green	22.50
Ink, Rectangular, Penholders, Similar To C-511, Clear	2.00
Ink, Rideout & Co., Umbrella, Label, Open Pontil, Similar To C-131, Amber	90.00
Ink, Round, Amber, 1 7/8 In.	7.00
Ink, Round, BIMAL , Dug, Cobalt	2.00
Ink, Round, Cobalt Blue, 3 1/8 In.	4.00
Ink, Round, Flaring Lip, Aqua, C-359	4.00
Ink, Round, Pontil, Light Green, 7 1/2 In.High, C-1027	
Ink, Round, Rough Lip, Aqua, C-729	6.00
Ink, Round, 4 Dots, Cobalt	4.00
Ink, S.Fine Black Ink, Green, Open Pontil	165.00
Ink, S.Fine, Black Ink, Round, Open Pontil, Similar To C-192, Aqua	80.00
Ink, S.O.Dunbar, Taunton, Mass., Crude, Collared Lip, Aqua, Pint	37.50
Ink, S.O.Dunbar, Taunton, Mass., Master, Spout, Similar To C-755, Aqua	32.50
Ink, S.O.Dunbar, Taunton, Mass., Similar To C-755 Center, Aqua, 7 1/2 In.	10.00
Ink, S.O.Dunbar, Taunton, Umbrella, Label, O.P., Similar To C-115, Aqua	65.00
Ink, S.O.Dunbar, Umbrella, Label, Aqua, C-161	22.50
Ink, S.S.Stafford's Inks, Embossed In Square, Pouring Lip, Cobalt Blue	10.00
Ink, S.S.Stafford's Inks, Made In U.S.A.Embossed, BIMAL , Cobalt Blue, Qt.	28.00
Ink, S.S.Stafford's, Clear, 1/2 Pint	6.00
Ink, S.S.Stafford's, Pour Spout	12.00
Ink, Sanford Mfg.Co., Embossed On Base, 4 Oz., Clear, 4 3/4 In.High	35.00
Ink, Sanford Patent Applied For, Embossed On Base, Label, Aqua, 2 In.High	20.00

Ink, **Sanford Universal**, Label, Round, Similar To C-370, Aqua	3.00
Ink, **Sanford 39 Ink**, Embossed On Base, Aqua, 2 3/8 In.High	8.00
Ink, **Sanford**, Patent Date 1911, Pouring Spout, Labels, Brown, Quart	8.50
Ink, **Sanford's Chicago**, Label, Round, Clear, C-730	2.00
Ink, **Sanford's Fountain Pen Inks**, Square Base, Similar To C-447, Clear	10.00
Ink, **Sanford's Ink & Library Paste**, Pint	4.50
Ink, **Sanford's Inks & Pastes**, Handle, Pottery, No Lid, Gallon	6.00
Ink, **Sanford's M.F.G.Co.**, Label, Rectangular, Clear, C-540	6.00
Ink, **Sanford's 217**, Patent, Embossed, BIMAL , Clear, 1 1/2 Oz.	15.00
Ink, **Sanford's**, Clear .... *Illus*	3.50
Ink, **Sanford's**, Cone, Amber	8.00
Ink, **Sanford's**, Embossed On Base, ABM , Clear, 2 9/16 In.High	12.00
Ink, **Sanford's**, Embossed On Base, BIMAL , 3 5/16 In.High	12.00
Ink, **Sanford's**, Embossed On Base, Plus 39-4, Aqua, 2 1/2 In.High	8.00
Ink, **Sanford's Inkwell**, Embossed On Base	2.00
Ink, **Sanford's**, Milk Glass	3.00
Ink, **Sanford's**, Round, Amber, Quart	6.00
Ink, **Schoolhouse**, Square, Cobalt Blue, 3 In.High	12.00
Ink, **Senate Ink Company**, Barrel, Clear	65.00
Ink, **Sheared Lip**, Swirled Body, Sunburst Bottom	10.00
Ink, **Shepard & Allen's Fluid**, Master, Label, Pouring Spout, Amber, C-893	30.00
Ink, **Signet Ink**, Paper Label, Clear, 2 7/16 In.High	12.00
Ink, **Signet**, Embossed, Ground Top, ABM, Cobalt, 6 In.	8.00
Ink, **Signet**, Master, Label, Cobalt	12.00
Ink, **Snow's Acid Proof Writing Fluid**, Master, Spout, Similar To C-894, Blue	17.50
Ink, **Soapstone**, 8 Sides, C-1640	35.00
Ink, **Spencerian**, Master, Stoneware, Brown, 27 In.High, C-1015	100.00
Ink, **Square**, Amber, Similar To C-1495	25.00
Ink, **Square Base**, C.1900, Cobalt Blue	3.00
Ink, **Square**, BIMAL , Dug, Cobalt	2.00
Ink, **Square**, Cobalt Blue	1.00 To 2.45
Ink, **Square**, Handmade Pouring Lip, Aqua	4.50
Ink, **Square**, Penholders, Stain, Green, C-507	10.00
Ink, **Stafford's Carmine Non-Copying**, Square, Clear, 2 1/8 In.High	9.00
Ink, **Stafford's Commercial Ink**, Aqua .... *Illus*	22.00
Ink, **Stafford's Commercial**, Inkstand Type, Place For 2 Pens, Aqua, 2 1/8 In.	22.00

Ink, Teakettle
24 Ribs, Clear, C-1226
See Page 147

Ink, Log Cabin, Kensington, C-677
See Page 143

Ink, Sanford's, Clear

Ink, Patent 1876, Light Blue, 5 In.
See Page 144

Ink, **Stafford's Master Ink**, Pour Lip, Aqua, Pint	12.00
Ink, **Stafford's New Black**, Cone, Label, Similar Shape To C-73, Clear	25.00
Ink, **Stafford's Universal**, Cone, Label, Similar To C-98, Aqua	3.00
Ink, **Stafford's Universal**, Label, Round, Similar To C-377, Aqua	5.00
Ink, **Stafford's Writing Fluid**, Commercial Ink, Stopper, Cobalt Blue	12.00
Ink, **Stafford's**, Cobalt, Quart	10.00
Ink, **Stafford's**, Cobalt, 6 In.Tall	10.00
Ink, **Stafford's**, Embossed Vertically, Pouring Lip, Teal Blue Green	110.00
Ink, **Stafford's**, Embossed, Paper Label, Blue Black Office	8.00
Ink, **Stafford's**, Embossed, Pouring Lip, Tapered, Emerald Green	47.00
Ink, **Stafford's**, Label, Round, Similar To C-317, Aqua	3.00
Ink, **Stafford's**, Master, Cobalt, Pint	7.00
Ink, **Stafford's**, Master, Embossed, Made In Usa, 9 In.High	28.00
Ink, **Stafford's**, Master, Label, Spout, Similar To C-896, Stain, Blue Green	15.00
Ink, **Stafford's**, Master, Pouring Spout, Similar To C-897, Green, 9 1/2 In.	15.00
Ink, **Stafford's**, Master, Pouring Spout, Similar To C-901, Blue, 6 In.High	7.50
Ink, **Stafford's**, Round, Label, Similar Shape To C-370, Amber	17.50
Ink, **Stafford's**, Round, Label, Similar To C-317, Aqua	5.00
Ink, **Stafford's**, Round, Similar To C-318, Stain, Aqua	2.00
Ink, **Stafford's**, Vertical Line Between Double Ringed Base, Round, Blue	8.50
Ink, **Standard Ink Co.**, Buffalo, N.Y., Master, Stoneware, Gray, Gallon	22.00
Ink, **Standard Violet**, Label, Square, Similar To C-441, Aqua	6.00
Ink, **Stickwell & Co.**, Embossed, 8 Panels, Bimal, Aqua, 3 1/16 In.High	20.00
Ink, **Stoddard**, Cone	85.00
Ink, **Stoddard**, Umbrella, Olive Amber	85.00
Ink, **Stoddard**, Umbrella, Open Pontil, Amber	65.00
Ink, **Stoddard**, Umbrella, Pontil, Amber	75.00
Ink, **Stylographic**, Label, Round, Aqua, C-159	8.00
Ink, **Superior Black**, Cone, Label, Similar To C-97, Aqua	2.00
Ink, **Superior Black**, Igloo, Label, Similar Shape To C-647, Aqua	12.50
Ink, **Superior Fluid**, Igloo, Label, Similar Shape To C-647, Aqua	20.00
Ink, **Superior**, Label, Open Pontil, Similar To C-196, Light Green	30.00
Ink, **Superior**, Umbrella, Label, Open Pontil, Similar To C-125, Aqua	27.50
Ink, **Superior**, Umbrella, Label, Pontil, Similar To C-147, Aqua	20.00
Ink, **T.David's & Co.**, Round, Similar To C-269, Aqua	7.50
Ink, **T.H.A.D.David's Co.**, N.Y., Label, Square, Aqua, C-413	7.50
Ink, **Taylor's Ink**, Umbrella, Union Ink Co., Mass., 8 Sided, Aqua	45.00
Ink, **Taylor's**, Igloo, Label, Similar Shape To C-647, Aqua	26.00
Ink, **Taylors Ink**, Umbrella, Ground Pontil, 8 Sided *Illus*	45.00
Ink, **Teakettle**, Amber, 2 In.High, C-1263	180.00
Ink, **Teakettle**, Aqua	150.00
Ink, **Teakettle**, Aqua, 1 3/4 In.High, C-1281	50.00
Ink, **Teakettle**, Barrel Shape, C.Harrison Hard Cider Campaign, Cold Green	255.00
Ink, **Teakettle**, Barrel, Blue, 2 In.High, C-1285	240.00
Ink, **Teakettle**, Barrel, Similar To C-1285, Green, 2 In.High	210.00
Ink, **Teakettle**, Blown, Green, 7 1/2 In.High, C-1252	95.00
Ink, **Teakettle**, Blue, 2 In.High, C-1254	160.00
Ink, **Teakettle**, Blue, 2 In.High, C-1255	120.00
Ink, **Teakettle**, Brass Collar & Cap, Similar To C-1285, Sapphire Blue	300.00
Ink, **Teakettle**, Clear, 1 In.High, C-1248	27.50
Ink, **Teakettle**, Double Font, Clear, 6 In.High, C-1276	85.00
Ink, **Teakettle**, Double Font, Green, 3 In.High, C-1272	340.00
Ink, **Teakettle**, Emerald Green	170.00
Ink, **Teakettle**, Gold Decoration, Clear, 7 1/2 In.High, C-1245	70.00
Ink, **Teakettle**, Gold Decoration, Similar Shape To C-1266, Blue, 2 In.High	200.00
Ink, **Teakettle**, Light Green, 2 In.High, C-1268	60.00
Ink, **Teakettle**, Octagonal With Stepped Top, Brass Collar, Dark Amethyst	250.00
Ink, **Teakettle**, Opalescent, Shape Similar To C-1265, 1 3/4 In.High	70.00
Ink, **Teakettle**, Polished Pontil, Similar To C-1271, Stain, Clear, 2 In.High	35.00
Ink, **Teakettle**, Pottery, 2-Tone Tan	110.00
Ink, **Teakettle**, Raised & Painted Decoration, Opalescent, 3 In.High, C-1277	190.00
Ink, **Teakettle**, Raised & Painted Design, Opalescent, 2 In.High, C-1233	180.00
Ink, **Teakettle**, Raised Design, Similar To C-1278, Clear, 2 In.High	75.00
Ink, **Teakettle**, Shape Similar To C-1261, Amber, 2 In.High	130.00
Ink, **Teakettle**, Shape Similar To C-1261, Blue, 1 3/4 In.High	170.00
Ink, **Teakettle**, Similar To C-1235, Citron, 2 In.High	160.00

Ink, **Teakettle**, Similar To C-1248 Except Larger, Clear, 7 1/2 In.High	60.00
Ink, **Teakettle**, Similar To C-1254, Bruise On Rib, Green, 2 In.High	75.00
Ink, **Teakettle**, Similar To C-1255, Clear, 1 1/2 In.High	65.00
Ink, **Teakettle**, Similar To C-1261, Amber, 2 In.High	170.00
Ink, **Teakettle**, Similar To C-1261, Green, 2 In.High	130.00
Ink, **Teakettle**, Similar To C-1265, Green, 2 In.High	120.00
Ink, **Teakettle**, Similar To C-1271, Amber, 2 In.High	130.00
Ink, **Teakettle**, Stain, Aqua, 2 In.High	50.00
Ink, **Teakettle**, Star Shape Design On Top, Blue, 2 In.High, C-1267	230.00
Ink, **Teakettle**, 8 Concave Sides Between Sets Of 3 Vertical Ribs, Amethyst	225.00
Ink, **Teakettle**, 8 Concave Sides, Similar To C-1255, Kelly Green	190.00
Ink, **Teakettle**, 8 Sided, 11 Stars In Gold Leaf On Panels, Brass Top, Blue	210.00
Ink, **Teakettle**, 24 Ribs, Clear, C-1226 .... *Illus*	400.00
Ink, **Thaddeus & Davids & Co.**, New York, Est.1825, Stopper, Cobalt Blue	22.00
Ink, **Thaddeus & Davids & Co.**, Umbrella, Pontil, Aqua	48.00
Ink, **Thaddeus & Davids & Co.**, Umbrella, Pontil, 8 Sided .... *Illus*	30.00
Ink, **Thaddeus & Davids & Co.**, Umbrella, Rolled Lip, 8 Sided, Aqua	30.00
Ink, **Thaddeus Davis Ink**, Salem, Mass., Pouring Spout, Green	225.00
Ink, **Thomas Ink's On Cap**, Round, Clear, C-732	2.00
Ink, **Thomas Unrivaled**, Umbrella, Label, Similar To C-161, Aqua	27.50
Ink, **Thomas**, L.H., Quart	11.00
Ink, **Thos.L.Harris**, Claremont, N.H., Master, Pouring Lip, Olive Amber	300.00
Ink, **Three Mold**, Geometric Pattern, Open Pontil, Olive Amber	100.00
Ink, **Tin & Brass Holder**, Round, Clear	15.00
Ink, **Toybard's**, Igloo, Label, Similar Shape To C-647, Aqua	15.00
Ink, **Traveler's**, Square, Tin Box, Similar To C-1689	5.00
Ink, **Traveler's**, Whalebone, C-1677	50.00
Ink, **Traveling**, Composition Case, 2 Bottles	10.00
Ink, **Traveling**, Wood & Leather Case, 2 Bottles	10.00
Ink, **Traveling**, Wood Case, 2 Bottles	10.00 To 20.00
Ink, **Turtle**, Cardinal Bird On Dome, Aqua	60.00
Ink, **Turtle**, Cardinal Bird On Dome, Stain	50.00
Ink, **Turtle**, Domed Top, Citron, C-636	220.00
Ink, **Turtle**, Embossed Bird, Aqua	40.00
Ink, **Turtle**, Embossed Bird, Dug, Stain	40.00
Ink, **Turtle**, Embossed Bird, Similar To C-638, Aqua	40.00
Ink, **Turtle**, Embossed, Cardinal, Aqua	42.00
Ink, **Turtle**, J.I.M., Clear .... *Color*	XX.XX
Ink, **Turtle**, Similar To C-641, Light Green	80.00
Ink, **Turtle**, Similar To C-641, Rough Lip, Aqua	8.00
Ink, **Turtle**, 8 Sided, Similar To C-639, Aqua	12.50
Ink, **Turtle**, 12 Panels, Aqua	18.00
Ink, **Umbrella**, Amber	5.00
Ink, **Umbrella**, Amethyst	3.00
Ink, **Umbrella**, Apple Green	25.00
Ink, **Umbrella**, Aqua	3.00 To 18.00
Ink, **Umbrella**, Aqua, G.Oven's, 2 5/8 In. .... *Illus*	48.00
Ink, **Umbrella**, Aqua, 2 3/4 In.	8.00
Ink, **Umbrella**, Cobalt, Open Pontil .... *Color*	XX.XX
Ink, **Umbrella**, Dark Amber .... *Color*	XX.XX
Ink, **Umbrella**, Dark Olive Green	100.00
Ink, **Umbrella**, Embossed N.Y.On Base, Aqua	15.00
Ink, **Umbrella**, G.Owen's Permanent Black Record Ink, Aqua	40.00
Ink, **Umbrella**, Octagon, Open Pontil, Light Green	28.00 To 34.50
Ink, **Umbrella**, Open Pontil, Aqua	15.00 To 25.00
Ink, **Umbrella**, Open Pontil, Aqua, 12 Sided	35.00
Ink, **Umbrella**, Open Pontil, Olive Amber	100.00
Ink, **Umbrella**, Open Pontil, Olive Green, C-133	90.00
Ink, **Umbrella**, Open Pontil, Similar To C-127, Aqua	15.00
Ink, **Umbrella**, Open Pontil, Similar To C-129, Green	55.00
Ink, **Umbrella**, Open Pontil, Similar To C-129, Light Green	60.00
Ink, **Umbrella**, Open Pontil, Similar To C-133, Rough Spot, Olive Green	60.00
Ink, **Umbrella**, Open Pontil, Similar To C-135, Amber	65.00
Ink, **Umbrella**, Open Pontil, Similar To C-137, Smaller Size, Blue	280.00
Ink, **Umbrella**, Open Pontil, Similar To C-145, Amber	70.00
Ink, **Umbrella**, Open Pontil, Similar To C-145, Olive Green	70.00

Ink, Umbrella, Open Pontil, Teal Blue 48.00
Ink, Umbrella, Panels, Similar To C-178, Aqua 35.00
Ink, Umbrella, Pontil, Aqua, 2 1/4 X 2 1/4 In. 15.00
Ink, Umbrella, Pontil, Burst Bubble, Olive Green 65.00
Ink, Umbrella, Pontil, Medium Green 45.00
Ink, Umbrella, Similar To C-177, Small, Aqua .... 5.00 To 7.50
Ink, Umbrella, Similar To C-177, Stain, Aqua 9.00
Ink, Umbrella, Similar To C-179, Aqua 9.00
Ink, Umbrella, Stain, Open Pontil, Aqua 10.00
Ink, Umbrella, Steel Pen, Label, Similar To C-161, Aqua 6.00
Ink, Umbrella, 6 Sided, Olive Amber, C-173 & 174 .... 70.00
Ink, Umbrella, 8 Sided, Aqua, 2 1/2 In.High 27.00
Ink, Umbrella, 12 Sided, Open Pontil, Similar To C-151, Amber 100.00
Ink, Umbrella, 12 Sided, Open Pontil, Similar To C-151, Aqua 20.00
Ink, Umbrella, 12 Sided, Open Pontil, Similar To C-151, Small Size, Green 90.00
Ink, Umbrella, 12 Sided, Pontil, Light Green 16.00
Ink, Umbrella, 16 Panels, Open Pontil, Similar To C-153 & 154, Olive Amber 140.00
Ink, Umbrella, 16 Sided, Open Pontil, Olive Green 180.00
Ink, Underwood Black, Label, Green, C-288 .... 16.00
Ink, Underwood Inks, Master, Pouring Spout, Similar To C-913, Blue, 8 In.High 30.00
Ink, Underwood's Everlasting Bank, Cobalt Blue, 32 Ozs. .... *Illus* 25.00
Ink, Underwood's Inks, Metal Top, Label, Cobalt 25.00
Ink, Underwood's Inks, 8 Sided, Similar To C-562, Aqua 12.50
Ink, Underwood's, Beehive Shape, Round, Stain, Aqua, C-598 .... 20.00
Ink, Underwood's, Embossed One Side, Cobalt Blue, 8 1/4 In.High 125.00
Ink, Underwood's, Embossed, Pen Ledge On Both Sides, Aqua, 2 1/16 In.High 27.00
Ink, Underwood's, Embossed, 2 3/4 In.High 27.00
Ink, Underwood's, Master, Cobalt, Quart 45.00
Ink, Underwood's, Master, Pouring Spout, Similar To C-913, Blue, 8 In.High 22.50
Ink, Underwood's, Master, Pouring Spout, Similar To C-914, Blue, 9 1/2 In. 22.50

Ink, Underwood's
Everlasting Bank,
Cobalt Blue, 32 Ozs.

Ink, Ward's Fountain Pen,
Label, Clear, 3 In.High
See Page 149

Ink, Underwood's, Pouring Spout, Cobalt, Quart 40.00
Ink, Underwood's, Round, Stain, Aqua, C-331 .... 7.00
Ink, Union Ink Co., Springfield, Mass., Embossed, Aqua, 1 7/8 In.High 55.00
Ink, W.Allen & Co., N.Y., Ledger Inks, Pottery, Pouring Spout 9.00
Ink, W.E.Bonney, Barrel 12.00
Ink, W.E.Bonney, Barrel, Aqua 17.50
Ink, W.E.Bonney, Barrel, Label, Similar To C-657, Rough Lip, Aqua 35.00
Ink, W.E.Bonney, Barrel, Open Pontil, Similar To C-653, Aqua 55.00
Ink, W.E.Bonney, Barrel, Pouring Spout, Label, Aqua 115.00
Ink, W.E.Bonney, Barrel, Similar To C-653, No Pontil, Aqua 20.00
Ink, W.E.Bonney, Cone, Label, C-39 & 40 .... 30.00
Ink, W.E.Bonney, Embossed On Side, Aqua, 2 In. 25.00
Ink, W.E.Bonney, Embossed, Aqua, 2 1/2 In.High 30.00
Ink, W.E.Bonney, Embossed, Long Neck, Aqua, 2 5/8 In.High 30.00
Ink, W.E.Bonney, Embossed, Oval Shape, Label, Aqua 60.00

Ink, **W.E.Bonney**, Master, Aqua, 7 1/2 In.High, C-801	110.00
Ink, **W.E.Bonney**, Master, Barrel, Pouring Spout, Similar To C-660, Aqua, 6 In.	70.00
Ink, **W.E.Bonney**, Master, Barrel, Similar To C-661, Aqua, 7 In.High	65.00
Ink, **W.E.Bonney**, Master, Pouring Spout, Similar To C-661, Aqua, 7 In.High	85.00
Ink, **W.E.Bonney**, Round, Similar To C-238, Aqua	12.50
Ink, **W.E.Bonney**, South Hanover, Mass., Embossed, Square, 2 1/2 In.High	20.00
Ink, **W.E.Bonney**, Square, Similar To C-393, Aqua	7.00
Ink, **W.S.Brakenbridge**, Norwich, Ct., Pontil, Chipped Lip .... *Illus*	100.00
Ink, **Ward's Fountain Pen**, Label, Clear, 3 In.High .... *Illus*	7.50
Ink, **Ward's**, Boston, Master, Pouring Spout, Similar To C-918, Blue Green	14.00
Ink, **Ward's**, Embossed, Pouring Spout, Deep Green, 7 3/4 In.High	90.00
Ink, **Ward's**, Pouring Spout, Similar To C-337, Green, 4 1/2 In.High	35.00
Ink, **Washington Bust**, Screw Cap, Blue	6.75
Ink, **Water's**, Troy, N.Y., Umbrella, Aqua	125.00
Ink, **Water's**, Troy, N.Y., Umbrella, Open Pontil, Aqua, C-132	160.00
Ink, **Waterlow & Sons Limited**, Scarlet, English, Pottery .... *Illus*	6.50
Ink, **Watermans & Sanfords**, Clear	3.00
Ink, **White Friar's**, Candied End, Stopper, Signed	55.00
Ink, **Wood's Black Ink**, Portland, Cone, Open Pontil, Similar To C-12, Aqua	20.00
Ink, **Wood's Black Ink**, Portland, Embossed, Conical, Isabella G.W., N.J.	60.00
Ink, **Wooden Sander**, C-1669	20.00
Ink, **Worden's**, Round, Metal Container, Similar To C-347, Aqua	8.00
Ink, **3 In.**, Cobalt Blue .... *Color*	XX.XX
Ink, **8 Sided**, Pontil, Crude, Almost Black Green, 2 1/2 In.High	110.00
Ink, **12 Sided**, Open Pontil, Similar To C-547, Olive Amber	85.00
Ink, **12 Sided**, Open Pontil, Similar To C-550, Aqua	20.00
Ink, **12 Sided**, Shape Similar To C-550, Light Green	17.50
Ink, **16 Sided**, Rough Pontil, Dark Amber, 2 In.High	135.00
Ink, **24 Rib Mold**, Pontil, Clear, 2 1/2 In.High	400.00
Jack Daniel, **Apple Brandy**, Lem Motlow .... *Illus*	20.00
Jack Daniel, **Corn Whiskey**, 14 Years Old, No.7 .... *Illus*	17.00
Jack Daniel, **Distiller**, Old No.7, Battleship Maine .... *Color*	XX.XX
Jack Daniel, **Distillery**, Tenn., Fluted Neck, No.7 In.Circle, Clear	12.00
Jack Daniel, **No.7**, Square, Clear, Quart	8.00
Jack Daniel, **Old Time Distillery** .... *Illus*	15.00
Jack Daniel, **Tennessee Whiskey**, Screw Top .... *Illus*	6.00
Jack Daniel, **Uncle Jack's**, No.7 .... *Illus*	14.00
Jack Daniel, **W.T.& C.D.Gunter**, No.7 & Address, Clear, Pint	15.00
Jar, **American Porcelain**, Aqua, Two Quart	25.00
Jar, **Battery**, Francis Keil & Son, Reliance, 6 1/2 In. .... *Illus*	12.00
Jar, **Candle**, Open Pontil, Tin Cover, Clear	18.00
Jar, **Candy**, Country Store, Greek Key Pattern, Clear	8.00
Jar, **Globe Tobacco Company**, Detroit, Pat.Oct.10th, 1882, Barrel Shape, Amber	20.00
Jar, **Ground Mouth**, Screw Top, Cobalt Blue, 1/2 Pint	18.50
Jar, **Ground Top**, Tin Cover, 1/2 Gallon	6.00
Jar, **Honey**, Blown, 3 Mold, Midwestern, C.1830, Swag Pattern, Clear	95.00
Jar, **Love Candy Co.**, Embossed Heart & Arrow, Fruit Tablets, Aqua	75.00
Jar, **Molded**, Blue, 11 1/2 In.High	20.00
Jar, **Pickle**, Goofus Glass, Painted Gold With Red Grapes, 7 In.	6.00
Jar, **Pittsburgh**, Covered, Applied Blue Rings, Blue Finial, Blown	170.00
Jar, **Pomade**, Millefiori, Lid, Blue	20.00
Jar, **Pottery**, Miniature, Marked C.Price, Bristol	10.00
Jar, **Tobacco**, Carter's Spanish Mixture, Collared Neck, Medium Green	80.00
Jar, **Tobacco**, Globe, Barrel	22.00
Jar, **Tobacco**, Globe, Pat.Oct.10th, 1882, Amber .... 16.00 To 20.00
Jar, **Tobacco**, Lapalina, Cover	8.00
Jar, **Tobacco**, Silver Bulldog On Lid	15.00
Jar, **Wide Mouth**, Signed On Bottom, Molded, Aqua	7.50
Jug, **Cahart & Brother**, Handle, Amber, Quart	300.00
Jug, **Cahart & Brother**, New York, Handle, Red Amber, Quart	260.00
Jug, **Chestnut Grove**, Sealed, Open Pontil, Amber	150.00
Jug, **Collared Neck**, Deep Red Amber	17.50
Jug, **Cork Stopper**, Iron & Wooden Handle, Amber, 2 Gallon	3.75
Jug, **Dewars Scotch**, Doulton, Ceramic, Brown Glaze, Quart	45.00
Jug, **Flora Temple**, Handled, Dated 1859, Crude String Lip, Puce, Quart	200.00

Ink, Waterlow & Sons Limited,
Scarlet, English, Pottery
See Page 149

Jack Daniel,
Apple Brandy, Lem Motlow
See Page 149

Jack Daniel, Corn Whiskey,
14 Years Old, No.7
See Page 149

Jack Daniel,
Tennessee Whiskey, Screw Top
See Page 149

Jack Daniel, Old Time Distillery
See Page 149

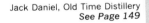

Jack Daniel, Uncle Jack's, No.7
See Page 149

Jar, Battery, Francis Keil & Son,
Reliance, 6 1/2 In.
See Page 149

Jug, Handled, Puce Amber, String Lip, Quart, Dated 1859	200.00
Jug, Handled, Amber, Pint	25.00
Jug, Handled, Banded Mouth, Midwestern, Medium To Dark Amber, 14 In.High	575.00
Jug, Handled, Open Pontil, Amber, Pint	25.00

Jug, **Macy & Jenkins**, N.Y., Amber, 9 1/2 In.Tall 12.00
Jug, **Pure Malt Whiskey**, Bourbon Co., Handle, Amber, Pint 110.00
Jug, **R.B.Cutter**, Handle, Amber, Pint 170.00
Jug, **S.M.& Co.**, Handled, Open Pontil, Whittled, Amber 165.00
Jug, **S.M.& Co.**, New York, Handle, Pint 200.00
Jug, **Star Whiskey**, Handle, Amber, Pint 210.00
Jug, **The Old Mill**, Handle, Amber, Pint 450.00
Jug, **Whitney Glassworks**, Handle, Amber, Quart 170.00

*Kamotsuru Sake Brewing Company of Japan has made sake for
centuries. In 1965 the first of their decanters were imported to the
United States.*

Kamotsuru, God of Longevity, 1965 .... 12.50
Kamotsuru, God of Wealth, Daokoku 16.50
Kamotsuru, God of Wealth,Hotei 16.50
Kamotsuru, Goddess of Art,1965 .... 12.50

*Kord Distilleries of Czechoslovakia have bottled liqueurs in decanters
for many years.*
Kord, Coach, 1948 .... 50.00
Kord, Decanter, Bagpipe, 1950 .... 40.00
Kord, Dolphin, 2 Compartment 15.00
Kord, Hunter's Lady, Glass, 1958 .... 18.00
Kord, Wild Geese, 1951, Full 45.00
Kummel Bear, See also Figural
Kummel, Bear, Black, Olive Amber 35.00
Kummel, Bear, Green 35.00
Kummel, Gilka, Green 45.00
Kummel, Russian, Label Shows 3 Horses, Sled, 1896 In Base, Wine Shape 30.00
Lady's Leg, Blob Top, Aqua 10.00
Lady's Leg, Boker's Label 65.00
Lady's Leg, Burst Bubble, Olive Green, 12 In.High 11.00
Lady's Leg, E.W.Inc., Hexagonal, Milk Glass, White, 7 3/4 In. 18.00
Lady's Leg, Green 46.00
Lady's Leg, Hay, Amber 10.00
Lady's Leg, Hay, Red Amber 13.00
Lady's Leg, Olive Green 45.00
Lady's Leg, Turn Mold, Dark Green 30.00
Lady's Shoe, High Top, Clear, 4 1/2 In. 4.50
Laird's, Soldier, New Jersey, Blue 20.00
Lalique, Atomizer, 6 Nudes In Relief, Signed 45.00
Lalique, Perfume, Stopper Is Pair Sculptured Birds In Flight, Signed 55.00
Larsen, Ship, Frosted 20.00
Larsen, Ship, Glass, Large 10.95
Larsen, Viking Ship 45.00
Lestoil, Flask, Dark Green 3.00
Lestoil, Flask, Amber 2.00
Lestoil, Flask, Amethyst 2.00
Lestoil, Flask, Green 2.00
Lestoil, Flask, Light Green 3.00
Lestoil, Flask, Smokey Amethyst 3.00

*Lionstone Distilleries has made three series of porcelain bottles to hold
their bourbon. The bottles are all figurals, a single man for each bottle.
Each figure represents a character of the Old West. These are limited-
edition bottles.*
Lionstone, Al Unser No.1 .... 25.00
Lionstone, Annie Christmas .... 19.00 To 23.50
Lionstone, Annie Oakley .... 20.50 To 23.95
Lionstone, Bar Scene, No.1 .... 100.00
Lionstone, Bar Scene, No.2 .... 100.00
Lionstone, Bar Scene, No.3 .... 100.00
Lionstone, Bar Scene, No.4 .... 100.00
Lionstone, Bartender .... 26.50 To 36.95
Lionstone, Belly Robber .... *Illus* 21.15
Lionstone, Bluebird, Wisconsin 27.95

Lionstone,
Belly Robber, Vol. III
See Page 151

Lionstone,
Circuit Riding Judge, Vol. II
See Page 153

Lionstone,
Country Doctor, Vol.I
See Page 153

Lionstone,
Frontiersman, Vol. III
See Page 153

Lionstone,
Jesse James, Vol.I
See Page 153

Lionstone,
Mountain Man, Vol. III
See Page 153

Lionstone,
Railroad Engineer, Vol. II
See Page 153

Lionstone,
Stagecoach Driver, Vol. III
See Page 153

Lionstone, Call House Madam	20.50
Lionstone, Camp Cook	19.50 To 34.95
Lionstone, Camp Follower	20.50 To 23.95
Lionstone, Cardinal, Indiana	29.95
Lionstone, Casual Indian	11.50 To 22.95
Lionstone, Cavalry Scout	11.50 To 22.95
Lionstone, Chinese Laundryman	20.50 To 23.95
Lionstone, Circuit Riding Judge	*Illus* 19.50
Lionstone, Country Doctor	*Illus* 24.50
Lionstone, Cowboy	11.50 To 29.95
Lionstone, Cherry Valley Club, Gold Handle	35.00
Lionstone, Frontiersman	*Illus* 21.50
Lionstone, Gentleman Gambler	11.50 To 22.95
Lionstone, Gold Panner	24.95 To 34.95
Lionstone, Highway Robber	17.95 To 34.95
Lionstone, Jesse James	*Illus* 19.50
Lionstone, Johnny Lightning	12.50 To 22.00
Lionstone, Madame	23.95
Lionstone, Meadowlark	19.95 To 24.95
Lionstone, Mint Bar Scene	400.00
Lionstone, Mint Bar Scene, With Nude	500.00
Lionstone, Mountain Man	*Illus* 26.95
Lionstone, Proud Indian	11.50 To 12.95
Lionstone, Quail, Gambels	19.95 To 32.50
Lionstone, Railroad Engineer	*Illus* 19.50
Lionstone, Renegade Trader	23.50 To 34.95
Lionstone, Riverboat Captain	19.50
Lionstone, Roadrunner	27.50 To 49.95
Lionstone, Sheepherder	27.95 To 36.95
Lionstone, Sheriff	11.50 To 19.50
Lionstone, Sod Buster	17.50 To 19.50
Lionstone, Squawman	19.50 To 34.95
Lionstone, Stagecoach Driver	*Illus* 25.95
Lionstone, STP Turbo Car	11.50
Lionstone, STP Turbo Car, Gold And Platinum, Pair	70.00
Lionstone, Swallow, Gold	27.50
Lionstone, Swallow, Silver	44.65
Lionstone, Telegraph Operator	20.50 To 23.95
Lionstone, Vigilante	14.50 To 22.95
Lionstone, Wells Fargo Guard	17.50 To 19.75
Lionstone, Woodhawk	19.50 To 34.95
Liqueur, Anis Margarita	4.00
Liqueur, Anisette, Papillon Embossed, Full	4.00
Liqueur, Anton Riemerschmid, Cherry With Rum, Label, Stamp, Full	3.00
Liqueur, Anton Riemerschmid, Liqueur Deluxe, Label, Stamp, Full	3.00
Liqueur, Bar, Blackberry, Enameled, Clear, Quart	12.50
Liqueur, Benedictine, BIMAL	4.50
Liqueur, Benedictine, 1958	2.00
Liqueur, Benedictine, 1968	2.00
Liqueur, Blackberry Julep	2.00
Liqueur, Bols, Dancing Ballerina, Clear	20.00
Liqueur, Bols, Tulip, Labels, Full	30.00
Liqueur, Bralatta	2.00
Liqueur, Brizard Apry	2.50
Liqueur, Brizard Creme De Menthe	4.00
Liqueur, Brooklyn, Reliable Cordials, N.Y., Crema Caffee, Clear, Fifth	10.00
Liqueur, Cherry Heering, Royal Copenhagen, 1856, White, Raised Flowers	40.00
Liqueur, Cherry Julep	2.00
Liqueur, Clark's California Cherry Cordial, Amethyst	15.00
Liqueur, Coco-Marianna, Paris, Squat, Dark Green	5.00
Liqueur, Cusenier, Peach	6.00
Liqueur, Du Bouchett, Curacao, Label, Stamp, Blue, 5 In.	10.00
Liqueur, EK Cordials, Melbourne & Sidney, Australia, Sun Purpled	35.00
Liqueur, French Cherry Marnier	5.95
Liqueur, Galliano, Labels, Gallon, 27 In.High	22.00
Liqueur, Giacomo Casanova	4.00

Liqueur, Grand Marnier, Silver & Gold Decoration, Green, Pint	8.00
Liqueur, Lemon Horehound Rock & Rye, Oblique Embossing, Amethyst	5.00
Liqueur, Mesimarja, Nectorberry, Finnish	2.60
Liqueur, Millefiori Cucchi	2.50
Liqueur, Peppermint, Bar, Graf Distilling Co., Clear *Illus*	12.50
Liqueur, Pond's Rock & Rye, Square, Swirl Neck, Clear, Fifth	5.00
Liqueur, Pond's Rock & Rye, Square, Swirl Neck, Sun Colored Amethyst, Fifth	5.00
Liqueur, Suomuurain, Cloudberry, Finnish	2.60
Liqueur, Vallet, Opaque	3.00
Liqueur, 3 Section, Cognac, Creme-De-Menthe, Gin	4.00

Luxardo bottles were first used in the 1930s to bottle the Italian liqueurs.
The firm was founded in 1821. Most of the Luxardo bottles found today
date after 1943. The dates given are the first year the bottle was made.

Luxardo, Amphora, Pink & White	10.00
Luxardo, Alabaster Fish, 1960	35.00
Luxardo, Amphora, Deruta, Majolica, 1956	50.00
Luxardo, Amphora, Deruta Cameo, 1959	55.00
Luxardo, Amphora, Dragon, Majolica, 1953	55.00
Luxardo, Amphora Mazzo, Majolica, 1954	50.00
Luxardo, Amphora, Primavera, Label, No Stopper, 1958	25.00
Luxardo, Amphora, Ruby & Gold, 1958	55.00
Luxardo, Amphora, Springbok, Majolica, 1952	60.00

Liqueur, Peppermint, Bar, Graf Distilling Co., Clear

Luxardo, Amphora, White & Gold Faun, 1958	40.00
Luxardo, Amphora, White & Gold Griffon, 1958	50.00
Luxardo, Ampulla, Venetian Glass, 1959	15.00
Luxardo, Apothecary Jar, Majolica, 1960	15.00
Luxardo, Apple, Majolica, 1960	8.00
Luxardo, Ashtray, Fighting Cocks, Majolica, 1962	20.00
Luxardo, Ashtray, Mosaic, Green, 1959	10.00
Luxardo, Autumn Leaves, Majolica, 1952	50.00
Luxardo, Autumn Wine Pitcher, 1958	60.00
Luxardo, Baby Amphora, 1956	15.00
Luxardo, Babylon, Majolica, 1960	22.50 To 25.00
Luxardo, Bacchus	16.00
Luxardo, Bantu, Majolica, 1962	25.00
Luxardo, Baroque, Gold, Ruby, Amphora, 1951	45.00 To 55.00
Luxardo, Baroque, Gold, Turquoise, Majolica, 1952-55	45.00 To 55.00
Luxardo, Barrel, Majolica, 1968	15.00
Luxardo, Black & Green Ampulla, Majolica, 1958	60.00
Luxardo, Blue & Gold Amphora, Majolica, 1968	25.00
Luxardo, Brizantina, Majolica, 1959	30.00
Luxardo, Brocca, Majolica, 1958	50.00
Luxardo, Buddha, Brown, Majolica, 1962	22.00
Luxardo, Buddha, Gray, Majolica, 1962	20.00

Luxardo, Buddha, Majolica, 1961	28.00
Luxardo, Calypso Girl, Majolica, 1962	10.50 To 15.00
Luxardo, Candlestick, Alabaster, Venetian Glass, 1961	30.00
Luxardo, Cellini Urn, Molded, Glass, Silver, 1968	18.95
Luxardo, Cellini Vase, Venetian Glass, 1958	19.00 To 22.00
Luxardo, Cellini, 1958	30.00
Luxardo, Cherry Basket, Majolica, 1960	32.00
Luxardo, Chess Pieces, Majolica, 6, 1959	300.00
Luxardo, Classical Fragment, Majolica, 1961	25.00
Luxardo, Clock, Venetian Glass, 1960	9.50
Luxardo, Cocktail Shaker, Venetian Glass, 1957	19.00
Luxardo, Coffee Carafe, Majolica, 1962	15.50
Luxardo, Congo, Majolica, 1960	22.50
Luxardo, Cucciolo Puppy, Venetain Glass, 1961	24.00
Luxardo, Curva Vaso, Venetian Glass, 1961	30.00
Luxardo, Decanter, Blue Fiammetta, 1957	20.00
Luxardo, Decanter, Diana, Majolica, 1956	55.00
Luxardo, Decanter, Dogal Silver, Green, Gondola, 1952-55	30.00
Luxardo, Decanter, Dogal Silver, Green, Gondola, 1956	20.00
Luxardo, Decanter, Dogal Silver, Ruby, Buildings, 1956	20.00
Luxardo, Decanter, Dogal Silver, Ruby, Lady, 1952-55	30.00
Luxardo, Decanter, Dogal Silver, Smoke, Gondola, 1956	20.00
Luxardo, Decanter, Dogal Silver, Smoke, Gondolier, 1952-55	25.00
Luxardo, Decanter, Dogal Silver, Smoke, Neck Bands, Gondola, 1957	20.00
Luxardo, Decanter, Euganean Bronze, Majolica, 1952-55	60.00
Luxardo, Decanter, Euganean Copper, Majolica, 1952-55	60.00
Luxardo, Decanter, Sheraton, Silver, Brown, 1957	20.00
Luxardo, Decanter, Silver Amethyst, 1957	20.00
Luxardo, Decanter, Silver Jade, 1957	20.00
Luxardo, Decanter, Silver, Blue, 1952-55	20.00
Luxardo, Decanter, Silver, Brown, 1952-55	20.00
Luxardo, Decanter, Silver, Green, Floral, 1952-55	20.00
Luxardo, Decanter, Venetian Gold Wine Leaf, 1958	25.00 To 30.00
Luxardo, Decanter, Venetian Gold, Green, 1952-55	30.00
Luxardo, Decanter, Venetian Gold, Rose, 1952-55	30.00
Luxardo, Decanter, Venetian Gold, Violet, 1952-55	30.00
Luxardo, Decanter, Venetian Merletto, 1957	30.00
Luxardo, Decanter, Venetian Silver, Green, Flecked, 1952-55	30.00
Luxardo, Decanter, Venetian Silver, Violet, 1952-55	30.00
Luxardo, Decanter, Vermilion Firmmetta, 1957	30.00
Luxardo, Decanter, White & Gold, Glass, 1952	400.00
Luxardo, Dolphin, Venetian Glass, 1959	50.00
Luxardo, Doughnut, Venetian Glass, 1959	7.00
Luxardo, Duck, Green, Venetian Glass, 1960	40.00
Luxardo, Duck, Surrealist, 1952-55	60.00
Luxardo, Eagle, Onyx, 1970	48.00
Luxardo, Egyptian, Majolica, 1959	15.00
Luxardo, Egyptian, Majolica, 1968	12.50
Luxardo, Etruscan, Dark Brown, Majolica, 1959	50.00
Luxardo, Faenza, 1956	7.00
Luxardo, Fiori, Majolica, 1956	60.00
Luxardo, Fish, Alabaster, Venetian Glass, 1960	30.00
Luxardo, Fish, Venetian Glass, Green & Gold, 1960	23.00
Luxardo, Fish, Venetian Glass, Ruby, 1961	24.00
Luxardo, Florentine, Majolica, 1956	45.00 To 50.00
Luxardo, Forget-Me-Not, 1959	40.00
Luxardo, Fruit Miniatures, 6, 1960	50.00
Luxardo, Fuso, Majolica, 1959	30.00
Luxardo, Gambia, Majolica, 1961	10.50
Luxardo, Gazelle, Surrealist, 1952-54	60.00
Luxardo, Giara, Majolica, 1959	30.00
Luxardo, Gondola, Majolica, Minature, 1959	7.00
Luxardo, Gondola, Majolica, Miniature, 1960	7.00
Luxardo, Gondola, Majolica, 1959	30.00
Luxardo, Gondola, Majolica, 1960	30.00
Luxardo, Goose, Alabaster, Venetian Glass, 1960	23.00

Luxardo, Grapes, Majolica, 1960	8.00
Luxardo, Marabou, Surrealist, 1957	60.00
Luxardo, Mayan, Majolica, 1960	21.00
Luxardo, Medieval Palace, 1952	8.00
Luxardo, Miss Luxardo, 1970	16.00
Luxardo, Nacreous, Majolica, 1957	40.00
Luxardo, Nubian, Majolica, 1959	15.00
Luxardo, Nubian, Miniature, Majolica, 1959	5.00
Luxardo, Opal, Majolica, 1957	40.00
Luxardo, Oriental Screen, Majolica, 1961	25.00
Luxardo, Owl, Onyx, 1970	48.00
Luxardo, Paestum, Majolica, 1959	6.00
Luxardo, Paestum, Miniature, 1959	5.00
Luxardo, Pagliacci, Venetian Glass, 1959	20.00
Luxardo, Pear, Majolica, 1960	7.00
Luxardo, Penguin, Venetian Glass, 1968	24.00
Luxardo, Pheasant, Black, Venetian Glass	100.00
Luxardo, Pheasant, Red, Clear, Venetian Glass, 1960	34.50
Luxardo, Pheasant, Red, Gold, Venetian Glass, 1960	24.00
Luxardo, Pierrot, Signed Tile, Majolica, 1959	61.00
Luxardo, Pitcher, Deruta, Majolica, 1953	60.00
Luxardo, Pitcher, Dragon, Majolica, 1958	60.00
Luxardo, Pompeiian, Majolica, 1956	49.95
Luxardo, Puppy, Venetian Glass, 1960	24.00
Luxardo, Purple & Gold Urn, 1958	30.00
Luxardo, Safari, Majolica, 1960	22.50
Luxardo, Santa Maria, 1970	16.00
Luxardo, Silhouette, 1961	40.00
Luxardo, Sir Lancelot, Majolica, 1962	20.00 To 22.00
Luxardo, Slave Girl, Majolica, 1960	38.00
Luxardo, Spugnato, Majolica, 1956	50.00
Luxardo, Squirrel, Venetian Glass, 1968	28.00
Luxardo, Strusca, Light Brown, Majolica, 1959	40.00
Luxardo, Sudan Africa, Majolica, 1960	17.95
Luxardo, Swan, Surrealist, 1952-55	60.00
Luxardo, Tamburello, Majolica, 1959	25.00
Luxardo, Tapa Print	7.00
Luxardo, Torre Azzura, Majolica, 1961	20.00
Luxardo, Torre Bianca, Majolica, 1962	15.00
Luxardo, Torre Rosa, Majolica, 1962	15.00
Luxardo, Torre Tinta, Majolica, 1962	20.00
Luxardo, Tower Of Flowers, Majolica, 1968	20.00
Luxardo, Tower Of Fruit, Majolica, 1968	20.00
Luxardo, Trio, Majolica, 1956	100.00
Luxardo, Turkey, Miniature, Majolica, 1961	15.00
Luxardo, Two Compartment, Majolica, 1955	50.00
Luxardo, Uciello Pitcher, Majolica, 1958	50.00
Luxardo, Urn, Gray & Gold, 1958	30.00
Luxardo, Urn, Warrior, Majolica, 1956	50.00
Luxardo, Vasella Romana, 1957	55.00
Luxardo, Venetian Cannon, Ceramic	15.00
Luxardo, Venus De Milo, Majolica, 1959	27.50
Luxardo, Venus Di Milo, Miniature, Majolica, 1959	5.00
Luxardo, Venus Di Milo, 1971	14.00
Luxardo, White Topaz, Majolica, 1952-55	50.00
Luxardo, Wobble Bottle, Venetian Glass, 1957	35.00
Luxardo, Zebra, Surrealist, 1957	45.00 To 60.00
Luxardo, Zodiac, Onyx, 1970	19.95
Mc Cormick, Aging Barrel, 1968	6.95
Mc Cormick, Air Race Decanter, Pylon	14.95
Mc Cormick, Bluebird, Missouri	21.95 To 24.95
Mc Cormick, Jupiter 1960 Locomotive	12.45
Mc Cormick, Jupiter 1960 Mail Car	10.45
Mc Cormick, Jupiter 1960 Passenger Car	12.45
Mc Cormick, Jupiter 1960 Wood Tender	10.45
Mc Cormick, Kansas City Chiefs	49.95 To 79.95

Medicine, Ayer's Hair Vigor, Paper Cover

Medicine,
Lydia Pinkham
Vegetable Compound, 8 In.

Medicine,
Dr.Miles Nervine,
7 1/2 In.

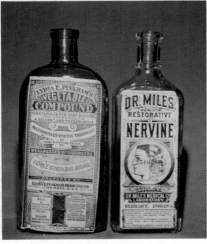

Medicine,
Dr.Sweets, BLK ,
Oil, Rochester, N.Y., Pontil

Medicine,
I Coverts Balm Of Life,
Olive Green, Pontil

Medicine, Dr.Wistar's Balsam Of
Wild Cherry, Pontil

Milk Glass,
Hartwig Kentorowicz,
9 1/2 In.

Milk Glass,
Sazerac Aromatic Bitters
11 In.

Medicine, Shaker Extract Of Roots,
5 1/2 In., Clear

Milk Glass, Klondyke Flask,
Gold Nugget, Painted

Miniature,
Old Bob Burton
Pure Rye Whiskey,
3 1/2 In.

Miniature,
Compliments Of
The Duquesne, 3 In.

Miniature,
Helmet Rye,
2 1/2 In.

Miniature,
Cambridge Springs,
Mineral Water, 2 1/2 In.

Miniature, Motto Jug,
Detrick Distilling, 4 1/2 In.

Miniature, Motto Jug,
Detrick Distilling, 5 In.

Soda, Eagle,
Cobalt Blue

Soda,
S.Smiths, 7 In.,
Cobalt Blue

Soda, Taylor
Never Surrenders,
Cobalt Blue

Soda,
Elmers Medicated,
Cobalt Blue

Poison, Not To Be Taken, Cobalt, 6 In.

Seal, The Old Mill, Whitlock And Company

Nursing, Columbia Nursing Bottle

Nursing, Our Baby's,
Pat.U.S.Office April, 1875

Nursing,
The Empire Nursing Bottle

Soda, Grape Smash,
Clear, Glass Label, 12 In.

Soda, Orange Julep,
Clear, Glass Label

Soda, J.R.Donald,
Newark, N.J., 7 In.,
Cobalt Blue

Soda,
Union Glassware,
Philadelphia, Cobalt Blue

Soda, Seitz And Bros., Soda, Union Glassworks,
Easton, Pa., 7 In., Cobalt   J & A Dearborn, Cobalt

Whiskey, Hiram Ricker & Sons, Inc., Facsimile

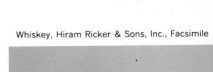

Water, Round Lake Mineral Water,
Saratoga County, N.Y.

Whiskey, Casper's, North Carolina

Whiskey, Wharton's,
Chestnut Grove,
1850, 9 1/2 In.

Whiskey, Wharton's,
Wharton, N.Y.,
9 1/2 In.

Whiskey, Old Kentucky Valley,
1861, Inside Screw

Apollo 14, Aqua, 1971   Apollo 15, Green, 1971

W.C.Fields,   Jean Harlow,   Humphrey Bogart,
Aqua, 1972   Topaz, 1972   Green, 1971

Wheaton Commemoratives

Christmas, Green, 1971   Christmas, Topaz, 1972

Andrew Jackson,   Thomas Jefferson,   Ulysses S.Grant,   Herbert C.Hoover,
Green, 1971   Ruby, 1970   Topaz, 1972   Aqua, 1972

Mc Cormick, Kansas City Royals .... 12.95 To 16.50
Mc Cormick, Missouri Sesquicentennial, Ceramic 14.95
Mc Cormick, Missouri Sesquicentennial, Glass .... 11.45 To 14.95
Mc Cormick, Pirate, No.1, Porcelain, 1/2 Pint 16.95
Mc Cormick, Pirate, No.2, Porcelain, 1/2 Pint 13.95
Mc Cormick, Pirate, No.3, Porcelain, 1/2 Pint 13.95
Mc Cormick, Pirate, No.4, Porcelain, 1/2 Pint 13.95
Mc Cormick, Pirate, No.5, Porcelain 1/2 Pint 13.95
Mc Kenna, Jug, Fifth Size 5.95
Mc Kenna, Jug, Miniature 1.95

*Medicine bottles held all of the many types of medications used in past
centuries. Most of those collected today date from the 1850-1930 period.
Bitters, sarsaparilla, poison, and a few other types of medicine are listed
under their own headings.*

Medicine, A Mineral From The Earth 5.00
Medicine, A.A.Cooley, Olive Green 80.00
Medicine, Alexander's Cure, Labels 12.00
Medicine, Alexander's Cure, Labels, Contents 15.00
Medicine, Alexander's Safe Cure For Malaria, Amber .... 7.00 To 10.50
Medicine, Allen's Botanical Cough Syrup, Label, Contents, Aqua 5.00
Medicine, Allenrhu For Rheumatism & Neuritis, Clear, Pint .... 5.00 To 8.00
Medicine, Alvas Brazilian Specific, Aqua 85.00
Medicine, American, Coventry, Auburn, N.Y., Compound, Aqua, 7 1/2 In.High 14.00
Medicine, Anderson's Poor Man's Cough Cure, Haze Inside, Aqua 5.50
Medicine, Armour's Vigoral, Chicago, Squat, Wide Mouth, Amber 3.00
Medicine, Aromatic Schnapps, Olive Green 15.00
Medicine, Athieu's Cough Syrup 5.00
Medicine, Ardui Woman's Relief, Embossed, Label .... 3.00 To 5.00
Medicine, Ayer's Ague Cure, Aqua 6.50
Medicine, Ayer's Ague Cure, BIMAL , Iridescent, Aqua, 7 In.Tall 5.00
Medicine, Ayer's Ague Cure, Contents, Sealed Package 8.00
Medicine, Ayer's Cherry Pectoral 3.00
Medicine, Ayer's Cherry Pectoral, Embossed, Pontil, Aqua .... 15.00 To 30.00
Medicine, Ayer's Cherry Pectoral, Light Green 18.00
Medicine, Ayer's Hair Vigor 12.00
Medicine, Ayer's Hair Vigor, Ball Stopper, Peacock Blue .... 18.00 To 30.00
Medicine, Ayer's Hair Vigor, BIM , Blue .... 10.00 To 17.00
Medicine, Ayer's Hair Vigor, Label, Aqua 61.00
Medicine, Ayer's Hair Vigor, Paper Cover .... *Color*   XX.XX
Medicine, Ayer's Hair Vigor, Paper Label, 7 In. .... *Illus*   8.00
Medicine, Ayer's Hair Vigor, Stopper 7.50
Medicine, B.A.Fahnestock's Vermifuge, Round, Shaved Lip, Open Pontil, Aqua 10.00
Medicine, B.Denton's Healing Balsam, Octagon 24.00
Medicine, Bachelor's Hair Dye, No.1 .... 15.00
Medicine, Bachelor's No.1 Liquid Hair Dye, 3 In.Square, Open Pontil 9.50
Medicine, Baker's Great American Specific, Maine .... *Illus*   12.00
Medicine, Baker's Liniment For Animals, Rectangular, Tin Top, Clear 4.50
Medicine, Baker's Vegetable Bladder & Liver Cure 300.00
Medicine, Baldpate Hair Tonic 5.00
Medicine, Baldwin's Celery Pepsin & Dandelion Tonic, Amber 17.50
Medicine, Balm Of Beauty, For The Complexion, Stain, Open Pontil, 5 In.High 24.00
Medicine, Barker Moore & Mein Medicine Co., Aqua 5.00
Medicine, Barry's Tricopherous For The Skin & Hair, Pontil, Aq .... 10.00 To 18.00
Medicine, Bauer's Cough Cure, Aqua 2.50
Medicine, Bear's Oil, Pontil, Aqua 7.50
Medicine, Bell Schnapps, Label, Amber 27.50
Medicine, Benne's Pain Killing Magic Oil, Slug Plate, Aqua 5.00
Medicine, Berlin Series, Aqua 5.00
Medicine, Blown, 10 Panel, Bluish, 4 In. 5.00
Medicine, Bonpland's Fever And Ague Remedy 18.00
Medicine, Booth's Hyomei, Dry Air Cure For Catarrh, Asthma, Bronchitis 7.50
Medicine, Boswell & Warner's Colorific, Rectangular, Beveled, Dark Amber 7.00
Medicine, Botanic Blood Balm, Box, Label, Amber, Quart 5.00
Medicine, Brant's Indian Pulmonary Balsam, Open Pontil, Aqua ...... 15.00 To 42.50
Medicine, Brant's Purifying Extract, Snap Case 17.00

Medicine,
Ayer's Hair Vigor,
Paper Label, 7 In.
See *Page 157*

Medicine,
Buchu-Gin, Kidney &
Liver Troubles, Green
See *Page 159*

Medicine,
Baker's Great American
Specific, Maine
See *Page 157*

Medicine, Carter's Spanish Mixture, Olive Green, 8 In.
See *Page 159*

Medicine,
Champlin's Liquid Pearl,
Milk Glass, 5 In.
See *Page 159*

Medicine,
Citrate Of Magnesia,
Clear, 8 In.High
See *Page 159*

Medicine, Cod Liver Oil, Reed,
Carnrick, & Andrus, Cobalt
See *Page 159*

Medicine, Dr.Browder's Compound
Syrup & Indian Turnip
See *Page 160*

Medicine, Brioschi, Label, Contents, Cobalt	10.00
Medicine, Bromo-Seltzer	2.00
Medicine, Bromo Seltzer & Syrup Of Figs, Cobalt Blue	6.50
Medicine, Bromo Seltzer, Cobalt, 8 In.	6.00
Medicine, Bromo Seltzer, Green	17.50
Medicine, Brown's Instant Relief For Pain, Embossed, Aqua, 5 1/4 In.	3.50
Medicine, Brown's Young American Liniment	4.00
Medicine, Buchu-Gin, Kidney & Liver Troubles, Green *Illus*	38.00
Medicine, Buckhout Dutch Liniment, Open Pontil, Aqua	130.00
Medicine, Burma Turpentine	.98
Medicine, Buxton's Rheumatic, Embossed, Label, Aqua	10.00
Medicine, By Dr.Gordak Only, Jelly Of Pomegranate Preparate, Aqua	15.00
Medicine, C.A.Richards & Co., Amber	15.00
Medicine, C.Brinckerhoff's Health Restorative, Open Pontil, Olive Green	120.00
Medicine, C.T.Whipple Garget Cure, Aqua	7.00
Medicine, C.W.Merchant's, Lockport, N.Y.	25.00
Medicine, Calder's Dentine, Cork, Clear, 3 In.	4.00
Medicine, Caldwell's Syrup Of Pepsin, Embossed, Corker, Aqua	2.00
Medicine, Caldwell's Syrup Pepsin, Monticello, Ill., 3 In. High	3.00
Medicine, California Tooth Tablet, Milk Glass, Metal Top	50.00
Medicine, Capilania Hair Restorative, Extended Neck, Snap Case, Aqua	8.00
Medicine, Carter's Spanish Mixture, Olive Green, 8 In. *Illus*	75.00
Medicine, Cary's Cough Cure Syrup, Aqua	8.50
Medicine, Castor Oil, Cobalt, 8 In.High	7.50
Medicine, Castor Oil, Paper Label, Push-Up Base, Rough Pontil, Clear	15.00
Medicine, Catarrh Snuff	4.50
Medicine, Celery Compound, Labels, Amber	25.00
Medicine, Chamberlain's Balsam, Blown In Mold	4.00
Medicine, Chamberlain's Cough Remedy	3.00
Medicine, Chamberlain's Liniment, Paper Labels	12.50
Medicine, Champlin's Liquid Pearl, Milk Glass, 5 In. *Illus*	12.00
Medicine, Cheney's Expectorant, BIMAL	3.00
Medicine, Chesebro's Liquid Corn Plaster, Round, Cobalt Blue, 2 1/8 In.	.99
Medicine, Chinese Opium, Miniature, Hand Blown, Embossed, Bubbly, 2 In.	2.25
Medicine, Cholera Specific, Stoddard, Three Mold, Clear	3.00
Medicine, Citrate Magnesia, Porcelain Stopper	2.50
Medicine, Citrate Of Magnesia, Clear, 8 In.High *Illus*	3.25
Medicine, Citrate Of Magnesia, Glass Stopper, Wire Bail, Clear	5.00
Medicine, Citrate Of Magnesia, Milk Glass	5.50
Medicine, Clock's Excelsior Hair Restorer, Embossed, Aqua	3.00
Medicine, Cod Liver Oil, Fish, ABM , Amber	5.00
Medicine, Cod Liver Oil, Fish, Amber, 9 1/2 In.	8.50 To 18.00
Medicine, Cod Liver Oil, Reed, Carnrick, & Andrus, Cobalt *Illus*	110.00
Medicine, Coffeen's Liniment No.2, Open Pontil, Dug, Aqua, 4 1/4 In.	6.50
Medicine, Cold Press Castor Oil, Cylinder, Long Neck, Label, Deep Cobalt	21.00
Medicine, Coltsfoote Expectorant, Label, Box & Circular	5.00
Medicine, Connell's Brahmnical Moonplant E.Indian Remedies, Pint	37.50
Medicine, Constitutional Beverage, Cabin Shape, Amber	55.00
Medicine, Cook's Hair Invigorator, Lewiston, Me., Aqua	28.00
Medicine, Cough Syrup, Bites All The Way Down, 8 1/2 In.	12.00
Medicine, Cramer's Cure, Sample	4.00
Medicine, Cramer's Kidney & Liver Cure, Sample	6.50
Medicine, Criswell's Bromo Pepsin	4.00
Medicine, Curling's Citrate Of Magnesia, Cobalt	20.00
Medicine, Cuticura Cure, Large	4.00
Medicine, Cuticura Cure, Small	6.00
Medicine, Cuticura System Of Blood & Skin Purification, 2 Labels, Aqua	13.00
Medicine, Cuticura System Of Curing Constitutional Humors	4.00 To 7.00
Medicine, Cuticura System Of Curing Constitutional Humors, Aqua	3.50
Medicine, Cuticura System Of Curing Constitutional Humors, 7 1/2 In.	6.00
Medicine, D.Evan's Camomile Pills, Pontil	6.00
Medicine, Dalby's Carminative	15.00
Medicine, Dalton's Sarsaparilla & Nerve Tonic, Aqua	15.00
Medicine, Davis Vegetable Pain Killer, Label, Open Pontil, Dated 1854, Aqua	35.00
Medicine, Davis Vegetable Pain Killer, Pontil	22.00
Medicine, Dead Shot Vermifuge, Pontil	10.00

Medicine, Deschien Syrup, Paris Embossed Label, Cobalt 35.00
Medicine, Diabetes Cure, Embossed, 16 Oz. 40.00
Medicine, Donnell's Rheumatic Liniment, Rectangular, Contents, Label, Aqua 1.85
Medicine, Dr.A.Boschee's German Syrup, Contents, Flyer In Original Box 3.00
Medicine, Dr.A.Roger's Liverwort Tar & Canchalagua, New York, Aqua 42.00
Medicine, Dr.Ashbough's Wonder Of The World, Pittsburgh, Pa., Aqua 6.00
Medicine, Dr.B.J.Kendall's Quick Relief, Embossed, Label, Contents, Box 3.00
Medicine, Dr.Browder's Compound Syrup & Indian Turnip .... *Illus* 75.00
Medicine, Dr.C.Bouveris' Buchi Gin 5.50
Medicine, Dr.C.C.Roc's Liver, Neuralgic & Rheumatic Cure 10.00
Medicine, Dr.C.K.Donnell's Indian Remedies, Lewiston, Me., Embossed, Clear 7.00
Medicine, Dr.C.W.Roback's, Iron Pontil 125.00
Medicine, Dr.C.W.Roback's Scandinavian Blood Purifier, Cincinnati, O., Aqua 125.00
Medicine, Dr.Caldwell's Laxative Senna, Embossed, Contents, Box, & Circular 8.00
Medicine, Dr.Caldwell's Syrup Of Pepsin & Laxative, Embossed 1.00
Medicine, Dr.Caldwell's Syrup Of Pepsin, Aqua, 3 In.High 4.50
Medicine, Dr.Caldwell's Syrup Of Pepsin, Embossed, Corker, Aqua 2.00
Medicine, Dr.Campbell's Hair Invigorator, Open Pontil, Aqua 27.50
Medicine, Dr.Corhams Gray Hair Restorer 4.50
Medicine, Dr.Craig's Kidney Cure, Embossed Kidney, Cloud In Base, Amber 150.00
Medicine, Dr.Crook's Wine Of Tar .... 10.00 To 12.00
Medicine, Dr.Cumming's Vegetine 9.95
Medicine, Dr.Daniel's Colic Drops 3.00
Medicine, Dr.Daniel's Osteroccus Nerve & Muscle Liniment 5.00
Medicine, Dr.Daniel's Veterinary Colic Drips, Clear .... 3.00 To 5.00
Medicine, Dr.Davis Depuritive, Improved Pontil, Green 260.00
Medicine, Dr.Evan's Camomile Pills, Open Pontil, Flanged Mouth, Cloudy 7.50
Medicine, Dr.F.S.Forsha Alterative Balm, Aqua, 6 3/4 In. 5.00
Medicine, Dr.Fenner's Golden Relief 3.50
Medicine, Dr.Fenner's Kidney & Backache Cure 30.00
Medicine, Dr.Fenner's People's Remedies, Amber 15.00
Medicine, Dr.Fenner's People's Remedies, U.S.A., 1872, 1898 .... 3.00
Medicine, Dr.Fenner's Pleasant Syrup, 1870 .... 7.50
Medicine, Dr.Fitch, Broadway, New York, Open Pontil 25.00
Medicine, Dr.Flint's Remedie, Label, Embossed, Full, Amber 15.00
Medicine, Dr.Fordak, Jelly Of Pomegranate, Aqua 110.00
Medicine, Dr.G.A.Zimmerman's Easy To Take Castor Oil, BIMAL, Cobalt 8.00
Medicine, Dr.Gilbert's Gas-Tro-Ma 4.00
Medicine, Dr.Gould's Pin Worm Syrup 5.00
Medicine, Dr.Graves' Heart Regulator, Cures Heart Disease 7.50
Medicine, Dr.Green's Nervura 8.00
Medicine, Dr.H.Kelsey, Lowell, Mass., Applied Top, O.P., Stained, 6 1/2 In. 6.00
Medicine, Dr.H.Kelsey, Lowell, Mass., BIMAL, Aqua, 6 3/4 In. 7.00
Medicine, Dr.Ham's Invigorator, Cylinder, Amber, 7 In.High 6.00
Medicine, Dr.Hamilton's Syrup Of Blackberry & Sassafras, Oval, Aqua 20.50
Medicine, Dr.Hardy's Medical Pain Destroyer, Embossed, Label, Full, Aqua 5.00
Medicine, Dr.Harter's Iron Tonic, Amber, 9 1/4 In. 10.00
Medicine, Dr.Harter's Soothing Drops 7.00
Medicine, Dr.Hartshorn's Cordial For Diarrhea, Aqua .... *Illus* 4.50
Medicine, Dr.Hawk's Universal Stimulant, Aqua 4.00
Medicine, Dr.Hayne's Arabian Balsam, 12 Panels 4.00
Medicine, Dr.Hess Colic Remedy, Labeled Cannabis Indica, Contents, Amethyst 8.00
Medicine, Dr.Higgin's Great Antalgica, Paper Label, Aqua, 6 1/2 In. 13.50
Medicine, Dr.Hoffman's Celebrated German Liniment, 6 1/4 In. 4.00
Medicine, Dr.Ingham's Nervene, Open Pontil 15.00
Medicine, Dr.J.G.B.Siegert & Hijos, BIMAL , Dug, Whittled, 3 Mold, Green 4.00
Medicine, Dr.J.Larivier's Female Health Regulator, Aqua 8.00
Medicine, Dr.J.Pettit's Canker Balsam, Sheared Neck, O.P., Aqua, 3 1/8 In. 15.00
Medicine, Dr.J.S.Clark's Balsam For The Throat & Lungs, 8 3/4 In. 5.00
Medicine, Dr.J.W.Bull's Baby Syrup, A.C.Meyer & Co., Dated May 1, '99, Aqua 5.95
Medicine, Dr.J.W.Polands, White Pine Compound, Aqua .... *Illus* 7.50
Medicine, Dr.James Cannabis Indica, Aqua 37.50
Medicine, Dr.Jayne's Alternative, Open Pontil, Aqua 15.00
Medicine, Dr.Jayne's Carminative Balsam, Pontil, Aqua 10.00
Medicine, Dr.Jayne's Expectorant, Aqua 2.50
Medicine, Dr.Jayne's Expectorant, Embossed Pontil 26.00

Medicine, Dr.Jayne's Expectorant, Open Pontil, Aqua	16.50
Medicine, Dr.Jayne's Expectorant, Pontil, Dug	12.50
Medicine, Dr.Jayne's Expectorant, Stain, Open Pontil, Aqua	15.00
Medicine, Dr.Jayne's Hair Tonic, 4 In.	9.50
Medicine, Dr.Jayne's Tonic Vermifuge, Pontil, Aqua	35.00
Medicine, Dr.Jayne's Tonic Vermifuge, The Strength Giver	3.00
Medicine, Dr.Kendall's Elixir, Free Sample, Label, Aqua	3.00
Medicine, Dr.Kendall's Kidney & Liver Cure, Label, Box	5.00
Medicine, Dr.Kennedy's Favorite Remedy, Applied Lip, Clear	3.00
Medicine, Dr.Kennedy's Medical Discovery, Aqua, 9 In. _Illus_	4.00
Medicine, Dr.Kennedy's Medical Discovery, Open Pontil, Aqua	37.50
Medicine, Dr.Kennedy's Medicinal Discovery, Roxbury, Mass., Green, 8 In.High	37.50
Medicine, Dr.Kennedy's Rheumatic Dissolvent, Embossed, Label	4.50
Medicine, Dr.Kilmer's Cure, Aqua, 7 In.	3.00
Medicine, Dr.Kilmer's Cures, Sample	1.50
Medicine, Dr.Kilmer's Female Remedy	12.00 To 19.00
Medicine, Dr.Kilmer's Oceanweed Heart Remedy, Aqua _Illus_	30.00

Medicine, Dr.Hartshorn's Cordial For Diarrhea, Aqua
See Page 160

Medicine, Dr.J.W.Polands, White Pine Compound, Aqua
See Page 160

Medicine, Dr.Kennedy's Medical Discovery, Aqua, 9 In.

Medicine, Dr.Kilmer's Oceanweed Heart Remedy, Aqua

Medicine, Dr.Kilmer's Swamp Root Cure, BIMAL , Dug, Aqua	2.00
Medicine, Dr.Kilmer's Swamp Root Cure, Specific, 8 1/4 In.High	1.00 To 3.50
Medicine, Dr.Kilmer's Swamp Root Kidney & Liver Cure, 7 In.Aqua	3.50
Medicine, Dr.Kilmer's Swamp Root Kidney, Liver, & Bladder Cure	3.50
Medicine, Dr.Kilmer's Swamp Root, Green	4.00
Medicine, Dr.Kilmer's U & O Anointment, Binghamton, N.Y., Sample, Clear	3.00
Medicine, Dr.Kilmer's U & O Anointment, Ground Lip, Aqua, Screw Top, Aqua	5.00
Medicine, Dr.King's New Discovery For Consumption, BIMAL , Dug, Aqua	3.00
Medicine, Dr.King's New Discovery For Coughs & Colds, Aqua	4.00
Medicine, Dr.King's New Discovery, Chicago, Ill., Trial Size, Aqua	4.50
Medicine, Dr.King's New Life Pills, Clear, 2 1/2 In.High	3.00
Medicine, Dr.Langley's 99 Union, Aqua	18.00
Medicine, Dr.Larookah's Indian Vegetable Pulmonic Syrup, Applied Top	8.00
Medicine, Dr.Lesure's Family Liniment, Keene, N.H.	4.00
Medicine, Dr.M.M.Fenner, Fredonia, N.Y., 1904, Trial Size, Amber	4.75
Medicine, Dr.M.M.Fenner's Kidney & Backache Cure, Short Neck, Amber	23.50
Medicine, Dr.Marshall's Catarrh Snuff	3.00
Medicine, Dr.Mc Clane's American Worm Specific	18.00
Medicine, Dr.Mc Clean's Strengthening Cordial & Blood Purifier	12.50 To 15.00
Medicine, Dr.Mc Mumm's Elixir Of Opium, Open Pontil, Aqua, 4 In	7.50 To 12.50

Medicine, Dr.Mile's Heart Treatment, Label, Contents, ABM 6.00
Medicine, Dr.Mile's Medical Co. 2.00
Medicine, Dr.Mile's Nervine, Label, 1906, 8 In. .... *Illus* 2.50
Medicine, Dr.Mile's Nervine, 7 1/2 In. .... *Color* XX.XX
Medicine, Dr.Mile's New Heart Cure, Embossed, Aqua, 8 1/4 In. .... 5.00 To 6.00
Medicine, Dr.Mile's Remedy For The Heart, Aqua, 8 1/4 In. 4.50
Medicine, Dr.Mile's Restorative Blood Purifier, Aqua, 8 1/4 In. 6.50
Medicine, Dr.Miller's Soothing & Healing Balsam, Sheldonville, Mass., Aqua 10.00
Medicine, Dr.Miller's Vegetable Expectorant, Labeled 6.00
Medicine, Dr.Morse's Celebrated Syrup 19.95
Medicine, Dr.Ordway's Pain Destroyer, Pontil, Clear .... *Illus* 25.00
Medicine, Dr.Ordway's Pain Destroyer, 1850, 12 Sided, Label, Aqua, 5 1/2 In. 15.00
Medicine, Dr.Peter's Oleoid 3.00
Medicine, Dr.Pierce, Embossed R.V.Pierce, M.C., Aqua, 8 1/2 In.High 4.00
Medicine, Dr.Pierce's Favorite Prescription, Deep Bluish Aqua Aqua, 8 In. 3.00
Medicine, Dr.Pierce's, Embossed, Whittled, Aqua, 8 1/2 In.High 4.00
Medicine, Dr.Pinkham's Emmenagogue, Pontil, Aqua, 6 In. .... *Illus* 60.00
Medicine, Dr.Pitcher's Castoria 2.00
Medicine, Dr.Poland's White Pine Compound, Sparkly Aqua 8.50
Medicine, Dr.Pollard's Bile Corrector, Open Pontil, Label 20.00
Medicine, Dr.Porter, New York, Embossed Pontil .... 15.00 To 18.00
Medicine, Dr.R.C.Flower's Lung Cordial, Panel With Label, Boston, Amber 4.00
Medicine, Dr.Richmond, For Sanitarium, Patee House Hotel, Flint 5.00
Medicine, Dr.Ring's New Discovery 3.00
Medicine, Dr.Roback, Swedish Remedy, 8 Sided, Pontil 6.00
Medicine, Dr.S.A.Weavers Canker & Salt Rheumatic Syrup, Oval, Aqua 17.00
Medicine, Dr.S.B.H.& Co. 4.00
Medicine, Dr.S.F.Stowe's Ambrosial Nectar, Pat.May 22, 1866, Amber, Pint 9.00
Medicine, Dr.S.Pitcher & Co. Substitute For Castor Oil 10.00
Medicine, Dr.Sage's Buffalo Catarrh Remedy, 2 In. 3.00
Medicine, Dr.Sage's Catarrh Remedy, Contents, Aqua 3.00
Medicine, Dr.Sanford's Liver Invigorator, Aqua, 7 3/4 In. .... 3.00 To 3.75
Medicine, Dr.Seth Arnold's Cough Killer, Embossed Pontil 16.00
Medicine, Dr.Seth Arnold's Cough Killer, Whittled, Aqua, 8 In.High 12.00
Medicine, Dr.Shoop's Family Medicines, Square, 7 1/2 In.Clear 3.00
Medicine, Dr.Shoop's Family, Square, Aqua 3.50
Medicine, Dr.Swayne's Syrup Of Wild Cherry, Pontil 15.00
Medicine, Dr.Sweets, BLK , Oil, Rochester, N.Y., Pontil .... *Color* XX.XX
Medicine, Dr.Syke's New England Liver Tonic & Bilious Annihilator, Amber 10.00
Medicine, Dr.Thacher's Liver & Blood Syrup, Amber, 8 1/2 In. 5.50
Medicine, Dr.Thompson's Eye Water, New London, Conn., Embossed, Aqua, 4 In. 2.00
Medicine, Dr.Thomson's Great English Remedy, Embossed, ... 20.00
Medicine, Dr.Tobias Venetian Liniment 3.00
Medicine, Dr.W.B.Caldwell's Syrup Pepsin, Clear .... *Illus* 10.00
Medicine, Dr.Wistar's Balsam Of Wild Cherry, Phila., 8 Sided .... 15.00 To 40.00
Medicine, Dr.Wistar's Balsam Of Wild Cherry, Pontil .... *Color* XX.XX
Medicine, Dr.Wistar's Balsam Of Wild Cherry, Sealed Package, 2 Oz. 4.00
Medicine, Dr.Wistar's Balsam Of Wild Cherry, Sealed Package, 4 Oz. 4.00
Medicine, Dr.Zimmerman's Easy To Take Castor Oil, Jamestown, Pa., Cobalt 6.50
Medicine, Dr's Atomizer, Free-Blown, 5 In.High 13.00
Medicine, Drey's Emulsion, Contents, Boxed 3.00
Medicine, Electric Brand Laxative, Label, Contents, Amber, Pint 8.00
Medicine, Elepizone Cure 30.00
Medicine, Elixir Of Calisaya, Blown In Mold 6.00
Medicine, Ely's Cream Balm For Catarrh & Hay Fever 4.00
Medicine, Ely's Cream Balm, Small Size 3.00
Medicine, Eno's Fruit Salts, Glass Stopper 5.00
Medicine, Eno's Fruit Salts, Stopper, Light Green 4.50
Medicine, Esgood's, Embossed, India Cholagogue, 5 Oz. 9.00
Medicine, Evan's, Pontil 10.00
Medicine, F.W.Greenhalge Fifty Cent Hair Restorer, Oval, Aqua 4.50
Medicine, Fahnestock's Vermifuge, Round, Open Pontil, Aqua, 4 In. 10.00
Medicine, Fellow's Syrup Of Hypophosphites 3.00
Medicine, Firwein, Tilden & Co., N.Y., Blue, 7 1/2 In. .... *Illus* 20.00
Medicine, Foley Kidney & Bladder Cure 8.50
Medicine, Foley's Cure, Sample 3.00

Medicine, Foley's Honey & Tar Compound .... *Illus*	2.00
Medicine, Foley's Kidney & Bladder Cure, Amber, 9 1/4 In.	10.00
Medicine, Foley's Kidney Cure, Embossed, Label, Amber, 7 3/8 In.	12.00
Medicine, Foley's Kidney Cure, Embossed, Label, Contents, Boxed	7.00
Medicine, Foley's Kidney Cure, Sample	8.00
Medicine, Folger's Olosaonian, Pontil	15.00
Medicine, Forestine Kidney Cure, Label	16.50
Medicine, French Remedy For Colds, Throat, Embossed, Haze, Clear	6.50
Medicine, G.W.Merchant, Lockport, N.Y., Stained, Green, 5 In.High	10.00
Medicine, Galen's Restorative Elixir, Label, Open Pontil, Aqua	25.00
Medicine, Garget Cure, C.T.Whipple, Prop., Portland, Me., Aqua .... 4.50 To 7.00
Medicine, Gargling Oil, Cobalt Blue	10.00
Medicine, Gargling Oil, Lockport, N.Y., Cobalt, 5 In.High .... *Illus*	14.00

Medicine,
Gargling Oil, Lockport,
N.Y., Cobalt, 5 In.High

Medicine,
Dr.Pinkham's
Emmenagogue,
Pontil, Aqua, 6 In.
See Page 162

Medicine, Dr.Ordway's
Pain Destroyer,
Pontil, Clear
See Page 162

Medicine, Firwein,
Tilden & Co., N.Y.,
Blue, 7 1/2 In.
See Page 162

Medicine, Dr.W.B.Caldwell's Syrup
Pepsin, Clear
See Page 162

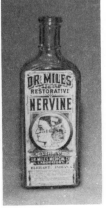

Medicine,
Foley's
Honey & Tar
Compound

Medicine, Dr.Mile's Nervine,
Label, 1906, 8 In.
See Page 162

Medicine, **Gargling Oil**, Lockport, N.Y., Green 8.00
Medicine, **Genuine Essence**, Embossed Pontil 16.00
Medicine, **Genuine Essence**, Open Pontil, Rectangular, Embossed, Dug, Aqua 7.50
Medicine, **Germene**, Cures Sick Blood, Label, Contents, Box & Flyer 3.00
Medicine, **Gibb's Bone Liniment**, 8 Sided, Pontil, 4 On Base, Olive Green 200.00
   Medicine, **Gin**, see Gin
Medicine, **Glover's Imperial Mange Cure**, Amber 5.00
Medicine, **Goelicke's Matchless Sanative**, Free-Blown, Dated 1836, Aqua 7.50
Medicine, **Gold Medal Harlem Oil**, Label, Embossed 2.00
Medicine, **Granular Citrate Of Magnesia**, Glass & Lead Screw Cap, Cobalt 8.00
Medicine, **Gray's Balsam**, Embossed, Corker 1.50
Medicine, **Great Dr.Kilmer's Cure**, Specific, Aqua, 8 1/4 In. 6.00
Medicine, **Great Dr.Kilmer's Swamp Root Kidney**, Liver & Bladder Cure 6.00
Medicine, **Groder's Botanic Dyspepsia Syrup**, Paper Label 6.00
Medicine, **Grove's Chill Tonic**, Contents 3.00
Medicine, **Grove's Tasteless Chill Tonic**, Embossed 1.00
Medicine, **Grover Graham's Dyspepsia Cure**, Clear 5.00
Medicine, **H.H.H.**, Back D.D.J., 1868, The Celebrated, Aqua .... *Illus* 5.50
Medicine, **H.H.H.Horse Medicine**, Aqua 8.00
Medicine, **H.Lake's Indian Specific**, Open Pontil .... 65.00 To 80.00
Medicine, **H.Oldfield Embossed**, Octagonal, 2 Piece Mold, C.1800, Green 50.00
Medicine, **Hadacol**, 20 Oz., Full & Boxed 3.75

Medicine, H.H.H., Back D.D.J., 1868, The Celebrated, Aqua

Medicine, **Hagan's Magnolia Balm**, Milk Glass 12.00
Medicine, **Hair Balsam**, Blob Top, Olive Green 5.00
Medicine, **Hair Oil**, Made In St.Joseph, Label, Red Oil Contents, 6 1/2 In. 2.00
Medicine, **Hale's Honey Of Horehound & Tar**, Embossed, Label, Aqua 7.00
Medicine, **Hall's Catarrh Cure**, Aqua .... 2.00 To 3.00
Medicine, **Hall's Hair Renewer**, Peacock Blue 32.00
Medicine, **Halls**, Sicilian Hair Renewer, Label, 6 1/2 In. 10.00
Medicine, **Hamlin's Wizard Oil**, Embossed, Corker, Aqua 2.00
Medicine, **Hanford's Celery Cure**, Cures Rheumatism, Neuralgia, Insomnia 18.00
Medicine, **Hanford's Extracts**, Syracuse, Embossed, Corker 1.50
Medicine, **Harper Method Tonic For The Hair**, Martha Matilda Harper 4.00
Medicine, **Harriet's Discovery Cure For Diabetes**, Contents, Package 17.00
Medicine, **Hart's Swedish Asthma Cure**, Amber .... 3.00 To 8.00
Medicine, **Hart's Swedish Asthma Cure**, Embossed, Amber 12.00
Medicine, **Haskin's Nervine**, BIMAL, Dug, Aqua 4.00
Medicine, **Haskin's Nervine**, Binghamton, N.Y., Aqua, 8 1/4 In. .... 4.00 To 7.50
Medicine, **Hay's Hair Health**, Amber, 6 1/2 In. 4.00
Medicine, **Hay's Hair Health**, Embossed, Corker 1.50
Medicine, **Hayne's Genuine Arabian Balsam** 1.00
Medicine, **Healy & Bigelow Indian Sagwa** 6.50
Medicine, **Hick's Capudine For Headaches**, Colds, Gripp, Corker, Amber 5.00
Medicine, **Himalaya Kola Compound Asthma Cure**, Square, Amber 7.00

Medicine, **Holman's Nature's Grand Restorative**, Open Pontil, Aqua	30.00
Medicine, **Hood's Liver Pills Cure**, Aqua	3.00
Medicine, **Hood's Pills**, For Liver Ills, Flask	4.00
Medicine, **Hood's Pills**, Liver Ills, Clear	3.50
Medicine, **Horse Spavin Remedy**	6.00
Medicine, **Humphrey's Homeopathic Veterinary**, Embossed Horse's Head	4.00
Medicine, **Humphrey's**, Ogdensburg, Pontil, Aqua	5.00
Medicine, **Hunt's Liniment**, C.E.Stanton	20.00
Medicine, **Hunt's Liniment**, Open Pontil, Green	22.00
Medicine, **I Coverts Balm Of Life**, Olive Green, Pontil .... *Color*	XX.XX
Medicine, **Imperial Magnesia Laxative**, Embossed Boy Running, Aqua	5.00
Medicine, **Improved Champion Liniment**	7.00
Medicine, **Indian Sagwa**, Aqua .... 11.95 To	15.00
Medicine, **Iron & Nux In Munyon's Paw Paw**, Applied Mouth, ABM , Amber	9.00
Medicine, **J.B.Wheatley's Compound Syrup**, Ky., Embossed, Aqua, 1/2 Pint	22.50
Medicine, **J.B.Wheatley's Compound Syrup**, Ky., Embossed, Green, 1/2 Pint	22.50
Medicine, **J.J.Maher & Co. Proprietors**, Augusta, Maine, Amber, Pint	3.00
Medicine, **Jarmuth's Beef Wine & Iron**, 8 In., Aqua Ovals	5.00
Medicine, **Jelly Of Pomegranate & Dr.Fordak**, Open Pontil, Aqua	110.00
Medicine, **John Smith**, Kentucky Glass Works, Aqua	35.00
Medicine, **John Wyeth & Bros.**, Dose Cap, Label, Cobalt Blue	11.00
Medicine, **John Wyeth & Bros.**, Embossed, Cap, Cobalt Blue, 10 1/4 In.	35.00
Medicine, **Johnson's American Anodyne Liniment**, Embossed Pontil	18.00
Medicine, **Johnson's American Anodyne Liniment**, Round, Aqua, 4 1/4 In.High	.65
Medicine, **Johnson's American Anodyne Liniment**, Round, Aqua, 6 1/2 In.High	.65
Medicine, **Johnson's American Anodyne Liniment**, Round, BIMAL, Aqua	3.00
Medicine, **Johnson's Chill & Fever Tonic**, BIMAL, Dug, Turning Purple	3.00
Medicine, **Johnson's Chill & Fever Tonic**, Clear	3.00
Medicine, **Ka Ton Ka**, The Great Indian Remedy, Applied Lip, Clear	6.00
Medicine, **Kalo Compound For Dyspepsia**, Embossed, Corker, Aqua	2.00
Medicine, **Keeley's Chloride Of Gold Cure For Drunkeness**, Stain, Clear	85.00
Medicine, **Keeley's Cure Drunkeness**, Sun Colored	45.00
Medicine, **Keeley's Cure Tobacco Habit**, Sun Colored	55.00
Medicine, **Kemp's Balsam For Throat & Lungs**	4.00
Medicine, **Kemp's Cough Balsam**, Aqua, 2 1/2 In.High	3.00
Medicine, **Kemp's Cough Balsam**, Woodward, Sampler, 2 1/2 In.High	4.00
Medicine, **Kendall's Quick Relief**	5.00
Medicine, **Kendall's Spavin Cure For Human Flesh**, Poison Label, Aqua	6.00
Medicine, **Kendall's Spavin Cure**, Amber .... 2.00 To	6.00
Medicine, **Kendall's Spavin Cure**, Slight Film, Aqua	3.00
Medicine, **Kendall's Spavin Cure**, 12 Panels, Amber .... 4.00 To	6.00
Medicine, **Kennedy's Favorite Remedy**	3.50
Medicine, **Kennedy's Medical Discovery**, Snap Case	8.00
Medicine, **Kennedy's Medicinal Discovery**	4.00
Medicine, **Kennedy's Sarsaparilla & Celery Compound**, Amber	17.50
Medicine, **Kerry's Balsam**, Embossed, Corker	1.50
Medicine, **Kickapoo Cough Cure**	5.75
Medicine, **Kickapoo Indian Sagwa**, Labels, Aqua	10.95
Medicine, **Kickapoo Oil**	4.00
Medicine, **Kickapoo Sagwa Stomach**, Liver, & Kidney Renovator, Aqua, 8 1/2 In.	20.00
Medicine, **Kickapoo Sagwa Tonic**, Label, Full, Boxed, & Instructions	15.00
Medicine, **Klinck's Catarrh & Bronchial Remedy**, A Sure & Safe Cure, Box	3.00
Medicine, **Koenig's Nervine**, Corker, Label	2.50
Medicine, **Ky.State Dental Assoc.Clyco Thymoline**, Ground Stopper, 7 In.	18.00
Medicine, **Lactopeptine**, Square, Blue, Pint .... 15.00 To	17.50
Medicine, **Laley's Kidney Cure**, Sample	3.00
Medicine, **Laxol**, A.J.White, N.Y., Patent 1894, 3 Sided, Blue	3.95
Medicine, **Laxol**, Blue, 7 In.High .... *Illus*	7.00
Medicine, **Lindsey's Blood Plus Searcher**, Pittsburgh, Deep Blue Aqua	18.00
Medicine, **Lindsey's Blood Searcher**, Marked Hollidaysburg, Applied Lip, Aqua	35.00
Medicine, **Liquid Opodeldoc**, Embossed, Flared Top, Cylinder, O.P., 4 1/2 In.	5.00
Medicine, **Liquid Opodeldoc**, Pontil, Aqua, 3 In.	7.00
Medicine, **Little Doctor Medicine**, The	2.00
Medicine, **Liverade**, Boxed, Clear .... *Illus*	1.50
Medicine, **Lockport Gargling Oil**	8.00
Medicine, **Lockport Gargling Oil**, Broken Bubble On Reverse, Green, 7 In.High	25.00

Medicine,
Laxol, Blue, 7 In.High
See Page 165

Medicine, Liverade, Boxed, Clear
See Page 165

Medicine,
Mellin's Baby Food,
Screw Top, Small Size

Medicine, Lockport Gargling Oil, Cobalt	9.00
Medicine, Lockport Gargling Oil, Green	8.00 To 9.00
Medicine, Log Cabin Cough & Consumption Remedy, Small Size	95.00
Medicine, Log Cabin Extract, Label	75.00
Medicine, Log Cabin Scalopine, Iridescent, Dug	75.00
Medicine, Lydia E.Pinkham, Clear	3.00
Medicine, Lydia Pinkham's Vegetable Compound, 8 In. .... *Color*	XX.XX
Medicine, Lydia Pinkham's, Label, Aqua	7.00
Medicine, Lydia Pinkham's, 1906, 95 Percent Label	4.50
Medicine, Lyon's Celery Tonic, Label, Aqua	6.00
Medicine, Lyon's For The Hair, Kathairon, Embossed Pontil	20.00
Medicine, Lyon's Kathairon For The Hair, N.Y., Rectangular, Dug, Aqua, 6 In.	16.00
Medicine, Lyon's Kathairon For The Hair, Sealed Package	6.00
Medicine, Made For Patee House Hotel, Dated 1882-1885, Flint	5.00
Medicine, Magic Mosquitoe Bite Cure	8.00
Medicine, Magnesia, Dated 1906, Light Blue	4.00
Medicine, Magnetic Liniment, Albany, German	9.00
Medicine, Malaria Specific, Blown In Mold, Labeled	5.00
Medicine, Mansfield & Hurd New Discovery, Cobalt, 7 1/2 In.High	22.50
Medicine, Mansfield's Mississippi Cordial For Diarrhea	3.50
Medicine, Marsden's Asiatic Cholera Cure, Label, Contents, Revenue Stamp	20.50
Medicine, Maywood's Prescription For Irregular Menstruation, Aqua	5.00
Medicine, Mcclean's Strengthening Cordial, A & D.H.C.	15.00
Medicine, Mccombie's Compound Restorative, Pontil	25.00
Medicine, Mckesson Cod Liver Oil, Full & Labeled	12.00
Medicine, Medicinal Solution Of Pyrozone, Glass Stopper	7.00
Medicine, Meelress Wine Of Cardui, Embossed, Corker, Aqua	2.00
Medicine, Melcher's Schnapps, Label, Green	32.50
Medicine, Mellin's Baby Food, Screw Top, Small Size .... *Illus*	4.00
Medicine, Mexican Mustang Liniment, Blown In Mold, Open Pontil, Aqua	8.00
Medicine, Mexican Mustang Liniment, Brooklyn, N.Y., Amethyst	5.00
Medicine, Min-O-Compound Laxative	3.50
Medicine, Minard's Liniment, Half Paneled	3.00
Medicine, Moones, Emerald Oil, Labled, Embossed	2.00
Medicine, Morris, Otsego County, New York, S.S.Seely, Embossed Pontil	20.00
Medicine, Mother's Relief, Graphite Pontil, Blue Green	150.00
Medicine, Moxie Nerve Food, Aqua, Quart	4.00

Medicine, Moxie Nerve Food, Lowell, Mass., Blob Top 5.00
Medicine, Mrs.S.A.Allen's World's Hair Restorer 15.00
Medicine, Mrs.Winslow's Soothing Syrup, Aqua 3.00
Medicine, Mrs.Winslow's Soothing Syrup, BIMAL, Dug, Aqua 2.00
Medicine, Mrs.Winslow's Soothing Syrup, Curtis & Perkins, Aqua, 5 In. 12.00
Medicine, Mrs.Winslow's Soothing Syrup, Embossed Pontil 15.00
Medicine, Mrs.Winslow's Soothing Syrup, Full 7.50
Medicine, Mrs.Winslow's Soothing Syrup, Round, Pontil, Aqua, 3 In. 6.50
Medicine, Mulford's Extract, Oval, Amber 5.00
Medicine, Munyon's Inhaler, Cures Colds, BIMAL , Emerald Green, 4 1/4 In. 10.00
Medicine, Munyon's Paw Paw Tonic, Full, Boxed, & Instructions, Amber 12.00
Medicine, Mysterious Pain Cure 8.75
Medicine, N.Wood & Co., Portland, Me., Embossed Label Castor Oil, Aqua 5.00
Medicine, Naptha Syrup, Pontil, Aqua 15.00
Medicine, Nash's C.C.D.For Temporary Loose Bowels 3.50
Medicine, Nash's Chill Tonic With Laxative 4.00
Medicine, National Remedy Co., Embossed, Corker 1.50
Medicine, National Remedy Co., N.Y., Aqua 3.00
Medicine, Neill's Pain Destroyer 5.00
Medicine, Nerve & Bone Liniment, Clear 3.50
Medicine, Nerve & Bone Liniment, Round, Open Pontil, Aqua 13.50
Medicine, Newell's Vegetable Pain Reliever 6.00
Medicine, Not-A-Bite, Black Fly & Mosquito Lotion, Embossed, Clear 3.00
Medicine, Nubian Tea For The Liver, Embossed, Label, Dark Amber 37.50
Medicine, Nuxated Iron 3.50
Medicine, O-Sa-To Tonic Indian Laxative, Relieves Many Ills, Corker, Clear 18.50
Medicine, Old Dominion Wheat Tonic, A.M.Bininger & Co., N.Y., Square, Amber 27.50
Medicine, Olmsted Constitutional Beverage, Stain, Yellow Green 190.00
Medicine, One Minute Cough Cure, Aqua 2.50
Medicine, One Minute Cure, Clear 4.00
Medicine, Opium, Open Pontil, Aqua 6.00
Medicine, O'Rourke & Hurley Druggists, Little Falls, New York 7.50
Medicine, Otto's Cure 4.00
Medicine, Owen's Pink Mixture, Blood Colored 6.50
Medicine, Ozomulsion, Amber, 5 1/4 In.High 3.00
Medicine, Ozomulsion, Dark Amber 3.00
Medicine, P.P.P.Prickley Ash Pokercot Potassium, The Great Blood Purifier 25.00
Medicine, Paine's Celery Compound, Amber .... 3.50 To 8.00
Medicine, Paine's Celery Compound, BIMAL, Dug, Amber 4.00
Medicine, Paine's Celery Compound, Label, Dark Amber 7.50
Medicine, Paine's Celery Tonic, Square Sided, Amber 4.50
Medicine, Paine's Celery, Embossed Celery On Panel, Label 25.00
Medicine, Parker's Hair Balm, Amber 5.00
Medicine, Parker's Hair Balsam, BIMAL, Dug, Amber 4.00
Medicine, Peptenzyme, Label & Contents, Cobalt, 3 In. 7.00
Medicine, Perfect Health For Kidney & Liver Diseases, Embossed Man, Amber 72.50
Medicine, Perry's Hungarian Balm For The Hair, Aqua, 5 3/4 In. 18.50
Medicine, Peruvian Syrup, Open Pontil, Stain 17.50
Medicine, Physician's Sample Siphon Kumysgen Bottle, Cobalt Blue 75.00
Medicine, Pinch Bottle, 4 Panels, Open Pontil 10.00
Medicine, Pinex, Embossed, Corker 1.50
Medicine, Piso's Cure For Consumption, Amethyst 4.00
Medicine, Piso's Cure For Consumption, Aqua .... 2.00 To 3.50
Medicine, Piso's Cure For Consumption, BIMAL , Dug, Clear 2.00
Medicine, Piso's Cure For Consumption, Emerald 3.50
Medicine, Piso's Cure For Consumption, Emerald Green 4.50
Medicine, Pitcher's Castoria, The Kind The Baby Cries For, Aqua 3.00
Medicine, Pitcher's Livura, Nashville, Tenn. 10.00
Medicine, Polar Star Cough Cure, Embossed Star, Clear, Miniature 7.00
Medicine, Polar Star Diarrhea Cure 8.00
Medicine, Pond's Chill & Fever Cure, Frog, Amber 12.00
Medicine, Pond's Extract, Embossed, Corker 1.50
Medicine, Pond's Extract, Embossed, 90 Per Cent Label, ABM , Aqua 10.00
Medicine, Pond's Kidney & Liver 32.50
Medicine, Porter's Cure Of Pain, Clear 4.00
Medicine, Portus Cure Of Pain, Aqua 2.00

Medicine, **Portus Cure Of Pain**, Clear	2.00
Medicine, **Professor I.Hubert's Malvina Lotion**, Toledo, Ohio, Milk Glass	15.00
Medicine, **Professor W.H.Peeke's Medicine**, Stain	8.00
Medicine, **Professor Wood's Hair Restorative**, Open Pontil, Aqua, 7 1/4 In.	22.50
Medicine, **Psychine**, Greatest Of Tonics, Label, Box, & Circular	5.00
Medicine, **Pure Lemon Acid**, Round, Open Pontil, Dug, Aqua, 3 1/4 In.	16.00
Medicine, **Puritannia**, Oval, Cobalt, 7 In.High	5.00
Medicine, **Quick Stop For Headache**	3.50
Medicine, **R.R.R.Radway & Co.**, Aqua	5.50
Medicine, **R.R.R.Radway & Co.**, Embossed Pontil	13.00
Medicine, **R.R.R.Radway & Co.**, Ent'd Accor'd To Act Of Congress, Embossed	17.50
Medicine, **R.R.R.Radway & Co.**, Light Green, 5 1/2 In.	3.50
Medicine, **R.R.R.Radway's Ready Relief**, 50 Cents	35.00
Medicine, **R.R.R.Radway's Resolvent**, Open Pontil, Aqua	35.00
Medicine, **Radam's Microbe Killer**, Embossed Skeleton, Amber	25.00 To 65.00
Medicine, **Ramon's Rub**	2.00
Medicine, **Rawleigh's**, Embossed, Corker, Amber	2.00
Medicine, **Rawleigh's**, Trademark, Label, Contents, Clear	4.00
Medicine, **Rectangular**, Open Pontil, Flat	4.00
Medicine, **Reed & Carnick**, Peptenzyne, Cobalt, 8 5/8 In.High	6.00
Medicine, **Reed's Apothecary**, Milk Glass, 5 In.	15.00
Medicine, **Reed's Gilt Edge Tonic**, 1878, Rectangular, BIMAL , Amber	28.00
Medicine, **Reed's Gilt Edge Tonic**, 1878, Rectangular, BIMAL , Honey Amber	28.00
Medicine, **Rev.W.Clarke's European Cough Remedy**	12.00 To 25.00
Medicine, **Robt.Turlington**, Balsam Of Life, Jany, London On Sides, 2 5/8 In.	8.50
Medicine, **Roche's Embrocation For The Hooping Cough**, Square, Clear	9.00
Medicine, **Roger's Canchalagua**, Open Pontil, Aqua	30.00
Medicine, **Rohrer's Expectoral**, Amber	65.00
Medicine, **Rohrer's Expectoral Wild Cherry Tonic**, Amber ... *Illus*	150.00
Medicine, **Root's German Ointment**, 512 Broadway, N.Y., Embossed Pontil	20.00
Medicine, **Royal Gall Remedy**, Amber, 7 1/2 In.	8.00
Medicine, **Royal Hair Restorer**, Cobalt	35.00
Medicine, **Ru-Bin-Ol**, Label, Contents, Clear, 6 In.	3.00
Medicine, **Rubifoam For The Teeth**, Embossed, Label, Sample, Clear, 2 1/4 In.	2.50
Medicine, **Rucker's Triena Laxative**	2.50
Medicine, **Rudolph's Wolf Schnapps**, Amber	20.00
Medicine, **Rufford Chemical Works**, Blue Green	9.00
Medicine, **Rush's Buchu**	10.00
Medicine, **Rushton's Cod Liver Oil**, Aqua	10.00
Medicine, **S.C.Dispensary**, Ding Inside, Sun Colored Amethyst	13.00
Medicine, **Sagwa**, Aqua, 8 1/2 In.	4.00
Medicine, **Sallade Magic Mosquito Bite Cure**, Aqua	9.00
Medicine, **Sanborn's Kidney & Liver Vegetable Laxative**, Amber, 10 In.High	70.00
Medicine, **Sanderson's Blood Renovator**, Milton, Vt., Oval, Pontil, Dark Aqua	75.00
Medicine, **Sanford's Radical Cure**, Cobalt Blue	18.00 To 30.00
Medicine, **Sanitol For The Teeth**	7.00
Medicine, **Sanitol For The Teeth**, Rectangular, Milk Glass	11.50 To 14.00
Medicine, **Sauler's Extracts**, Embossed, Corker	1.50
Medicine, **Saymen's Vegetable Liniment For Catarrh & Colds**	30.00
Medicine, **Schenck's Pulmonic Syrup**, Philadelphia, Aqua, Pint	6.00 To 15.00
Medicine, **Schenck's Pulmonic Syrup**, 8 Sided	6.50
Medicine, **Schenck's Seaweed Tonic**, Aqua, 9 In.	7.50 To 22.00
Medicine, **Scott's Emulsion With Lime & Soda**, Aqua, Embossed Ma	3.00 To 6.00
Medicine, **Seabury's Cough Balsam**, Aqua, 4 1/2 In.Tall	3.50
Medicine, **Seven Sisters**, Swayback	8.00
Medicine, **Shaker Digestive Cordial**, A.J.White, New York, Clear Panel	15.00
Medicine, **Shaker Extract Of Roots**, Aqua, 5 In.High ... *Illus*	16.00
Medicine, **Shaker Extract Of Roots**, 5 1/2 In., Clear ... *Color*	XX.XX
Medicine, **Shaker Fluid Extract Valerian**, Flared Lip, O.P., Stain, 3 3/4 In.	16.00
Medicine, **Shaker Syrup No.1**	18.95
Medicine, **Sharp & Dohme Lapactic Pill**, Corker, Amber	4.00
Medicine, **Shell & Scroll Design**, Pontil, Light Blue	200.00
Medicine, **Sherk's Bitter Tincture Of Roots**, Aqua	50.00
Medicine, **Shiloh's Catarrh Remedy**, Glass Injector, Boxed	1.00
Medicine, **Shiloh's Consumption Cure**	5.00
Medicine, **Shiloh's Consumption Cure**, Leroy, N.Y., Aqua	4.50

Medicine, Rohrer's Expectoral
Wild Cherry Tonic, Amber
See Page 168

Medicine, Shaker Extract Of Roots,
Aqua, 5 In.High
See Page 168

Medicine, **Shirley Universal Renovator**, Open Pontil	40.00
Medicine, **Simmon's Liver Regulator**	4.50
Medicine, **Simmon's Liver Regulator**, Aqua	7.50 To 10.00
Medicine, **Simmon's Liver Regulator**, 3 Recessed Front Panels, Ice Blue	7.50
Medicine, **Sloan's Sure Colic Cure**, Aqua	3.50
Medicine, **Sloan's Sure Colic Cure**, Clear	4.00
Medicine, **Smith's Vegetable Hair Tonic**, 5 1/2 In.	18.50
Medicine, **South Carolina Dispensary**, Clear, Quart	3.00
Medicine, **Sowmen Verenpuhdistus**, Finnish Blood Purifier, Clear, 5 1/4 In.	8.50
Medicine, **Sparks For Kidney & Liver Diseases**, Amber	75.00
Medicine, **Spavin Cure**	4.00
Medicine, **Spohn's Distemper Cure**, Clear	3.00
Medicine, **Spohn's Distemper Cure**, Epizotic & Glut	4.00
Medicine, **Sporker Perfect Health For Kidney & Liver Diseases**, Amber	100.00
Medicine, **Squibb's**, 8 Sided, Cobalt, Quart	15.00
Medicine, **Stephen Infallible Liniment**, Open Pontil, Aqua	14.00
Medicine, **Stowe's Ambrosia**, Lime Green	15.00
Medicine, **Strong**, Cobb & Co., Wholesale Druggists, Cleveland, O., Blue	40.00
Medicine, **Swain's Panacea**, Est.1820, St.Louis, Mo.	18.00
Medicine, **Swain's Panacea**, Green	20.00
Medicine, **Swain's Panacea**, Label, Contents, Aqua	23.00
Medicine, **Swain's Panacea**, Light Emerald Green	40.00
Medicine, **Swain's Panacea**, Philadelphia, Emerald Green, 7 3/4 In.High	78.50
Medicine, **Swain's Panacea**, Philadelphia, Paneled, Olive Green	85.00
Medicine, **Swain's Panacea**, Rectangular, Open Pontil, Aqua	150.00
Medicine, **Swanson's Rheumatic Cure**, Aqua	6.00
Medicine, **Sweet Oil**, The Moxham Pharmacy, Johnstown, Pa., Amber	4.50
Medicine, **T.J.Dunbar & Co.Schnapps Cordial**, Label, Green	40.00
Medicine, **Thayer's Emulsion**, Full, Label, Boxed, Aqua	12.00
Medicine, **Thayer's Sulphur & Lead Hair Restorer**, Label, Contents	3.00
Medicine, **Thompson's Original Wild Cherry Phosphate**	*Illus* 18.00
Medicine, **Tiger Oil Cure**, Clear	6.00
Medicine, **Tiger Oil**, Cures Pain, Aqua	9.00
Medicine, **Tonsilline**, Embossed Giraffe	3.00
Medicine, **Trask's Magnetic Ointment**	2.00
Medicine, **True's Elixer**	.75
Medicine, **Tu Sand**, Shaped Like Hood's Sarsaparilla	18.50
Medicine, **Turlington's Balsam Of Life**, King's Patent	*Illus* 5.00
Medicine, **Turlington's Balsam**, Fiddle Shape, Front & Back Embossed, Clear	5.00
Medicine, **Turlington's Balsam**, Fiddle Shape, One Side Embossed, Clear	3.00
Medicine, **Turlington's Balsam**, The King's Patent, Acorn, Contents	25.00
Medicine, **Turlington's Balsam**, Violin Shape, Aqua, 2 1/4 In.High	8.00
Medicine, **Turlington's**, King's Patent, Open Pontil, Aqua	32.50
Medicine, **U & O Anointment**, Threaded Ground Top, Aqua	3.50
Medicine, **Udolpho Wolfe's Schiedam Aromatic Schnapps**, Pontil, Dark Green	32.50

Medicine,
Van Arsdale's
Myrrholphean For
Hair, Aqua
See Page 171

Medicine,
Thompson's Original Wild Cherry Phosphate
See Page 169

Medicine,
W.H.Bull Herbs &
Iron, Amber, 10 In.
See Page 171

Medicine, Turlington's Balsam Of Life, King's, Patent
See Page 169

Medicine, Warner's Log Cabin Extract, Boxed, Brown
See Page 171

Medicine,
Warner's Log Cabin Liver Pills, Clear, 2 In.
See Page 171

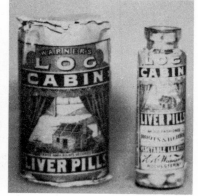

Medicine, **United States Medicine Co.**, New York, Aqua 3.50
Medicine, **Universal Cough Syrup**, Label 3.00
Medicine, **Van Arsdale's Myrrholphean For Hair**, Aqua .... *Illus* 22.50
Medicine, **Van Arsdale's Myrrholphean For The Hair**, N.Y., Oval, Aqua 13.50
Medicine, **Vaughn's Vegetable Mixture**, Aqua 22.50
Medicine, **Vegetable Pulmonary Balsam**, Contents, Box 3.00
Medicine, **Veterinarian's Office**, Square, Cork, Amber, 13 In.Tall, Set Of 3 .... 35.00
Medicine, **Vogeler's Violet Triple Extract Cut In Bottle**, Round, Clear 22.00
Medicine, **W.E.Mann**, Bangor, Me., Sample, Aqua 4.00
Medicine, **W.H.Bull Herbs & Iron**, Amber, 10 In. .... *Illus* 10.00
Medicine, **Wakefield's Blackberry Balsam** 3.00
Medicine, **Wakeles Cameline**, Cobalt 6.50
Medicine, **Walt's Kidney & Liver**, Amber 22.50
Medicine, **Warner's Log Cabin Extract**, Boxed, Brown .... *Illus* 75.00
Medicine, **Warner's Log Cabin Extract**, Label, Carton, & Corkscrew 90.00
Medicine, **Warner's Log Cabin Hops & Buchi Remedy** 140.00
Medicine, **Warner's Log Cabin Liver Pills**, Clear, 2 In. .... *Illus* 6.00
Medicine, **Warner's Log Cabin Liver Pills**, Label, Contents .... 6.00 To 12.00
Medicine, **Warner's Remedies Co.**, Sample 40.00
Medicine, **Warner's Reverse Safe**, Sample 60.00
Medicine, **Warner's Safe Co.**, ABM, Aqua, 12 1/2 Oz. 15.00
Medicine, **Warner's Safe Co.**, BIMAL, Amber, 12 1/2 Oz. 11.00
Medicine, **Warner's Safe Cure**, Amber, Embossed .... 10.00 To 25.00
Medicine, **Warner's Safe Cure Co.**, Sample, Embossed, Dug, Amber 20.00
Medicine, **Warner's Safe Cure**, Melbourne, Australia, Amber 35.00
Medicine, **Warner's Safe Cure**, Rochester, New York, 8 Oz. 27.50
Medicine, **Warner's Safe Cure**, Sample 20.00
Medicine, **Warner's Safe Diabetes Cure**, Embossed 38.00
Medicine, **Warner's Safe Diabetes Cure**, Label 45.00
Medicine, **Warner's Safe Kidney & Liver Cure**, Amber 10.00
Medicine, **Warner's Safe Kidney & Liver Cure**, Blob Top, Light Amber 14.00
Medicine, **Warner's Safe Kidney & Liver Cure**, Double Collar 10.00
Medicine, **Warner's Safe Kidney & Liver Cure**, Label, Amber 17.50
Medicine, **Warner's Safe Kidney & Liver Cure**, Left Hinge 60.00
Medicine, **Warner's Safe Kidney & Liver Cure**, Reversed Safe, Smoky Amber 55.00
Medicine, **Warner's Safe Kidney & Liver Cure**, Sample 28.00
Medicine, **Warner's Safe Kidney & Liver Cure**, Stain, Amber 5.00
Medicine, **Warner's Safe Kidney & Liver Remedy**, Amber, 16 Oz. 19.50
Medicine, **Warner's Safe Kidney & Liver Remedy**, Blob Top, Amber, Large Size 17.00
Medicine, **Warner's Safe Kidney & Liver Remedy**, Blob Top, Amber, 16 Oz. 18.00
Medicine, **Warner's Safe Liver Pills**, Log Cabin 5.00
Medicine, **Warner's Safe Liver Pills**, Wrapper Marked Warner's Log Cabin 42.50
Medicine, **Warner's Safe Lon L Cure** 9.00
Medicine, **Warner's Safe Nervine**, Amber .... 35.00 To 43.00
Medicine, **Warner's Safe Nervine**, 8 Oz. 36.00
Medicine, **Warner's Safe Remedies Co.**, Amber, 12 1/2 Oz. 16.00
Medicine, **Warner's Safe Remedies Co.**, Amber, 6 Oz. .... 22.00 To 25.00
Medicine, **Warner's Safe Remedies Co.**, Aqua, 12 1/2 Oz. 20.00
Medicine, **Warner's Safe Remedies Co.**, Clear, 1/2 Pint 20.00
Medicine, **Warner's Safe Remedies Co.**, Honey Amber 18.00
Medicine, **Warner's Safe Remedies Co.**, Label, Aqua 15.00
Medicine, **Warner's Safe Remedies Co.**, Stain, Clear 25.00
Medicine, **Warner's Safe Remedy Co.**, ABM , Amber 4.95
Medicine, **Warner's Safe Rheumatic Cure**, Amber 40.00
Medicine, **Warner's Safe Tonic** 87.50
Medicine, **Warner's Safe Tonic**, Dug 87.50
Medicine, **Warner's Tippecanoe** 125.00
Medicine, **Warners Safe Cure**, Animal 300.00
Medicine, **Watkins**, Embossed, Corker, Aqua 2.00
Medicine, **West Electric Cure**, Stopper, Electrical Unit, Cobalt 25.00
Medicine, **Westmoreland's Calisaga Tonic**, Amber 22.00
Medicine, **Whipple Garget Cure**, Clear 3.50
Medicine, **Wilson's Pulmonary Cherry Balsam**, 12 Sided, Aqua 3.00
Medicine, **Wire Grass Liver & Kidney Medicine**, C.1880, Label 2.50
Medicine, **Wishart's**, Pine Tree Tar Cordial, Embossed, Label, Amber .... 25.00 To 50.00
Medicine, **Wishart's**, Pine Tree Tar Cordial, Embossed, Label, Green .... 25.00 To 50.00

Medicine, Wishart's Pine Tree Tar Cordial, Emerald Green	40.00
Medicine, Wishart's Pine Tree Tar Cordial, Stain, Light Green	22.50
Medicine, Wistar's Balsam Of Wild Cherry, Aqua	12.50
Medicine, Witch Hazel Cream, Green	6.00
Medicine, Witsell's Chill Tonic, Boxed	4.00
Medicine, Wm.R.Warner Medallion, N.Y., St.Louis, Amber	15.00
Medicine, Wm.R.Warner Sample, N.Y., St.Louis	8.00
Medicine, Wm.R.Warner's Co.Philadelphia, Cobalt Blue, Round, 6 In.Tall	4.00
Medicine, Wm.Radam's Microbe Killer, Amber, Square, 10 In.Tall	25.00 To 65.00
Medicine, Wolfe's Aromatic Schnapps, Citron	12.50
Medicine, Wolfe's Aromatic Schnapps, Label, Olive Green	8.50 To 15.00
Medicine, Wolfstirn's Rheumatic & Gout Remedy, Embossed, N.J., Aqua	7.25
Medicine, Wolfstirn's Rheumatic & Gout Remedy, Hoboken, N.J., Aqua, 2 Oz.	1.45
Medicine, Wyeth & Bros.Collyrium, Eye Cup, Labeled, Cobalt	16.00
Medicine, Wyeth & Bros.Malt Extract, Blown In Mold	4.00
Medicine, Wyeth & Bros., Cobalt Blue, 1/2 Gallon	7.00
Medicine, Wyeth & Bros., Dose Cap, Embossed, Cobalt Blue, 5 3/4 In.	5.00
Medicine, Wyeth & Bros., Johann Hoffmann, Whittled, BIMAL, Dug, Green	4.00
Medicine, Zoller's Kidney Remedy, Embossed, Label & Contents, Amber	19.00
Metaxa, Royal Greek Guard, Blue Coat	19.95
Metaxa, Royal Greek Guard, Red Coat	19.95
Midwestern, Globular, Aqua, 11 In.High	110.00
Midwestern, Globular, Greenish Aqua, 11 In.	45.00
Midwestern, 32 Swirled Ribs, Sunken Pontil, Blue Aqua	75.00
Milk Glass, Armour & Company, Chicago, Vertically Embossed, 2 Flat Sides	23.00
Milk Glass, Hartwig Kentorowicz, 9 1/2 In. Color	XX.XX
Milk Glass, Klondyke Flask, Gold Nugget, Painted Color	XX.XX
Milk Glass, Sazerac Aromatic Bitters, 11 In. Color	XX.XX
Milk Glass, Secrete De Beaute D'Eugenie In Circle, L F Marshall, 12 Sided	32.00

Milk bottles were first used in the 1880s. The characteristic shape and printed or embossed wording identify these bottles for collectors.

Milk, A.G.Smalley, Tin Top, Quart	12.50
Milk, Absolutely Pure, Hot & Co., N.Y., Clear, 8 1/2 In. *Illus*	55.00
Milk, AGS & Co.1898, Metal Bands, Clamp & Handle	45.00
Milk, Alaskan	2.00
Milk, Anglo-Swiss Condensed, Embossed Girl, 1900-10, Amber	25.00
Milk, Applied Top, Bubbles, Amber	14.00
Milk, Baby Face, Cream Top, Quart	3.00
Milk, Baby Face, Double, Round, Embossed, Pint	5.00
Milk, Baby Face, Double, Round, Embossed, Quart	5.00
Milk, Baby Face, Double, Round, Embossed, 1/2 Pint	3.00
Milk, Baby Face, Double, Round, Painted, Pint	4.00
Milk, Baby Face, Double, Round, Painted, Quart	4.00
Milk, Baby Face, Double, Round, Painted, 1/2 Pint	2.50

Milk, Absolutely Pure,
Hot & Co., N.Y., Clear,
8 1/2 In.

Milk, Good Will Dairy Co.,
Pittsburgh, Pa., Brown, Quart
See Page 173

Milk, **Baby Face**, Double, Square, Embossed, Pint	5.50
Milk, **Baby Face**, Double, Square, Embossed, Quart	4.50
Milk, **Baby Face**, Double, Square, Embossed, 1/2 Pint	3.00
Milk, **Baby Face**, Double, Square, Painted, Pint	3.50
Milk, **Baby Face**, Double, Square, Painted, Quart	4.00
Milk, **Baby Face**, Double, Square, Painted, 1/2 Pint	2.50
Milk, **Baby Face**, Single, Round, Embossed, Pint	4.50
Milk, **Baby Face**, Single, Round, Embossed, Quart	4.00
Milk, **Baby Face**, Single, Round, Embossed, 1/2 Pint	3.00
Milk, **Baby Face**, Single, Round, Painted, Pint	3.50
Milk, **Baby Face**, Single, Round, Painted, Quart	3.50
Milk, **Baby Face**, Single, Round, Painted, 1/2 Pint	2.50
Milk, **Baby Face**, Single, Square, Embossed, Pint	4.00
Milk, **Baby Face**, Single, Square, Embossed, Quart	4.50
Milk, **Baby Face**, Single, Square, Embossed, 1/2 Pint	2.50
Milk, **Baby Face**, Single, Square, Painted, Pint	3.00
Milk, **Baby Face**, Single, Square, Painted, Quart	3.00
Milk, **Baby Face**, Single, Square, Painted, 1/2 Pint	2.50
Milk, **Beach**, Lakeview Terrace, No.1053, Fairbanks, Alaska, Painted, Embossed	5.00
Milk, **Bellview Dairy**, Syracuse, N.Y., Painted Farm Scene, 1/2 Pint	1.00
Milk, **Bellview Dairy**, Syracuse, N.Y., 1/4 Pint	1.50
Milk, **Bellview Dairy**, Syracuse, N.Y., 1/3 Quart	1.50
Milk, **Big Elm Dairy Co.**, Emerald Green, Quart	125.00
Milk, **Borden's**, Picture & Date, Amber, 1/2 Gallon	1.90
Milk, **Borden's**, Signature & Picture, Square, Amber, Quart	3.50
Milk, **Brookfield**, Baby Face, Double, Square, Painted	6.00
Milk, **Brookfield**, Baby Face, Single, 1/2 Pint	7.00
Milk, **Brookfield**, Double Baby Face, Square, Painted	6.00
Milk, **Burr Daisy**, Clinton, Conn., Amber, Quart	5.00
Milk, **Chicago Sterling Milk Co.**, Zinc Cap, Light Green, Quart	6.00
Milk, **Chisholm**, Minn., Amber	3.50
Milk, **Cloverdale Farms**, Binghamton, N.Y., 1934, Amber	20.00
Milk, **Cop-The-Cream**, Round, Embossed, Quart	4.50
Milk, **Cop-The-Cream**, Round, Painted, Quart	4.00
Milk, **Cop-The-Cream**, Square, Embossed, Quart	4.50
Milk, **Cop-The-Cream**, Square, Painted, Quart	4.00
Milk, **Cottage Cheese Jar**, Embossed	1.50
Milk, **Cottage Cheese Jar**, Painted	1.00
Milk, **Cream Separator**, Round, Embossed	5.00
Milk, **Cream Separator**, Round, Embossed, Painted	5.00
Milk, **Cream Separator**, Square, Embossed	5.00
Milk, **Cream Separator**, Square, Embossed, Painted	5.00
Milk, **Cream Top**, Quart	2.00
Milk, **Crown Top**, Embossed, West Virginia	2.00
Milk, **Curles Neck Dairy**, Inc., Baby Face, Square, Embossed, Quart	5.50
Milk, **Dairylee**, Baby Face, Double, Square, Painted	6.00
Milk, **Dairylee**, Double Baby Face, Square, Painted	6.00
Milk, **Drink Ideal Milk**, Double Baby Face, Square, Painted	6.00
Milk, **Drink Ideal**, Baby Face, Double, Square, Painted	6.00
Milk, **Embossed Tonopah**, Nevada, Clear, 1/4 Pint	3.50
Milk, **Embossed**, Tin Lid & Closure, 1/2 Pint	3.00
Milk, **Embossed**, West Virginia	2.00
Milk, **Embossed**, Whittled, Bubbles, 1878 Patent, Green	100.00
Milk, **Embossed**, 1/3 Quart	1.50
Milk, **Fargo**, Square, Painted, Cream Top, Quart	.75
Milk, **Gail Borden**, Amber, Quart	3.50
Milk, **Gail Borden**, Embossed Borden, 1/2 Gallon	8.50
Milk, **Gail Borden**, White Printing, Amber, Quart	8.50
Milk, **Gascoyne Dairy**, Lockport, N.Y., Embossed, Cream Separator, Round, Quart	12.00
Milk, **Good Will Dairy Co.**, Pittsburgh, Pa., Brown, Quart _Illus_	40.00
Milk, **Home Dairy Co.**, Embossed Full-Size Cow, Tin Top, Clear, 1/4 Pint	15.00
Milk, **It Whips**, Cream Top	3.00
Milk, **Jersey Crown Dairy**, Hayward, Cal., Square, Yellow Paint, Pint	10.00
Milk, **Jersey Crown Dairy**, Hayward, Cal., Square, Yellow Paint, 1/2 Pint	1.00
Milk, **Jug**, Square, Green, 1 Gallon	25.00
Milk, **Liberty Milk Co.**, Buffalo, N.Y., Round, Embossed, 1/2 Pint	5.00
Milk, **Liberty Milk Company With Statue Of Liberty On Back**, 1/2 Pint	5.00

Milk, **Lightning Closure**, Pint	25.00
Milk, **Little Jersey Farm**, Marshfield, Mass.	8.00
Milk, **Mesaba Dairy**, Chisholm, Minn., Amber, Quart	4.00
Milk, **Mickey Mouse**, Picture Painted	3.50
Milk, **Minnesota**, Amber, Quart	4.00
Milk, **Missouri Pacific**	2.00
Milk, **Musgrave's Tower Farm**, Embossed, Baby Face	12.00
Milk, **Orange Lettering**, Amber, Quart	1.75
Milk, **Orange Lettering**, Clear, Pint	1.00
Milk, **Painted**, 1/3 Quart	1.00
Milk, **Parkside Dairy**, E.Rochester, N.Y., Painted, Square, Milkmaid, Amber	2.25
Milk, **People's Dairy**, 1934, Amber	30.00 To 40.00
Milk, **Peters' Dairy**, Cow's Head, Clear, Pint	1.50
Milk, **Peveley**, Embossed, Quart	.50
Milk, **Queen City Dairy**, Cream Top, Embossed, Pint	4.50
Milk, **Queen City Dairy**, Cream Top, Embossed, Quart	3.00 To 3.50
Milk, **Queen City Dairy**, Cream Top, Embossed, 1/2 Pint	4.50
Milk, **Red Paint**, Wire Bail, Gallon	4.00
Milk, **Round**, Embossed, Amber	12.00
Milk, **Round**, Embossed, Amber, Quart	12.00
Milk, **Round**, Embossed, Emerald Green, Quart	20.00
Milk, **Round**, Embossed, Pint	.50
Milk, **Round**, Embossed, Quart	1.00
Milk, **Round**, Embossed, Tin Closure, Pint	5.50
Milk, **Round**, Embossed, Tin Closure, Quart	5.50
Milk, **Round**, Embossed, Tin Closure, 1/2 Pint	8.00
Milk, **Round**, Embossed, Tin Closure, 1/4 Pint	8.50
Milk, **Round**, Embossed, 1/2 Pint	1.00
Milk, **Round**, Embossed, 1/4 Pint	1.15
Milk, **Round**, Embossed, 10 Oz.	1.00
Milk, **Round**, Embossed, 12 Oz.	.75
Milk, **Round**, Painted, Pint	.25
Milk, **Round**, Painted, 1/2 Pint	.50
Milk, **Round**, Painted, 1/4 Pint	.75
Milk, **Round**, Plain, Tin Closure, Pint	4.50
Milk, **Round**, Plain, Tin Closure, Quart	5.00
Milk, **Round**, Plain, Tin Closure, 1/2 Pint	6.00
Milk, **Round**, Plain, Tin Closure, 1/4 Pint	8.00
Milk, **Royal Farms Dairy**, Cop The Cream, Clear, 9 In. *Illus*	5.00
Milk, **Ruby Red**	20.00
Milk, **Square**, Embossed, Amber, Quart	1.25
Milk, **Square**, Embossed, Pint	.50
Milk, **Square**, Embossed, Quart	.70
Milk, **Square**, Embossed, 1/2 Pint	1.00
Milk, **Square**, Embossed, 1/4 Pint	1.00
Milk, **Square**, Painted, Amber, Quart	1.00
Milk, **Square**, Painted, Pint	.25
Milk, **Square**, Painted, 1/2 Pint	.25
Milk, **Square**, Painted, 1/4 Pint	.60
Milk, **Thatcher**, East, Pint	15.00
Milk, **Thatcher**, East, Quart	20.00
Milk, **Thatcher**, Pint	25.00
Milk, **Thatcher**, Quart	40.00
Milk, **Thatcher**, West, Pint	25.00
Milk, **Thatcher**, West, Quart	40.00
Milk, **Turner Centre Creamery**, Ornate Monogram, Pinball Shape, Tin Top	10.00
Milk, **Turner Centre**, Monogram Only, Tin Top, 1/2 Pint	8.00
Milk, **V.M.& I.C.Cos Milk-O**, Amber, Quart	15.00 To 20.00
Milk, **V.M.& I.C.Cos Milk-O Embossed**, Amber	10.00
Milk, **V.M.& I.C.Cos Milk-O**, In 3 Lines, Embossed, Dug, Quart	15.00
Milk, **V.M.& I.C.Cos Milk-O**, In 3 Lines, Embossed, Dug, 1/2 Pint	10.00
Milk, **Van Hornesville Dairy**, Ribbed Neck, Cecil C.Harrad, N.Y.	2.50
Milk, **Weckerle**, Embossed, Green, Quart	85.00
Milk, **Weckerle**, Green, Quart	75.00
Milk, **Wendt's Dairy**, Cream Top, Square, Painted, Quart	1.75
Milk, **West Frankfort**, Illinois, Quart	1.50

Miniature, A Wee Scotch, German .... *Illus*	15.00
Miniature, Acme, Embossed	2.50
Miniature, Amethyst, 3 3/4 In.Tall	25.00
Miniature, Anis Escarchado Mexico, Embossed, Cork	4.00
Miniature, Apothecary Jar	15.00
Miniature, Apricot Cordial .... *Illus*	4.00
Miniature, Baby Bottle, Ceramic, Whiskey Giveaway, Made In Germany	30.00
Miniature, Ballantine's New P.S.A., Scotch, Embossed, Label	2.50
Miniature, Ballantine's, Scotch, Embossed, Flat	3.00
Miniature, Bell Royal Vat, Scotch, Embossed, 12 Yrs.Old	2.50
Miniature, Bell's Scotch, Embossed, Bell Shape	3.00
Miniature, Beneagles, Castle	6.50
Miniature, Beneagles, Deer, Flask	6.50
Miniature, Beneagles, Monster	8.50
Miniature, Beneagles, Pheasant, Flask	6.50
Miniature, Beneagles, Pike	3.25
Miniature, Beneagles, Tower Bridge, Paperweight	3.25
Miniature, Beneagles, Trout, Flask	6.50
Miniature, Black & White, Scotch, Embossed, Tall	3.00
Miniature, Blindfolded Pig, The .... *Illus*	35.00
Miniature, Borghini, Cardinal	3.50
Miniature, Borghini, Cat	3.50
Miniature, Borghini, Penguin	3.50
Miniature, Bottles Of America, Bar Scene, 6 In Case	96.00
Miniature, Bourbon Springs, Violin Shape .... *Illus*	6.00

Milk, Royal Farms Dairy,
Cop The Cream, Clear, 9 In.
See Page 174

Miniature, Apricot Cordial

Miniature, A Wee Scotch, German

Miniature,
Bourbon Springs,
Violin Shape

Miniature,
Blindfolded Pig, The

Miniature, Bowler	*Illus*	15.00
Miniature, Bull, Blown		12.00
Miniature, Cambridge Springs, Mineral Water, 2 1/2 In.	*Color*	XX.XX
Miniature, Castle Walk	*Illus*	30.00
Miniature, Cat, Blown		7.25
Miniature, Cavalier		20.00
Miniature, Chess Piece, Bishop, Ubaldo, Wine		7.00
Miniature, Chess Piece, King, Ubaldo, Wine		9.00
Miniature, Chess Piece, Knight, Ubaldo, Wine		7.00
Miniature, Chess Piece, Pawn, Ubaldo, Wine		6.00
Miniature, Chess Piece, Queen, Ubaldo, Wine		9.00
Miniature, Chess Piece, Rook, Ubaldo, Wine		7.00
Miniature, Chivas Regal, Scotch, Embossed, Florida Stamp, Cork		3.50
Miniature, Compliments Of The Dusquesne, 3 In.	*Color*	XX.XX
Miniature, Crown Distilleries Co., Whiskey, Inside Threads		28.00
Miniature, Cuban Banana Liqueur, Embossed		5.00
Miniature, Cuban Pina Liqueur, Embossed		5.00
Miniature, Cunnington Soda		2.50
Miniature, Cusenier Liqueur, France, Embossed, Cork		6.00
Miniature, Dancer, Tango, German		50.00
Miniature, Dancer, Turkey Trot, German		50.00
Miniature, Deer, Holland, 1971	*Illus*	4.00
Miniature, Dice, Blown		12.00
Miniature, Dickel, Powder Horn		2.35
Miniature, Dog & Bottle, His Master's Breath, Japanese		10.00
Miniature, Dog Biting Girl, Just A Little Nip, Japanese		10.00
Miniature, Dog, Blown	7.25 To	12.00
Miniature, Dog With Bandaged Tail, All's Well That Ends Well, Japanese		10.00
Miniature, Dog, Bols Blown Glass		9.00
Miniatute, Dr.Pepper, World War II , Embossed, 3 In.High		2.00
Miniature, Drioli, Cherry Log, 1969		3.25
Miniature, Drioli, Donkey, Ceramic, 1970		5.00
Miniature, Drioli, Elephant, Ceramic, 1970		5.00
Miniature, Drioli, English Range, 1969		3.25
Miniature, Drioli, Last Chance Bar Scene, Six Pieces, Frame		90.00
Miniature, Drioli, Merchant, Ceramic, 1970		5.00
Miniature, Drioli, Oriental Range, Three Piece, Ceramic, 1970		5.00
Miniature, Drioli, Striped Jug, Italy, 1958	*Illus*	8.00
Miniature, Drioli, Turkey, Ceramic, 1970		5.00
Miniature, Drioli, Vase, Amphora, Ceramic, 1970		5.00
Miniature, Drioli, Vase, 1969		3.25
Miniature, Drioli, Venus De Milo, Ceramic, 1970		5.00
Miniature, Drunk, Tall, Japanese		10.00
Miniature, Duck, Blown		7.25
Miniature, Duck, Manhattan	*Illus*	7.00
Miniature, Duckling, Blown		12.00
Miniature, Fanta, Threaded Design, Label, Full & Capped		.50
Miniature, Fiddle Shape, Hand-Painted Matador, Spain, Crema Bananas, Cork		15.00
Miniature, Fish, Blown		12.00
Miniature Fred Stern, BIMAL, Black Glass, 4 1/2 In.High		8.50
Miniature, Gaelic Old Smuggler, Scotch, Embossed, Cork		5.00
Miniature, Galliano, Soldier		3.25
Miniature, Garnier, Butterfly		4.50
Miniature, Garnier, Cardinal		4.50
Miniature, Garnier, Day Peacock		4.50
Miniature, Garnier, Goldfinch		4.50
Miniature, Garnier, Jack Of Clubs, Flask		4.50
Miniature, Garnier, Jack Of Hearts, Flask		4.50
Miniature, Garnier, King Of Clubs, Flask		4.50
Miniature, Garnier, King Of Hearts, Flask		4.50
Miniature, Garnier, Leaf		4.50
Miniature, Garnier, Madagascar		4.50
Miniature, Garnier, Mockingbird		4.50
Miniature, Garnier, Partridge		4.50
Miniature, Garnier, Queen Of Clubs, Flask		4.50
Miniature, Garnier, Queen Of Hearts, Flask		4.50

Miniature, Garnier, Roadrunner		4.50
Miniature, Garnier, Robin		4.50
Miniature, Garnier, Spanish Tobacco		4.50
Miniature, Garnier, Swallowtail		4.50
Miniature, Garnier, Vase, Biarritz		4.50
Miniature, Garnier, Vase, Blue Delft		4.50

Miniature, Policeman, Stop
See Page 181

Miniature, Bowler
See Page 176

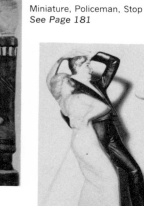

Miniature, Castle Walk
See Page 176

Miniature, Tango
See Page 181

Miniature,
Deer, Holland, 1971
See Page 176

Miniature,
Drioli, Striped Jug,
Italy, 1958
See Page 176

Miniature, Duck, Manhattan
See Page 176

Miniature, George Washington, Cobalt, 4 In.
See Page 178

Miniature, **Garnier**, Vase, Centaur	4.50
Miniature, **Garnier**, Vase, Deauville, Pink Delft	4.50
Miniature, **Garnier**, Vase, Pegasus	4.50
Miniature, **Garnier**, Vase, Strasbourg	4.50
Miniature, **George Washington Bust**	10.00
Miniature, **George Washington**, Cobalt, 4 In. _Illus_	4.00
Miniature, **Giffard Vase**, Blue Petit	5.25
Miniature, **Giffard Vase**, Coffeepot	5.25
Miniature, **Giffard Vase**, Red Amphora	5.50
Miniature, **Gin**, Case, Olive Green, 3 1/2 In.	50.00
Miniature, **Girl Climbing On Flask**, A Wee Bit Of Scotch, Japanese	10.00
Miniature, **Girl In Champagne Glass**, Giveaway, 6 In.High	25.00
Miniature, **Girl**, Serving _Illus_	29.00
Miniature, **Golden Horseshoe**	8.95
Miniature, **Golden Rooster**	8.95
Miniature, **Grant's**, Evaporated, Scotch, Embossed	2.50
Miniature, **Grant's**, Scotch, Embossed, Cork, Triangle	5.00
Miniature, **Guckerheimer**	3.50
Miniature, **Hardy**	7.00
Miniature, **Harold's Club**, Reno Nevada In White Enamel	.50
Miniature, **Helmet Rye**, 2 1/2 In. _Color_	XX.XX
Miniature, **Himbeer**, German, Pear	2.25
Miniature, **Himbeer**, German, Raspberry	2.25
Miniature, **His Masters Breath**, German _Illus_	15.00
Miniature, **Horse**, Blown	12.00
Miniature, **Hot Water Bottle** _Illus_	22.00
Miniature, **Hunter**	4.00
Miniature, **Inca**, Pisco's No.2	1.10
Miniature, **Irish Mist**, Soldier	6.25
Miniature, **Ivanoff**	12.50
Miniature, **Johnnie Walker**, Scotch, Black Label, Embossed	5.00
Miniature, **Johnnie Walker**, Scotch, Red Label, Embossed	5.00
Miniature, **Jug**, Schroffen Enzian, Boy On Fence _Illus_	3.50
Miniature, **Jug**, Schroffen Enzian, Flowers _Illus_	3.50
Miniature, **King William**, Scotch, Embossed	3.00
Miniature, **King's Ransom**, Scotch, Embossed	4.00
Miniature, **Kiss Snookums** _Illus_	35.00
Miniature, **Kord Horse's Head**	10.00
Miniature, **Larson**, Viking Ship, Frosted	6.75
Miniature, **Larson**, Viking Ship, Limoges	10.75
Miniature, **Laurel**	7.00
Miniature, **Laurel & Hardy In A Car**	8.00
Miniature, **Lincoln Portrait**, China, C.A.R., Canteen	24.00
Miniature, **Luxardo**, Ashtray With Horse, Green Mosaic, 1959	6.00
Miniature, **Luxardo**, Bison _Illus_	6.50
Miniature, **Luxardo**, Gambia, 1968	4.00
Miniature, **Luxardo**, Gondola, 1968	4.00
Miniature, **Luxardo**, Nubian, 1968	4.00
Miniature, **Luxardo**, Paestum, 1968	4.00
Miniature, **Luxardo**, Venus De Milo, 1968	4.00
Miniature, **Luxardo**, Wild Boar _Illus_	6.50
Miniature, **Maggio's**, Chess Bishop	6.25
Miniature, **Maggio's**, Chess Castle	6.25
Miniature, **Maggio's**, Chess King	10.25
Miniature, **Maggio's**, Chess Knight	6.25
Miniature, **Maggio's**, Chess Pawn	4.25
Miniature, **Maggio's**, Chess Queen	10.25
Miniature, **Maggio's**, Dog & Cat, Amber	4.75
Miniature, **Maggio's**, Dog & Cat, Sitting On Dice, Lampost Between	10.25
Miniature, **Maiden Holding Dog & 7 Bottles**, A Little Scotch, Japanese	20.00
Miniature, **Map Of Argentina**	10.00
Miniature, **Martin's**, Evaporated, Scotch, Embossed	1.50
Miniature, **Mc Kearin G III -12**, Blown In Mold, Clear, 2 5/8 In.High	35.00
Miniature, **Milk**, Highland Park Dairy, Wooden Holder, 2 _Illus_	15.00
Miniature, **Mirinda Soda**	2.50
Miniature, **Mobana Monkey**	4.00

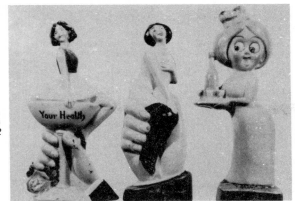

Miniature,
Your Health
See Page 182

Miniature,
Present For You, A
See Page 181

Miniature,
Girl, Serving
See Page 178

Miniature,
His Masters Breath, German
See Page 178

Miniature, Kiss Snookums
See Page 178

Miniature, Hot Water Bottle
See Page 178

Miniature, Jug,
Schroffen Enzian,
Boy On Fence
See Page 178

Miniature, Jug,
Schroffen Enzian,
Flowers
See Page 178

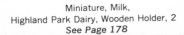

Miniature, Luxardo, Bison
See Page 178

Miniature, Milk,
Highland Park Dairy, Wooden Holder, 2
See Page 178

Miniature, Luxardo, Wild Boar
See Page 178

Miniature, One Of The Boys

Miniature, **Motto Jug**, Ceramic, Sample, Brown & White Glaze	10.00
Miniature, **Motto Jug**, Detrick Distilling, 4 1/2 In. .... *Color*	XX.XX
Miniature, **Motto Jug**, Detrick Distilling, 5 In. .... *Color*	XX.XX
Miniature, **Mouse**, Blown	7.25
Miniature, **Old Bob Burton Pure Rye Whiskey**, 3 1/2 In. .... *Color*	XX.XX
Miniature, **Old Charter**	2.50
Miniature, **Old Forester**	2.00
Miniature, **Old Grand Dad**, Flat, Embossed	4.00
Miniature, **Old Rarity**, Scotch, Embossed, Cork	3.00
Miniature, **Old Thompson**, Scotch, Embossed, Florida Stamp	3.00
Miniature, **One Of The Boys** .... *Illus*	29.00
Miniature, **Orange Crush**	2.50
Miniature, **Owl**, Blown	12.00
Miniature, **Pabst Beer**, Embossed	3.00
Miniature, **Parker Rye N.M.Uri & Co.**, Crock Stenciled Under Glaze	25.00
Miniature, **Passport**, Scotch, Embossed	2.00
Miniature, **Paul Jones Rye**	8.00
Miniature, **Pelican**, Blown	12.00

Miniature, Pinch Bottle, Scotch, Embossed	3.50
Miniature, Policeman, Just A Little Nip, Japanese	10.00
Miniature, Policeman, Stop *Illus*	15.00
Miniature, Present For You, A *Illus*	22.00
Miniature, Queen's Castle Scotch Barrel, Blue	3.25
Miniature, Queen's Castle Scotch Barrel, Brown	3.25
Miniature, Queen's Castle Scotch Barrel, Gray	3.25
Miniature, Queen's Castle Scotch Barrel, Green	3.25
Miniature, Queen's Castle Scotch Barrel, White	3.25
Miniature, Queen's Castle Scotch Barrel, Yellow	3.25
Miniature, Queen's Castle Scotch Barrels, Set Of 6	25.00
Miniature, Red Horse Whisky, Kick Up, Hand Blown, Cork	25.00
Miniature, Rynbende, Ancient Urn	4.99
Miniature, Rynbende, Blue Delft	4.00
Miniature, Rynbende, Bulldog	17.00
Miniature, Rynbende, Candlestick	4.00 To 5.00
Miniature, Rynbende, Cat, Black	1.00
Miniature, Rynbende, Cat, White	10.00
Miniature, Rynbende, Churn	4.00 To 5.00
Miniature, Rynbende, Duck, Blown	4.00 To 5.00
Miniature, Rynbende, Dutch Town House	4.50
Miniature, Rynbende, Fox, Blown	4.00
Miniature, Rynbende, Goose, Blown	4.00
Miniature, Rynbende, Hare, Blown	4.00
Miniature, Rynbende, House, KLM , No.20, 1940s	10.00
Miniature, Rynbende, House, KLM , No.22, 1940s	10.00
Miniature, Rynbende, House, KLM , No.23, 1940s	10.00
Miniature, Rynbende, House, KLM , No.24, 1940s	10.00
Miniature, Rynbende, House, KLM , No.25, 1940s	10.00
Miniature, Rynbende, House, KLM , No.26, 1940s	10.00
Miniature, Rynbende, House, KLM , No.27, 1940s	10.00
Miniature, Rynbende, Jug, No.4	4.00
Miniature, Rynbende, Jug, No.44	4.00
Miniature, Rynbende, Jug, Square, No.39	4.00
Miniature, Rynbende, Kangaroo, Blown	4.00
Miniature, Rynbende, Oil Lamp	4.00 To 5.00
Miniature, Rynbende, Owl, Blown	4.00
Miniature, Rynbende, Pelican, Blown	4.00 To 4.99
Miniature, Rynbende, Penguin, Blown	4.00
Miniature, Rynbende, Sea Lion, Blown	4.00
Miniature, Rynbende, Shoe	4.00 To 4.90
Miniature, Rynbende, Swan, Blown	4.00 To 4.99
Miniature, Rynbende, Windmill	4.00 To 4.99
Miniature, Rynbende's, Embossed	8.00
Miniature, Scotchman With Glass, Old Scotch, Japanese	10.00
Miniature, Senorita	30.00
Miniature, Shark, Blown	12.00
Miniature, Ship, Viking	10.00
Miniature, Spanish Matador	10.00
Miniature, Spanish Senorita	10.00
Miniature, Spirit Of Hollywood, German *Illus*	14.00
Miniature, Sprite, Case Of 24	9.90
Miniature, Sprite, Hobnail, Emblem, Filled & Capped, Green	.50
Miniature, Stulz Brothers, Pumpkinseed	45.00
Miniature, Sunnybrook	1.50
Miniature, Tango *Illus*	30.00
Miniature, Teacher's Highland Cream, Scotch, Embossed, Colorado Stamp, Cork	10.00
Miniature, The Hollenden, Pumpkinseed, Cleveland, Ohio	45.00
Miniature, Thorne's, Scotch, Embossed	2.00
Miniature, Vat 69, Scotch, Embossed, Cork	4.00
Miniature, Viking Ship, China	12.50
Miniature, Viking Ship, Glass	8.50
Miniature, Vodka, Explorer, Embossed	12.00
Miniature, Whiskey, Ceramic, Just A Little Nip *Illus*	12.50
Miniature, Whiskey, Ceramic, The Nineteenth Hole *Illus*	12.50
Miniature, Whiskey, Duffy's Malt, Amber, 4 In.High	15.00

Miniature, Whiskey, First Prize World's Fair Old Times, Clear 5.00
Miniature, Whiskey, Good Old O C B, Winchell & Davis Imp.Co., N.Y., Pottery 24.00
Miniature, Whiskey, Old Kaintuck, Clear, 3 3/4 In.High 8.00
Miniature, Whiskey, Paul Jones, Blob Seal 8.00
Miniature, Whiskey, Red Top 6.00
Miniature, Whiskey, Taylor Williams 4.00
Miniature, Your Health .... *Illus* 25.00
Moses, Amber, Quart 45.00
Moses, Aqua 95.00
Moses, Ball Stopper, Amber 25.00
Moses, Facsimile, Clear, Quart 15.00
Moses, Honeymoon, Emerald Green, Quart .... 30.00 To 45.00
Moses, Poland Spring, Aqua 58.00
Moses, R-61 9s 5, Clear 10.00
Moses, Screw Cap, Green, Quart 15.00
Moses, 1 Cup Water Facsimile 29.50

Nursing bottles were first used in the second half of the 19th century.
They are easily identified by the unique shape and the measuring units that
are often marked on the sides.
Nursing, Acme Nursing Bottle Embossed, Bladder Type 12.00

Miniature, Whiskey,
Ceramic, Just A Little Nip
See Page 181

Miniature, Whiskey,
Ceramic, The Nineteenth Hole
See Page 181

Miniature, Spirit Of Hollywood, German
See Page 181

Nursing, Bulldog,
Clear, 5 1/2 In.High
See Page 183

Nursing, Elephant,
Clear, 5 1/2 In.High
See Page 183

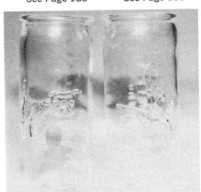

Nursing, **Baby Embossed**, Clear 14.00
Nursing, **Betty Jane Nurser Embossed** 3.50
Nursing, **Bulldog**, Clear, 5 1/2 In.High .... *Illus* 3.75
Nursing, **Bunny On Front**, Small Bunnies, Clear, 6 1/2 In.High 6.50
Nursing, **Burr's Medallion**, Flask, Shaped With Profile On Front, Stain, Aqua 27.50
Nursing, **Burr's Patent**, Nov.26, 1872, Corseted, Embossed, Stained, Aqua 22.50
Nursing, **Clapps**, Embossed, Amber 7.00
Nursing, **Columbia Nursing Bottle** .... *Color* XX.XX
Nursing, **Columbia**, Clear 8.00
Nursing, **Elephant**, Clear, 5 1/2 In.High .... *Illus* 3.75
Nursing, **Elephant**, Embossed, Wide Mouth 3.00
Nursing, **Flask Shape**, Oval, Embossed Ounces & Scale, Clear 3.00
Nursing, **Franklin** 4.50
Nursing, **Franklin Baby** 4.50
Nursing, **Graduated** 4.00
Nursing, **Hand Blown**, Flask Shape, Clear, 8 Oz. 2.00
Nursing, **Happy Baby & Baby Embossed** 3.50
Nursing, **Happy Baby**, 8 Oz. .... *Illus* 4.00
Nursing, **Lyric**, Embossed, 10 Oz. 4.00
Nursing, **Naked Full Length Baby & 3 Nurses On Side**, Embossed 3.50
Nursing, **Novac**, Nov.7, 1911, 7 1/2 In. .... *Illus* 8.00

Nursing, Happy Baby, 8 Oz.

Nursing, Novac,
Nov.7, 1911, 7 1/2 In.

Nursing, **Our Baby's**, Pat.U.S.Office April, 1875 .... *Color* XX.XX
Nursing, **Rabbits**, Embossed, Clear, 7 Oz. 4.50
Nursing, **Safe Grip Oval**, Armstrong, 8 Oz. 2.50
Nursing, **Sonny Boy** 3.00
Nursing, **The Best Patent**, Sept.1, '91, Hole In Both Ends 15.00
Nursing, **The Empire Nursing Bottle** .... *Color* XX.XX
Nursing, **Turtle Shape**, C.1890 .... 10.00
OBR , **National Hockey League Series**, Boston Bruins 14.95
OBR , **National Hockey League Series**, Chicago Black Hawks 14.95
OBR , **National Hockey League Series**, Detroit Red Wings 14.95
OBR , **National Hockey League Series**, Minnesota North Stars 14.95
OBR , **National Hockey League Series**, New York Rangers 14.95
OBR , **National Hockey League Series**, St.Louis Blues 14.95
OBR , **Transportation Series**, Balloon 11.95
OBR , **Transportation Series**, Fifth Avenue Bus .... 9.95 To 12.45
OBR , **Transportation Series**, Pierce Arrow .... 9.95 To 11.95
OBR , **Transportation Series**, Prairie Schooner .... 9.95 To 11.95
OBR , **Transportation Series**, River Queen .... 10.95 To 11.95
OBR , **Transportation Series**, Santa Maria 12.45
OBR , **Transportation Series**, Titanic .... 12.00 To 12.45
Oil & Vinegar, **Cambridge**, Urn, Etched Floral Swag & Oil & Vinegar, Clear 19.00
Oil & Vinegar, **Cut Glass**, Signed Hawkes 18.00
Oil & Vinegar, **Cut Glass**, Signed Hawkes, Sterling Top, June 20, 1916 .... 65.00
Oil & Vinegar, **Cut Glass**, 8 In.High, Pair 7.00

Oil & Vinegar, Pressed Glass, 7 1/2 In.Tall, Pair	22.00
Oil, Battery, Thomas A.Edison Signature, Clear, 4 1/4 In.High	1.50 To 4.00
Oil, Dill Machine Co., Norristown, Pa., Embossed 'shoo-Fly', Clear	4.50
Oil, Hemlock Oil Co., Derry, N.H., Clear, 5 3/4 In.	2.00 To 4.00
Oil, Huffman	5.00
Oil, Kerosene, Quick Neal, Embossed	2.50
Oil, Omega, Refired Lip	3.00
Oil, Penzoil, Amber	2.00
Oil, Sewing Machine, Clear	2.50
Oil, Sewing Machine, Embossed, Contents, Label, Clear, 5 In.High	1.10
Oil, Sewing Machine, 6 1/2 In.	8.00
Oil, Shell Motor, Clear, Quart	5.90
Oil, Shell, Embossed Shell Emblem, Guaranteed Delivers One Quart, Clear	9.00
Oil, Shell, Embossed, Cylindrical, ABM , Clear, 14 1/2 In.	15.00
Oil, Standard Oil Company, An Ohio Corporation	5.00
Oil, 3 In 1, Purple, 4 In.High	2.00
Old Crow, Chess Set	275.00
Old Crow, Chessman, Bishop, Dark	6.00
Old Crow, Chessman, Bishop, Light	5.00
Old Crow, Chessman, Castle, Dark	6.00
Old Crow, Chessman, Castle, Light	5.00
Old Crow, Chessman, Knight, Dark	6.00
Old Crow, Chessman, Knight, Light	5.00
Old Crow, Chessman, Pawn, Dark	14.00
Old Crow, Chessman, Pawn, Light	12.00
Old Crow, Chessman, Queen, Dark	6.00
Old Crow, Chessman, Queen, Light	5.00
Old Crow, Doulton	65.00
Old Fitzgerald, Cabin Still, American Cup, Special	18.95
Old Fitzgerald, Cabin Still, Blarney Bottle	3.00
Old Fitzgerald, Cabin Still, Blarney Stone, 1970	10.00
Old Fitzgerald, Cabin Still, California	10.95
Old Fitzgerald, Cabin Still, Candlelight, Pair, 1956	20.00
Old Fitzgerald, Cabin Still, Candlestick, 1961	5.95
Old Fitzgerald, Cabin Still, Coat Of Arms	2.00
Old Fitzgerals, Cabin Still, Crown	6.95
Old Fitzgerald, Cabin Still, Decanter, Colonial	6.00
Old Fitzgerald, Cabin Still, Decanter, Deer Browsing, 1967	6.00
Old Fitzgerald, Cabin Still, Decanter, Dog, Pointing Setter	14.00
Old Fitzgerald, Cabin Still, Decanter, Duck	9.00
Old Fitzgerald, Cabin Still, Decanter, Flagship	6.49
Old Fitzgerald, Cabin Still, Decanter, Florentine	7.95 To 10.00
Old Fitzgerald, Cabin Still, Decanter, Four Seasons	5.00
Old Fitzgerald, Cabin Still, Decanter, Gold Coaster	12.95 To 14.00
Old Fitzgerald, Cabin Still, Decanter, Gold Web, 1953	18.00
Old Fitzgerald, Cabin Still, Decanter, Jewel, 1952	7.95
Old Fitzgerald, Cabin Still, Decanter, Monticello, Thomas Jefferson, White	2.50
Old Fitzgerald, Cabin Still, Decanter, Trout, 1969	6.00
Old Fitzgerald, Cabin Still, Diamond, 1961	9.95
Old Fitzgerald, Cabin Still, Fleur-De-Lis, 1962	9.00
Old Fitzgerald, Cabin Still, Goose	2.95
Old Fitzgerald, Cabin Still, Hillbilly, Pint, 1954	30.00
Old Fitzgerald, Cabin Still, Hillbilly, Quart, 1954 _Illus_	40.00
Old Fitzgerald, Cabin Still, Hillbilly, 1939	150.00
Old Fitzgerald, Cabin Still, Hillbilly, 1956	39.50
Old Fitzgerald, Cabin Still, Hillbilly, 1969	5.95
Old Fitzgerald, Cabin Still, Hunting, West Virginia	14.95
Old Fitzgerald, Cabin Still, Irish Patriots	12.00
Old Fitzgerald, Cabin Still, Leprechaun, 1968	20.00
Old Fitzgerald, Cabin Still, Lexington	5.00
Old Fitzgerald, Cabin Still, Memphis, 1969	10.95
Old Fitzgerald, Cabin Still, Ohio State	14.95
Old Fitzgerald, Cabin Still, Pheasant	11.00
Old Fitzgerald, Cabin Still, Pheasant, Rising	15.00
Old Fitzgerald, Cabin Still, Quail	7.95
Old Fitzgerald, Cabin Still, Ram	2.95

Old Fitzgerald, Cabin Still, Rebel Yell	10.95
Old Fitzgerald, Cabin Still, Richwood West Virginia	14.95
Old Fitzgerald, Cabin Still, Rip Van Winkle, 1971 .... *Illus*	14.95
Old Fitzgerald, Cabin Still, Sons Of Erin, 1969	10.00
Old Fitzgerald, Cabin Still, South Carolina, 1970	10.95
Old Fitzgerald, Cabin Still, Texas Longhorn, Stizler Weller	10.00
Old Fitzgerald, Cabin Still, Tournament, 1963	9.00
Old Fitzgerald, Cabin Still, Tree Of Life	10.00
Old Fitzgerald, Cabin Still, Vermont	12.95
Old Fitzgerald, Cabin Still, Weller Masterpiece, 1963	29.95
Old Fitzgerald, Texas Longhorn, Stizler Weller	10.00
Old Hickory, Andrew Jackson, 1956	17.50
Old Mr.Boston, Bust, Gold	6.50
Old Taylor, see Whiskey, Old Taylor	
Old Taylor, Castle	3.95
Onion, 1710, Black	35.00
Paste, Sanford's Library, For Mounting Photographs .... *Illus*	4.00
Pepper Sauce, Aqua, 8 1/2 In.High	9.50
Pepper Sauce, Blue Green	22.00
Pepper Sauce, Bull's-Eyes, Oval At Front, Cobalt Blue To Purple	150.00
Pepper Sauce, C.C.O.& Co., Paper Label, Clear, 7 1/2 In. .... *Illus*	10.00
Pepper Sauce, C.C.O., Pat.Sept.28, 1875, 15 Ridged	12.00
Pepper Sauce, Cathedral, Applied Top, Green, 8 1/2 In.High	45.00
Pepper Sauce, Cathedral, Aqua, 9 In. .... *Illus*	35.00
Pepper Sauce, Cathedral, Blown, Aqua, 8 In. .... *Illus*	58.00

Old Fitzgerald, Cabin Still,
Hillbilly, Quart, 1954
See Page 184

Old Fitzgerald,
Cabin Still,
Rip Van Winkle, 1971

Pepper Sauce,
C.C.O.& Co.,
Paper Label,
Clear, 7 1/2 In.

Paste, Sanford's Library,
For Mounting Photographs

Pepper Sauce,
Cathedral, Aqua, 9 In.

Pepper Sauce,
Cathedral, Blown, Aqua, 8 In.

Pepper Sauce, Cathedral, Crude Bent Neck, Aqua, 8 1/2 In.High	14.00
Pepper Sauce, Cathedral, Haze On 2 Panels, Aqua, 9 In.Tall	18.00
Pepper Sauce, Cathedral, Light Green	30.00
Pepper Sauce, Cathedral, Open Pontil, Light Green	30.00
Pepper Sauce, Cathedral, Rough Pontil, Stain, 8 1/2 In.High	29.00
Pepper Sauce, Cathedral, Sparkling	7.00
Pepper Sauce, Cathedral, Windows, Deep Aqua	30.00
Pepper Sauce, Cathedral, 4 Sides, Aqua, 8 1/2 In.Tall	45.00
Pepper Sauce, Cathedral, 6 Gothic Panels, Open Pontil, Clear, 8 3/4 In.High	35.00
Pepper Sauce, Cathedral, 6 Sided, Applied Lip, Aqua, 8 3/4 In.High	12.00
Pepper Sauce, Cathedral, 6 Sided, Aqua, 9 In.Tall	40.00
Pepper Sauce, Cathedral, 6 Sided, Gothic Windows, Aqua, 8 1/2 In.	13.00
Pepper Sauce, Eight Vertical Panels, Open Pontil, Aqua	12.00
Pepper Sauce, Fluted, Embossed Wells, Miller & Provost, Open Pontil, Aqua	50.00
Pepper Sauce, Fluted, Open Pontil, Aqua .... 17.50 To	20.00
Pepper Sauce, Fluted, Open Pontil, Stain, Clear	17.50
Pepper Sauce, Fluted, 6 Sided, Aqua, 8 In.High	9.00
Pepper Sauce, Gothic Arch, Octagonal, Aqua Blue	30.00
Pepper Sauce, Green Spiral, Aqua	18.50
Pepper Sauce, Oval, Clear	3.50
Pepper Sauce, Oval, 20 Rings	8.00
Pepper Sauce, Pat.Applied For, Ridgy, Emerald Green	17.50
Pepper Sauce, Pontil, Aqua, 7 1/2 In. .... *Illus*	28.50
Pepper Sauce, Ridgy, Aqua	10.00
Pepper Sauce, Ridgy, Blue Green	17.00
Pepper Sauce, Ridgy, Green	20.00
Pepper Sauce, Ringed	3.50
Pepper Sauce, Ringed, Blown In Mold, Applied Lip, Green	9.75
Pepper Sauce, Ringed, Clear, 9 In.	7.00
Pepper Sauce, Roped Corners, Roselike Flower On 3 Sides, Clear	10.50
Pepper Sauce, Spiral Ridge, Pat.App.For 18--, Aqua .... *Illus*	25.00
Pepper Sauce, Twenty Ring, Aqua	10.00
Pepper Sauce, Vertical Ribbed, 3 Ring, Clear	6.00
Pepper Sauce, Wah-Wah	4.00
Pepper Sauce, 6 Indented Panels Tapering From Base To Neck, Aqua, 8 In.	12.50
Pepper Sauce, 8 Ribbed, Pontil	17.50
Pepper Sauce, 8 Sided, 3 Rings On Neck, Open Pontil, Aqua	32.00
Pepper Sauce, 20 Rings	8.00
Pepper Sauce, 21 Rings	4.00
Pepper Sauce, 24 Rings, Round, Aqua	5.00
Perfume, Amber, Glass Blown, Stopper, Enameled Floral, Pink, White & Green	30.00
Perfume, Amberina, Footed, Ground Stopper, Etched Design, 6 1/4 In.High	32.00
Perfume, Atomizer, Cut Crystal, 3 In.	7.00
Perfume, Atomizer, Gold-Plated Crackle Glass, 3 1/4 In.	9.00
Perfume, Atomizer, Iridescent, Marked	6.75
Perfume, Baccarat, Acid Etched Design, Signed, 5 1/2 In.High	28.00
Perfume, Baccarat, Amber Swirl, Signed	45.00
Perfume, Baccarat, Diamond Shape, Cut & Polished Ribs, Stopper, 3 In.Tall	15.00
Perfume, Baccarat, Embossed Pattern, Blue Trim, Signed, 6 1/4 In.High	30.00
Perfume, Baccarat, Paperweight, Cut & Polished Diamonds, Diamond Stopper	40.00
Perfume, Baccarat, Swirl, Clear To Cranberry To Amberina, 5 In.High	48.00
Perfume, Betty Boop	12.00
Perfume, Blown, White Enamel, Tulip Stopper	8.00
Perfume, Bohemian, Applied Ring Around Neck, Enameled Decor, Stopper	75.00
Perfume, Bristol, Enameled Bird & Flowers, Stopper, Blue, 9 In.Tall	20.00
Perfume, Bristol, Pedestal, Decorated, Opalescent, Blown Stopper	15.00
Perfume, Brule-Parfum, Louis XVI Ormolu Mounted, Enameled, C.1750, Pair	950.00
Perfume, Bulbous, Embossed Circle For Label, Emerald Green	7.00
Perfume, C.W.Laird, N.Y., Milk Glass, 5 In.High .... *Illus*	10.00
Perfume, Cambridge, Helio, Marked Devilbiss Atomizer	35.00
Perfume, Cameo Glass, Brown Floral On Cream, Signed Ciarama	137.00
Perfume, Cameo, English, Lay Down, Carved, Citron Ground	350.00
Perfume, Celeste Blue Stopper, Tall, Inverted Cone Shape	140.00
Perfume, Charlie McCarthy, 3 In.	6.00
Perfume, Cloth Case, Clear	2.00

Pepper Sauce, Pontil,
Aqua, 7 1/2 In.
See Page 186

Perfume, C.W.Laird, N.Y.,
Milk Glass, 5 In.High
See Page 186

Pepper Sauce, Spiral Ridge,
Pat.App.For 18--, Aqua
See Page 186

Perfume, Colgate, Blown In Mold	10.00
Perfume, Cranberry Glass, Cut Stopper	25.00
Perfume, Crystal, Octagonal, Frosted Intaglio Cut Flower & Foliage, Stopper	24.00
Perfume, Cut Glass, Bulbous, Matching Stopper, 5 1/4 In.High	38.00
Perfume, Cut Glass, Colonial Pattern, Pink Enamel Sterling Stopper	35.00
Perfume, Cut Glass, Etched Frosted Poppy On Stopper, 4 1/2 In.High	15.00
Perfume, Cut Glass, Faceted Cut Knob, 5 1/2 In.Tall	23.00
Perfume, Cut Glass, Faceted Stopper, 4 3/4 In.High	22.50
Perfume, Cut Glass, Horn Shape, Hinged Sterling Top	15.00
Perfume, Cut Glass, Rose Color, 4 1/2 In.	12.50
Perfume, Cut Glass, Signed Czech., 1 1/2 In.Tall Stopper, Amber	15.00
Perfume, Cut Glass, Square Star Cut Base, Stopper, 8 In.High, Pair	20.00
Perfume, Cut Glass, Stopper, Amethyst & Clear, 8 1/4 In.	45.00
Perfume, Cut Glass, Thumbprint On Stopper	14.00
Perfume, Devilbiss, Atomizer, Bulbous, Cable, Gold-plated Top, Vaseline	22.00
Perfume, Devilbiss, Atomizer, Cut Glass, Stemmed, Etched Flowers, Gold Top	150.00
Perfume, Devilbiss, Signed, Bulb, Blue	12.00
Perfume, Devilbiss, Silver Scrolled Collar, Stopper, Jade, Black	31.00
Perfume, Doggie, Black Celluloid Hat, 2 1/2 In.High	5.00
Perfume, Encased In Metal	4.50
Perfume, Evening In Paris, Purse Size, Cobalt	3.00
Perfume, Fancy Design, Label, Open Pontil, Clear, 3 In.	15.00
Perfume, Fancy, Clear, 3 In.	5.00
Perfume, Figural, Puppy, Full	4.00
Perfume, Flask, Jet Black	20.00
Perfume, Florida Water, Murray And Lanman, 9 In. *Illus*	12.00
Perfume, Florida Water, Stevens & Stevens Co., 9 In. *Illus*	10.00
Perfume, Francis Whittemore, Stopper Enclosing Blue Rose	225.00
Perfume, Frosted, Ground Glass Stopper, Label, Boxed	15.00
Perfume, Frosted, Rose, Butterfly Stopper, Made In France	12.50
Perfume, Galle, Frosted Rose Ground, Brown Floral, 2 Acid Cuttings, Signed	165.00
Perfume, Heisey, Signed, Amethyst, 7 In.	25.00
Perfume, Hobnail, Green, Pair	35.00
Perfume, Hobnail, Opalescent, White	8.50
Perfume, Kaziun, Upright Pink Lily, Cut Facets, Blue Ground	285.00
Perfume, Kewpie, China, Germany, 2 1/2 In.High	8.00
Perfume, Laird Perfumery, Milk Glass	8.50
Perfume, Lalique, Atomizer, Pink, Molded Roses, Open Rose Stopper, 4 1/2 In.	35.00
Perfume, Lalique, Lotus Flower, Signed, Pair	60.00

Perfume, Florida Water,
Murray And Lanman, 9 In.
See Page 187

Perfume, Florida Water,
Stevens & Stevens Co., 9 In.
See Page 187

Perfume, **Lalique**, Nude, Signed, Oval, 14 In.High	110.00
Perfume, **Lalique**, Nude, Signed, 8 1/3 In.High	110.00
Perfume, **Lalique**, Nude, Signed, 2 Nudes On Stopper, 7 1/3 In.High	90.00
Perfume, **Lalique**, Open Rose Form, Satin, Butterfly Stopper, Signed	35.00
Perfume, **Lalique**, Prism Sides & Shoulders, Frosted Shell Stopper, Pair	18.00
Perfume, **Lalique**, Round, Cut Clear, Stopper Is Lady, 8 1/2 In.High	60.00
Perfume, **Lalique**, Stopper Is Pair Of Birds In Flight, Signed	55.00
Perfume, **Lavender**, Dated 1936	3.00
Perfume, **Louis D'Or Of France**, 1/2 Oz.	3.00
Perfume, **Mary Gregory**, Oval, Brass Cap, Chain, & Ring, Girl, Sapphire Blue	45.00
Perfume, **Mellier's**, Round, BIMAL , Ground Neck, Ball Stopper, 10 In.High	10.00
Perfume, **Minton**, Pear Shape, Enameled Lilies Of The Valley, C.1830	60.00
Perfume, **Moser**, Atomizer, Intaglio Cut, Violet Panels, Gold Top	45.00
Perfume, **Moser**, Intaglio Cut, Tulip Panels, Faceted Stopper, 5 In.Tall	52.50
Perfume, **Pairpoint**, Paperweight Style, Stopper, 7 1/2 In.	15.00
Perfume, **Palmer**, Emerald Green	5.00
Perfume, **Paperweight Type**, Bird Stopper, Clear, 6 In.High	8.00
Perfume, **Paperweight**, Blown, Signed St.Clair, Dated	20.00
Perfume, **Parfum**, Ground Glass Stopper, Label, C.L.C.Co. Embossed	10.00
Perfume, **Persian**, Flask, Birds, Flowers, & Fish In Black Under Blue Green	28.00
Perfume, **Pressed Glass**, Stopper	6.50
Perfume, **Rose Geranium**, Pat.March, 1870, Barrel, Labels, Aqua	15.00
Perfume, **Sandwich**, Ribbed, Double Collar, Clear	50.00
Perfume, **Sandwich**, Ribbed, Single Collar, Clear	50.00
Perfume, **Secret De Beaute**, Cherub, Milk Glass, 4 1/2 In. *Illus*	37.50
Perfume, **Silver Overlay**, Carnation Pattern, Emberald Green	30.00
Perfume, **Silver Overlay**, Chrysanthemums, Blown, Emerald Green	135.00
Perfume, **Silver Overlay**, Engraved Initials G.E.H., Emerald Green	40.00
Perfume, **Silver Overlay**, Engraved Initials M.S., Emerald Green	15.00
Perfume, **Silver Overlay**, 3 In.	11.00
Perfume, **Solon Palmer**, Dated May 28, 1867, Ground Stopper, Label, 9 In.	20.00
Perfume, **Solon Palmer**, Tapered Oval, Emerald Green	7.00
Perfume, **Stain Glass**, Decorated Front, Sterling, Dark Green, 5 In. High	40.00
Perfume, **Sterling Silver**, Round, Amethyst On Lid, Funnel	16.50
Perfume, **Sterling**, Miniature, Etched Leaf, Funnel	20.00
Perfume, **Steuben**, Verre De Soie, Green Jadelike Stopper	55.00
Perfume, **Steuben**, Verre De Soie, Melon Shape, Iridescent Blue Frame Stopper	55.00
Perfume, **Vantine's Indian**, Label, 4 3/4 In.Tall	2.25
Perfume, **Venetian Glass**, Square, White Latticinio, Goldstone Panels	35.00
Perfume, **Verre De Soie**, Cerise Ruby Stopper, Ball Shape, Flat Base	145.00
Perfume, **Vial**, Mercury, Orange Stripe, Mercury Stopper	8.75
Persian Type, Crooked Neck, Applied Glass At Neck, O.P., Light Blue Green	8.00
Pickle, **Albany Glass Works**, Fancy Design Improved Pontil, Aqua	160.00
Pickle, **Baird's Pickles**, Glasgow, 6 Panels, Embossed, Green	10.00
Pickle, **Bristol**, 12 1/2 In.Tall	14.75
Pickle, **Bunker Hill**, Aqua	5.00

Pickle, Bunker Hill, Embossed Monument	12.00
Pickle, Bunker Hill, Embossed, Label, Amber, Pint	14.00
Pickle, Bunker Hill, Embossed, Label, Pint	7.50
Pickle, Bunker Hill, Mineral Stain, Amber, 8 1/4 In.	45.00
Pickle, Bunker Hill, Skilton & Foote, Gilded	15.50
Pickle, Bunker Hill, Skilton & Foote, Round, Whittled, Citron	29.00
Pickle, Bunker Hill, Skilton, Foote & Co., Golden Amber, 7 1/2 In.High	19.00
Pickle, Cathedral, Aqua	45.00 To 85.00
Pickle, Cathedral, Aqua, Gallon	50.00
Pickle, Cathedral, Aqua, 8 1/2 In.High *Illus*	34.00
Pickle, Cathedral, Dark Aqua, 14 In.Tall	75.00
Pickle, Cathedral, Extended Teardrops From Neck, Aqua, Large Size	70.00
Pickle, Cathedral, Light Aqua, 12 In.Tall	65.00
Pickle, Cathedral, Light Green, 11 1/2 In.High	35.00
Pickle, Cathedral, Six Panel, Green, 13 1/2 Gallon	75.00
Pickle, Cathedral, Square, Light Green, 2 Quart	35.00
Pickle, Cathedral, Stain, Gallon	20.00
Pickle, Cathedral, 2 1/2 In.Square, 9 In.Tall	7.00
Pickle, Cathedral, 3 1/2 In.Square, Aqua, 13 1/2 In. Tall	40.00
Pickle, Cathedral, 3 1/2 In.Square, Aqua, 15 In.Tall	45.00

Perfume, Secret De Beaute,
Cherub, Milk Glass, 4 1/2 In.
See Page 188

Pickle, Cathedral,
Aqua, 8 1/2 In.High

Pickle, Cathedral, 4 Sided, Aqua, 11 3/4 In.High	40.00
Pickle, Cathedral, 4 Sided, Deep Aqua, 11 In.High	32.50
Pickle, Cathedral, 6 Sided, Light Green, 2 1/2 Quart	45.00
Pickle, Cathedral, 6 Sided, Ornate, Gallon	42.00
Pickle, East India	25.00
Pickle, Goofus Glass, Embossed Cable Handles, Painted Daisies, 12 1/2 In.	8.00
Pickle, Goofus Glass, Rose Embossed, Amethyst, Pint	8.50
Pickle, Goofus Glass, Rose Embossed, Amethyst, Quart	8.50
Pickle, Goofus Glass, Rose Embossed, Amethyst, 1/2 Pint	10.50
Pickle, Gothic Arch, Embossed Crown On Base, Aqua, 7 In.	6.50
Pickle, Gothic Arch, Embossed Crown On Base, Aqua, 12 In.	8.75
Pickle, Gothic Arch, Embossed Crown On Base, Aqua, 7 In.	6.50
Pickle, Gothic Arch, Flared Lip, 6 Sided, Light Amethyst, 13 1/2 In.Tall	50.00
Pickle, Gothic Arch, Rolled Lip, Diagonal Mold, 3 1/8 In.Square, Green	150.00
Pickle, Hayward's Military	15.00
Pickle, Ivy Leaves, Oval Panels, Square, Graphite Pontil, 10 3/4 In.	78.00
Pickle, J.M.Clark, Ridgy At Base, Apple Green	5.50
Pickle, M.A.Gedney Pickling Co., The, Amethyst, Pint	3.00
Pickle, Paneled Forget-Me-Not, Cover	25.00
Pickle, Panels & Flowers Design, Clear, 13 In.Tall	50.00
Pickle, Plain Panels, Stain, Aqua, 2 Quart	5.00
Pickle, Rowat & Co., Aqua	10.00
Pickle, Rowat & Co., Glasgow, Regd.No.13-2762 On Sides, Square, Light Green	10.00
Pickle, Stoddard Glass, Clover Leaf, Red Amber	125.00

Pickle, Stoddard, Clover Leaf, Dark Amber	60.00
Pickle, Three Mold, Vase Shape, Embossed Flowers, 10 In.Tall, Aqua	25.00
Pickle, Three Mold, Vase Shape, 10 In.Tall, Golden Amber	50.00
Pickle, 3 Mold, Embossed Floral, Vase Type, C.1870, Blue Aqua, 15 In.	59.00
Pickle, 4 Sided, Aqua, 14 In.High	10.00
Pictorial Bottle Review, Antique Peddler, Lido Markets Label	39.50
Pinch, Inset Neck, Pewter Top, Cobalt Blue	140.00
Pinch, Semi, Swirled To Right, Pewter Top, Cobalt Blue	90.00
Pinch, Swirled To Right, Pewter Top, Blue	90.00

Poison bottles were usually made with raised designs so the user could feel the danger in the dark. The most interesting poison bottles were made from the 1870s to the 1930s.

Poison, Amber, 3 1/2 In.High	2.00
Poison, B.P.Co., Triloids Poison, Cobalt	10.00
Poison, British Admiralty Arrow, Ribbed, Cobalt, 16 Oz.	10.00
Poison, Cobalt, Set Of 4, BIMAL , 3 1/2 In.To 6 1/4 In.	65.00
Poison, Coffin, Cobalt, 7 1/2 In.High	45.00
Poison, Coffin, Label, Cobalt, 3 1/2 In.High	22.00
Poison, Coffin, Label, Contents, Cobalt	10.00
Poison, Collared Neck, New England, Hobnail, Clear, 6 In.	45.00
Poison, Covered With Pearl Dots, Green, 1/2 Pint	70.00
Poison, Embossed Lid, Clear, 6 In.Tall	4.00
Poison, Embossed, Dug, Amber	2.00
Poison, Embossed, Eight Sided, Dug, Cobalt	6.00
Poison, Embossed, Glass Lid, Clear, 6 In.Tall	4.00
Poison, Embossed, 6 Sided, Cobalt, 3 1/2 In.High	7.00
Poison, F.A.Thompson, Detroit, Coffin Flask, Amber	60.00
Poison, Jar, Clear	2.00
Poison, Lattice & Points, Round, Burst Bubble On Lip, Green, 4 1/2 In.High	8.00
Poison, Lattice, BIMAL , Green, 4 1/2 In.	10.00
Poison, Moberly Lade, B.C., Canada, Cobalt	10.00
Poison, Norwich, IGA, Cobalt, 8 In.High *Illus*	60.00
Poison, Not To Be Taken, Cobalt, 6 In. *Color*	XX.XX
Poison, O.K.	25.00
Poison, Owl, Cobalt, 2 7/8 In.High	8.00
Poison, Owl, Triangular, Cobalt	25.00
Poison, Pearl Shape Pattern, Aqua, Small Size	50.00
Poison, Quilted, Stopper, Cobalt Blue	22.50
Poison, Sawtooth Patterns, Clear	50.00
Poison, Skull & Crossbones On 2 Sides, Beveled Corners, Cobalt, 3 1/4 In.	10.00
Poison, Skull & Crossbones, Embossed, Dug, Amber	5.00
Poison, Square, Cobalt	3.50
Poison, Three Corner, Amber	2.60

Poison, Norwich, IGA,
Cobalt, 8 In.High

Poison, Tincture Of Iodine, Embossed Skull & Crossbones, Cobalt	12.50
Poison, Triangle, Amber	2.30
Poison, Trilet's, Cobalt	4.00
Poison, Triloid's, Cobalt Blue	4.50 To 12.00
Poison, Triloid's, Triangle, Hobnail Corners, Cobalt	10.00
Poison, Wyeth, Blue, 2 1/4 In.	5.00
Poison, 3 Corner With Ridges, ABM , Amber	3.00
Porter, C.1760, Bulbous Neck	40.00
Porter, 10 In.	45.00
Royal Doulton, Commemorative, Black Don, 1937	45.00
Royal Doulton, Don, 1938, Full, Pair	35.00
Royal Doulton, Hot Water, London, Ceramic, Screw Cap, Leather Washer, Quart	25.00
Royal Doulton, Sandeman	35.00
Royal Doulton, Zorro, England	50.00
Rum, Carioca Eggnog, Frosted	2.50
Rum, Carioca, Lampshade	6.00
Rum, Carioca, Oxen & Cart, Tan, 1938	6.50
Rum, Carioca, Oxen & Cart, White, 1938	6.50
Rum, Carioca, Oxen & Cart, 1938	6.50
Rum, Carioca, Oxen & Cart, Miniature, 1935	14.95
Rum, Carioca, Oxen & Cart, Miniature, 1940	14.95
Rum, Carioca, Pirates & Treasure Chest, Miniature, 1935	14.95
Rum, Carioca, Pirates & Treasure Chest, Miniature, 1940	14.95
Rum, Doubloon Ron Virgin	2.50
Rum, Encrusted, Open Pontil, Green, Quart	7.00
Rum, Escarchado	3.50
Rum, Free-Blown, 1790-1800, Deep Kickup, Open Pontil, Black Glass, Quart	90.00
Rum, I.F.Hoffman & Sons, Rotterdam Embossed At Bottom, Dark Olive Green	35.00
Rum, Jug, Jamaica, Handled, Open Pontil, Label, Amber	35.00
Rum, Pontil, Olive Amber	5.00
Rum, Pontil, Olive Green, Quart	8.00
Rum, Ron Bocoy	2.50
Rum, Seaver's Joint & Mirror Liniment, Label, Olive Green, 8 1/2 In.High	10.00
Rum, Very Old Medford Rum On Label, Wicker Case, Amber, Quart	1.00
Sacajawea, Captain Meriwether Lewis	32.00
Sacajawea, Captain William Clark	30.00
Sacajawea, With Papoose	19.95
Saddle, Persian, Teal Blue, 7 1/2 In.High	11.00
Sandwich Glass, Blown, Deep Blue Green, 4 In.High	32.50

Sarsaparilla bottles must be marked with the word sarsaparilla to be collected. Most date from 1840 to 1900.

Sarsaparilla, A.D.& C.Co's Best Extract	39.50
Sarsaparilla, A.H.Bull, Hartford, Open Pontil	20.00
Sarsaparilla, Allen's Co., Woodfords, Maine, Rectangular, Clear, Medium Size	12.00
Sarsaparilla, Allen's, Oval, Aqua	12.00
Sarsaparilla, Atlas Medicine Co., Henderson, N.C., Embossed, Amber, 9 In.	100.00
Sarsaparilla, Ayer's	4.00
Sarsaparilla, Ayer's Compound, Applied Mouth	12.00
Sarsaparilla, Babcock, Amber	20.00
Sarsaparilla, Bell's, Bangor, Me., Aqua	15.00
Sarsaparilla, Bell's, Bangor, Me., Pottery, Jug	37.50
Sarsaparilla, Bristol's Genuine, Embossed, Dug, BIMAL , Aqua	12.00 To 25.00
Sarsaparilla, Brown's For Kidneys, Liver, & Blood, Embossed, Aqua	6.00
Sarsaparilla, Brown's, Aqua	5.00 To 8.00
Sarsaparilla, Bull's, Pontil	20.00
Sarsaparilla, Charles Langley's	30.00
Sarsaparilla, Dalton's Sarsaparilla & Nerve Tonic, Aqua	7.95 To 15.00
Sarsaparilla, Dalton's, Belfast, Maine, Contents, Label, Box	4.00 To 10.00
Sarsaparilla, Dalton's, Boxed, Aqua, 10 In.	*Illus* 10.00
Sarsaparilla, Dana's	2.00 To 2.80
Sarsaparilla, Dana's, Aqua	1.00 To 6.00
Sarsaparilla, Dana's, Bangor, Me., Embossed, Aqua	15.00
Sarsaparilla, Dana's, Belfast, Maine, BIMAL , Stain, Aqua, 9 In.Tall	6.00
Sarsaparilla, Dana's, Blown In Mold	6.00

Sarsaparilla, Dalton's,
Boxed, Aqua, 10 In.
See Page 191

Sarsaparilla,
Yager's Compound
Extract, Brown
See Page 193

Sarsaparilla, **Dana's**, Cloudy	1.25
Sarsaparilla, **Dr.Abott's Compound Extract Of**, Label, Aqua	19.00
Sarsaparilla, **Dr.Cronk's Sarsaparilla Beer**, Crockery, 12 Sided	35.00
Sarsaparilla, **Dr.Cronk's Sarsaparilla Beer**, Pottery, Age Cracks, Gray	32.00
Sarsaparilla, **Dr.Fenner's Peoples Remedy**, Aqua	25.00
Sarsaparilla, **Dr.Green's**	23.00
Sarsaparilla, **Dr.Guysott's Compound Extract Of Yellow Dock &**, Aqua, Green	85.00
Sarsaparilla, **Dr.Guysott's**, Aqua, Pontil	50.00 To 75.00
Sarsaparilla, **Dr.Pierce's**, Label, Contents	9.50
Sarsaparilla, **Dr.Scott's**, A.A.Shepherd, Rockland, Me., Label, Aqua	3.00 To 20.00
Sarsaparilla, **Dr.Thomson's**, Great English Remedy	35.00
Sarsaparilla, **Dr.Townsend's**, Albany, N.Y., Pontil, Olive Green	57.50
Sarsaparilla, **Dr.Townsend's**, Albany, N.Y., Stain, Emerald Green	42.00
Sarsaparilla, **Dr.Townsend's**, Improved Pontil, Green	55.00
Sarsaparilla, **Dr.Townsend's**, Olive Green	85.00
Sarsaparilla, **Dr.Townsend's**, Snap Case Pontil, Olive Green	59.00 To 70.00
Sarsaparilla, **F.Brown**, Boston, Sarsaparilla On Tomato Bitters, Aqua	87.50
Sarsaparilla, **Foley's**, Amber	12.50
Sarsaparilla, **Gooch's**	10.00
Sarsaparilla, **Goodwin Indian Vegetable &**, Aqua	140.00
Sarsaparilla, **Green Mountain Sarsaparilla Compound**, Aqua	41.00
Sarsaparilla, **Hood's**	2.00 To 3.00
Sarsaparilla, **Hood's**, Apothecaries, Aqua, 7 In.Tall	35.00
Sarsaparilla, **Hood's**, Apothecaries, 9 In.	4.00
Sarsaparilla, **Hood's**, Aqua	1.00
Sarsaparilla, **Hood's**, BIMAL , Dug, Aqua	3.00
Sarsaparilla, **Hood's**, Cloudy	1.25
Sarsaparilla, **Hood's**, Label, Contents	9.50
Sarsaparilla, **Hood's**, Rectangular, Aqua, 9 In.High	2.45
Sarsaparilla, **Hood's**, Trial Size, Clear, 7 In.High	9.00
Sarsaparilla, **J.V.Babcock**, Gold Medal, Amber	32.00
Sarsaparilla, **John Bull**, BIMAL , Large Size	25.00
Sarsaparilla, **John Bull**, Extract Of, Louisville, Ky., Aqua	35.00
Sarsaparilla, **John Bull**, Extract Of, Louisville, Ky., Stain, Aqua	19.00
Sarsaparilla, **John Bull**, Hand Blown, Aqua	75.00
Sarsaparilla, **Joy's**, Rectangular, San Francisco, Aqua	19.00
Sarsaparilla, **Kennedy's Sarsaparilla & Celery Compound**, Amber	17.50
Sarsaparilla, **King's**, 80 Percent Label, Aqua	10.00
Sarsaparilla, **Leon's**, Aqua	15.00
Sarsaparilla, **Masury's**, Cloudy	47.00
Sarsaparilla, **Murray's**, Burnham, Me., Label, Aqua	15.00
Sarsaparilla, **Radway's Sarsaparillian Resolvent**, Box, Insert	22.00 To 45.00
Sarsaparilla, **Radway's Sarsaparillian Resolvent**, Embossed, Blue Green	27.50
Sarsaparilla, **Radway's Sarsaparillian Resolvent**, Improved Pontil, Aqua	15.00
Sarsaparilla, **Rush's**, Cloudy, Aqua	10.00

Sarsaparilla, Rush's, Embossed, Aqua 12.00
Sarsaparilla, Sand's, Cloudy, Aqua, Pint 52.50
Sarsaparilla, Sand's, Pontil, Aqua, 6 In.Tall 37.00
Sarsaparilla, Sand's, Stain, Aqua 52.00
Sarsaparilla, Sarsaparilla & Celery Phosphate, Labels 1.50
Sarsaparilla, Skoda's, Amber .... 22.75 To 25.00
Sarsaparilla, Skoda's Wolfville Discovery, Amber, 9 In. 22.50
Sarsaparilla, Syruper's Sarsaparilla Co.Compound Syrup Of, Amber, 32 Oz. 5.00
Sarsaparilla, The People's Favorite, Label, Amber 15.00
Sarsaparilla, Warner's Log Cabin, Embossed, Label .... 65.00 To 85.00
Sarsaparilla, Warner's, Log Cabin, 90 Percent Label 85.00
Sarsaparilla, World's Columbian, Clear .... 38.00 To 50.00
Sarsaparilla, Yager's Compound Extract, Brown .... *Illus* 35.00
Sarsaparilla, Yager's, Burst Surface Bubble 24.00
Scent, Blown, 3 Mold, Ribbed, Sandwich, Clear, 5 1/2 In. 20.00
Scent, Chinese, Ta Ching Chi Ching Mein Chih, C.1796-1820 .... 25.00
Scent, Cut Glass, Sterling Cap, Purse Size 14.00
Scent, Galle, Onion Shape, Thistle Spray In Pink & Brown, Amber 140.00
Scent, Iridescent, Pedestal Foot 9.00
Scent, Mc Kearin 241, Polished Lip & Pontil, Deep Blue 110.00
Scent, Mc Kearin 241, Sandwich Glass, Flint No.28, Fiery Opal 30.00
Scent, Mc Kearin 241, Sandwich Glass, Flint No.30, Blue 38.00
Scent, Mc Kearin 241, Sandwich Glass, Flint No.31, Blue 35.00
Scent, Mc Kearin 241, Sandwich, Pewter Cap, Deep Violet Blue 40.00
Scent, Stiegel Type, Blown From 24 Rib Mold, Pennsylvania, C.1760 .... 95.00
Scent, 3 Mold Type, C.1830, Emerald Green 150.00
Seal, A.S.C.R., Pontil, Olive Amber, Quart 42.50
Seal, AH , Gin, Amber, Quart 32.50
Seal, AH , Gin, Olive Amber, Quart .... 17.50 To 25.00
Seal, Arenenbe & Co., Olive Green, Quart 5.00
Seal, B.B.Co., Patent On Shoulder, Three Mold, Rickett's Glass Works, Green 50.00
Seal, Beven Lebela-Amsterdam, Olive Amber, Quart 20.00
Seal, Bininger, New York, Pontil, Olive Amber, Quart 420.00
Seal, Bootz Amsterdam, Amber, Quart 77.00
Seal, Coat Of Arms, Pontil, Olive Amber, Quart 65.00
Seal, DBD, Pontil, Olive Amber, Quart .... 15.00 To 35.00
Seal, D.Sears, Green, Quart 30.00
Seal, D.Sears, Pontil, Green, Quart 30.00
Seal, Dasilvas Port, Olive Amber, Quart 7.50
Seal, DBDW , Pontil, Olive Amber, Quart 27.50
Seal, Doneraile House & 8-Point Sunburst, H Rickett's & Co., Bristol, Black 75.00
Seal, Doneraile House, H.Ricketts Glass Works, Olive Green 32.50
Seal, Emanuel College, Black Glass 60.00
Seal, Falling Star, Label, Green, 2 Quart 15.00
Seal, G.H., Pontil, Olive Amber, Quart 90.00
Seal, Hotel De Paris Monte Carlo, Olive Green, Quart 7.00
Seal, Maltese Cross, Olive Amber, Quart 4.00
Seal, Mc Kearin 221-3, Embossed Applied Seal, 1717, N.Wells, London, Black 425.00
Seal, Mc Kearin 221-6, Applied Embossed Seal, P.Palmer, C.1730, Black, Quart 43.00
Seal, Mc Kearin 221-8, Embossed H.H.C., Tilts, C.1770, Black, Quart 74.00
Seal, N In Wreath, Green, Quart 1.00
Seal, P F Heering, Applied Ribbon, Dip Mold, Amber To Red Amber 38.00
Seal, P.S., Pontil, Olive Amber, 2 Quart 70.00
Seal, R.Lenox, Pontil, Olive Amber, Quart 60.00
Seal, Rev.J.B.Melhuish, Bristol Glass Works, Pontil, Olive Green, Quart 35.00
Seal, Rev.J.B.Melhuish, Open Pontil, Olive Green 60.00
Seal, Sam Archer, Pontil, Olive Amber, Quart 70.00
Seal, Sir Wm.Strickland, Pontil, Olive Amber, Quart 65.00
Seal, The Old Mill, Whitlock And Company .... *Color* XX.XX
Seal, Two Coats Of Arms, Olive Amber, Quart 5.00
Seal, Valitro, Clear, Pint 2.00
Seal, Vandenbergh & Co., Gin, Olive Amber, Quart 25.00
Seal, W.Ludlow, Pontil, Olive Amber, 2 Quart 200.00
Seal, Xavier De Lestapis, 1865, Green, Quart 3.00
Seal, 1875, Green, Quart 3.00
Seal, 1875, Olive Green, Quart 7.50

Seal, 1881 Special, Kopke Co., Olive Amber, Quart	4.00
Seltzer, Blue, 12 In.High	5.00
Seltzer, Ebony Beverage Co., Electric Blue	15.00
Seltzer, Etched Glass, Siphon	4.00
Seltzer, Fluted, Pewter Top, Siphon, Vaseline Glass	15.95
Seltzer, Harris Home Service, Brooklyn, Sapphire Blue	16.00
Seltzer, Label, Peacock Blue	4.00
Seltzer, Maiden's Blush Pink, 12 In.Tall	5.00
Seltzer, Pewter Top & Tubes, Hourglass Shape, Green	10.00
Seltzer, Pewter Top & Tubes, Made In Austria, Heavy Bottom, Blue Green	8.50
Seltzer, Pewter Top & Tubes, Round, Forest Green	6.00
Seltzer, Pewter Top & Tubes, Tapered, Made In Czechoslovakia, Blue	15.00
Seltzer, Pewter Top & Tubes, 10 Sided, Crystal Clear	7.00
Seltzer, Pewter Top & Tubes, 10 Sided, Emerald Green	7.50
Seltzer, Pewter Top, C.1800	2.00
Seltzer, Saratoga, Blue Green	100.00
Seltzer, Saratoga, Green	100.00
Seltzer, Siphon, Fluted, Sapphire Blue	9.00
Seltzer, Siphon, Hourglass Shape, Golden Amber	11.50
Seltzer, Ten Sided, Pewter Top, Siphon, Emerald Green	8.50
Seltzer, Ten Sided, Pewter Top, Siphon, Golden Amber	9.50
Seltzer, Ten Sided, Pewter Top, Siphon, Sapphire Blue	8.50
Seltzer, Vaseline Glass, Fluted, Pewter Top, Siphon	15.95
Shoe Polish, Bixby Embossed On Base, BIMAL , Aqua, 2 1/2 In.High	8.00
Shoe Polish, Bixby's Royal Polish, Embossed Patented 6, 83, BIMAL, Aqua	31.00
Shoe Polish, Eclipse, Green Amber	7.50
Shoe Polish, Gilt Edge Dressing, Pat.May 15, 1890, Aqua *Illus*	11.00
Shoe Polish, Howdy Doody	3.00
Shoe Polish, Shulife, Green Amber	7.50

Shoe Polish, Gilt Edge Dressing, Pat.May 15, 1890, Aqua

Shoe Polish, Stoddar Shoe Blacking, Oliver Amber, Pontil	35.00
Shoe Polish, Whittemore, Embossed, Label	7.00
Smelling Salts, Bullet Shape, 8 Sided, Emerald Green	4.00
Smelling Salts, Mc Kearin No.18, Blown In Mold, Aqua	20.00

Snuff bottles have been made since the eighteenth century. Glass, metal, ceramic, ivory, and precious stones were all used to make plain or elaborate snuff holders.

Snuff, Agate, White & Brown Pebbles Throughout, Green Stopper, Black	45.00
Snuff, Black, 4 1/2 In.Tall	15.00
Snuff, Carnelian & Metal Stopper, Smoky Crystal	85.00
Snuff, Carved Coral	80.00
Snuff, Carved Ivory, Scenic	37.50
Snuff, Chinese, Blue With Overlay Of Opal, Gold, Shell, & Turquoise, 3 In.	115.00
Snuff, Chinese, Brass, Inlaid Enamel, Champleve, 3 3/4 In.	120.00

Snuff, Chinese, Carved Agate, Natural Inclusion To Form Monkey In Cave 500.00
Snuff, Chinese, Carved Amber, 3 1/4 In.High 250.00
Snuff, Chinese, Carved Amethyst, Carved In Shape Of Monkey, 2 1/2 In. 300.00
Snuff, Chinese, Carved Cinnabar, 2 3/4 In.High 110.00
Snuff, Chinese, Carved Hornbill Beak, 4 1/4 In.Long X 3 1/3 In.High 625.00
Snuff, Chinese, Carved Ivory, Inscribed Scene On Reverse, 3 In. 10.00
Snuff, Chinese, Carved Ivory, 3 In.High 25.00
Snuff, Chinese, Carved Lapis Lazuli, 2 1/4 In. 230.00
Snuff, Chinese, Carved Opal, 2 1/4 In.High 225.00
Snuff, Chinese, Carved Peking Glass, Imperial Yellow, 3 In.High 100.00
Snuff, Chinese, Carved Peking, 6-Color Overlay, Floral, Carnelian, 1776-1808 .... 700.00
Snuff, Chinese, Carved Rattan Root, Black Coral, 2 1/2 In.High 25.00
Snuff, Chinese, Cloisonne, 4 1/4 In.High 65.00
Snuff, Chinese, Crystal, Inlaid Design, Natural Fracture, 2 5/8 In. 175.00
Snuff, Chinese, Fossilized Mammoth Tooth, 2 5/8 In. 375.00
Snuff, Chinese, Gourd, Engraved Scene On Front, Poem On Reverse, 2 3/4 In. 150.00
Snuff, Chinese, Hardstone Stopper, Spoon 19.95
Snuff, Chinese, Jade Stopper, Spoon 19.95
Snuff, Chinese, Laminated Shell, 2 1/2 In.High 35.00
Snuff, Chinese, Malachite, Carved With Dragon On Front, 2 3/4 In. 185.00
Snuff, Chinese, Mongolian, Inlays Of Coral & Turquoise, 3 1/4 In. 150.00
Snuff, Chinese, Mother-Of-Pearl, Inscribed Scenes On Front & Back 35.00
Snuff, Chinese, Mother-Of-Pearl, Overlay Designs, 3 In. 145.00
Snuff, Chinese, Pebble Jade, 2 3/4 In.High 75.00
Snuff, Chinese, Peking Glass, Inside Painting, 4 In.High 15.00
Snuff, Chinese, Reticulated Metal, Turquoise & Coral On Stopper, Screws In 175.00
Snuff, Chinese, Teakwood, Silver Inlay, 2 3/4 In.High 35.00
Snuff, Chinese, Zoisite, Ruby, Ruby Carved To Form 2 Swans, 2 3/8 In.High 175.00
Snuff, Cloisonne, Ching Dynasty 74.95
Snuff, Doc Marshall's, Blown In Mold, Open Pontil, Aqua .... 8.00 To 20.00
Snuff, Doc Marshall's, Embossed Pontil 22.00
Snuff, E.Roome, Open Pontil, Green 110.00
Snuff, E.Roome, Troy, New York, Bubbles, Dark Green 75.00
Snuff, Embossed Dutch Scene, Milk Glass, 5 1/2 In.High 8.50
Snuff, Helme's Railroad Mills, Amber, 3/4 Quart 10.00
Snuff, Interior Painted, Turquoise Stopper, Signed 35.00
Snuff, J.A.Gilka, Berlin, Reddish Type 14.00
Snuff, Jar, Heman 8.00
Snuff, Jar, Olive Amber, Blown 42.50
Snuff, Jar, Pontil, Olive Green 30.00
Snuff, Jar, Sheared Top, Olive Green 12.50
Snuff, Lapis Lazuli, Relief Carving Of Flowers & Animals 270.00
Snuff, Maccoboy, Paper Label, Rough Pontil, 4 1/4 In.High 125.00
Snuff, Mc Kearin 227, No.10, Beveled Corners, Open Pontil, Olive Green 38.00
Snuff, Mother-Of-Pearl, Ivory Panel On Each Side, Carved Tiger 65.00
Snuff, Mouth, Large Size 4.00
Snuff, Octagonal, Applied & Rolled Collar, Olive Green, 5 7/8 In. 160.00
Snuff, Octagonal, Applied Ring Around Neck, Dark Olive Green, 6 3/4 In. 65.00
Snuff, Octagonal, Rolled Lip, Offset Neck, Dark Olive Green, 5 In.High 100.00
Snuff, Olive Green, Round 50.00
Snuff, Open Pontil, Beveled Corners, Light Green 36.00
Snuff, Open Pontil, Bright Green 29.50
Snuff, Open Pontil, Flared Top, Dark Green, 2 1/2 In.High 32.50
Snuff, P.Lorillard, Jar, BIMAL, Ground Top, Dated Lid, Amber .... 8.00 To 12.00
Snuff, Painted Inside, Figures, Grasshoppers, Cabbages, & Beets 37.50
Snuff, Peking Glass, Painted From Inside 32.50
Snuff, Peking Glass, Red, Gray, & Green Veining, Jade Stopper 55.00
Snuff, Pitkin, Flaring Lip, Square, Olive Green, 6 1/16 In.High 165.00
Snuff, Pitkin, Octagonal, Flanged Lip, Light Olive Green, 6 5/8 In.High 165.00
Snuff, Porcelain, Red Lacquer 16.50
Snuff, Porcelain, Stopper, 3 In.High 12.95
Snuff, Rectangular, Crude, Green 20.00
Snuff, Rounded Shoulders, Chamfered Corners, 2 7/8 In.Square, Olive Amber 135.00
Snuff, Rounded Shoulders, Chamfered Corners, 3 2/7 In.Square, Olive Amber 135.00
Snuff, Rounded Shoulders, Diagonal Mold Line, Olive Green, 4 5/16 In.High 125.00
Snuff, Rounded Shoulders, Rough Pontil, Olive Green, 4 1/2 In.High 115.00

Snuff, Square, Open Pontil, Contents, Amber 35.00
Snuff, Weyman's 7.00

Soda bottles held soda pop or Coca-Cola or other carbonated drinks. Many soda bottles had a characteristic blob top. Hutchinson stoppers and Codd ball stoppers were also used.

Soda, see also Water

Soda, A.& D.H.C., Blob Top, Dug, Aqua 5.50
Soda, A.C.Gilligan, Cincinnati, Ohio, Eagle, Clear .... *Illus* 15.00
Soda, A.J.Nevers, Norway, Me., Blob Top, Fluted Bottom, Aqua 6.00
Soda, Adams & Sons, Halstead, Three Flowers In Center, 8 3/4 In.Embossed 4.15
Soda, Arkansas, Razorback Hog Embossed 5.00
Soda, Atlanta, Ga., Blob Top, Embossed 2.95
Soda, Atlanta, Ga., Blob Top, Embossed, Dug 2.95
Soda, Atlanta, Hutchinson, Embossed 3.00
Soda, Aunt Ida, Embossed, Green 4.00
Soda, Azule, Bear, Aqua 25.00
Soda, Azule, Bear, Light Green 45.00
Soda, Bay City, Cobalt 35.00
Soda, Benjamin D.Gall, Miniature, Steam Power Mineral Water Works, Aqua 16.50
Soda, Bill Mills, Honey Amber, Squat 12.00
Soda, Binder Bros., Yankton, S.D. .... .75
Soda, Blob Top, Blue Green 20.00
Soda, Blob Top, Dug, Aqua 3.50
Soda, Blob Top, Round Bottom 2.00
Soda, Blob Top, Torpedo 3.25
Soda, Boonerock Ginger Ale, Figure Of Daniel Boone Shooting Gun, Green 2.25
Soda, Bottling Works, Marion, Ohio, Hutchinson 12.00
Soda, Brownie, Embossed, Clear 8.00
Soda, Buffalo Ginger Ale, 2 Buffalo Heads Embossed, Clear 1.75
Soda, C.& K.Eagle Soda Works, Sac City 35.00
Soda, C.C.& Co., Blob Top, Aqua 6.00
Soda, C.L.Kornahrens, Charleston, S.C., Blob Top, Dug, Aqua 8.00
Soda, C.R.Wigert, Burlington, Ia., C.1870, Aqua 4.00
Soda, Canada Dry Water 5.00
Soda, Canada Dry, Carnival, White 6.00
Soda, Canada Dry, Carnival, Yellow 6.00
Soda, Canada Dry, Dated 1923, Label, Carnival Glass, Marigold 22.00
Soda, Canada Dry, Dated 1923, Label, Carnival Glass, White 22.00
Soda, Canada Dry, Dated 1926, Label, Carnival Glass, Marigold 22.00
Soda, Canada Dry, Dated 1926, Label, Carnival Glass, White 22.00
Soda, Canada Dry, Lyndon B.Johnson, Label 50.00
Soda, Canada Dry, Paper Label 3.00
Soda, Canal, Dover, Hutchinson's, Blob Top, Aqua 5.00
Soda, Cantrell & Cochrane, Dublin, Medicated Aerated Water, Round Bottom 6.00
Soda, Carnation, Embossed 2.98
Soda, Carnation, Enameled On Front 2.98
Soda, Carnival Glass, Marigold 19.00
Soda, Carpenter & Cobb, Knickerbocker Soda Water, Saratoga Springs, Cobalt 75.00
Soda, Centennial, 1925, Carnival 12.00
Soda, Champagne Mead, Aqua 35.00
Soda, Charles Bauer, Laporte, Ind., Blob Top, Dug, Cobalt Blue 32.50
Soda, Cliquot Club, Aqua, 10 In. 5.00
Soda, Comstock Gove & Co., Canal Street, Boston, Aqua, Blob Top 8.00
Soda, Constitutional Beverage, Amber 20.00
Soda, Coppahaunk Ginger Ale Springs, Embossed Indian, ABM , Aqua 5.00
Soda, Crown Top, Embossed, West Virginia 2.00
Soda, Crown Top, Milk Glass 6.00
Soda, Crown Top, Round Bottom 1.00
Soda, Crystal Soda Co., Windber, Pa., Stopper, Light Green, Hutchinson 3.50
Soda, Crystal Soda Water Co., Patented Nov.12, 1872, Cobalt 60.00
Soda, Crystal Spring, Barnet, Hutchinson 5.00
Soda, D.Brown, Graphite Pontil, Green, 6 1/2 In. .... *Illus* 65.00
Soda, D.J.Whelan Troy, New York, Hutchinson 6.00
Soda, Distilled Soda Water Co.Of Alaska, Blob, Hutchinson, Embossed 35.00
Soda, Donald Duck 5.00

Soda, D.Brown,
Graphite Pontil,
Green, 6 1/2 In.
See Page 196

Soda, A.C.Gilligan, Cincinnati, Ohio, Eagle, Clear
See Page 196

Soda, **Dr.Pepper**, Clock	1.50
Soda, **Drink L.A.W.5 Cents**, Quenches The Thirst, Pewter Top	5.00
Soda, **E.Ottenville**, Nashville, Tenn., Blob Top, Cobalt	50.00
Soda, **E.Sheehan**, 1880, Augusta, Ga., Embossed, Blob Top, Amber	12.00
Soda, **E.W.F.Rice & Co.**, Boston, Blob Top, Iron Pontil, Cornflower Blue	70.00
Soda, **Eagle Soda Works**, Sac City, Miniature, Whittled, Tapered, Cobalt Blue	35.00
Soda, **Eagle**, Blob Top, Green	100.00
Soda, **Eagle**, Cobalt Blue .... *Color*	XX.XX
Soda, **Eight Sided**, Glob Collar, Green	45.00
Soda, **Elmers Medicated**, Cobalt Blue .... *Color*	XX.XX
Soda, **Embossed**, Crown Top	2.00
Soda, **Embossed**, Iron Pontil, Tapered Collar, Stain, Emerald Green	19.00
Soda, **Emerald Green**	7.50
Soda, **English**, Screw-In Stopper, Embossed	5.00
Soda, **Eye-Se**, Embossed, Clear	4.00
Soda, **Fanta**	1.10
Soda, **Fanta**, Miniature, Coca-Cola Product, Threaded Design, Capped & Filled	.50
Soda, **Fanta**, Miniature, Threaded Design, Fanta Label, Filled & Capped	.50
Soda, **Fanta**, Miniature, Threaded Design, 3 In.Tall	4.00
Soda, **Five Points**, Embossed, Clear	4.00
Soda, **G.A.Tole**, Litchfield, Ill., Blob Top, Aqua	12.50
Soda, **G.Cemenden**, Pontil, Green	35.00
Soda, **Gardner Bros.**, Greencastle, Indiana, Heavy	3.00
Soda, **Ginger Ale**, Boonerock, Daniel Boone Shooting Gun, Emerald Green	2.25
Soda, **Ginger Ale**, Boonerock, Embossed Daniel Boone Shooting, Emerald	2.25
Soda, **Ginger Ale**, Boonerock, Painted, Aqua	1.25
Soda, **Ginger Ale**, Buffalo, Embossed Buffalo Heads, Clear	1.75
Soda, **Ginger Ale**, Hutchinson Type, Norway, Me., Aqua	6.00
Soda, **Ginger Ale**, Meincke & Ebbenwein, 1882, Savannah, Ga., Amber	25.00
Soda, **Ginger Beer**, Debossed J.Stoechert, New Ulm, Pottery, Sand Color	12.00
Soda, **Ginger Beer**, Pottery, Embossed Name	3.50
Soda, **Ginger**, Stoneware, Screw-In Stopper, English, Marked	4.00
Soda, **Grape Smash**, Clear, Glass Label, 12 In. .... *Color*	XX.XX
Soda, **Henry Kuck Savannah**, Green	13.00
Soda, **Henry Kuck**, Emerald	22.00
Soda, **Henry Lubbs**, 1885, Emerald	22.00
Soda, **Hires** Porcelain Cap, Embossed, Tall	7.00
Soda, **Hires Root Beer**	7.00
Soda, **Hires**, Blob Top	5.00
Soda, **Hutchinson**, Aqua, Quart	8.00
Soda, **Hutchinson**, Atlanta, Embossed, BIMAL, Dug	3.00
Soda, **Hutchinson**, Eagle	10.50
Soda, **Hutchinson**, Embossed Pennsylvania	5.00
Soda, **Hutchinson**, Hand Blown, Wire Loop Controlled Rubber Gasket, Aqua	4.50

Soda, Hutchinson, New Jersey	3.25
Soda, Hutchinson, Rubber Gasket, Aqua	4.50
Soda, I Brownell, New Bedford, This Bottle Never Sold, Blob Top, Cobalt	48.00
Soda, Independent Bottling Works, Chicago, Blob Top, Blue Green	2.00
Soda, Ingalls Bros., Portland, Maine, Applied Top, Light Green, 7 In.High	30.00
Soda, J.A.Dearborn, N.Y., Iron Pontil, Medium Cobalt	30.00
Soda, J.Cosgrove, Charlston, Monogram	40.00
Soda, J.H.Rymer, Applied Collar, Inside Threads, Aqua	9.00
Soda, J.Hindle & Co., Applied Collar, Inside Threads, Green	12.00
Soda, J.Lyon, Newark, Ohio	12.00
Soda, J.P.Benjamin, 13 State St., N.Y., Union Glass Works, Blob, Cobalt	70.00
Soda, J.R.Donald, Newark, N.J., 7 In., Cobalt Blue *Color*	XX.XX
Soda, J.Rowens, Parkesburg, Pa., Green, 7 1/2 In. *Illus*	75.00
Soda, J.Wise, Allentown, Pa., 6 1/2 In. *Color*	XX.XX
Soda, Jackson's Napa, Aqua	5.00
Soda, James Ray, Savannah, Ga., Blob Top, Aqua	5.50
Soda, John Graf, Blob Top, Hutchinson Stopper, Green	5.00
Soda, John L.Gebhardt, Boston, Blob Top, Dark Green, 10 In.	9.00
Soda, John Ryan Excelsior Soda Works, Ga., Blob Top, Graphite Pontil, Cobalt	40.00
Soda, John Ryan, Excelsior, Union Glass Works, Blob Top	28.00
Soda, Jos.Allgair, Sayerville, N.J., Aqua, 9 In., Hutchinson	5.00
Soda, Keys, Burlington, N.J., Blob Top, Dug, Pontil, Green	39.50
Soda, Kimball & Co., Pontil, Blob Top, Dug, Cobalt Blue	39.50
Soda, L & R Morton, Improved Pontil, Encrusted, Green, 1/2 Pint	21.00
Soda, L.Werbach, Milwaukee, Blob Top, Cobalt	35.00
Soda, Lancaster Glass Works, N.Y., Blob Top, Pontil, Cobalt	40.00
Soda, Levi Bender, Williamsport, Pa., Blob Top	7.50
Soda, Lime Cola, Embossed, Clear	4.00
Soda, Lock Haven, Pa., 10 Sided, Blown In Mold, Aqua, Hutchinson	7.00
Soda, M.Mc Cormack, Blob, Cobalt	32.50
Soda, M.Mc Cormack, Stain, Amber	19.00
Soda, Marion Bottling Works, Embossed, Marion, Kansas, Applied Crown Top	2.00
Soda, Marion Bottling Works, Marion, Kans., Applied Crown, Embossed	2.00
Soda, Maui Soda Works, Embossed, Blob Top	12.00
Soda, Mission Dry, Black Glass	2.50
Soda, Mission Orange, Black Amethyst	8.00
Soda, Mobile, Ala., Blob Top, Embossed	2.95
Soda, Mobile, Ala., Blob Top, Embossed, Dug	2.95
Soda, Moshers Steam Bottling Works, Pa., 10 Panels, Clear, Hutchinson	12.00
Soda, Moxie Nerve Food, Aqua, Quart	4.00
Soda, Moxie, Applied Label, 7 Oz.	8.00
Soda, Moxie, Green	3.50
Soda, Moxie, Inscribed On Front & Back, 7 Oz., Aqua, 8 In.Tall	2.00
Soda, Moxie, Star On Base, Aqua	3.00
Soda, Moxie's, Brown Top, Label, Aqua, Blob Top, 7 Oz.	3.00
Soda, Murray Bottling Works, Muncy, Pa., Blob Top, Aqua	6.00
Soda, N.S.D.A.1967 Convention, Enameled Scenes Of Houston, Cobalt	10.00
Soda, Nesbitt Orange, Square, July 20, 1920, Amber	6.00
Soda, New Orleans & Complete Street Address, Bluish Green, Embossed	5.00
Soda, Nu-Icy, Embossed, Clear	4.00
Soda, Olmstead Constitutional Beverage, Cloudy, Yellow Green	190.00
Soda, Olney, Ills., Gravitating Stopper, Blob Top, Dug, Aqua	10.50
Soda, One Tall One, Ohio, June 21, 1927, Clear *Illus*	4.00
Soda, Orange & Lemon Crush	3.00
Soda, Orange Crush, Amber	1.00
Soda, Orange Crush, Full, Label	11.00
Soda, Orange Julep, Clear, Glass Label *Color*	XX.XX
Soda, Owen Casey, Eagle Soda Works, Sac City	40.00
Soda, P.F.Heering, Blob Top, Whittled, Amber	30.00
Soda, Pacific Soda Works, Glassen & Co., S.F., Aqua	20.00
Soda, Parrot, Independence, Mo., Embossed Parrot	4.95
Soda, Paul Pohl, Chicago, Ill., Blob Top, Dug, Amber	24.50
Soda, Pepsi-Cola, Amber	22.50
Soda, Pepsi-Cola, Birmingham, Ala., Amber	35.00
Soda, Pepsi-Cola, Embossed	5.00
Soda, Pepsi, Light Amber	30.00

Soda, J.Rowens, Parkesburg,
Pa., Green, 7 1/2 In.
See Page 198

Soda, One Tall One,
Ohio, June 21, 1927, Clear
See Page 198

Soda, **Pepsi**, Straight Letters, Embossed	5.00
Soda, **Perrin's Apple Ginger**, Amber	80.00
Soda, **Pfaff & Hanscom**, Boston, P & H On Reverse, Aqua	8.00
Soda, **Pittsburgh Bottling House**, Squat, Aqua	14.00
Soda, **Quinan & Studer**, 1888, Savannah, Ga., Cobalt	22.00
Soda, **R.C.Cola**, Applied Label, 12 Oz.	2.00
Soda, **Root Beer**, Amber	35.00
Soda, **Root Beer**, Brown	15.00
Soda, **Ross's**, Belfast, Round Bottom, Applied Lip	5.00
Soda, **Ross's**, Belfast, Round Bottom, Cloudy	3.50
Soda, **Round Bottom**, Blob Top	3.00
Soda, **Round Bottom**, Crown Top	1.00
Soda, **Royal Crown Cola**, 25 In.Tall	6.00
Soda, **Russ**, Harrisburg, Pa., Aqua, Pint	5.00
Soda, **S.F.Glass Works**, Aqua	15.00
Soda, **S.Smiths**, 7 In., Cobalt Blue *Color*	XX.XX
Soda, **Schmuck's Ginger Ale**, Cleveland, Ohio, Aqua	5.00
Soda, **Seitz And Bros.**, Easton, Pa., Embossed, Blob Top, Green	12.50
Soda, **Seitz And Bros.**, Easton, Pa., 7 In., Cobalt *Color*	XX.XX
Soda, **Seitz**, Easton, Pa., S On Back, Green	12.00
Soda, **Selino Orange Flower Water**	1.00
Soda, **Seven-Up**, Front Enamel, Amber	10.00
Soda, **Seven-Up**, Painted Label, Amber	7.00
Soda, **Seven-Up**, Squat, Amber	9.00
Soda, **Sprite**	1.10
Soda, **Sprite**, Miniature, Filled, Capped, Case Of 24	9.00
Soda, **Sprite**, Miniature, Hobnail, Emblem, Filled & Capped, Green, 3 In.Tall	.50
Soda, **Sprite**, Miniature, Hobnail, Green, Filled & Capped	.50
Soda, **Spur**	8.50
Soda, **Standard Bottling Works**, Aqua, Pint	3.00
Soda, **Star Boy**, Cathedral, Dated, Aqua, 7 Oz.	2.25
Soda, **Star Boy**, Cathedral, Dated, Aqua, 9 Oz.	2.25
Soda, **Star Boy**, Cathedral, Dated, Green, 7 Oz.	2.25
Soda, **Star Boy**, Cathedral, Dated, Green, 9 Oz.	2.25
Soda, **Star Brand Super Strong With Star**, Marble Stopper, Aqua	7.45
Soda, **Sunnybrook Bottling Works**, Suffolk, Peanuts Embossed, Clear	5.00
Soda, **Sunnybrook Bottling Works**, Suffolk, Va., Pat'D Oct.1929, Clear	5.00
Soda, **Superior**, Eagle & Shield, Flags, Emerald Green	160.00
Soda, **Tampa**, Fla., Blob Top, Embossed	2.95
Soda, **Tampa**, Fla., Blob Top, Embossed, Dug	2.95
Soda, **Taylor Never Surrenders**, Cobalt Blue *Color*	XX.XX
Soda, **Teal**, A.C., Westlake, Star, Auburn, N.Y., Agw, 1876 On Base, Cobalt	28.00
Soda, **The Original 3 Cent Drink**, Embossed, Green, 6 Oz.	5.00
Soda, **Thos.Maher**, Crude Slug Plate, Green, 7 In.Tall	25.00

Soda, Thos.Maher, Embossed, Iron Pontil, Slightly Cloudy, Emerald Green	25.00
Soda, Thos.Maher, Sunburst, Savannah, Geo., Emerald Green	30.00
Soda, Torpedo, Blob Top, Hazy	3.00
Soda, Torpedo, Schweppes, Blob Top	10.00
Soda, Turkey Coke, Embossed	27.50
Soda, Uncle Jo, Embossed, Amber	4.00
Soda, Union Glassware, Philadelphia, Cobalt Blue .... Color	XX.XX
Soda, Union Glassworks, J & A Dearborn, Cobalt .... Color	XX.XX
Soda, Utah, Crown Top	3.00
Soda, W.E.Brockway, N.Y., Green, Iron Pontil	48.00
Soda, W.Eagle Vestry Varick, Aqua	10.00
Soda, W.Garrison, Louisville, Blob, Aqua, Iron Pontil	34.50
Soda, Western, Deer's Head	4.50
Soda, Wintle & Sons, Blob Top, Honey	12.50
Soda, Wm.Fanning, Monroeville, Ohio, Hutchinson	12.00
Soda, York Wine & Spirit Co., St.Helen's Square, York, Corker, Embossed	3.50
Soda, Zetz 7-Up Bottling Co., Inc., Sparkling Water, New Orleans, Enamel	15.00
Soda, 10 Sided, Pontil, Cobalt	125.00
Southern Comfort, Limoges Signed	750.00
Spirit, Cylinder, Black Glass, Olive Amber, Quart	5.00
Spirit, France, 4 Way	15.00
Spirit, Kidney Shape, Ring Around Sheared Mouth, Olive Amber, 7 1/4 In.High	8.00
Spirit, Made In France, 4 Parts	28.00
Spirit, Open Pontil, Bubbles, Clear Grass Green	29.00
Spirit, Pint	12.50
Spirit, Pontil, Olive Green, 10 1/2 In.High	10.00
Spirit, Westford, Scarred Pontil, Red Amber, Pint	10.00
Spirit, Whiskey Shape, Blue	40.00
Spirit, 3 Mold, Black Glass, Quart	6.00
Spirit, 3 Mold, Push-Up Pontil, Blue Color Base, Pint	10.00
Stiegel Type, Case, Applied Neck, Cut Decoration, Penn., C.1767, Clear	200.00
Stiegel Type, Cordial, Enameled Bell Ringer Figure, Ground Stopper	150.00
Stiegel Type, German Words On Back, Red, Blue, & Yellow .... Illus	180.00
Stoddard, Free-Blown	15.00
Stoneware, Jug, Pear, B.Edmonds & Co., Charlestown, Brown Glaze	50.00
Stoneware, 3 Liters, 14 In.High	11.50
Strikow, Totem Pole	10.00
Three Mold, Arnas, Amber	4.00
Three Mold, Ellensville Glass Works, Cylinder, I.P., Olive Green, 11 1/2 In.	19.00
Three Mold, H.Ricketts Glass Works On Base, Bristol, Pontil, Olive Amber	13.00
Three Mold, Olive, 12 In.	4.50
Three Mold, Pulled Neck, Olive Green	275.00
Three Mold, Refired Pontil, Black	5.00
Three Mold, Weeks & Potter, Boston, Inside Screw Threads, Amber, Quart	10.00

Stiegel Type, German Words On Back,
Red, Blue, & Yellow

Three Mold, Whitney Glass Works On Base, Inside Screw, Glass Stopper, Amber	16.00
Three Mold, Whitney Glass Works, Cylinder, Patent On Shoulder, Aqua, 11 In.	13.00
Three Mold, Whitney Glass Works, Glassboro, N.J. Embossed On Base, Citron	10.00
Three Mold, Whittled, R.Cooper & Co., Portobello Embossed On Base, Olive	10.00
Three Part Mold, Dyottville Glass Works, Phila.On Base, Patent, Amber	20.00
Tobacco, Globe Tobacco Company, Detroit, Pat.Oct.10, 1882, Tin Cover, Amber	25.00
Tobacco, P.Lorillard, Amber	11.50
Toilet Water, Blown, Expanded Collar, Clear	10.00
Toilet Water, Mc Kearin G I-29, Cobalt Blue, 1/2 Pint	150.00
Toilet Water, Milk Glass	11.00
Toilet Water, Milk Glass, Enameled Floral, Blue	30.00
Toilet Water, Ribbed, Single Collar On Neck, Amethyst	200.00
Toilet Water, Sandwich, Double Ring Neck, Stopper, Cobalt Blue	140.00
Toilet Water, Sandwich, Ribbed, Single Collar, Stopper, Cobalt Blue	140.00
Vaseline Glass, Opal Stripes, Small Size	60.00
Vial, Wooden, Stopper, 2 1/2 In.High	1.25
Vinegar, Apple Juice, Panel Duffy, 1842, Amber, 6 3/4 In.	6.00
Vinegar, Champion's, Australia, Sun Purpled, 13 In.	30.00
Vinegar, White House, Embossed White House, Aqua	10.00
Vinegar, White House, Embossed, Gallon	8.00
Vinegar, White House, Embossed, Pint	4.00
Vinegar, White House, Embossed, Quart	4.00
Vinegar, White House, Embossed, 1/2 Gallon	5.00
Vinegar, White House, Embossed, 1/2 Pint	10.00
Vinegar, White House, Floral Pattern, Vase Form, ABM , Clear	8.50
Vinegar, White House, Globe Shape, Emerald Green, Quart	12.00
Vinegar, White House, Pour Spout, Pat.1909, Quart	12.00
Water, see also Soda	
Water, Abilene Natural Cathartic, Amber	2.00
Water, Canute Water Embossed, Rectangular, Amber	10.00
Water, Congress Empire Springs, Saratoga, New York	25.00
Water, Empire Spring, Quart	16.00
Water, Gettysburg Katalysine, Emerald Green, Quart	24.00
Water, Hathorn Spring	25.00

Mineral water was first bottled about 1828 in the United States.
Embossed bottles that held mineral spring waters are usually the only ones
included in this category.
Mineral water bottles held the fresh natural spring waters favored for
health and taste. Most of the bottles collected today date from the 1850-
1900 period. Many of these bottles have blob tops.

Water, Mineral, Alburgh Springs, Amber, Quart	75.00
Water, Mineral, Aqua De Florida	3.00
Water, Mineral, Artesian Spring Co., Ballston, N.Y., Emerald Green, Pint	35.00
Water, Mineral, Ballston Spa Artesian Spring Co., Green, Pint	30.00
Water, Mineral, Bear Lithia, Embossed Polar Bear, 1/2 Gallon	19.00
Water, Mineral, Beaverdam Bottling Co., Beaver On Bottom, Aqua	3.00
Water, Mineral, Bedford, Saratoga Type, Iron Pontil, Amber, Pint	175.00
Water, Mineral, Buffalo Lithia, Embossed Women, Aqua, 10 In. 8.00 To	16.00
Water, Mineral, Buffalo Lithia, Whittled, 1/2 Gallon, Aqua	8.50
Water, Mineral, Carlsbad L.S. on Bottom, Applied Collar, Round, Green, Quart	6.95
Water, Mineral, Cascadian Spring Co., Grandview, N.Y., Embossed, Aqua, Gallon	20.00
Water, Mineral, Chemung Spring, Indian, Embossed, Aqua, Gallon	35.00
Water, Mineral, Clark & Co., Highly Whittled, Quart	45.00
Water, Mineral, Clark & White Large C, Near Black, Quart	34.50
Water, Mineral, Clark & White Spring, Green	22.00
Water, Mineral, Clark & White Spring, Whittled, Dark Green, Quart	29.00
Water, Mineral, Clark & White, C.N.Y., Dark Emerald, Pint	24.50
Water, Mineral, Clark & White, Emerald Green, Pint	25.00
Water, Mineral, Clark & White, New York, Olive Green	20.00
Water, Mineral, Clark & White, New York, Pontil, Olive Green	35.00
Water, Mineral, Clark & White, Olive Green, Quart	17.50
Water, Mineral, Clark & White, Pint	16.00
Water, Mineral, Clark & White, Quart, Emerald Green	35.00
Water, Mineral, Codd, Embossed 1890, England	11.00
Water, Mineral, Congress & Empire Co., Saratoga, N.Y., Whittled, Green	27.50

Water, Mineral, Congress & Empire Spring Co., Contents, Green, Pint 20.00
Water, Mineral, Congress & Empire Spring Co., Emerald Green, Pint 20.00
Water, Mineral, Congress & Empire Spring Co., Green, Pint 15.00
Water, Mineral, Congress & Empire Spring Co., Light Green 15.00
Water, Mineral, Congress & Empire Spring Co., Saratoga, N.Y., Emerald, Pint 37.50
Water, Mineral, Congress & Empire Spring Co., Saratoga, N.Y., Emerald, Quart 18.00
Water, Mineral, Congress & Empire Spring Co., Saratoga, N.Y., Olive, Pint 18.00
Water, Mineral, Congress & Empire, Green, Quart 27.00
Water, Mineral, Congress & Empire, Hotchkiss & Sons 24.00
Water, Mineral, Congress & Empire, Large C, Saratoga, Green, Pint 19.50
Water, Mineral, Congress Spring Co., Pint, Emerald Green 20.00
Water, Mineral, D.A.Knowlton, Saratoga, N.Y., Black, Quart 26.00
Water, Mineral, E.P.Shaw & Co., Gold Medal Award, Wakefield 3.00
Water, Mineral, E.P.Shaw, Wakefield, Gold Medal Award, London, 1903 .... 3.00
Water, Mineral, E.P.Shaw, Wakefield, 7 In. 3.00
Water, Mineral, E.P.Shaw, Wakefield, 9 1/2 In. 3.00
Water, Mineral, Embossed Wootan Wells, Tex., Blood Purifier, Aqua 20.00
Water, Mineral, Friedrichshall Oppell & Cr. 5.00
Water, Mineral, G.W.Merchant, Lockport, New York, Green 55.00
Water, Mineral, G.W.Weston & Co., Saratoga Type, Dark Olive Green 60.00
Water, Mineral, G.W.Weston & Co., Saratoga, N.Y., Olive Green, Quart 375.00
Water, Mineral, Gettysburg Katalasine, Emerald Green, Quart 40.00
Water, Mineral, Geyser Spring, Pint 24.00
Water, Mineral, Guilford Mineral & Spring, Vt., Green, Quart 29.00
Water, Mineral, Guper Spring, The Saratoga Spouting Spring, Aqua 20.00
Water, Mineral, Hanbury Smith, Olive 45.00
Water, Mineral, Hanbury Smith, Vichy Water, Aqua 15.00
Water, Mineral, Haskin's Spring Co., Shutesbury, Mass., Emerald Green, Quart 85.00
Water, Mineral, Hathorn Spring, Amber, Quart .... 18.00 To 25.00
Water, Mineral, Hathorn Spring, Emerald Green 25.00
Water, Mineral, Hathorn Springs, Olive Amber 20.00
Water, Mineral, Hathorn Springs, Pint, Emerald Green 27.00
Water, Mineral, Hathorn Springs, Saratoga, N.Y., Black, Pint 15.00
Water, Mineral, Hathorn Springs, Saratoga, N.Y., Black, Quart 15.00
Water, Mineral, Hathorn Springs, Saratoga, N.Y., Green 25.00
Water, Mineral, Highrock Congress Springs, C & W, Rock In Center, Oiled 25.00
Water, Mineral, Holmes & Co., Pontil 30.00
Water, Mineral, Honesdale Glass Works, Graphite, Emerald 45.00
Water, Mineral, Honeymoon, Poland Spring, Green 16.00
Water, Mineral, Hopkins' Chalybete, Baltimore, Saratoga Type, Blue Green, Pt. 37.50
Water, Mineral, Hotchkiss & Sons, Spring Water, Dark Green 28.00
Water, Mineral, Improved, Blue 40.00
Water, Mineral, John Clarke, New York, 3 Piece Mold, Dark Olive Amber, Quart 85.00
Water, Mineral, John Clarke, Pontil, Olive Amber, Quart 42.50
Water, Mineral, John Ryan, Excelsior Union Glass Works 38.75
Water, Mineral, John Ryan, Excelsior, Savannah, Ga., Union Glass Works, Cobalt 32.50
Water, Mineral, Kernan & Co. 12.00
Water, Mineral, Kissingen, Hanbury Smith 45.00
Water, Mineral, Laurential L.Sylva, Montreal, Clear, 2 Quart 12.50
Water, Mineral, Lynch & Clark, New York, Olive Amber 115.00
Water, Mineral, Lynch & Clark, Olive Amber, Pontil, Pint 75.00
Water, Mineral, Madden Co., Clarendon Springs, Round Bottom, 7 In.High 3.00
Water, Mineral, Mardela Springs, Mardela, Md. 7.00
Water, Mineral, Meincke Ebberwein, Cobalt, 8 In. 25.00
Water, Mineral, Middletown Healing Springs, Grays & Clarke, Amber, Quart 30.00
Water, Mineral, Minnehaha Natural Spring, Light Aqua .... *Illus*   20.00
Water, Mineral, Missisquoi Springs, Amber, Quart 30.00
Water, Mineral, Moses, H.Ricker & Sons, Poland Spring, Maine, Aqua, Quart 40.00
Water, Mineral, Moses, H.Ricker & Sons, Poland Spring, Maine, Clear, Quart 25.00
Water, Mineral, Moses, H.Ricker & Sons Proprietors, Poland, Aquamarine 75.00
Water, Mineral, Oak Orchard Acid Springs, Lockport, N.Y., Green, Quart 33.00
Water, Mineral, Olympia Water Co., Mineral Wells, Tex., BIMAL , Aqua, Gal. 10.00
Water, Mineral, Pequot Spring, Glastonbury, Conn., Clear, 5 Pints 6.00
Water, Mineral, Pluto, America's Physic, Embossed, Aqua 3.50
Water, Mineral, Pluto, Embossed Devil, French Lick, Ind., Aqua, Quart 10.00

Water, Mineral, Poland Spring, Honeymoon, Green, Quart 12.50
Water, Mineral, Red Saratoga Springs, Green, Pint 35.00
Water, Mineral, Saratoga & Empire Springs, Whittled, Emerald, Quart 25.00
Water, Mineral, Saratoga Spring, Green, Pint 19.00
Water, Mineral, Saratoga Spring, Green, Quart 24.00
Water, Mineral, Saratoga Type, 1820-40, Iron Pontil, Olive Green 50.00
Water, Mineral, Saxlehener, Label, Green 3.00
Water, Mineral, St.Leon Spring, Light Green 62.50
Water, Mineral, St.Regis, Massena Springs, Black Glass, Quart 60.00
Water, Mineral, Star Spring Co., Amber, Pint 30.00
Water, Mineral, Star Spring Co., Misshaped, Olive Green 15.00
Water, Mineral, Star Spring Co., Saratoga, N.Y., Amber 35.00
Water, Mineral, Sterling Springs, Hancock Michigan 9.50
Water, Mineral, Superior, Union Glassworks, Harrisburg, Green 230.00
Water, Mineral, Superior, Union Glassworks, Phila., Blue 130.00
Water, Mineral, Sweetwater Springs, Cal., 1/2 Gallon 4.50
Water, Mineral, Veronica Medicinal Spring Water, Amber, Quart 6.00
Water, Mineral, Veronica Medicinal Spring, Square, BIMAL , 10 1/2 In. 4.00
Water, Mineral, Vichy, Hanbury Smith, Embossed, Emerald Green, 7 In. 35.00
Water, Mineral, Waukesha Imperial Spring Co., Green .... *Illus* 1.50
Water, Mineral, Whelan Troy, 1881, Hutchinson, Embossed Tulips 12.75
Water, Mineral, White Rock Mineral Spring Co., Brown .... *Illus* 1.75

Water, Mineral,
Minnehaha Natural Spring,
Light Aqua
See Page 202

Water, Mineral,
White Rock
Mineral Spring Co., Brown

Water, Mineral,
Waukesha Imperial Spring Co., Green

Water, Moses, see Figural, Moses., Whiskey, Hiram Ricker
Water, Oak Orchard, Acid Springs, H.W.Bostwich 35.00
Water, Pewter Neck & Top, White & Green Enameled Floral, Cobalt Blue 37.50
Water, Pluto, Devil Embossed, French Lick, Indiana, Cork Top, Aqua, Quart 10.00
Water, Round Lake Mineral Water, Saratoga County, N.Y. .... *Color* XX.XX
Water, Royal Crystal, Pressed Glass 15.00
Water, Shanon Sulphur, Pint 31.00
Water, Sno-Top, Distilled, Label, Clear 4.00
Water, Spring, Seal Rock Spring Water, Silas Gurnery, Boston, Blue, Quart 55.00
Water, Teepee 15.00
Water, Vartray Crystal, Blob Top, Clear, 1/2 Gallon 9.50
Wedgwood, Sandman, Left 11.95
Wedgwood, Sandman, Right 11.95

Wheaton Company was established in 1888. The firm made hand-blown and pressed glassware. In 1938 automatic equipment was added and many molded glass items were made. Wheaton-Nuline now makes all types of containers for pharmaceuticals and cosmetics and foods, as well as gift shop antique-style bottles.

Wheaton Commemorative, Abraham Lincoln, Topaz, 1968		7.00 To 30.00
Wheaton Commemorative, Andrew Jackson, Green, 1971	Color	10.00
Wheaton Commemorative, Apollo 11, Blue, 1969		20.00 To 35.00
Wheaton Commemorative, Apollo 12, Ruby, 1969		30.00 To 40.00
Wheaton Commemorative, Apollo 13, Burley, 1970		5.00 To 12.00
Wheaton Commemorative, Apollo 14, Aqua, 1971	Color	5.00
Wheaton Commemorative, Apollo 15, Green, 1971	Color	5.00
Wheaton Commemorative, Apollo 16, Iridescent Flint, 1972		5.00
Wheaton Commemorative, Benjamin Franklin, Aqua, 1970		5.00 To 16.00
Wheaton Commemorative, Betsy Ross, Ruby, 1969		5.00 To 12.00
Wheaton Commemorative, Billy Graham, Green, 1970		5.00 To 12.00
Wheaton Commemorative, Charles A.Lindbergh, Blue, 1968		5.00 To 12.00
Wheaton Commemorative, Charles Evans Hughes, Blue, 1971		5.00 To 7.00
Wheaton Commemorative, Christmas, 1971, Green Frosted, 1971		7.00
Wheaton Commemorative, Christmas, Unfrosted, 1971	Color	10.00
Wheaton Commemorative, Christmas, Topaz, 1972	Color	5.00
Wheaton Commemorative, Democrat, Donkey, Green, 1968		10.00 To 16.00
Wheaton Commemorative, Democrat, Mcgovern, Eagleton, 1972		10.00
Wheaton Commemorative, Democrat, Mcgovern, Shriver, 1972		10.00
Wheaton Commemorative, Douglas Macarthur, Amethyst, 1968		5.00 To 11.00
Wheaton Commemorative, Franklin D.Roosevelt, Green, 1967		10.00 To 25.00
Wheaton Commemorative, General Patton, Aqua, 1971		5.00
Wheaton Commemorative, George Washington, Frosted Flint, 1969		5.00 To 12.50
Wheaton Commemorative, Helen Keller, Frosted Flint, 1970		5.00
Wheaton Commemorative, Herbert C.Hoover, Aqua, 1972	Color	5.00
Wheaton Commemorative, Humphrey Bogart, Green, 1971	Color	5.00
Wheaton Commemorative, Jean Harlow, Topaz, 1972	Color	5.00
Wheaton Commemorative, John F.Kennedy, Blue, 1967		30.00 To 50.00
Wheaton Commemorative, John Paul Jones, Green, 1970		5.00
Wheaton Commemorative, Lee W.Minton, Blue, 1971		10.00
Wheaton Commemorative, Martin Luther King, Amber, 1968		10.00 To 32.00
Wheaton Commemorative, Paul Revere, Blue, 1971		5.00 To 8.00
Wheaton Commemorative, President Eisenhower, Green, 1969		6.00 To 35.00
Wheaton Commemorative, Republican, Elephant, Topaz, 1968		10.00 To 16.00
Wheaton Commemorative, Republican, 1972		10.00
Wheaton Commemorative, Robert E.Lee, Green, 1969		5.00 To 10.00
Wheaton Commemorative, Robert F.Kennedy, Green, 1968		10.00 To 24.00
Wheaton Commemorative, Sheriff's Association, Blue, 1971		15.00
Wheaton Commemorative, Theodore Roosevelt, Blue, 1970		5.00 To 12.50
Wheaton Commemorative, Thomas Edison, Blue, 1969		5.00 To 12.00
Wheaton Commemorative, Thomas Jefferson, Ruby, 1970	Color	5.00
Wheaton Commemorative, Ulysses S.Grant, Topaz, 1972	Color	5.00
Wheaton Commemorative, W.C.Fields, Aqua, 1972	Color	5.00
Wheaton Commemorative, Will Rogers, Topaz, 1969		5.00 To 10.00
Wheaton Commemorative, Woodrow Wilson, Blue, 1969		5.00 To 17.50
Wheaton Products, Mini Set, Presidential No.1		12.50
Wheaton Products, Mini Set, Presidential No.2		12.50
Wheaton Products, Mini Set, Presidential No.3		12.50
Whimsey, Glass Blower's, Amethyst		15.00

Whiskey bottles came in assorted sizes and shapes through the years. Any container for whiskey is included in this category.

Whiskey, A.& D.H.C., 3 Mold, Whittled, Amber, Quart		6.95
Whiskey, A.J.Gilka, Whittled, 2 Figures On Bottom, Green, Quart		35.00
Whiskey, A.J.Wintle & Sons, Bill Mills, Mr.Ross, Amber, 6 1/2 In.High		3.00
Whiskey, A.J.Wintle & Sons, Bill Mills, Mr.Ross, 7 In.High		3.00
Whiskey, A.J.Wintle & Sons, Bill Mills, Mr.Ross, 8 In.High		3.00
Whiskey, A.M.Bininger, Handled Urn, Amber, Pint		425.00
Whiskey, Ballantine, see Ballantine		
Whiskey, Bininger & Co., Old London Dock, Olive	Illus	49.00

Whiskey, Bininger & Co., Old London Dock, Olive
See Page 204

Whiskey, Bininger, Barrel, Smooth Base 105.00
Whiskey, Bininger, 19 Broad, 1849, Old Kentucky Bourbon, Barrel, Amber 160.00
Whiskey, Aboossur Bourbon, Label, Aqua, Quart 2.00
Whiskey, Adolph Marcus Von Butow, Germany, Gilka Shape 12.00
Whiskey, Albion, Maryland, Lamden, Thompson & Co., Baltimore, 1/2 Pint 3.50
Whiskey, Altschul Distilling Co., Embossed, Corker, Clear 2.50
Whiskey, Altschul, Springfield, Ohio, Embossed Barrel, Quart 4.50
Whiskey, Ambrosial, Seal, Jug, Handled, Pontil, Amber, Quart 80.00
Whiskey, Americus Club, Flask, Amber, 1/2 Pint 6.00
Whiskey, Americus Club, Fluted Neck, Sun-Colored Amethyst, Quart 15.00
Whiskey, Americus Club, Pure, Flask, Screw Type, Amethyst, Pint 5.00
Whiskey, Ancient Age Bourbon, Round 2.00
Whiskey, Apostles, 6, Embossed, Stain, Yellow Amber, Quart 45.00
Whiskey, Arcade Grocery Co.Clear, Quart 10.00
Whiskey, Autocrat, Square, Sun-Colored Amethyst, Pint 10.00
Whiskey, B.F. & Co., New York, Dogs & Game, Ceramic, Brown, Pint 75.00
Whiskey, Bald Eagle 7.75
Whiskey, Baltimore Rye, 1808, Jug, Ceramic, Spout, Unglazed, Banding, Quart 3.00
Whiskey, Banjo, Clear, 5th Size 8.00
Whiskey, Bar, Aaa Lexington Club, Enameled, Polished Pontil, Clear, Quart 6.00
Whiskey, Bar, Bailey's, Enameled, Clear, Quart 9.00
Whiskey, Bar, Black Swan Cabinet, Enameled, Clear, Quart 12.50
Whiskey, Bar, Burwood, White Enamel, Cylindrical 9.00
Whiskey, Bar, Cascade Whiskey In White Enamel 15.00
Whiskey, Bar, Clark's Pure Rye, Enameled, Clear, Quart 10.00
Whiskey, Bar, Crystal Glen Rye, Enameled, Clear, Quart 2.00
Whiskey, Bar, Decanter, -M&t-Xxx, Enameled, Polished Pontil, Clear, Pint 1.00
Whiskey, Bar, Decanter, Aaa Scotch, Enameled, Clear, Quart 1.00
Whiskey, Bar, Decanter, B & B Rye, Enameled, Clear, Pint 2.00
Whiskey, Bar, Decanter, Bailey's, Polished Pontil, Clear, Quart 4.00
Whiskey, Bar, Decanter, Beaver Rye, Enameled, Clear, Pint 2.00
Whiskey, Bar, Decanter, Bouquet, Polished Pontil, Stain, Clear, Pint 2.00
Whiskey, Bar, Decanter, Calvert's Pure Rye, Enameled, Clear, Quart 6.00
Whiskey, Bar, Decanter, Columbia, Enameled, Clear, Quart 1.00
Whiskey, Bar, Decanter, Douglas Club, Enameled, Stain, Clear, Quart 6.00
Whiskey, Bar, Decanter, Finche's Golden Wedding, Enameled, Clear, Pint 1.00
Whiskey, Bar, Decanter, Hewitt, Enameled, Clear, Quart 2.00
Whiskey, Bar, Decanter, Highland Special Rye, Enameled, Clear, Quart 6.00
Whiskey, Bar, Decanter, Hollywood, Enameled, Polished Pontil, Clear, 1/2 Pint 5.00
Whiskey, Bar, Decanter, Hunter, Polished Pontil, Clear, Pint 3.00
Whiskey, Bar, Decanter, Jack Silver Bourbon, Enameled, Clear, Pint 3.00
Whiskey, Bar, Decanter, Maryland Club, Enameled, Clear, Quart 3:00
Whiskey, Bar, Decanter, Maywood Rye, Enameled, Clear, Pint 2.00
Whiskey, Bar, Decanter, Moonlight, Enameled, Clear, Quart 3.00

Whiskey, Bar, Decanter, Norris, Enameled, Clear, 1/2 Pint 1.00
Whiskey, Bar, Decanter, Old Canteen, Enameled, Clear, Quart 2.00
Whiskey, Bar, Decanter, Old Cliff, Polished Pontil, Clear, Pint 4.00
Whiskey, Bar, Decanter, Old Joe Gideon, Crackle Glass, Clear, Pint 4.00
Whiskey, Bar, Decanter, Old Mason Rye, Enameled, Clear, Quart 7.00
Whiskey, Bar, Decanter, Rock & Rye, Enameled, Clear, Quart 4.00
Whiskey, Bar, Decanter, Rye, Enameled, Clear, Quart 2.00
Whiskey, Bar, Decanter, Rye-Lee & Co., Enameled, Clear, Quart 1.00
Whiskey, Bar, Decanter, Sherwood Pure Rye, Enameled, Clear, Pint 3.00
Whiskey, Bar, Decanter, Sterling's Malt, Enameled, Clear, Quart 2.00
Whiskey, Bar, Decanter, Sunny Brook, The Pure Food, Enameled, Clear, Pint 5.00
Whiskey, Bar, Decanter, Wellbrock, Enameled, Polished Pontil, Clear, 1/2 Pint 5.00
Whiskey, Bar, Delmar Club, Enameled, Stain, Clear, Quart 2.00
Whiskey, Bar, Enameled 14.00
Whiskey, Bar, Epstein Fine Old Rye, Enameled, Clear, Quart 4.00
Whiskey, Bar, Fine Gibson, Enameled, Polished Pontil, Clear, Quart 4.00
Whiskey, Bar, Fluted, Emerald Green, Quart 35.00
Whiskey, Bar, Fountain Spring, White Enamel, Cylindrical 16.00
Whiskey, Bar, Gold Spring, Enameled, Clear, Quart 7.50
Whiskey, Bar, Hayner's Combination Stopper, Clear, Quart .... 3.00 To 12.00
Whiskey, Bar, J.W.Palmer, Enameled, Polished Pontil, Clear, Quart 9.00
Whiskey, Bar, Kentucky Reserve, Enamel, Pinch, Stopper 15.00
Whiskey, Bar, Lincoln Club, Enameled Lettering, Clear 15.00
Whiskey, Bar, Lynch Standard, Enameled, Clear, Quart 3.00
Whiskey, Bar, Maryland Club, Enameled, Polished Pontil, Clear, Quart 10.00
Whiskey, Bar, Monmouth Cave, Picture, Enameled, Stain, Clear, Quart 30.00
Whiskey, Bar, Montreal Brand Malt Rye Made In Louisville, Ky., Enameled 14.00
Whiskey, Bar, Mulherin's Old Rye, Enameled, Stain, Clear, Quart 9.00
Whiskey, Bar, Myer's Monongahela, Polished Pontil, Etched, Clear, Quart 7.00
Whiskey, Bar, Old Hermitage Bourbon, Enameled, Clear, Quart 7.00
Whiskey, Bar, Old Joe Gideon, Enameled, Clear, Quart 17.00
Whiskey, Bar, Old Transylvania, Enameled, Polished Pontil, Clear, Quart 12.50
Whiskey, Bar, Peewee, Enameled, Clear, Quart 15.00
Whiskey, Bar, Sherwood Rye, Polished Pontil, Enameled, Clear, Quart 4.00
Whiskey, Bar, Spring Garden Rye, Enameled, Clear, Quart 8.00
Whiskey, Bar, Tucker Rye, Enameled, Polished Pontil, Clear, Quart 12.50
Whiskey, Bar, W.N.Walton's Pat.Sept.23, 1862, Old Rye In Sunken Panel, Amber 165.00
Whiskey, Barclay 76 Pure Rye, Loon Pouring, Cut Stars Design, Enameled 25.00
     Whiskey, Beam, see Beam
Whiskey, Beech Hill Co., Cincinnati, Ohio, Amber, Quart 10.00
Whiskey, Bell Of Anderson, Embossed, Milk Glass 77.00
Whiskey, Bell's Scotch, Ceramic Bell, Brown Glaze, Quart 4.00
Whiskey, Belle Of Anderson, Milk Glass 150.00
Whiskey, Bennett & Carroll, Pitts., Pa., Pontil, Amber, Quart 130.00
Whiskey, Berry's Diamond Wedding, Boston, 3 Embossed Barrels, Clear, Quart 15.00
Whiskey, Bf & Co., Dogs & Game, Handled, Ceramic, Mottled Brown, Pint 75.00
Whiskey, Bininger Regulator Bourbon, Label, Pontil, Amber, Pint 290.00
Whiskey, Bininger Regulator, Stain, Pontil, Amber, Pint 190.00
Whiskey, Bininger, Barrel, Pontil, Amber, Pint 130.00
Whiskey, Bininger, Barrel, Pontil, Amber, Quart 130.00
Whiskey, Bininger, Handled Jug, Label, Amber, Pint 120.00
Whiskey, Bininger's Old Kentucky Bourbon, Amber, Quart 50.00
Whiskey, Bininger's Old Kentucky Bourbon, 1848, Brown .... *Illus* 47.00
Whiskey, Bininger's, Old Kentucky Bourbon, 1849 Reserve, Olive Green 45.00
Whiskey, Bininger's Traveler's Guide, Amber, 1/2 Pint 140.00
     Whiskey, Black & White, see also Black & White
Whiskey, Black & White-Embossed, 3 Mold, Green, Quart 15.00
Whiskey, Black Cat On Label, Olive Amber, Quart 2.00
Whiskey, Black Swan Cabinet, Clear, Quart 12.50
Whiskey, Blake's 7.75
Whiskey, Blanchard Farrar & Co., Handled, Frosted, Clear, Pint 8.00
Whiskey, Blown, Handled, Amber 60.00
Whiskey, Bond & Co., Amber, Quart 11.00
Whiskey, Bonded Belmont, Bell Shape 4.00
Whiskey, Bonnel & Co., Ky., Glass Stopper, Clear, 1 1/4 Quart 6.00
Whiskey, Bonnie Castle, Ceramic Jug, Tan & Cream Glaze, Quart 11.00

Whiskey, Booz, E.G., Old Cabin, Amber, Quart	130.00
Whiskey, Bouquet, Ceramic Jug, Brown & White Glaze	6.00
Whiskey, Bouquet, Jug, Ceramic, Brown & Gray Glaze, Quart	2.00
Whiskey, Bourbon Supreme, Williamsburg	12.00
Whiskey, Brook, Stopper Pulls Out Tiny Pencil	4.50
Whiskey, Brookville Distilling Co., Cincinnati, Ohio, Embossed, Clear, Quart	50.00
Whiskey, Brown-Forman Co., Distillers, Ky., Flask, Clear, 1/2 Pint	3.00
Whiskey, Brown-Forman Co., Distillers, Louisville, Ky., Amethyst, 1/2 Pint	9.50
Whiskey, Brown, Applied Seal Embossed Nathan's Bros., Phila., 1863	16.00
Whiskey, Buchanan's Black & White, Double Lip, Honey Amber, Quart	12.00
Whiskey, Buffet Cocktails On Label, Amber, Quart	2.00
Whiskey, Burgerspital On Seal, Amber, Quart	12.50
Whiskey, Burke's, Pinch Bottle, Enameled, Open Pontil, Clear, Quart	5.00
Whiskey, Burlington Pure Rye, H.Weil & Sons, Ky., Square, Clear, Quart	10.00
Whiskey, Bushmills	8.00
Whiskey, C.B.Seeley & Sons, Inc., Embossed, Aqua, 11 1/4 In.	8.00
Whiskey, C.H.Graves, Non Federal Law, Amber	6.50
Whiskey, C.H.Moore Old Bourbon & Rye, Jesse Moore & Co., Ky., Stain	32.00
Whiskey, C.Hallahan, Clear, Quart	3.50
Whiskey, C.O.Taylor On Base, Non Federal Law, Amber	9.50
Whiskey, C.R.Gibson, Salamanca, N.Y., Flask, Clear, Quart	5.00
Whiskey, C.W.Chestnut Grove, Handled, Seal, Pontil	125.00
Whiskey, Cahart & Brother, N.Y.On Seal, Handled Jug, Pontil, Red Amber, Quart	260.00
Whiskey, California, Improved Pontil, Bubbles	45.00
Whiskey, Callahan, Amethyst, 12 1/8 In.High	7.45
Whiskey, Canada Buffalo Club	10.00
Whiskey, Canada Malt Rye, Amber, Pint	28.00
Whiskey, Canadian Club, Label, Amber, 1/2 Pint	1.00
Whiskey, Canadian Club, Labeled, Pumpkin Seed, Clear, 3 3/8 In.	8.00
Whiskey, Canadian Club, 1940	4.00
Whiskey, Canadian Lord Calvert	2.50
Whiskey, Canadian Rye, Label, Clear Pint	2.00
Whiskey, Carlton Pure Rye, Label Under Glass, Clear, Quart	35.00
Whiskey, Carroll & Carroll, San Francisco, 4-Piece Mold, C.1870, Amber	65.00
Whiskey, Casper Co., N.Carolina, Stoneware, Jug, 2 Gallon	25.00
Whiskey, Casper's, Embossed, Faulty Mold, Cobalt	150.00
Whiskey, Casper's, Made By Honest N.C.People, Cobalt *Illus*	185.00
Whiskey, Casper's, North Carolina *Color*	XX.XX
Whiskey, Cattos, Flask, Green, Quart	12.00
Whiskey, Cattos, Oval, ABM , Olive Green	8.00
Whiskey, Cattos, Script, Oval, Green, Fifth	12.00
Whiskey, Cerruti Mercantile Co., Calif., Fluted Shoulders, BIMAL, Amber	38.00

Whiskey, Casper's,
Made By Honest
N.C.People, Cobalt

Whiskey,
Bininger's Old Kentucky Bourbon, 1848, Brown
See Page 206

Whiskey, Champlin's, Milk Glass, Pearl	10.00
Whiskey, Chapin & Gore Sour Mash, Amber, Pint	25.00
Whiskey, Chapin & Gore Sour Mash 1867, Barrel, Amber	39.00 To 50.00
Whiskey, Chapin & Gore, Paneled, Glass Stopper, Amber	25.00
Whiskey, Charles & Co., Label, Amber, Quart	2.00
Whiskey, Charles Nelson, Nashville, Tenn., Clear, Quart	9.00
Whiskey, Chas.Dennehy & Co., Chicago, Rectangular, Amber, Quart	10.00
Whiskey, Chase & Duncan, N.Y., Sun-Colored, 7 In. *Illus*	30.00
Whiskey, Chequer's Scotch	2.00
Whiskey, Chestnut Grove, CW , Jug, Handled, Amber	176.00
Whiskey, Chestnut Grove, CW , Jug, Handled, Chestnut, Flat, Open Pontil	150.00
Whiskey, Chestnut Grove, Jug, Handle, Amber, Pint	85.00
Whiskey, Chestnut Grove, Label, Pontil, Amber, Quart	170.00
Whiskey, Chevalier Old Castle, Inside Screw, Amber, 1/5	25.00

Whiskey, Chase & Duncan, N.Y., Sun-Colored, 7 In.

Whiskey, City Liquor Store, Ceramic Jug, Glazed, Quart	2.00
Whiskey, Clark's Pure Rye, Clear, Quart	10.00
Whiskey, Claymore Scotch, Ceramic Jug, Spout, Doulton, Scottish Figure	40.00
Whiskey, Club 45	2.50
Whiskey, Colebrook & Co.Rye, 9 In.High	3.00
Whiskey, Columbia, Enameled, Pinch Bottle, Clear, Pint	2.00
Whiskey, Cooper's Malt Whiskey, Amber	20.00
Whiskey, Cooper's Malt Whiskey, Round, Stain, Amber	15.00
Whiskey, Corby's Reserve	3.00
Whiskey, Corker, Amethyst, Pint	2.65
Whiskey, Corker, Amethyst, Quart	3.65
Whiskey, Crown Distilleries Co., Inside Threads, Quart	30.00
Whiskey, Crown Distilleries Co., Round, Inside Screw, 5th, Amber	25.00
Whiskey, Crutch Rye, Rectangular, Amber, Quart	12.00
Whiskey, Cunningham & Ihmsen, Pitts., Pa., Patent On Shoulder, Honey Amber	14.00
Whiskey, Cutter A No.1	35.00
Whiskey, Cutter Crown	15.00
Whiskey, Cutter Extra	75.00
Whiskey, Cutter OK	75.00
Whiskey, Cyrus Noble, Quart, 11 In.High	7.45
Whiskey, Dallemond & Co.Inc., Chicago, Amber, Quart	5.50 To 7.00
Whiskey, Dallenmand, Amber, Quart	20.00
Whiskey, Dant, see Dant	
Whiskey, Decanter, Calvert Maryland Pure Rye, White Enamel, Cut Glass	17.50
Whiskey, Decanter, Free-Blown, Pittsburgh, Aqua, Gallon	100.00
Whiskey, Decanter, O.F.C., Cut Glass, Gold Letters	16.50
Whiskey, Decanter, Usher's, Ceramic, Coronation, Copeland Spode, Green, Quart	17.50
Whiskey, Deep Spring, Tenn., Three-Piece Mold, Amber	16.00
Whiskey, Deep Spring, Tennessee, ABM , Amber, Quart	3.50
Whiskey, Dewar's Scotch, Ceramic, Jug, Spout, Doulton, Figure, Brown, Quart	45.00

Whiskey, **Dewar's**, Label, Square, Olive, Quart 12.00
Whiskey, **Diamond Wedding**, Clear, Quart 5.00
Whiskey, **Don Quixote** 10.00
Whiskey, **Donnelly Rye Full Quart**, Rectangular, Inside Screw, Amber 40.00
Whiskey, **Double Eagle**, Pittsburgh, Quart, Aqua 47.50
Whiskey, **Doulton Lambeth**, Viking Ship 25.00
Whiskey, **Doulton**, Lambeth, England, Marked, Brown Ship On Front 50.00
Whiskey, **Duffy Malt**, Patent Aug.24, 1886, Amber 15.00
Whiskey, **Duffy's Malt**, Amber, Quart .... 3.50 To 7.00
Whiskey, **Duffy's Malt**, Applied Mouth, Amber, Quart 5.00
Whiskey, **Duffy's Malt**, Baltimore 12.00
Whiskey, **Duffy's Malt**, Bottom Embossed Date 1886, Amber 4.50
Whiskey, **Duffy's Malt**, Golden Amber, 10 In.High, ABM 6.00
Whiskey, **Duffy's Malt**, Label 15.00
Whiskey, **Dunbar's**, Green, Quart 8.00
Whiskey, **Dyottville Glass Works**, Amber, Quart 15.00
Whiskey, **Dyottville Glass Works**, Cylinder, Green 10.00
Whiskey, **Dyottville Glass Works**, Improved Pontil, Olive Amber, Quart 27.50
Whiskey, **Dyottville Glass Works**, Iron Pontil 28.00
Whiskey, **Dyottville Glass Works**, Olive Amber, Quart 27.50
Whiskey, **Dyottville Glass Works**, Olive Green, Quart 13.00
Whiskey, **Dyottville Glass Works**, Three Mold, Amber 8.00
Whiskey, **Dyottville Glass Works**, 3 Mold, Patent On Shoulder, Green, Quart 22.00
Whiskey, **E.Gray**, Clear, Quart 6.00
Whiskey, **E.P.Shaw**, Wakefield, Gold Medal Award, London, 1903, 6 In.High 3.00
Whiskey, **E.P.Shaw**, Wakefield, 7 In.High 3.00
Whiskey, **E.P.Shaw**, Wakefield, 9 1/2 In.High 3.00
Whiskey, **Elk's**, Elk's Head, Ceramic, 2-Tone Brown Glaze, 5 In. 12.00
Whiskey, **Epstein Fine Old Rye**, Clear, Quart 4.00
Whiskey, **Ezra Brooks, see Ezra Brooks**
Whiskey, **F.Chevalier Co.**, Inside Threads, Old Castle, Amber .... 19.00 To 25.00
Whiskey, **F.Chevalier**, San Francisco, Flask, Amber 6.50
Whiskey, **Ferdinand Westheimer & Sons**, Cincinnati, Ohio, Amber, Pint 5.00
Whiskey, **Ferdinand Westheimer & Sons**, Cincinnati, Ohio, Amber, 1/2 Pint 5.00
Whiskey, **Figge-Doyle Co.**, Milwaukee, Round, Amber, Quart 24.00
Whiskey, **Finest Old Highland**, Ceramic, Brown Glaze, Quart 10.00
Whiskey, **First Prize World's Fair Old Times**, Clear, Quart 20.00
Whiskey, **Flask**, Alderney Old Rye, Clear, Quart 4.00
Whiskey, **Flask**, Coffin, J.H.Cutter, Old Bourbon, Portland, Ore., Amber 125.00
Whiskey, **Flask**, Cortwright Whiskey On Label, Clear, 1/2 Pint 1.00
Whiskey, **Flask**, Embossed, Wicker, Sun-Colored Amethyst, Quart 15.00
Whiskey, **Flask**, Freiberg Meyer Co., Amber, 1/2 Pint 1.00
Whiskey, **Flask**, Genuine Distilled Protection, Clear, 1/2 Pint 26.00
Whiskey, **Flask**, Green River, Traveler 22.00
Whiskey, **Flask**, Haddox Wines & Liquors On Label, Aqua, 1/2 Pint 1.00
Whiskey, **Flask**, Jackson & Co., Olive Green, 1/2 Pint 52.50
Whiskey, **Flask**, Merry Christmas On Label, Clear, 1/2 Pint 2.00
Whiskey, **Flask**, Montezuma Rye On Label, Silver Basketwork Case, Clear, Pint 2.00
Whiskey, **Flask**, Old Joe Gideon, Gold Medal Winner Embossed, Amber, Pint 15.00
Whiskey, **Flask**, Pepper Sour Mash Whiskey On Label, Clear, 1/2 Pint 1.00
Whiskey, **Flask**, Picnic, Delport Whiskey On Label, Amber, 1/4 Pint 1.00
Whiskey, **Flask**, Picnic, Rye Whiskey On Label, Clear, 1/4 Pint 5.00
Whiskey, **Flask**, Pocket, Wharton's, Blue, 1/4 Pint 200.00
Whiskey, **Flask**, Pumpkin Seed, Cobweb, Sun-Colored Amethyst, Pint 15.00
Whiskey, **Flask**, Quaker Maid, Amber, 1/2 Pint 12.00
Whiskey, **Flask**, Robertson's Scotch, Green, Quart 4.00
Whiskey, **Flask**, Swirl Ribbed Pattern Lower Half, Clear, 7 1/2 In.High 6.00
Whiskey, **Flask**, Taylor & Williams, Sun-Colored Amethyst, Pint 4.00
Whiskey, **Flask**, Warranted Flask Shape, Apple Green, Quart 7.00
Whiskey, **Flask**, Wm.Jackson & Co., Olive Green, Quart 55.00
Whiskey, **Flask**, Wm.Penn Rye On Label, Green, Quart 5.00
Whiskey, **Fleischmann Co.**, Round Ceramic Jug, Handle, Blue, Quart 10.00
Whiskey, **Fleischmann's Pure Rye**, Clear 8.50
Whiskey, **For Good Indians**, Red Chief Baltimore Rye, Stain, Clear, 12 3/8 In. 45.00
Whiskey, **Forbes Fine Whiskeys**, Ceramic Jug, Cream Glaze 2.00
Whiskey, **Forest Lawn**, Bulbous, Pontil, Green, Pint 140.00

Whiskey, Forest Lawn, JVH, Bulbous, Squatty Onion Shape, C.1840, Green	225.00
Whiskey, Four Roses, Decanter, Pottery, Embossed Train Depot, People	20.00
Whiskey, Four Roses, Embossed Roses & Paul Jones & Co., Ky., Amber, Quart	22.00
Whiskey, Four Roses, Embossed, Amber, Pint	7.00
Whiskey, Four Roses, Miniature, Embossed, Dug, Amber	4.00
Whiskey, Four Roses, Paul Jones Co., Embossed Roses, Quart	10.00
Whiskey, Fred Raschen Co., Sacramento, Cal., Round, Stain, Amber, 5th	20.00
Whiskey, Friedman Keiler, Paducah, Ky., Fluted, Amber, 1/2 Pint	7.00
Whiskey, Fuddy's Malt, Rochester	4.75
Whiskey, G.O.Taylor, Old Bourbon, Boston, 1873, Coffin, Labels, Amber, Pint	16.00
Whiskey, Gaelic Old Smuggler's, Label, Green, Quart	6.00
Whiskey, Gaelic Old Smuggler's, Labels, Amber, Quart	7.00
Whiskey, Geo.Bieler & Sons, Brookfield Rye, 1/2 Pint	15.00
Whiskey, Geo.Wissman, Sacramento, Metal Screw Cap, Flask, Amber, 1/2 Pint	9.00
Whiskey, George Holley, Ltd., Nottingham, Raised Sheaf Of Wheat	3.00
Whiskey, George Washington Bust, Rye, 1930s	11.00
Whiskey, Gibb's Special, Amethyst, Quart	16.50
Whiskey, Gibb's Special, James Gibb, S.F., Cal., Amethyst, Quart	16.50
Whiskey, Gibson's Xxxx Rye, 1930s	4.00
Whiskey, Gibson's, Amber, Quart	3.00
Whiskey, Gibson's, For Invalids & Connoisseurs, Red Lion Hotel, Clear	15.00
Whiskey, Gillespy's Old Cabin Home Bourbon, Handled Jug, Label, Amber, Pint	150.00
Whiskey, Gin, Applied Light Blue Seal, Embossed Schiedam, Clear	18.00
Whiskey, Gininger's Old Kentucky Bourbon, Amber, Quart	50.00
Whiskey, Gininger's Old Kentucky Bourbon, Green	75.00
Whiskey, Glen Garry, Ceramic Jug, Brown Glaze, Quart	5.00
Whiskey, Glen Garry, Ceramic, Jug, Double Handle, Spout, Glazed, Quart	3.00
Whiskey, Glenco Brand Scotch, Ceramic Jug, Brown & Gray Glaze, Quart	17.00
Whiskey, Gold Spring, Clear, Quart	7.50
Whiskey, Gold Spring, Pinch Bottle, Enameled, Clear, Pint	3.00
Whiskey, Golden Gate All Rye, Stain, Amber, Quart	8.00
Whiskey, Golden Heart Fire Copper Pure Rye, Amber, Fifth	26.00
Whiskey, Golden Star, Jug, Ceramic, Sample, Brown Glaze	10.00
Whiskey, Golden Wedding, Carnival Glass, Marigold, Salesman's Sample	45.00
Whiskey, Golden Wedding, Carnival Glass, Marigold, 1/10 Pint	10.00
Whiskey, Golden Wedding, Carnival Glass, Pint	10.00
Whiskey, Golden Wedding, Carnival Glass, 1/2 Pint	7.00 To 14.00
Whiskey, Golden Wedding, Carnival, Quart	14.00
Whiskey, Golden Wedding, Carnival, Quart	14.00 To 22.50
Whiskey, Graef's Canteen, Green, Pint	120.00
Whiskey, Greeley's Bourbon, Barrel, Puce	140.00
Whiskey, Greeting, Theodore Netter *Color*	XX.XX
Whiskey, Guinness, Regular	4.00
Whiskey, Guinness, 1959, Anniversary	6.00
Whiskey, H.F.& B., N.Y., Fluted, Red Amber, Pint	160.00
Whiskey, H.F.& B., N.Y., Fluted, Yellow Amber, Pint	160.00
Whiskey, H.G.Co.On Base, Blown In Mold, Applied Lip, Black Glass	7.50
Whiskey, H.Gardner, West Bromwick, 7 1/2 In.High	3.00
Whiskey, H.Kirk, Embossed Indian, Non Federal Law, Amber	8.75
Whiskey, H.W.Hespenheide, Wholesale Liquor Dealers, Pa., Square, Clear, Quart	8.50
Whiskey, H.W.Huguley Co., 134 Canal St., Boston, Full Quart, Round, Label	7.95
Whiskey, Haig & Haig, Pinch Bottle, Etched, Clear, Quart	2.00
Whiskey, Hannis Distilling Co., Amber, 1/2 Pint	6.00
Whiskey, Hannis Distilling Co., Pat.Mar.25, 1890, Rectangular, Amber, Pint	8.00
Whiskey, Hanover, Pinch Bottle, Enameled, Clear, Pint	3.00
Whiskey, Hartwig Kantorowicz, Nachf Shulz Marke Berlin, Lady's Leg Neck	18.00
Whiskey, Harvard Rye, Clear, Pint	6.00
Whiskey, Hawkins' Rye, Slug Plate, Full Quart Back, Rectangular, Aqua	35.00
Whiskey, Hawthorne Club Whiskey, Sample, Onion Shape, Clear, 2 1/2 In.	15.00
Whiskey, Hayne's	5.00
Whiskey, Hayner Distilling Co., Dayton, Ohio & St.Louis, Mo., Quart	12.00
Whiskey, Hayner Distilling Co., Ohio, Clear, 11 In. *Illus*	4.00
Whiskey, Hayner, Decanter, Lock Type, Lavender	11.50
Whiskey, Hayner, Distillery, Troy, Ohio, Clear, Quart	3.00
Whiskey, Hayner, Full Label, Cork, Quart, Clear	10.00
Whiskey, Hayner, Lock, Box 290, Dayton, O., Stone Jug, Quart	15.00

Whiskey, Hayner Distilling Co., Ohio, Clear, 11 In.
See Page 210

Whiskey, **Hayner's Distillery**, Troy, O., Amethyst	3.75
Whiskey, **Hayner's Distillery**, Troy, Ohio, Haze, Amber, Quart	5.00
Whiskey, **Hayner's**, Amethyst, Quart	12.50
Whiskey, **Hayner's**, BIMAL , Dug, Clear	4.00
Whiskey, **Hayner's**, Clear, Quart	2.75
Whiskey, **Hayner's**, Embossed, Label	6.75
Whiskey, **Hayner's**, Non Federal Law, Amber	9.50
Whiskey, **Hayner's**, Troy, Ohio, Patent Nov.30, 1897, Quart	10.00
Whiskey, **Hayner's**, BIMAL , Dug, Clear	4.00
Whiskey, **Heather Blossom Pure Old Malt**, Providence, R.I., Honey Amber	15.00
Whiskey, **Heather Dew Scotch**, Ceramic Jug, Label, Brown & Gray	2.00 To 7.00
Whiskey, **Heather Dew Scotch**, Stoneware, 2 Handles, Jug	20.00
Whiskey, **Heaven Hill**, Old Kentucky Home, House	3.95
Whiskey, **Henry Mc Kenna**, Scotch, Jug	10.00
Whiskey, **Herman Cramer**, 6 Sided, Green	14.00
Whiskey, **Highland**, Ceramic Jug, Brown Glaze, Quart	10.00
Whiskey, **Highland**, Special, Jug	50.00
Whiskey, **Hildebrandt & Posner & Co.**, San Fransicso, California, Round, Stain	20.00
Whiskey, **Hiram Ricker & Sons**, Inc., Facsimile *Color*	XX.XX
Whiskey, **Hiram Ricker**, Moses, Facsimile, Amber	12.00
Whiskey, **Holland Bros.**, Clear, Quart	6.00
Whiskey, **Hollywood**, Amber, Quart	5.00 To 10.00
Whiskey, **Hollywood**, Cylinder, Amber, Quart	12.00
Whiskey, **Hollywood**, Cylinder, Burst Base Bubble, Amber, Quart	8.00
Whiskey, **Holtz Freystadt Co.**, N.Y., Jug, Handled, Round, Amber	20.00
Whiskey, **Homers California Ginger Brandy**	4.00
Whiskey, **House Of Lords**, Clear, 8 1/4 In.High	6.00
Whiskey, **Huguley**, Non Federal Law, Amber	6.50
Whiskey, **Hurley**, Clear, Quart	6.00
Whiskey, **I.F.Cutler**, E.Martin & Co., San Francisco, Cal., Round, 5th	20.00
Whiskey, **I.Goldberg**, Distiller, 12 Sided, Amber, 2 Quart	30.00
Whiskey, **I. W. Harper, see I.W.Harper**	
Whiskey, **Imperial Club Pure Rye**, Ceramic Jug, Brown & White Glaze, Quart	12.50
Whiskey, **Imperial Club**, Pinch Bottle, Enameled, Clear, Pint	6.00
Whiskey, **Imperial**, Bubbles, Applied Mouth, Dark Green, Quart	12.00
Whiskey, **Imperial**, Bubbles, Olive Green, Quart	4.50
Whiskey, **Ivanof**, Drunk Russian, Rye, 1930s	7.00
Whiskey, **J.A.Gilka Berlin**, Schutzen No.9, Rectangular, Blob Top, Red Amber	15.00
Whiskey, **J.C.& Co.**, 1847, Non Federal Law, Amber	9.50
Whiskey, **J.C.Cutter's Old Bourbon**, Crown, A.P.Hotaling	12.00
Whiskey, **J.C.Schnell's Sour Mash Kiln Dried Grain**, Jug, Stone, Quart	30.00
Whiskey, **J.E.Danaher**, Albany, N.Y., Amber, Quart	20.00
Whiskey, **J.F.T.Rye**, Label, Amber, Quart	10.00
Whiskey, **J.H.Cutter Old Bourbon**, 'A No.1', A.P.Hotaling & Co.	30.00
Whiskey, **J.H.Cutter Old Bourbon**, A.P.Hotaling & Co., Western, Amber, Quart	45.00

Whiskey, J.H.Cutter Old Bourbon, Trademark C, Amber, 12 In.	150.00
Whiskey, J.H.Cutter Pure Old Rye, C.P.Moorman Manufacturer, Ky., Dug, Amber	30.00
Whiskey, J.Reiger & Co., Amethyst, Quart	7.00
Whiskey, J.Reiger & Co., Kansas City, Clear, Quart	8.00
Whiskey, J.Waterman, Phila., Pontil, Amber, Quart	75.00
Whiskey, J. W. Dant, see Dant	
Whiskey, Jack Daniel, see Jack Daniel	
Whiskey, Jack Dempsey, 1930	13.00
Whiskey, James Buchanan Distillery, ABM	8.00
Whiskey, James Hawker, Porcelain, Ship Labels, Copeland Spode, White, Quart	6.00
Whiskey, Jaranson Full Measure, Seattle, Washington, Embossed, Amber, Quart	21.00
Whiskey, Jas.Pepper, Amber, 1/2 Pint	8.00
Whiskey, Jesse Moore Hunt Co., San Francisco, Center Antler, Amber, Fifth	15.00
Whiskey, Jesse Moore Hunt, Calif & Ky., Elk's Horn Trademark, Amber	20.00
Whiskey, Jesse Moore, Old Bourbon, Horns	12.00
Whiskey, Jesse Moore, Sole Agent	25.00
Whiskey, Jim Beam, see Beam	
Whiskey, John Gillon, King William Vi	8.00
Whiskey, John Ryan, Clear, Quart	6.00
Whiskey, John W.O'Connor's Premium XXXX Monongahela Rye, Ga., Amber, Quart	125.00
Whiskey, Johny Walker, Square, Australia, Sun-Purpled	15.00
Whiskey, Jonas F.Brown, JFB Monogram, Flask, Strap, Rectangular, Clear	5.00
Whiskey, Jones, Blob Seal, Amber	7.50
Whiskey, Jos.A.Magnus, Amber, 1/2 Pint	5.00
Whiskey, Jos.A.Magnus, Embossed Dragon, Pint	4.50
Whiskey, Joseph Seagram & Sons, Book, Amber, Quart	12.00
Whiskey, Jug, A.Hatke & Co., Stoneware, Gallon	25.00
Whiskey, Jug, Blanchard Far & Co., Boston, Handled, Frosted & Clear	38.00
Whiskey, Jug, Carhart & Brothers On Seal, Handled, Amber, Quart	300.00
Whiskey, Jug, Coronation, Ceramic, Brown Glaze, Quart	4.00
Whiskey, Jug, Greybeard Stone, Label, Mitchell Bros.	20.00
Whiskey, Jug, Handle, Bulbous, Pontil, Puce	112.00
Whiskey, Jug, Handle Cutter Type, Flat Top, Rounded String Collar	46.00
Whiskey, Jug, Spring Lake Hand Made Sour Mash, Klein Bros., K.T.K.China	75.00
Whiskey, Jug, Sprinkle Whiskey Wants Your Business, Embossed, Clear, Gallon	8.00
Whiskey, Kellerstraus, St.Louis, Mo., Clear, Quart	6.00 To 18.00
Whiskey, Kellerstraus, Sample, Label	8.50
Whiskey, Kellerstraus, Sun-Colored Amethyst, Quart	9.00
Whiskey, Kellogg's Nelson Co.Extra Kentucky Bourbon, Amber	47.00
Whiskey, Kellogg's Wilmerding, Loewe, San Francisco, Inside Thread	25.00
Whiskey, Kentucky Moonshine Sour Mash, Pat.Aug 11, 1891, Pottery, Jug, Gal.	125.00
Whiskey, Keystone Rye, Jug, Ceramic, Brown & Gray Glaze, Quart	4.00 To 11.00
Whiskey, Keystone, Applied Mouth, Dated 1854, Amber, Quart	15.00
Whiskey, King Leo, Pinch Bottle, Enameled, Clear, Pint	2.00
Whiskey, King William, Scotch, Metal Snap	3.50
Whiskey, Kream Pure Rye, Amber	5.00
Whiskey, Kueka Vintage, Clear, Quart	6.00
Whiskey, L.Greenbaum Crescent Club, Flask, Amber, Quart	20.00
Whiskey, Lenox, Pinch Bottle, Enameled, Clear, Pint	4.00
Whiskey, Levaggi Company, San Francisco, California, Rectangular, Amber	25.00
Whiskey, Lewin Mercantile Co.Cor.16th & Larimer Sts.Colo., Jug, Cream	10.00
Whiskey, Lewis & Clark Expedition, Pair	29.90
Whiskey, Life Plant, Embossed Eagle, Amber, Pint	12.00
Whiskey, Lillianthal, San Francisco	75.00
Whiskey, Lincoln Club, Clear, 12 In. *Illus*	6.00
Whiskey, Lion Mother, White	14.00
Whiskey, Lionstone, see Lionstone	
Whiskey, Louis Taussig, Cal., Inside Screw, Sun-Colored Amethyst, Quart	20.00
Whiskey, Louis Taussig, San Francisco, Inside Threads, Clear, Fifth	5.00
Whiskey, M.Salzman Co., Vertical Script, Rectangular, Amber, 1/5 Gallon	15.00
Whiskey, Mackinlay's Scotch, Jug, Ceramic, Doulton, Green & Brown	8.00
Whiskey, Macy & Jenkins, Honey Amber	31.00
Whiskey, Macy & Jenkins, N.Y., On Base, Jug, Handled, Round, Amber	10.00 To 20.00
Whiskey, Macy & Jenkins, Stain, Dark Amber	23.00
Whiskey, Maggi, Non Federal Law, Amber	6.50
Whiskey, Magnolia, Lady's Leg, Amethyst, Quart	7.00

Whiskey, **Manhattan Club**, Sole Agent 60.00
Whiskey, **Manhattan**, Bar Bottle, Enameled, Clear, Quart 5.00
Whiskey, **Mast Head Scotch**, Jug, With Thistle, Gray & Brown 4.00
Whiskey, **Maybrook H & T Whiskey**, Loon Pouring, Enameled 22.00
Whiskey, **Mc Donald & Cohn**, San Francisco, Full Quart In Slant Writing, Amber 25.00
Whiskey, **Mc Donald's**, Ceramic Jug, Gray Glaze, 2 Quart 7.00
Whiskey, **Mc Henry**, 1812, Amber, Quart 3.00
Whiskey, **Mc Kenna**, Jug, Straight 1.10
Whiskey, **Meadville Rye**, Ceramic Jug, Brown & White Glaze, Quart 8.00
Whiskey, **Meier's Crock**, Rye, 1930s 4.00
Whiskey, **Meredith's Diamond Club Pure Rye**, Ohio, Handled, KT & K 16.00
Whiskey, **Merry Christmas & Happy New Year**, Lady On Barrel, Rooster, Clear 45.00
Whiskey, **Merry Christmas**, Flat Barrel, Clear, Pint 30.00
Whiskey, **Merry Christmas**, Happy New Year, Flat Barrel, Aqua, 1/2 Pint 41.00
Whiskey, **Michaelis & Trotman**, N.Y. On Seal, Handled, Amber, Quart 82.50
Whiskey, **Midget**, Spider & Web Mason, Quart 15.00
Whiskey, **Miller's Gamecock**, Boston, Clear, Pint 5.00
Whiskey, **Miller's Gamecock**, Stain, Aqua, 1/2 Pint 2.00
Whiskey, **Millionaire Club**, Cylindrical Shape, Green, Quart .... 8.00 To 30.00
Whiskey, **Milton Hardy Old Rye**, Amber, Quart 4.00
Whiskey, **Minnehaha Laughing Water**, Jug, Ceramic, Glazed, Blue Transfer, Quart 32.50
Whiskey, **Monongahela**, Label, Handle, Jug, Pontil, Amber, Quart 75.00
Whiskey, **Monongahela**, Label, Handled, Jug, Pontil, Amber, Pint 95.00
Whiskey, **Monro's**, Ceramic Jug, Spout, Brown & White Glaze, Quart 8.00
Whiskey, **Monroe's King Of Kings Scotch**, Jug, Gray & Brown 10.00
Whiskey, **Montreal Brand Malt Rye**, Enameled, Pinch Bottle, Clear, Pint 2.00
Whiskey, **Morgan's Maryland Rye**, It's Pure That's Sure, Sheared Lip 19.00
Whiskey, **Mt.Vernon Pure Rye**, Cook & Bernheimer Co., Lady's Leg Neck, Amber 18.00
Whiskey, **Mt.Vernon Pure Rye**, Patent March 25th, 1892 On Base, Amber 10.00
Whiskey, **Mt.Vernon**, Rye, 1930s 4.00
Whiskey, **Mt.Vernon**, Square, Amber, Quart 10.00
Whiskey, **Munro Dalwhinnie**, Scotland, Square, Light Olive Green 50.00
Whiskey, **N.M.Uri & Co.**, Louisville, Ky., Amber, Quart 15.00
Whiskey, **N.M. URI**, Non Federal Law, Amber 6.50
Whiskey, **Naranjas**, Ceramic, Mexico 3.00
Whiskey, **Neal's Ambrosia**, Seal, Blue, Quart 190.00
Whiskey, **Newman's Pat.'76**, Pewter Shot Cap, Clear, Quart 27.50
Whiskey, **Nordhausen Kornschnapps**, Ceramic Jug, Brown Glaze, Quart 15.00
Whiskey, **Nordhausen Kornschnapps**, Ceramic Jug, Glazed, Quart 10.00
Whiskey, **O.Blake Bourbon**, Barrel, Clear 8.00
Whiskey, **O.Blake Rye**, Barrel, Clear 8.00
Whiskey, **O'Donnel's Old Irish**, Belfast, Crockery, Applied Handle, 1/4 Gallon 25.00
Whiskey, **O'Keefe's Pure Malt**, N.Y., Pottery Jug, Handle, Tan & Brown, Quart 8.50
Whiskey, **Okolona On Label**, Clear, 1/2 Pint 2.00
Whiskey, **Old Bridgeport Rye**, 1918 .... 7.00

Whiskey, Lincoln Club, Clear, 12 In.
See Page 212

Whiskey, Old Buck Sportsmen's Favorite, Clear, Quart	5.00
Whiskey, Old Bushmills Distillery Co., Pure Malt, Est'd 1784, Aqua	8.00
Whiskey, Old Bushmills, Embossed Still In Front, Aqua, Quart	25.00
Whiskey, Old Bushmills, Irish	3.50
Whiskey, Old Bushmills Distillery, Embossed Still, Aqua	10.00
Whiskey, Old C.H.Moore Bourbon & Rye, Jesse Moore Hunt Co., Amber, Fifth	20.00
Whiskey, Old Capitol Pure Rye, A.Graf & Co., St.Louis, Stone, Quart	35.00
Whiskey, Old Capitol Pure Rye, Ceramic, White Glaze, Quart	12.00
Whiskey, Old Cascade Tenn. Sour Mash	8.00
Whiskey, Old Club House, Handled Jug, Label, Amber, Pint	25.00
Whiskey, Old Columbia Pure Rye, Brown, 4 1/2 In.High .... *Illus*	30.00
Whiskey, Old Continental, Acorn, Pottery, Jug	10.00
Whiskey, Old Continental, Amber, Quart	40.00
Whiskey, Old Continental, Jug, Complimentary, 1/4 Pint	9.50
Whiskey, Old Crow, see also Old Crow	
Whiskey, Old Crow, Pinch Bottle, Enameled, Shot Glass Stopper, Clear, Quart	2.00
Whiskey, Old Crow, Royal Doulton	75.00
Whiskey, Old Dearborn, Pinch Bottle, Enameled, Clear, Pint	3.00
Whiskey, Old Drum, Drum Shape	5.00
Whiskey, Old Drum, Label, Embossed As Drum, Amber, Quart	23.00
Whiskey, Old Echo Springs, 7 Yr., Straight	1.35
Whiskey, Old Fitzgerald, see Old Fitzgerald	
Whiskey, Old Forester, Bottled 1946-50, Round, Sample, Amber	1.50
Whiskey, Old Grandad, Wathen's Distiller, 1788, Medicinal Tonic	150.00
Whiskey, Old Gum Spring, Jug, Complimentary, 1/4 Pint	10.00
Whiskey, Old Hickory	21.00
Whiskey, Old Irish Whisky, Mitchell & Belfast, Crest, Aqua, Imperial Quart	25.00
Whiskey, Old Irish, Jug, Ceramic, Tan & Gray With Transfer, Quart	4.00
Whiskey, Old Joe Gideon, Clear, Quart	17.00
Whiskey, Old Kentucky Distiller's Co., Covington, Ky., Clear, Quart	5.00
Whiskey, Old Kentucky Valley, 1861, Inside Screw .... *Color*	XX.XX
Whiskey, Old Kentucky, Covington, Ky., Quart	12.00
Whiskey, Old Mckenna, Jug, Ceramic, Sample, Brown & Gray Glaze	8.00
Whiskey, Old Mill, Medallion, Jug, Handled, Pontil, Amber, Pint	450.00
Whiskey, Old Mr.Boston, Decanter, Swirled, Fluted, Pedestal Base, Clear	9.00
Whiskey, Old Mr.Boston, Gold Bust	6.50
Whiskey, Old Mr.Boston, Nebraska, Gold Trophy, No.1 Football Players	22.50
Whiskey, Old Quaker Rye, Frosted, 1930s	5.00
Whiskey, Old Quaker, Embossed, Clear, Quart	3.50
Whiskey, Old Republic, Clear, Quart	3.00
Whiskey, Old Santee Corn, Clear, Quart	15.00
Whiskey, Old Scotch Malt Whiskey, Jug, Ceramic, Glazed, Blue Transfer, Quart	9.00
Whiskey, Old Smuggler, Cork, Kick Up	6.00
Whiskey, Old Smuggler, Gaelic, Black Glass, Quart	10.00
Whiskey, Old Smuggler, Gaelic, Embossed Base, 3 Mold, Green, Quart	15.00
Whiskey, Old Sour Mash Whiskey, L.G.Co. On Base, Lyndeboro, Gold Amber, Pint	27.50
Whiskey, Old Taylor, Castle, 1967 .... *Illus*	4.95
Whiskey, Old Times, Canteen, Clear, Pint	9.00
Whiskey, Old Times, Clear, Pint	9.00
Whiskey, Old Times, Pinch Bottle, Enameled, Clear, Pint	2.00
Whiskey, Old Times, Wicker, Labels, Aqua, Quart	2.00
Whiskey, Old Tub, Cork	90.00
Whiskey, Old Wheat, Pontil, Olive Amber, 2 Quart	260.00
Whiskey, Onion, Dutch, Black Glass	37.50
Whiskey, Onion, Dutch, C.1700, Stubby Neck, Green	50.00
Whiskey, Onion, Pontil	30.00
Whiskey, Oregon Importing Co., Portland, BIMAL, Amber, Quart	27.00
Whiskey, Oregon Importing Co., Portland, BIMAL, Clear, Quart	27.00
Whiskey, Orient Pure Rye, Label, Three-Part Mold, Honey Amber	20.00
Whiskey, P.Chapman, P.C.Kirkstall, 9 In.High	3.00
Whiskey, Parker Old Style, Ceramic, Jug, Cream Glaze, Quart	11.00
Whiskey, Paul Jones Pure Rye, Blob Seal .... 8.00 To	15.00
Whiskey, Paul Jones Whiskey, Seal, Wicker Case, Amber, Quart	10.00
Whiskey, Paul Jones, Amber	15.00
Whiskey, Paul Jones, Miniature, BIMAL, Dug, Amber	8.00
Whiskey, Paul Jones, Wicker With Handle, Stopper, Chain, Red Amber, Quart	13.00

Whiskey, Old Columbia Pure Rye,
Brown, 4 1/2 In.High
See Page 214

Whiskey, Old Taylor, Castle, 1967
See Page 214

Whiskey, Pearl Wedding, Label, Wicker Case, Clear, Quart	1.00
Whiskey, Perkins & Stearns, Amber	12.50
Whiskey, Perrine's Barley Malt, Cylinder, Blob Top, Short Neck, Amber	7.00
Whiskey, Personal Service, Sherman Hotel, Chicago, 1870s, Etched, Set Of 4	50.00
Whiskey, Pett's Bald Eagle, Clear, Quart	6.00
Whiskey, Peewee, Enameled, Clear, Quart	15.00
Whiskey, Pikes Peak, Old Rye, Pint, Aqua	47.50
Whiskey, Pikesville Rye, 1930s	4.00
Whiskey, Planter Rye, Registered Ullman & Co., Ohio, Deep Amethyst, 1/2 Pint	10.00
Whiskey, Porter Rye, Ceramic Jug, Brown & Gray Glaze, 1/2 Pint	4.00
Whiskey, Pottery, Barrel, Dated 1807, Initials W.G., Brown & Green	210.00
Whiskey, Pottery, Square, Fancy	12.00
Whiskey, Prussian Helmet, Label, Embossed Seidel & Co., Amber	100.00
Whiskey, Pure Fulton, Aqua, Gallon	5.00
Whiskey, Pure Malt Whiskey Bourbon Co., Handle, Amber	140.00
Whiskey, Quaker Maid, Flask, Amber, Pint	18.00
Whiskey, Quaker Maid, Honey, 1/2 Pint	8.95
Whiskey, Queensdale Whiskey On Label, Amber, Quart	1.00
Whiskey, R.B.Cutter's, Handled Jug, Pontil, Amber, Pint	170.00
Whiskey, R.B.Cutter's, Louisville, Ky., Tapered, Handled, Whittled, Amber	66.00
Whiskey, R.B.Cutter's Bourbon, Jug, Handled, Iron Pontil, Red Amber	155.00
Whiskey, R.F.Hoffman, Ceramic Jug, Sample, Brown & Gray Glaze	10.00
Whiskey, R.G.Tullidge & Co.Pure Pop Corn Whiskey, Est.1868, SCA , Quart	75.00
Whiskey, Red Top Rye, Amber, Quart	12.00
Whiskey, Red Top Rye, Cylindrical, Embossed, Green, Pint	75.00
Whiskey, Red Top Rye, Pint, Amber	8.95
Whiskey, Red Top Rye, Stain, Green	45.00
Whiskey, Redville Rye, 1930s	4.00
Whiskey, Rheinstrom Brothers, Eagle, Yellow Amber, Quart	20.00
Whiskey, Rieger, Blown In Mold, Open Pontil	3.00
Whiskey, Rittenhouse Rye, 1930s	3.50
Whiskey, Roanoke Rye, Shea Bocqueraz Co., Dark Slug Plate, BIMAL , Amber	34.00
Whiskey, Robert Steel, Amber, Quart	8.00
Whiskey, Rock And Rye, Enameled, Clear, Quart	4.00
Whiskey, Roderich, DHW, Old Highland, Ceramic Jug, Spout, Quart	9.00
Whiskey, Roehling & Schultz, Cabin, Labels, Amber	145.00
Whiskey, Rose Valley, Label, Clear, 1/2 Pint	1.00
Whiskey, Roth & Co., Full Quart, Calif.Inside Screw, Fluted, BIMAL, Amber	38.00
Whiskey, Roth & Co., Full Quart, San Francisco, California, Round, Amber	30.00
Whiskey, Roth & Co., San Francisco Guaranteed Full Quart, Lawton Rye, Amber	15.00
Whiskey, Rothenberg Co., San Francisco, Calif., Amber	18.00
Whiskey, Royal Blend, Ceramic Jug, Tan & White Glaze, Quart	11.00
Whiskey, Royal Doulton Commemorate, Elizabeth II, Scotch	35.00

Whiskey, Royal Handmade Sour Mash, Aqua, Quart	5.00
Whiskey, Russell Distilling Co., Newark, N.J., Flask, Clear, 1/2 Pint	3.00
Whiskey, Ruxton Rye, 1930s	4.00
Whiskey, S.A.Wertz, Philada, Superior, Old Rye, Applied Lip, Amber, Quart	45.00
Whiskey, S.C.Boehm & Co., N.Y., 1876, Embossed, Clear, Quart	8.00
Whiskey, S.C.Dispensary, Embossed Tru, Whittled, Finish Lip, Clear, Quart	75.00
Whiskey, S.Grabfelder & Co., Distillers, Louisville, Clear, Pint	3.00
Whiskey, S.Grabfelder & Co., Dist., Louisville, Ky., Amber, 1/2 Pint	5.00
Whiskey, S.Grabfelder & Co., Distillers, Louisville, Ky., Amber, Pint	5.00
Whiskey, S.Hyde, Script, Wines & Liquors, Seattle, Wash., Amber, Quart	22.50
Whiskey, S.M.& Co., N.Y., Handled Jug, Pontil, Amber, Pint	200.00
Whiskey, S.M.& Co., N.Y., Handled Jug, Pontil, Stain, Amber, Pint	190.00
Whiskey, S.N.Weil & Co., Cincinnati, Ohio, Clear, Quart	10.00
Whiskey, S.P.Giancomini, Calif., Cylinder, Honey Amber, Fifth	25.00
Whiskey, S.W.Branch Grocer, Savannah, Ga., Banded Union Oval, Amber, Pint	15.00
Whiskey, Sack's Sons, Amber, Quart	7.00
Whiskey, Sam Bass, Baltimore, Md., Square, Indented Panels, Amber	22.00
Whiskey, Sample Huguley's, Canal Street, Boston	6.00
Whiskey, Sandeman, Royal Doulton, Coronation Crest, 1937	27.00
Whiskey, Sandy Mcdonald, Oval, Amber	10.00
Whiskey, Schilee & Sons, Columbus, Ohio, Embossed Coat Of Arms, Aqua, Quart	7.00
Whiskey, Scotch, Porcelain, Keg, Contents, White With Banding	8.00
Whiskey, Scotch, Porcelain Keg, White With Banding	5.00 To 7.00
Whiskey, Seagrams, 1933	3.00
Whiskey, Sheehan's Malt, Clear, Quart	2.00
Whiskey, Sherbrook, Rye, 1930s	4.00
Whiskey, Sherman Rye, Hildebrandt Posner & Co. Inc., San Fransisco, Amber	25.00
Whiskey, Sherwood Rye, Enameled, Clear, Quart	4.00
Whiskey, Silver Tip, Big Spring Distilling Co., Ky., Clear, 1/2 Pint	5.00
Whiskey, Sir R.Burnett & Co., London, England, Aqua, Fifth	10.00
Whiskey, Sold For Medicinal Purposes Only, Paper Label, Screw Cap	4.50
Whiskey, South Carolina Dispensary & Tree, Amber, Quart	310.00
Whiskey, Southern Queen, Feathered Shoulders, Amber, Quart	29.00
Whiskey, Spider Web Embossed, Rye, 1930s	6.00
Whiskey, Spider Web, Screw Cap	12.50
Whiskey, Splaine, Clear, Quart	6.00
Whiskey, Spring Garden Rye, Clear, Quart	8.00
Whiskey, Spruance Stanley & Co., Dated On Embossed Horseshoe 1869, Amber	38.00
Whiskey, Star, Jug, Handled, Pontil, Amber, Pint	210.00
Whiskey, Taylor & Williams, In., Ky., Flask, Sun-Colored, 1/2 Pint	4.00
Whiskey, Taylor & Williams, Sun-Colored Amethyst, Quart	5.00
Whiskey, Teakettle, Embossed, Amber	175.00
Whiskey, Tennessee Centennial, 1769-1969, Bobwhite	4.95
Whiskey, Tennessee Sour Mash, Cascade	7.50
Whiskey, Theodore Netter, Phila., Barrel, Clear, 1/2 Pint	6.00
Whiskey, Three Mold, Embossed Crown	15.00
Whiskey, Three Mold, Patent On Shoulder, I.P., Teal Green, Quart	38.50
Whiskey, Tiffany Club, Fluted, Lion On Front, Sun Colored Amethyst, Quart	25.00
Whiskey, Traveler's, Cased, Shot Glass Stopper, Railway Companion Label	3.00
Whiskey, Tucker Rye, Clear, Quart	12.50
Whiskey, Tullamore Dew, Irish, Jug, Green Handles, Gray	10.00
Whiskey, Turnbull's Favorite Club Scotch, Jug, Gray & Brown	10.00
Whiskey, Twin Seal, Rye	13.50
Whiskey, U.S.Mailbox Rye, Label, Clear, Quart	100.00
Whiskey, Union, Rye, A & DHC , Pittsburgh, Aqua, Quart	45.00
Whiskey, Usher's, Ceramic, Coronation, Decanter, Copeland Spode, Blue, Quart	15.00
Whiskey, Vally, Eight-Sided, Amber, Pint	335.00
Whiskey, Very Old Corn Whiskey, Handled, Clear, Pint	15.00
Whiskey, Victoria Club, Chicago, Fancy, Clear, 1/2 Pint	12.50
Whiskey, W.C.Mc Donnell & Co., Amber, Quart	10.00
Whiskey, W.H.Jones & Co., Importers, Boston, Flask, Strap, Clear, Quart	12.00
Whiskey, W.J.Van Schuyver & Co.Inc., Portland, Ore., Inside Screw, Amber	20.00
Whiskey, W.L.S. Cricket Ball, Rye, 1930s	5.00
Whiskey, Walker's Kilmarnock, Embossed Base, Square, Abm, Sea Green, Fifth	5.00
Whiskey, Warranted Flask, Gold Amber, Quart	10.00
Whiskey, Waterman, J., Philadelphia, Amber, Quart	75.00

Whiskey, Wedderburn's Wines & Liquors, Ceramic Jug, Sample, Brown & White 6.00
Whiskey, Weeks & Potter, Inside Screw Cap, Amber, Quart 15.00
Whiskey, Weeks Glassworks, Red Amber 130.00
Whiskey, Wharton's, Chestnut Grove, 1850, 9 1/2 In. .... *Color* XX.XX
Whiskey, Wharton's, Jug, Handled, Amber, Quart 260.00
Whiskey, Wharton's, Warton, N.Y., 9 1/2 In. .... *Color* XX.XX
Whiskey, Wharton's, 1850, Chestnut Grove, Cobalt Blue 225.00
Whiskey, Whiskey & Sheaf Of Rye, Jug, Handled, Etched, Clear, Pint 10.00
Whiskey, White & Mc Kay, Bagpipe Man 11.95
Whiskey, White Horse, Embossed White Horse, Amber, Quart 5.00
Whiskey, White Horse, Green, Quart 6.50
Whiskey, White Oak, E.R.Betterton & Co., Distillers, Round, Amber, Quart 85.00
Whiskey, Whitney Glass Works, Glass Stopper, Amber, Quart 15.00
Whiskey, Whitney's Glass Works, Olive Green 22.00
Whiskey, Whyte & Mackay, Glasgow, 3 Mold, Crude, Aqua, Quart 7.50
Whiskey, Wicker Case, Green, Quart 5.00
Whiskey, Wild Turkey, 86 Proof, 7 Yr., Straight 1.10
Whiskey, Wild Turkey, 101 Proof, Straight 22.00
Whiskey, William C.Bass, Louisville, Clear, Quart 3.50
Whiskey, Wm.Frank & Son, Pitts. On Base, 3 Mold, Amber, Quart 6.95
Whiskey, Wm.Hone Liquors, Savannah, Ga., Amber 75.00
Whiskey, Wolf Creek Rye, 1930s 4.00
Whiskey, Woman's Portrait Under Glass, Clear, 1/2 Pint 30.00
Whiskey, Wooden, 14 In. 15.00
Whiskey, Woodford, Pinch Bottle, Enameled, Clear, Pint 3.00
Whiskey, Wright & Taylor Distillers, Ky., Rectangular, Amber, Quart 12.00
Whiskey, Wright & Taylor, Amber, Quart .... 8.00 To 10.00
Whiskey, Wright & Taylor, Bimal, Dug, Amber, Quart 4.00
Whiskey, Wright & Taylor, Distillers, Quart 12.00
Whiskey, Y.P.M., Embossed, Label 14.00
Whiskey, Ye Monks Whiskey, Jug, Ceramic, Label, Brown & White, Quart 2.00
Whiskey, Zeigler Rye, Jug, Handled, Etched, 1860, Polished Pontil, Clear, Pint 11.00
Whiskey, 3 Mold, BIMAL, Dug, Amber, Quart 2.00
Whiskey, 3 Mold, BIMAL, Dug, Clear, Quart 2.00
Whiskey, 4 Section, Stopper, Clear, 12 1/2 In.High 28.00
Wine, A.M.Smith 1907, California Wine Depot, 1872, Flask, Clear, Quart 12.00
Wine, A.M.Smith 1907, California Wine Depot, 1872, Flask, SCA , Pint 12.00
Wine, A.M.Smith 1907, California Wine Depot, 1872, Flask, SCA , 1/2 Pint 12.00
Wine, Amber 1.00
Wine, Birchmead, Kelsey & Co., N.Y., Aug.28, 1877, Aqua .... *Illus* 150.00
Wine, Blob Top, Spun, Cobalt, Quart 65.00
Wine, Blue Hock, 11 In. 7.00
Wine, Bowling Pin Shape, FR, Seal, Tubular Pontil, Olive Green 100.00
Wine, Brocton, Square Collar, Embossed Grape Cluster, Clear, Quart 5.00
Wine, Brotherhood Wine Co., Registered On Shoulder, Clear, Quart 4.00

Wine, Birchmead, Kelsey & Co., N.Y., Aug.28, 1877, Aqua

Wine, Deep Kick Up, Pontil, Long Neck, Sheared Top, Applied Ring, Green	23.00
Wine, Embossed Seal, Green	9.00
Wine, France, Cupid With Clock On Shoulders, 14 In.High, Modern	2.75
Wine, Free-Blown, Ring Collar, Improved Pontil, Olive Green	14.00
Wine, French, Depose, Frosted Hand Holding Percussion Pistol, Open Pontil	95.00
Wine, Garrett & Co., 25 Oz.	8.00
Wine, Garrett, Sample	12.00
Wine, Green Hock, Crude Lip, 13 In.	6.00
Wine, Hammondsport Wine Co., Square, Aqua, Quart	6.50
Wine, Hammondsport, N.Y., Grapes, Aqua, Quart	9.00
Wine, Hock, Amber	4.00
Wine, Hock, Applied Mouth, Red Amber	7.00
Wine, Hock, Cobalt, 9 In.High	50.00
Wine, Hock, Label, Red Amber, 14 In.Tall	4.00
Wine, Hock, Teal Blue	4.00
Wine, Hyde In Script, Seattle, Wash., Full Measure, Amber, Quart	22.50
Wine, Italian, Aqua, 10 In.Tall, Pair	4.00
Wine, James & Co., Wine Merchants, Bascomb, 9 In.High	3.00
Wine, Jug, Porcelain, Man's Face, Brown Nightcap	85.00
Wine, Jug, Spanish, C.1700, 13 In.High	250.00
Wine, Kick Up, Seal On Shoulder, Aqua	7.00
Wine, Lafite Bordeaux On Seal, Sheared Lip, Applied Ring, Kick Up, Green	12.00
Wine, Moch, Upset Bottom, Turn Mold, Applied Ring Around Mouth, Amber	10.00
Wine, Mogen David, Soldiers, Cannon, Set Of 5	66.00
Wine, Open Pontil, Olive Green, Quart	8.00 To 15.00
Wine, Port, Keg, Porcelain, Contents, White With Banding	10.00
Wine, Porter, JCC In Seal, Bubbly, Olive Green, 10 In.Tall	75.00
Wine, Porter, Pontil, 1/2 Pint	35.00
Wine, Pure Port, Medicinal Use, 3 Piece Mold, Citron	5.00
Wine, Sherry, Porcelain Keg, Contents, White With Banding	8.00
Wine, Snake Around Neck, Green, 9 In.	20.00
Wine, Tester, Emerald Green	7.50
Wine, Tester, Turn Mold, Olive Green	15.00
Wine, Tester, Vial, Sheared Mouth, Pontil, Green	10.00
Wine, The Onion, Onion Rib, Flare Base, Creased Neck, Green, 13 In.High	37.50
Wine, Vino Banderia, Woman From Spain, Ceramic	35.00
Zanesville Type, Ohio, Club Shape, Broken Swirl, 8 In. *Illus*	650.00
Zanesville, Chestnut, Golden Amber *Illus*	210.00
Zanesville, Chestnut, 24 Swirled Ribs, Amber *Illus*	230.00
Zanesville, Globular, Broken Swirl, Deep Aqua, 8 In.High	1700.00
Zanesville, Globular, Deep Amber, 8 In.High	350.00
Zanesville, Globular, Folded Color, Bluish Aqua, 11 1/4 In.	70.00
Zanesville, Globular, Honey Amber, 12 In.High	1300.00
Zanesville, Globular, Onion Shape, Aqua, 9 1/4 In.	110.00
Zanesville, Globular, Plain, Deep Amber, 9 1/2 In.High	150.00
Zanesville, Globular, Swirled To Left, Amber, 7 5/8 In.High	275.00
Zanesville, Globular, Swirled To Left, Amber, 8 1/4 In.High	275.00
Zanesville, Globular, Swirled To Left, Aqua, 7 In.High	175.00
Zanesville, Globular, Swirled To Left, Aqua, 8 3/4 In.High	120.00
Zanesville, Globular, Swirled To Left, Black Amber, 7 3/4 In.High	450.00
Zanesville, Globular, Swirled To Left, Black Amber, 8 1/4 In.High	550.00
Zanesville, Globular, Swirled To Left, Honey Amber, 8 In.High	400.00
Zanesville, Globular, Swirled To Left, Red Amber, 7 3/4 In.High	400.00
Zanesville, Globular, Swirled To Left, Red Amber, 8 3/8 In.High	200.00
Zanesville, Globular, Swirled To Right, Amber, 8 1/4 In.High	475.00
Zanesville, Globular, Swirled To Right, Aqua, 7 3/4 In.High	175.00
Zanesville, Globular, Swirled To Right, Yellow Amber, 8 In.High	400.00
Zanesville, Globular, Swirled, Golden Amber, 7 1/2 In.High	1100.00
Zanesville, Globular, Swirled, Green, 8 In.High	700.00
Zanesville, Globular, 24 Ribs Swirled To Left, Aqua, 7 1/2 In.High	125.00
Zanesville, Globular, 24 Ribs Swirled To Right, Amber, 8 In.High	200.00
Zanesville, Globular, 24 Ribs Swirled To Right, Aqua, 7 1/2 In.	95.00
Zanesville, Globular, 24 Ribs Swirled To Right, Aqua, 7 3/8 In.High	90.00
Zanesville, Globular, 24 Ribs Swirled To Right, Aqua, 8 In.	85.00
Zanesville, Globular, 24 Ribs Swirled To Right, Aqua, 9 In.	65.00
Zanesville, Globular, 24 Ribs Swirled To Right, Dark Amber, 8 In.	310.00

Zanesville, Globular, 24 Ribs Swirled To Right, Medium To Deep Amber 325.00
Zanesville, Globular, 24 Ribs Swirled, Dark Amber 200.00
Zanesville, Globular, 24 Ribs Swirled, Medium Amber, 7 1/8 In. 200.00
Zanesville, Globular, 24 Ribs, Red Amber, 7 5/8 In. .... *Illus* 500.00

Zanesville Type, Ohio,
Club Shape, Broken Swirl, 8 In.
See Page 218

Zanesville, Globular, 24 Ribs,
Red Amber, 7 5/8 In.

Zanesville, Chestnut,
24 Swirled Ribs, Amber
See Page 218

Zanesville, Chestnut,
Golden Amber
See Page 218